VISUAL
Rhetoric

To our students

VISUAL Rhetoric

A Reader in Communication and American Culture

Lester C. Olson
University of Pittsburgh

Cara A. Finnegan
University of Illinois at Urbana-Champaign

Diane S. Hope
Rochester Institute of Technology

editors

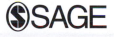

Los Angeles • London • New Delhi • Singapore

For information:

SAGE Publications, Inc.
2455 Teller Road
Thousand Oaks, California 91320
E-mail: order@sagepub.com

SAGE Publications India Pvt. Ltd.
B 1/I 1 Mohan Cooperative Industrial Area
Mathura Road, New Delhi 110 044
India

SAGE Publications Ltd.
1 Oliver's Yard
55 City Road
London EC1Y 1SP
United Kingdom

SAGE Publications Asia-Pacific Pte. Ltd.
33 Pekin Street #02-01
Far East Square
Singapore 048763

Printed in the United States of America

Library of Congress Cataloging-in-Publication Data

Visual rhetoric: a reader in communication and American culture / Lester C. Olson, Cara A. Finnegan, Diane S. Hope.
      p. cm.
Includes bibliographical references and index.
ISBN 978-1-4129-4919-4 (pbk.)
  1. Visual communication—United States. 2. Communication—Political aspects—United States.
3. United States—Politics and government. I. Olson, Lester C. II. Finnegan, Cara A. III. Hope, Diane S.

P93.5.V568 2008
302.2'22—dc22   2007041866

This book is printed on acid-free paper.

08 . 09   10   11   12   10 9 8 7 6 5 4 3 2 1

Acquisitions Editor:	Todd R. Armstrong
Editorial Assistant:	Aja Baker
Production Editor:	Astrid Virding
Copy Editor:	Gillian Dickens
Typesetter:	C&M Digitals (P) Ltd.
Proofreader:	Dennis Webb
Indexer:	David Prout
Cover Designer:	Candice Harman
Marketing Manager:	Carmel Schrire

CONTENTS

Alternate Table of Contents I: Media   vii

Alternate Table of Contents II: Chronology   xi

List of Illustrations   xiii

Preface   xv

Foreword. Visual Rhetorical Studies: Traces Through Time and Space   xxi
    Bruce E. Gronbeck

Visual Rhetoric in Communication: Continuing Questions and Contemporary Issues   1
    Lester C. Olson, Cara A. Finnegan, and Diane S. Hope

SECTION I: Performing and Seeing   **15**

1. The Performative Dimension of Surveillance: Jacob Riis' *How the Other Half Lives*   21
    Reginald Twigg

2. Embodying Normal Miracles   41
    Nathan Stormer

3. Recognizing Lincoln: Image Vernaculars in Nineteenth-Century Visual Culture   61
    Cara A. Finnegan

4. "What Lips These Lips Have Kissed": Refiguring the Politics of Queer Public Kissing   79
    Charles E. Morris III and John M. Sloop

SECTION II: Remembering and Memorializing   **99**

5. The Rhetoric of the Frame: Revisioning Archival Photographs in *The Civil War*   105
    Judith Lancioni

6. Representative Form and the Visual Ideograph:
    The Iwo Jima Image in Editorial Cartoons   119
    Janis L. Edwards and Carol K. Winkler

7. Reproducing Civil Rights Tactics:
    The Rhetorical Performances of the Civil Rights Memorial   139
    Carole Blair and Neil Michel

8. Remembering World War II: The Rhetoric and Politics of
    National Commemoration at the Turn of the 21st Century   157
    Barbara A. Biesecker

9. Public Identity and Collective Memory in
    U.S. Iconic Photography: The Image of "Accidental Napalm"   175
    Robert Hariman and John Louis Lucaites

SECTION III: Confronting and Resisting   **199**

10. The Precarious Visibility Politics of Self-Stigmatization: The Case of HIV/AIDS Tattoos   205
    Dan Brouwer

11. Encountering Visions of Aztlán: Arguments for Ethnic Pride,   227
    Community Activism, and Cultural Revitalization in Chicano Murals
    Margaret R. LaWare

12. The Guerrilla Girls' Comic Politics of Subversion   241
    Anne Teresa Demo

13. Behold the Corpse: Violent Images and the Case of Emmett Till   257
    Christine Harold and Kevin Michael DeLuca

SECTION IV: Commodifying and Consuming   **273**

14. The Force of Callas' Kiss: The 1997 Apple Advertising Campaign, "Think Different"   279
    Ronald E. Shields

15. "Put Your Stamp on History": The USPS Commemorative Program
    Celebrate the Century and Postmodern Collective Memory   295
    Ekaterina V. Haskins

16. Memorializing Affluence in the Postwar Family:
    Kodak's Colorama in Grand Central Terminal (1950–1990)   313
    Diane S. Hope

SECTION V: Governing and Authorizing   **327**

17. Benjamin Franklin's Pictorial Representations of the   333
    British Colonies in America: A Study in Rhetorical Iconology
    Lester C. Olson

18. Presidential Rhetoric's Visual Turn: 357
    Performance Fragments and the Politics of Illusionism
    Keith V. Erickson

19. Mediating Hillary Rodham Clinton: Television News   375
    Practices and Image-Making in the Postmodern Age
    Shawn J. Parry-Giles

20. "To Veil the Threat of Terror": Afghan Women and the   393
    <Clash of Civilizations> in the Imagery of the U.S. War on Terrorism
    Dana L. Cloud

Afterword: Look, Rhetoric!   413
    Thomas W. Benson

Index   417

About the Editors   431

About the Contributors   433

Alternate Table of Contents I

Media

Note: Some essays appear more than once in this table of contents.

Advertising Photography

The Force of Callas' Kiss: The 1997 Apple Advertising Campaign, "Think Different" / *Ronald E. Shields* — 279

Memorializing Affluence in the Postwar Family: Kodak's Colorama in Grand Central Terminal (1950–1990) / *Diane S. Hope* — 313

Billboards

The Guerrilla Girls' Comic Politics of Subversion / *Anne Teresa Demo* — 241

The Force of Callas' Kiss: The 1997 Apple Advertising Campaign, "Think Different" / *Ronald E. Shields* — 279

Memorializing Affluence in the Postwar Family: Kodak's Colorama in Grand Central Terminal (1950–1990) / *Diane S. Hope* — 313

Bodies

"What Lips These Lips Have Kissed": Refiguring the Politics of Queer Public Kissing / *Charles E. Morris III and John M. Sloop* — 79

The Precarious Visibility Politics of Self-Stigmatization: The Case of HIV/AIDS Tattoos / *Dan Brouwer* — 205

The Guerrilla Girls' Comic Politics of Subversion / *Anne Teresa Demo* — 241

Behold the Corpse: Violent Images and the Case of Emmett Till / *Christine Harold and Kevin Michael DeLuca* — 257

"To Veil the Threat of Terror": Afghan Women and the <Clash of Civilizations> in the Imagery of the U.S. War on Terrorism / *Dana L. Cloud* — 393

Books

The Performative Dimension of Surveillance: Jacob Riis' *How the Other Half Lives* / *Reginald Twigg* — 21

Remembering World War II: The Rhetoric and Politics of National Commemoration at the Turn of the 21st Century / *Barbara A. Biesecker* — 157

BROADSIDES/NEWSPAPERS

The Guerrilla Girls' Comic Politics of Subversion / *Anne Teresa Demo*   241

Benjamin Franklin's Pictorial Representations of the British Colonies in America:
A Study in Rhetorical Iconology / *Lester C. Olson*   333

Presidential Rhetoric's Visual Turn: Performance Fragments and the Politics of Illusionism /   357
Keith V. Erickson

CARTOONS

Representative Form and the Visual Ideograph: The Iwo Jima Image in Editorial Cartoons /   119
Janis L. Edwards and Carol K. Winkler

Benjamin Franklin's Pictorial Representations of the British Colonies in America:
A Study in Rhetorical Iconology / *Lester C. Olson*   333

DOCUMENTARY FILM

Embodying Normal Miracles / *Nathan Stormer*   41

FEATURE FILM

"What Lips These Lips Have Kissed": Refiguring the Politics of Queer Public Kissing /   79
Charles E. Morris III and John M. Sloop

Remembering World War II: The Rhetoric and Politics of National Commemoration
at the Turn of the 21st Century / *Barbara A. Biesecker*   157

ILLUSTRATIONS

"Put Your Stamp on History": The USPS Commemorative Program
Celebrate the Century and Postmodern Collective Memory / *Ekaterina V. Haskins*   295

MAGAZINES

Recognizing Lincoln: Image Vernaculars in Nineteenth-Century Visual Culture /   61
Cara A. Finnegan

"What Lips These Lips Have Kissed": Refiguring the Politics of Queer Public Kissing /   79
Charles E. Morris III and John M. Sloop

"To Veil the Threat of Terror": Afghan Women and the <Clash of Civilizations>
in the Imagery of the U.S. War on Terrorism / *Dana L. Cloud*   393

MEMORIALS

Reproducing Civil Rights Tactics: The Rhetorical Performances of the
Civil Rights Memorial / *Carole Blair and Neil Michel*   139

Remembering World War II: The Rhetoric and Politics of National Commemoration
at the Turn of the 21st Century / *Barbara A. Biesecker*   157

PHOTOJOURNALISM

The Performative Dimension of Surveillance: Jacob Riis' *How the Other Half Lives* /   21
Reginald Twigg

The Rhetoric of the Frame: Revisioning Archival Photographs in *The Civil War* /   105
Judith Lancioni

Public Identity and Collective Memory in U.S. Iconic Photography: The Image of
    "Accidental Napalm" / *Robert Hariman and John Louis Lucaites*   175

Behold the Corpse: Violent Images and the Case of Emmett Till /   257
    Christine Harold and Kevin Michael DeLuca

Presidential Rhetoric's Visual Turn: Performance Fragments and the
    Politics of Illusionism / *Keith V. Erickson*   357

"To Veil the Threat of Terror": Afghan Women and the <Clash of Civilizations>
    in the Imagery of the U.S. War on Terrorism / *Dana L. Cloud*   393

PLACE

"What Lips These Lips Have Kissed": Refiguring the Politics of Queer Public Kissing /   79
    Charles E. Morris III and John M. Sloop

Encountering Visions of Aztlán: Arguments for Ethnic Pride, Community Activism and
    Cultural Revitalization in Chicano Murals / *Margaret R. LaWare*   227

Memorializing Affluence in the Postwar Family: Kodak's Colorama in
    Grand Central Terminal (1950–1990) / *Diane S. Hope*   313

PORTRAIT PHOTOGRAPHY

Recognizing Lincoln: Image Vernaculars in Nineteenth-Century Visual Culture /   61
    Cara A. Finnegan

"Put Your Stamp on History": The USPS Commemorative Program
    Celebrate the Century and Postmodern Collective Memory / *Ekaterina V. Haskins*   295

STAMPS

"Put Your Stamp on History": The USPS Commemorative Program
    Celebrate the Century and Postmodern Collective Memory / *Ekaterina V. Haskins*   295

TELEVISION COMMERCIALS

The Force of Callas' Kiss: The 1997 Apple Advertising Campaign, "Think Different" /   279
    Ronald E. Shields

TELEVISION DOCUMENTARY

The Rhetoric of the Frame: Revisioning Archival Photographs in *The Civil War* /   105
    Judith Lancioni

Presidential Rhetoric's Visual Turn: Performance Fragments and the Politics of Illusionism /   357
    Keith V. Erickson

TELEVISION NEWS

Presidential Rhetoric's Visual Turn: Performance Fragments and the Politics of Illusionism /   357
    Keith V. Erickson

Mediating Hillary Rodham Clinton: Television News Practices and Image-Making in the
    Postmodern Age / *Shawn J. Parry-Giles*   375

Alternate Table of Contents II

Chronology

1750–1900

Benjamin Franklin's Pictorial Representations of the British Colonies in
America: A Study in Rhetorical Iconology / *Lester C. Olson*   333

The Performative Dimension of Surveillance: Jacob Riis' *How the Other Half Lives* /
Reginald Twigg   21

Recognizing Lincoln: Image Vernaculars in Nineteenth-Century Visual Culture /
Cara A. Finnegan   61

1900–1960

Memorializing Affluence in the Postwar Family: Kodak's Colorama in
Grand Central Terminal (1950–1990) / *Diane S. Hope*   313

Behold the Corpse: Violent Images and the Case of Emmett Till /
Christine Harold and Kevin Michael DeLuca   257

1960–1990

Representative Form and the Visual Ideograph: The Iwo Jima Image in Editorial Cartoons /
Janis L. Edwards and Carol K. Winkler   119

Encountering Visions of Aztlán: Arguments for Ethnic Pride, Community Activism
and Cultural Revitalization in Chicano Murals / *Margaret R. LaWare*   227

Public Identity and Collective Memory in U.S. Iconic Photography: The Image of
"Accidental Napalm" / *Robert Hariman and John Louis Lucaites*   175

The Guerrilla Girls' Comic Politics of Subversion / *Anne Teresa Demo*   241

Embodying Normal Miracles / *Nathan Stormer*   41

Reproducing Civil Rights Tactics: The Rhetorical Performances of the Civil
Rights Memorial / *Carole Blair and Neil Michel*   139

Presidential Rhetoric's Visual Turn: Performance Fragments and the Politics of Illusionism /
Keith V. Erickson   357

1990–present

The Rhetoric of the Frame: Revisioning Archival Photographs in *The Civil War* /
Judith Lancioni   105

Mediating Hillary Rodham Clinton: Television News Practices and Image-Making in the
Postmodern Age / *Shawn J. Parry-Giles*   375

The Precarious Visibility Politics of Self-Stigmatization: The Case of HIV/AIDS Tattoos /   199
Dan Brouwer

Remembering World War II: The Rhetoric and Politics of National Commemoration
at the Turn of the 21st Century / *Barbara A. Biesecker*   157

The Force of Callas' Kiss: The 1997 Apple Advertising Campaign, "Think Different" /   279
Ronald E. Shields

"Put Your Stamp on History": The USPS Commemorative Program *Celebrate the
Century* and Postmodern Collective Memory / *Ekaterina V. Haskins*   295

"To Veil the Threat of Terror": Afghan Women and the <Clash of Civilizations>
in the Imagery of the U.S. War on Terrorism / *Dana L. Cloud*   393

"What Lips These Lips Have Kissed": Refiguring the Politics of Queer Public Kissing /
Charles E. Morris III and John M. Sloop   79

LIST OF ILLUSTRATIONS

Cover image, *Communication Quarterly*   15
"Bohemian Cigarmakers at Work in a Tenement"   28
"Mountain Eagle, and his Family of Iroquois Indians"   31
"Black and Tan Dive on Broome Street"   32
"'Washing Up' in the Newsboys' Lodging House"   35
"The Earliest Portrait of Abraham Lincoln"   61
Gran Fury "READ MY LIPS" poster   86
Tim Molloy and Brian Duck Celebrate Their Wedding Reception   91
Washington, D.C., Inside the Lincoln Memorial   99
"Wait!"   123
"THE CLOSET"   123
"New Hampshire"   127
"PREMIUM"   129
[No title], Bill Shorr   130
[No title], Steve Benson   131
Civil Rights Memorial, Montgomery, Alabama   143
Civil Rights Memorial, Montgomery, Alabama   143
Civil Rights Memorial, Montgomery, Alabama   143
Civil Rights Memorial, Montgomery, Alabama   144
Civil Rights Memorial, Montgomery, Alabama   144
Civil Rights Memorial, Montgomery, Alabama   146
Civil Rights Memorial, Montgomery, Alabama   146
World War II Memorial, Washington, DC   157
Women in Military Services of America Memorial   167
"Accidental Napalm"   178
Kim Phuc and child   183
"Veritatis Vietnam"   186
"Soldiers of Misfortune"   187
"Pittsburgh, 1916"   199
Street view of Casa Aztlán   234
Close-up of mural front of Casa Aztlán   235
"La marcha," Casa Aztlán   236
"Do women have to be naked . . . ?"   250
"George Bush, 'The Education President'"   251
"Lasso Yourself a Western Vacation!"   273
Colorama in Grand Central Terminal   314
Christmas Carolers Colorama   318

Farm Scene and Family Snapshots Colorama   319
Lake Placid Colorama   320
Monument Valley, Arizona Colorama   322
"The Opposition"   327
"JOIN, or DIE"   334
"MAGNA Britannia: her Colonies REDUC'D"   335
"MAGNA Britania her Colonies REDUC'D" (broadside)   336
"BRITTANNIA MUTILATED"   337
"JOIN, or DIE" (Constitutional Courant)   340
["Patriotic Capitalist Mourns"]   399
["From Shadow into Light"]   399
["Eye Contact: Schoolgirl in Afghanistan"]   399
["Half Devil and Half Child"]   400
["Hyper-Mediated Women's Liberation"]   400
"*Defining Visual Rhetorics* Cover Image"   415

PREFACE

Visual Rhetoric: A Reader in Communication and American Culture is designed for teachers, scholars, and students with an interest in the visual aspects of rhetorical theory, history, and criticism. We have designed this reader for those who wish to teach visual rhetoric either as a stand-alone course or as a component in another course, such as visual communication or rhetorical criticism. Despite the rise of interest in visual rhetoric over the past several years, we have observed that a number of factors make it difficult for teachers to know exactly where to begin when seeking to introduce students to the area. First, within the communication discipline, what has come to be called the study of "visual rhetoric" has also been termed variously the study of the rhetoric of symbolic action, rhetorical dimensions of media, rhetoric of nonoratorical forms, celluloid rhetoric, rhetorical iconography or iconology, or electronic rhetoric, just to name a few. Furthermore, scholars may also describe their work as the "rhetoric of" a genre or medium, such as prints, paintings, maps, documentary, photography, cartoons, comics, posters, film, television, advertisements, sculpture, architecture, or textiles. Another factor making the teaching and learning of visual rhetoric difficult is the scattered range of disciplinary locations where rhetorical aspects of the visual have been engaged, among them American studies, art history, communication, English, rhetoric and composition, history, media, and visual studies. Finally, both within the field of communication and without, researchers have proceeded with more or less consciousness of how rhetoric's rich and diverse history provides valuable conceptual resources for analyses of symbolism. When we realized that currently there is no textbook that gathers together exemplary essays originally published elsewhere and demonstrates a firm grasp of the development of visual rhetoric in the communication discipline, we decided to create one. Visual Rhetoric: A Reader in Communication and American Culture offers teachers and students of visual rhetoric alike a firm foundation from which to begin their own investigations into visual rhetoric.

ORGANIZATION AND FEATURES OF THE BOOK

The book's central purposes are to offer a narrative of visual rhetoric scholarship in the communication discipline and teach key rhetorical actions by featuring exemplary essays representing a range of approaches for studying visual rhetoric in U.S. culture. Although the study of visual rhetoric in communication has a long history and is currently burgeoning, its substantive contributions have not yet been systematically interpreted as a vital part of the field's past and present. While teachers and students of communication study the visual in a variety of contexts—for example, conducting research into media effects or engaging in the teaching and learning of media production techniques—in most communication departments, the study of rhetoric as persuasive, public communication is still presumed to be largely grounded in oral speech and written text. Our choice to focus on visual rhetoric scholarship in the communication discipline, then, offers students of communication an additional way to understand how the visual is vital to communicating in public life.

In this volume, we frame the development of rhetoric's attention to the visual in several ways. In the Foreword to the volume, Bruce Gronbeck comments on the long history of visual rhetoric, reminding us that rhetoric's ongoing and sustained attention to visuality goes back to ancient conceptions of rhetoric. In the Introduction, the editors explore the nearly half-century of intellectual and institutional attention to the relationship between rhetoric and the visual in the communication discipline and highlight key developments in that scholarship from 1950 to the present. In the Afterword, Thomas Benson reflects on past and present relationships between rhetorical criticism and visual rhetoric. Taken together, these introductory and concluding materials offer students and teachers a substantive orientation to the ways that scholarship on visual rhetoric has developed in the discipline of communication. While we recognize that a rich body of work on visual rhetoric has developed in allied disciplines such as English and composition studies, and we reference that work throughout this book, as communication scholars, we are especially interested in presenting teachers and students with ways to understand visual rhetoric from a communication perspective.

One way that we foreground a communication perspective is by organizing the book around what we term "rhetorical actions." Rhetorical actions are actions that humans perform when they use symbols to persuade or invite cooperation from others. The rhetorical actions that we feature here are by no means unique to visual rhetoric but represent a variety of ways that we communicate in public life, be they oral, textual, or visual (or, more likely, some combination of all of these). Our choice to focus on rhetorical action as an organizing scheme offers several advantages. First, it links the scholarship featured in the book to the broader interests of the field of rhetoric as a whole. By linking practices of visual rhetoric to rhetorical action more generally, we mean to show teachers and students that visuality is not distinct from, but rather fully integrated in, our practices of everyday persuasion. A second advantage of the focus on rhetorical action is

that such an approach illuminates for scholars who study the visual in related fields how a specifically rhetorical approach to the study of visuality may be usefully different from other approaches.

The bulk of the book is devoted to five groups of essays, each of which features a specific pair of related rhetorical actions: performing and seeing, remembering and memorializing, confronting and resisting, commodifying and consuming, and governing and authorizing. An essay introducing each section orients students to the featured rhetorical actions, provides an introduction to each of the essays in that section, offers a set of discussion questions, and lists suggestions for further reading. Each unit opens with a provocative image that appears without comment to prompt discussion, focus critical awareness, and encourage engagement with the visual as rhetoric. Within each section, the essays are presented in chronological order by original publication date.

Why these specific rhetorical actions? On one hand, these actions emerged organically from our editorial process. As we reviewed the wealth of published work on visual rhetoric and considered essays for inclusion in the volume, we noted and tracked those rhetorical actions that seemed to emerge as central concerns for the authors. Yet as we worked, we realized that we were finding these rhetorical actions because these actions are ones frequently of interest to those who study all forms of rhetoric, not just visual rhetoric. One needs only to browse through the major research journals in rhetorical studies to see that scholars who work with oral or written texts of rhetorical criticism are often interested in the very same rhetorical actions we identified and use here. Such overlap should not be surprising, because the rhetorical actions we feature are all broad forms of symbolic action that help to constitute our rhetorical world. While the pairs of rhetorical actions we highlight are by no means exhaustive of the wide variety of rhetorical actions scholars are typically interested in, they do tap into important relationships and issues of abiding concern to scholars of rhetoric and communication.

Our criteria for selection of essays reflected our desire to foreground scholarship engaging both rhetoric and visuality. By *visuality,* we mean not just images or visual media but the totality of practices, performances, and configurations of the visual. Although the term *visual rhetoric* now surfaces regularly in essays and books in multiple disciplines, scholarship that considers both visuality and rhetoric in depth and in their relationship to each other is often easily lost among that which treats visual media without substantive engagement of rhetoric's rich range of conceptual and theoretical resources or, at the other extreme, treats the rhetoric of media texts without substantive engagement with what is actually *visual* about certain media. Against this backdrop, we have collaboratively selected essays in which concepts from the rich, diverse lexicon of rhetoric are featured substantively in their relationship to visual experience. Each selected essay is a case study that engages an instance of visual communication or series of examples; puts them in social, political, and cultural context; and addresses broader conceptual and theoretical implications for the study of rhetoric. The primary criterion for an essay's inclusion in the volume was its overall quality as a model that has abiding value for learning about visual rhetoric. Additional criteria reflected in our selections include the essay's overall excellence, its usefulness and accessibility for upper-level undergraduate and graduate students, its explicit and sustained attention to visuality, its coherent use of rhetorical concepts or theoretical concerns, its clear writing style, and its value as a compelling case study. We also considered it important that the collection as a whole include a range of media, discuss both historical and contemporary cases, cover a wide range of scholarly approaches and methods for handling primary materials, and attend substantively to issues of sex, gender, race, sexuality, and class.

We have restricted our selections to those essays focused on U.S. culture and have done this for a few reasons. The first of these is our belief that visual rhetoric, like all rhetoric, is culturally situated. By *culturally situated,* we mean that visual rhetoric is particularized by ways of seeing that have been developed, learned, and produced by specifically "American" experiences, history, and ideologies. As we pondered the meanings of "visual rhetoric" that emerged for us while we prepared this book, we were reluctant to extend our interpretations to symbolic actions as they might be contextualized in other visual cultures. Our second consideration was that the great majority of publications on visual rhetoric by U.S. scholars are focused on symbolic actions in the United States. Perhaps this reflects a disciplinary parochialism, but just as likely it reflects legitimate caution on the part of rhetorical critics who rightly recognize that not all visual cultures are the same.

The vernacular usage designating U.S. cultural imperatives as "American" is, of course, problematic and thus deserves comment here. North, South, and Central America host a number of nations and indigenous cultures—each vastly different from the United States and from one another. Each nation is an integral part of the American continents, but none other than the United States describes its culture solely as "American." In addition, no other culture has permeated global narratives with the degree of power that propels the visual culture of the United States. In this book, then, *American* reflects vernacular use and recognizes the hegemony implied by the term. The complicated meaning of *American* is inherently a part of U.S. culture, and our use reflects that awareness. Our choice to focus on visual rhetoric in the U.S. context means that we did have to set aside a group of excellent essays that move visual rhetoric scholarship beyond domestic borders and offer valuable insights into global issues.

With this collection of essays, we certainly have not exhausted the well of valuable scholarship on visual rhetoric in the field of communication; indeed, that we engaged in a lengthy deliberative process in order to select essays for this volume points to the outstanding quality and quantity of scholarship in this area. Furthermore, our choice to focus specifically on the rhetorical actions of public communication required us also to set aside studies of visual rhetoric from allied fields such as art history, English, and composition. Fortunately, much of that excellent work is available in other anthologies; we encourage teachers and students to turn to the substantive bibliography in the introduction chapter for examples of related approaches to visual rhetoric. In short, we have had to leave out more than we have put in. While this is disappointing, it is also exciting because it allows us to suggest further avenues for teachers and students to explore. To facilitate explorations beyond the essays in this book, in each of the sections we offer suggestions for further reading designed to expand the range of available resources and invite users of the reader to follow up on issues of specific interest to them.

Among the distinctive features of this book is that it offers alternate tables of contents. While we assume that most users of the book will want to use the primary organizational scheme of rhetorical actions, we also offer two additional tables of contents that reorganize the essays to feature groupings of them suitable for varied audiences, students, and courses. Teachers who wish to adopt the book as a component in courses on rhetorical criticism or visual communication, for example, and prefer to emphasize the rhetorical aspects of specific media may wish to use Alternative Table of Contents I that organizes our selections by medium (e.g., television, photography). Teachers in art history, history, or American studies programs may wish to consult Alternative Table of Contents II that organizes our selections chronologically by historical period.

Another distinctive feature of the book is that some essays are more richly illustrated here than when they were originally published. One essay that was originally published without illustrations has them supplied here, while others are accompanied by additional illustrations that did not appear in the original published versions. We were pleased to work with the authors of these essays to offer these additional illustrations to readers.

ACKNOWLEDGMENTS

We have many people to thank for helping us realize our vision for this book. Most important, we offer a huge thanks to Todd Armstrong and his colleagues at Sage, especially Sarah Quesenberry and Katie Grim; they have been enthusiastic, encouraging, patient, and committed partners in this project. Many others helped bring this book to fruition as well. In mid-2005, we posted queries on the CRTNET and H-Rhetor e-mail lists, asking teachers to share their experiences of the visual rhetoric and communication courses they teach. The more than 30 responses we received were invaluable in helping us formulate our initial proposal to Sage. In addition, we wish to thank the following for generously replying to our request to suggest essays for the volume: Sue Barnes, Thomas W. Benson, Barbara A. Biesecker, David S. Birdsell, Carole Blair, Barry Brummett, Robin R. Means Coleman, Kevin Michael DeLuca, Anne Teresa Demo, Bonnie J. Dow, Janis L. Edwards, Sonja K. Foss, Thomas S. Frentz, Bruce E. Gronbeck, Robert Hariman, Kathleen Hall Jamieson, Henry P. Krips, John Louis Lucaites, Martin J. Medhurst, Paul Messaris, Charles E. Morris III, Michael M. Osborn, Catherine H. Palczewski, Shawn J. Parry-Giles, Dann L. Pierce, Carol A. Stabile, Robert E. Terrill, and Kathleen J. Turner. The reviewers who reviewed the proposal and the manuscript for Sage offered crucial feedback, and we are grateful for their help and suggestions. These include Catherine Ann Collins, Willamette University; Kristie S. Fleckenstein, Florida State University; Robert Hariman, Northwestern University; Keith Kenney, University of South Carolina; Marc Leverette; Colorado State University; Julianne H. Newton, University of Oregon; and Matthew J. Sobnosky, Hofstra University. Our undergraduate and graduate students at Rochester Institute of Technology, University of Pittsburgh, and University of Illinois at Urbana-Champaign "road-tested" many of the essays as well as the organizational scheme, and we thank them for helping us determine what worked in the classroom. The William A. Kern Endowment for Research in Communications at the Rochester Institute of Technology has contributed much to this project, both intellectually and financially. In addition to making possible several important conferences on visual communication and rhetoric over the past decade, the Kern Endowment provided necessary and generous financial support for image acquisition and permissions. Thanks to Cassandra Shellman, RIT's Administrative Assistant to the Endowed Chairs, for all her work on this project. We thank the publishers of the original essays for permission to reproduce those essays in this volume. We also extend our thanks to those authors whose excellent work appears here, as well as the many others whose excellent work we unfortunately were unable to include. We offer special thanks to contributors Bruce Gronbeck and Tom Benson, both of whom have devoted their distinguished careers to exploring rhetoric in all of its complex forms. Their pioneering insights on rhetoric, visuality, and political communication have made this book possible in more ways than one. Last, we editors wish to thank one another for an immensely rewarding and pleasurable collaboration. From the selection of essays to the devising of the organizational scheme to the writing of the editorial apparatus, each of the editors contributed equally to the project; the sequence of names on the cover reflects only the order in which we committed to the effort. As we ponder the hundreds of e-mails and hours of phone calls and meetings it took to get this book to completion, we also know that we had a lot of fun. It is our hope that the book reflects not only the effort but also the energy, enthusiasm, and intellectual engagement that we experienced while preparing it.

Lester C. Olson

Cara A. Finnegan

Diane S. Hope

FOREWORD

VISUAL RHETORICAL STUDIES

Traces Through Time and Space

BRUCE E. GRONBECK

The things of which there can be sight, hearing, and learning—these are what I especially prize. (55)

Eyes are more accurate witnesses than ears. (101a)

Heraclitus, *Fragments* (Harris, n.d.)

In our time, civic and cultural spectacle has been captured through print, photo-reproductive, and digital technologies. Public, politically and culturally sensitive spectacle has been framed in static media (handbills, posters, photographs, transparencies, faxed displays) as well as mechanically and electronically mobilized images (film, television, digital media, etc.). Because of the explosion of mediated spectacle and the public's seemingly insatiable hunger for it, the 19th and 20th centuries in the West have been called *ocularcentric* (Jay, 1994), or eye centered. The popularity and power of static and moving images in political and social life, their work in ethical-moral judgment of humanity's moments of inhumanity, and their place in what we know and share with each other (social epistemology) make what we see central to the contemporary world.

Yet, we must not assume that the idea of seeing is believing (and knowing and interpreting and judging) has arisen suddenly in the West. As the comments from Heraclitus (6th-century BCE) suggest, the ancient world likewise was fascinated with sight and seeing. Diogenes of Sinope (4th-century BCE) was perhaps the first great master of performance art, acting out his beliefs and critiques as one of the Cynics of Athens: To be seen acting publicly was to embody an argument. Or, consider Plato's allegory of the cave from Book 7 of *The Republic* as an argument about sight-centered knowledge: Seeing not the shadows of objects cast on a cave wall by an inferior light source (fire), but the objects themselves observed in bright superior light (sunshine), became a primal Western story whose moral is clear: Direct observation of the world is the surest guide to truth, allowing us to avoid confusing what is real with what is merely simulation (Jay, 1994, p. 478).

Even Aristotle's treatise on memory, *De memoria et reminiscentia* (McKeon, 1941), reflects the special virtues of vision in human life. In that short treatise, he contrasts recalling, or brute remembering, with reminiscing, wherein the scene is brought back to thought replete with human actions, emotions, motivations, status differences, and outcomes. According to Aristotle, humans use *phantasmata,* mental images or pictures, in the construction of memory (Sisko, 1997; cf. Vance, 1979). Longinus, too, in *Peri Hypsous* or *On the Sublime,* in seeking to define sublimity in oral and written discourse, takes recourse to the visual (Fyfe, 1960): "Weight, grandeur, and energy in writing are very largely produced, dear pupil, by the use of images . . . [where] you seem to see what you describe and bring it vividly before the eyes of your audience" (sec. 15, p. 171).

We could continue moving through the Greek and Roman worlds to find knowing and believing grounded in seeing and the visualized. In Greek, the words *theoria* or knowledge and *theoros* or witness are rooted in sight. The Latin *imago* comes from the infinitive "to see," even the English word *evidence* derives from *e-videre* or "out of or from seeing," and a *speculum* or mirror suggests that spectators are reflecting what they see. The experience of seeing in the West anchors both individual and collective accounts of shared opinions (*doxa*) and truth (*episteme*). (For more such arguments, see Jay, 1994, chap. 1, tracing these ideas through Western history.)

Rituals of sacred and secular spectacle and power likewise were well developed in postclassical Europe. The medieval church, as well as its ikons, dialogic liturgy, vestments, pageantry, the various cycles (Wakefield, York, Chester, N-town, etc.) of religious plays (*Middle English Plays,* n.d.), and architecture, all served as *visibilia* (Vance, 1979, p. 375), or visual evidence of the Church's powers to demand, to validate and judge, and even to confer identity upon those who lived within its sphere. Civic collective

witnessing was equally focused on status and authority: the use of public punishments, including outdoor executions and bodily display (Bleackley & Lofland, 1977); heraldry and its symbolic representations of familial units and status; Elizabeth I's grand tour of England after her accession to the crown, dressed in spun glass and traveling in gilded carriages so as to garner charisma, the power of light (Geertz, 1977); and, of course, the public lifestyle and stylings of the personage, chateaux, and cultural institutions of *Le Roi Soleil,* the sun king Louis XIV. Such spaces, images, rituals, and bodily performances all contributed to strong, reciprocal interdependence between the Church and communicant, between the State and citizen.

Yet, as deeply rooted in Western philosophies of thought (epistemology), social structure (ideology), and identity (subjectivity) as ocularcentrism is, scholars of communication have only begun to scratch the surface of the political and social implications of ocularcentrism. Visual rhetorical studies have been centered predominantly in the public performances and visual technologies of 20th-century politics. The remainder of this foreword will review briefly the rise of visual media and their uses in (especially) American politics and conclude with an equally concise consideration of where visual rhetoric stands in relation to the grand history of rhetoric understood as featuring oral and written composition.

VISUAL MEDIA OF/IN POLITICS

We begin with posters. In the early 20th century, artists all but perfected the poster as an effective medium of political communication. Thanks to metal plates and color lithography as well as large-format presses, posters reached their apex as a political tool in World War I (Rossi, 1969, p. 17; cf. Fern, 1985). They comprised a versatile print medium, running in size (not counting stamps) from handbills to prints capable of decorating public spaces: the walls of town squares, later billboards. An argument can be made—and has been (Schnapp, 2005)[1]—that posters were "hailing" devices that called to viewers, encouraging them to be active citizens and helping Western modernist states complete their evolution into democracies. Posters could call citizens to participatory actions, depict leaders at work in their name and for their causes, and conceive of idyllic new worlds if citizens worked to achieve major reforms and even revolutions. They likewise could warn of the consequences of failure, inscribe their enemies with evil motives and scandalous acts, and make fear of failure a prod to extraordinary actions. Few words (usually), simple pictures, and larger-than-life actors and actions in the examples of wall-sized posters marked them as dynamic, even outrageous, modes of public, political persuasion.

Equally important to turn-of-the-century politics was the photographed image. Photography was an antebellum technology that became much more publicly powerful with the coming of dry-plate processing in 1878, the halftone printing system (c. 1880) for turning pictures into narrow monochromatic strips to ease printing, the commercially viable rotary printing press (1910), and the wirephoto machine (1911) that permitted pictures to be transported via telephone (Lacayo, 1990). These developments allowed books and newspapers to print photographs economically, making them a genuinely mass medium and hence relevant to politics generally.[2] The realism of photos, in combination with eyewitness journalism, created a potent rhetorical combination: The sense that photographic images and journalistic words are materially or experientially grounded made them feel like transparent windows on the world.

Then came the technical development that made those images move: film, first silent then sounded. When the government got into film-making in the second decade of the 20th century, films were put to government use. The Department of the Interior distributed a film about the Pima Indian reservation in 1911; the Civil Service Commission, one on meritocracies in 1912; and the Committee for Public Information, a series of films on wartime preparedness in 1915 and 1916 (*Documentary Film Classics,* 1980; Ward, 1985). Then, as the political agenda of government offices was combined with the romantic, anthropological feel of early documentaries, Depression-era government films such as *The Plow That Broke the Plains* (1936), which advocated environmentally sensitive agricultural practices, and *The River* (1938),

which examined the TVA dams project, offered information and argument clothed in transcendent musical scores, poetic narration, and soul-searing images (Barnouw, 1974; Ellis, 1989; MacCann, 1973). Romance yielded to investigative reportage in the television "white papers" and news documentaries of the 1950s and 1960s (Curtin, 1996), though that sense of imagaic transparency did not disappear with the mere change of mass medium (Rosteck, 2005).

Television actually advertised itself as a "window on the world" (*Television,* 1996), constructing the likes of Walter Cronkite, Chet Huntley, David Brinkley, Howard K. Smith, and other television journalists as those who could expertly interpret what we saw outside. TV gave us representations that encompassed multiple media (words, images, sounds), offering viewers a complex mix of fictional, nonfictional, and commercial narratives and experiences; it was almost like the medium itself was an extension of our bodies and environments. Television felt like both a window and a door for those who sat around their sets to watch a few programs before going to bed after the evening news, weather, and sports. Viewers felt like they were inviting into their homes lovable Lucy and Ricky Ricardo, the Cartrights on *Bonanza,* and most of the rest of the folks you still can watch on the Nickelodeon channel.

Television practiced a double surveillance: Citizens watched a world they thought they lived in and, in turn, thanks to rating services, were watched for signs of taste, preference, and demographic characteristics, all important to advertisers. In its heyday, television was the center of the American political economy (e.g., Parenti, 1993; Schudson, 1995), as consumer culture erupted in the 1950s and 1960s and as we were taught what politics is and concerns through TV news, documentaries, special events such as the 1963 Kennedy assassination and funeral, the 1968 Martin Luther King Jr. and Robert Kennedy killings, the "living-room war" in Vietnam (Arlen, 1969), the 1977 *Roots* miniseries, and more.

The position of television as absolutely dominant in collective, ocularcentric, American political life, however, is being challenged in our time. Not only has the Big Three networks' influence in news and entertainment been eroded by cable and satellite channels, but computerized conduits, thanks to digitalization and the growing accessibility of World Wide Web content, are occupying more and more of the weekly media consumption in American households.

The WWW's home in the world of visual-rhetorical media is many-chambered. The Web is in fact an information highway, with photos, musical-video collages, photo-shopped images, and several forms of streaming live and archived video cruising up and down its roads, with places to stop to chat, to IM with Webcams and cell phones, and to jointly construct digitalized visual masterpieces interactively with others. Its revolutionary rhetorical capabilities create open-source politics with the help not only of listservs—so central to the World Trade Organization protests (DeLuca & Peeples, 2002)—but, now, a fully functional blogosphere (Keren, 2006; more generally, see Chadwick, 2006; Cornfield, 2004; Jenkins & Thorburn, 2003). The political poster may have put bodies on roads by calling people to assemble in a time and place, but the Internet virtualizes minds and bodies, then distributes them out of the reach of institutionalized controls (at least so far). The potential for a radically new visual rhetoric is today being operationalized, incident by incident, election by election. Time can be stretched or compressed; space can be recontoured or evaporated. The eye cannot trust, the mind cannot verify, what it sees. PhotoShop and Java (for now) rule!

CICERO WOULD HAVE BEEN A BLOGGER

And so, what are we to make of the ocularcentric West, with its eye-biased epistemology, the relationships between its centers of power and its citizenries performed in show-biz fashion, and its communication media ever expanding their influence on daily life? What should the place of visual rhetorical studies be in our intellectual and social lives?

To take on the first question, scholars of rhetoric have come to understand that visual rhetorical studies is not parasitic on traditional rhetoric, rhetoric as conceived of as the arts of oral and written discourse. As I noted above, visuality always has been integral to rhetorical consciousness—Kennedy's (1963) term—since

the inception of written texts treating oral interaction. The Western intellectual heritage marks visual rhetorical studies as a sprawling field composed of examinations of embodiment, performance, visual representations, and now even virtual copresence and coaction. Traditional oral and written rhetorical practice always has had a visual dimension to or aura about it. Delivery (*actio*) was one of the canons of classical rhetoric, and Cicero's *Brutus* contains great accounts of courtroom histrionics that were part of forensic oratory. And as we have seen, visualization was foundational to ancient language use. Cicero circulated speeches that he never delivered just to empower his ideas, much like a blogger today distributes diatribes and calls-to-action.

As the teaching of rhetoric became scientized as part of modernist thought around the turn of the 19th century in Western Europe, the Latin conception of *elocutio* as the clothing of ideas in language was transformed into the sciences of presenting them publicly via voice, countenance, gesture, and body. The elocutionary sciences of chironomia (descriptive gesturing), chirologia (emotional gesturing), proxemics (body positioning), facial display, and bodily action became elements of a general theory of harmony: public communication as requiring the perfect harmonization of soul, mind, and body, of thought, language, and movement, for people to fully understand each other (Gronbeck, 1998). The coming of dramaturgical studies, wherein communication transactions are understood as involving complementary role-play and face work (Goffman, 1959), made interpersonal communication absolutely and unremittingly holistic. "The visual" never stands alone but rather lives in a web of signification (Geertz, 1973, p. 5) that includes the symbolic coding of place, time, situation, and multiple communication media.

This volume, therefore, is extending and making concrete the eddies and currents in the flow of visual rhetorical studies, especially in our time. The editors are pursuing here, admittedly, a foreshortened history of visual rhetoric because recent scholarship has seen the eruption of new thinking, substantively and methodologically, in this subject matter. The field is still stumbling over itself to be freed from rhetorical thinking that conceives of visual matters as "nonoratorical" (Tompkins, 1969), thereby constructing visuality in opposition to oral communicative traditions. But the essays in this volume go a long way toward reminding us that understanding visuality should not be an "add-on" but rather central to how we understand ourselves in the world.

By organizing a series of essays around rhetorical actions—performing and seeing, remembering and memorializing, confronting and resisting, commodifying and consuming, governing and authorizing—the editors have put primary stress on what always must be a focus of rhetorical studies: the range of powers that discourse can leverage in cultural life. This volume stands as testament to the breadth of the ocularcentric subjectivities that engaged even Heraclitus, Diogenes, and Plato and of the range of life experiences and effectivities in the human personal, social, economic, and political spheres that are centered on the visual.

NOTES

1. The "Crowds Project," built by Jeffrey T. Schnapp, director of the new Stanford Humanities Lab, and his colleague Leah Dickerman, is an exhibition of posters and a multimediated book-resource-event of grand proportions, driving toward conclusions that play around the idea of "the people as the cornerstone of the legitimacy of modern nation states, their institutions, and laws" (Schnapp, 2005, p. 13), embodied in various categories of posters, "exploring [their] potentially transformative impact" as "information technologies" (Schnapp, 2005, Acknowledgements, n.p.). Many aspects of the project are available at http://revolutionarytides.stanford.edu/withflash.html.

2. The first political uses of photographed images, however, came from an older technology—the magic lantern slide. Magic lanterns were the first screen technology, as 3.25 × 4.00-inch glass slides were projected via an illuminating box. As the light source went from candles and oils to limelight and then electric lamps, the projected images became larger, clearer, and, with photographs, more realistic. Magic lantern shows were used by political reformers such as Jacob Riis in the late 19th century when giving speeches for social and political change (e.g., Gronbeck, in press; Stange, 1989).

REFERENCES

Arlen, M. J. (1969). *Living-room war.* New York: Viking.

Barnouw, E. (1974). *Documentary: A history of the non-fiction film.* New York: Oxford University Press.

Bleackley, H., & Lofland, J. (1977). *State executions viewed historically and sociologically: The hangmen of England and "the dramaturgy of state executions."* Patterson, NJ: Patterson Smith.

Chadwick, A. (2006). *Internet politics: States, citizens, and new communication technologies.* New York: Oxford University Press.

Cornfield, M. (2004). *Politics moves online: Campaigning and the internet.* New York: Century Foundation Press.

Curtin, M. (1996). *Redeeming the wasteland: Television documentary and the cold war.* New Brunswick, NJ: Rutgers University Press.

DeLuca, K. M., & Peeples, J. (2002). From public sphere to public screen: Democracy, activism, and the "violence" of Seattle. *Critical Studies in Media Communication, 19*(2), 125–151.

Documentary film classics, produced by the United States government [Films]. (1980). Washington, DC: National Archives and Records Service.

Ellis, J. (1989). *The documentary idea: A critical history of English-language documentary film and video.* Englewood Cliffs, NJ: Prentice Hall.

Fern, A. (1985). *Off the wall research into the art of the poster.* Chapel Hill, NC: Hanes Foundation.

Fyfe, W. H. (Trans.). (1960). *Aristotle; "Longinus"; Demetrius.* The Loeb classical library. Cambridge, MA: Harvard University Press.

Geertz, C. (1973). *The interpretation of culture.* New York: Basic Books.

Geertz, C. (1977). Centers, kings and charisma. In J. B. David & T. N. Clarke (Eds.), *Culture and its creators* (pp. 150–171). Chicago: University of Chicago Press.

Goffman, I. J. (1959). *The presentation of self in everyday life.* Garden City, NY: Doubleday.

Gronbeck, B. E. (1998). *Paradigms of speech communication studies: Looking back toward the future.* Carroll C. Arnold lecture, National Communication Association. Boston: Allyn & Bacon.

Gronbeck, B. E. (in press). Jacob Riis and the doubly material rhetorics of his politics. In J. L. Lucaites & B. Biesecker (Eds.), *Rhetoric, materiality, and politics.* New York: Peter Lang.

Harris, W. (n.d.). *Heraclitus: The complete philosophical fragments*. Retrieved November 2, 2006, from http://community-middlebury.edu/~harris/Philosophy/Heraclitus.html.

Jay, M. (1994). *Downcast eyes: The denigration of vision in twentieth-century French thought*. Berkeley: University of California Press.

Jenkins, H., & Thorburn, D. (Eds.). (2003). *Democracy and new media*. Cambridge: MIT Press.

Kennedy, G. A. (1963). *The art of persuasion in Greece*. Princeton, NJ: Princeton University Press.

Keren, M. (2006). *Blogosphere: The new political arena*. Lanham, MD: Lexington Books.

Lacayo, R. (1990). *Eyewitness: 150 years of photojournalism*. New York: Time/Oxmoor House.

MacCann, R. D. (1973). *The people's films: A political history of U.S. government motion pictures*. New York: Hastings House.

McKeon, R. (Ed.). (1941). *The basic works of Aristotle*. Chicago: University of Chicago Press.

Middle English plays: The texts. (n.d.). Retrieved November 2, 2006, from http://www.luminarium.org/medlit/playtexts.htm.

Parenti, M. (1993). *Inventing reality: The politics of the mass media* (2nd ed.). New York: St. Martin's.

Rossi, A. (1969). *Posters*. New York: Hamlyn.

Rosteck, T. (2005). *See it now confronts McCarthyism: Television documentary and the politics of representation*. Tuscaloosa: University of Alabama Press.

Schnapp, J. T. (Ed.). (2005). *Revolutionary tides: The art of the political poster 1914–1989*. Milan, Italy: Skira Editore.

Schudson, M. (1995). *The power of news*. Cambridge, MA: Harvard University Press.

Sisko, J. I. (1997). Space, time, and phantasms in Aristotle's *de memoria* 2, 452B7–225. *Classical Quarterly, 47*(1), 167–175.

Stange, M. (1989). *Symbols of ideal life: Social documentary photography in America 1890–1950*. New York: Cambridge University Press.

Television: Window on the world [Television broadcast]. (1996). Malibu, CA: Center for Media Literacy.

Tompkins, P. (1969). The rhetorical criticism of non-oratorical forms. *Quarterly Journal of Speech, 55*(4), 431–439.

Vance, E. (1979). Roland and the poetics of memory. In J. V. Harrai (Ed., Intro.), *Textual strategy: Perspectives in post-structuralist criticism* (pp. 374–403). Ithaca, NY: Cornell University Press.

Ward, L.W. (1985). *The motion picture goes to war: The U.S. government film effort during World War I*. Ann Arbor, MI: UMI Research Press.

VISUAL RHETORIC IN COMMUNICATION

Continuing Questions and Contemporary Issues

LESTER C. OLSON, CARA A. FINNEGAN, AND DIANE S. HOPE

A news photograph. A memorial. A television documentary. Protesters taking to the streets. A digital video circulated on the World Wide Web. The contemporary U.S. public sphere seems dominated by visual images, visual artifacts, visual performances, and other commands to "look." Yet for every instance of 21st-century visual communication that we encounter—the digital video, the Web page, the newest memorial built in Washington, D.C.—we could also name countless historical examples of visual communication: the cave painting, the humble political print, the 19th-century daguerreotype. Our contemporary period is not unique in being dominated by images; in *every* historical period, images have been an influential presence in the public sphere. Public images often work in ways that are rhetorical; that is, they function to persuade. If we wish fully to understand the role of rhetorical communication in the United States, we

should open ourselves up to the multiple and marvelous ways that rhetoric can be visual.

This book explores the role of visual images, artifacts, and performances of looking in the U.S. public sphere. We call these explorations "visual rhetoric" to acknowledge the powerful role that visuality plays in shaping our public symbolic actions. The essays in this book take up examples that date from the 18th century to contemporary times. They analyze a variety of forms of visual communication, from photographs, prints, television documentary, and film to stamps, advertisements, and tattoos. And they explore the breadth of symbolic actions that constitute rhetorical communication: performing and seeing, remembering and memorializing, confronting and resisting, commodifying and consuming, and governing and authorizing. By embracing a critical perspective that links visuality and rhetoric, locates the study of visual rhetoric within a disciplinary framework of communication, and

---

EDITORS' NOTE: Students and teachers interested in exploring narratives of the development of scholarship in visual rhetoric beyond the one we offer here will wish to consult Olson (2007) as well as Hope (2006), which situates visual rhetoric against the backdrop of visual communication; Prelli (2006), which positions visual rhetoric against the backdrop of rhetorical theories of display; and Gregg (1985), which situates visual rhetoric against the backdrop of studies of symbolic inducement.

explores the role of the visual in the cultural space of the United States, we argue that the study of visual rhetoric is of vital importance for students of communication interested in understanding the dynamics of public persuasion.

We offer an approach to the study of visual rhetoric grounded in three assumptions. First, unlike some who would wish to separate or isolate word from image, we believe that, in practice and in principle, words and images are oftentimes mixed together in rhetorically interesting ways. To study visual rhetoric, then, means not to study images or artifacts in isolation from larger textual or performative contexts in which an audience might encounter them, but rather in precise relation to those contexts that give them shape and meaning. Our second assumption is perhaps best expressed by Bruce Gronbeck, who, in the Foreword to this volume, observes that "visuality always has been integral to rhetorical consciousness." While the traditional approaches to rhetoric that students often encounter in communication classrooms tend to focus on oratorical or written texts, Gronbeck reminds us that the visual per se is by no means absent from even our most ancient traditions of rhetorical pedagogy (see also Kjeldsen, 2003; O'Gorman, 2005). Thus, visual rhetoric should not be viewed as a supplement to more traditional "talk and text" approaches to rhetoric, but rather as integral. Finally, this book assumes and illustrates that scholarship in visual rhetoric is strongest when it combines the conceptual resources of the rhetorical tradition itself—the lexicon of terms that rhetorical scholars have developed over time to help them understand the nature and functions of persuasive communication—with the conceptual resources developed by scholars in other fields. While scholars in other fields may or may not explicitly employ the vocabulary of rhetoric, they often display in their work what Gronbeck calls "rhetorical consciousness," an awareness of the ways that persuasive communication is context dependent, contingent, and often strategically crafted by agents with particular purposes in mind.

Given these grounding assumptions about visual rhetoric, it should be clear that an abiding interest in rhetoric itself lies at the core of this book. For that reason, we have organized the book around what we call "rhetorical actions,"

which we define as those actions that humans perform when they use symbols to persuade or invite cooperation from others. While we offer alternate tables of contents that illustrate how the book might be used to explore examples of various media (such as photography or television) or to study U.S. visual rhetoric chronologically, our primary interest lies in helping students see how visual rhetoric affects the whole range of our activities in public life: how we perform, how we see (both literally and metaphorically), how we remember, how we memorialize, how we confront, how we resist, how we consume, how we commodify, how we govern, and how we authorize. By sorting exemplary analyses of visual rhetoric in public life into this wide variety of rhetorical actions, we present a perspective on visual rhetoric that shows how the visual is foundational to communication.

In the rest of the introduction chapter that follows, we offer a definition of visual rhetoric and highlight some reasons for studying visual rhetoric. Next, we describe the development of scholarship on visual rhetoric, focusing primarily on how it evolved in the field of communication since 1950. We then explore various conceptual resources for the study of visual rhetoric, including those from within the rhetorical tradition as well as from the humanities more generally. Finally, we explain the organizational scheme of the book, which places rhetorical actions in the foreground. Ultimately, *Visual Rhetoric: A Reader in Communication and American Culture* stands as an argument not just for the importance of studying visual rhetoric but for the importance of studying it in a certain way: acknowledging that images and texts are always related in context, accepting that the visual has traditionally been a part of the field of rhetoric, and embracing a range of conceptual resources that may be mobilized to help us understand how we perform, see, remember, memorialize, confront, resist, consume, commodify, authorize, and govern in U.S. culture.

A DEFINITION OF VISUAL RHETORIC

A growing group of scholars in communication and related disciplines (especially English and composition studies) has become interested in the visual dimensions of rhetoric. For example, several recent and important essay collections have contributed to the evolving scholarly framework for what has come to be called "visual rhetoric" (Handa, 2004; Hill & Helmers, 2004; Hope, 2006; Prelli, 2006). Although not every essay in this book features the term, we have chosen *visual rhetoric* from among other possibilities because it seems to best and most directly name our interest in the "contested terrain" of visual studies (Finnegan, 2004, p. 235; see also Olson, 2007). Although rhetoric is commonly assumed to focus on language acts, the essays in this volume document how rhetorical actions frequently comprised both verbal and visual symbols. The scholars represented here understand that visual rhetoric occupies a central place within the interconnected dynamics of civic, cultural, and social discourses. As the essays in this book illustrate vividly, the resources of rhetorical theory and criticism can be used to enrich the study of visual actions. At the same time, the essays also show how the field of rhetorical studies may benefit from more sustained engagement with visual artifacts and actions.

Because *visual rhetoric* links two terms that appear to be distinct and that sometimes are even opposed in academic research, it is useful briefly to uncouple *visual* from *rhetoric* to better understand each term. *Visual* implies the cultural practices of seeing and looking, as well as the artifacts produced in diverse communicative forms and media. Visual media, images, and pictorial messages permeate the culture. We associate them with aesthetic expression and pleasure, emotional response, and both fine art and popular culture. Image makers use visualizations to record, document, investigate, instruct, report, thrill, excite, entertain, sell, and often to persuade. In contrast, by definition, *rhetoric* as practice and theory concerns persuasive symbolic actions primarily. Rhetoric seeks and creates public audiences through symbolic identifications situated in specific historical times, places, and contexts (Burke, 1950/1969). Rhetors and their acts manifest *agency,* which we may define as the ability and competence to act "in a way that will be recognized or heeded by others in one's community" (Campbell, 2005, p. 3).

Reconnected, the two terms in our broad definition of visual rhetoric name those symbolic actions enacted primarily through visual means, made meaningful through culturally derived ways of looking and seeing and endeavoring to influence diverse publics. Visual means may include photography, film, posters, cartoons, bodies, drawings, demonstrations, memorials, emblems, advertisements, illustrations, television, and computer screens—in short, any and all communicative forms and media apprehended primarily through vision. Visual rhetoric invites complex responses from viewers, often spontaneous and immediate, but just as frequently, of lingering and reflective consideration. Audience engagement with visual rhetoric may reinforce, challenge, or restructure commonly held assumptions and values and may guide individual choices and collective actions. Indeed, visual rhetoric helps constitute the ways we know, think, and behave.

Like other forms of rhetoric, visual rhetoric addresses diverse public audiences through processes of production, circulation, apprehension, reception, and consumption. Visual rhetoric seeks and produces communities of viewers, spectators, witnesses, and participants through actions visualized in various forms. In the context of visual rhetoric, rhetorical critics are particularly interested in how images' influence on viewers are "shaped by a variety of contexts: the contexts of photographic conventions, of fashion, of hair styles, of political debate, of social myths, and so on" (Benson & Frandsen, 1976/1982, p. 28). Yet scholars of visual rhetoric know that while visual images, artifacts, and performances have considerable power to shape the world, viewers and spectators are hardly passive; rather, they co-create meaning along with the artifacts themselves. Thus, rhetorical critics typically ask, "What kinds of audiences are constructed by specific rhetorical acts?"

WHY STUDY VISUAL RHETORIC?

Why should students of communication, rhetoric, and American culture care to think specifically about the kinds of symbolic actions we designate here as visual rhetoric? Why might students of rhetoric extend the scope of their studies beyond the speeches and texts that have dominated rhetorical scholarship for decades?

Because rhetorical critique is concerned with how symbolic actions influence and construct "reality" for diverse publics, it is past time that we acknowledge fully the pervasive presence of visual actions in rhetorical studies, research, and curricula. Where early scholarship tended to ask how, if at all, the resources of rhetoric were useful for analyzing, interpreting, and assessing visual media, more recent work has asked how understanding culturally shaped practices of viewing might be useful for reenvisioning the field of rhetoric. We are inclined to think that it is important to hold those two questions in constant relationship to each other. If you believe, as we do, that the most important rhetorical theories of the past tended to engage the most consequential developments of their time, then theorizing visual rhetoric holds considerable promise for the present and future.

As the essays collected here demonstrate, communication technologies including photography, television, film, and digital media are used to produce, reproduce, and circulate visual images in order to influence publics. Instances of visual rhetoric in the form of advertising, civic engagement, political spectacle, and entertainment dominate the cultural landscape. Studying visual rhetoric trains us to discriminate the commercial from the civic, the propagandistic from the democratic, and the sentimental from the memorable, and it may even increase citizen involvement in the processes of government and community.

Another reason for studying visual rhetoric concerns the professional demands of careers in communication. As Thomas Benson points out in the Afterword to this volume, rhetorical critics typically do not guide students in the production of visual rhetoric. Yet many students of rhetoric go on to work in areas that center on the production of images, such as political campaigns, advertising, and Web design. Others will work for private, public, corporate, or not-for-profit institutions that increasingly rely on visual messages. Studying visual rhetoric will broaden the ways that students think about the messages they may be asked to produce in the future. Likewise, knowledge of visual rhetoric is useful for future professionals in government, law, education, and medicine.

Yet further reasons to study visual rhetoric arise out of recent and extraordinary technological developments in digital and Internet technologies.

These rapid, ongoing changes in the ways we communicate have profound ramifications for both the theory and practice of communication. The skills of critical analysis that students develop through the study of visual rhetoric train students to have a more discerning eye when it comes to digital media and the Internet. In addition, the study of visual rhetoric may inform their own personal and professional efforts to use such technologies in their own communication. Furthermore, appreciation and understanding of digital media requires students to know something about how more established media such as photography and film work. Even the language of digital imaging is often patterned on the language of analog media. Users of the popular imaging software PhotoShop, for example, manipulate digital tools that "crop," "dodge," and "burn," all traditional darkroom practices done by hand. Training in visual rhetoric encourages students to see these and other parallels. Thus, the student interested in digital media benefits from the study of visual rhetoric even when that rhetoric is not explicitly tied to digital technology.

Finally, traditional "talk and text" rhetoric has not always been an option for groups marginalized by class, race, gender, sex, or sexuality. With limited access to traditional forms of communication used to govern and authorize civic action, such groups have had to turn instead to forms of social action embodied more visually, such as marches, rallies, street theater, emblems, posters, cartoons, murals, and demonstrations. For groups with limited access to media and power, visual rhetoric has been a traditional and indispensable means of establishing agency and taking civic action. As a result, the study of visual rhetoric is of particular significance for understanding challenges to power hierarchies in the United States.

A Narrative of the Development of Visual Rhetoric Scholarship in Communication

In the United States, the interest in visual rhetoric since 1950 grew out of a range of intellectual, social, political, and technological developments. Among the intellectual roots is Kenneth Burke's important *A Rhetoric of Motives,* initially published in 1950. In that book, Burke defined rhetoric as symbolic action in ways that raised several possibilities for subsequent scholarship across the humanities (Burke, 1950/1969). Burke's broad interest in symbolic action may have inspired scholars to think about the symbolic in ways especially important for understanding *visual* symbols. For example, in communication, Sol Worth and Larry Gross explored what they called "symbolic strategies," inquiring, "How do we distinguish 'natural' from 'symbolic' events, and how do we assign meaning to them?" (Worth & Gross, 1974, p. 27), while Richard B. Gregg employed the expression "symbolic inducement," a term likewise influenced by Burke (Gregg, 1984, 1985).

Attempting to broaden rhetoric's traditional focus on speeches and texts, other scholars defined an area of rhetoric by exploring what it was not: oratory or verbal communication. For example, Phillip K. Tompkins (1969) wrote a book review essay in which he explored the "rhetorical criticism of non-oratorical forms" (p. 431), while Haig A. Bosmajian (1971) published the influential *The Rhetoric of Nonverbal Communication,* a collection of readings that explored "the turn to ritual, ceremony, symbols, demonstrations; the dependence upon communication, which takes us beyond words" (p. vi).

By the early 1970s, the field of rhetoric as a whole was rethinking its approach to theory and criticism, and this rethinking had important implications for the study of visual rhetoric. A collaborative statement authored by scholars who attended two meetings sponsored by the Speech (now National) Communication Association set up priorities that led to further advances in visual rhetoric. Titled "Report of the Committee on the Advancement and Refinement of Rhetorical Criticism" and commonly known as the "Wingspread" report, the document was later published in a book called *The Prospect of Rhetoric* (Bitzer & Black, 1971). The report argued that "rhetorical criticism must broaden its scope to examine the full range of rhetorical transactions; that is, informal conversations, group settings, public settings, mass media messages, picketing, sloganeering, chanting, singing, marching, gesturing, ritual, institutional and cultural symbols, cross cultural transactions, and so forth" (Sloan et al., 1971, p. 225).

As Thomas W. Benson, a participant in the project, asserts in the Afterword to this book, the report was important because it "stimulated new ways of thinking about 'traditional' rhetoric." This collective statement, along with earlier intellectual contributions, set the academic scene for subsequent work by communication scholars on what today is regularly referred to as visual rhetoric.

Additional roots nourishing the development of visual rhetoric scholarship were political and social. One of the reasons rhetorical scholars in 1971 were interested in expanding their notion of rhetoric was because they were increasingly aware of the complexities of the world around them. Scholars noted the tactics of sit-ins, marches, and rallies of civil rights activists and their adoption by anti-Vietnam War protesters, radical feminists, and activists in the overarching "counterculture" of the 1960s. Observing these rhetorical dynamics, they began to recognize that rhetorical theory offered important analytical tools for approaching the challenges to perceived injustice where they increasingly occurred—in the street—and where they were seen by most of the public—on television. Furthermore, they argued that omission of "nonoratorical" or "nonverbal" forms of rhetorical action from study constrained rhetorical studies and threatened it with irrelevance to the major issues of the day.

The ongoing development of highly visual media technologies with profound ramifications for communication also deepened academic interest in visual rhetoric. Both older media such as photography, film, and television and newer media such as the World Wide Web and digital technology transformed the ways in which speeches and other messages were recorded and conveyed to their audiences. These same technologies made visual evidence (both historical and contemporary) increasingly available to scholars for study. Perhaps implicitly inspired by Marshall McLuhan's (1964) famous claim that "the medium is the message," rhetorical scholars began to focus on the study of a particular visual medium. By the mid-to-late 1970s, for example, Bruce Gronbeck was concentrating on what he has variously called "celluloid rhetoric" or "electronic rhetoric," nomenclature that, at once, concentrates both on a specific range of media and a particular historical period (Gronbeck, 1978). In that same work, Gronbeck also explored what he called "genres of documentary," especially featuring programming on television and film (Gronbeck, 1978). Thomas W. Benson's early work on "the rhetoric of film" likewise featured a specific medium (Benson, 1974, 1980), as did Kathleen J. Turner's (1977) rhetorical perspective on comics. Such approaches according to medium remain relevant today. The rise of digital media and the Internet has generated extraordinary interest among scholars and produced a substantive and quickly changing literature in multiple disciplines (e.g., Cartwright, 1995; Chun, 2005; Handa, 2004; Kowal, 2002; Manovich, 2001; Mirzoeff, 2002; Nakamura, 2007; Sturken & Cartwright, 2001; Warnick, 2002). In addition, aspects of visual rhetoric have also been characterized by other terms such as the *rhetoric of material culture* (Dickinson, Ott, & Aoki, 2006; Olson, 1991; Rohan, 2004), *rhetoric of cultural performance* (Katriel, 1987; Pezzullo, 2003, 2007), and *rhetoric of popular culture,* a concept exemplified by Barry Brummett's (1991) important book, *Rhetorical Dimensions of Popular Culture.*

Some early scholarship emphasized visual rhetoric produced by individual agents. This work often focused on a specific artist's oeuvre—for example, Diego Rivera's murals (R. L. Scott, 1977); Judy Chicago's visual art installation, "The Dinner Party" (Foss, 1988); and Frederick Wiseman's documentary films (Anderson & Benson, 1991; Benson, 1980; Benson & Anderson, 1989/2002). This approach has also continued with more recent studies of individual figures, such as Lester Olson's work on images produced by Benjamin Franklin (Olson, 1987, 2004).

An important edited collection of work appeared in 1984 with Martin J. Medhurst and Thomas W. Benson's *Rhetorical Dimensions in Media: A Critical Casebook* (1984/1991), which firmly established that varieties of media, including television, film, graphic arts, magazines, and, later, advertising and architecture (included in a 1996 supplement to the second edition), were open to rhetorical analysis. The reader positioned case studies on individual media against "classic" essays in rhetorical theory in order to demonstrate how rhetorical interpretation could be used to analyze media. The editors' introductory review of the relationship between "rhetoric" and "poetic" (Medhurst & Benson, 1984, pp. ix–xxiii) and the substantive

bibliography of germane books and essays are important resources for anyone wishing to become familiar with scholarship on visual rhetoric before the mid-1980s (Medhurst & Benson, 1984, pp. 365–407).

One of the ambivalent results of these intellectual, political, social, and technological influences on the development of visual rhetoric scholarship was a tendency to focus on the relatively recent past. While during this period traditional rhetorical scholarship embraced studies of both the past and the present, early visual rhetoric studies offered few explorations of visual rhetoric before the 20th century. Such a focus may have been shaped by the 1971 report itself; although it argued that historical scholarship should not be denigrated, the report also declared that rhetoric scholarship should show "a deep concern for the pressing problems of our time" (Sloan et al., 1971, p. 225). Nevertheless, important exceptions to visual rhetoric's presentism did emerge during this time, most notably Lester Olson's (1983) work on Norman Rockwell's paintings and his extensive studies of the visual and material culture of the colonial era (Olson, 1987, 1990, 1991, 2004), as well as Medhurst and Benson's (1981) study of the New Deal–era documentary film, *The City.* As several essays in this volume illustrate (including those of Olson, Finnegan, Lancioni, and Twigg), visual rhetoric scholarship today increasingly features artifacts of the more distant past as well as those of the present.

In summary, a number of intellectual, social, political, and technological forces influenced the rise of visual rhetoric studies within the discipline of communication. At the same time that the study of rhetoric in departments of communication was becoming more hospitable to visual rhetoric, parallel transformations in the humanities increasingly favored attention to the visual as well. The following section of the chapter explores some of these.

VISUAL RHETORIC'S RELATIONSHIP TO VISUAL STUDIES IN THE HUMANITIES

The methods of visually oriented disciplines such as art history have long appealed to rhetoric scholars interested in looking outside of the field for intellectual resources for the study of visual rhetoric. For example, some scholars of visual rhetoric have turned to the important work of Erwin Panofsky, who in writings such as *Studies in Iconology* (1939) and *Meaning in the Visual Arts* (1955) defined his art-historical approach as "iconology," a method that involved study of the form of the art work, incorporation of one's cultural knowledge about the content or subject matter of the work, and a reconstruction of the cultural history in which the work participated. Such an approach resonated for rhetoric scholars in the early 1980s, who employed terms for visual rhetoric drawn largely from art history and designated specific art-historical techniques in the analysis of visual texts (e.g., Medhurst, 1982; Olson, 1991).

Apart from art history, however, the embrace of visuality in the humanities would happen more gradually. The first step was a transformation that occurred in the mid-20th century and is commonly referred to as "the linguistic turn." While scholars of rhetoric have always recognized that language is central to the human experience, in the humanities more generally, this recognition did not fully emerge until well into the 20th century. Beginning in the mid-20th century (with important antecedents before), the "linguistic turn" in philosophy and social theory (advanced by philosophers such as Ludwig Wittgenstein and Richard Rorty) posited language as constitutive of reality rather than merely descriptive of it. Many rhetorical scholars enthusiastically embraced the linguistic turn in the 1970s and 1980s because, in part, it validated what they already believed: that language is contingent and constitutive—that is, *rhetorical*— rather than grounded in objective "reality" or "truth." Indeed, rhetorical scholar Dilip Gaonkar has observed that strands of an "implicit rhetorical turn" may be found in the work of many important philosophers of the late 20th century, such as Jürgen Habermas, Michel Foucault, Thomas Kuhn, and Jacques Lacan (Gaonkar, 1999, p. 203). Gaonkar (1999) suggested that this work was "groping for a vocabulary that could adequately characterize the tropological and suasory aspects of the discursive practices that remain occluded from disciplinary consciousness" (p. 203)—a vocabulary that rhetoric offers. Gaonkar thus termed this rhetorical turn "implicit" because its authors

show little or no awareness of rhetorical theory, though they do possess what he terms a "rhetorical consciousness" that embraces the contingency of language (p. 210).

A similar dialectic of awareness/unawareness exists with regard to rhetoric in the context of a subsequent "turn" in the humanities, what W. J. T. Mitchell (1994) termed the "pictorial turn." During the last third of the 20th century, a variety of social theorists, art historians, and visual studies scholars offered up a range of concepts that scholars now see as central to the study of visuality and the elaboration of a "pictorial turn." Mitchell argues that the pictorial turn is similar to the earlier linguistic turn in that it, too, marks a transformation in the humanities. What is different is that the pictorial turn is "postlinguistic," evolving not on the basis of language but of visuality. For Mitchell, the pictorial turn is marked by both a "rediscovery of the picture as a complex interplay between visuality, apparatus, institutions, discourse, bodies, and figurality" and a "realization that *spectatorship* (the look, the gaze, the glance, the practices of observation, surveillance, and visual pleasure) may be as deep a problem as various forms of *reading* (decipherment, decoding, interpretation, etc.)" (p. 16). As Mitchell frames it, the seeds of the pictorial turn were planted and cultivated in the humanities through the work of a variety of thinkers (among them semiotician Charles S. Peirce, art historian Nelson Goodman, philosopher Jacques Derrida, and a group of critical social theorists called the Frankfurt School) who did "not begin with the assumption that language is paradigmatic for meaning" (p. 12). These and other scholars encouraged us to reconsider the presumed dominance of language, reminding us that the visual may not always be reducible to language.

In positing the pictorial turn, then, Mitchell was attempting to pull together a number of strands of scholarship that were woven through philosophy, social theory, and the visual arts in the late 20th century. For example, the concept of "visuality" that Mitchell invokes in the above quotation emerged in the 1980s as an important term for historians of art interested in going beyond studies of artists and art objects to explore the ways in which vision itself is historically and socially constructed. Scholars such as Hal Foster, Jonathan Crary (1988, 1990), and

Martin Jay (1988, 1993) emphasized in their scholarship that vision is not merely natural or physical but social and situated. As Foster (1988) put it, visuality conceives of "sight as a social fact," not just a "physical operation" (p. ix). That is, they argued that we "see" in particular ways because we grow up in cultures that teach us to see in those ways.

In scholarship related to the pictorial turn, we can find traces of the earlier dialectic of awareness/unawareness of rhetoric noted earlier. What Mitchell marked as key aspects of the pictorial turn are precisely its *rhetorical* dimensions, though he did not name them as such. Mitchell wanted us to understand that pictures, like language, are forms of communication that are created by a variety of forces, institutions, and historical circumstances; this is what he means when he urges us to "rediscover" the picture as an "interplay" of forces. He also wanted us to recognize that audiences' experiences of pictures are conditioned by the ways that they are taught to see and consume images; this is what he means by encouraging us to recognize the "problem" of spectatorship. Like the theorists of the "implicit rhetorical turn" mentioned above, for the most part, Mitchell and other thinkers tied to the pictorial turn do not employ the lexicon of rhetoric in their explorations of visuality. What they do offer, however, is a "rhetorical consciousness" in precisely the sense that Gaonkar (1999) used the term: Mitchell and other theorists and thinkers of the visual implicitly recognize the rhetorical dimensions of our experience of vision and images and encourage us to explore the multiple ways that pictures and audiences interact.

In sum, it is important to remember that the development of visual rhetoric in the discipline of communication has been characterized by the use of concepts drawn *both* from traditional rhetoric and the humanities more generally. In the following section, we explore the results of the development of visual rhetoric by considering briefly those conceptual resources available to students of visual rhetoric.

Conceptual Resources for the Study of Visual Rhetoric

The essays collected together in this book draw on a range of conceptual resources as they examine the symbolic actions of visual rhetoric. Some scholars rely primarily on a conceptual framework drawn from rhetorical studies itself, while others explore instances of visual rhetoric using concepts derived primarily from other disciplinary fields. Most of the studies of visual rhetoric featured in this volume, however, combine attention to the conceptual resources of rhetoric with recognition of the broader resources available in the humanities more broadly.

Scholars of visual rhetoric draw on a range of conceptual resources from the rhetorical tradition, which provides a rich vocabulary of terms for analyzing and understanding symbolic acts of persuasion in context. Visual rhetoric scholars turn to concepts related to argumentation as they explore symbolic actions as *visual argument* (e.g., Balter-Reitz & Stewart, 2006; Birdsell & Groarke, 1996; Jensen, 2006; Lake & Pickering, 1998; LaWare, 1998; Palczewski, 2002, 2005; Shelley, 1996). Visual rhetoric scholars rely on concepts tied to the ancient rhetorical tradition, such as the *enthymeme* (e.g., Finnegan, 2001, 2005) or the notion of *topoi* (e.g., Olson, 1987). They explore the visual aspects of *common rhetorical devices* such as depiction (e.g., Osborn, 1986), metaphor (e.g., Danto, 1981; Kaplan, 1990), and other rhetorical figures (e.g., B. Scott, 2004; Tom & Eves, 1999; Van Mulken, 2003; Willerton, 2005). Not surprisingly given his powerful influence on studies of symbolic action, visual rhetoric scholars find several of Kenneth Burke's concepts useful, including his discussions of the *tragic and comic frame* (e.g., Demo, 2000), the *psychology of form* (e.g., Foss, 1986), *identification* (e.g., Olson, 1983), and *representative anecdote* (e.g., Clark, 2004), to name just a few. They also turn to more recently theorized concepts in rhetorical studies, such as the *ideograph,* first introduced by Michael McGee (e.g., Cloud, 2004; Edwards & Winkler, 1997; Palczewski, 2005); the *image event* (Delicath & DeLuca, 2003; DeLuca & Peeples, 2002); *rhetorical circulation* (Finnegan, 2003; Olson, 2004); and the *iconic photograph* (Hariman & Lucaites, 2001, 2002, 2003, 2007).

As these and the numerous other examples we could include illustrate, visual rhetoric scholarship has been enriched and extended by the conceptual resources of the rhetorical tradition itself. Yet scholarship in visual rhetoric has also been and continues to be productively animated by conceptual resources found in the humanities more generally. As we noted above, while this realm of scholarship may not invoke the rhetorical tradition explicitly, it frequently is "rhetorically conscious"; that is, it recognizes that visual images, artifacts, and performances are always situated in complex circumstances of viewing, interpreting, and consuming. Visual rhetoric scholarship frequently draws on the work of important transdisciplinary thinkers who explored the broad implications of our cultural experiences in terms that resonate with an interest in visual culture (e.g., Barthes, 1977, 1981; Benjamin, 1968, 1985; Berger, 1972; Deleuze, 1994; Peirce, 1992, 1998; Sontag, 1977). Visual rhetoric scholars also explore and use terms developed by theorists interested in understanding the complex dynamics of the act of viewing itself. Examples of attention to the act of viewing include Laura Mulvey's notion of *the gaze* (Mulvey, 1989), Michel Foucault's discussions of *surveillance* and *panopticism* (Foucault, 1977) and *heterotopia* (Foucault, 1986), and Jacques Lacan's psychoanalytic discussion of the *mirror stage* (Lacan, 2006). Visual rhetoric scholars sometimes turn to the work of thinkers who theorize the politics of contemporary capitalist media culture, such as Guy Debord's theory of *spectacle* (Debord, 1995) and the media theories of Gilles Deleuze and Félix Guattari (e.g., Deleuze & Guattari, 1987). Also frequent is attention to thinkers who explore the social and political power of a culture's "meta-narratives" of seeing, such as Christian Metz's idea of the *scopic regime* (Metz, 1982). Finally, scholars interested in the dynamics of visual culture incorporate important recent work on digital culture such as Lev Manovich's discussions of *new media* (Manovich, 2001). While it is difficult to chronicle here the full range of conceptual resources available in the interdisciplinary realm of visual studies, several helpful anthologies exist to help scholars, students, and teachers grasp some of the key thinkers and concepts in this vast and continually changing area of research (e.g., Evans & Hall, 1999; Handa, 2004; Mirzoeff, 2002; Sturken & Cartwright, 2001).

Our attempt to review the concepts and theories potentially relevant to visual rhetoric studies is only cursory here, but we hope that this brief discussion has demonstrated the diversity of conceptual resources available to rhetorical critics doing work in visual rhetoric. Throughout the essays collected in this book, rhetorical critics routinely turn to the ideas and concepts explored by visual studies scholars from outside of the discipline of communication as they attempt to understand particular cases of visual rhetoric. Indeed, one of the things that makes the work featured in this book so exciting is that the authors creatively combine concepts from the rhetorical tradition with those from other areas of the humanities in ways that offer new and exciting potential for reenvisioning rhetoric for our own time.

KEY RHETORICAL ACTIONS FEATURED IN THIS BOOK

While individual instances of rhetorical practice might differ to the extent that they are more or less textual, oratorical, or visual, what is common to all rhetorical acts is that they mobilize symbols to influence diverse publics. Each of the five sections of this volume presents essays that exhibit a sustained focus on those symbolic actions central to public and private life. Performing and seeing, remembering and memorializing, confronting and resisting, commodifying and consuming, governing and authorizing—these pairs of actions name many of the ways that visual rhetoric invites American audiences to understand and negotiate civic, social, and cultural life. With this broad commitment to rhetorical action in mind, and these five pairs of actions in particular, we have grouped 20 carefully chosen essays that reveal persistent and interconnected ways that people, institutions, and audiences seek to influence and create lines of identification with others. We expect that the combinations and juxtapositions of the essays presented here will result in open-ended, generative conversations and reflections about both the featured examples of visual rhetoric and the five pairs of rhetorical actions themselves.

In order to encourage open-ended exploration of the rhetorical actions, each section is introduced with a single image chosen to in some way "speak" to the rhetorical actions in that section. We offer little commentary and no analysis of these five examples of visual rhetoric because we want instead to encourage scholars, students, and teachers to engage the images directly: to contemplate their potential meanings in the context of their time and circumstance, to think about the various ways they exemplify each rhetorical action, to ferret out those rhetorical concepts pertinent to understanding the image as an attempt to persuade, and to discover the public audiences for each act. We encourage you to appreciate the depth and variety of visual rhetoric through these examples.

Section I, "Performing and Seeing," opens with a graphic design produced in 1976 by Lanny Sommese for a cover of *Communication Quarterly,* an academic journal of communication studies, and features case studies by Reginald Twigg, Nathan Stormer, Cara A. Finnegan, and Charles E. Morris III and John M. Sloop. Each of the essays in the section focuses on rhetorical actions that invite audiences to perform and to see in certain ways (and not others). These authors' studies of visual practices such as observing, examining, viewing, and displaying highlight the ways that we use ritual performance to communicate things such as culture, race, sex, gender, class, sexuality, and social norms. The essays' attention to the rhetorical action of "seeing" underscores how even routine performances of everyday life may depend on visual inferences.

Section II, "Remembering and Memorializing," presents a few of the many ways that Americans have visualized public memories of the past in order to define their relationships to the present. A 1943 image of the Lincoln Memorial produced by a photographer working for a U.S. government agency opens the section, which includes essays by Judith Lancioni, Janis L. Edwards and Carol K. Winkler, Carole Blair and Neil Michel, Barbara Biesecker, and Robert Hariman and John Louis Lucaites. Each essay illustrates how acts of remembering and memorializing invite audiences to remember certain historical events and persons (and forget others), to remember them in specific ways, and to memorialize them in particular forms.

Section III, "Confronting and Resisting," opens with a political cartoon titled "Pittsburgh, 1916," rendered by Robert Minor and initially published in 1916 in the American socialist magazine *The Masses.* The section includes essays by Dan Brouwer, Margaret R. LaWare,

Anne Teresa Demo, and Christine Harold and Kevin Michael DeLuca. These essays examine moments in which those resisting domination or confronting oppression have turned to visual rhetoric as a source for power. The essays show how agents, especially marginalized ones, may use the rhetorical actions of confronting and resisting to challenge established norms and institutions and refute hierarchies of power and privilege.

Section IV, "Commodifying and Consuming," emphasizes ways that visual rhetoric is deeply embedded in the ways we buy, sell, and use products, ideas, beliefs, and social relationships. The section opens with an image of a Pennsylvania Railroad poster produced by an unknown artist, probably in the late 1930s, and includes essays by Ronald E. Shields, Ekaterina V. Haskins, and Diane S. Hope. The essays collectively illustrate how rhetorical actions quite commonly invite publics to commodify experiences of all kinds. They indicate that instances of "commodifying and consuming" are often also nostalgic rhetorics of remembering and memorializing, thus opening a productive discussion of the relationships among commodification, nostalgia, memory, and consumption practices.

Section V, "Governing and Authorizing," commences with an image of an oil painting, "The Opposition," produced by William Gropper in 1942 and includes essays by Lester C. Olson, Keith V. Erickson, Shawn J. Parry-Giles, and Dana L. Cloud. In each of their essays, the authors examine the relationship of visuality to the rhetoric of high-profile institutions and officials to emphasize how visual rhetoric informs the symbolic activities of warranting, justifying, or sanctioning leaders' practices.

Visual rhetoric research is robust and diverse in focus. The essays selected for this book are representative of the broad range of topics that have been featured in visual rhetoric scholarship in the communication discipline in recent years. In particular, studies of marginalized communities, human bodies, the environment, science and technology, war, memorials and museums, photojournalism, and institutional and corporate power figure prominently. Readers will notice that these topics emerge again and again in the essays we feature here as well as in the suggestions for further reading at the end of each section. Notice also that these topics cut provocatively across the whole range of rhetorical actions we feature in the book. For example, questions of science and technology appear in the "performing and seeing" section (e.g., Stormer's discussion of reproductive technology and film) and also in the "commodifying and consuming" section (e.g., Shields's essay on Apple Computer's advertising strategies and Hope's discussion of the Kodak Colorama installations). War emerges as a recurring topic in the "commodifying and consuming" section (e.g., Hope's analysis of postwar affluence in the Kodak Colorama), the "remembering and memorializing" section (e.g., Hariman and Lucaites's analysis of a Vietnam War photograph and Biesecker's study of World War II memory), and the "governing and authorizing" section (e.g., Cloud's essay on photographs from Afghanistan). And nearly all of the sections feature essays that deal in some way with the experiences of marginalized communities. We encourage scholars, teachers, and students to notice such connections and explore ways that these and other topics recur across the rhetorical actions we feature. In some cases, we offer guidance in the form of suggested pairings of essays from one section with essays from another. As our suggested pairs of readings indicate, the essays relate to each other in multiple ways and implicitly promise vigorous future directions for studies in visual rhetoric.

In summary, the study of visual rhetoric is an intellectual movement both broad and deep in that it spans multiple disciplines and engages the most influential communication technologies. The essays collected in this volume are organized around the perspective that, above all, rhetoric is symbolic action. We hope the "conversations" between the rhetorical critics represented here inspire you to join their discussion in your own study of visual rhetoric.

REFERENCES

Anderson, C. A., & Benson, T. W. (1991). *Documentary dilemmas: Frederick Wiseman's "Titicut Follies."* Carbondale: Southern Illinois University Press.

Balter-Reitz, S. J., & Stewart, K. A. (2006). Looking for Matthew Shepard: A study in visual argument field. In D. S. Hope (Ed.), *Visual communication: Perception, rhetoric, and technology* (pp. 111–126). Cresskill, NJ: Hampton Press/RIT Cary Graphic Arts Press.

Barthes, R. (1977). *Image—music—text.* New York: Hill & Wang.

Barthes, R. (1981). *Camera lucida: Reflections on photography* (R. Howard, Trans.). New York: Hill & Wang.

Benjamin, W. (1968). The work of art in the age of mechanical reproduction. In *Illuminations: Essays and reflections* (E. Jephcott, Trans.) (pp. 217–251). New York: Schocken.

Benjamin, W. (1985). A small history of photography. In *One Way Street and other writings* (E. Jephcott & K. Shorter, Trans.) (pp. 240–257). London: Verso.

Benson, T. W. (1974). Joe: An essay in the rhetorical criticism of film. *Journal of Popular Culture, 8*(3), 608–618.

Benson, T. W. (1980). The rhetorical structure of Frederick Wiseman's *High School. Communication Monographs, 47*(4), 233–261.

Benson, T. W., & Anderson, C. (2002). *Reality fictions: The films of Frederick Wiseman.* Carbondale: Southern Illinois University Press. (Original work published 1989)

Benson, T. W., & Frandsen, K. D. (1982). *An orientation to nonverbal communication.* Palo Alto, CA: Science Research Associates. (Original work published 1976)

Berger, J. (1972). *Ways of seeing.* London: BBC.

Birdsell, D. S., & Groarke, L. (Eds.). (1996). Toward a theory of visual argument [Special issue]. *Argumentation and Advocacy, 33*(1–2), 1–39, 56–80.

Bitzer, L. F., & Black, E. (Eds.). (1971). *The prospect of rhetoric: Report of the National Developmental Project, sponsored by Speech Communication Association* (pp. 220–227). Englewood Cliffs, NJ: Prentice Hall.

Bosmajian, H. (1971). *The rhetoric of nonverbal communication.* Glenview, IL: Scott, Foreman.

Brummett, B. (1991). *Rhetorical dimensions of popular culture.* Tuscaloosa: University of Alabama Press.

Burke, K. (1969). *A rhetoric of motives.* Berkeley: University of California Press. (Original work published 1950)

Campbell, K. K. (2005). Agency: Promiscuous and protean. *Communication and Critical/Cultural Studies, 2*(1), 1–19.

Cartwright, L. (1995). *Screening the body: Tracing medicine's visual culture.* Minneapolis: University of Minnesota Press.

Chun, W. (2005). *Control and freedom: Power and paranoia in the age of fiber optics.* Cambridge: MIT Press.

Clark, G. (2004). *Rhetorical landscapes in America: Variations on a theme from Kenneth Burke.* Columbia: University of South Carolina Press.

Cloud, D. L. (2004). "To veil the threat of terror": Afghan women and the <clash of civilizations> in the imagery of the U.S. war on terrorism. *Quarterly Journal of Speech, 90*(3), 285–306.

Crary, J. (1988). Modernizing vision. In H. Foster (Ed.), *Vision and visuality* (pp. 29–49). New York: New Press.

Crary, J. (1990). *Techniques of the observer: On vision and modernity in the nineteenth century.* Cambridge: MIT Press.

Danto, A. C. (1981). *The transfiguration of the commonplace.* Cambridge, MA: Harvard University Press.

Debord, G. (1995). *The society of the spectacle.* New York: Zone Books.

Deleuze, G. (1994). *Difference and repetition* (P. Patton, Trans.). New York: Columbia University Press.

Deleuze, G., & Guattari, F. (1987). *A thousand plateaus: Capitalism and schizophrenia* (B. Massumi, Trans.). Minneapolis: University of Minnesota Press.

Delicath, J. W., & DeLuca, K. M. (2003). Image events, the public sphere and argumentative practice: The case of radical environmental groups. *Argumentation, 17,* 315–333.

DeLuca, K. M., & Peeples, J. (2002). From public sphere to public screen: Democracy, activism, and the "violence" of Seattle. *Critical Studies in Media Communication, 19*(2), 125–151.

Demo, A. T. (2000). The Guerrilla Girls' comic politics of subversion. *Women's Studies in Communication, 23*(2), 133–157.

Dickinson, G., Ott, B. L., & Aoki, E. (2006). Spaces of remembering and forgetting: The reverent eye/I at the Plains Indian Museum. *Communication and Critical/Cultural Studies, 3*(1), 27–47.

Edwards, J. L., & Winkler, C. K. (1997). Representative form and the visual ideograph: The Iwo Jima image in editorial cartoons. *Quarterly Journal of Speech, 83*(3), 289–310.

Evans, J., & Hall, S. (1999). *Visual culture: The reader.* Thousand Oaks, CA: Sage.

Finnegan, C. A. (2001). The naturalistic enthymeme and visual argument: Photographic representation in the "skull controversy." *Argumentation and Advocacy, 37*(3), 133–150.

Finnegan, C. A. (2003). *Picturing poverty: Print culture and FSA photographs.* Washington, DC: Smithsonian Books.

Finnegan, C. A. (2004). Review essay: Visual studies and visual rhetoric. *Quarterly Journal of Speech, 90*(2), 234–247.

Finnegan, C. A. (2005). Recognizing Lincoln: Image vernaculars in nineteenth-century visual culture. *Rhetoric & Public Affairs, 8*(1), 31–57.

Foss, S. K. (1986). Ambiguity as persuasion: The Vietnam Veterans Memorial. *Communication Quarterly, 34*(3), 326–340.

Foss, S. K. (1988). Judy Chicago's *The Dinner Party:* Empowering women's voice in visual art. In B. Bate & A. Taylor (Eds.), *Women communicating: Studies of women's talk* (pp. 9–26). Norwood, NJ: Ablex.

Foster, H. (Ed.). (1988). *Vision and visuality.* New York: New Press.

Foucault, M. (1977). *Discipline and punish: The birth of the prison.* New York: Vintage.

Foucault, M. (1986). Of other spaces. *Diacritics, 16*(1), 22–27.

Gaonkar, D. P. (1999). Rhetoric and its double: Reflections on the rhetorical turn in the human sciences. In J. L. Lucaites, C. M. Condit, & S. Caudill (Eds.), *Contemporary rhetorical theory: A reader* (pp. 194–212). New York: Guilford.

Gregg, R. B. (1984). *Symbolic inducement and knowing: A study in the foundations of rhetoric.* Columbia: University of South Carolina Press.

Gregg, R. B. (1985). The criticism of symbolic inducement: A critical-theoretical connection. In T. W. Benson (Ed.), *Speech communication in the twentieth century* (pp. 41–62, 380–383). Carbondale: Southern Illinois University Press.

Gronbeck, B. E. (1978). Celluloid rhetoric: On genres of documentary. In K. K. Campbell & K. H. Jamieson (Eds.), *Form and genre: Shaping rhetorical action* (pp. 139–161). Falls Church, VA: Speech Communication Association.

Handa, C. (Ed.). (2004). *Visual rhetoric in a digital world: A critical sourcebook.* New York: Bedford–St. Martin's.

Hariman, R., & Lucaites, J. L. (2001). Dissent and emotional management in a liberal-democratic society: The Kent State iconic photograph. *Rhetoric Society Quarterly, 31*(3), 5–31.

Hariman, R., & Lucaites, J. L. (2002). Performing civic identity: The iconic photograph of the flag raising on Iwo Jima. *Quarterly Journal of Speech, 88,* 363–392.

Hariman, R., & Lucaites, J. L. (2003). Public identity and collective memory in U.S. iconic photography: The image of "accidental napalm." *Critical Studies in Media Communication, 20*(1), 35–66.

Hariman, R., & Lucaites, J. L. (2007). *No caption needed: Iconic photographs, public culture, and liberal democracy.* Chicago: University of Chicago Press.

Hill, C. A., & Helmers, M. (Eds.). (2004). *Defining visual rhetorics.* Mahwah, NJ: Lawrence Erlbaum.

Hope, D. S. (Ed.). (2006). Introduction: Identity and visual communication. In D. S. Hope (Ed.), *Visual communication: Perception, rhetoric and technology: Papers from the William A. Kern Conferences in visual communication* (pp. 1–27). Cresskill, NJ: Hampton Press/Rochester Institute of Technology Cary Graphic Arts Press.

Jay, M. (1988). Scopic regimes of modernity. In H. Foster (Ed.), *Vision and visuality* (pp. 3–27). New York: New Press.

Jay, M. (1993). *Downcast eyes: The denigration of vision in twentieth century French thought.* Berkeley: University of California Press.

Jensen, R. E. (2006). The eating-disordered lifestyle: Imagetexts and the performance of similitude. *Argumentation and Advocacy, 42*(1), 1–18.

Kaplan, S. J. (1990). Visual metaphors in the representation of communication technology. *Critical Studies in Mass Communication, 7*(1), 37–47.

Katriel, T. (1987). Rhetoric in flames: Fire inscriptions in Israeli youth movement ceremonials. *Quarterly Journal of Speech, 73*(4), 444–459.

Kjeldsen, J. E. (2003). Talking to the eye: Visuality in ancient rhetoric. *Word and Image, 19*(3), 133–137.

Kowal, D. M. (2002). Digitizing and globalizing indigenous voices: The Zapatista movement. In G. Elmer (Ed.), *Critical perspectives on the Internet* (pp. 105–126). Lanham, MD: Rowman & Littlefield.

Lacan, J. (2006). *Écrits: The first complete edition in English* (B. Fink, H. Fink, & R. Grigg, Trans.). New York: W. W. Norton.

Lake, R. A., & Pickering, B. A. (1998). Argumentation, the visual, and the possibility of refutation: An exploration. *Argumentation, 12*(1), 79–93.

LaWare, M. R. (1998). Encountering visions of Aztlán: Arguments for ethic pride, community activism, and cultural revitalization in Chicano murals. *Argumentation and Advocacy, 34*(3), 140–153.

Manovich, L. (2001). *The language of new media.* Cambridge: MIT Press.

McLuhan, M. (1964). *Understanding media: The extensions of man.* New York: Routledge and Kegan Paul.

Medhurst, M. J. (1982). *Hiroshima, mon amour:* From iconography to rhetoric. *Quarterly Journal of Speech, 68*(4), 345–370.

Medhurst, M. J., & Benson, T. W. (1981). *The City:* The rhetoric of rhythm. *Communication Monographs, 48*(1), 54–63.

Medhurst, M. J., & Benson, T. W. (1991). *Rhetorical dimensions in media: A critical casebook.* Dubuque, IA: Kendall/Hunt. (Original work published 1984)

Metz, C. (1982). *The imaginary signifier: Psychoanalysis and the cinema.* Bloomington: Indiana University Press.

Mirzoeff, N. (2002). *The visual culture reader* (2nd ed.). London: Routledge.

Mitchell, W. J. T. (1994). The pictorial turn. In *Picture theory: Essays in verbal and visual representation* (pp. 11–34). Chicago: University of Chicago Press.

Mulvey, L. (1989). *Visual and other pleasures.* Bloomington: Indiana University Press.

Nakamura, L. (2007). *Digitizing race: Visual cultures of the Internet.* Minneapolis: University of Minnesota Press.

O'Gorman, N. (2005). Aristotle's phantasia in the *Rhetoric*: Lexis, appearance, and the epideictic function of discourse. *Philosophy and Rhetoric, 38*(1), 16–40.

Olson, L. C. (1983). Portraits in praise of a people: A rhetorical analysis of Norman Rockwell's icons in Franklin D. Roosevelt's "Four Freedoms" campaign. *Quarterly Journal of Speech, 69*(1), 15–24.

Olson, L. C. (1987). Benjamin Franklin's pictorial representations of the British colonies in America: A study in rhetorical iconology. *Quarterly Journal of Speech, 73*(1), 18–42.

Olson, L. C. (1990). Benjamin Franklin's commemorative medal, *Libertas Americana:* A study in rhetorical iconology. *Quarterly Journal of Speech, 76*(1), 23–45.

Olson, L. C. (1991). *Emblems of American community in the revolutionary era: A study in rhetorical iconology.* Washington, DC: Smithsonian Institution Press.

Olson, L. C. (2004). *Benjamin Franklin's vision of American community: A study in rhetorical iconology.* Columbia: University of South Carolina Press.

Olson, L. C. (2007). Intellectual and conceptual resources for visual rhetoric: A re-examination of scholarship since 1950. *Review of Communication, 7*(1), 1–20.

Osborn, M. (1986). Rhetorical depiction. In H. W. Simons & A. A. Aghazarian (Eds.), *Form, genre, and the study of political discourse* (pp. 79–107). Columbia: University of South Carolina Press.

Palczewski, C. H. (2002). Argument in an off-key. In T. Goodnight (Ed.), *Arguing communication and culture: Selected papers from the twelfth NCA/AFA Conference on Argumentation: 2001* (Vol. 1, pp. 1–23). Washington, DC: National Communication Association.

Palczewski, C. H. (2005). The male Madonna and the feminine Uncle Sam: Visual arguments, icons, and ideographs in 1909 anti-woman suffrage postcards. *Quarterly Journal of Speech, 91*(4), 365–394.

Panofsky, E. (1939). *Studies in iconology: Humanistic themes in the art of the Renaissance.* New York: Oxford University Press.

Panofsky, E. (1955). *Meaning in the visual arts: Papers in and on art history.* Garden City, NY: Doubleday.

Peirce, C. S. (1992). *The essential Peirce, selected philosophical writings, Volume 1 (1867–1893)* (N. Houser & Christian Kloesel, Eds.). Bloomington: Indiana University Press.

Peirce, C. S. (1998). *The essential Peirce, selected philosophical writings, Volume 2 (1893–1913).* Bloomington: Indiana University Press.

Pezzullo, P. C. (2003). Resisting "National Breast Cancer Awareness Month": The rhetoric of counterpublics and their cultural performances. *Quarterly Journal of Speech, 23*(3), 345–365.

Pezzullo, P. C. (2007). *Toxic tourism: Rhetorics of pollution, travel, and environmental justice.* Tuscaloosa: University of Alabama Press.

Prelli, L. J. (Ed.). (2006). *Rhetorics of display.* Columbia: University of South Carolina Press.

Rohan, L. (2004). I remember mamma: Material rhetoric, mnemonic activity, and one woman's turn-of-the-twentieth-century quilt. *Rhetoric Review, 23*(4), 368–387.

Scott, B. (2004). Picturing irony: The subversive power of photography. *Visual Communication, 3*(1), 31–59.

Scott, R. L. (1977). Diego Rivera at Rockefeller Center: Fresco painting and rhetoric. *Western Journal of Speech Communication, 41*(2), 70–82.

Shelley, C. (1996). Rhetorical and demonstrative modes of visual argument: Looking at images of human evolution. *Argumentation and Advocacy, 33*(1), 53–68.

Sloan, T. O., Gregg, R. B., Nilson, T. R., Rein, I. J., Simons, H. W., Stelzner, H. G., & Zacharias, D. W. (1971). Report of the committee on the advancement and refinement of rhetorical criticism. In L. F. Bitzer & E. Black (Eds.), *The prospect of rhetoric: Report of the National Developmental Project, sponsored by Speech Communication Association* (pp. 220–227). Englewood Cliffs, NJ: Prentice Hall.

Sontag, S. (1977). *On photography.* New York: Farrar, Straus & Giroux.

Sturken, M., & Cartwright, L. (2001). *Practices of looking: An introduction to visual culture.* New York: Oxford.

Tom, G., & Eves, A. (1999). The use of rhetorical devices in advertising. *Journal of Advertising Research, 39*(4), 39–42.

Tompkins, P. K. (1969). The rhetorical criticism of non-oratorical works. *Quarterly Journal of Speech, 55*(4), 431–440.

Turner, K. J. (1977). Comic strips: A rhetorical perspective. *Central States Speech Journal, 28*(1), 24–35.

Van Mulken, M. (2003). Analyzing rhetorical devices in print advertisements. *Document Design, 4*(2), 114–128.

Warnick, B. (2002). *Critical literacy in a digital era: Technology, rhetoric, and the public interest.* Mahwah, NJ: Lawrence Erlbaum.

Willerton, R. (2005). Visual metonymy and synecdoche: Rhetoric for stage-setting images. *Journal of Technical Writing and Communication, 35*(1), 3–31.

Worth, S., & Gross, L. (1974). Symbolic strategies. *Journal of Communication, 24*(4), 27–39.

SECTION I

PERFORMING AND SEEING

The essays featured in this section shed light on performing and seeing as symbolic actions that recur in visual rhetoric. Performing is a commonplace activity featured in a substantial body of visual rhetoric scholarship. Regularly ritualized in everyday life, performances may express, convey, and reproduce gender or sex roles, racial classifications and stereotypes, and economic class. Public performances can affirm and transmit culture by bringing groups of people together in community or by driving them apart. Consequently, students of visual rhetoric may wish to consider how doing certain deeds expresses or conveys varied meanings from the perspectives of diverse participants or onlookers. For example, something as apparently simple as a public kiss can be a greeting between friends, an expression of affection or love, a featured symbolic act during a marriage ceremony, a taken-for-granted display of privileged status, or an act of public resistance and protest defying discrimination and social injustice. Our interpretation of the meaning of the kiss will depend on who performs the kiss; its ritual, institutional, or cultural circumstances; and the participants' and onlookers' perspectives.

In thinking critically about performing as a symbolic activity, students of visual rhetoric may find it useful to ask some general questions: Who is authorized to perform the symbolic actions being viewed or conducted (e.g., a marriage ceremony, a kiss in a public space, or a declaration of a state of war among nations)? Who is included or subjected to the symbolic

Figure 1 *Communication Quarterly* 24(2) 1976 cover image.

SOURCE: Used here by permission of the Eastern Communication Association and with courtesy of the artist, Lanny Sommese.

actions being performed? Who is excluded by law or discouraged by custom from engaging in certain performances? Whose social standing and economic resources are enhanced and, on the other hand, whose are diminished or undermined by public performances of symbolic actions? How might public and private conduct depend on the location or space for the performance? In what ways are relationships of power, authority, or place in a social order reproduced through public performances? In what respects might some viewers actively identify with a public performance, while others may not or, worse, feel offended and alienated by it?

Many researchers who feature performing in visual rhetoric have been influenced by Kenneth Burke's recognition in his voluminous writings that all human activity is symbolic (Burke, 1950/1969). As he put it in many places in his ouevre, "Things move, persons act" (Burke, 1972, p. 21). These scholars tend to view human activity and interaction as a drama rich in meaningful significance, and they believe that human performances reflect a certain degree of human agency, however much performers' actions are conditioned and shaped by socialization and culture. Other scholars of performance explore how human identity itself is composed largely of symbolic performances rather than tied to nature or biology. For example, many scholars feature Judith Butler's (1993) depiction of performance, wherein the very act of doing ritualized deeds conveys meanings, such as affirming one's sex, gender, sexuality, race, or economic class by means of one's public conduct. Still other scholars draw on J. L. Austin's (1962) and John R. Searle's (1969) writings concerning speech acts, where utterances are treated as deeds with public consequences and, in the case of utterances that they call "performatives," do or enact what they say. For instance, participating in or witnessing the exchange of vows during a wedding ceremony—when authorized by the appropriate official representing a recognized religion or state—changes the relationship between the couple, while transforming others in the community in their relationship to them. Sociologist Pierre Bourdieu's (1991) writings concerning "habitus" also surface in some visual rhetoric scholarship concerned with performance, because Bourdieu's work emphasizes the powerful ways that ritual and socialization influence symbolic actions.

By *seeing,* we refer to a wide range of human activities such as observing, examining, viewing, watching, showing, displaying, imagining, envisioning, visualizing, or making visible. Seeing happens sometimes through firsthand observation or at other times through the use of familiar tools (such as pencil, ink, or crayon) or special optical equipment and digital technologies (from photography, film, and television to stethoscopes, probes, ultrasound, and electron microscopes). Essays in this section regularly question the assumption that "seeing equals knowing" and complicate the idea that viewing provides access to self-evident, virtually unmediated insight or truth. In addition, much of the scholarship on seeing focuses on the often power-laden relationships between the observer and the observed.

Students of visual rhetoric will wish to contemplate certain basic questions concerning seeing: In what ways might the apparently simple activity of viewing others, objects, and landscapes be conditioned by custom, socialization, and culture? How and why are certain visual images recorded, preserved, or conveyed to specific audiences, while others are discarded, considered taboo, or simply ignored altogether? In what respects do presumptions about what is private and public inform each viewer's gaze and, consequently, her or his beliefs concerning the propriety of either watching or being seen? How, if at all, do such presumptions impinge on whose cultures, which social groups, and what performances are visible and invisible in public? Who is seen by whom, in which locations or sites, by what means, and for what reasons?

One dominant theme in the essays featured here is that of *visibility.* The onlooker's gaze can sometimes make invisible groups and practices become visible; sometimes that visibility involves the problematic acts of surveillance and voyeurism, which can turn another person into an object of study in ways that contribute to her or his dehumanization. In contrast, other essays in this section illustrate how the act of deliberately making one's culture or social group visible and public can serve as meaningful resistance to bias, discrimination, and social injustice and enable public dissent and resistance. Other themes in this section include the role of science and visual technologies in visualizing human biology and character. Key communication concepts that recur in the essays on seeing include *the gaze, surveillance,* the *scopic drive* to see and to be seen, the *panopticon,* and *voyeurism.* Scholars who feature such concepts often draw on the insights of Walter Benjamin, Michel Foucault, Sigmund Freud, and Jacques Lacan, among others.

Reginald Twigg's essay, "The Performative Dimension of Surveillance: Jacob Riis' *How the Other Half Lives,*" focuses on Jacob Riis's activities of observing, describing, and photographing working-class people's lives. Twigg explains that during the late 19th century, the visual conventions of realism activated by photography influenced all facets of culture, including law and science. Twigg contrasts the performance of "taking" a picture through photography with "making" one in earlier periods to call attention to how photography appeared to make the production of art increasingly democratic. His essay illustrates how socialized conventions condition the very activities of seeing and the assumed value of what is worth viewing.

Twigg's essay is a case study of Jacob Riis's photographs of working-class people in *How the Other Half Lives.* He contends that these photographs performed varieties of surveillance and voyeurism because they enabled people from within financially secure and comfortable classes to see into the lives and working conditions of what were pejoratively called the "dangerous classes": the working poor and recent immigrants. Financially comfortable viewers were able to derive pleasure—sometimes erotic, other times from experiencing their own relative privilege and dominance—from consuming images of the working poor. Riis's images offered viewers pleasurable visual fictions of race, sex, gender, sexuality, and class; viewers used these photographs of the working class in oftentimes fictionalized ways to manage and control them. Ultimately, Twigg argues, the photographs helped the financially comfortable classes to define their own identities as well. In addition to being considered in the context of the other essays in this section, Twigg's essay could be paired with Dan Brouwer's essay, "The Precarious Visibility Politics of Self-Stigmatization: The Case of HIV/AIDS Tattoos" (in Section III), because Brouwer also explores the relationship between surveillance and vulnerable communities.

The next essay in this section treats performing and seeing in the public practice and popular representations of scientific inquiry. Nathan Stormer's essay, "Embodying Normal Miracles," studies the uses of visual technologies for enlargement or magnification of images of human reproduction in a pro-life film titled *The Miracle of Life,* featuring photography by Lennart Nilsson. Stormer traces historical changes in how technology has been used to limit or enhance vision, from early historical

uses of convicted prisoners' bodies for anatomical examinations and pictorial illustrations through more recent technologies such as the stethoscope, probe, ultrasound, and the electron microscope. He explores how technology has enhanced viewers' abilities to see aspects of life processes that had not been previously subject to human viewing.

Even though photographic imagery may seem to make nature evident in what viewers might experience as objective, self-evident, or virtually unmediated insight or truth, Stormer underscores how unrecognized presumptions concerning gender roles, human sexuality, and reproduction surface in the language used to describe the images. Stormer points out, for instance, how the visual portrayals of human hormones in the documentary were entirely visual representations without any scientific basis. He then turns attention to how gender socialization informs the documentary film narrator's ways of naming the sperm's "penetration" of the egg (rather than, say, its "envelopment"), thereby employing stereotyped codes and types of masculine and feminine courtship performances. Emphasizing that the documentary film offers a thoroughly rhetorical performance rather than objective, scientific truth, Stormer underscores the value of considering how technological, social, and institutional practices of visualization affect our cultural experience of human reproduction.

In addition, Stormer generalizes that medical professionals, as a result of their disciplinary training, tend to view human health as a cluster of bodily norms concerning such factors as size, weight, age, sex, race, class, tissues, fluids, chemical composition, dietary habits, and the like. In other words, health professionals see the human body in ways conditioned heavily by their socialization. With regard to how socialization produces such powerful presumptions, Stormer's essay may be paired with Diane S. Hope's essay, "Memorializing Affluence in the Postwar Family: Kodak's Colorama in Grand Central Terminal (1950–1990)" (in Section IV), which studies how Kodak commodified ideas about family socialization in order to induce consumption of its products.

Whereas Stormer's essay focuses on performing and seeing in the context of seemingly tangible claims about science, knowledge, or truth, the next essay in this section explores how something as intangible as character was imbued with viewable presence in a 19th-century photograph of Abraham Lincoln. In "Recognizing Lincoln: Image Vernaculars in Nineteenth-Century Visual Culture," Cara A. Finnegan concentrates on how audiences talked about the visible evidence of Lincoln's character in a youthful photograph of him published in *McClure's* magazine in 1895. Finnegan examines a series of letters to the editor that commented on the photographic image, which was reproduced from an 1840s daguerreotype of the young Lincoln not seen by the wider public until 1895. By using their implicit understanding of portrait photography and the pseudo-science of physiognomy, viewers performed interpretations of the photograph that Finnegan calls "image vernaculars," arguments grounded in viewers' beliefs that a photograph could convey character. Finnegan argues that those who responded to the photograph constructed a memory of Lincoln that fit with the social and political needs of their present by emphasizing Lincoln's heroic and supposedly singularly "American" identity. Such arguments, Finnegan contends, were persuasive in a period when elite citizens of a rising global empire were anxious about the fate of "American" identity. In her analysis, Finnegan extends the idea of performance to encompass those by audiences. In doing so, she broadens the landscape of visual rhetoric to include not only visual artifacts themselves but also what she terms "visual culture," the historically situated beliefs about vision and images that influence audiences' practices of looking. Finnegan's essay could be paired with Judith Lancioni's essay, "The Rhetoric of the Frame: Revisioning Archival Photographs in *The Civil War*" (in Section II), inasmuch as both essays explore how historical photographs were recirculated through later technologies and reinterpreted by subsequent audiences.

The last essay in this section features performing and seeing in its relationship to the politics, heritage, and culture of vulnerable communities. Charles E. Morris III and John M. Sloop's essay, "'What Lips These Lips Have Kissed': Refiguring the Politics of Queer Public Kissing," underscores how discrimination and social injustice may enforce invisibility; how only certain varieties of visibility might be condoned, permitted, or authorized by mainstream culture; and how performing and seeing sometimes can become a means of protest, dissent, and social activism. The essay examines public visibility of queer sexuality and AIDS activism through an examination of performances of same-sex kissing. Illustrated by posters such as Gran Fury's "READ MY LIPS," which were displayed in public places and reproduced on T-shirts to organize "kiss-ins," as well as in newspaper accounts and photographs of same-sex civil unions and marriages, "queer kissing" in public spaces is a symbolic performance that enacts confrontation and resistance by deliberately disrupting taken-for-granted norms. Kissing in public, as Morris and Sloop portray it, is a sustained illustration of how certain varieties of visibility may be performed in public to the exclusion of others. While public kissing ordinarily appears familiar and unthreatening when performed by opposite-sex couples, it becomes a provocative, political activity when performed by a couple of the same sex, especially by two men. Audiences' responses to such performances are oftentimes affective and visceral rather than rational, resulting in some cases in disciplinary punishment. Becoming visible to others through queer public kissing, the authors contend, allows gay men to enact a performance of resistance to discrimination and social injustice.

In their attention to how public queer kissing is a performance of the body, Morris and Sloop illustrate how public kissing is a form of "body rhetoric," which has become a major focus of interest in visual rhetoric scholarship (Hauser, 1999; Selzer & Crowley, 1999). As a study of body rhetoric, Sloop and Morris's essay could be paired with Anne Teresa Demo's essay, "The Guerrilla Girls' Comic Politics of Subversion" (in Section III) to explore symbolic acts that depend heavily on making a community's invisible presence visible.

There is an abundance of excellent visual rhetoric scholarship on performing and seeing. Students of visual rhetoric who wish to learn more about performing and seeing in scientific inquiry may wish to consult Cameron Shelley's

(1996) essay, "Rhetorical and Demonstrative Modes of Argument: Looking at Images of Human Evolution," which examines the roles of these symbolic actions in what might be called scientific persuasion or rhetoric of science. For further insight into how mainstream culture may condone or tolerate only a limited range of visibility, Bonnie Dow's (2004) essay, "Fixing Feminism: Women's Liberation and the Rhetoric of Television Documentary," would be a useful supplemental reading. See the suggestions for further reading at the end of this section for additional work in this area.

Discussion Questions

1. After reading these essays, how would you characterize the ramifications of performing and seeing for shaping or influencing attitudes and beliefs in public life?

2. All of the essays explore the relationship between those doing the viewing and those people or objects being viewed. In each of the essays, how would you describe relationships of power between the viewer and the viewed?

3. The role of technology is another common theme in this section. Explore how the essays discuss the role of visual technology. What are the ramifications for visual rhetoric of technologies that enhance vision? In what ways do such technologies transform our experience of seeing?

4. According to these essays, in what ways do notions of public and private influence how performances make the invisible visible, or transform what some might consider a private deed into a public deed or spectacle? In your opinion, what factors are important when considering whether image makers should make the invisible and private either visible or public? Why?

5. Based on the readings in this section, what factors might lead one to question the assumption that seeing equals knowing or that viewing provides access to self-evident or unmediated truth? Other than the factors mentioned in the essays, what additional reasons, if any, occur to you for questioning those assumptions?

REFERENCES

Austin, J. L. (1962). *How to do things with words.* Cambridge, MA: Harvard University Press.

Bourdieu, P. (1991). *Language and symbolic power* (J. B. Thompson, Ed.; G. Raymond & M. Adamson, Trans.). Cambridge, MA: Harvard University Press.

Burke, K. (1969). *A rhetoric of motives.* Berkeley: University of California Press. (Original work published 1950)

Burke, K. (1972). *Dramatism and development.* Barre, MA: Clark University Press.

Butler, J. (1993). *Bodies that matter: On the discursive limits of sex.* New York: Routledge.

Dow, B. J. (2004). Fixing feminism: Women's liberation and the rhetoric of television documentary. *Quarterly Journal of Speech, 90*(1), 53–80.

Hauser, G. A. (Ed.). (1999). Body argument [Special issue]. *Argumentation and Advocacy, 36*(1–2), 1–100.

Searle, J. R. (1969). *Speech acts.* London: Cambridge University Press.

Selzer, J., & Crowley, S. (Eds.). (1999). *Rhetorical bodies.* Madison: University of Wisconsin Press.

Shelley, C. (1996). Rhetorical and demonstrative modes of visual argument: Looking at images of human evolution. *Argumentation and Advocacy, 33*(1), 53–68.

SUGGESTIONS FOR FURTHER READING

Brummett, B., & Duncan, M. C. (1994). Twin peaks: Using theory in two analyses of visual pleasure. In B. Brummett (Ed.), *Rhetoric in popular culture* (pp. 179–198). New York: St. Martin's.

Krips, H. (1999). *Fetish.* Ithaca, NY: Cornell University Press.

Stabile, C. A. (1992). Shooting the mother: Fetal photography and the politics of disappearance. *Camera Obscura, 28*, 179–205.

1

THE PERFORMATIVE DIMENSION OF SURVEILLANCE

Jacob Riis' How the Other Half Lives

REGINALD TWIGG

In 1890, William Dean Howells, then editor of the *Atlantic Monthly,* claimed enthusiastically that "the time is coming, I hope, when each new author, each new artist, will be considered, not in his proportion to any other author or artist, but in his relation to the human nature, known to us all, which it is his privilege, his high duty, to interpret."[1] Though ostensibly addressed to writers and artists, this statement's greatest significance lies in the way it articulates a broader social, cultural and historical transformation, one in which artistic and literary representations perform a central function. "Realism," as Howells and his contemporaries termed this new attitude toward aesthetic practice, signifies new ways of seeing not only in art and literature but in virtually every facet of late nineteenth-century social life from law enforcement to pedagogy and medicine to the emergent social sciences. From the realist perspective, the artist's or writer's relation to the world was not substantially different from that of the scientist or physician—all of whom were increasingly understood as observers whose task it was to survey and document human behavior. This flattening of received distinctions between aesthetic, scientific, and other socio-cultural practices points to the ways in which art and literature actively participate in the construction of cultural meanings and social relations.

The broader implications of the realist turn are profoundly illustrated in the growing importance Americans from the mid-nineteenth century to the present ascribe to photography. On one level, new photo-reproductive technologies seemingly democratized the production of art, since nearly anyone who could afford to could acquire the ability to "take" pictures.[2] *Taking* a picture is a distinct perceptual process from *making* one. Critical theorist Walter Benjamin notes that "for the first time in the process of pictorial reproduction, photography freed the hand of the most important artistic functions which henceforth devolved only upon the eye

SOURCE: Twigg, R. (1992). The performative dimension of surveillance: Jacob Riis' *How the other half lives. Text and Performance Quarterly, 12,* 305–328. © National Communication Association.

looking into a lens."[3] Photography, as Benjamin so acutely observes, is a process of looking, of discovering a seemingly objective reality which the photographer captures. This relation between the photographer and reality erases the degree to which photographs generate the very reality they claim to discover. Throughout much of its history the authority of photographic realism has rested precisely on the ability of the photo to present images of reality seemingly free of interpretation. Yet photographic meaning comes from the complex webs of signification in which the image is embedded. Consequently, the practice of photography is best understood as a social text—a critical site where the meaning(s) of reality are constantly challenged and destabilized.

Because of the seemingly transparent relation photography bears to reality, its evidential authority and textuality has received much recent critical attention.[4] The ability to erase its own textuality is precisely what makes photography so relevant to performance studies. Photography is above all a signifying practice that generates, rather than transmits, meaning. Its rhetorical appeal comes from its often explicit denial that any active performance of interpretation is necessary. Photographs, nonetheless, are interpretations rhetorically and poetically charged by their ability to "write" reality in ways that *appear* politically neutral.[5] As moments of discourse, photographic texts circulate and negotiate meanings intertextually in ways that actively engage and reconfigure their socio-historical contexts. "Intertextuality," Beverly Long and Mary Strine observe, "fosters a way of being in the world that assumes all of us bring something complex to our experiences, that we are capable of acting, of engaging others, including texts, and not simply reacting to them."[6] To understand photographs intertextually excavates their operations as interpretations, including the ways in which they deny themselves as interpretations.

Post-structuralists, particularly those informed by Foucault, point out that all knowledge statements are politically charged interpretations where self and Other, knowledge and power, are functions of discourse. Discursive practices generate identity as a social text continually reshaped and reformed in the performance of discourse itself.[7] Looking at oneself and others through the camera performs these very functions by situating the viewing subject in a relation of power with the objectified Other. Susan Sontag describes this process as voyeuristic: "While the others are passive, clearly alarmed spectators, having a camera has transformed one person into something active, a voyeur: only he has mastered the situation."[8] The semiotic process by which we produce and read documentary photography is a performance of self identity effectuated by the unstable and politically charged representations of Otherness.

By the late nineteenth century, documentary photography was appropriated as a means of surveying and managing groups subordinated by race, class and gender. Drawing on the realism of photography, a new social reform literature emerged to make the surveyed Other available for dominant-class inspection.

The pivotal figure in this new activity was Jacob A. Riis, whose book of collected photographs, statistics, and highly moralized rhetoric, *How the Other Half Lives: Studies Among the Tenements of New York,* provided one of the most comprehensive images of the working classes—the "Other Half"—to his middle-class audiences. Riis' widespread appeal came, according to Maren Stange, from the effectiveness with which his text merged photographic images with other discursive techniques: "Allowing his meanings to emerge only as photographs were appreciated in a rhetorical framework created by their interaction with captions, texts, and with his authority as presenter and narrator, Riis made each image a rich carrier of specific ideological messages."[9] More specifically, as Abigail Solomon-Godeau put it, Riis' use of multiple discursive forms "could be seen to converge within a dense matrix of bourgeois social anxieties and the need to assuage them," producing a matrix that "was constituted by the threat posed by large numbers of poor, unassimilated recent immigrants, the spector of social unrest, the use of photography as a part of the larger enterprise of surveillance, containment, and social control, and the imperatives of 'Americanization.'"[10] Riis' effectiveness came from his ability to co-articulate race, gender, and class identities—perform them—through his text, and, by doing so, to construct a narrative of "American" identity based upon the mutually-reinforcing exclusions these categories produce.

How the Other Half Lives reveals the ways in which documentary photography, read intertextually, problematizes the politically innocent relation between documentary discourses and reality posed by modernist theories of the image. By focusing on the ways in which this text articulates its historical context, we gain greater insights into the implications of seeing social texts as performative enactments of cultural values and social struggles. Moreover, *How the Other Half Lives* provides a poignant illustration of the ways in which documentary photography and other modes of "objective" discourse are thoroughly rhetorical, in fact are rhetorically powerful because they can disguise their own rhetoricity. This essay explores the implications of photography as performance on a number of levels. First, it situates and explores the implications of documentary as a form of surveillance; second, it explores how Riis' text co-articulates and subtly interconnects race, gender, and class identity; finally, it explicates the ways in which the voyeurism of *How the Other Half Lives* simultaneously activates and contains the human body as a site of desire and opposition.

THE POETICS AND POLITICS OF SURVEILLANCE

The realist photography of Riis and his contemporaries emerged as a representational practice during the gradual but profound transformation Michel Foucault terms the "formation of a disciplinary society."[11] With the birth of modern institutions of medicine, education, law enforcement, and the "social" sciences came the development of disciplinary apparatuses that, taken together, operate to constitute humans as objects of knowledge, and, in the process, discipline, punish, and ultimately control the body as a site of opposition. The techniques, tools, or methods by which academic disciplines and other institutional discourses produce knowledge—methods such as rigorous observation, normalizing judgment, and examination—are also, simultaneously, techniques through which power is exercised.[12] Discipline enacts and produces relations of power, Foucault adds, because

"discipline fixes; it arrests or regulates movements; it clears up confusion; it dissipates compact groupings of individuals wandering about the country in unpredictable ways; it establishes calculated distributions."[13] By fixing and regulating movements, disciplinary techniques construct social positions into which humans, as disciplined subjects, are located and managed. In the process, these techniques draw attention away from the power relations they construct by presenting themselves as rational, objective categories of "knowledge."

Surveillance is the primary technique through which disciplinary mechanisms exercise power. The act of observing, which simultaneously performs the discursive operations of looking and classifying, constructs the observer as subject and the observed as object, the latter "incorporeally transformed," as Deleuze and Guattari suggest, into a thing and subjected to the power implied in the observer's gaze.[14] This transformation is performed at the moment of looking where the observer assumes the right to speak for and classify the observed Other. In the performative ritual of surveillance, the surveyed Other is silenced because he or she is, Foucault points out, "seen, but he [or she] does not see; he [or she] is the object of information, never a subject in communication."[15] This process of surveillance, then, produces the surveyed Other as a text, and, by doing so, appropriates Otherness itself as a function of signification. As an object of knowledge, the surveyed Other is a discursive construct, whose body-as-text becomes a rich carrier of meaning.[16] In this way the discourse of photographic realism literally writes the human body into a manageable system of signification that flattens human experience into categories of knowledge such as race, gender, and class.

The politics of surveillance were most concretely performed in administrative practices of industry and law enforcement where discipline became necessary in the making of productive labor and consumer forces. However, immigrants from rural areas and other countries did not assimilate quickly enough to maximize the profits of industrial corporations. Unassimilated, they could not function properly as good consumers or laborers and consequently threatened the social order of American capitalism. It was here that information-gathering techniques of the knowledge disciplines had a significant influence; for the techniques of surveillance such as the gathering of statistics, monitoring living conditions, collecting census data—in short, making immigrant and working classes visible—could transform "alien" populations into an exploitable labor and consumer force. At the same time, the accumulation of capital created a greater urgency for effective law enforcement, since private property had become essential as the basis of social order. Because the accumulation of capital depends upon exploitative class inequalities—the low pay, long hours, and horrific working conditions of the factories—the threat of labor unrest was constantly present. The Haymarket incident of 1886 and the Pullman Strike in 1894 serve as important reminders. Just as the techniques of surveillance operated to produce a docile labor force, they could provide ways of managing and controlling potential political opposition to the dominant order by observing, scrutinizing, and monitoring the working classes. The close interworkings of surveillance thus produced an order in which "discipline is the unitary technique by which the body is reduced as a 'political' force at least cost and maximized as a useful force."[17]

Seen in this context, documentary photography functioned as a powerful realist rhetoric and became, Benjamin claims, "standard evidence for historical occurrences, and acquire[d] a hidden political significance."[18] Ironically, the source of documentary photography's political power as a "realist" representational genre was its poetic force. Photographs need explanations that provide directions for reading them: they could neither speak for themselves nor refer directly to any specific context. Captions and other literary devices generated contexts from which photos derived their meanings, embedding them in complex matrices of other texts and discourses.[19] In this regard, photographs are metonyms, signs whose meanings are produced only by associations with other signs. Figure 3, for example, would shock audiences only to the degree that they would fear miscegenation; for the black hand on the white woman's shoulder poses substantial problems for a culture committed, as Victorians were, to categorical and racial "purity." Hence the photograph's relation to the

world it represents is by the conventions of reading only; its metonymy is based on arbitrarily derived, yet thoroughly ideological associations.

The "documentary realism"[20] of *How the Other Half Lives* was an attempt to provide stable, monologic images of reality through photographic and narrative portraits of urban slum life. In subtle, yet ideologically powerful ways, documentary realism poetically transformed the surveyed other into a manageable, containable, and usable fiction who, in the process, was politically marginalized. Contained in this fiction, however, were points of instability and social anxiety, which ascribed to realism the purpose of providing, in Amy Kaplan's words, "fiction to combat the functionality of everyday life."[21] In its surveillance of the other through texts like *How the Other Half Lives,* the bourgeoisie at the turn of the century performed their own identities by the strategic appropriation of Otherness—a fiction produced as an imaginary anchor for bourgeois identity.

RIIS' PERFORMANCE OF RACE/GENDER/CLASS IDENTITY

Jacob A. Riis, a Danish immigrant, first studied the tenements of New York as a police reporter for the New York *Tribune* in 1877.[22] It was not until 1887 that he began to make his journeys into the tenements with a camera. From that time through the first decade of the twentieth century, Riis shot or collected hundreds of photos of tenement life in New York. In 1890, he published *How the Other Half Lives,* a compilation of photographs, statistics, demographic charts, narratives of his "adventures" in the "ghettos," and highly moralized rhetoric designed to draw attention to New York's tenements and their inhabitants. Riis also gave a series of slide lectures, often with musical accompaniment, in which he combined the book's ideological treatment with humor and melodrama to produce highly moralized entertainment for his middle-class audiences. In both of its manifestations, Riis' text provided a tour of New York's "dark continent," its "Other Half," knowledge of whom had seemed unnecessary until the time they posed a threat to social order: "Long ago it was said that 'one half of the world does not know how the other half lives.' That was true then. It did not know because it did not care."[23] The language of this passage, as well as that of the book's title, reflects, on one level, a fear of the "Other Half" since, as Stange observes, "he recoiled from workers and working-class culture, especially when he saw that culture's potential for solidarity in opposition to the individualist and entrepreneurial values of the middle class."[24]

On another level, however, that fear cannot be separated from the self-confirmatory function the "Other Half" performed for the middle classes. In many ways, Riis' textual construction of the Other was a subtle performance of bourgeois self identity that served to stabilize race, gender, and class sensibilities in an age when cultural diversity deeply problematized homogeneous conceptions of "American" identity. These categories of identity are simultaneously encoded in the very operations of his surveillance, a gaze whose configurations of power produce the "Other Half" in tenement inhabitants' bodies. In this way, Riis generated a narrative of "national" identity whose central features universalize middle-class values that, Anita Levy observes, "offered a model of the individual detached from social and economic circumstances, anchored instead to internal features of the self or of the body that were more amenable to educational, normalizing, or therapeutic interventions that involved little, if any, significant political or economic change."[25]

The Disciplinary Gaze: Naturalizing Social Stratification

Much of the rhetoric of *How the Other Half Lives* expresses middle-class anxiety about the political threat of the "Other Half" but frames that anxiety in a managerial discourse that renders the Other visible for public inspection and regulation. In the conclusion of the book, for example, Riis warns his audiences that "as the crowds increase, the need *of guiding this drift into safe channels* becomes more urgent."[26] The highlighted language here expresses the class interests of channeling the Other into living patterns that are "safe," that is, "useful" to the middle classes. Fear punctuated the concern that New York's "Other Half" comprised the greater

proportion of its population: "To-day three-fourths of its people live in the tenements. . . . We know that there is no way out; that the 'system' that was the evil offspring of public neglect and private greed has come to stay, a storm-centre forever of our civilization. Nothing is left but to make the best of a bad bargain."[27] While this introductory passage draws attention to the fact that the "urgency" of the "tenement problem" results from public neglect, Riis carefully channels the subsequent anxiety into a terministic frame where important political questions about the justice or morality of social inequality are deflected. The assumed permanence of the tenement naturalizes the ghetto as a transhistorical fact, hence erasing it as a political consequence of the entrepreneurial and individualist values he shares with his audience.

Making the "best of a bad bargain," as the rest of the book suggests, involved reforms based upon the middle-class conceptions of social justice that do not eliminate ghettos, but rather shape them into more useful components of the economic system. The final words of the book provide a clear sense of the urgency of treating this issue, while containing the audience's anxiety within a framework of dominant cultural values:

> The sea of a mighty population, held in galling fetters, heaves uneasily in the tenements. . . . If it rise once more, no human power may avail to check it. The gap between the classes in which it surges, unseen, unsuspected by the thoughtless, is widening day by day. . . . I know of but one bridge that will carry us over safe, a bridge founded upon justice and built of human hearts. I believe that the danger of such conditions as are fast growing up around us is greater for the very freedom which they mock.[28]

In these lines Riis deploys the hierarchical social relations between the surveyor and the surveyed Other in ways that subtly configure the Other as an inhuman force that "heaves uneasily in the tenements" while the dominant class acts through its "human power," a relation he punctuates in the final sentence as the danger encircling "us," his audiences, as "they" mock the "freedom" of his own class. This passage is a clear example of what the rest of *How the Other*

Half Lives rhetorically performs: the naturalization of social stratification as a hierarchical relation between human and inhuman social conditions, one between the seeing subject and the seen object. More subtly, Riis' gaze produced a distinction between the public and private domains whereby the making of the "Other Half" publicly visible helps to protect the private interests of his audiences. Indeed, so long as the "Other Half" can be made visible, yet unable to return the gaze, their political power can be checked.

While this initial explication shows that Riis appropriated Otherness in a dialectic that defined middle-class cultural identity, closer scrutiny can explain how the textual construction of Otherness articulates that identity in multiple, yet interconnected layers of race, gender, and class. On one level, surveillance genders its relations between observer and observed. In his critical history of documentary photography, John Tagg explains that, "in the terms of such discourses, the working classes, colonized peoples, the criminal, poor, ill-housed, sick or insane were constituted as passive—or, in this structure, 'feminised'—objects of knowledge." In this process, he suggests, when others are "subjected to a scrutinizing gaze, forced to emit signs, yet cut off from command of meaning, such groups were represented as, and wishfully rendered, incapable of speaking, acting or organising for themselves."[29] By penetrating the depths of tenement experience and making it visible to the viewing public, Riis' text ascribed a passive, "feminine" role to the "Other Half," a role he reinforced with the attitude that "guidance into safe channels" is a benevolent paternalistic act. In this way, surveillance constructs gender roles as subject positions one occupies in the act of looking.[30] The objectified position women often occupy in patriarchal culture is directly analogous to the position of the colonized Other in disciplinary culture; for patriarchy and colonialism are both concrete practices of surveillance that produce the surveyed Other as a gendered, that is, passive, "feminine" object observed by an active, "masculine" subject.[31]

Surveillance simultaneously "racializes" its relations between observer and observed. Riis most clearly invoked "race" in his concern over

what he characterized as the tenement inhabitants' steady erosion of "American" identity. At one point, for example, he directly stated his concern thus: "The one thing you vainly ask for in the chief city of America is a distinctively American community. There is none; certainly not among the tenements."[32] In these moments Riis simultaneously raised a fear of cultural diversity and offered a textual strategy for its containment. Interestingly enough, cultural diversity becomes a danger when Riis coded it as degeneration: "[Americans] are not here. In their place has come this queer conglomerate mass of heterogeneous elements, ever striving and working like whiskey and water in one glass, and with the like result: final union and a prevailing taint of whiskey."[33] Unless clear physical and conceptual boundaries are maintained, Riis suggested here, the "purity" of what he saw as the most superior of races—"Americans"—will be destroyed, with the effect of "tainting" all of humanity. What is really at stake here is the authority upon which social inequalities are naturalized and maintained. This authority is evidenced by his scientific language, a discourse that maintains a strict social separation between the viewer (Riis and his audiences) and the objectified Other. As long as the Other remains objectified (here expressed as "elements" of water and whiskey), s/he poses little threat to the authority of Riis' discourse and the exclusions it maintains. Seen in the context of the other passages cited in this study, the distinctive "American community" Riis envisioned was founded on a particular and inflexible set of traditions and values that worked to the advantage of particular class interests.

Thus, the disciplinary gaze with which Riis "feminized" the people of the tenements also saw the cultural differences of the tenement districts as differences in "race." And, at the same time, differences in race provided naturalized explanations for class differences, especially when grounded in the emerging idioms of biology and heredity. Riis' explanation for why the Chinese and laundry—a paradigm of working-class service labor—go so well together should suffice as an illustration: "[Neatness] is the distinguishing mark of Chinatown, outwardly and physically. It is not altogether by chance the Chinaman has chosen the laundry as his distinctive field. He is by nature as clean as the cat, which he resembles in his traits of cruel cunning and savage fury when aroused."[34] Notice that Riis sees the connection between a person and a type of labor as a physical one, and, by implication, resemblances between the Chinese and cats is subtly reduced to a physical one. Needless to say, seeing social inequalities in this light draws attention away from their political nature: if one's social position is biologically, not culturally determined, it does not appear to be political. In this way, Riis' coding of working class bodies produced class distinctions as a function of biology whereby their subordinated position was doubly naturalized as they became feminized objects of a gaze that classified differences as products of "race."

Riis' invocation of aesthetic sensibility also converged relations of race, gender, and class, but in ways that extended and supported the evolutionary arguments his text assumes. For evolutionist discourses, aesthetic sensibility is evidence of the highest stage of social evolution, a stage that posited art and beauty as transcendence and mastery over the body.[35] His discussion of the superiority of Germans to the Irish provides a clear illustration and is worth quoting at length:

His garden goes with him wherever [the German] goes. Not that it represents any high moral principle in the man; rather perhaps the capacity for it. He turns his saloon into a shrubbery as soon as his back-yard. But wherever he puts it in a tenement block it does the work of a dozen police clubs. In proportion as it spreads the neighborhood takes on a more orderly character. As the green dies out of the landscape and increases in political importance, the police find more to do. Where it disappears altogether from sight, lapsing into a mere sentiment, police-beats are shortened and the Force patrols double at night.[36]

On one level, this use of the aesthetic is disciplinary: it maintains social order without the use of force. Also, as the passage points out, aesthetic sensibility disciplines because it draws attention away from politics, thereby making the *individual* responsible for his or her own social position. On another level, it justifies the use of force on the body. Its logic is thus: police force

is necessary to discipline those "races" who cannot discipline themselves.

On yet another level, this disciplinary structure depends centrally on the objectification of the body by the transcendent paternalistic gaze of the middle classes. Morality, Riis contended, transcends the body in ways that justify rigid, even violent discipline as in the best interest of the Other. Consequently, as "every blade of grass, every stray weed, every speck of green, has been trodden out, as must inevitably be every gentle thought and aspiration *above* the *mere* wants of the *body* in those whose moral natures such home surroundings are to nourish."[37] People marginalized by race, gender, and class, by this logic, have not "evolved" beyond their own bodies. As Riis concludes, "tenement-houses have no aesthetic resources. If any are to be brought to bear on them, they must come from the outside."[38] By implication, those subordinated by the subtle interworkings of race, gender, and class are reduced to mere bodies "naturally inferior" to white middle-class men whose duty it is to *look over* them.

Domesticating the "American" Family

Many of the images Riis associated with the tenements, both in his photos and his anecdotes, presented the working classes as subversive of what increasingly came to define dominant cultural values. These images invoked gender roles as pivotal in the maintenance of the middle-class ideal of the "American" family. In one of his photos (see Figure 1) Riis presented a portrait of what he termed "Bohemian cigarmakers at work in their tenement."[39] While on the surface this image looks benign—merely a hard-working family earning its living—its metonymy contains many elements subversive of middle-class ideals.

Initially, Riis' caption directs a reading which emphasizes the domestic sphere's function as a comfortable environment separate from the factory: here the home is a place of labor, a rather direct extension of the factory. Such an image rubs against the grain of a culture in which the perceptual boundaries between the domestic and labor spheres were becoming rigidly guarded. For many Victorians, the home was increasingly seen as a safe environment, one that

Figure 1   Bohemian Cigarmakers at Work in a Tenement.

SOURCE: The Jacob A. Riis Collection, #147. Museum of the City of New York.

provided refuge from the toils of the workplace. This boundary is violated by the image of each member of the family involved in the production of cigars. The children, presumably, must surrender play or school time in order to help the family earn a living. Each family member participates in the same economic activity, suggesting in its subtlety that the "domestic" activities of the family are dysfunctional: the gendered roles between mother, father and children become indistinguishable from each other. In such a setting, the clearly-demarcated boundaries around gender and age roles are subverted. At a deeper level, this subversion has serious consequences, primarily the subversion of "family." If the woman spends nearly every waking hour at work for money, this is done directly at the expense of the "proper" supervision of the family. In other words, this image affiliated itself to an ideology in which women's

labor should remain in domestic operations, hence hidden, while men's labor provides the support of the family. Such a subversion, Riis suggested in many places, is destructive of "the family," meaning the traditionally-defined nuclear family, and is a central contributory factor to juvenile delinquency and other crimes. In this way, his "Bohemian" subjects were appropriated to naturalize the middle-class family and its attendant gender, generational, and age relations by "illustrating" the "dangers" of any subversion of it.

The rhetorical power of this image was intensified when coupled with Riis' articulation of the domestic ideology of his time. This ideology not only feared working women, but did so because it saw domesticated women as pivotal in the maintenance of social order. For middle-class audiences, Levy observes, the ideal home of the nineteenth century revolved "around the figure of the domestic female, who becomes dependent upon the male for economic sustenance."[40] Not only does this ideal envision women as politically and economically powerless; it posits the properly domesticated wife as the agent through which the working and living activities of working-class men could be regulated and rendered useful. For this reason, Riis claimed the Chinese could become "useful" only by domestication: "Rather than banish the Chinaman, I would have the door opened wider—for his wife; make it a condition of his coming or staying that he bring his wife with him."[41] By servicing the health and personal needs of the working man, the domestic wife makes him more productive. Hence, as Levy succinctly explains, "since bad habits and not the extremities of economic exploitation 'curse' the working-class population, what better place to control those habits than in the home?"[42] In this context, the "Bohemian" wife Riis presents us is multiply subversive. She is working side by side with her husband, violating the expectation that women's labor must remain spatially and physically separate from men's, as well as the expectation that her labor supports, not duplicates, his. Neglecting her "wifely" duties, she was held responsible for the destruction of her family's moral, physical, and spiritual "health."

Even more powerful was the way in which Riis deployed the image of the "working girl." Quoting the report of the Working Women's Society, Riis framed his audiences' fear of working women: "It is simply impossible for any woman to live without assistance on the low salary a saleswoman earns, without depriving herself of real necessities. . . . It is inevitable that they must in many instances resort to evil."[43] While the report did provide economic explanations for prostitution, its discourse framed and located these conditions in the physiognomy of deviant female sexuality, thereby naturalizing women's class subordination as the result of their "degenerate nature." One explanation Riis advanced for women's wages provides a good illustration: "The pay they are willing to accept all have to take."[44] Since working women were seen as willing to accept low wages, they, as individuals, were responsible for their conditions. In another passage Riis pointed out that "girls with the love of youth for beautiful things,

with this hard life before them—who will save them from the tempter?"[45] Taken together these statements suggest that working women's fate was attributable to their weak natures, since, as the quote makes clear, they need external guidance in order to stay on the right path.

Here economic explanations were not as important to Riis' text as the discourses they cued. His paternalism was grounded in the nineteenth-century assumption that women had a "natural" proclivity for prostitution because, as the "weaker sex," women were coded closely with blacks. In this way, as Sander Gilman succinctly explains, images of prostitutes derived their ethos from subtle alignments with images of black women: "It is thus the inherent fear of the difference in the anatomy of the Other which lies behind the synthesis of images. The Other's pathology is revealed in anatomy. It is the similarity between the black and the prostitute—as bearers of the stigmata of sexual difference and, thus, pathology—which captured the late nineteenth century."[46] Put simply, Riis' fear of working women naturalized their social subordination by invoking a discourse in which women were "racialized"—"naturally" subordinated by biological traits directly connected to those of blacks. Hence the paternalism of Riis' rhetoric drew its authority from its ability to engage a discourse in which women's subordination is imagined as a result of their racial—that is, biological, physiognomic—"degeneracy." Seen in this light the image of the Bohemian family in Figure 1 was dangerous to Riis' audiences because of its textual and ideological connections with the image of Womanhood presented in Figure 3. These images, when combined with the domestic ideology of middle-class Victorians, naturalized race, gender, and class subordination as an effect of individual anatomical nature. Needless to say, women with any more power than that accorded to proper domesticity could easily be seen as destructive to the "American family," indeed of the entire race of "Americans" that middle-class audiences so vigorously guarded.

Constructing an "American" Identity

At the same time, *How the Other Half Lives* relied heavily upon classification schemes to categorize individuals into easily manageable units that, interestingly, reduce all cultural differences into racial distinctions clearly discernable by color. For example, early in the book, Riis sketches a graph of ethnicity, assigning colors to different cultures, while simultaneously commenting on the moral problem such "races" present:

> A map of the city, colored to designate nationalities, would show more stripes than on the skin of a zebra, and more colors than any rainbow. The city on such a map would fall into two great halves, green for the Irish prevailing in the West Side tenement districts, and blue for the Germans on the East Side. But intermingled with these ground colors would be an odd variety of tints that would give the whole the appearance of an extraordinary crazy-quilt.[47]

This assignation of colors strategically contained Otherness in two ways. First, color metaphors clarify because they arrange all differences visually on a spectral continuum. Yet, as metaphors, colors also abstract the meanings of difference by moving them to a different conceptual level and again making them "concrete" by the visual images attached to them. These metaphors become rhetorically powerful because "they do not draw attention to themselves as metaphors, and thus do not invite us to decode them consciously."[48] This power is intensified when such meanings become commonsensical—that level of understanding we take to be natural, unquestionable, upon which we do not reflect. In this way, constructed race differences become naturalized within the conceptual framework of the dominant culture as empirically verifiable categories, in the process erasing themselves as metaphors.

Second, coloring ethnic groups produces a manageable system through which Otherness could be contained. It enables Riis' text to put clear boundaries around the various groups that compose the "Other Half" and arrange them, first in theory, then in practice, in a social hierarchy devised by the observing class. In this way his text can easily define cultural, now racial, differences as "impurities" that "stain" the urban landscape: " . . . the black mark will be found overshadowing to-day many blocks on the East Side, with One Hundredth Street as the

centre, where colonies of them have settled recently."[49] The very language of the description constructs African-Americans as evil or degenerate, especially when the dialectical black-white metaphor is invoked. Such linguistic dehumanization further vilified African-Americans because they were reduced to a "black mark" whose "colonies" bear a closer relation to those of insects than people. By writing Otherness into this system of signification Riis' text could demonstrate his own moral, intellectual, and cultural superiority over the Other. Negation, which so clearly attends this system, was the means through which Riis and his audiences performed their individual and "American" identities. The *act* of negation simultaneously performs self affirmation, making identity a function of what it denies.

By positioning the bourgeois subject, as one who "transcended" the contingencies of the body, Riis' text provided a particular lens through which his audiences could view the "Other Half." One photograph in particular illustrates the process by which Riis' text generated an "American" identity. In a picture of an Iroquois family, the truly "native" inhabitants of New York (see Figure 2), Riis somewhat ironically provided evidence for his claim that there is no "distinctively American community." In this picture is a poignant reminder of the consequences of American colonial expansion: the taking over of Iroquois land and the absorption or nullification of their own culture into that which now inhabits that land. For example, the Iroquois family performed the same laborious tasks many of Riis' pictures portray; whatever skills they had in their native culture were quickly transformed into exploitable labor while other less useful traditions and customs were nullified or marginalized. Here the Iroquois are presented for the judgment of the scrutinizing gaze, one that invades the privacy of their home without apology or explanation. They are made to appear as a "sight"—an image of the "Other Half"—posing for the camera's gaze while denied the ability to return it. While they may look back at the camera, our consumption of the image, the photograph, takes control of its meaning out of their hands. By moving all of these images freely from one context to another, Riis' text makes images exchangeable commodities whose meanings are purchased for the price of the book or the lecture. Silenced except for their status as objects, this family is appropriated as evidence for the categorical distinctions and the meanings the viewing audience ascribes to them.

But while most of Riis' subjects never looked at the camera, Mountain Eagle's daughter does—even smiles at it. If possession of the image entails looking without apology at people who, by virtue of their subordinated social position, cannot look back, how can we explain this image? For Riis' audiences, this image could be seen as both subversive and affirming of middle-class ideals: her look activates fears of women—especially women of Other "races"—with sexual and labor power, and then calls for its containment within domestic ideology. Seen next to her brother, who is reclining and playing a violin, her image would be coded as "evidence" of the laziness and lack of scruples with which Riis' audiences characterized socially-subordinated groups at the turn of the century. In this process, the power of her look is channeled

into a justification for paternalistic guidance of the tenements. If this image of her sexuality was subversive, its subversion must be managed by the discourse in which it was framed. Powerfully coded by her race, gender, and class, her negation or control becomes an enactment of bougeois identity.[50]

Once again, the discursive formations in which the *viewer* positions this image produce its meanings. The discourse of surveillance, in which this image became embedded, appropriates it as "objective" evidence of the degeneracy of the Other, in need of paternalistic control. What is clearly denied in this discourse is the way in which her Otherness is politically constructed; and an awareness of the material circumstances of her marginality is deflected. What is affirmed is the superiority of the observer (both Riis and his audiences) who carries, among other things, the presumed right to look.

In another instance Riis offers a peek into a "black-and-tan dive in 'Africa.'"[51] The history of popular images of black men needs little

Figure 2 Mountain Eagle, and his family of Iroquois Indians.

SOURCE: The Jacob A. Riis Collection, #281. Museum of the City of New York.

elaboration. What made this image so rhetorically powerful, however, was the appearance of a white woman with a black hand on her shoulder (see Figure 3). This image is accompanied in the text by a curious passage in which Riis claimed "the [color] line may not be wholly effaced while the name of the negro, alone among the world's races, is spelled with a small *n*."[52] This characterization reduces African-Americans to the lowest of all humans, a characterization common to nineteenth-century anthropological and other scientific discourses, discourses that similarly demonized Hottentots as the lowest of all human "races."[53] Moreover, these discourses naturalized social inequalities between self and Other in the same terms as Riis uses here: "Natural selection will have more or less to do beyond a doubt in every age with dividing the races; only so, it may be, can they work out together their highest destiny."[54] By locating African-Americans at the bottom of the "race" hierarchy and attributing this position to "natural selection," Riis' text set a critical standard for race hierarchy and simultaneously erased its

own politics. The audience is shown the "bottom" of the human condition as a product of primitive or degenerate nature. More importantly, the presence of a white woman made this image frightening for its viewers because it activated deeply-ingrained fears of miscegenation. She was thus positioned as the "weak link" between the races, and her looking down indicates both shame and the turn-of-the-century belief that mixing the "races" somehow "lowers" the quality of "mankind."[55]

At another level, the image's ideological power came from its ability to activate cultural stereotypes of women as overly promiscuous and dangerous in any realm other than the domestic sphere. Possessed by virtue of the black hand on her shoulder, her position as an object of male sexual power is not open for question; her ability to be possessed is what makes her dangerous to the dominant culture. Her dirty face, raggy clothes and dishevelled hair mark her class affiliations with the black man as well: given the marginal status blacks have in contemporary culture, not to mention at the turn of the

Figure 3   Black and Tan Dive on Broome Street, circa 1889.

SOURCE: The Jacob A. Riis Collection, #281. Museum of the City of New York.

century, it was nearly impossible ever to escape poverty. In this image *How the Other Half Lives* brings together all of the fears of the dominant culture into the operations of surveillance; for the "bottom" of human existence, the completely Other, so to speak, fuses all categories of marginalization. To the degree that the poor white woman is brought into the possession of the obviously poor black man, this image argues that a flattening of distinctions of race, gender, and class is the worst of all possible conditions. She becomes the bearer of her race, and, in doing so, becomes dangerous when anywhere but the privatized sphere of the "proper" home.

This point of convergence is pivotal to the ideological power of Riis' text. In its complex operations, the disciplinary gaze genders, racializes, and class(ifies) the Other at the moment of its performance; for race, gender, and class are socially constructed, not natural, categories politically deployed in the performative rituals of surveillance. The conceptual distance between the observer and the observed Other makes these operations possible because its attendant hierarchy conveys on the observer the seemingly natural right to name, categorize, and ultimately control the Other. Differences of race, gender, and class are objectified in analogous ways, equally marginalized under the gaze. As depositories of Otherness, these categories perform identity in multiple layers of negation when brought together. Profoundly intertextual, the metonymy of Riis' text produced compelling images of Otherness through its complex affiliations with many interconnected hegemonic discourses. At the same time, it channeled these images into the production of bourgeois identity that functioned through the negation of all that was inscribed in the textually generated Other. By providing a *form* for middle-class anxieties, Riis' textualization of the "Other Half" *performed* his audiences' individual and cultural identity, an identity bound inextricably to the performance of the gaze.

CLASS VOYEURISM AND THE PERFORMANCE OF DESIRE

The conceptual distance necessary for the operation of surveillance inevitably produces a feeling of alienation and weightlessness in the observer, primarily because the fiction of a transcendent gaze is accomplished only by the rigorous denial of the body. With the body no longer serving as a referent for experience or as an anchor to the material world, life loses its center of gravity. One consequence is that gender, race, and class identity are unstable, constantly revised in the ongoing processes through which we continually engage texts. A second consequence is that texts become vitally important as anchors of experience and identity. Often acting as substitutes for physical experiences, texts are critical sites in modern culture where identity is performed. Finally, documentary texts like *How the Other Half Lives* can provide a deferred sense of unity between body and seeing subject by allowing their audiences to look upon Other bodies. While the spectacle of the Other in *How the Other Half Lives* constructs the Other as an object of fear and contempt, it also produces the body of the Other as an object of desire. In this sense, Riis' text is a "keyhole vocabulary," a discourse of voyeurism.[56] Through this voyeurism Riis attempts to negotiate the complex interworkings of class boundaries and transgressions that animate cultural performances and social rituals.

In *The Politics and Poetics of Transgression*, Peter Stallybrass and Allon White argue that the construction of social distinctions carries with it the desire to transgress them. Various social and textual practices implicitly sexualized the exotic Other, whose bodily images imbue surveillance with the pleasures of peeping through the keyhole.[57] Sexual relations between master and servant, for example, produce an illusory transgression of social and economic distinctions because the sexual act occurs between two bodies. However, this transgression is an illusion precisely because sexuality is infused with power relations; the sexual act still, perhaps even more profoundly, objectifies the subaltern.[58] In quite similar fashion, surveillance imbues the act of looking at Others with sexual power. Objectification is simultaneously a sexual and political act whereby the Other is rendered naked and vulnerable in the performance of the gaze. As passive objects offered up to the transcendent gaze, a gaze that invades the most private and vulnerable moments, Others are put on display and visually consumed.

John Berger explains that "to be nude is to be seen naked by others and yet not recognized for oneself. A naked body has to be seen as an object in order to become a nude. (The sight of it as an object stimulates the use of it as an object.) Nakedness reveals itself. Nudity is placed on display."[59] A body does not have to be physically naked to be a nude, since, as Berger notes, "nudity is a form of dress."[60] Rather, the Other is sexualized as a nude by the way in which the viewer composes and consumes the image. For example, compare the young woman in Figure 2 with nudes of the nineteenth century or even images of women in present-day advertising. Her pose is very similar to the sexualized female in the iconography of the past two centuries. Her sexuality is put on display just as easily as her impoverished condition. But the discourse in which her image is embedded encodes her poverty as the result of her sexuality. Berger continues: "But it would seem that nakedness has a positive visual value in its own right: we want to *see* the other naked: the other delivers to us the sight of themselves and we seize upon it—sometimes quite regardless of whether it is for the first time or the hundredth."[61] Surveillance, then, imagines Otherness in the nude, offering it up for political, social, and sexual consumption. In this way sexual pleasure is derived from the control of the Other's image, while, simultaneously, images of the body out of control become sites where the destablizing tendencies of desire threaten social order. This tension, according to Stallybrass and White, animates the boundaries between self and Other.

Riis' documentary served similar ends; for bourgeois audiences sought to anchor their own sexuality in images of the Other, into whom the instabilities of sexual desire could be projected and managed. In fact, Riis' obsession with the "Other Half" in the tenements could be explained as a metonymic projection of bourgeois anxiety/desire. Stallybrass and White explain that "whilst the 'low' of the bourgeois body becomes unmentionable, we hear an ever increasing garrulity about the *city's* 'low'—the slum, the ragpicker, the prostitute, the sewer—the 'dirt' which is 'down there.' In other words," they continue, "the axis of the body is transcoded through the axis of the city, and whilst the bodily low is 'forgotten,' the city's low becomes a site of obsessive preoccupation, a preoccupation which is itself intimately conceptualized in terms of discourses of the body."[62] In the metonymy of Riis' images of the slums is a dialectics of bourgeois disgust and desire, where the erotics of forbidden zones and dangerous classes subtly permeates the rhetoric of disgust. Disgust is a way of channeling desire, just as the slum is a way of channeling anxiety about one's own body. Riis' text provides a plethora of examples of this activity, especially in his numerous pictures and descriptions of people caught in their sleep or in the act of bathing. The brutality of its representation is central to its appeal because the sense of "realism" it generated could maintain the objectifying distance necessary to channel desire into disgust. Ironically, the distanciation of self and Other performed in the gaze produces both disgust and desire: each is an effect of alienating subjectivity from the body.

The performance of the gaze is eroticized further in its rigid enforcement of the boundaries between private and public activities and spaces. Like race, gender, and class categories, the public-private dichotomy so prevalent in nineteenth- and twentieth-century discourse is a construction that serves particular political interests. In the previous section I suggested that much of Riis' rhetoric serves to naturalize woman's "place" as in the home, by implication producing an idealized public sphere in which male interests are universalized as "the public interest." This subjection of women and other marginalized groups is critically dependent upon the enforcement of rigid boundaries between public and private spaces. Privatized, women remain objects of discourse, rarely able to speak: we talk *about* the private; the private does not speak.[63] The gaze thus complicates the boundaries between the public and private spheres—making the private publicly visible to a "public" abstracted and interiorized in the private interests/anxieties/desires of the transcendental subject. The erasure of the private from many forms of discourse makes it a source of mystery, access to which is an exclusive privilege. In its treatment of the tenements as a hidden mystery to be explored by the camera, *How the Other Half Lives* is a thoroughly voyeuristic text. So much of it is devoted to the penetration of the most intimate moments of human existence. As Riis readily admits, many of his photos were taken by breaking into tenements after midnight in order to "catch" people in their beds.

A particularly stunning example of Riis' prying into the private activities of his subjects can be seen in his photo of newsboys' washing up for dinner (see Figure 4). Here Riis' camera invades one of the most "private" moments in American bourgeois culture, bathing. Prominently displayed in the center of this shot is a faceless half-dressed boy removing his shirt, an image which exposes the body to audiences who, ironically, increasingly covered up their own bodies. This invasion constitutes a momentary transgression of public-private boundaries yet contains this transgression within a moralized rhetoric suggesting that the activities in lodging-houses, like the one pictured here, help these young people "to grow up self-supporting men and women safe from the temptations and the vice of the city."[64] In the interplay of these two messages the stern and repressive morality of Victorian audiences could be validated and "safely" transgressed through a gaze that is both controlling and voyeuristic.

This voyeurism serves two distinct but interrelated purposes. First, the viewer's penetration into the bathroom was justified by the disciplinary motives driving Riis' rhetoric. Having access to the most private moments of people's lives is one of the most effective disciplinary practices precisely because it opens *every* human action up for surveillance. Thus, as Riis points out, "it is the settled belief of the men who conduct [newsboy lodging houses] that soap and water are as powerful moral agents in their particular field as preaching, and they have experience to back them."[65] Soap and water, from this perspective, is the disciplinary agent of the middle class, one that disciplines through denial and repression: the clean body is less "visible" than the dirty one because it does not activate the senses. Cleaning disciplines the body by hiding it, denying its presence. "The

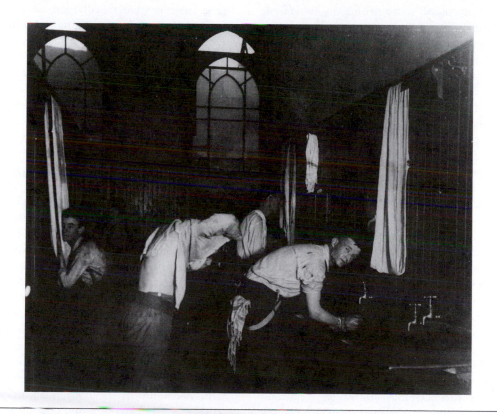

Figure 4 "Washing Up" in the Newsboys' Lodging House.
SOURCE: The Jacob A. Riis Collection, #164. Museum of the City of New York.

police and soap," write Stallybrass and White, "were the antithesis of the crime and disease which supposedly lurked in the slums, prowling out at night to the suburbs; they were the agents of discipline, surveillance, purity."[66]

Second, soap and water are combined with the gaze because we are looking across class boundaries: in this discourse it is the poor who are watched. At this moment, the objects of our gaze become eroticized. Because these boys are of the "underclass," their image is made available to the viewers. Bathing transgresses class boundaries temporarily in that it is a "universally" desirable ritual for the bourgeoisie. A positive image to its middle-class viewers, this photo collapses class boundaries temporarily with the effect of providing bourgeois audiences a chance to watch themselves in this most private moment. With soap and water washing away the "disgusting" barrier of dirt, we are left with an image of clean, hence "desirable," bodies. Interestingly, the auspices of the disciplinary gaze do not control this desire completely. The moment of transgression is subversive. Foucault makes the point clear: "But sexuality, through thus becoming an object of analysis and concern, surveillance and control, engenders at the same time an intensification of each individual's desire for, in and over his body."[67] Hence, while this image performs the disciplinary function of making the poor visible, the activity and space presented are destabilizing because they make the audience's own private activities erotically available to them. Needless to say, the "desirability" of what is presented here has multiple, interconnected meanings, not the least of which is the production of a desirable body.

The value of Riis' documentary realism for bourgeois audiences was tied to its ability to provide the illusion of an intense experience without any of its attendant risks. While erotic desires could be raised by these images, more often than not these desires were contained by the distanciating gaze and "disgust." While activating such desires, the "balcony" rhetoric of *How the Other Half Lives* produced a strategy to deflect desire into the visual pleasure of the text. In his autobiography Riis identifies his textual "excursionism" as decidedly advantageous over direct experience: "The beauty of looking into these places without actually being present there is that

the excursionist is spared the vulgar sounds and odious scents and repulsive exhibitions attendant upon such a personal examination."[68] Stallybrass and White point out that "the tram, the railway station, the ice rink, above all the streets themselves, were shockingly promiscuous. And the fear of that promiscuity was encoded above all in terms of the fear of being touched." Consequently, "contagion and 'contamination' become the tropes through which city life was apprehended."[69] Since bodily contact was seen as contaminating, the significance of visual experience was intensified, serving simultaneously as a means of control and as a substitute for direct experience. "From the balcony, one could gaze, but not be touched."[70] Riis made experiences of Otherness safe by enforcing the distance between his viewers and his subjects, allowing viewers to penetrate the darkest spaces of the tenements without leaving their viewing contexts. His audiences were thus transformed into tourists who followed the map he, as the guide, laid out for them; and as such, they could only be observers whose subjects were visually and ideologically packaged for them. Consequently, the sensational vulgarity of Riis' account served to provide only vicarious, hence contained, pleasures for a class whose bodily experiences of reality were becoming increasingly regulated and displaced.

This textualization of experience takes the control of meaning out of the hands of those colonized by the text. Instead, meaning is largely controlled by the expert whose own discourse morally and politically, as well as physically, separates his audience from the tenements. Here, then, is where textual experiences become most insidious. As texts like *How the Other Half Lives* drive the production of a specific body of knowledge about Others, the meanings they naturalize make it possible for "experts" to continue producing statements about "ghettos" and other marginal spaces and people without ever having to enter them. The "Other Half" is a textual construction whose images have rather direct political consequences, namely their literal ghettoization in the discursive practice of surveillance.

Riis' semiotic of the body, then, operated textually as an object of desire and knowledge to be managed and contained through the disciplinary gaze. Though the working class body was inscribed with the status of inferiority (Riis' accounts of disease, stench, fatigue, and above all sobriety draw attention to this), it can also be seen as a site of resistance. John Fiske writes, "the struggle for control over the meanings and pleasures (and therefore the behaviors) of the body is crucial because the body is where the social is most convincingly represented as the individual and where politics can best disguise itself as human nature."[71] The bourgeoisie sought to repress the working class body because it could resist the dominant order, but in the end the bourgeoisie needed the body as the textual link to authenticate its own sense of identity. Thus, disgust not only can produce class identity by what it excludes, but the body out of control can also deeply threaten the ontological foundations of distinctions. Fiske explains that "cleanliness is order—social, semiotic, and moral (it is, after all, next to godliness)—so dirt is disorder, is threatening and undisciplined. The body is inherently 'dirty': all its orifices produce dirt—that is, matter that transgresses its categorical boundary, that contaminates the separateness of the body, and therefore its purity as a category."[72] In its textual operations, the body is transformed into a containable abstraction. While the body may be a vital site from which to oppose a particular social order, the modern techniques of surveillance can discipline and punish it without the direct use of force. And yet while the gaze offers the body of the Other up visually as something to be controlled, subversive moments appear, thus producing the text as a site of struggle. This struggle suggests that domination, like resistance, is enacted in the moment of performance—never given, never stable, never final.

CLOSING THOUGHTS

How the Other Half Lives, in its complex discursive operations, was a late nineteenth-century strategy for managing cultural diversity. Through the controlling gaze of the camera and documentary description, the bourgeoisie sought to contain and transform these differences into usable units of production and consumption. Whether this strategy was successful is a matter for speculation. Though bourgeois political power was increasingly solidified by the turn of the century, it was often exercised through the direct use of force. Violence against organized labor continued and even intensified after the turn of the century, often pitting government troops against strikers. The racist sentiments of the time shortly thereafter developed into the nationwide revival of the Ku Klux Klan, which widened its attack to include nearly every point of difference from ethnicity to religion to social class.[73] Viewed in this context, Riis' documentary realism can be seen as part of a larger struggle to transform nationalist anxiety into a manageable system of signification, thereby maintaining the unstable hegemony of the ruling classes. Riis' realism, read in its intertextual relations with other realist texts, as well as the economic, legal, scientific, and anthropological discourses of its time, was a critical site in which Otherness could be both textualized and performatively engaged. *How the Other Half Lives* performed a semiotics of race, gender, and class identity that ultimately naturalized these differences as a "real" hierarchy, producing and justifying hostility against cultural differences. This ideology of difference is only just now being seriously challenged by multiculturalist academicians and activists who have done much to raise critical awareness of the politics of seemingly "objective" information-gathering practices.

At a deeper level, however, *How the Other Half Lives,* like any other text, contained numerous points of instability; for the wealthy needed the vulgarity of the working class body in order to authenticate its own, albeit vicarious, experience. Here the body became a site of resistance precisely because the bourgeois desire for intense experiences made its regulation a shaky practice. Ironically, the very instrument of power for the bourgeoisie—the controlling gaze—could itself provide only voyeuristic experiences of the body. To gaze on the vulgar body and to transform it into a text is only to experience it visually. Consequently, the visual experience of such hegemonic texts functions to channel desires in ways that contain them as a threat to the social order, hence reproducing in the bourgeoisie the alienation their performance of identity sought to escape or transcend.

NOTES

1. Howells, William Dean, "Criticism and Fiction," *Documents of Modern Literary Realism,* ed. George J. Becker (Princeton: Princeton UP, 1963) 145.

2. John Tagg, *The Burden of Representation* (Amherst: The U of Massachusetts P, 1988) 66.

3. Walter Benjamin, "The Work of Art in the Age of Mechanical Reproduction." First published in 1936, this essay appears in a collection of his essays entitled *Illuminations,* trans. Harry Zohn (New York: Schocken Books, 1969) 219.

4. For examples of this trend, see Carol Squires, ed. *The Critical Image* (Seattle: Bay P, 1990). See also Richard Bolton, ed. *The Contest of Meaning: Critical Histories of Photography* (Cambridge: MIT P, 1989).

5. Specifically, close examination of the root words of "photograph," "photo" and "graph," reveals that photography itself is a discourse, literally. Jacques Derrida points out, the graphic is "read, or it is written" (3) in *Margins of Philosophy,* trans. Alan Bass (Chicago: U of Chicago P, 1972). To the degree that photography is a writing of images, it is a mode of communication not substantively distinct from other communicative forms. The difference is one of function. That is, photography appropriates a discursive space distinct yet necessarily interactive with other modes of discourse. The importance of visual texts for performance studies is discussed by Sonja K. Foss in "Review Essay: Visual Imagery as Communication," *Text and Performance Quarterly* 12 (1992): 85–90.

6. Beverly Whitaker Long and Mary Susan Strine, "Reading Intertextually: Multiple Mediations and Critical Practice." *Quarterly Journal of Speech* 75 (1989): 474.

7. For relevant discussions of these issues, see Jacques Derrida, *Writing and Difference,* trans. Alan Bass (Chicago: U of Chicago P, 1978). See also, Michel Foucault, *The Order of Things: An Archeology of the Human Sciences,* trans. R. D. Laing (New York: Vintage Books, 1970). Jean Baudrillard goes further in flattening the distinction between text and performer by suggesting that human bodies and subjectivities are textual performances: "With the television image—the television being the ultimate and perfect object for this new era—our own body and the whole surrounding universe becomes a control screen." See "The Ecstasy of Communication" (trans. John Johnston) in ed. Hal Foster, *The Anti-Aesthetic: Essays on Postmodern Culture* (Seattle: Bay P, 1983) 127.

8. Susan Sontag, *On Photography* (New York: Dell Publishing Co., 1977) 10. Another comprehensive treatment of the relations between looking and voyeurism can be found in Marianna Torgovnick, *Gone Primitive: Savage Intellects, Modern Lives* (Chicago: U of Chicago P, 1990), Chs.1, 2.

9. Maren Stange, *Symbols of Ideal Life: Social Documentary Photography in America 1890–1950* (New York: Cambridge UP, 1989) 2.

10. Abigail Solomon-Godeau, *Photography at the Dark: Essays on Photographic History, Institutions, and Practices* (Minneapolis: U of Minnesota P, 1981) 175.

11. Michel Foucault, *Discipline and Punish: The Birth of the Prison,* trans. Alan Sheridan (New York: Vintage Books, 1979) 193.

12. Foucault 170–194. In the interests of clarity, the present study uses the term "discipline" as Foucault does, to signify a number of overlapping phenomena. Academic disciplines as fields of study constitute one such usage of the term. However, this usage is inseparable from the activity of discipline and punishment; for all of these activities seek to normalize or standardize behavior, whether in the rubric of producing research or maintaining social order. Disciplines, in short, produce both knowledge and order.

13. Foucault 219.

14. Gilles Deleuze and Félix Guattari, *A Thousand Plateaus: Capitalism and Schizophrenia* (Minneapolis: U of Minnesota P, 1987) 109.

15. Foucault 200.

16. Sander Gilman explicates the appalling results of textualizing the body of the Other in "Black Bodies, White Bodies: Toward an Iconography of Female Sexuality in Late Nineteenth-Century Art, Medicine, and Literature," *"Race," Writing, and Difference,* ed. Henry Louis Gates, Jr. (Chicago: U of Chicago P, 1985) 223–261. Similarly, Dwight Conquergood explores the role of ethnography in constructing and resisting the "Other" as an object of knowledge in "Poetics, Play, Process, and Power: The Performative Turn in Anthropology," *Text and Performance Quarterly* 1 (1989): 82–88. See also his "Rethinking Ethnography: Towards a Critical Cultural Poetics," *Communication Monographs* 58 (1991) 179–194.

17. Foucault 221.

18. Benjamin 226.

19. See Tagg 144–148.

20. Tagg 99.

21. Amy Kaplan, *The Social Construction of American Realism* (Chicago: U of Chicago P, 1988) 20.

22. Stange 1.

23. Jacob A. Riis, *How the Other Half Lives: Studies Among the Tenements of New York* (1890; New York: Dover Publications, Inc., 1971) 1.

24. Stange 4.

25. Anita Levy, *Other Women: The Writing of Class, Race, and Gender, 1832–1898* (Princeton: Princeton UP, 1991) 27. Though Levy's study focuses on English sociological discourse of the mid-nineteenth century, this passage appropriately describes Riis' strategic deployment of middle-class values.

26. Riis 226 (emphasis added).

27. Riis 1.

28. Riis 229.

29. Tagg 11.

30. John Berger makes this point deftly in *Ways of Seeing* (London: British Broadcasting System Books, 1977) 47: "One might simplify this by saying: *men act* and *women appear.* Men look at women. Women watch themselves being looked at. This determines not only most relations between men and women but also the relation of women to themselves. The surveyor of woman in herself is male: the surveyed female. Thus she turns herself into an object— and most particularly an object of vision: a sight." For an elaboration of the panoptic operations of gender, see Sandra Lee Bartky, "Foucault, Femininity, and the Modernization of Patriarchal Power," *Femininity and Domination: Studies in the Phenomenology of Oppression* (New York: Routledge, 1990) 63–82.

31. Jane Miller, in her insightful discussion of the convergences of race, class, and gender, explains the connection between the colonizing gaze and "feminization" thus: "To undermine the economy, the sovereignty and the culture of another people is, above all, to undermine the identity and integrity of its male citizens. That has often involved the theft of their women, as part of a process which is to be thought of as infantilization or, ultimately, as feminization. The question remains: why does such an analysis not entail a concern for women's loss of political and economic status, in itself?" *Seductions: Studies in Reading and Culture* (Cambridge: Harvard UP, 1991) 118. Miller answers this question by pointing out that colonization is fused with the imagery of sexual penetration: "A prevailing imagery of penetration, of stamina and of the eventual discovery of the strange and the hidden merge the colonizing adventure definitively with the sexual adventure" (117). In a nutshell, the penetration of Other spaces is both rape and colonization. For

another discussion of how gender is a discursive production, rather than a natural quality, see Hélène Cixous, "The Laugh of the Medusa," *The Critical Tradition: Classic Texts and Contemporary Trends,* ed. David H. Richter (New York: St. Martin's P, 1989) 1090–1118. For a discussion of the ways in which colonialism and patriarchy converge, see Gayatri Chakravorty Spivak, "Three Women's Texts and a Critique of Imperialism," in Gates 262–280.

32. Riis 19.

33. Riis 19.

34. Riis 80.

35. For relevant examples of these discourses, see John Fiske's *The Discovery of America Vols. 1 & 2,* (Boston: 1895). See also W. A. Croffut. *The Vanderbilts and the Story of Their Fortune* (New York: 1886). A particularly informative example is Andrew Carnegie's "The Gospel of Wealth," *Words that Made American History Since the Civil War,* 3rd ed. Vol. 2, ed. Richard N. Current et al. (Boston: Little, Brown, & Co., 1962) 123–133. For an elaboration of the pervasive operations of this discourse, see Jackson Lears, *No Place of Grace: Antimodernism and the Transformation of American Culture 1880–1920* (New York: Pantheon, 1981) Ch. 1.

36. Riis 124–126.

37. Riis 124 (emphasis added).

38. Riis 124.

39. Riis 109.

40. Levy 33.

41. Riis 83.

42. Levy 34.

43. Riis 183.

44. Riis 183.

45. Riis 124.

46. Gilman 256.

47. Riis 22.

48. John Fiske, *Introduction to Communication Studies,* 2nd ed. (New York: Routledge, 1990) 94.

49. Riis 22.

50. On the multivalent effects of her triple stigma, Sander Gilman elaborates: "The 'white *man's* burden' thus becomes his sexuality and its control, and it is this which is transferred into the seed to control the sexuality of the Other, the Other as sexualized female. The colonial mentality which sees 'natives' as needing control is easily transferred to 'woman'—but woman as exemplified by the caste of the prostitute. This need for control was a projection of inner fears; thus, its articulation in visual images was in terms which described the polar opposite of the European male" (256).

51. Riis 115.

52. Riis 115.

53. For a thorough discussion, see Gilman.

54. Riis 115.

55. The fear of miscegenation is very clearly performed in D. W. Griffith's 1915 film *The Birth of a Nation* where the Ku Klux Klan's violent enforcement of racial segregation is seen as the critical moment in which "America" as a nation is unified against the "common" enemy of "the black man" and is thus "born." The assumption that racial differences are natural is considerably complicated in Charles W. Chesnutt's 1901 novel, *The Marrow of Tradition* (Ann Arbor: Ann Arbor Paperbacks, 1969), in which realist and naturalist techniques are invoked to show that the social distinctions between races are arbitrarily derived. Both narratives suggest to a large degree that the "nation" is defined by rigid, often violent, enforcement of race, gender, and class exclusions. While Griffith's film celebrates this conception of "America," Chesnutt sees racism as the morally debilitating "marrow" of "American" tradition.

56. Torgovnick 4.

57. Peter Stallybrass and Allon White, *The Politics and Poetics of Transgression* (Ithaca: Cornell UP, 1986) Ch. 4.

58. Stallybrass and White 149–150. A similar discussion of the issue appears in Kenneth Burke, *A Rhetoric of Motives* (Berkeley: U of California P, 1969) 168–169.

59. Berger 54.

60. Berger 54.

61. Berger 58.

62. Stallybrass and White 145.

63. For elaborations of this argument see Susan Willis, *A Primer for Daily Life* (New York: Routledge, 1991) Ch. 5. See also Mary Ryan, *Women in Public: Between Banners and Ballots, 1825–1880* (Baltimore: The Johns Hopkins UP, 1990).

64. Riis 160.

65. Riis 156.

66. Stallybrass and White 134.

67. Michel Foucault, "Body/Power," *Power/Knowledge: Selected Interviews and Other Writings 1972–1977,* ed. Colin Gordon (New York: Pantheon, 1980) 56–57.

68. Stange 16.

69. Stallybrass and White 135.

70. Stallybrass and White 136.

71. John Fiske, *Understanding Popular Culture* (Boston: Unwin Hyman, 1989) 70.

72. Fiske, *Understanding* 99.

73. For a relevant discussion see John Higham, *Strangers in the Land: Patterns of American Nativism 1860–1925* (New York: Atheneum, 1970) 264–330.

2

EMBODYING NORMAL MIRACLES

NATHAN STORMER

Broadly speaking, at the juncture of the "body" and the "population," sex became a crucial target of a power organized around the management of life rather than the menace of death.

—M. Foucault, *The History of Sexuality*

The following film, The Miracle of Life, *is about the process of human reproduction. Please use discretion when choosing to view the program.*

—narrator, *The Miracle of Life*

You are warned of the miracle and the danger of "the extraordinary process" you are about to see. Abruptly, you find yourself falling into the ocean like Icarus. Once submerged in the "shallow, primordial sea," the descent continues into the genetic material of a cell. The images are stunning, colorful, and translucent. Suddenly you are pulled out of microscopic flesh and informed of the genetic similarity of all life on earth only to be plunged back into the flesh, this time into a woman's reproductive organs. In "a microscopic world of beautiful" oranges, reds, pinks, and blues "deep inside ourselves," you travel with a torpid egg from the ovary, through muscular gathers of the fallopian tube, to the fertile plain of the uterus. The remarkable process of ovulation is detailed and quantified as you proceed: time, distance, size, magnification, and risk are reported. Leaving the uterus, you then traverse a man's reproductive organs on an elliptical return to the egg. Worming your way down the urethra, you pass the tissues and glands that will help you return, finally entering the seminiferous tubules where you meet many sperm. Again beautifully composed, everything is quantified and named. Witnessing a thermal profile of an erection, you then accompany the sperm through an ejaculation. Once in the vagina, you and the intrepid sperm embark on a "perilous journey," overcoming incredible obstacles, suffering losses at every step, until you return to penetrate the egg. You watch cells double and redouble, scrutinizing the periodic emergence of fetal fingers, toes,

SOURCE: Stormer, N. (1997). Embodying normal miracles. *Quarterly Journal of Speech, 83*(2), 172–191. © National Communication Association.

and facial features until a new person is born. In phenomenally magnified, brilliantly colored images that recede and swell, the floating, swimming, breathing "miracle of life" has been embodied before you.[1]

In 1983, PBS broadcast the Emmy-Award winning *The Miracle of Life,* "the first filmed record of human conception photographed by Lennart Nilsson." The film has been re-broadcast, is available on video, and has been an educational tool in classrooms.[2] Born in 1922 in Sweden, Nilsson is a photographer of biology and a pioneer in the imaging of reproduction. Beginning in 1951, after viewing two-month old fetuses, he began a series of works celebratory of life and of visualization. Now famous for the image of a fetus that graced *Life*'s cover in 1965, Nilsson has produced numerous scientific photographs, "but his greatest subject, and his continuing lifetime project, is based on the way he sees a mother's womb–not as a social battleground but as a 'very interesting' world in which a magical process occurs" (Van Biema 46). Nonetheless, Nilsson's images have found a place in the conflicted discourse about abortion on anti-abortion placards, silhouettes on billboards, and so on.[3] According to historian Barbara Duden, Nilsson's work buttresses the anti-abortion position that life begins at conception because ostensibly we can *see* life forming (*Disembodying*).

The considerable attention paid Nilsson's imagery as proof of life illustrates how the rhetorical act of visualizing reproduction brings biology into the orbit of politics. His filmed account of reproduction, though unparalleled in visual splendor, tells a common story of the egg and the sperm found in scientific textbooks. That narrative follows gendered stereotypes of pursuit and consummation by the male of the female.[4] Because Nilsson sets the standard for visualizing this process and because his images follow the common narrative, his film is a touchstone for visual rhetoric about procreation. Further, because his images are readily employed by anti-abortion advocates, Nilsson's work sits at a crossroads between the bio-medical and anti-abortion communities' discourses on "life." This is significant not only because it raises questions about biology as a way of knowing, but also because pro-choice and pro-life advocates rely on biology to understand reproduction. Catholic prelates, United States politicians, and Planned Parenthood members stand on the same biological ground when discussing bodily rights and procreation and, if Nilsson's film is indicative, that ground is not as level as one might assume.[5]

Taking Nilsson's film as a leading exemplar of bio-medical discourse on reproduction, I argue that his imagery is a form of "pro-life" rhetoric, one that has broader implications than that term might imply. In his work, life is rhetorically embodied by naturalizing gendered sexual conventions and by erasing the social context in which those conventions were formed. Maintaining life becomes procreative sexuality, a coupling that provides a first premise for the social management of reproduction and the normalization of sexual behavior. In Nilsson's vision of reproduction, a broad "pro-life" perspective on sexuality is concretized as medical truth in a representation of the body. As I use the term, then, "pro-life" refers to an outlook that deems the creation of human life a value that supersedes cultural and individual considerations and that centralizes life's worth in reproductive structures and practices.

After some prefatory remarks on life as a modern social construct, I establish my criticism in three sections. The first is a brief history of bio-medical perception of the body and the rhetorical maneuver of naturalizing "truths" in the body via scientific observation. I also note Nilsson's position in this tradition. The second section applies these principles of visual rhetoric to an exegesis of *The Miracle of Life*. Based on the similarities between the video and an anatomy lesson, I describe in detail the ways in which gender and sexuality are naturalized in seemingly objective commentary on human biology. The final section discusses the pro-life politics of biology in this video and its possible ramifications. I note the explicit connection between environmental discourse about life on earth and life in the body. Through reproduction, the individual body is yoked to the species body.

With this essay, I am joining a conversation about the population politics of pregnancy. Following in the footsteps of feminist critics of scientific discourse such as Alice Adams, Barbara Duden, Barbara Ehrenreich and Deidre English, Evelyn Fox Keller, Emily Martin, Rosalind

Petchesky, and Londa Schiebinger, I offer a feminist criticism of the construction of gender and sexuality in *The Miracle of Life*.[6] I am interested in the way that scientific metaphors and methods of visualization construe our bodies because, historically, individual bodily rights have been undercut by discourses of biological determinism, whether through measurements of skull size, genetic explanations of sexuality, or neurological models that justify institutionalization.[7] My intent is to highlight how contemporary knowledge of reproduction is rhetorical and how such rhetoric invites identifications with a particular form of population politics.[8] By doing so, I hope to create greater space for development of alternate articulations of the body.[9] Although I contend that it is not possible to have a pure, neutral description of the body, it is possible and necessary to debate the merits of different descriptions and to acknowledge their social ancestry and effects. When considering definitions of life and our bodily rights in terms of sexual practices, we should question established truths carefully because rhetoric such as Nilsson's is often unwittingly accorded the status of absolute proof.

This film draws much of its status from biology's station as the science of "life." Historian Barbara Duden writes, "Life as a substantive notion appears a good century after the final demotion of Aristotle as the great science teacher, or about two thousand years after his death. In 1801 Jean-Baptiste Lamarck introduced the term *biology* into the French language. The new science defined 'life' as its object" (emphasis in original, *Disembodying* 103). As the field gained prominence over the last two centuries, the creative force of the universe shifted from nature to reproductive life. It is not a difficult transition to make because the term nature is derived from nascitura, or birthing, such that "woman's pregnancy is the eminent analogy to nature's constant action" (Duden, *Disembodying* 105). As a science, biology's task has been the systematic articulation of life's embodiment, "successively searching for this organization [life] in tissues, then cells, then protoplasm, then the genetic code, and by now . . . in morphogenetic fields" (Duden, *Disembodying* 103). The vague, mysterious presence of "life" in all of existence is its power. Life is the primordial essence of all being from which each living

thing descends as a momentary individuation of that essence (Foucault, *Order* 278). Biology presumes an unseen fabric that connects individuals to the world like visible links in a great chain of invisible ontology that supersedes us.

In this modern biological context I argue that *The Miracle of Life* is a pro-life film in ways not revealed by the typical vernacular of abortion politics. Nilsson's video is an instance of anti-abortion discourse sedimented in the naturalistic and objective language of biology and medicine. Put another way, the bio-medical discourse that makes Nilsson's video sensible to us is also embedded in a system of power that constructs the reproductive body as an anchor for society. An imperative to maximize life, a pro-life mandate in its broadest sense, permeates this video and is a counterweight to more brutal tendencies in anti-abortion discourse. As one sociologist writes, "those who call themselves 'pro-life' choose to present themselves not with images of living children . . . but with images which reduce life to 'pulp' or 'bloody mass'" (Frank 77). This is true if one looks to films that provide grisly records of abortions, such as *The Silent Scream* and *Eclipse of Reason,* or to placards of aborted fetuses at rallies. Anti-abortion rhetoric is a discourse obsessed with untimely, unwarranted death; however, anti-abortion discourse is equally obsessed with life to the extent that images such as Nilsson's offer proof that abortion is murder. That is, abortion is death only if we can see embodied life in the womb. These images form a dialectic of life and death such that bio-medical discourse on reproduction is necessarily intertwined in the believability and intelligibility of anti-abortion rhetoric.

To explain how systems of power are rhetorically enmeshed in the production of a knowledge of life, I turn to the work of Michel Foucault. His historical and theoretical writings are invaluable for understanding the intersections of bio-medical discourse, vision, and sexuality. In *The Birth of the Clinic*, Foucault argues that life and death have played a mutually defining role in the modern medical profession's quest for control over vitality (144–145).[10] Early knowledge of life was predicated on morbidity, thereby making "Death . . . the great analyst" (144). Pathological anatomy came to define medical perception and institutions after the Enlightenment, replacing earlier symptomatic knowledges of the humors with a systematic embodiment of illness in tissue. Anatomists and physicians dissected the newly deceased, sometimes executed criminals, to find the seats of disease as opposed to the ancient pathological analysis of bile, blood, and so on. The presumption was that death operated as a mirror to life such that one could infer conditions in the living body by inverting the progress of decay in a corpse (Adams 136; Duden, *Skin*). As a way of knowing, morbidity presumed the doctor to be reading backward through death and across life.

In part, the early premise that death was a reversal of life was shaped by technological limitations of the gaze (Adams 136). Autopsies and anatomical dissection have to be done after death, which prohibits seeing life at work. Ironically, life "hides and envelops" while death "opens up to the light of day the black coffer of the body" (Foucault, *Birth* 166). With the advent of the stethoscope, probe, ultrasound, and the electron microscope, however, the medical gaze has opened the living body. Just as death became *"embodied in* the *living bodies* of individuals" given its location in diseased flesh, life too is embodied through its location in the reproductive organs (emphasis in original, Foucault, *Birth* 196). In other words, there has been a shift from one term of the dialectic to the other so that knowledge now reads through life and across death. In the words of Alice Adams,

> Developments in mammalian embryology in the nineteenth century and the study of genetics in the twentieth describe a backward movement through the lifetime of the individual. Instead of focusing on the moment of death as the revelatory moment, now the clinical gaze focuses on the first moments of life.... In its search for the roots of life, the clinical gaze shifts from the corpse to the living embryo. (136–137)

Viewing *The Miracle of Life* as part of the biological endeavor to make invisible life visible is significant because, in the modern context, the exercise of power is authorized by life to operate on and through bodies. In the introduction to *The History of Sexuality,* Foucault explains that "a normalizing society is the historical outcome of a technology of power centered on life" (144). He invokes his theory of power developed in *Discipline and Punish* wherein he argues that societal power is enacted through ever-increasing institutional surveillance of, and ultimately self-surveillance by, the individual. Individuals are socialized through institutionalized discourses whether biological, sexual, clinical, penal, or otherwise, and produce a normal society by conformity. We all function as "police" of sorts, continually checking our behavior against the cultural codes to which we adhere.[11] Echoing feminist commentaries that date to Mary Wollstonecraft, Foucault argues that bodies are sites on and through which disciplinary power operates in that we subject bodies to constant scrutiny and employ them in broad patterns of choreographed ritual (Bordo, "Feminism"; Foucault, *Discipline*). Further, he connects the "penality of the norm" to the powerful, invisible notion of life as the authorization for disciplinary practices. He contends that contemporary technologies of power operate "no longer to kill, but to invest life through and through" (*Sexuality* 139). Individual bodies are organized in relation to the "social body which needs to be protected, in a quasi-medical sense" (Foucault, "Body/Power" 55). Conceptually, it is a shift from discussing the Body Politic, wherein "the state or society was imagined as a human body . . . to the politics of the body" wherein population politics are the politics (Bordo, *Weight* 21).[12]

Exercises of power, however, are "never seamless but are always spawning new forms of culture and subjectivity, new opportunities for transformation" (Bordo, *Weight* 27). In his later work, Foucault believed "dominant forms and institutions are continually being penetrated and reconstructed by values, styles, and knowledges that have been developing and gathering strength, energy, and distinctiveness 'at the margins'" (Bordo, *Weight* 27–28). Accordingly, "true" biological discourses about reproduction are central instruments in the operation of power and, necessarily, contested. Reproductive knowledge is part of the medical socialization of sexuality because sexuality offers "a means of access both to the life of the body and the life of the species," and, thus, is the key to population politics (Foucault, *Sexuality* 146). Sexuality is a means for "disciplining the body" in terms of procreative practices and for "regulating the population" by normalizing reproduction (Foucault, *Sexuality* 46). Popular bio-medical discourse about reproduction, as illustrated by this analysis, helps normalize sexuality. To that extent, I am addressing the political work tacitly present in the discursive practices by which bio-medical knowledge is produced. As an exemplar of those practices, Nilsson's imagery is implicated in that political work. I am neither addressing Nilsson's conscious intent nor assigning an explicit agenda to the medical profession; rather, I am criticizing everyday rules for making knowledge and the consequences of those rules for society. By joining the feminist critique of reproductive knowledge, I am participating in the resistance to that form of dominance.

In the Flesh

The history of medical representation, particularly anatomical depictions, has been a process of creating virtual bodies in lieu of corporeal ones. The medical gaze produces a discursive body that is a visualization of knowledge. Instead of confirming a body's essential being, medical vision articulates it. From this perspective, as a form of visual rhetoric that bestows concreteness on images, medical imagery actively constructs the essence of reproductive sexuality. As I argue, *The Miracle of Life* participates in that rhetoric.

The watchful, judgmental eye of the medical profession is trained to see the "normal" individual. That individual is constituted by norms of size, weight, age, sex, race, socio-economic position, tissues, fluids, cell structure, chemical composition, dietary habits, and so forth. The modern subject is tabled, psychodemographed, *contained*. That is, she or he is predefined (Rajchman 92). In the practice of seeing, the properly disciplined gaze makes this normal, modern, medical subject "visible" (Crary 16). This collapse of knowing into seeing is Foucault's basic argument about the medical gaze in *The Birth of the Clinic:* "the genesis of the manifestation of the truth is also the genesis of the knowledge of the truth" (110). Thus, the medical "picture's only role is to divide up the visible within an already given

conceptual framework," that of the modern, normal body (113).

Foucault calls the enactment of seeing-as-knowing the "speaking eye" (*Birth* 114). His emphasis on the speaking position is only half the story, however. Duden contends that as consumers of authoritative images we have become quite compliant, accustomed to visualizing "on command" to the point that we have a "strange mistrust of our own eyes, a disposition to take as real only that which is mechanically displayed in a photograph, statistical curve, or a table" (*Disembodying* 17). In his 1990 interview in *Life,* Nilsson echoes this claim: "Life is stronger than death; it is much stronger, *and you see it here*" (emphasis mine, Van Biema 46). Barbara Maria Stafford concurs with Duden, arguing in *Body Criticism* that the Enlightenment marks the revolutionary emergence of a visual culture mediated by textual interpretation. As a result, the wholesale internalization of "seeing as knowing" in modernity creates an "illusion that we forget is an illusion" as Nietzsche might say, or what Duden calls "misplaced concreteness" (*Disembodying* 20). This misplacement is a key feature of the power of normality because it hides power's operation: "Disciplinary power . . . is exercised through its invisibility; at the same time it imposes on those whom it subjects a principle of compulsory visibility" (Foucault, *Discipline* 187). The ways in which we make "truth" are so transparent that we "are 'prisoners' of the self-evidence of one *way* of seeing" (emphasis in original, Rajchman 94).

Moreover, we have come to desire the act of knowing sexuality. Foucault writes, "We have at least invented a different kind of pleasure: pleasure in the truth of pleasure, the pleasure of knowing that truth, of discovering and exposing it, the fascination of seeing it and telling it, of captivating and capturing others by it, of confiding it in secret, of luring it out in the open—the specific pleasure of the true discourse on pleasure" (*Sexuality* 71). Nilsson is no exception to this fascination, as he and his co-author Lars Hamberger indicate in their 1990 book of reproductive images, *A Child is Born:* "The more scientists have learned about the beginning of human life, the greater the wonder has become" (15). Nilsson and Hamberger consciously shift attention from their role in the production of "miraculous" images: "At the center of our story, however, is neither technology nor modern medicine but the enduring miracle of pregnancy and birth" (15). In the *Life* interview, Nilsson abdicates any responsibility for embodying life: "Look at the pictures. I am not the man who shall decide when human life started. I am a reporter, I am a photographer" (Van Biema 46). Nonetheless, he has devoted his life to the pleasure of knowing the lyrical magic of procreation. He is visualizing life's apparent truth and the sexuality by which it is maintained, and we too are held by that magic. Absenting himself from the process of visualization is simply a manifestation of desiring a self-evident sex.

The effect of this medical visioning often is discussed in terms of Foucault's comment that history has destroyed the body and Baudrillard's theory of simulacra.[13] The body has achieved a "purely *rhetorical* existence"; it has become a floating metaphor that no longer need refer to a corporeal body to have significance (emphasis in original, Kroker & Kroker 21; Stafford 26). Through medical technology and practice, the interior of the body has become its exterior, and the discourse of the disciplined, normalized individual has been embodied in that public interior. Rhetorically forged by the "speaking eye," this virtual body is the anchor for a powerful medical discourse about life.

The "speaking eye" is especially apparent in Nilsson's work. Employing electron microscopy, he creates images by what Duden calls "*photogeny*" (*Disembodying* 18). Digitally constructed pictures are generated by lightwaves, not imprinted by light on a receptive surface as is the case with *photo*graphy.[14] In the free-wheeling rhetorical space of a virtual body, digital imagery dramatically expands our ability to visualize even as it remains within the prison of "self-evidence." Consider the extended hormonal interlude in *The Miracle of Life*. Early in the video, images of hormones that have been dyed and crystallized appear. Reminiscent of sequences from Disney's *Fantasia,* beautiful streaks of blue ice cascade across the screen as peaceful music overlays the scene. We are told that these are hormones. What is left out is that hormones do not exist or function anywhere in the body as they appear in this image. Yet because they are visualized and named, the virtual embodiment of a hormone is now seen as

self-evident. Moreover, the processes of life are embodied in these virtual hormones. The narrator informs us that sex hormones control the entire reproductive cycle. "Normal" human reproduction is beyond our control, made primal and essential by virtue of its embodiment.

I call attention to this particular image because it demonstrates the desire of the "speaking eye" to command our vision and the degree to which the corporeal body cannot be viewed in any objective, neutral fashion. The other bodily images in the film are realistic (if considerably magnified) simulations of bodily tissues or fluids. In contrast, as a piece of crystalline artwork the image of the hormone has absolutely no biological status. Ostensibly we now "know" what hormones look like, and the urge to breed has been made concrete in the most abstract of aesthetics. More important, under the authoritative medical gaze, the beauty of the body appears at the expense of the body. Literally, the hormone was destroyed to make this image. In a moment of technological narcissism, Nilsson stuns the viewer with his prowess. The rest of the film is no less pleasurable to view, but the scientific realism of the other images hides the libidinal desire to see, the "lust of the eye" as Duden calls it (*Disembodying* 15–16). In this hormonal moment, the consummatory desire to see (and, thus, to know) emerges from behind its scientific mask. The corporeal body is a literal palette on which Nilsson paints the desired virtual body.

Indeed, all representations of the body rely on the corporeal body as a palette. My point in stressing the constructedness of the film's imagery is not to allude to a truer body that Nilsson has forsaken but to draw attention to the casuistry we necessarily engage in when making sense of our bodies. *The Miracle of Life* is a masterwork of bodily representation that concretizes a set of images as the flesh itself. Consequently, the symbolic action effected by mistaking the film for the body enables one to critique the merits of Nilsson's interpretation in terms of a system of power that takes life as a justifying term.

VAST MICROCOSMS

In *The Miracle of Life,* in a chronology of ovulation, ejaculation, fertilization, and gestation, we are sheparded through the male and female reproductive organs and informed about the various parts and their respective functions. In that sense, the film is an anatomy lesson; however, it is not the dissection of a corpse. Nonetheless, both forms of representation share a logic. The differences from and similarities to the traditional anatomy lesson allow us to discern the embodiment of life in Nilsson's work and how the video participates in systems of power. To highlight the interconnection of power and modes of creating corporeal images, one can compare the less sophisticated pathological anatomy of old to the contemporary benchmark images in *The Miracle of Life*. The shared perspective of old and new methods demonstrates how constructions of the body are entwined with power.

As mentioned earlier, the rise of pathological anatomy changed medical perception. It also changed how we know our bodies—now we are always anatomized. Just as we imagine boundary lines between nations, we extend demarcations between parts of the body beneath the skin, projecting anatomical models we have learned. This logic has been in operation for many centuries as Jonathan Sawday noted in his study of a particular Renaissance dissection. The great anatomist Andreas Vesalius was discoursing on the anatomy of a man, still living, who was to be dissected: "The man who is still alive as Vesalius speaks has already been conceptually anatomised. Objectified, he is to be the passive recipient—a blank drawing page—of anatomical knowledge" (115). To early anatomists the virtual body depicted in atlases was more "real" than the flesh and bone of whomever was before them. Rembrandt's *The Anatomy Lesson of Dr. Nicolas Tulp,* a painting in which many famous surgeons are depicted attending a lesson by Dr. Tulp, is indicative of this visual paradigm. Art historian Francis Barker notes the significance of the collective gaze within the painting: "No eye within the painting sees the body. The scientific gaze, the perspective of natural philosophy, may be organized around the corpse, but not in order to see it. The lines of sight can be easily traced. They return from the surgeons to we who look (how real we are), or they run to the anatomy atlas open at the foot of the corpse" (77). Barker comments that this averted gaze harks back to the medieval tradition of announcing the lesson from a text without ever examining the corpse or without a corpse entirely. "The corpse . . . becomes, unseen, the absent aspect of the modern body, from which the gaze and the trajectory of discourse are averted" (80). In place of the corporeal body, "a new identity was created. The new identity is that of the scientific subject" (Sawday 116). In the present context of a body turned inside out by ultrasound, x-rays, and electron microscopy, I would argue it is now a working assumption within our culture that anatomical knowledge is synonymous with our interior (Kroker & Kroker). In that regard, the anatomy lesson is a central example of the displacement of the unruly corporeal body and the embodiment of the disciplined normal one.

In *The Miracle of Life,* there is a subtle nod to the tradition of announcing the lesson from the anatomical atlas that, on the surface, would seem to bring the gaze back to the body and away from the image. It is, in fact, only another instance of looking away from the lived body. Prior to the presentation of the female and male reproductive organs we are shown a very simple drawing of each. Accompanied by narration, the process of ovulation and fertilization is illustrated on the female anatomy and the process of sperm maturation and ejaculation on the male. After the mini-lesson about the female reproductive system, we shift to a highly magnified image of the ovary in which the organ occupies much of the frame. The narrator informs the viewer that this is "the ovary itself." Similarly, after the male system is illustrated, we are taken inside "the urethra itself like moles in a tunnel of tissue. Throughout the film, ontological claims about the reality of the images are habitual, signified by the phrase "this is" preceding descriptions. In particular, when DNA molecules are presented we are told in reverent tones that the images are the thing: "these are the DNA molecules themselves," and life's essence is in these virtual molecules. A similar moment occurs when the egg is finally fertilized. "Never before" have the initial cell divisions of a new organism been witnessed.

The apparent shift from the image to the corporeal body is reinforced by the juxtaposition of crude images of reproduction with phenomenally detailed, magnified images of tissues and organs "themselves." These are simply different orders of simulacra touted as image versus reality. In a false return to the corporeal body, the virtual body achieves a still more privileged status as "reality." Interestingly, interspersed with ontological statements about reality are awed remarks about the degree of magnification that makes these images possible. Magnifications range from thousands of times for grosser features to "half a million" when viewing new cell division. Stafford documents the eighteenth-century process by which magnifying technologies were elevated, on the platform of empiricist and rationalist Enlightenment philosophies, to a status of truer than true vision. Magnification is not at odds with seeing the truth in this film; it is a requisite to do so. Echoing Duden's remark that we no longer trust our own vision, the naked eye is simply not sufficient.

The inconsistency of the magnification, shifting thousands of degrees at a time, reinforces the veracity of the visuals as well. Image after image in the video is presented in roughly equivalent size in the center of the screen, with occasional perspective given to sperm or egg in relation to other organs or each other. As we are shown a looming ovary, egg, or testicle, magnifications are recited by the "speaking eye" but they are difficult to process against, say, the image of a large flagellum protruding from an egg. Even relations to everyday objects (the fallopian tube is the "width of two strands of hair," the egg is the size of "a grain of sand") are not helpful against a backdrop of gargantuan cells, molecules, and tubules. The ever-varying magnification creates an infinite rhetorical space in which size becomes truth and, in a virtuoso performance of power hiding its mechanisms, the confusing visual equivalences mask the way of seeing that makes them equivalent. The most pertinent example is in the habitual attention paid the sperm cell. As Naomi Pfeffer argues, "focusing on sperm as individual actors in fertilisation leads to confusion about the function of the vast numbers expended in one ejaculate" (41). One could imagine a film wherein the individual sperm is not the center of attention and where the function of ejaculation in relation to ovulation, rather than the fate of man's seed, is the focal point.[15] In Nilsson's film, magnification that parses the ejaculate into millions of individuals (as opposed to one egg) reinforces a Social

Darwinistic drama, aggrandizes ejaculation, and makes the single fertilizing hero visible.

The role of magnification in creating the effect of truth is equally important in articulating space. With the rise in popularity of early modern dissections, death became inexhaustibly legible in the textual space of the anatomized body. It was localized in time and space by its embodiment in diseased tissues, muscles, and organs with the boundaries of this inner space limited only by the refinement of distinctions (Foucault, *Birth* 142, 158–159). That is, the more finely one parsed the body, the more sites one created for medical commentary and intervention. Today, the embodiment of life's truth has become inexhaustibly legible through microscopic vivisection. The vastness of the living inner space Nilsson explores is bounded only by the degree of magnification available.

In *The Miracle of Life,* magnified vivisection is an act of intense scrutiny that, in effect, forces the flesh to "confess" the heterosexual essence of its vitality and, simultaneously, to normalize that sexuality. Generally, the narration and imaging of the film inscribe heterosexual norms of fertility in structures such as eggs, sperm, hormones, and ovarian fluids, and in actions such as movement. It is an archetypal example of what anthropologist Emily Martin calls "a scientific fairy tale" in that masculinized and feminized structures enact the stereotypical pursuit of a man for a woman (486).

For example, masculine and feminine virtues are encoded in the egg and sperm. In the first fifteen minutes of an hour-long program, the passive egg is "released" from the ovary, "drawn in" by the fringes of the fallopian tube and "moved along" by its muscle contractions. The stage has been set for a drama as the egg now "waits" for the sperm. From this point in the video until fertilization (approximately thirty-five minutes), the sperm is the active lead character. Redoubtable sperm, complete with sugar-based "fuel packets," swim upstream through the "extraordinary activity" of the flagellum whose function is to deliver the sperm "quickly and precisely" to "penetrate" the egg. The background for the heroic sperm drama is one of hostile environments, which require the sperm to persevere against great odds. In the testicles, sperm are attacked by antibodies and, thus, rely on "nurse cells" that "protect and nourish" up to 150 sperm until they are ready to embark on their treacherous journey (the androgyny within the testicle not withstanding). Once ejaculated, the sperm enter the acid environment of the vagina, which is "dangerously inhospitable" to these "unwelcome" "potential enemies" as evidenced by one-quarter of the sperm dying immediately. This is a narrative of attrition, laid out in terms of obstacles and risks: antibodies in the vagina take their toll; some sperm lose their way to the cervix; others take the wrong fallopian road once in the uterus; and downward currents resist sperm progress throughout. Resourceful sperm, however, coagulate initially and later bunch up to prevent attrition, and some even stay behind as a "potential back-up." "If they find the egg at all," only fifty or so sperm out of an initial 200 to 300 million will finish the journey. Once arrived, the sperm release enzymes that "dissolve" the egg's surface so as to force entry. It is a Social Darwinistic story overwhelmingly concerned with the journey of the sperm replete with unlucky, defective, and stupid sperm being weeded out. The miracle is heightened by a crescendo of risk and survival culminating in successful fertilization.

The grammar of these events is not a "truth" awaiting discovery. Among several examples, Martin considers the "penetration" metaphor prevalent in reproductive rhetoric. She points out that the egg coat (zona pellucida) has a ligand molecule (ZP3) that binds with receptor proteins on the sperm. The egg holds the sperm to it. Further, the egg may be described as enveloping the sperm rather than being penetrated (495–496). Pfeffer shares Martin's concern, contending that biological discourse overwhelmingly portrays male reproductive organs as relatively free of disease and in terms of triumphant sperm. Female reproductive systems are attributed more functions (justifying greater intervention) and as diseased. It is not accidental that there is no male counterpart to gynecology (Pfeffer 32–36). There is no single story of the body that is free of connotation; accordingly, it is worth the effort to consider the ramifications of the ones on which we rely.

The codification of masculine and feminine traits in bodily structures not only brings reproductive organs into a circuit of connotations, it also reifies a social order in "life itself." In *The Miracle of Life,* the gendered narrative is the vehicle through which we tour the anatomy of female and male reproductive organs and discover life in particular tissues and fluids. The oceans are the original "cradle of life." By analogy, the ovarian fluid encasing the egg follicle prior to ovulation is "the water of life" because it has the same salt content as the ocean. Cells, generally, are the foundation of life with the DNA inside being "the essence of life." Without the chromosomes that carry this "precious genetic" material, life would be impossible. Cell replication is, thus, the replication of life. Egg and sperm are special, of course, because only in fertilization can new life be formed. Overseeing this whole process are hormones that "control" the reproductive ability of both sexes. Still more important, within hours of fertilization we are "permanently" coded male and female by our estrogen or testosterone levels. Life as a concept is embodied as the ability and imperative to procreate.

Once embodied, life's force may be regimented and restrained. In *Discipline and Punish,* Foucault argues that one of the features of the normalizing gaze is the hierarchical partitioning of space so that interventions may be organized and observation maintained (141-143, 170–192).[16] In *The Miracle of Life,* individual pieces in the reproductive puzzle are identified and ranked in terms of their proximity to life's headwaters. In descending order of importance: hormones control the creation of life; DNA is life; sperm create new combinations of life (DNA) by finding the egg; cells carry DNA and replicate it in order to be alive; and all other cells and fluids (such as nurse cells, ovarian fluids, fuel packets, erectile tissues, and fallopian muscle) nourish life. Life is contained and ordered, then, in its biological "cells."

Life in these virtual bodies is further disciplined by its adherence to a program requiring a series of events that "assures the elaboration of the act itself. . . . Power is articulated directly onto time; it assures its control and guarantees its use" (Foucault, *Discipline* 149–160, 152, 160). As the brief outline of the narrative indicates, ovulation begins a sequence that seemingly requires erection, penetration, and ejaculation. An in-coitus ejaculation is represented (the photo-generative feat no doubt warranted the cautionary statement preceding the video) and becomes a mandatory punctuation of reality, a logic of arrangement that gives meaning to disorderly events (Hall). In a video that celebrates life, we are informed that eggs and sperm "die" if they go unused and letting them die runs counter to the narrative of creating the most precious value of life. After insemination, the steadfast sperm inexorably produce the miracle of fertilization. Again, all forms of sex that do not culminate in life are unmiraculous or aberrant because they do not conform to the truth of the narrative. Put differently, if life works in a mutually defining dialectic with death and if life is valorized as a miracle, not to participate in carrying on the miracle is to be caught in a web of negative associations with death.

The normalization of procreation is reinforced by a sequence, just prior to the vivisection of an erection, in which male and female jazz dancers perform an abstracted dance of "courtship." The narrator informs us that no one really understands arousal but that visual and tactile stimulation cause excitation, which in turn leads to an erection and ejaculation. Biological imperatives overwrite sexuality, normalizing procreative heterosexual behaviors. Recall the primacy given hormones over the reproductive cycle. The truth of sex is that ovulation commands fertilization because it has been seen and embodied, whereas courtship is unknowable and lacks biological specificity except as it relates to stimulation and hormonal states. As a program of events and of television, reproduction is perfectly disciplined in time. The virtual bodies replay the drama in the same way in the same sequence, thus normalizing the knowledge of reproduction through its re-enactment.

The Miracle of Life, then, is an anatomy lesson that produces a miraculous truth as Nilsson normalizes it. It makes life visible and disciplined in a patchwork of spatially equivocated body parts, ordered by function, and organized to maximize the value of life. The public interior of these piecemeal virtual bodies is perfectly disciplined, produced to be reproductive. As Foucault remarks, "disciplinary coercion establishes in the body the constricting link between an increased aptitude and an increased domination" (*Discipline* 138), and this body is miraculous at breeding.

The place of *The Miracle of Life* within disciplinary systems of power is worth noting because it illustrates an evolution of the anatomy lesson, from early dissection to microscopy, that reflects some potential limitations of recent criticism of reproductive biology. Unlike the last two centuries, dissection was formerly science *and* punishment. Certain criminals, as part of their sentence, were to be dissected as a last humiliation. Conveniently, this also provided a stock of corpses for scientific pursuits. Sawday notes that early modern and Renaissance culture connected "anatomical investigation and the final tearing apart of the criminal body after death" (116). Rembrandt's *Anatomy Lesson,* for example, is a depiction of juridical dissection, or "the exercise of a jurisdiction over the body of [a criminal], an act of penal and sovereign domination" (Barker 74). Dissection was part of punishment up to the eighteenth century as evidenced by a 1752 act of English Parliament "directing that the bodies of persons executed for murder be hung in chains or be handed over to the surgeons for dissection" (Forbes 490). In the early modern period, anatomists were part of the penal system.

In this vein, many contemporary feminist critics argue that medical technologies, particularly fetal imaging, effect a form of sovereign punishment on a woman's body by erasing, skinning, or generally disembodying her (Adams; Duden; Kroker & Kroker; Manion; Petchesky; Rothman). This overlooks the place of pathological anatomy in discourses on normality and its participation in a less rigid form of disciplinary power. Even in its early days, there was a shift among anatomists to the more rhetorically appealing project of science. In an effort to overcome the contradictions of a punishing medical science, anatomists began to enlist the corpses' help in their drawings. For example, in *Historia de la Composición del Cuerpo Humano,* published in 1556 by Juan de Valverde de Amusco, a Spanish anatomist, there are self-dissecting corpses. In one drawing a man is holding his flesh in one hand and a knife in the other, literally having skinned himself. In a series of abdominal illustrations, men pull away various layers of their own abdominal walls. "Not only is the anatomist not involved in an act of punitive violation, but . . . the corpse is working, in conjunction with the anatomist, towards a shared end . . . the corpse *desires* dissection" (emphasis in original, Sawday 123). These are the ultimate in disciplined, docile bodies that foretell the emergence of disciplinary power in anatomical study.

The contemporary focus on the symbolic flaying of women draws attention from the more flexible form of power of the medically normalized body that is represented by *The Miracle of Life*. On one hand, a juridical, authoritarian form of power *is* at work in medicine as indicated by involuntary sterilizations and other invasive procedures authorized by physicians.[17] Further, Horkheimer and Adorno argue that, "abstraction, the tool of the Enlightenment, treats its objects as did fate . . . it liquidates them" (13). Abstraction of the body into imagery is liquidation of a sort. On the other hand, liquidation does not address the willingness of many women to be monitored, to have their interior made exterior. It also does not account for the liquidation of the man's body in reproductive images. In Nilsson's video, the stunningly visualized, gendered, microscopic space embodies the imperative to procreate at the cellular level. In a culture where bio-medical visualization is almost unquestioned, these images reinforce the verity of patriarchal and heterosexualized norms. For instance, that the man has a duty to impregnate the woman is factualized. There is no discussion of customs of fertility management, in which every culture has engaged throughout history. Because women have been coerced into bearing children in a variety of ways in our history, the lack of discussion of the cultural ramifications of breeding and the naturalized motif of heterosexuality reinforce a patriarchal ideology of compulsory procreation.[18] Also, in light of the narrative of risk and attrition, homosexuality is factualized as unprocreative and a threat to the miracle of life. Through the truth of the medical gaze, power sounds out a biological "confession of the flesh" in ways that reverberate beyond the immediate act of liquidation. Therefore, a critique of authoritarian aspects of the medical vivisection of women should also take into account the disciplining of women to medical practices and the ways in which a seemingly identical vivisection of men inscribes sexualized power. My point is that power does not stop with the "knife," and that we must ask, "What normative work is accomplished by this discourse?"

CONTRACTUAL OBLIGATIONS

Concentric environments for life are created as we are tutored on reproductive anatomy in a funhouse of brightly colored, animalistic organs and cells. The interiors of bodies become public environments for reproduction while the world outside those bodies is made into the environment for their procreation. In terms of the power to foster life, the focus on our public interior in the film is about normalizing procreational politics in individual bodies while the focus on the world environment is about managing the species body. Tying both these environments together is a discourse about the ocean and life's seed, DNA, which permeates both the individual and the species body. As Duden and Foucault have observed, life links bio-medical discourses about reproduction and environmentalism together in ways that have serious import for the functioning of power. In this final section, I address the ways in which the dominant discourse on reproduction that reduces gender and sexuality to physiology, which *The Miracle of Life* typifies, promotes a pro-life politics in the broadest sense.

I delineated the construction of a microenvironment of reproductive systems in the previous section. Both the male and female threaten the sperm as it travails to reach the egg. The hierarchy of space and tissues imprinted on these virtual bodies makes the sperm the prime actor and all else "scenery" for the sperm's triumph. The passive representation of the egg as the "destination" for sperm makes it part of the scenery as well. What is interesting about this interior environment is how barren it is. Time, except as it orders the completion of fertilization, is absent. Space, except as it organizes fertilization, is absent. Social institutions are erased. Finally, although we view a set of parents at the very end of the film, the generic construction of all individuals' genitals erases the social identity of the participants. Only sex as cast in a gendered drama remains as biologically natural.

Oddly, the drama of procreation played out on the austere stage of biology enacts a cellular version of the Original Position argued by John Rawls. In his canonical text, *A Theory of Justice,* Rawls argues the intellectual necessity of a hypothetical position prior to the formation of a social contract wherein the principals are ignorant of their generation, social status, culture, and any particular knowledge that might lead to unfair and therefore unjust decisions (120). General, static knowledge of economic and political theory is necessary, however, for the participants to make the best "rational plan for life" (137). Only behind this Veil of Ignorance can purely rational, just contracts be made (136–142). In an apotheosis of Enlightenment ideals, Rawls makes ignorant innocence a precondition that guarantees the rational achievement of the well-being of the social body.

In the world of reproduction there are beings capable of such ignorance. The egg and the sperm are "aware" of their surroundings in *The Miracle of Life,* and they respond accordingly. Further, sperm, represented as proactive agents, make rational decisions based on the economy and politics of the woman's reproductive system. They swim hard and fast, coagulate, bunch up, and leave behind reserves in tactical sexual politics. Likewise, they are genetically aware of the dangerous economy they enter, so they come in droves. Upon fertilization, the two parties have conceived a new order, a rationally planned life. Also, they have conceived, in innocence, a just creation. Whereas Rawls's theory is predicated on what, to my ears at least, is an impossible hypothetical state, the act of reproduction as represented in *The Miracle of Life* replicates the Original Position strikingly well.

The significance of the parallel I have drawn is apparent when taken in conjunction with the film's portrayal of the macro-environment. From its beginning, *The Miracle of Life* connects all beings together in a tableau of life. The introductory segment, prior to the anatomy lesson of the female, establishes an unbroken, evolutionary chain of being from the first protozoan to humans. After being told that the oceans are "the cradle of life" and shown the structure of DNA, we are informed that this same genetic material connects all beings such as a protozoan, an elephant, a palm tree, or a human. Life escapes the individual's reproductive space because it is embodied in all space. Later, after we have perused the anatomy of males and females, the narrator uses the premise of a life fabric to collapse the individual's body into the species body. Deformed, abnormal sperm appear, and the maladies from which they suffer are detailed. They are weak and devoured, or have

two heads, no head, a defective tail, two tails, and so on. The narrator states that minor fluctuations in temperature due to environmental factors cause such deformities: "overcrowding, stress, smoking, chemical pollution of air and water, occupational hazards, radiation, poor nutrition," even "tight jeans." The implicit commentary (consistent with the drama of heroic attrition) is that the environment threatens life by deforming sperm. That forty percent of sperm are habitually inadequate is not relevant; deformities presume an outside threat (Pfeffer 33). "Despite such obstacles," however, "humans have been successfully reproducing for millions of years." The drama of risk and threat is carried into the larger environment.

The connection between the interior environment of reproduction and the external environment of "modern life" is strengthened by a discourse reminiscent of undersea nature films. The story begins with a descent into the ocean; a connection is drawn between all beings *in water,* and a man and woman swim "above" us. As the woman passes overhead, a rough outline of her reproductive system emerges from her pelvis, and we are shown a magnified image of an ovary. As the anatomy lesson proceeds, images of cells and tissues are represented in motion, in various fluids, often against a neutral or blank background. The subtle sound of fluid in motion, much like the ocean, is a common background to many of these images. This is especially true for images of sperm, always swimming, or shots of the fallopian tube waving on the pelvic sea floor like a great sea cactus. A more explicit connection is drawn when salt water, "the water of life," is located in the ovarian fluid encasing the egg follicle. These images are like the sea flora and fauna of a Jacques Cousteau program. Moreover, we are positioned to view these reproductive critters in much the same manner as a Cousteau film—in their natural habitat, frequently illuminated in a dark space. The most striking example, perhaps, is when the camera confronts a mid-term fetus that tries to push the camera away. The wily fetus has been spotted and flushed.

The pervasiveness of an undersea documentary motif subtly reinforces the link of the individual to the species as well as the environmental threat posed at both levels. Nature films, for which the Cousteau series set the tone and standard "as the first [popular] regularly scheduled television program with a strong message concerning ecology" (Shaheen 93), are almost unconsciously concerned with depicting the environment in danger. Stylistically, to rely on the register of nature films implicitly connotes that same concern. It is a way of seeing that is peculiar to an ecological discourse centered on "the essence of life" (Shaheen 100). Reproductive bodies, as represented in this film, still dwell in the sea of life from which they evolved.

To return to Rawls, understanding the representation of life as a tapestry of individuals by way of his theory illustrates two strategies by which governance is authorized. First, life *is* the social contract. At the level of individual bodies, life is conceived in innocence, in an Original Position, and, therefore, is filled with the social promise innocence entails. At the level of the species body, we already are involved in the contract of life by virtue of our "successful reproduction" and our genetic bond with lowly protozoans. The miracle of life is that the species contract is born anew, in innocence, with each fertilization. Second, life is constructed as a kind of generative irony. At the level of the individual or species, life threatens life. In reproductive anatomy, antibodies and defense systems attack sperm and try to prevent fertilization, yet these cells owe their life to fertilization. Similarly, the environmental hazards of "modern life" threaten the health of reproductive systems and, thus, the further germination of modern life. In order to fulfill the contract of life, governance is marshaled to protect life against itself. The more life is fostered, the more the rational plan for life is threatened, and so on. The management of the life of the "population comes to appear above all else as the ultimate end of government" (Foucault, "Governmentality" 17). In the dialectic of life-death, a politics of life presumes simple embodied existence as the authorization for social administration and camouflages its "political economy" within that existence. Life swallows death; life speaks it. If the dialectic is understood as life threatening itself, existence inherently justifies its own benevolent bondage.

Rawls's innocently engendered contract also clarifies the means by which governmental power is hidden. Life, as conceptualized in *The Miracle of Life,* creates an empty reproductive environment that bears no mark of civilization except its visualization. Reproductive technologies are completely absent from the narrative although it is now uncommon to have a pregnancy without some kind of medical procedure—ultrasound, episiotomy, drug treatment, fetal surgery, and so forth (Gregg; Rothman; Stanworth). In fact, more and more pregnancies are conceived through fertility technologies like in-vitro fertilization (Stanworth 6–7). The need for greater debate on the potential dangers of reproductive technology both for control and physical harm to the patients has raised a chorus of voices (Adams; Rothman; Gregg; Manion; Stanworth; Zuskar; among others). The great benefits that reproductive medicine has wrought are not without negative consequences. In the face of a mythologized, naturalized, virtually embodied reproduction, however, it is hard for those voices to be heard. Policies and practices that influence procreation generally are also missing from the film even though many of those policies create the stress and pollution that threaten life. The naturalized contract to reproduce represented in *The Miracle of Life* not only displaces authority onto life as it authorizes power over life, but it also makes power permanently *innocent* and, therefore, predicated on justice.

The legal system, of course, epitomizes this just exercise of power for life by sanctioning punishment and intrusion. Feminist critics commonly note that fetal rights have increased since the eighties at the expense of pregnant women's rights. For example, pregnant women have been prosecuted on the grounds that they have put their in utero "babies" at risk (Bordo *Weight,* 81–82). These are, of course, intrusions of power after conception. Sociologist Rose Jones documents the emergence of exclusionary policies in businesses, since the seventies, based on risks to fertility generally such as lead poisoning. Laws for negligence are sensitized to protect women's fertility such that discriminating against women is "less costly" (more profitable) (45). In an extension of the power of surveillance, genetic screening for potentially "high-risk" workers can be justified on similar grounds (48). Individuals, once embodied as reproductive systems vital to the species body, are open to intervention on the just premise of protecting unrealized innocent contracts. The limits of intervention are boundless dependent on when one marks life's beginning, as Nilsson illustrates: "Maybe the first moment of human life, it starts with a kiss" (Van Biema 46).

BACK TO THE BEGINNING, BACK TO THE BLANK PAGE

In *The Miracle of Life,* sexualized power is normalized in three intertwining, mutually dependent ways. The truth of life and our sexualized desire to know it, to see it, is anchored in the ether of virtual bodies. As the "speaking eye" articulates the truth of those bodies, the virtual flesh that comes to embody procreative sexuality "confesses" its miraculous normality and its natural imperative. Simultaneously, the interior and exterior environments for reproduction are made hostile so that nature's innocent, living contract is threatened. As biological discourse writes its interior, the corporeal body is lost in the sense of the body being pre-cultural or natural. Thus, in the video, generalized bodies of females and males are disciplined to breed the species body in hyper-real anatomical images; concurrently, governance of reproduction is authorized by a genetically encoded social contract that perpetually threatens self-immolation.

At all three levels the discursive operation of power is hidden. In Nilsson's wondrous film, the pleasure of viewing sexuality in a marvel of light and knowledge masks the powerfully interested techniques that produce the images. The miracle of life is self-evident; just "look at the pictures." In a false return to the corporeal body, the scrutinous naming of parts and sequences of procreation, the glorified seeing of every pre-defined detail of life's embodiment makes procreational politics natural and unquestionable. The miraculous, in a disciplinary sleight of hand, is made normal. Finally, justifying authority on the grounds that life poses a threat to itself provides a cloak of natural innocence for social management.

I think the key maneuver in the rhetoric of this video, then, is the embodiment of normal miracles. The "miracle of life," reproduction, is a central means of social power in the modern era. The normalizing and maintenance of that miracle is what I refer to when I argue that population politics are the basic topos of the modern social order. If one were to look for commonality across different types of pro-life discourse, this would be a good starting point—the mundane miracle that requires careful custodial management to preserve its miraculous nature. This may afford us a means to criticize pro-life discourse other than through the rhetoric of "choice" or rebukes of authoritarian reproductive policies. Addressing the bio-medical authority that is used to substantiate the desired normality of reproduction is vital to allow a broader critique of the *knowledge* created by, and supportive of, an anti-abortion culture.

I have attempted to place what we mean by pro-life in a wider context of bio-medical, visual, and disciplinary authority and to illuminate the discursive backdrop for much of abortion rhetoric.[19] Understanding how a seemingly neutral discourse like biology can support a specific system of power creates a space in which to debate the effects of our common understanding of reproduction on the political structure of our society. The current model of reproduction, as indicated by Nilsson's film, naturalizes a politics that submerges bodily rights in the imperative of conceiving more human beings. If we are to generate a knowledge of procreation that takes into account the lived bodies of a broad range of people (who engage in a plethora of practices for managing fertility or who practice non-reproductive sex), then we must bring culture into our discourse on biology, and we must acknowledge that physiology does not and should not dictate custom, either directly or implicitly. But to do so we must first remove the shroud of unquestioned truth that conceals the rhetoric of biological discourse. We must recognize that knowledge of reproduction is not neutral but is humanly crafted and, therefore, laden with values. Unless and until we de-naturalize the truth of the visual image and recognize the symbolic force of the "speaking eye," we cannot renegotiate our understanding of the body or debate the politics invested in it.

NOTES

1. All uncited textual references in this paper are taken from the video itself or its jacket notes.

2. I have attempted to contact PBS and the video distributor about the video's popularity (rental

information, sales, any feedback from educators they may have received) and have been repeatedly ignored. I am aware from anecdotal evidence from high school teachers (from several regions of the country) that the video is commonly used in biology classes and from discussions with students of mine that many people are familiar with the video.

3. For example, in Minnesota the outline of a fetus quite similar to the one Nilsson has popularized is the standard image for Pro-Life Minnesota. Adams states that images of fetuses that Nilsson has generated have appeared on placards (141–142).

4. Anthropologist Emily Martin, an often-cited commentator on the metaphors and discourse of reproductive science, surveyed the major textbooks for undergraduate and medical students at Johns Hopkins (texts which are widely employed throughout the country). Compared to her synthesis of these textbooks, *The Miracle of Life* replicates their basic narrative of reproduction perfectly. Thus, it is squarely within the mainstream of bio-medical discourse on reproductive biology. See Martin, 485–501. Her essay is a model of criticism of scientific discourse.

5. For example, Cardinal Ratzinger, in 1987, proclaimed the zygote was a human brother and relied on biological concepts to bolster his argument about life at conception (Duden, *Disembodying* 21–22). Abortion rights advocates just as quickly employ information on the non-human character of an early term fetus to indicate life does not begin at conception.

6. I realize there are numerous varieties of feminist scholarship. I proceed along a social constructivist path, one that recognizes the inseparable intersection of the symbolic realm and the non-symbolic in all aspects of human enterprise. In relation to the scholars cited, my analysis is most similar to Petchesky's critique of *The Silent Scream* and Duden's work on the body as a social object, although all of these authors influenced how I think of science and its relation to culture. For more explication on a social constructivist form of feminist scholarship, see Scott.

7. For example, the skeletal proportions of woman were offered as justification that women were intended to fulfill prevailing gender roles of the 18th and 19th century (Schiebinger, "Skeletons"). We should not assume that discourses on sexuality are any less culturally bound today, although they are undoubtedly different in their assumptions. See Gallagher and Laqueur; Gould; Tavris; Schiebinger, *Nature's Body* and *The Mind Has No Sex?*

8. My argument parallels Kenneth Burke's claim that delineating "pure" science from "interested" science is a rhetorical maneuver of the first order. I embellish this idea by looking at the images of the body themselves and not the professed allegiances of the rhetors involved.

9. As yet, I am not aware of any fully-developed alternate descriptions of reproductive biology, nor is there a need to start from scratch. To re-vision a way of describing biology does not necessarily mean that we must begin anew. The feminist critique of science is still relatively young and different models, ones that do not re-inscribe patriarchal norms in biology, are still being formulated. Emily Martin argues that the few attempts to explain fertilization differently than the norm of textbooks still attribute gender stereotypes to cells and structures. Part of the difficulty is that we need a better analysis of the ways in which culture is currently written into biology. Better and richer alternatives will be able to grow only after we have de-naturalized explanations offered by contemporary textbooks and educational films.

10. Edward Schiappa has addressed this issue from the standpoint of logical definition; see "Arguing About Definitions."

11. Foucault is not claiming individuals are simply mass-produced as colorless automatons from a culture factory—quite the opposite. One of the compelling points of his theory of power is that it presumes social cohesion is maintained by an intricate web of diverse individual practices and, almost paradoxically, a broad pattern of conformity that emerges from this diverse practice. Susan Bordo, philosopher and social critic, expressed this point eloquently in *Unbearable Weight:* "For Foucault, modern (as opposed to sovereign) power is non-authoritarian, non-conspiratorial, and indeed non-orchestrated; yet it nonetheless produces and normalizes bodies to serve prevailing relations of dominance and subordination" (26–27). To understand this power arrangement, we must imagine power as diffusely enacted rather than singularly possessed. Also, we must imagine power as patterns of domination that permeate every facet of our lives in historically specific formations, rather than as chaotic or random events (Bordo 26–27). In short, our agency is actively molded from within ourselves and within a whole nexus of social relations. As a result, I am not trying to make a "big brother" indictment of Nilsson or bio-medical texts generally. Instead, I am trying to illuminate patterns and

practices in the production of biological knowledge (which Nilsson's film exemplifies) that implicitly serve the deployment of a broad-based pro-life ideology.

12. In the first volume of *The History of Sexuality,* Foucault describes this connection of the individual body to the species body via practices that emphasize life: "One might say that the ancient right to *take life* or *let live* was replaced by a power to *foster* life or *disallow* it to the point of death. . . . Now it is over life, throughout its unfolding, that power establishes its domination. . . . In concrete terms, starting in the seventeenth century, this power over life evolved in two basic forms. . . . One of these poles—the first to be formed, it seems—centered on the body as a machine: its disciplining, the optimization of its capabilities, the extortion of its forces, the parallel increase of its usefulness and its docility, its integration into systems of efficient and economic controls, all this was ensured by the procedures of power that characterized the *disciplines:* an *anatamo-politics of the human body.* The second, formed somewhat later, focused on the species body, the body imbued with the mechanics of life and serving as the basis of the biological processes: propagation, births and mortality, the level of health, life expectancy and longevity, with all the conditions that can cause these to vary. Their supervision was effected through an entire series of interventions and *regulatory controls: a bio-politics of the population . . .* a power whose function was perhaps no longer to kill, but to invest life through and through" (emphasis in original, 138–139).

13. For more discussion on the historical process of inscribing the body, see Baudrillard; Foucault, "Nietzsche, Genealogy, History"; Grosz; Kroker & Kroker; Ostrander.

14. Discussing Nilsson's photo spread in *Life* magazine in 1990, Duden states that the electron microscope is not used "to verify a biological theory but to create a semblance of natural science representing his own visualization of 'the beginning of human life'" (*Disembodying* 18). Electron microscopy is used because molecules are too small to reflect light, being shorter than the wavelengths of light energy. We are seeing "a collage of digital measurements made by the interference of electron bundles with molecules" (18). The verification that the digitized measurements correspond to human genetic material happens in another procedure such that "Nilsson would not be a bit less convincing if he had used the results of scanning

ultramicroscopy on tissues of any other species" (18). Of course, Nilsson did not use non-human bodily material. The point is that we are not seeing life, nor even a photographic reflection of life (in and of itself a highly rhetorical thing). We are seeing a digitized interpretation of theories of biological life. Although Nilsson uses some photographic images in the film, the wondrous representations that make the invisible visible are digitized.

15. Martin provides an example wherein Nilsson presented an electron micrograph at a conference of a multitude of tiny sperm surrounding a very large egg. He titled it, "Portrait of Sperm." Martin remarks that this is like presenting a picture of a dog and calling it "Portrait of a Flea" (491).

16. In *Discipline and Punish,* Foucault is talking about the surveillance of people in institutional settings. This video is an artifact of such discipline. I am extending Foucault's argument by demonstrating the recording of surveillance as a programmed form of discipline.

17. Sterilization abuse, for instance, "is not a new development. Beginning in the nineteenth century, people known as *eugenicists* tried to popularize the idea that social problems such as crime and poverty could be eliminated by preventing certain 'unfit' people from having children," according to the latest edition of *The New Our Bodies, Ourselves* (Boston Women's, in footnote, 301). In the contemporary context, "since 1974, women have revealed and studies have documented a terrible pattern of sterilization abuse. Victims of sterilization abuse are usually poor or black, Puerto Rican, Chicana or Native American, often with little or no understanding of English. Sometimes physicians consider women mentally unfit. Physicians pressure women into giving consent during labor or childbirth; welfare officials threaten the loss of benefits if women refuse; no one informs women that the operation is permanent. Black women in the South are all too familiar with the 'Mississippi appendectomy,' in which the fallopian tubes are tied or the uterus is removed without them [*sic*] knowing it" (emphasis in original, Boston Women's Collective, 301). Legally, as of the 1988, fourteen states permitted involuntary sterilization, seven of which "specifically mentioned mentally retarded people" (Brantlinger 33; Davis).

18. These strategies range from medical procedures such as S. Weir Mitchell's rest cure to the structure of divorce law. The body of literature that deals

with compulsory motherhood is vast. For a few pieces, consider de Beauvoir's *The Second Sex,* Ehrenreich and English's *For Her Own Good,* Gordon's *Woman's Body, Woman's Right,* Rich's "Compulsory Heterosexuality," and Smith-Rosenberg's *Disorderly Conduct.*

19. I have stressed the textual element of power's operation to the exclusion of material manifestations, as per Susan Bordo's critique that theories of discursive free-play sidestep the concrete effects of power (*Weight* 38). My choice is intentional in that I want [to] reveal the internal mechanisms and external implications of a very significant body of imagery as epitomized by *The Miracle of Life.* This is only a step. What should follow are analyses of how these texts are physically produced, encountered, and internalized.

REFERENCES

Adams, Alice. *Reproducing the Womb: Images of Childbirth in Science, Feminist Theory, Literature.* Ithaca: Cornell UP, 1994.

Barker, Francis. "Into the Vault." *The Tremulous Private Body: Essays on Subjection.* London: Methuen, 1984. 71–112.

Baudrillard, J. "Simulacra and Simulations: Disneyland." Trans. Paul Foss, et al. *Jean Baudrillard: Selected Writings.* Ed. Mark Poster. Stanford, CA: Stanford UP, 1988. 166–184.

Beauvoir, Simone de. *The Second Sex.* Trans. and ed. H. M. Parshley. 1952. New York: Vintage Books, 1989.

Bordo, Susan. "Feminism, Foucault, and the Politics of the Body." *Up Against Foucault: Explorations of Some Tensions Between Foucault and Feminism.* Ed. Caroline Ramazanoglu. Padstow, Cornwall: T. J. P., 1993. 179–202.

Bordo, Susan. *Unbearable Weight: Feminism, Western Culture, and the Body.* Berkeley: U of California P, 1993.

Boston Women's Health Book Collective. *The New Our Bodies, Ourselves: Updated and Expanded for the '90's.* New York: Simon & Schuster, Inc., 1992 rev.

Brantlinger Ellen. *Sterilization of People with Mental Disabilities: Issues, Perspectives, and Cases.* Westport, CT: Auburn House, 1995.

Burke, Kenneth. *A Rhetoric of Motives.* New York: Prentice Hall, 1950.

Crary, Jonathan. *Techniques of the Observer: On Vision and Modernity in the Nineteenth Century.* Cambridge, MA: MIT, 1990.

Davis, Susan, ed. *Women Under Attack: Victories, Backlash and the Fight for Reproductive Freedom.* Boston: South End P, 1988.

Duden, Barbara. *Disembodying Women: Perspectives on Pregnancy and the Unborn.* Cambridge: Harvard UP, 1994.

Duden, Barbara. *The Woman Beneath the Skin: A Doctor's Patients in Eighteenth-Century Germany.* Cambridge: Harvard UP, 1991.

Eclipse of Reason. Prod. Charles Warren. Dir. R. Anderson. Writ. Bernard Nathanson. Nar. Charlton Heston. Video. Bernadell, Inc. 1987.

Ehrenreich, Barbara and Deidre English. *For Her Own Good: 150 Years of Experts' Advice to Women.* Garden City, NY: Anchor Books, 1978.

Forbes, Thomas. "To be Dissected and Anatomized." *Journal of the History of Medicine and Allied Sciences* 36 (1981): 490–492.

Foucault, Michel. (1973). *The Birth of the Clinic: An Archaeology of Medical Perception.* Trans. A. M. Sheridan Smith. 1963. New York: Vintage Books, 1994.

Foucault, Michel. "Body/Power." Trans. Colin Gordon, et al. *Power/Knowledge: Selected Interviews & Other Writings, 1972–1977.* Ed. Colin Gordon. New York: Pantheon, 1980. 55–62.

Foucault, Michel. *Discipline and Punish: The Birth of the Prison.* Trans. Alan Sheridan. 1975. New York: Vintage Books, 1979.

Foucault, Michel. "Governmentality." *M/F: A Feminist Journal* 3 (1979): 5–21.

Foucault, Michel. *The History of Sexuality: An Introduction, Vol. 1.* Trans. Robert Hurley. 1976. New York: Vintage Books, 1990.

Foucault, Michel. "Nietzsche, Genealogy, History." Trans. Donald Bouchard and Sherry Simon. *Language, Counter-Memory, Practice: Selected Essays and Interviews.* Ed. Donald Bouchard. Ithaca: Cornell UP, 1977. 136–164.

Foucault, Michel. *The Order of Things: An Archaeology of the Human Sciences.* 1970. New York: Vintage Books, 1994.

Frank, Arthur W. "For a Sociology of the Body: An Analytical Overview." *The Body: Social Process and Cultural Theory.* Ed. Mike Featherstone, et al. London: Sage, 1991. 36–102.

Gallagher, Catherine and Thomas Laqueur, eds. *The Making of the Modern Body: Sexuality and Society in the Nineteenth Century.* Berkeley: U of California P, 1987.

Gordon, Linda. *Woman's Body, Woman's Right: Birth Control in America.* 1976. New York: Penguin Books, 1990 rev.

Gould, Stephen Jay. *The Mismeasure of Man.* 1981. New York: Norton, 1996 rev.

Gregg, Robin. "'Choice' as a Double-Edged Sword: Information, Guilt and Mother-Blaming in a High-Tech Age." *Women & Health* 20.3 (1993): 53–73.

Grosz, Elizabeth. *Volatile Bodies: Toward a Corporeal Feminism.* Bloomington: Indiana UP, 1994.

Hall, Stuart. "The Rediscovery of 'Ideology': Return of the Repressed in Media Studies." *Society, Culture, and the Media.* Ed. Michael Gurevitch, et al. London: Methuen 1982. 56–90.

Horkheimer, Max and Theodor Adorno. *Dialectic of Enlightenment.* Trans. John Cumming. 1944. New York: Continuum, 1993.

Jones, Rose. "The Politics of Reproductive Biology: Exclusionary Policies in the United States." *Births and Power: Social Change and the Politics of Reproduction.* Ed. W. Penn Handwerker. Boulder: Westview, 1990. 39–51.

Keller, Evelyn Fox. *Secrets of Life, Secrets of Death.* New York: Routledge, 1990.

Kroker, Arthur and Marilouise Kroker. "Theses on the Disappearing Body in the Hyper-Modern Condition." *Body Invaders: Panic Sex in America.* Ed. Arthur Kroker and Marilouise Kroker. New York: St. Martin's P, 1987. 20–34.

Manion, Elizabeth. "A Ms.-Managed Womb." *Body Invaders: Panic Sex in America.* Ed. Arthur Kroker and Marilouise Kroker. New York: St. Martin's P, 1987. 193–200.

Martin, Emily. "The Egg and the Sperm: How Science Has Constructed a Romance Based on Stereotypical Male-Female Roles." *Signs: Journal of Women in Culture and Society* 16 (1991): 485–501.

The Miracle of Life. Photo. Lennart Nilsson. Prod. Bebe Nixon. Video. Crow Publishers, Inc., 1983.

Nilsson, Lennart and Lars Hamberger. *A Child is Born.* New York: Delacorte P, 1990.

Ostrander, Gregg. "Foucault's Disappearing Body." *Body Invaders: Panic Sex in America.* Ed. A

Kroker and M. Kroker. New York: St. Martin's P, 1987. 169–182.

Petchesky, Rosalind Pollack. "Fetal Images: The Power of Visual Culture in the Politics of Reproduction." *Feminist Studies* 13 (1987): 263–292.

Pfeffer, Naomi. "The Hidden Pathology of the Male Reproductive System." *The Sexual Politics of Reproduction.* Ed. Hilary Homas. Brookfield, VT: Gower, 1985. 30–45.

Rajchman, Jonathan. "Foucault's Art of Seeing." *October* 44 (1988): 89–117.

Rawls, John. *A Theory of Justice.* Cambridge, MA: Belknap P, 1973.

Rich, Adrienne. "Compulsory Heterosexuality and Lesbian Existence." *Signs* 5 (1980): 631–660.

Rothman, Barbara Katz. *Recreating Motherhood: Ideology and Technology in a Patriarchal Society.* New York: W. W. Norton, 1989.

Sawday, Jonathan. "The Fate of Marysas: Dissecting the Renaissance Body." *Renaissance Bodies: The Human Figure in English Culture, c. 1540–1660.* Ed. Lucy Gent and Nigel Llewellyn. London: Reaction Books, 1990. 111–135.

Schiappa, Edward. "Arguing About Definitions." *Argumentation* 7 (1993): 403–417.

Schiebinger, Londa. *Nature's Body: Gender in the Making of Modern Science.* Boston: Beacon P, 1993.

Schiebinger, Londa. *The Mind Has No Sex? Women in the Origins of Modern Science.* Cambridge: Harvard UP, 1989.

Schiebinger, Londa. "Skeletons in the Closet: The First Illustrations of the Female Skeleton in Eighteenth Century Anatomy." *The Making of the Modern Body: Sexuality and Society in the Nineteenth Century.* Ed. Catherine Gallagher and Thomas Laqueur. Berkeley: U of California P, 1987. 42–82.

Scott, Joan. *Gender and the Politics of History.* New York: Columbia UP, 1988.

Shaheen, John. "The Documentary of Art: 'The Undersea World of Jacques Cousteau.'" *Journal of Popular Culture* 21 (1987): 93–101.

Silent Scream. Prod. and Dir. Jack Duane Dabner. Writ. Donald S. Smith. Nar. Bernard Nathanson. Video. American Portrait Films, 1984.

Smith-Rosenberg, Carroll. *Disorderly Conduct: Visions of Gender in Victorian America.* New York: Oxford UP, 1985.

Stafford, Barbara. *Body Criticism: Imaging the Unseen in Enlightenment Art and Medicine.* Cambridge: MIT, 1993.

Stanworth, Michelle. Introduction. *Reproductive Technologies: Gender, Motherhood, and Medicine.* Ed. Michelle Stanworth. Minneapolis: U of Minnesota P, 1987. 1–9.

Tavris, Carol. *The Mismeasure of Woman.* New York: Simon & Schuster, Inc., 1992.

Van Biema, David. "Master of an 'Unbelievable, Invisible World.'" *Life* 13.10 (1990): 44–46.

Zuskar, Deborah M. "The Psychological Impact of Prenatal Diagnosis of Fetal Abnormality: Strategies for Investigation and Intervention." *Women & Health* 12.1 (1987): 91–103.

3

RECOGNIZING LINCOLN

Image Vernaculars in Nineteenth-Century Visual Culture

CARA A. FINNEGAN

In 1895 *McClure's* magazine published a newly discovered image, the earliest known photograph of Abraham Lincoln. Revealed to the American public nearly 50 years after its creation, the daguerreotype reproduction featured a Lincoln few had seen before: a thirtysomething, well-groomed middle-class gentleman (see photo). The image was received with great delight by readers of the magazine. Brooklyn newspaper editor Murat Halstead rhapsodized,

> This was the young man with whom the phantoms of romance dallied, the young man who recited poems and was fanciful and speculative, and in love and despair, but upon whose brow there already gleamed the illumination of intellect, the inspiration of patriotism. There were vast possibilities in this young man's face. He could have gone anywhere and done anything. He might have been a military chieftain, a novelist, a poet, a philosopher, ah! a hero, a martyr—and yes, this young man might have been—he even was Abraham Lincoln![1]

THE EARLIEST PORTRAIT OF ABRAHAM LINCOLN.
From a daguerreotype taken when Lincoln was about forty; owned by his son, the Hon. Robert T. Lincoln, through whose courtesy it is here reproduced for the first time.

Figure 1 The earliest portrait of Abraham Lincoln.

SOURCE: *McClure's,* November 1895, 482.

SOURCE: Finnegan, C. A. (2005). Recognizing Lincoln: Image vernaculars in nineteenth-century visual culture. *Rhetoric & Public Affairs, 8*(1), 31–58, published by Michigan State University Press.

General Francis A. Walker, president of MIT, wrote similarly but more plainly of the photograph: "The present picture has distinctly helped me to understand the relation between Mr. Lincoln's face and his mind and character, as shown in his life's work. . . . To my eye it *explains* Mr. Lincoln far more than the most elaborate line-engraving which has been produced."[2]

The photograph hardly seems to inspire such broad claims or florid prose. Indeed, at first glance it is difficult to glean what exactly Walker thinks it might "explain." The image is not particularly unusual save for the later fame of its subject. Cropped by *McClure's* to highlight Lincoln's head and shoulders and reproduced in the pictorialist style of the era, the image is nevertheless a standard-issue early daguerreotype: its pose stiff and formal, body and head held firm to accommodate the long exposure times of 1840s photography.[3] Yet in this utterly conventional image Halstead and Walker claim to see the seeds of Lincoln's greatness.

Those who wrote letters to the magazine in response to the photograph engaged in similar discourse. Viewers saw in the image not only a Lincoln they recognized physically, but one whose psychology and morality they recognized too. To the contemporary eye, claims such as these seem overblown. In today's saturated image culture, portraits—especially portraits of the well-known—are not taken to be windows to the soul nor keys to understanding mythic greatness.[4] Yet for viewers in the late nineteenth century, photographs such as the Lincoln image were understood in precisely these ways. For those of us interested in the rhetorical history of American visual culture, it makes sense to ask why.

The definition of "visual culture" is a subject of much debate, but at base the concept of visual culture recognizes that visuality frames our experience and acknowledges "that vision is a mode of cultural expression and human communication as fundamental and widespread as language."[5] Roland Barthes presaged the concept of visual culture in his germinal 1961 essay, "The Photographic Message," in which he observed that a photograph's "period rhetoric" needs to be understood as an aspect of the image's connoted message.[6] Art historian Michael Baxandall wrote of the "period eye" of Quattrocento Italian painting, and Svetlana Alpers invoked the term specifically in her groundbreaking study *The Art of Describing: Dutch Art in the Seventeenth Century.*[7] In the American context, some scholars have written of the 1930s as a "documentary decade," a visual culture in which relatively distinct modes of visualization of "the real" (such as documentary photography and film) dominated public discourse.[8] Scholarship of this sort argues that we should neither ignore an era's visual culture nor assume that we know what it is. Rather, the construction of rich rhetorical histories requires careful, situated investigation of the social, cultural, and political work that visual communication is made to do.

In this essay I model one way of accomplishing such investigation by turning critical attention to what I am calling *image vernaculars* of late nineteenth-century visual culture. Those who responded in writing to the *McClure's* photograph tapped into myths about Lincoln circulating during the late nineteenth century. Yet readers' responses to the photograph suggest that their use of these myths was tied more closely to what Baxandall calls "visual skills and habits" than it was to Lincoln the man.[9] When *McClure's* viewers claimed to "recognize" Lincoln, they were relying upon their social knowledge about photography and exhibiting their comfort with "scientific" discourses of character such as physiognomy and phrenology. Armed with this specific yet implicit way of talking about photographs—an image vernacular—viewers not only treated the photograph as evidence of Lincoln's moral character, they used it to elaborate an Anglo-Saxon national ideal type at a time when elites were consumed by fin-de-siècle anxieties about the fate of "American" identity. Below I define image vernaculars and explore what their study offers public address scholarship. Then I turn to the case of the Lincoln daguerreotype reproduced in *McClure's* and show how those who responded to the photograph deployed image vernaculars of late nineteenth-century visual culture to make rhetorical sense of what they saw.

IMAGE VERNACULARS AND PUBLIC ADDRESS STUDIES

Image vernaculars are the enthymematic modes of reasoning employed by audiences in the context of specific practices of reading and viewing in visual cultures.[10] Enthymemes (arguments in which one or more premises are suppressed or assumed) are not abstract, universalist modes of argument but rather are context-bound and tied to the everyday experiences of audiences.[11] Enthymemes are a powerful mode of argument because they are constructed using the audience's tacit social knowledge; describing something as "Photoshopped," for example, requires that audiences know of this readily available digital imaging software. The power of the enthymeme lies in the fiction that its unstated premise, at once invisible and transparent, is "natural" rather than context-bound; it is simply something that "everybody knows." In addition, enthymemes are powerful because they grant audiences agency. The audience is not merely a witness to the argument, but a participant in its creation. When I describe image vernaculars as *enthymematic modes of reasoning,* then, I mean to invoke both aspects of the enthymeme's power. As ways of talking about images that utilize the inventional resources of particular visual cultures, image vernaculars are tacit topoi of argument that viewers employ creatively in specific rhetorical situations. Unlike some conceptions of visual culture that suggest our experience of the visual realm is determined by the overwhelming force of ideology, the concept of image vernaculars preserves a necessary space for agency by theorizing the ways that viewers mobilize images as inventional resources for argument. The critic studying image vernaculars thus avoids the extremes of either assuming that people's responses to images are, on the one hand, merely eccentric, or, on the other hand, an inevitable product of ideology that leaves no room for the agency of rhetorical actors. Image vernaculars make available a fruitful middle space for critical engagement.

The study of image vernaculars also attunes us to a rhetorical history of photography for which rhetoricians and photography historians have insufficiently accounted. Rhetorical scholars are increasingly turning attention to public address in its visual forms and exploring how visual discourse functions as public address.[12] But those of us who study visual rhetoric have yet to devote much attention to public address *about* the visual. If we seek to understand the artifacts of particular visual cultures, it makes sense to pay attention to how rhetorical expression taps into, shapes, and contests the norms of those visual cultures. Fortunately, as scholars of rhetoric and argumentation, we are uniquely positioned with the critical resources with which to do so.

In "Photography: The Emergence of a Keyword," Alan Trachtenberg argues somewhat paradoxically that what is missing from the history of photography is attention to language. Scholars have done a good job of constructing the history of photography as a medium, a technology, and an art, but they have not connected these histories to "a history of picturing photography in the medium of language."[13] Trachtenberg aims to correct this omission by tracing the social and cultural emergence of "photography" as a keyword in the public discourse of nineteenth-century Americans. He deftly shows how early photography functioned not only as a mass medium, a technology, and an art, but also as a rhetoric: a metaphor, an image, an idea.[14] Trachtenberg's critical approach is a familiar one to rhetorical historians; indeed, his desire to construct what he calls a "history of verbalizations" about photography might well constitute a good definition of what public address studies do best: construct histories of the ways that publics verbalize their relationships to people, issues, artifacts, and ideas. As the social knowledge that informs how we respond to images and use them as inventional resources, image vernaculars constitute a readily available medium for reclaiming the lost history of photography's "verbalizations."

Photographs of Abraham Lincoln are particularly fascinating in this regard because of the staggering force of the Lincoln mythos. Throughout his career, but particularly after his assassination, Lincoln was (and remains) a potent but contested visual icon. Lincoln was one of the earliest and arguably one of the most photographed political figures of the middle nineteenth century.[15] By the close of the nineteenth century, he began to surpass George Washington as the political icon of the republic.[16] Today, in academia and in popular culture, Lincoln is big business.[17] In rhetorical studies, of course, he remains one of our most cherished subjects, though visual representations of Lincoln remain largely unexplored territory for rhetoricians.[18] But exploration of Lincoln iconography can be fruitful territory. Indeed, Lincoln was probably the only American whose image could produce the kind of public response that tapped directly into contested meanings of national identity in the late nineteenth century. As Barry Schwartz argues, in the 50 or so years following his death, "Lincoln was not elevated . . . because the people had discovered new facts about him, but because they had discovered new facts about themselves, and regarded him as the perfect vehicle for giving these tangible expression."[19] Strictly speaking, then, this is not an essay about Abraham Lincoln but an essay about how people used the image vernaculars of their own visual culture to make sense of Lincoln and, as a result, of their evershifting national identity.

THE *MCCLURE'S* LINCOLN

The image in question was published in *McClure's* to accompany the first in a series of articles on the life of Abraham Lincoln, penned by Ida Tarbell. Tarbell is best known today as the Progressive Era muckraking journalist who exposed corporate corruption at the Standard Oil Company.[20] Like many of her generation, Tarbell had a passing fascination with Lincoln; one of her most vivid childhood memories was witnessing her parents' grief upon his death.[21] As the foundation for her life of Lincoln, Tarbell relied heavily on the biographers who had known him most intimately.[22] But her series went beyond the familiar tales—it delivered new facts, documents, and images in an era when people had begun to conclude that there was nothing new to learn about Lincoln. She traveled to Kentucky, Indiana, and Illinois, interviewing people who had known Lincoln in person and consulting court records, newspapers, and other archival resources that previous Lincoln biographers had neglected.[23]

The Tarbell series would cement the early success of *McClure's,* a middlebrow literary magazine barely three years old. Publisher S. S. (Samuel Sidney) McClure founded the magazine in 1893 in the belief that a cheap, illustrated literary magazine could succeed. Seeing a gap between the working-class *People's Literary Companion* and the higher-end elitism of periodicals like *Century, Harper's,* and *Scribner's,* Sam McClure sought to create an affordable mainstream periodical squarely positioned for the middle-class reader.[24] McClure's efforts were made easier by technical developments in image reproduction. The halftone process appeared in the 1880s; by the 1890s it was in wide use by magazines.[25] Halftone, combined with the availability of cheaper glazed paper, made it possible for publishers like McClure to provide an inexpensive, yet lavishly illustrated, product.[26]

McClure's promised that its Lincoln series would "publish fully twice as many portraits of Lincoln as have ever appeared in any *Life,* and we shall illustrate the scenes of Lincoln's career on a scale never before attempted."[27] Readers responded. Between its first issue in 1893 and the first installment of Tarbell's Lincoln series in November 1895, the circulation of the magazine rose from eight thousand to well over one hundred thousand readers per month.[28] For the November issue, Sam McClure sought to make a heavily publicized splash with one of the most vivid Tarbell discoveries: a previously unpublished photograph of the late president made when he was a much younger man.

During the course of her research Tarbell met Robert Todd Lincoln, the only surviving child of the president. Robert Lincoln guarded his father's legacy closely and famously battled with many of Lincoln's biographers. He did not provide Tarbell with much (his personal papers, which included a wealth of hitherto unknown information related to his father, were not made available to researchers until 1947),[29] but he did show her a daguerreotype that he said was the earliest known photograph of his father.[30] Tarbell was shocked at what she saw. The photograph looked like Lincoln, but one the public had never seen before. Previously known photographs of Lincoln dated only as far back as the late 1850s, well into Lincoln's public career and middle age. The most famous of these early images was made by photographer Alexander Hesler in 1857. Known as the "tousled hair" portrait, it portrayed a strong but rather disheveled Lincoln.[31] This new but older image would allow *McClure's* readers to encounter Lincoln as a much younger and more dignified-looking man. While the 1857 "tousled hair" photograph figured Lincoln as a raw frontier lawyer having what may only be described as a bad hair day, this new image showed a youthful, dignified, reserved Lincoln. Tarbell recalled, "It was another Lincoln, and one that took me by storm."[32]

Access to the daguerreotype was thus quite a coup. Sam McClure decided the image should be published as the frontispiece of Tarbell's first article in November 1895. The magazine proudly trumpeted its find: "How Lincoln Looked When Young can be learned by this generation for the first time from the only early portrait of Lincoln in existence, a daguerreotype owned by the Hon. Robert T. Lincoln and now first published, showing Lincoln as he appeared before his face had lost its youthful aspect."[33] While forgery of Lincolniana was common, this image was not a fake; coming from Lincoln's own son, readers would not doubt its authenticity.[34] McClure promoted the photograph for all it was worth.

The image is a cropped version of a quarter-plate, three-quarters-length-view daguerreotype most likely made in the mid-to-late 1840s. The *McClure's* version isolates Lincoln's head and shoulders and frames him in a fuzzy pictorialist haze common to magazine reproductions of portraits in the 1890s. Yet editors also used an elaborate line drawing to frame the image, perhaps attempting to signal to viewers its daguerrean origins (see photo on p. 61). The differences between the two images should be of interest, for not only were 1890s viewers encountering an 1840s photograph, but they were encountering it framed in a decidedly 1890s fashion.

To be specific, what *McClure's* readers encountered in the pages of the magazine was a halftone reproduction of a photograph of a daguerreotype. Most photographic reproductions of images, especially photographic reproductions of photographs, are viewed simply as transparent vehicles for communication of the earlier image. But art historian Barbara Savedoff warns against the assumption of transparency: "We are encouraged to treat reproductions as more or less transparent documents. But of course, photographic reproductions are not really transparent. They transform the artworks they present."[35] Daguerreotypes, in particular, are dramatically transformed in the process of reproduction.[36] The mirrored daguerreotype image is meant to be directly and intimately engaged by the viewer, literally manipulated by hand in order for the mirrored image to come into view.[37] Photographic reproductions of daguerreotypes thus lose both their magical mirrored quality and the visual depth of the original.[38] The photographic reproduction of Lincoln necessarily removed the image from its association with daguerreotypy (despite the editors' attempt to "frame" it) and transformed it into an image more familiar to late nineteenth-century magazine readers. *McClure's* viewers' experiences of the photograph were thus several steps removed from an encounter with the "magical" aura of the daguerreotype. This conceptual distance makes viewers' effusive responses to the image initially all the more surprising. What exactly was it about the photograph, no longer a magical daguerreotype but a run-of-the-mill halftone illustration, that produced such passionate discourse? As we shall see, the image's potency had a lot to do with cultural understandings of what portrait photographs were believed to communicate to viewers in 1895.

Sam McClure was right that the photograph would draw immediate attention to Tarbell's series. Circulation swelled to 175,000 for the first of Tarbell's articles in the series and then catapulted to 250,000 for the second installment in December.[39] Circulation numbers were not the only sign of interest in the series. A number of readers responded specifically to the photograph itself. The December 1895 issue featured a full four pages of letters, the January 1896 issue two more. As noted earlier, *McClure's* was intended to be a low-cost, middle-class magazine of letters, more affordable and "popular" than other magazines of the day such as *Scribner's* or *Harper's*. Yet curiously, the majority of letters published in response to the photograph were not from these middle-class readers but from those who represented the era's intellectual elite: university professors, Supreme Court justices, former associates of Lincoln.[40] Judging from the content of the letters and the identities of the letter writers, McClure must have sent advance copies of the photograph and its accompanying text to members of the eastern political and scholarly establishment.[41] His motivations for doing so were likely manifold: to drum up interest in the upcoming Tarbell series, to show his confidence in the authenticity of the image by testing it out before "experts," and to solicit elite responses in order to signal to *McClure's* readers the "proper" way to interpret the photograph. When I discuss the letters below, it is important to keep in mind that those whose responses to the photograph were published in the pages of *McClure's* were not necessarily the same readers who would have purchased the magazine on the newsstand or subscribed to it at home. This disjuncture, as we shall see, becomes important for understanding the particular image vernaculars upon which letter writers relied when making rhetorical sense of the *McClure's* Lincoln.

"VALUABLE EVIDENCE AS TO HIS NATURAL TRAITS . . ."

Overwhelmingly, letter writers discussed the photograph not as a material object of history, nor as an artful example of a technology no longer in use, but in terms of the kind of evidence it offered about its subject. In interpreting the photograph's significance, they deployed image vernaculars that tapped into culturally available narratives about photography and character in complex and fascinating ways.

None of the writers disputed the identity of the photograph as Lincoln, though a few did have trouble seeing a resemblance to the man they remembered from history. The Hon. David J. Brewer, associate justice of the Supreme Court of the United States, wrote, "The picture, if a likeness, must have been taken many years before I saw him and he became the central figure in our country's life. Indeed, I find it difficult to see in that face the features with which we are all so familiar."[42] Similarly, Charles Dudley Warner of Hartford had a hard time seeing his recollected Lincoln in the photograph: "The deep-set eyes and mouth belong to the historical Lincoln, and are recognizable as his features when we know that this is a portrait of him. But I confess that I should not have recognized his likeness . . . the change from the Lincoln of this picture to the Lincoln of national fame is almost radical in character, and decidedly radical in expression."[43]

Brewer's and Warner's difficulties mirrored Tarbell's own reported experience of first viewing the photograph—it *was* radical, a Lincoln no one had ever seen before. Yet most viewers reported the opposite. A colleague from Lincoln's younger years wrote, "This portrait is Lincoln as I knew him best: his sad, dreamy eye, his pensive smile, his sad and delicate face, his pyramidal shoulders, are the characteristics which I best remember . . . This is the Lincoln of Springfield, Decatur, Jacksonville, and Bloomington."[44] Henry C. Whitney, identified in the magazine as "an associate of Lincoln's on the circuit in Illinois," wrote, "It is without doubt authentic and accurate; and dispels the illusion so common (but never shared by me) that Mr. Lincoln was an ugly-looking man." Implying perhaps the famed roughness of Lincoln's frontier habits, Whitney concluded bemusedly, "I never saw him with his hair combed before."[45]

Many of the correspondents in *McClure's* noted the absence of "melancholy" in Lincoln's face, a characteristic of many of the later presidential-era portraits. John C. Ropes of New York City wrote, "It is most assuredly an interesting portrait. The expression, though serious and earnest, is devoid of the sadness which characterizes the later likenesses." And Woodrow Wilson, then professor of finance and political economy at Princeton, noted, "The fine brows and forehead, and the pensive sweetness of the clear eyes, give to the noble face a peculiar charm. There is in the expression the dreaminess of the familiar face without its later sadness."[46] Similarly, Herbert B. Adams, professor of history at Johns Hopkins University in Baltimore, wrote, "The portrait indicates the natural character, strength, insight, and humor of the man before the burdens of office and the sins of his people began to weigh upon him."[47]

Some readers saw in the photograph shades of Lincoln's future greatness, a man whose rise to prominence was literally prefigured in his visage. John T. Morse, biographer of Lincoln, Jefferson, and Adams, among others, wrote to the magazine, "I have studied this portrait with very great interest. All the portraits with which we are familiar show us the man as *made;* this shows us the man *in the making;* and I think every one will admit that the making of Abraham Lincoln presents a more singular, puzzling, interesting study than the making of any other man known in human history."[48] Morse went on to note that he had shown the portrait to several people without telling them who it was: "Some say, a poet; others, a philosopher, a thinker, like Emerson. These comments also are interesting, for Lincoln had the raw material of both these characters very largely in his composition. . . . This picture, therefore, is valuable evidence as to his natural traits."[49]

This initial, cursory reading of the letters reveals that writers connected the surface aspects of the image to prevailing cultural myths about Lincoln. Merrill D. Peterson argues that five myths or themes have dominated our national public memory of Lincoln: the Great Emancipator, the Man of the People, the First American, the Self-Made Man, and the Savior of the Union.[50] While overall the themes have remained relatively stable, not all eras embraced each of these Lincolns. Recalling Schwartz's contention that each era invents the Lincoln it needs, we should expect that viewers of the 1890s would see in the *McClure's* photograph a Lincoln who fit their unique needs and interests. Thus the interesting question is not which myths about Lincoln were invoked, but rather *how* and *why* they were invoked. To answer these questions we must dig deeper, moving beyond Lincoln to take up the letters in light of late nineteenth-century visual culture.

The letters are striking for the way that they negotiate the complex temporality of the photograph. Lincoln has been dead for nearly 30 years, the photograph itself is nearly 50 years old, yet the letter writers write in the present tense: the image *"is Lincoln,"* it *"explains"* Lincoln. The ontology of the photograph permits such a slippage, of course, for via the photograph Lincoln is persistently present despite his absence. Importantly, this temporal ambiguity enables readers to engage the image actively. Rather than simply noting the photograph's existence as a document of the past, *McClure's* readers activated the image in their own present. In doing so, they did not assume that the photograph spoke for itself but transformed it into a playful space for interpretation.

In particular, the topoi of *character* and *expression* come across strongly in the letter writers' remarks—specifically, character as revealed in expression. The photograph is uniformly read as offering evidence about Lincoln's character. Lincoln's face is "noble"; both his eyes and his smile are "pensive." His brow is "fine" and illuminated with "intellect"; his eyes are read alternately as "clear" and "dreamy." Several correspondents explicitly compared this early image of Lincoln with ones more familiar to them. While later images offered a "sad" Lincoln, this image avoided such melancholy; the younger Lincoln is merely "serious and earnest." The collective image of Lincoln constructed by these readings is a man for all people, alternately a dreamy romantic and a strong patriot, a "pensive" intellectual and an insightful empath, a manly "military chieftain" and a feminized figure of "sweetness" and delicacy. Letter writers grounded their arguments in the assumption that there was a direct correspondence between Lincoln's image and his "natural traits"—between, as General Walker so tellingly put it, "Mr. Lincoln's face and his mind and character." In making such arguments, *McClure's* readers employed image vernaculars grounded in the relationship between photographic portraiture and popular nineteenth-century discourses of physiognomy and phrenology.

THE PHOTOGRAPHIC PORTRAIT

By the end of the nineteenth century, Miles Orvell argues, photography was an increasingly "intrusive presence in society."[51] Viewers of the Lincoln photograph could scarcely remember a time when photography did not exist. What appeared in 1839 as a unique, nonreproducible object was by the early 1890s endlessly reproducible as an artifact of mass culture. The photographer, who in the early 1840s was as much a chemist as a businessperson, had by the 1890s become also an artist, a journalist, and most strikingly, an amateur hobbyist. Cameras became increasingly portable while exposure times decreased, so much so that Eadweard Muybridge was able to literally stop time in his movement studies of the late 1880s.[52] The first Kodak camera, which would revolutionize the average person's relationship to photography, entered the market in 1889; by 1896 George Eastman's company had sold more than one hundred thousand of them.[53] Until the late 1880s, photographs had to be turned into engravings in order to be circulated in mass media. The invention of the halftone process enabled magazine and newspaper publishers to bring photographs more directly to readers. By the turn of the century photographs were ubiquitous at home in the magazines and newspapers middle-class families read and in the albums of family photographs they carefully tended.

In the nearly 50 years between the creation of the Lincoln daguerreotype and its reproduction in *McClure's,* then, photography was dramatically transformed: "No longer regarded as a mysterious hybrid with unclear application and unknown potential, photography at the age of fifty was an accepted fact of modern life, and photographers and photographic images were commonplace."[54] Late nineteenth-century viewers of the *McClure's* Lincoln brought with them a history of reading and viewing practices influenced by these transformations. Embedded in a visual culture in which photography very much took center stage, they creatively employed image vernaculars that reflected their acquired (but seemingly intuitive) understanding of the rhetoric of the photograph—especially the photographic portrait.

In the nineteenth century, portraits were thought to be *ekphrastic*—that is, they were believed to reveal or bring before the eyes something vital and almost mysterious about their subjects.[55] It was assumed that the photographic portrait, in particular, did not merely "illustrate" a person but also constituted an important locus of information about human character. Art historian David M. Lubin observes, "Even though a portrait purports to allow us the close observation of a single, localized, individual, we discern meaning in it to the extent that it appears to *reveal* something about general human traits and social relationships."[56] Even after changes in photographic technology after the Civil War enabled more idiosyncratic, spontaneous images, the prevailing rhetoric of photography preferred a more formal style of portraiture thought to say something more general about human nature.

As *loci* of generalizable information about character, portraits educated common people about the virtues of the elites and warned them against the danger of vice; thus they served as a way of educating the masses about what it meant to be a virtuous citizen. Images such

as the large daguerreotypes made by Mathew Brady in his New York and Washington, D.C., studios at mid-century provided visitors not only with an afternoon's stroll and entertainment, but with "models for emulation."[57] Brady's galleries functioned as citizenship training of a sort, offering a democratic space for viewing a democratic art that paradoxically perpetuated elitist definitions of virtue: "Viewing portraits of the nation's elite could provide moral edification for all its citizens who needed to learn how to present themselves as good Americans in a quest for upward mobility."[58] *Gallery of Illustrious Americans,* a book featuring exquisite lithographs made from the Brady studio's daguerreotypes of national luminaries, constructed the story of national destiny by offering the reading and viewing public "a space for viewing men in the guise of republican virtue: *gravitas, dignitas, fides.*"[59]

Visual discourses of morality did not just emphasize the virtuous civic elite, however. Just a few years after photography appeared, the portrait was already being used for the purposes of criminal identification and classification.[60] By the 1850s, the mug shot was a standardized genre that could be taught to police photographers. "Rogues' Galleries" began to appear in the urban centers of the United States and Western Europe, in which the faces of known criminals were put forth in a kind of "municipal portrait show" displayed in police headquarters to help solve and prevent crime.[61] Mug shots not only constituted products of a visual order of surveillance, but served simultaneously as elements of spectacle and moral education.[62]

Such education was possible because of the connection between portrait photography and "scientific" discourses such as phrenology and physiognomy, which connected physical attributes to moral and intellectual capacities. Allan Sekula argues, "we understand the culture of the photographic portrait only dimly if we fail to recognize the enormous prestige and popularity of a general physiognomic paradigm in the 1840s and 1850s."[63] Throughout the nineteenth century, "the practice of reading faces" was part of everyday life and remained so into the early twentieth century.[64] Whether it was images like Brady's *Gallery of Illustrious Americans* or those of the Rogues' Galleries, Americans were accustomed not only to reading the faces in photographs, but to making judgments about the moral character of their subjects. Viewers of the Lincoln photograph in *McClure's* paid close attention to the face, implying that in Lincoln's face may be found the key to his character. If we are to understand these kinds of assumptions, we need to trace how the portrait photograph circulated in a fin-de-siècle visual culture heavily influenced by the discourses of physiognomy.

PHYSIOGNOMY AND THE MORAL SCIENCE OF CHARACTER

Scholars have documented the nineteenth century's commitment to the formation of "character" as well as the popularity and prevalence of the "sciences" of phrenology and physiognomy. Karen Halttunen argues that during the bulk of the nineteenth century character formation was incredibly important to middle-class Americans, "the nineteenth-century version of the Protestant work ethic."[65] "Most importantly," Halttunen observes, "a man's inner character was believed to be imprinted upon his face and thus visible to anyone who understood the moral language of physiognomy."[66] The popular prominence of this language coincided with the birth of photography in the United States and Europe. The first volume of the *American Phrenological Journal* (produced by the Fowler brothers, Lorenzo and Orson, who popularized phrenology in the United States) was published in 1839—the same year the daguerreotype was introduced to the public.[67] While discourses of phrenology and physiognomy predated photography by many years, the introduction of photography gave them modern relevance and vigor.[68]

Allan Sekula calls phrenology and physiognomy "two tightly entwined branches" of the so-called moral sciences.[69] Conceived in the late eighteenth century by Johann Caspar Lavater and popularized in the United States and Europe in the nineteenth century, physiognomy involved paying attention to "the minuteness and the particularity" of physical details and making analogies between those details and the character traits they were said to illustrate.[70] Physiognomy was framed as a science of reading character "in which an equation is posited between facial type and the moral and personal qualities of the individual."[71] Similarly, phrenology was founded upon the belief that "there was an observable concomitance between man's mind—his talents, disposition, and character—and the shape of his head. To ascertain the former, one need only examine the latter."[72] Both "sciences" were, as Stephen Hartnett observes of phrenology, "essentially *hermeneutic* activities."[73] These interpretive practices "fostered a wide-ranging 'self-help' industry that . . . blanketed the nation with magazines and manifestoes intended to guide confused Americans through the multiple mine-fields of their rapidly changing culture."[74] Employing a circular rhetoric, both practices "drew on the moral and social language of the day in order to guarantee the claims made about human nature."[75]

Samuel R. Wells, a protégé (and brother-in-law) of the Fowler brothers, ran the publishing operation that helped to popularize their work. Wells believed that physiognomy, phrenology, and physiology constituted a tripartite "science of man."[76] Beginning in the 1860s, Wells wrote and published several books on physiognomy, including *New Physiognomy; or, Signs of Character, as Manifested through Temperament and External Forms, and especially in 'The Human Face Divine'* and the first of several volumes of *How to Read Character: A Handbook of Physiology, Phrenology and Physiognomy, Illustrated with a Descriptive Chart*. Wells argued in both texts that while the brain "measures the absolute power of the mind," the face may be understood as "an index of its habitual activity."[77] The Peircean language should not be lost on us here, for Wells treats the face as an index, a sign of the first order. The books outline in exquisite detail how to read faces in order to ascertain temperament and character; they discuss every facial feature, including mouth, eyes, jaw, chin, and nose, as well as hands and feet, neck and shoulders, movement, and even palmistry and handwriting analysis.

Such rhetorics tied a hermeneutic of the face to individuated aspects of morality as well as to broader typologies of national character. The practices of phrenology and physiognomy were not parlor-game fun; indeed, not many more steps were necessary for a full-blown discourse of eugenics.[78] These sciences of moral character enabled anxious Americans, especially those of the middle and upper classes, to use a language that placed themselves (as well as marginalized others) in "proper relation." And use this language they did. Historian Madeleine Stern observes, "Often without knowing precisely what they were saying, people spoke phrenology in the 1860s as they would speak psychiatry in the 1930s and existentialism in the 1960s."[79] The sciences of moral character constituted readily available image vernaculars for late nineteenth-century Americans.

"I Think We Can See in His Face . . ."

Turning back now to the Lincoln letters, we may see how these image vernaculars grounded the arguments made by the *McClure's* letter writers. The letter writers assume that the photograph's links to Lincoln's character are obvious; no one needs to make the case for reading Lincoln's face. The question is not whether the photograph shows a relationship between character and expression, but what specifically that relationship is. Descriptions of Lincoln's eyes as being "clear," for example, or his smile as being "pensive," are characterological references that would resonate for viewers familiar with physiognomic discourse. Perhaps the most vivid combination of discourse about Lincoln's character and expression may be found in the letter of Thomas M. Cooley of Ann Arbor, Michigan, former chief justice of the supreme court of Michigan, who began,

> I think it a charming likeness; more attractive than any other I have seen, principally perhaps because of the age at which it was taken. The same characteristics are seen in it which are found in all subsequent likenesses—the same pleasant and kindly eyes, through which you feel, as you look into them, that you are looking into a great heart. The same just purposes are also there; and, as I think, the same unflinching determination to pursue to final success the course once deliberately entered upon.[80]

Thus far Cooley's reading is similar to other correspondents' interpretations in its attention to physiognomic detail. Lincoln's face reveals not only "pleasant and kindly eyes," but eyes that signal a "great heart." His expression reveals "just purposes," as well as "unflinching determination." Here is a man, Cooley suggests, who can be relied upon to make the right decisions, a man who is thoughtful, determined, kind. The physiognomic image vernacular thus mobilized, Cooley goes on to elaborate what specifically the photograph reveals about Lincoln's character. Transcending temporal boundaries as only photographic interpretation can, Cooley reads the photograph in the present while speculating about a future that is already past. He constructs the meaning of the image in the conditional tense, even though from his point of view 50 years later there is no uncertainty:

> It seems almost impossible to conceive of this as the face of a man to be at the head of affairs when one of the greatest wars known to history was in progress, and who could push unflinchingly the measures necessary to bring that war to a successful end. Had it been merely a war of conquest, I think we can see in this face qualities that would have been entirely inconsistent with such a course, and that would have rendered it to this man wholly impossible. It is not the face of a bloodthirsty man, or of a man ambitious to be successful as a mere ruler of men; but if a war should come involving issues of the very highest importance to our common humanity, and that appealed from the oppression and degradation of the human race to the higher instincts of our nature, we almost feel, as we look at this youthful picture of the great leader, that we can see in it as plainly as we saw in his administration of the government when it came to his hands that here was likely to be neither flinching nor shadow or turning until success should come.[81]

This passage is extraordinary for the way it oscillates between the specifics of the image and imaginative generalities about Lincoln's character and behavior. The face that Cooley has already "read" for us is not the face of someone who is "bloodthirsty" or desirous of power; rather, this is the face of a man who will unflinchingly pursue a course of deliberate action. However (note the conditional tense), *if a war should come* (an eerie echo of Lincoln's Second Inaugural: "and the war came"), we can be assured that this man would only go to war for the right reasons; indeed, his face signals a character for which doing otherwise would be patently "impossible." This is not the face of a power-hungry, bloodthirsty "ruler of men," but of a benevolent, thoughtful, decisive leader: Lincoln, Savior of the Union.

Strikingly, Cooley goes a step beyond analysis of Lincoln's character to make quite another argument altogether: he actually argues that the war was not a war of conquest *precisely because the photograph does not reveal a man with such impulses:* "I think we can see in this face qualities that would have been entirely inconsistent with such a course." Cooley not only uses the photograph to articulate a vision of Lincoln as the Savior of the Union, he mobilizes it in the service of arguments about the nature of the war itself. Such a move is not possible without recourse to image vernaculars that enable him creatively to use the photograph as an inventional resource.

Cooley is not alone in reading Lincoln's image in this way. In fact, Lincoln figures prominently in the physiognomy literature. Samuel Wells's discussion of an engraved reproduction of a Lincoln photograph amounts to a near-complete physiognomic study of Lincoln, prefiguring Cooley's own remarks by nearly 30 years:

> This photograph of 1860 shows, not the face of a great man, but of one whose elements were so molded that stormy and eventful times might easily stamp him with the seal of greatness. The face is distinctively a Western face. . . . The brow in the picture of 1860 is ample but smooth, and has no look of having grappled with vast difficult and complex political problems; the eyebrows are uniformly arched; the nose straight; the hair careless and inexpressive; the mouth, large, good natured, full of charity for all . . . but looking out from his deep-set and expressive eyes is an intellectual glance in the last degree clear and penetrating, and a soul *whiter* than is often found among the crowds of active and prominent wrestlers upon the arena of public life, and far more conscious than most public men of its final accountability at the great tribunal.[82]

Reading the past of the Civil War into the present of the picture, Wells, like Cooley, uses the image vernacular of physiognomy to predict the future: this man with the "white soul" is destined for greatness in the face of heavy burdens. Lest the reader of *New Physiognomy* be unclear about the implications of his reading, Wells sums up: "The lesson . . . is one of morals as well as of physiognomy. Let any one meet the questions of his time as Mr. Lincoln met those of *his,* and bring to bear upon them his best faculties with the same conscientious fidelity that governed the Martyr-President, and he may be sure that the golden legend will be there in his features."[83]

While neither Cooley nor the other correspondents in *McClure's* write of Lincoln with the precise physiognomic detail found in the Wells account, the influence is there. Clearly, by the 1890s the discourses of physiognomy still offered a potent image vernacular. Furthermore, those who read the photograph mobilized the physiognomic image vernacular not only to claim Lincoln for their own era, but also to proclaim him as a new "American type" in an age of intense anxiety about the fate of Anglo-Saxon national identity.

"A NEW AND INTERESTING CHARACTER . . ."

Lincoln's physical appearance was a popular topic in the Gilded Age. Writers sought to construct a preferred image of Lincoln in the public mind; in doing so, they tied that image to broader questions about American national identity. In 1891 John G. Nicolay, Lincoln's former private secretary, published an essay in *Century* magazine called "Lincoln's Personal Appearance." Nicolay's stated goal in the essay was to dispel the persistent myth of Lincoln's ugliness.[84] Yet Nicolay was also interested in framing Lincoln as a new, distinctively "American" type. In defense of Lincoln's purported gawky ugliness, Nicolay quoted accounts that relied heavily on physiognomic detail. Sculptor Thomas D. Jones recalled to Nicolay that Lincoln's "great strength and height were well calculated to make him a peerless antagonist. . . . His head was neither Greek nor Roman, nor Celt, for his upper lip was too short for that, or a Low German. There are few such men in the world; where they came from originally is not positively known."[85] Nicolay constructed Lincoln as distinctly American, so much so that his ancestry was unimportant. Lincoln's Americanness could be found, Nicolay contended, in the frontier upbringing that exposed him to a variety of people and situations: "It was this thirty years of life among the people that made and kept him a man of the people—which gave him the characteristics expressed in Lowell's poem: 'New birth of our new soil; the first American.'"[86]

Viewers of the photograph in *McClure's* made similar arguments. Several letter writers argued that the Lincoln photograph revealed him as a distinctly American type, one whose physiognomy indicated a new stage in American characterological development. One of the *McClure's* letter writers was Truman H. (T. H.) Bartlett, identified by editors as an "eminent sculptor, who has for many years collected portraits of Lincoln, and has made a scientific study of Lincoln's physiognomy."[87] In his letter to *McClure's,* Bartlett observes that the photograph suggested the rise of a "new man":

> It may to many suggest certain other heads, but a short study of it establishes its distinctive originality in every respect. It's priceless, every way, and copies of it ought to be in the gladsome possession of every lover of Lincoln. Handsome is not enough—it's great—not only of a great man, but the first picture representing the only new physiognomy of which we have any correct knowledge contributed by the New World to the ethnographic consideration of mankind.[88]

Setting aside Bartlett's somewhat tortured prose, we see that for Bartlett (as for Nicolay), Lincoln's physical features signaled a marked shift in the social and cultural makeup of American man. While some might be content to tie the image to other physiognomic types ("other heads," as Bartlett so wonderfully puts it), Bartlett suggests that the "distinctive originality" of Lincoln's features signaled something entirely new. Twelve years later, Bartlett published in *McClure's* the study to which editors had alluded.[89] In "The Physiognomy of Lincoln," a highly detailed analysis of photographs and life masks of Lincoln's face and hands, Bartlett elaborated how Lincoln's physiognomy represented a distinct departure from those "other heads."

Classifying the "excellences of Lincoln's appearance" by analyzing both his facial expressions and his bodily movement, Bartlett contended that both constituted a new American type. He claimed to have shown the life masks and photographs to famous sculptors in France, including Rodin, who agreed with Bartlett that they illustrated "'a new and interesting character. . . . If it belongs to any type, and we know of none such, it must be a wonderful specimen of that type.' . . . 'It is a new man; he has tremendous character,' they said."[90] In all of these texts Lincoln is constituted not only in terms of his individual moral character, but in terms of his representativeness. Why was it so vital for *McClure's* readers—especially the elite letter writers—to connect Lincoln to this "new," uniquely American ideal? Their desire can in large part be traced to cultural anxieties about the changing character of the American citizenry at the end of the nineteenth century.

Anxiety consumed many elites during the Gilded Age. Many causes have been posited for this cultural "neurasthenia,"[91] including confusion about what it meant to be an American in the industrial age. Historian Robert Wiebe suggests that this confusion constituted nothing less than a national identity crisis: "The setting had altered beyond their [elites'] power to understand it and within an alien context they had lost themselves. In a democratic society who was master and who servant? In a land of opportunity what was success? In a Christian nation what were the rules and who kept them? The apparent leaders were as much adrift as their followers."[92] Attempts to grapple with these questions led elites to define American identity by emphasizing both what Americans were and what they were not.

The White Anglo-Saxon Protestant (WASP) cultural elite believed it had good cause to be worried about the future of American identity in the face of rising immigration and the threat of miscegenation. Jacob Riis's *How the Other Half Lives,* published in 1890, visualized these anxieties. Beginning in the late 1880s, Riis made photographs of New York's poor and their living conditions in the city's ghettoes, which he then shared in lantern slide lectures delivered to upper-class New York City audiences.[93] Writing of the cultural makeup of the New York tenements, Riis observed,

[T]here was not a native-born individual in the court. . . . One may find for the asking an Italian, a German, a French, African, Spanish, Bohemian, Russian, Scandanavian [*sic*], Jewish, and Chinese colony. . . . The one thing you shall vainly ask for in the chief city of America is a distinctively American community. There is none; certainly not among the tenements.[94]

The assumption grounding Riis's remarks is that there is, in fact, a "distinctively American community"—but it is one, by definition, of which these immigrants can not be a part.

During these years the United States also passed through a violent period of labor unrest, including most prominently the Haymarket Riot of 1886 and the bloody Pullman Strike of 1894. The voices of immigrants made themselves increasingly heard in these powerful labor movements, producing real fears of a violent class revolution. Anxious elites sought rhetorically to dissociate activist citizens from the identity of "American." After the incident at Haymarket Square in Chicago, one newspaper editorial pronounced, "The enemy forces are not American [but] rag-tag and bob-tail cutthroats of Beelzebub from the Rhine, the Danube, the Vistula and the Elbe."[95] Historian T. J. Jackson Lears observes, "Worry about . . . destruction by an unleashed rabble, always a component of republican tradition, intensified in the face of unprecedented labor unrest, waves of strange new immigrants, and glittering industrial fortunes."[96]

Many elites sought to alleviate their anxiety by embracing historical and "scientific" representations of American identity that articulated the "natural" dominance of a WASP ideal. They received help on a number of fronts. In 1893 at the World's Columbian Exposition in Chicago, historian Frederick Jackson Turner posited his influential "frontier thesis." Emphasizing the heroic, masculine traits of westward-moving pioneers, Turner argued that it was on the frontier that Americans had become Americans, forging a unique national identity apart from their European ancestry.[97] The frontier thesis provided a coherent reading "of the American past at a time of disunity, of economic depression and labor strife, of immigrant urban workers and impoverished rural farmers challenging a predominantly Anglo-Saxon Protestant economic and social elite."[98] It gave WASP elites a narrative

that acknowledged the dynamism of American cultural history but conveniently ignored difference and multiplicity. Similarly, genealogical organizations such as the Daughters of the American Revolution rose in response to perceived threats to "American civilization," making available "the consolidation of a *seemingly* stable, embodied, and racialized identity, one that conflated American borders with Anglo-Saxon bloodlines."[99] And eugenics discourse reached down from the rarified universe of science into the everyday lives of Americans, where it emphasized the importance of retaining a "pure" American identity in the face of the "threat" of the blending of the races.[100]

Physiognomy was used in these discourses to define those who were "real Americans" and those whose physiognomy revealed them to be dangerous threats to a pure American identity. In *New Physiognomy* Wells included a lengthy discussion of "The Anglo-American." Emphasizing Americans' genetic connections to the Anglo-Saxon, Celtic, and Teutonic "races," Wells observed that contemporary Americans differed strikingly in temperament and character from their European counterparts. As exemplars of this representative illustrious American, Wells offered up Cornelius Vanderbilt and Abraham Lincoln.[101] In Wells's complex rhetoric, Anglo-Saxon no longer stood for European, but for American. At the same time that Americans were being told there existed a uniquely American identity, then, this identity was declared to be threatened by the forces of social disorder. The physiognomic rhetoric constructing Lincoln as a "new and interesting character" reflected these broader tensions. Ironically, the Lincoln daguerreotype, no longer a mirror image itself, functioned as a mirror for these anxieties. Those who read the photograph employed image vernaculars that reflected back a Lincoln whose high moral character and apparently "American" genes fulfilled their need for a "distinctive" American type capable of mitigating the social anxieties of their age.

CONCLUSION

The goal of this essay has been to show how attention to image vernaculars—the enthymematic modes of reasoning employed creatively in particular visual cultures—enables us to construct rich rhetorical histories of American public address. The *McClure's* letter writers established the portrait photograph's worth as a vehicle for the communication of beliefs about individual and collective moral character. They constructed interpretations of the photograph that embodied contemporary tensions about the nature of America and Americans, the uniqueness of national character, and the boundaries of national morality. Attention to image vernaculars enables us to locate the cultural circulation of such anxieties in visual cultures of public address, illustrating how visual rhetoric constitutes powerful world-making discourse.

NOTES

1. "Miss Tarbell's Life of Lincoln," *McClure's,* January 1896, 208.

2. "The Earliest Portrait of Lincoln: Letters in Regard to the Frontispiece of the November McClure's," *McClure's,* December 1896, 112.

3. The photograph was most likely made in 1846 or 1847 in Springfield, Illinois, by local photographer N. H. Shepherd. See Charles Hamilton and Lloyd Ostendorf, *Lincoln in Photographs: An Album of Every Known Pose* (Norman: University of Oklahoma Press, 1963), 4–5.

4. Even an iconic figure such as John F. Kennedy does not inspire the specific kind of talk that the Lincoln image did. For a fascinating, if somewhat idiosyncratic, reading of photographs of John F. Kennedy and Jacqueline Kennedy, see David M. Lubin, *Shooting Kennedy: JFK and the Culture of Images* (Berkeley: University of California Press, 2003).

5. W. J. T. Mitchell, "Interdisciplinarity and Visual Culture," *Art Bulletin,* December 1995, 543. A good illustration of the multiple definitions of "visual culture" may be found in the infamous "Visual Culture Questionnaire" published in *October* 77 (Summer 1996): 25–70. See also James Elkins, *Visual Studies: A Skeptical Introduction* (New York: Routledge, 2003), 1–30.

6. Roland Barthes, "The Photographic Message," in *Image—Music—Text* (New York: Hill and Wang, 1977), 18.

7. Michael Baxandall, *Painting and Experience in Fifteenth-Century Italy* (Oxford, U.K.: Oxford University Press, 1972); Svetlana Alpers, *The Art of Describing: Dutch Art in the Seventeenth Century* (Chicago: University of Chicago Press, 1983).

8. See, for example, William Stott, *Documentary Expression and Thirties America* (Chicago: University of Chicago Press, 1973/1986); Miles Orvell, *The Real Thing: Imitation and Authenticity in American Culture, 1880–1940* (Chapel Hill: University of North Carolina Press, 1989); Cara A. Finnegan, *Picturing Poverty: Print Culture and FSA Photographs* (Washington, D.C.: Smithsonian Books, 2003).

9. Baxandall, *Painting and Experience,* 152.

10. On image vernaculars, see also Cara A. Finnegan, "Image Vernaculars: Photography, Anxiety, and Public Argument," *Proceedings of the Fifth Conference of the International Society for the Study of Argumentation,* ed. Frans H. van Eemeren et al. (Amsterdam: Sic Sat, 2003), 315–18. The concept "vernacular" appears elsewhere in rhetoric and photography scholarship. Although these uses of the term differ from my own (as well as from one another), they are related in that each invokes a sense of "vernacular" as unofficial, colloquial modes of communication. See Gerard Hauser, *Vernacular Voices: The Rhetoric of Publics and Public Sphere* (Columbia: University of South Carolina Press, 1999); Kent A. Ono and John M. Sloop, *Shifting Borders: Rhetoric, Immigration, and California's Proposition 187* (Philadelphia: Temple University Press, 2002); Geoffrey Batchen, "Vernacular Photographies," *History of Photography* 24, no. 3 (2000): 262–71.

11. In his translation of Aristotle's *Rhetoric,* George Kennedy articulates the enthymeme's role thusly: "rhetoric [forms enthymemes] from things [that seem true] to people already accustomed to deliberate among themselves" (Aristotle, *On Rhetoric,* trans. George Kennedy [New York: Oxford University Press, 1991], 41). See also the entry on the enthymeme in Thomas O. Sloane, ed., *Encyclopedia of Rhetoric* (New York: Oxford University Press, 2001), 247–50.

12. See Dana L. Cloud, "'To Veil the Threat of Terror': Afghan Women and the <Clash of Civilizations> in the Imagery of the U.S. War on Terrorism," *Quarterly Journal of Speech* 90 (2004): 285–306; Cori E. Dauber, "The Shot Seen 'Round the World: The Impact of the Images of Mogadishu on American Military Operations," *Rhetoric & Public Affairs* 4 (2001): 653–87; Kevin M. DeLuca, *Image Politics: The New Rhetoric of Environmental Activism* (New York: Guilford Press, 1999); Kevin M. DeLuca and Anne Teresa Demo, "Imaging Nature: Watkins,

Yosemite, and the Birth of Environmentalism," *Critical Studies in Media Communication* 17 (2000): 241–60; Finnegan, *Picturing Poverty;* John M. Murphy, "'Our Mission and Our Moment': George W. Bush and September 11th," *Rhetoric & Public Affairs* 6 (2003): 607–32; Lester C. Olson, *Benjamin Franklin's Vision of American Community: A Study in Rhetorical Iconology* (Columbia: University of South Carolina Press, 2004); Bryan C. Taylor, "'Our Bruised Arms Hung Up as Monuments': Nuclear Iconography in Post-Cold War Culture," *Critical Studies in Media Communication* 20 (2003): 1–34.

13. Alan Trachtenberg, "Photography: The Emergence of a Keyword," in *Photography in Nineteenth-Century America,* ed. Martha A. Sandweiss (Fort Worth and New York: Amon Carter Museum and Harry N. Abrams, 1991), 22.

14. Trachtenberg, "Photography," 22. On the daguerreotype as a rhetoric, see also Stephen John Hartnett, *Democratic Dissent and the Cultural Fictions of Antebellum America* (Urbana: University of Illinois Press, 2002), 132–72.

15. Charles Hamilton and Lloyd Ostendorf note that there are over one hundred extant photographs of Lincoln, more than 50 made before he became president, and more than 60 taken during his presidency. See Hamilton and Ostendorf, *Lincoln in Photographs,* ix–x.

16. Barry Schwartz traced references to both Lincoln and Washington in newspapers and in the *Congressional Record* from roughly 1865 to 1920. He found that references to Lincoln markedly increased after 1900 and soon thereafter surpassed references to Washington. See Barry Schwartz, *Abraham Lincoln and the Forge of National Memory* (Chicago: University of Chicago Press, 2000), 57–58, 78, 110–13. See also Marcus Cunliffe, "The Doubled Images of Lincoln and Washington," in *Gettysburg College,* 26th Annual Robert Fortenbaugh Memorial Lecture (Gettysburg College, Pa., 1988), 7–34; Merrill D. Peterson, *Lincoln in American Memory* (New York: Oxford University Press, 1994), 27–29.

17. On the consumer culture surrounding Lincoln, see Frank J. Williams and Mark E. Neely Jr., "The Crisis in Lincoln Collecting," in *Lincoln and Lincolniana,* ed. Harold Holzer (Providence, R.I.: Brown University Press, 1985), 79–96; Richard J. S. Gutman and Kellie O. Gutman, "Lincoln Dollars and Cents: The Commercialization of Abraham Lincoln," in Holzer, *Lincoln and Lincolniana,* 97–113. On the iconography of Lincoln in relation to questions of public memory more generally, see Peterson, *Lincoln in American Memory,* and Schwartz, *Abraham Lincoln.*

18. One exception is Brian Snee, "Shooting Lincoln: Rhetorical Dimensions in Historical Films" (Ph.D. diss., Pennsylvania State University, 2000). Harold Holzer is the foremost historian of the visual iconography of Lincoln. See Harold Holzer, *Lincoln Seen and Heard* (Lawrence: University Press of Kansas, 2000); Harold Holzer, Gabor S. Boritt, and Mark E. Neely, Jr., *The Lincoln Image: Abraham Lincoln and the Popular Print* (Urbana: University of Illinois Press, 2001); Harold Holzer, Gabor S. Boritt, and Mark E. Neely Jr., *Changing the Lincoln Image* (Fort Wayne, Ind.: Louis A. Warren/Lincoln Library and Museum, 1985). As evidence for Lincoln's continued relevance to rhetorical studies, see David Zarefsky, "The Continuing Fascination with Lincoln," *Rhetoric & Public Affairs* 6 (2003): 337–70.

19. Barry Schwartz, "The Reconstruction of Abraham Lincoln," in *Collective Remembering,* ed. David Middleton and Derek Edwards (London: Sage, 1990), 101.

20. Tarbell was already a veteran writer for *McClure's;* during its first year she wrote a popular series, "Life of Napoleon," for the magazine. On Tarbell see Kathleen Brady, *Ida Tarbell: Portrait of a Muckraker* (New York: Seaview/Putnam, 1984); see also Tarbell's autobiography, *All in a Day's Work* (New York: Macmillan Co., 1939).

21. Peterson, *Lincoln in American Memory,* 149.

22. In particular, Tarbell relied heavily on the recent work of Lincoln's former secretaries, John G. Nicolay and John Hay. See John G. Nicolay and John Hay, *Abraham Lincoln, A History* (New York: Century Co., 1890).

23. Brady, *Ida Tarbell,* 96–98; Peterson, *Lincoln in American Memory,* 150–52.

24. The monthly magazine first sold for 15 cents an issue (most similar magazines sold for 25 to 35 cents). McClure later cut the price to 10 cents. See Theodore Peterson, *Magazines in the Twentieth Century* (Urbana: University of Illinois Press, 1964), 6–7, 9–10.

25. On the importance of the halftone process to the circulation of photographs in print culture, see Robert Taft, *Photography and the American Scene* (New York: Dover, 1938), 427–41, 446.

26. Brady, *Ida Tarbell,* 92.

27. "Editorial Announcement," *McClure's,* November 1895, 483–84.

28. Peterson, *Magazines in the Twentieth Century,* 10.

29. Brady, *Ida Tarbell,* 98.

30. Brady, *Ida Tarbell,* 99; Peterson, *Lincoln in American Memory,* 151.

31. The "tousled hair" photograph was widely circulated after Lincoln's senate nomination. Lincoln wrote to a friend that he thought the photograph was "a very true one; though my wife and many others do not. My impression is that their objection arises from the disordered condition of the hair" (Hamilton and Ostendorf, *Lincoln in Photographs,* 6–7).

32. Quoted in Peterson, *Lincoln in American Memory,* 152; see also Tarbell, *All in a Day's Work,* 165–68.

33. "*McClure's* Magazine for 1895–6: How Lincoln Looked When Young," *McClure's,* November 1895, 3.

34. However, legend has it that despite its excellent provenance and strong resemblance to Lincoln, the family later was required to authenticate the image three times. See Harold Holzer, "Is This the First Photograph of Abraham Lincoln?" *American Heritage,* February-March 1994, 39–42. The daguerreotype eventually was donated by Robert Todd Lincoln's daughter to the Library of Congress. On forgery of Lincolniana in general, see Peterson, *Lincoln in American Memory,* 144–55, 291–98, 341; see also Holzer, *Lincoln and Lincolniana.*

35. Barbara Savedoff, *Transforming Images: How Photography Complicates the Picture* (Ithaca, N.Y.: Cornell University Press, 2000), 152.

36. On the history of daguerreotypes, see Beaumont Newhall, *The Daguerreotype in America,* 3d rev. ed. (New York: Dover Publications, 1976); Taft, *Photography and the American Scene,* 2–101.

37. See Trachtenberg, "Photography," 20; Susan S. Williams, *Confounding Images: Photography and Portraiture in Antebellum Fiction* (Philadelphia: University of Pennsylvania Press, 1997), 52; Alan Trachtenberg, "Likeness as Identity: Reflections on the Daguerrean Mystique," in *The Portrait in Photography,* ed. Graham Clarke (London: Reaktion Books, 1992), 177.

38. Savedoff, *Transforming Images,* 174.

39. Peterson, *Magazines in the Twentieth Century,* 10.

40. Of the first set of 12 letters published in the December 1895 *McClure's,* four are from members of the legal profession (including Supreme Court justices), five are from academics, and two are from newspaper editors.

41. Many correspondents began their letters by thanking McClure for sending an advance copy of the image; for example, C. R. Miller, editor of the *New York Times,* wrote on October 24, "I thank you for the privilege you have given me of looking over some of the text and illustrations of your new Life of Lincoln" ("The Earliest Portrait," 111).

42. "The Earliest Portrait," 111.

43. "The Earliest Portrait," 112.

44. "The Earliest Portrait," 110.

45. "The Earliest Portrait," 110.

46. "The Earliest Portrait," 111.

47. "The Earliest Portrait," 109.

48. "Miss Tarbell's," 206–7.

49. "Miss Tarbell's," 207.

50. See Peterson, *Lincoln in American Memory,* 27.

51. Miles Orvell, *The Real Thing: Imitation and Authenticity in American Culture, 1880—1940* (Chapel Hill: University of North Carolina Press, 1989), 101.

52. On Muybridge see Rebecca Solnit, *River of Shadows: Eadweard Muybridge and the Technological Wild West* (New York: Viking, 2003).

53. Michael L. Carlebach, *American Photojournalism Comes of Age* (Washington, D.C.: Smithsonian Institution Press, 1997), 18–19. An earlier invention of Eastman's, roll film, made the first Kodak cameras possible. The consumer would expose the roll of film, then mail the entire camera back to Kodak. The company would process the film and print its photographs, then send the photographs as well as the camera (reloaded with film) back to the consumer.

54. Sarah Greenough, "'Of Charming Glens, Graceful Glades, and Frowning Cliffs': The Economic Incentives, Social Inducements, and Aesthetic Issues of American Pictorial Photography, 1880–1902," in Sandweiss, *Photography in Nineteenth-Century America,* 259.

55. On the rhetoric of portrait photographs, see Graham Clarke, ed., *The Portrait in Photography* (London: Reaktion Books, 1992).

56. David M. Lubin, *Act of Portrayal: Eakins, Sargent, James* (New Haven, Conn.: Yale University Press, 1985), 3.

57. Trachtenberg, "Photography," 33.

58. Barbara McCandless, "The Portrait Studio and the Celebrity," in *Photography in the Nineteenth Century,* 49. See also Williams, *Confounding Images,* 19.

59. Alan Trachtenberg, *Reading American Photographs: Images as History from Mathew Brady to Walker Evans* (New York: Noonday Press, 1989), 48. Stephen Hartnett reads Brady's *Gallery* in light of the politics of the era, particularly debates about

slavery, and argues the images are examples of the "new genre of the daguerreotype as politician's tool" (Hartnett, *Democratic Dissent,* 152).

60. John Tagg, *The Burden of Representation: Essays on Photographies and Histories* (Minneapolis: University of Minnesota Press, 1988), 74. On the role of photography as an instrument of the state, see also Allan Sekula, "The Body and the Archive," *October* 39 (Winter 1986): 3–64; Suren Lalvani, *Photography, Vision, and the Production of Modern Bodies* (Albany, N.Y.: State University of New York Press, 1996), 87–137.

61. Harry Soderman and John J. O'Connell, *Modern Criminal Investigation,* 5th ed. (New York: Funk and Wagnall's, 1962), 71; Martha Merrill Umphrey, "'The Sun Has Been Too Quick for Them': Criminal Portraiture and the Police in the Late Nineteenth Century," *Studies in Law, Politics and Society* 16 (1997): 144. See also Trachtenberg, *Reading,* 28–29.

62. Martha Umphrey argues that one of the most popular late nineteenth-century texts on criminality, Thomas Byrne's *Professional Criminals of America* (1886), functioned as an ambivalent moral warning against criminal behavior because it both condemned and celebrated the most sensational forms of criminal activity (Umphrey, "'The Sun,'" 142). See also Sekula, "The Body and the Archive," 37–38.

63. Sekula, "The Body and the Archive," 12.

64. Orvell, *The Real Thing,* 16.

65. Karen Halttunen, *Confidence Men and Painted Women: A Study of Middle-Class Culture in America, 1830–1870* (New Haven: Yale University Press, 1982), 28.

66. Halttunen, *Confidence Men,* 40–41.

67. On the Fowlers see Madeleine B. Stern, *Heads and Headlines: The Phrenological Fowlers* (Norman: University of Oklahoma Press, 1971); see also O. S. Fowler, *Fowler's Practical Phrenology* (New York: Edward Kearney, 1846).

68. On relationships between phrenology/physiognomy and photography, see also Allan Sekula, "The Traffic in Photographs," *Art Journal* 41 (1981): 18–19; Sekula, "The Body and the Archive," 10–16; Hartnett, *Democratic Dissent,* 156–59.

69. Sekula, "The Body and the Archive," 11; Lucy Hartley, *Physiognomy and the Meaning of Expression in Nineteenth-Century Culture* (Cambridge, U.K.: Cambridge University Press, 2001), 2.

70. Hartley, *Physiognomy,* 127.

71. Orvell, *The Real Thing,* 14.

72. Stern, *Heads and Headlines,* x.

73. Stephen Hartnett, "'It Is Terrible to Possess Such Power!' The Critique of Phrenology, Class, and Gender in Hawthorne's 'The Birth-Mark,'" *Prospero* 5 (1998): 6.

74. Hartnett, "'It Is Terrible,'" 6.

75. Hartley, *Physiognomy,* 12.

76. Stern, *Heads and Headlines,* 212.

77. Samuel R. Wells, *How to Read Character: A Handbook of Physiology, Phrenology and Physiognomy, Illustrated with a Descriptive Chart* (New York: Fowler, Wells, and Co., 1888), 127.

78. Beginning in the late 1870s, Francis Galton made composite photographs that relied heavily on discourses of phrenology and physiognomy to construct typologies of criminality and deviance. Allan Sekula points out that Galton's "career was suspended between the triumph of his cousin Charles Darwin's evolutionary paradigm in the late 1860s and the belated discovery in 1899 of Gregor Mendel's work on the genetic ratio underlying inheritance" (Sekula, "Body and the Archive," 42). See also Orvell, *The Real Thing,* 92–94. On the rhetoric of eugenics in the twentieth century, see Marouf Arif Hasian Jr., *The Rhetoric of Eugenics in Anglo-American Thought* (Athens: University of Georgia Press, 1996).

79. Stern, *Heads and Headlines,* 214.

80. "The Earliest Portrait," 109.

81. "The Earliest Portrait," 109.

82. Samuel R. Wells, *New Physiognomy; or, Signs of Character, as Manifested through Temperament and External Forms, and Especially in 'The Human Face Divine'* (New York: Fowler and Wells, 1866), 550–51. Lincoln's Second Inaugural haunts Wells's text, too: "charity for all."

83. Wells, *New Physiognomy,* 552.

84. John G. Nicolay, "Lincoln's Personal Appearance," *Century,* October 1891, 932.

85. Quoted in Nicolay, "Lincoln's Personal Appearance," 933.

86. Nicolay, "Lincoln's Personal Appearance," 935, emphasis added. Nicolay is quoting the final line of James Russell Lowell's "Commemoration Ode," written for Harvard's graduation in the summer of 1865. See Peterson, *Lincoln in American Memory,* 32–33.

87. "Miss Tarbell's," 207.

88. "Miss Tarbell's," 207.

89. Truman H. Bartlett, "The Physiognomy of Lincoln," *McClure's,* August 1907, 390–407.

90. Bartlett, "Physiognomy," 399, 405.

91. On neurasthenia, see T. J. Jackson Lears, *No Place of Grace: Antimodernism and the Transformation*

of American Culture, 1880—1920 (Chicago: University of Chicago Press, 1981), 47–54; Alan Trachtenberg, *The Incorporation of America: Culture and Society in the Gilded Age* (New York: Hill and Wang, 1982), 47–48.

92. Robert Wiebe, *The Search for Order, 1877–1920* (New York: Hill and Wang, 1967), 43.

93. Jacob Riis, *How the Other Half Lives: Studies among the Tenements of New York* (New York: Dover, 1890/1971). See also Wiebe, *The Search for Order,* 88.

94. Riis, *How the Other Half Lives,* 19.

95. Quoted in Lears, *No Place of Grace,* 29.

96. Lears, *No Place of Grace,* 28.

97. Trachtenberg, *Incorporation,* 14.

98. Trachtenberg, *Incorporation,* 16.

99. Shawn Michelle Smith, *American Archives: Gender, Race, and Class in Visual Culture* (Princeton, N.J.: Princeton University Press, 1999), 136.

100. Even seemingly innocuous artifacts such as the baby book were developed as a cultural response to anxieties about the loss of American identity. Eugenicist Francis Galton promoted baby books to "those who care to forecast the mental and bodily faculties of their children, and to further the science of heredity" (quoted in Smith, *American Archives,* 125).

101. Wells, *New Physiognomy,* 409.

4

"What Lips These Lips Have Kissed"

Refiguring the Politics of Queer Public Kissing

Charles E. Morris III and John M. Sloop

In general, one may pronounce kissing dangerous. A spark of fire has often been struck out of the collision of lips that has blown up the whole magazine of virtue.

—*Anonymous, 1803[1]*

Kissing, in certain figurations, has lost none of its hot promise since our epigraph was penned two centuries ago. Its ongoing transformative combustion may be witnessed in two extraordinarily divergent perspectives on its cultural representation and political implications. In 2001, queer filmmaker Bruce LaBruce offered in Toronto's *Eye Weekly* a noteworthy rave of the sophomoric buddy film *Dude, Where's My Car?* One scene in particular inspired LaBruce, in which we find our stoned protagonists Jesse (Ashton Kutcher) and Chester (Seann William Scott) idling at a stoplight next to superhunk Fabio and his equally alluring female passenger.

Adolescent male jockeying ensues: "Fabio looks over contemptuously and revs his engine; Kutcher, behind the wheel, does the same. Fabio responds by putting his arm around his vixen; Kutcher rises to the challenge by placing his arm emphatically around Scott. Fabio then leans over and gives his girl a long, deep tongue kiss." What happens next, in LaBruce's exuberant judgment, is nothing short of revolutionary:

> The movie could have gone in infinite directions at this point, but amazingly Kutcher leans over and, gently and convincingly, delivers the lingering tongue to Scott. The actors neither overplay nor underplay the moment and show no visible

SOURCE: Morris, C. E., III, & Sloop, J. M. (2006). "What lips these lips have kissed": Refiguring the politics of queer public kissing. *Communication and Critical/Cultural Studies, 3*(1), 1–26. ISSN 1479-1420 (print)/ISSN 1479-4233 (online) © 2006 National Communication Association.

trace of disgust or regret afterward. I was almost in tears. This one scene does more to advance the cause of homosexuality than 25 years of gay activism.[2]

By stark contrast, Robert Knight, director of the rightwing Culture and Family Institute, responded in typical jeremiadic thunder to the Abu Ghraib scandal by warning of the "'Perfect Storm' of American cultural depravity," rooted in homosexuality and "advanced in the name of progress and amplified by a sensation-hungry media," that provides ample inducement for proliferating terrorism. According to his apocalyptic assessment:

> Imagine how those images of men kissing outside San Francisco City Hall after being "married" play in the Muslim world. We couldn't offer the mullahs a more perfect picture of American decadence. This puts Americans at risk all over the world, especially Christian missionaries who are trying to bring the Gospel to people trapped in darkness for millennia.[3]

What might appear as striking incommensurability between teen film and jihad is belied, in our judgment, by a shared focus on same-sex (specifically male) kissing that anchors and animates these consequential rhetorical visions. For obviously different reasons, both LaBruce and Knight conclude that from the collision of queer lips is sparked a conflagration sufficient to scorch the heteronormative order in U.S. public culture.[4] The perils and potentialities of such a project are the subject of our critical engagement, by means of which we emphasize the significance and urgency of same-sex kissing as at once cultural representation and a *political* imperative.

The sight of a similarly aged heterosexual couple kissing publicly might not be noticed at all or, if registered, would merely signify a largely sanctioned expression of mutual pleasure, affection, love. A gesture at once banal and iconic, the public kiss by members of the opposite sex represents metonymically the shared cultural embrace of heteronormative values and behavior. That same kiss between two men, however, constitutes a "marked" and threatening act, a performance instantly understood as contrary

to hegemonic assumptions about public behavior, and the public good, because it invites certain judgments about the men's *deviant sexual behavior* and its imagined encroachments, violations and contagions, judgments that inevitably exceed the mere fact of their having a mutually affirming encounter.[5]

Public kissing between men remains crucially problematic, we claim, despite current mainstream gay visibility, despite Frank Rich's claim in the *New York Times,* after witnessing the celebratory kiss between Marc Shaiman and Scott Wittman at the 2003 Tony Awards, that "Now the speed of both political and cultural change is accelerating, so much so that politicians who are flummoxed by homosexuality . . . are on a collision course with history."[6] We find it significant that this act can be simultaneously measured as readily for its daunting portents. As Otis Stuart concluded,

> Kissing is an act everybody knows, the sight everyone recognizes from personal experience. Onscreen and onstage, it's guaranteed common ground that goes to the gut of homophobia with a bloodcurdling message: *that* makes them human. Sexualizing and humanizing homosexuality, kissing could well be the last hinge in the closet door.[7]

We take a premise embedded in these varied judgments, namely kissing as a *queer juggernaut,* as the basis of our analysis. In doing so, we press beyond the basic acknowledgment that public kissing is an act rife with cultural meaning, a nodal point around which the common-sense understandings of sexuality can be understood and interrogated. We argue that man-on-man public kissing constitutes a paramount political performance, not sufficiently recognized as such in ongoing discussion and debate of gay visibility within GLBTQ communities, but understood accordingly by those who see it as a chief threat to heteronormativity and seek its discipline. We believe it vital to conceive of same-sex kissing as central to the prospects of a queer world and to reconsider the timing of its requisite escalating performance.

In this essay, we first highlight the specific act of man-on-man kissing as insufficiently mobilized within pro-gay logics of apolitical, incremental, and assimilationsist visibility. By contrast, in the second section, we consider the deployment of this kiss for its significance as a juggernaut in a broader project of queer world making, which requires an emphasis on visibility as cultural *and* political, as well as heightened attention to *kairos* in relation to critical visual mass. In the third section, we focus on ideological and political barriers to the creation of this kissing visual mass. Here, we examine homophobic discourses that seemingly treat all gay representation as political, disciplinary responses that dangerously undermine the queer ascendancy currently, perhaps prematurely, heralded. Finally, we conclude with relevant implications regarding same-sex kissing, the politics of visible pleasure, and their queer prospects.

When a Kiss Is Not a Kiss

Although we are generally, but not always, unaware of it during the embrace, each shared kiss is a "performative act," as Judith Butler would have it, an often unreflective performance which does not draw scrutiny because it "makes sense" within the ideology of contemporary U.S. culture.[8] Each public kiss between a man and woman serves as a reiteration and reaffirmation of heteronormativity.[9] It is, as Butler theorizes, an act of repetition, a ritualized product "under and through the force of prohibition and taboo," in which people are encouraged to reiterate expected social/sexual dynamics, steer away from unexpected or unwelcome social/sexual dynamics, and punish those who participate in such acts through social ostracism and other disciplinary means.[10] In short, most heterosexual kisses escape scrutiny not only because of their ubiquity but also because of their heteronormative reiteration. As Lauren Berlant and Michael Warner argue, "A complex cluster of sexual practices gets confused, in heterosexual culture, with the love plot of intimacy and familialism that signifies belonging to society in a deep and normal way. Community is imagined through scenes of intimacy, coupling, and kinship."[11]

It is important to emphasize that this complex cluster of meanings is historical and cultural rather than essential: public kissing could *mean* otherwise. Curiously, the performativity

and contingency of kissing is repeatedly acknowledged in public discussion,[12] yet cultural practices continue to maintain its heteronormative meanings. That is, although a database search of the words "public kiss" yields hundreds of popular press articles, including numerous histories of kissing—or its absence—in this and other cultures, most operate as if opposite-sex public kissing is not only normal but natural. We notice most heterosexual kisses no more than we do handshakes (of course, a *handshake* between a husband and wife might be noticeable). Although the meaning of the public kiss is historical and cultural, its rhetorical force, reiterated multiple times each day, materially grounds the assumption that it is a natural reaffirmation of proper gender behavior. By contrast, the sight of two men kissing necessarily disrupts visual and emotional, moral and political, fields of heteronormative expectation; same-sex kisses are therefore immediately marked, immediately suspect, and immediately susceptible to discipline because they are understood, often viscerally, as an unnatural and dangerous erotic expression—as exigent representation.

The Queer Media Celebration

Some might argue that blossoming gay visibility would seem to render such a perspective increasingly anachronistic. With the proliferation and sustained popularity of mediated gay depiction, there appears to be a growing consensus that homosexuality has become normal, that heteronormativity is yielding to the queer. As an issue of *Entertainment Weekly*, with the cast of *Queer Eye for the Straight Guy* on its cover, proclaimed, "So along with the Supreme Court's landmark *Lawrence v. Texas* ruling, the return of Elle Woods, and the emancipation of Ms. Liza Minnelli, it seems the nation may finally be ready to appreciate the finer delights of foie-gras mousse and pre-shave oil."[13] Television critic Carina Chocano has provocatively concluded, "*Queer Eye* is glastnost."[14]

The same-sex kiss, too, it seems, has come a long way since the "gay 1990s," a decade of occasioned but occluded kissing that was treated, as Larry Gross observes, "with all the delicacy and attention required for high-risk medical procedures."[15] It was, despite demonstrable gains, a decade in which Otis Stuart could note: "There's one thing you still don't see. If the current New York theater is a mirror held up to homosexuality, queers don't kiss. . . . Kissing is clearly gay theater's last taboo."[16] In the films *Philadelphia* and *Six Degrees of Separation,* Tom Hanks and Will Smith, both playing gay characters, refused to kiss their partners on screen. Smith purportedly heeded the advice of Denzel Washington, who admonished, "Don't you be kissing no man."[17] Although the producers of *Melrose Place* planned to feature a gay romantic kiss, network censors forced the camera to fade at the moment it occurred, a kiss implied but never shown.[18] The *New York Times* reported in 1996 that gay computer programmer Jacques Servin was fired after creating an Easter Egg that allowed players to see male characters kissing so as to expose the absence of homosexuality in video games.[19] In 1997, USA network's "Breaking the Surface" graphically depicted Olympic diver Greg Louganis' traumatic rape, but omitted any same-sex kissing.[20] One encountered that same year GLAAD's news alert service heralding as momentous a kiss shared by Tom Selleck and Kevin Kline in the problematic film *In and Out.*[21]

Without question, particularly in the past half-decade, representations of same-sex kissing have manifested in multiple cultural locations. Adam Sandler, in his 1999 teen film *Big Daddy,* prominently featured a gay couple as the best friends of straight protagonist Sonny Koufax, in one scene depicting them sharing a goodbye kiss; a friend's homophobic reaction to the couple's intimacy compelled Koufax's response, "That's what gay guys do, they kiss."[22] By 2000, the *Los Angeles Times* argued that the lack of public discussion about a kiss shared by Will and Jack on *Will & Grace* suggested that there was no longer anything shocking about gay publicity.[23] The rash of same-sex kissing on mainstream television shows such as *Spin City, That '70s Show, The Simpsons, Friends, It's All Relative,* and *Saturday Night Live* appears to substantiate such a claim. *Dawson's Creek* aired an episode in 2000 entitled "True Love," featuring Jack McPhee (Kerr Smith) engaged in the "first romantic kiss between two men"; Jack did so again in the 2003 series finale, projected five years into the future, in which he tells an elderly

couple who witnesses his kiss on the beach, "I'm just kissing my boyfriend!" to which the woman responds, "That's nice."[24]

MTV, long forward in its sexual representation, has unabashedly portrayed same-sex kissing on various seasons of *The Real World,* in its soap operas *Undressed* and *Spyder Games,* and in its public service campaigns "Do You Speak MTV" (2000) and "Fight For Your Rights: Take a Stand Against Discrimination" (2001). On Showtime's *Queer As Folk* and HBO's *Six Feet Under,* man-on-man kissing is but one of the recurrent displays of desire and affection that occur at home, on the street, in the local diner, and everywhere else. Pop singer Christina Aguilera was honored at the 2003 GLAAD Media Awards for depicting a romantic queer kiss in the video for her hit song "Beautiful." In Las Vegas, twice nightly, Cirque du Soleil's *Zumanity* features a "ferocious, lusty, lingering kiss, the explosive culmination and combination of all the varied emotions expressed in the movements that come before." Gay couples marrying in San Francisco and New York in 2004 found clips of their jubilant kisses broadcast on the nightly news.[25]

With such multiple representations in mind, we might triumphantly predict with Frank Rich that "the day when homosexuality threatens most heterosexuals seems to be passing in America."[26] The final acceptance of queer affectionate and erotic public display seems but an episode away. Such optimism, certainly worth savoring and nurturing, must be tempered and recast, however, by difficult questions related to sexuality, gender, and visibility that are presently obfuscated by ebullient punditry, undermining an activist orientation that understands public kissing *as tactically central and kairotic* rather than merely progressive.

Politics of Visibility

Our critically reflexive caution begins with Steven Seidman's perspective, which, in our judgment, remains apt despite the multiplication of queer kissing representations:

My sense is that, despite some dissent and conflict, there is a dominant culture that associates normal sexuality with sex that is exclusively between adults, that conforms to dichotomous gender norms, that is private, tender, caring, genitally centered, and linked to love, marriage, and monogamy. There is then a wide range of consensual adult practices that are potentially vulnerable to stigma and social punishment. . . . Individuals who engage in some of these acts will be scandalized as "bad citizens"; demands will be heard to use repressive or therapeutic interventions to protect good citizens from contamination—that is, being seduced, molested, or infected by disease-carrying sexual deviants.[27]

Crucial here is the *political* inflection given to an account of those who wish to defend and preserve heteronormativity. As we will demonstrate later, disciplinary responses to man-on-man kissing extend from a firm assumption that culture and politics are inextricably bound. The language employed by Richard Goldstein in his *Village Voice* article is telling: "Rather than reflecting a shift in acceptance, the new queer visibility may be fueling resentment. . . . To guys under duress, the glut of gay shows is yet another insurrection—and gay marriage is a fucking *coup d'état*. . . . It's crucial not to confuse a pop trend with a juggernaut."[28]

It is less clear whether those reveling in the ever-increasing mediated images of gays and lesbians, perhaps especially of same-sex kissing, sufficiently understand them within a context of "dissent and conflict," or rather are "confus[ing] a pop trend with a juggernaut," if the politics implied by the term juggernaut registers at all. The danger, as Suzanna Walters has argued, is that "we all carry with us a belief in a sort of causal connection between cultural visibility and political change, but I am convinced that, more often than not, there is actually a radical *disconnect* between the two."[29] This disconnect is articulated clearly in an interview Jeffrey Epstein conducted with seven of Hollywood's influential and openly gay executives. Paris Barclay claimed that there is not "anything more powerful" than television as, in Epstein's words, "the ultimate tool for social change." However, Bryan Fuller conceived of this tool as "mak[ing] them [mainstream audiences] comfortable with likeable gay characters in their living room—so they're not offensive and they don't make out on primetime—and little by little, you get leeway."

In response to Craig Zadan's reference to the "outrage" about the Shaiman/Wittman kiss at the 2003 Tony Awards, Ilene Chaiken observed, "It was before the really seismic shift that we're in the midst of right now."[30]

Queer visibility by these accounts is discernibly apolitical, without tactical vision, and its incrementalism obscures an understanding of *kairos* as a rhetorical imperative within this "seismic shift" of representation. With the exception of those portrayals on more exclusive outlets like MTV, Showtime or Cirque du Soleil, *mainstream* images of man-on-man kissing, unquestionably muscular in queer potential, are variously domesticated (comic displacement, quaint romantic but non-sexual plotting), short-circuited by assimilationist logic in which lips and tongues are not allowed to exert the same thrust as, say, impeccable grooming or wedding bands. Paul Rudnick's 1995 film *Jeffrey* astutely embodies the ongoing dilemma. In a gym-drenched, erotically charged exchange, sex-phobic protagonist Jeffrey (Stephen Weber) is tortured by the advances of the gorgeous Steve (Michael T. Weiss), who punctuates the moment with a question: "What would happen if I kissed you, right now?" Jeffrey resists then succumbs to Steve's passionate embrace. Subsequently, we witness another answer to the same question. Two young straight couples in a theater watching the movie react to the kiss, the women with longing sighs, their boyfriends with stunned expressions and sputterings of "Oh man, gross, disgusting." Jeffrey himself follows with a resounding "No!" and flees the gym. Rudnick, despite his insight, rather missed the point. He told the *Los Angeles Times,* "Actually, there is plenty of kissing between men within the first five seconds of the movie. We wanted to get it out of the way so that the audience would realize that 'Jeffrey' is not about some kind of shocking revelation."[31]

The politics of visibility are always a matter of great concern as marginalized and disciplined subjectivities gain representation through mass mediated texts and, as a result, larger access to a culture's dominant exchange of symbols. Is it better to be "marked" publicly as a way to alter perceptions about one's subjectivity in a positive manner, or are there more benefits to remaining "unmarked," outside of the strongest disciplinary gazes?[32] Is being publicly represented or marked necessarily a sign of progress, a cause for celebration? Moreover, once marked, how can the necessarily limited images be reshaped, rethought publicly? How does one engage in such a struggle?

In a sense, asking about the relative merits of being marked or unmarked is a moot question: there is no doubt that this is a high tide for queer representation. Rather than mull over the question of whether representation is desirable, we critically focus instead on the forms this visibility might take. As Walters persuasively argues, "There must be an invigorated concern with changes not only in the *quantity* of representation but in the *quality* as well. . . . It is the *quality* of this visibility that matters. More *Basic Instincts* or avoided prime-time kisses do not a social transformation make. The complexity and diversity of the gay and lesbian community needs to be *represented,* not promoted as simply heterosexuality with a twist."[33]

Cultural critics have repeatedly observed that, because advertisers want their commercial products to appeal to large numbers, mediated images and themes must necessarily be "comfortable" ones, reflecting commonsense expectations and shared ideological meanings. In the case of television, for example, images must fit visually and behaviorally within the acceptable expectations of most viewers. Fiske and Hartley refer to this as ideological clawback (i.e., the commercial nature of television encourages all potential changes in meaning to be "clawed back" toward the center); Celeste Condit simply notes that "television, or any mass medium, can do oppressive work solely by addressing the dominant audience that also constitutes the public."[34] In terms of our interests, we stress that current mass-mediated representations reflect predictable and comfortable understandings of gays and lesbians. It is neither the case that consumers have no control over meanings nor that mass-mediated representations are particularly regressive, rather that the needs of commercialism tend toward stability, to hold normative meanings in place.

Hence, a number of contemporary media scholars have detailed the ways in which contemporary GLBTQ representations have been constrained and recentered in the heteronormative imaginary. Helene A. Shugart has convincingly argued that mediated depictions of gay men have gained popularity only by virtue of being desexualized, depoliticized, and, indeed, heterosexualized, i.e., endowed with "decidedly conventional heterosexual signifiers."[35] Hemal Jhaveri observes that, despite their seemingly ubiquitous presence, "the representations of gay men have been disconcertingly one-dimensional. . . . Unfortunately, by only reinforcing perceptions that viewers are already comfortable with, a vast majority of these shows preserve the status quo rather than challenge it."[36]

The problem, then, is thinking beyond the idea that queer representation as an economic market is equivalent to political progress. Eric Clarke, while recognizing that there can be no "authentic" representation of gays and lesbians, asks that we think hard about "the terms on which this visibility will be offered, *and* the terms on which lesbians and gay men themselves attempt to achieve it" (emphasis ours).[37] Clarke's concern, which we share, is that "commercial publicity has nevertheless come to function as if it were a form of political representation that democratically recognizes and equitably circulates a constituency's civic value."[38]

Clarke observes that organizations like GLAAD and publications like *Out* and *The Advocate* congratulate the mass media industry for "positive" representations which are too often severely limited in the diversity of GLBTQ "types" one encounters, confined to that which is heteronormatively appealing.[39] How do we celebrate the existence of queers on television because of their value as a market group, if even a behavior so seemingly simple as a kiss is left unmarked? Or put differently, absent substantive representations of the kiss, do queers really exist? Again, as Clarke observes, "By viewing commercial value as if it were an appropriate principle for distributing equity, visibility politics aids in the culture industry's partial and distorted delivery of social enfranchisement."[40]

If "we" celebrate GLBTQ representation in mass-mediated texts as it currently exists, we misunderstand the importance of the kiss. To do so risks ceding the politics of representation substantially to those who prefer heteronormativity, those who perceive all such representation as "an agenda making homosexuality appear first normal, and then desirable."[41] That is, many gay progressives may not think of the man-on-man kiss as important tactically or temporally, and deliberately avoid it as overly confrontational, whereas anti-gay spokespersons most definitely grasp, with political inflection, its centrality to queer representation. Thinking solely in terms of visibility/invisibility, marked/unmarked or affirmative/regressive "restricts the kind of imaginative reach anti-homophobic efforts should have."[42]

The Gender Politics of Queer Kissing

Our emphasis on man-on-man kissing as the specifically requisite form of visibility raises equally complex and vexing issues regarding gender. Although gender bifurcation is obviously problematic, especially within a queer critique, we again underscore tactic and timing in claiming such kissing as a political "wedge" that is part of a larger project of queer world making. This perspective is grounded in Lisa Rosen's observation that, among proliferating same-sex display of affection, kissing women, long a staple in straight male erotic fantasy, are much more readily tolerated than kissing men, demonstrating "the different standards for women and men on TV . . . even straight women are more comfortable kissing than straight men are."[43]

We are not arguing that same-sex kisses between women are normalized. Indeed, the tumult created by women's kisses in Dodger Stadium and at a Boulder high school is indication enough that Rosen's generalization should be qualified. In both cases, discipline of same-sex kissing occurred despite the concurrent, unmarked practice of opposite-sex kissing several rows away and in the pages of the same yearbook.[44] But we would argue that representations of man-on-man kissing suffer stigma more severely and are perceived as a greater threat to heteronormativity. In part, we attribute this to the sexism that underwrites appropriations of women kissing. For example, the spectacle of Madonna kissing Britney Spears and Christina Aguilera at the 2003 MTV Music Awards suggests that a "lesbian" kiss fits comfortably, if contingently, within the heterosexual male gaze often containing it.[45]

Whereas depictions of women kissing borders on the cliché, argues Paul Rudnick, "When you see two guys kissing, it pretty much demonstrates they're not kidding. . . . It's seen as much more of a disruption of the world as we know it."[46] Conflating male and female gender representation dangerously misreads the depth of homophobia and sexism that lurks beneath the cultural surface of such "tolerance" and miscalculates the ferocity of the power struggle inherent to the queer world making that same-sex kissing might achieve.

In the following sections, we demonstrate how and why man-on-man kissing, far from having been normalized, constitutes a final front in the battle for a queer world, offering Gran Fury's "Read My Lips" campaign as one meaningful example of its productive mobilization. Because "Read My Lips" engages the anti-homophobic imaginary differently than so many contemporary accounts, we read it for its potential as a disruptive counterperformance. Finally, for the purposes of resisting "clawbacked" understandings of man-on-man kissing, we reveal the vigorous disciplining currently segregating and sanitizing matching lips.

READ MY LIPS:
THE IMPORTANCE OF BEING KISSED

As our survey of cultural representations suggests, the meaning of same-sex public kissing remains fraught with ideological conflict while being construed as virtually normalized. Consequently, one might question our aggressive call for its deeper politicization. Could one not reasonably argue that as long as sexual difference is legally sanctioned in private, and its intimate representation progressively populating the media, why insist on an activist stance? We respond by arguing for the significance of the man-on-man public kiss, deployed and read resistively, mobilized with a heightened sense of *kairos*,[47] because it effects a powerful affirmation for queer communities, functions as a "critical visual mass" more striking by saturation than accumulation, and could potentially queer the meaning of all public kissing, with potentially profound material and symbolic implications for the constitution of sexuality.[48]

Affirmation is, in our minds, the clearest immediate benefit for queer communities offered by the deeper politicization of same-sex kissing. Alfred Kielwasser and Michelle Wolf have revealed the endangerment resulting from a lack of representation in mainstream mediated texts: gay adolescents, without a model of what it is like to "come of age," often precariously understand themselves as aberrations.[49] For all queers, Pat Califia argues, the stakes are high: "Isolation begets invisibility, which perpetuates isolation and gives these variations [in sexual difference] a furtive and unattractive appearance to prospective members."[50]

Although our essay does not concern "public sex" as it has come to be understood, arguments about its rhetorical benefits and disciplinary costs have some applicability when paralleled with man-on-man public kissing. In William Leap's collection, *Public Sex/Gay Space,* a similar theme emerges: public (homo)sex has appeal, beyond the excitement possible exposure brings, precisely because it fulfills a deep need for self-affirmation of one's sexual identity.[51] For instance, Ira Tattelman notes of the appeal of bathhouses: "To make a sexual choice in front of others, who by their presence . . . applauded the ability to make these kinds of decisions, became an impetus for self-sufficiency, a redefinition of who the gay man is."[52] Califia argues that these bathhouses "taught gay men to see themselves as members of a common tribe with similar interests and needs."[53]

Similar claims have been made repeatedly regarding same-sex public kissing. Richard Meyer argues that such representations constitute "the power of queer desire . . . insisting that lesbians and gay men fight the efforts of the larger culture to render their sexuality—their desiring bodies—invisible."[54] The impetus for such representations, therefore, lies in its ability to signify unfettered, undiluted non-normative sexuality. As Frank Bruni observes, "Seeing a same-sex couple kiss makes it impossible for an observer to think about homosexuality only as an abstraction or to interpret warm interaction between two men or two women as something else— something less disturbing."[55]

Consider, for example, the 1988 image *Read My Lips* (Figure 1), wheat-pasted across Manhattan and then worn on T-shirts by countless queers throughout the successive decade. Created by Gran Fury, the New York collective comprised of ten artist members of ACT UP, *Read My Lips* announced ACT UP's kiss-in at 6th Avenue & 8th Street on April 29—the first of the "9 days of protest" coordinated nationally by a network of AIDS activist groups called AIDS Coalition to Network, Organize, and Win (ACT NOW)—to protest a variety of issues central to the epidemic.[56]

A black and white photograph depicts two uniformed sailor boys; hands clasped behind a partner's waist, around the other boy's neck— they could be slow dancing at the USO. Who they are is irrelevant, and what they wear serves only to punctuate the significance of their kiss: with heads cocked and eyes closed, prominent profiles display their concerted embrace, perhaps the ecstasy of a lover's emotional return from war. Absent an enlivened background, the sailors' kiss appears a studio pose, but provenance is not necessary to convey, nor does the contrivance of portraiture belie, what passionate lips say for themselves. Culture and politics are fused in this unyielding performance, represented and reiterated by those kissing on city streets with this

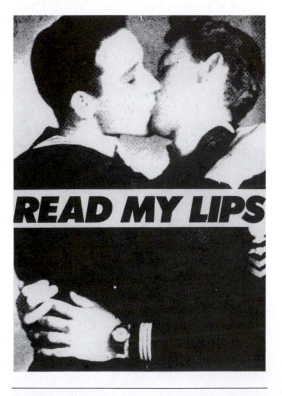

Figure 1 Gran Fury "READ MY LIPS" poster.

SOURCE: Avram Finkelstein.

image emblazoned on their chests, a beacon and battle plan for a queer world.

Gran Fury recast in explicit political fashion the declaration enacted in this vintage photograph of same-sex kissing by appending a banner across the center of the image: "READ MY LIPS." Reconfigured by the imperative voice, launched into public space, the photograph offered, in both word and deed, historically and presently, a direct challenge to heteronormativity. Meyer observes, "In *Read My Lips* . . . the representation of same-sex desire becomes an act of defiance because it is projected, with style and activist bravado, into the public sphere."[57] Its queer agenda, richly unfolding visually and epigrammatically before the gaze of a captivated, if not captive, spectator (who can resist the spectacle of the queer kiss?), was articulated by the fact-sheet handed out at the kiss-in, entitled "WHY WE KISS":

- **We kiss** in an aggressive demonstration of affection.
- **We kiss** to protest the cruel and painful bigotry that affects the lives of lesbians and gay men.
- **We kiss** so that all who see us will be forced to confront their own homophobia.
- **We kiss** to challenge repressive conventions that prohibit displays of love between persons of the same sex.
- **We kiss** as an affirmation of our feelings, our desires, ourselves.[58]

We might add another. Wheat-pasted as it was throughout the cityscape, with its emphatic banner both highlighting the patriotic and conscribing its audience, *Read My Lips* is *a queer recruitment poster.* It is not an entreaty—please take us—but rather an unequivocal declaration: we want you!

As *Read My Lips* exhibits, osculatory resistance ratchets up the intensity and stakes of "in your face" counterpolitics by its insistence on the centrality of the kiss, inscribing publicly the erotic abandon of mutual queer desire at the very moment matching lips touch. Shame, chief among the homophobic disciplinary arsenal, has been flouted, if not destroyed, by brazenly performing *flagrante delicto.* Shame, too long kindling in the foundation of the closet, now infused by defiant heat and a public airing,

becomes the chief fuel in a symbolic inversion of blazing criminality. Foremost, this inversion is an undomesticated public enactment of one's sexual difference, a declaration of the fundamental rightness of open erotic expression. There is no more visceral political manifesto.

In its transgressive occupation, violation of trenchant taboo, and inducement to expose erotophobia and homophobia, Kevin DeLuca argues, the queer kiss "turns the normalized terrain of heterosexuality into an alien landscape."[59] The ideological Richter scale registers queer kissing's tumultuous destabilization of the very grounding of the heteronormative order by making a spectacle of the invisible apparatus binding power, desire, and identity—displaying, in other words, "how thoroughly the local experience of the body is framed by laws, policies, and social customs regulating sexuality."[60] Familiar gestures instantiating heteronormativity by means of "proper public expression, loyal self-censorship, and personal discipline" now threaten to turn akimbo.[61] One's own lips might not be trusted absent such reiterative assurance and libidinous constraint.

In envisioning the transference of this activist perspective into the mainstream, it is imperative to recognize with Berlant and Warner that "the heteronormativity of U.S. culture is not something that can be easily rezoned or disavowed by individual acts of will, by a subversiveness imagined only as personal rather than as the basis of public-formation."[62] Rather than simply hoping for a world in which all "private acts" between adults are allowed, or in which same-sex public kissing is merely more acceptable, we espouse, as do Berlant and Warner, a "world making project" in which mass-mediated representations articulate sexuality differently, queering readings of all forms of intimacy and their public connections. In order to achieve a queer world, a "critical visual mass" of same-sex public kissing must exist, a rhetorical project that influences the meanings articulated by those acts. This entails not the incidental or domesticated man-on-man kiss (dis)located within an assimilationist and incremental logic of gay cultural visibility, but a politically robust calculation of representation in queer measures, in queer time. Such a calculation is articulated not by Max Mutchnick, co-creator of *Will &*

Grace, who argues that "these gay shows are a reflection of what everyone sees now in their jobs, in their families, in their schools," but rather by Russell T. Davies, creator of the original *Queer as Folk* for British *public* television:

> I recently got satellite television, and as I flicked through the 500 channels I was stopped by the image of Brian and Justin kissing on the American Queer as Folk. I thought, My God, that's not just two men kissing. It's two men I helped to create kissing. I was so pleased that it existed, because no matter how much we say there's more gay representation than before, it's still a wasteland. I hope the show runs and runs and runs.[63]

It is this reiterated sexual disruption, understood tactically and kairotically, that makes "Read My Lips" an enormously powerful queer mantra.

DISCIPLINING QUEER KISSES

"Read My Lips" as a queer world-making project is currently hampered by the apolitical, incremental, and assimilationist perspective adopted by gay and lesbian cultural agents. More dangerously, representations of queer kissing typically cause moral panic, conceived and disseminated in political as well as cultural terms, providing instant rationales and motivation for disciplinary action deployed to protect heteronormativity. Phillip Brian Harper observes, "Given this potential of the same-sex kiss to bespeak a homosexual identity for the persons who engage in it—and the threat to social status that such an identity generally constitutes—it is not surprising that extensive cultural safeguards have been constructed to short-circuit that potential in the contexts where such a kiss is likely to occur."[64]

In his classic ideological analysis, Goren Therborn suggests that when public behavior runs counter to dominant expectations, practitioners of this behavior meet with a variety of ideological, physical, and economic forms of discipline.[65] For example, two men kissing in public have often suffered verbal or physical bashing, meted out by those who find such behavior threatening. Or, a film or advertiser may lose revenue as people decide to stay away from representations they deem offensive. Or,

an actor obligated to kiss another man might disavow it, fearing damage to his professional future. Or queers, in a homophobic manifestation of realpolitik, police themselves to avoid any of these described scenarios.

One of the most common justifications for disciplinary practices is that same-sex kissing should be sequestered in order to protect children, implying that the kiss, especially performed by two men, is an affront to public morals, a prelude to molestation, or an act that persuasively "converts" or "recruits" children to homosexuality. For example, in a letter to the *L.A. Times* protesting a gay pride event, Cory Sheppard wrote, "It is up to all concerned heterosexuals to voice their opposition to the dangerously momentous surge of homosexual visibility. . . . It is only by keeping sexual perversities in the closet that our children have a chance at leading the kind of lives that we intend for them."[66] Sheppard explicitly claimed "little Jimmy" will be induced to experiment "with the neighbor's boy because he saw two men kissing in the park."[67] Similarly, after the Minneapolis *Star Tribune* published a story about same-sex kissing on television, letters to the editor complained: "My kids get the paper first. Guess I'll have to hide it from now on"; "Why should we have to screen the newspaper for our children?"; "We're trying to get young people to read the paper. Isn't it enough to have it on TV!"[68]

In addition to panicked moral framing of the "sexual nature" of same-sex kissing as a threat to children, its representation is also disciplined through legislation and economics. In 1990, the Illinois State Legislature debated a bill that sought to prohibit all billboards that depicted same-sex kissing.[69] According to Meyer, the bill emerged after Gran Fury received permission to display posters labeled "Kissing Doesn't Kill," which included pictures of three kissing couples—two of them same-sex couples—accompanied by a text that discussed the politics of AIDS research. When amfAR (The American Foundation for AIDS Research) asked Gran Fury to remove the accompanying text, only the images with the words "Kissing Doesn't Kill" were posted on buses and billboards in Chicago.[70] Without the accompanying texts, many people evidently read the ad as "advocacy" for homosexuality. Chicago City Aldermen argued that the posters had nothing to do with AIDS: "It has something to do with a particular lifestyle, and I don't think that is what the CTA (Chicago Transit Authority) should be in the business of promoting."[71] The bill passed the Illinois State Senate and was only defeated after heavy lobbying in the House.

Man-on-man kissing has also repeatedly met with economic discipline. Observing that one male actor left the cast of *Sunday, Bloody Sunday* rather than kiss another man, and that Harvey Fierstein had sought legal action against New Line Cinema when it attempted to cut a same-sex kiss from *Torch Song Trilogy* in order to sell it to television, Otis Stuart argued that "the problem, if not the reason, is the bottom line of a big-bucks industry."[72] Fox justified the erasure of the highly anticipated and controversial 1994 *Melrose Place* season finale male kiss by claiming, "We're in a business. . . .We'd have lost up to a million dollars by airing that kiss."[73] In 2004, the *Star Tribune* implicitly conveyed a similar motive when it refused to run an ad for Gay Pride that featured two men kissing, despite activists' claims that the paper runs such images of opposite sex couples.[74]

Even queer-friendly commercial media, cognizant of the limits of "tolerance" and the fragile link between projected public image and revenue, carefully police the type of sex that sells. Katherine Sender argues that

> marketers (and others who seek "positive images" of lesbians and gays) are particularly invested in a desexualized image of gayness to compensate for the fact that both queer and commercial forms of sexuality occur outside the charmed circle. Since an openly homosexual identity already puts gay and lesbian people on the outer limits, conforming to the inner circle in other respects—practicing monogamous, coupled, noncommercial, at-home, private, same-generation, vanilla sex—may recoup some moral capital for them, potentially gaining them broader social acceptance, access to economic and other resources, and protection from harassment.[75]

Most often, same-sex kissing, however "normative" we might think it to be, is out of bounds. Miller Brewing, for instance, which has embraced the "gay market" with a variety of gay-themed ads running in both queer and mainstream commercial locations, demonstrated how narrowly such boundaries must be drawn. In its

2001 Miller Lite commercial "Switcheroo," depicting flirtatious women sending a beer to a handsome man only to discover him holding hands with his boyfriend, an alternative ending with a man-on-man kiss was considered out of the question. Senior brand manager Tim McDougall claimed that, "In all of our ads, we're trying to get attention. But we don't want to shock people. One of our main messages is to be inclusive. We tested [Switcheroo] with all our consumers and felt no need to treat it special, or to bury or hide it. . . .We've gotten very positive feedback from people who like that the ad is not making judgments about gay people." That success, McDougall made clear, is contingent upon certain proscriptions: "We thought the kiss ending overshadowed the message and became shocking and sensational. We wanted to show the men in as normal a light as possible."[76] Sender's analysis eliminates any presumption that such caution is exclusive to the straight community.[77]

Where the dollar fails to curtail queer kissing, omission or disavowal constrains, distorts, or destroys such representation. Jeffrey Epstein wrote of the film *Murder By Numbers,* "Far more fascinating is the relationship between [Michael] Pitt's and [Ryan] Gosling's characters, which in several instances is so homoerotic, someone sitting next to me murmured, 'Would they just kiss and get it over with.'"[78] But the kiss, however much anticipated, never came. In films daring enough to exhibit men kissing, extra-textual interviews often reveal the labor expended to assure the public that it was indeed "only an act." Reflecting on his kiss with James Van Der Beek in *The Rules of Attraction,* Ian Somerhalder pronounced in *OUT,*

> We knew that it [the kiss] was an opportunity to do something that was very different and fuck with people, frankly. . . . We totally talked about it before, and the first thing we said is no tongue— definitely no tongue. . . . I have this crazy newfound respect for women. I don't ever plan on kissing a guy again, because it's so fucking scratchy.[79]

Similarly, in a *Los Angeles Times* article focusing on his kiss with Jonathan Walker in *Far from Heaven,* Dennis Quaid claimed that it could be screened because viewers knew that he was a committed heterosexual in his off-screen life.

Although Quaid may not have meant to sound homophobic, he reasoned by analogy that his ability to kiss a man on film is "like Nixon going to China. He was so staunchly anti-Communist he could go. I feel the same way. I'm a confirmed heterosexual."[80]

Finally, harassment, boycotts, and violence have also worked, if not to annihilate altogether same-sex kissing or discourses surrounding it, then to relegate it "elsewhere," to render it invisible. In 1993, the *Seattle Times* reported that police had "harassed, searched and threatened with arrest" a gay couple who were kissing on a Capitol Hill Street. The October 1995 *Guitar* magazine cover photo depicting a kiss between Red Hot Chili Peppers Flea and Dave Navarro provoked multiple retailers to refuse to sell the issue. Dave Triller, owner of "The Only Guitar Shop," told reporters that the photo "turned my stomach. I'm offended by two men kissing each other."[81] He added that when his son asked if the photo would be appropriate if it depicted a kiss shared by a man and a woman, he responded, "Sure, that's normal."[82] In 2000, a Delta flight nearly staged an emergency landing because two men refused to cease their kissing in the back row of the plane.[83] An art teacher in Texas was fired in 2001 for defending a student work that depicted same-sex kissing.[84] In its worst form, prohibition is achieved through the material and symbolic effects of violence. Representation of gay bashing conveys just how little is required of queers to attract a clenched fist. HBO's *Six Feet Under,* for instance, concluded its first season with the personal, familial, and communal paralysis (and death) that results from the savage disciplining of a hated gay kiss at an urban ATM.[85]

As an extended illustration of the confluence of disciplinary impulses that are evoked by the queer kiss, we offer the *St. Louis Post-Dispatch's* "Point of View" from June 5, 2000. There, one observed a wedding photograph, much like any other in this visual genre except that it depicted gay men kissing at their reception (Figure 2).[86] Unlike other wedding photographs in the local paper, however, this innocuous nuptial embrace met with more than passing glances.

Over the next week, the *Post-Dispatch* received more than 100 letters and phone calls concerning the troublesome photograph, with a large majority critical of the paper's decision to publish it. The reactions to the photograph reveal three predominant ideological perspectives/disciplinary strategies. First, readers framed the "general public" as both moral and heterosexual, hence, articulating gays as at once immoral and excluded from the "public interest." Second, multiple readers argued that the picture should not have been published because the *Post-Dispatch* is accessible by children, once again constituting same-sex kissing as not only "adult material," but also sexually persuasive. Third, the publication of a same-sex photo is repeatedly read as part of a political agenda, as opposed to the assumption that heterosexually framed photographs are natural rather than political.

A number of readers argued that the *Post-Dispatch* was working outside of "public interest" by publishing the photograph. M. Eliza Harris wrote, "I'm terribly saddened that this would be of public interest. . . . God is coming soon. I want to cry over this photograph and the idea of same-sex marriages and homosexuality."[87] Gene Carton averred, "To show a photograph of two gay men kissing at their wedding reception exceeds the bounds of decency,"[88] and Frank Baxendale argued, "It is bad enough that the *Post-Dispatch* continues to promote such aberrant lifestyles, but two men kissing, 'wedding' or not, is disgusting."[89] Using dramatic imagery, Anthony Galuska concluded that "America and its morals are going to hell in a handbasket, and you are helping weave the basket. How dare you publish a picture like this. . . . God does not condone this kind of atrocity."[90] Such comments not only align the "public interest" with heterosexuality (one could argue that such an articulation is the very definition of heteronormativity) but also articulate "public morality" with heterosexuality, leaving homosexuals, or, at the very least, homosexual acts, by definition outside of the public interest.

The editorial framing of this "wedding kiss" as an almost pornographic image, one from which children should be shielded, emerges repeatedly in letters that expressed fears that children can be, and have been, morally corrupted by this and similar representations. More than half of the nearly twenty letters published

Figure 2 Tim Molloy, 29 (left), and Brian Duck, 27, celebrate their wedding reception after a ceremony at a local church.

SOURCE: Photo by Laurie Skrivan, used with permission of the *St. Louis Post-Dispatch*.

by the *Post-Dispatch* voiced concern for "children." Bob Hawkins wrote, "Thank God, my children are too young to look at the paper," while another reader similarly asked, "What about the example we are setting for the children?"[91] Others expressed the same concern in a variety of ways: "It's no wonder today's kids . . . don't know what is right and what is wrong";[92] "for the sake of our children, don't make it appear that homosexuality is just another day at the office."[93] Again, the panic discourse here strategically articulated the same-sex kiss as a siren call of immorality. It is not simply fear that children might see an offensive image; rather, there is a terror that such an image will beckon and corrupt the innocents.

Finally, although within the logic of "common sense" press photographs of heterosexual weddings are accepted and expected, inclusion of this photograph depicting two men kissing is not only marked as immoral but always already read as a political agenda on the part of the publisher, and a dangerous one at that. Carton argued that *Post-Dispatch* editors published the gay wedding kiss as a means of extending their "liberal politics," and Baxendale asked, "Could not a less offensive picture have been chosen for your never-ending gay agenda?"[94] A caller to the paper protested, "I feel you are trying to force the public to accept this type of lifestyle."[95] In each of these comments, the man-on-man kiss is "marked" as political precisely because it transgresses "common sense": if such a photo is published, there must be a politics underwriting the marking of this aberrant wedding celebration.

In short, not only do *Post-Dispatch* readers understand or interpret the photograph as immoral, but they read homosexuality—or rather, they read a picture of two men kissing—as sexual temptation. We emphasize readers' reactions to this photograph as a note of critical caution. Although we may read public images as texts with potential to rework articulations of sexuality, same-sex kissing, and the performance of heteronormativity, we also must remain aware that the materiality of discourse operates as a powerful disciplinary constraint on such transformations.

In each of these cases, we witness multiple ways in which ideological, economic, and physical forces function "automatically" and politically to discipline same-sex kissing, to make it absent when possible, and to punish those who make it visible. From altered scripts to financially ruined films, from harassed or beaten couples to censored images, disciplinary procedures work. Moreover, they work not only on those who offend but also on those who might think about such behavior in the future. Although examples of transgressive images of man-on-man kissing are available, we must pause from simple celebratory readings to remember that kisses "matter" differently—and evoke different responses—depending on what lips these lips have publicly kissed.

SEALED WITH A KISS

As with literary and cultural criticism, our field has witnessed recent discussion of "body rhetorics" through explorations of the embodied dimensions of persuasion—by means of sharper focus on the materiality of body, how it forms and influences discourse, or an enhanced perspective on the ways in which (gendered, raced) bodies are understood rhetorically through meanings circulating in culture.[96] Given our investigation of public kissing between men, we find particularly relevant Gerard Hauser's work on the "body in pain."[97] Through such examples as Bobby Sand's starvation protest and women's narratives of sexual violence, Hauser asks us to consider how the pained body functions rhetorically: "What of the power of a body in pain to form deep and powerful identification among an audience that feels empathy for the sufferer's anguish? In addition to the utterly private and unshared physical experience of the body's own pain, there also are rhetorical and political dimensions to pain."[98] Indeed, not only does the body in pain influence the ways in which the pained subject understands her world and communicates to others, but the visible body in pain also functions rhetorically for others. Moreover, Hauser demonstrates, such rhetoric is shaped by our reading of the purposes of the pain, the gender and race of the body in pain, and the culture in which it is consumed.

In this analysis, however, our question concerns pain's rhetorical reversal in the "body in pleasure." We are not focusing specifically on the experience of pleasure (i.e., we extend beyond *plaisir* or *jouissance* as experienced) but rather on the ways in which a particular pleasurable bodily experience functions rhetorically when made public. "The queer body," Berlant and Freeman observe, "as an agent of publicity,

as a unit of self-defense, and finally as a spectacle of ecstasy—becomes the locus where mainstream culture's discipline of gay citizens is written and where the pain caused by this discipline is transformed into rage and pleasure."[99] Hence, in examining rhetorically those kisses shared and enjoyed by men, we offer an entry into a rhetoric of the body in pleasure. Although those visions of bodily pleasure operate for some viewers as affirmations of identity, for others, those same bodies—precisely because they are publicly in a state of pleasure—function as a bodily challenge to a culture of heteronormativity that dominates best when expressions of intimacy between men remain hidden and private, or are domesticated and disavowed in public.

The disruptive performances we have studied in this essay—these bodies in pleasure—constitute, therefore, what Berlant and Warner call "counterintimacy," the transmission of "the critical practical knowledge that allows such relations to count as intimate, to be not empty release or transgression but a common language of self-cultivation, shared knowledge, and the exchange of inwardness."[100] Inverting heteronormative intimacy in this manner enacts "parasitic and fugitive elaboration" such that exposing and resisting the "material and ideological conditions that divide intimacy from history, politics and publics" contributes to "queer world making." If the desire is not only to have queers on television but to affirm a wide variety of intimacies, then critics must continue to politicize dominant images and push for a visual critical mass of queer intimacy.

In the long view, we see this project as affirming Berlant and Warner's call for a queer criticism that does not simply "destigmatize those average intimacies, not just to give access to the sentimentality of the couple for persons of the same sex, and definitely not to certify as properly private the personal lives of gays and lesbians," but rather to "support forms of affective, erotic, and personal living that are public in the sense of accessible, available to memory, and sustained through collective activity."[101] In pursuing counterintimacy and queer world making, the critic must not only highlight the rhetorical strategies involved in representing the man-on-man public kiss as a body in pleasure but also expose the disciplinary mechanisms that strive to erase these images. To draw upon Foucault, we must see the critical readings of queer kissing as not simply explanatory but activist: "Knowledge is not made for understanding; it is made for cutting."[102]

NOTES

1. Edna St. Vincent Millay, "What Lips My Lips Have Kissed," *The Harp-Weaver and Other Poems* (New York: Harper & Brothers, 1923), 71; Anonymous, *Weekly Visitor or Ladies Miscellany,* April 1803, 203, http://www.bartleby.com/66/98/3598.html (accessed 9 June 2003).

2. Bruce LaBruce, "Dudes' Smooch Leads the Way," *Eye Weekly* [Toronto], 21 February 2001, www.eye.net/eye/issue_02.01.01/columns/feelings.html (accessed 15 July 2004). For an alternative reading of LaBruce's review, see Judith Halberstam, "Dude, Where's My Gender? or, Is There Life on Uranus?" *GLQ* 10.2 (2004): 308–12.

3. Robert Knight, "Iraq Scandal is 'Perfect Storm' of American Culture," *WorldNetDaily,* 12 May 2004, reprinted by Concerned Women for America, http://www.cwfa.org/articles/5663/CWA/misc/index.htm (accessed 15 July 2004).

4. For our purposes here, we understand "public culture" via those mass-mediated texts with the largest audiences; as such, texts—television, newspapers, film—must necessarily reflect the "common sense" understandings of large audiences. See Kent A. Ono and John M. Sloop, *Shifting Borders: Rhetoric, Immigration, and California's Proposition 187* (Philadelphia: Temple University Press, 2002), 1–25.

5. We recognize that the meaning of a public kiss is far more complex than hetero or homosexual. Change the age, race, physical attractiveness, type of kissing, or number of people involved, and of course the meaning of the kiss changes. Regardless of the combinations of people involved in "public kissing," however, it functions as a nodal point that illustrates the parameters of heteronormativity.

6. Frank Rich, "Gay Kiss: Business as Usual," *New York Times,* 22 June 2003, Section 2, p. 1.

7. Otis Stuart, "No Tongues, Please—We're Queer: The Same-Sex Kiss on the New York Stage," *The Village Voice* 2 February 1993, 90.

8. Butler's theses have become sufficiently widespread and familiar to most readers that we offer only a brief rehearsal here. For Butler, to say that

gender is "performative" is to suggest that—regardless of the physicality of gender—it is understood, or has meaning, through discourse or culturally accepted practices, including appearance, manners of speaking, occupational roles, choices of sexual partners, and so forth. Judith Butler, *Gender Trouble: Feminism and the Subversion of Identity,* 10th Anniversary Edition (New York: Routledge, 1999), 139. Moreover, given how heavily policed gender norms are in popular culture, Butler observes, bigender heterosexual behaviors become materialized, naturalized, as if they were essential rather than contingent. Performativity, then, cannot be understood outside of a process of iterability, a regularized and constrained repetition of norms: "This iterability implies that 'performance' is not a singular 'act' or event, but a ritualized production, a ritual reiterated under and through constraint, under and through the force of prohibition and taboo, with the threat of ostracism and even death controlling and compelling the shape of production." Judith Butler, *Bodies That Matter: On the Discursive Limits of Sex* (New York: Routledge, 1993), 95.

9. Butler, *Gender Trouble,* 139. Two points seem important here: first, to clarify that what we, and Butler, are discussing is the appearance of heterosexuality, not its essence. It does not matter if an "actual" male and female are kissing, as long as the kissing bodies appear to be a male and female. Second, we acknowledge that there are numerous male-female kisses that exist outside of normative expectations, that even within heteronormative culture there are marked and unmarked behaviors.

10. Butler, *Bodies That Matter,* 95.

11. Lauren Berlant and Michael Warner, "Sex in Public," in *Intimacy,* ed. Laurent Berlant (Chicago: University of Chicago Press, 2000), 318.

12. In searching for articles over the last decade on LexisNexis and other databases, we not only found hundreds of articles focusing on different types of public kisses, but encountered numerous discussions of the history of kissing worldwide [e.g., Frank Whelan, "Historically Speaking, A Kiss in Not Just a Kiss," *Los Angeles Times* 12 February 1989, 24, and "Did You Know?," *Sunday Telegraph* 27 April 1997, Local 3], expectations about future alterations in the meaning of kisses [Peter Johnson, "When a Man Greets a Man with a Kiss," *USA Today* 18 July 1989, 1D], the absence of public kissing in China [Anthony Blass, "Culture: Goodbye to Prudery," *Far Eastern Economic Review* 6 May 1993, 34], and Japan [Tim Easton, "A Scandalous Trend," *The Gazette* 2 October 1994, B5, T.R. Reid,

"The Puckering Stops Here," *Washington Post* 8 November 1994, Al, "Modest Japanese Begin Kissing Off Public Prudery," *Toronto Star* 23 December 1994, B7, Miki Tanikawa, "Japanese Young Couples Discover the Kiss," *New York Times* 28 May 1995, 139, Cameron W. Barr, "Japan Teens Pucker Up in Public Bowing's Out," *Christian Science Monitor* 17 February 1998, 1], the difference between public kissing in the U.S. and in the U.K. [Candida Crewe, "Kissing in Public," *The Times* 21 February 1998, Vicky Allan, "No Public Sex Please, We're British," *Scotland on Sunday* 9 April 2000, 19] or Mexico ["Kissing is a Very Public Sign of the Times in Mexico City," *St. Louis Post-Dispatch* 12 April 1998, D5]. For an historical overview of the meanings of kissing, see Adrianne Blue, *On Kissing: From the Metaphysical to the Erotic* (London: Victor Gollancz, 1996).

13. Nicholas Fonseca, "They're Here! They're Queer! And They Don't Like Your End Tables!" *Entertainment Weekly* 8 August 2003, 26.

14. Carina Chocano, "Sharper Image: Bravo's Queer Eye Gives the Makeover-Show Genre an Edge," *Entertainment Weekly* 8 August 2003, 62.

15. As Gross chronicles, there were unprecedented media representations of gays and lesbians during the 1990s, but displays of same-sex kissing were noteworthy in their absence, the camera angles that displaced and diminished them, and the contorted rationalizations offered by the executives forced to account for them. Larry Gross, *Up From Invisibility: Lesbians, Gay Men, and the Media in America* (New York: Columbia University Press, 2001), 85–93. See also Suzanna Danuta Walters, *All the Rage: The Story of Gay Visibility in America* (Chicago: University of Chicago Press, 2001); Steven Capsuto, *Alternate Channels: The Uncensored Story of Gay and Lesbian Images on Radio and Television* (New York: Ballantine, 2000).

16. Stuart, "No Tongues, Please—We're Queer," 90.

17. Frank Bruni, "Culture Stays Screen-Shy of Showing the Gay Kiss," *Detroit Free Press* 11 February 1994, reprinted in *The Columbia Reader on Lesbians & Gay Men in Media, Society, and Politics,* ed. Larry Gross & James D. Woods (New York: Columbia University Press, 1999), 327; Lynn Smith, "More than Just a Kiss," *Los Angeles Times* 10 November 2002, E1; Gary Morris, "When is a Kiss Not a Kiss?," *Bright Lights Film Journal,* http://www.brightlightsfilm.com/20/20_queerkiss.html (accessed 11 June 2003); Gary Morris, "Billy's Hollywood Screen Kiss," *Bright Lights Film Journal* http://www.brightlightsfilm.com/22/billyskiss.html (accessed 11 June 2003).

18. "Fox . . . Censorship is Un-American," GLAAD, 10 May 1994, http://www.glaad.org/publications/archive_detail.php?id=267& (accessed 9 June 2003); "Another Censored Kiss," GLAAD, 16 May 1994, http://www.glaad.org/publications/archive_detail.php?id=265& (accessed 9 June 2003).

19. "Man is Dismissed Over a Game's Gay Images," *New York Times,* 8 December 1996, Sec. 1, 46. The game manufacturer who fired the programmer claimed to have done so due to the "insertion of unauthorized material" in the game rather than because of the content of that material. However, such "unauthorized content," or Easter Eggs, are routinely inserted by programmers and expected by manufacturers.

20. Robert Bianco, "USA's Gay 'Tastes' Run to Rape, But Not Kissing," *Pittsburgh Post-Gazette* 20 January 1997, D6.

21. "The Kiss that Rocked the World", 10 October 1997, http://www.glaad.org/action/al_archive_ detail.php?id=1977(accessed 9 June 2003).

22. "Sandler's Big Daddy is Gay-Friendly," *GLAAD,* 17 June 1999, http://glaad.org/action/al_archive_detail.php?id=1535 (accessed 9 June 2003).

23. Paul Brownfield, "When a Kiss is Just a Kiss," *Los Angeles Times* 22 February 2000, F1.

24. Stephen Tropiano, "More Than Just a Kiss," *AlterNet.Org,* 3 June 2003, http://www.alternet.org/story.html?StoryID=16075 (accessed 9 June 2003); Rich, "Gay Kiss."

25. Mike Wilke, "Commercial Closet: Gay Ads Promote MTV," 9 November 1999, http://www.gfn.com/archives/story.phtml?sid=3621 (accessed 16 July 2003); "Language of Love," *Commercial Closet* (2000), http://www.commercialcloset.org/cgi-bin/iowa/portrayals.html?record=474 (accessed 6 June 2003); Richard Tate, "MTV Takes a Stand," *Advocate* 9 October 2001, p. 16; Rodger Streitmatter, "Real World Depicts the Real Gay World," *Gay Today* (2002), http://gaytoday.com/garchive/entertain/052002en.htm (accessed 9 June 2003); Tropiano, "More Than Just a Kiss"; Lynn Elber, "Solid Crossover Appeal Bolsters 'Queer As Folk,'" *The Los Angeles Times,* 4 January 2002, F38; "Christina Aguilera to be Honored at 14th Annual GLAAD Media Awards," *GLAAD,* 28 February 2003, http://www.glaad.org/media/release_detail.php?id=3283 (accessed 9 June 2003); Steve Freiss, "Cirque du So Gay," *Advocate,* 11 November 2003, 49.

26. Rich, "Gay Kiss: Business as Usual," 2.

27. Steven Seidman, *Beyond the Closet: The Transformation of Gay and Lesbian Life* (New York: Routledge, 2002), 17.

28. Richard Goldstein, "Get Back! The Gathering Storm Over Gay Rights," *The Village Voice* 6–12 August 2003, http://www.villagevoice.com/issues/0332/Goldstein.php (accessed 15 July 2004).

29. Walters, *All the Rage,* 15.

30. Jeffrey Epstein, "Gay Themes in Television," *The Hollywood Reporter* 26 March 2004, http://www.hollywoodreporter.com/thr/television/feature_display.jsp?vnu_content_id=1000473838 (accessed 15 July 2004).

31. Patrick Pacheco, "The Sound of Two Men Kissing Outlandish," *Los Angeles Times* 30 July 1995, 24.

32. For an argument concerning the benefits of remaining "unmarked," see Peggy Phelan, *Unmarked* (New York: Routledge, 1993).

33. Walters, *All the Rage,* 24.

34. John Fiske and John Hartley, *Reading Television* (New York: Methuen, 1978); Celeste Michelle Condit, "The Rhetorical Limits of Polysemy," *Critical Studies in Mass Communication* 6 (1989): 112.

35. Helene A. Shugart, "Reinventing Privilege: The New (Gay) Man in Contemporary Popular Media," *Critical Studies in Media Communication* 20 (March 2003): 67–91. For further discussion of heteronormative dilution, displacement, and distortion of queer mediated representation, see Kathleen Battles and Wendy Hilton-Morrow, "Gay Characters in Conventional Spaces: Will and Grace and the Situation Comedy Genre," *Critical Studies in Media Communication* 19 (2002): 87–105; Robert Alan Brookey and Robert Westerfelhaus, "Pistols and Petticoats, Piety and Purity: To Wong Foo, the Queering of the American Monomyth, and the Marginalizing Discourse of Deification," *Critical Studies in Media Communication* 18 (2001): 141–56; Bonnie J. Dow, "*Ellen,* Television, and the Politics of Gay and Lesbian Visibility," *Critical Studies in Media Communication* 18 (2001): 123–40; John M. Sloop, *Disciplining Gender: Rhetorics of Sex Identity in Contemporary U.S. Culture* (Amherst: University of Massachusetts Press, 2004).

36. Hemal Jhaveri, "Searching for a Real Gay Man," *PopPolitics* 22 October 2003, http://www.poppolitics.com/articles/2003-10-22-gaytv.html (accessed 15 July 2004).

37. Eric O. Clarke, *Virtuous Vice; Homoeroticism and the Public Sphere* (Durham: Duke University Press, 2000), 29. Michael Wilke, executive director of Commercial Closet Association, similarly observes, "I call it the 'Coors Effect.' On top of everything, you have to consider the political concerns of the gay community, which historically has not only been ignored but a maligned group." See Shelly Leachman, "Show Us the Love: Cable Company Ad's Same-Sex Smooch Reflects a Trend Among Businesses Chasing the Pink Buck," *Frontiers Newsmagazine* 19 July 2004, http://www.frontiersnewsmagazine.com/page.cfm?typeofsite=article&section=4&id=1149&sectionid=4 (accessed 30 July 2004).

38. Clarke, *Virtuous Vice,* 31.

39. Clarke, *Virtuous Vice,* 49.

40. Clarke, *Virtuous Vice,* 59.

41. A. William Merrell, vice-president on the executive committee of the Southern Baptist Convention, quoted in Bernard Weinraub and Jim Rutenberg, "Gay-Themed TV Gains a Wider Audience," *New York Times* 29 July 2003, A1.

42. Clarke, *Virtuous Vice,* 59.

43. Rosen, "The Kiss That Isn't Just a Kiss," 28.

44. Terry McDermott, "All Smiles After the Kiss Commotion," *The Los Angeles Times* 24 August 2000, B1; Monte Whaley, "Protesters Lock Lips at Boulder Kiss-In," *The Denver Post* 24 May A1.

45. We emphasize that any imprimatur currently bestowed upon a kiss between women constitutes a patriarchal, sexist gesture that has nothing to do with the pleasure and desire they might experience. Such "tolerance" is, in this manifestation, perfectly compatible with homophobia and should not be misperceived as a sign of the deterioration of heteronormativity or embrace of queerness. Controversy surrounding an Atlanta radio station's recent billboard advertisement depicting this kiss offers good evidence of our claim. See Sean Westmoreland, "From the Hub to Hollywood; Britney—Madonna Kiss Rocks VMA," *The Boston Herald* 29 April 2003, 15; Jeanette Walls, "Atlanta Just Says No to 'The Kiss,'" *MSNBC.Com* 20 October 2003, http://www.msnbc.com/news/970601.asp?0cv=CB20 (accessed 15 July 2004).

46. Lynn Smith, "More Than Just a Kiss," *The Los Angeles Times* 10 November 2002, E1.

47. For those unfamiliar with the term *kairos,* which refers to rhetorical—i.e., situationally contingent as well as strategically opportune and urgent—time and timing, see Phillip Sipiora and James S. Baumlin, ed., *Rhetoric and Kairos: Essays*

in History, Theory, and Praxis (Albany: SUNY Press, 2002).

48. Here, we extrapolate from arguments of Berlant and Warner. They suggest the importance of having geographic spaces—neighborhoods—with such a visible queer presence that a "critical mass" develops, hence giving the neighborhood a viable force as an economic and voting bloc. We are arguing that a "representational critical mass" of mediated scenes of man-on-man kissing would help provide similar argumentative force. Berlant and Warner, "Sex in Public," 326. For earlier discussion of this issue, see Scott Tucker, "Our Right to the World: Beyond the Right to Privacy," *Body Politic* (July/August 1982) in *The Columbia Reader on Lesbians & Gay Men in Media, Society, & Politics,* ed. Larry Gross & James D. Woods (New York: Columbia University Press, 1999), 575–83.

49. Alfred P. Kielwasser and Michelle A. Wolf, "Mainstream Television, Adolescent Homosexuality, and Significant Silence," *Critical Studies in Mass Communication* 9 (1992): 350–73.

50. Pat Califia, *Public Sex: The Culture of Radical Sex,* 2nd ed. (San Francisco: Cleis Press, 2000), 224.

51. William L. Leap, ed., *Public Sex/Gay Space* (New York: Columbia University Press, 1999).

52. Ira Tattelman, "Speaking to the Gay Bathhouse: Communicating in Sexually Charged Spaces," in *Public Sex/Gay Space,* ed. William L. Leap (New York: Columbia University Press, 1999), 73.

53. Califia, *Public Sex,* 7.

54. Richard Meyer, "This Is to Enrage You: Gran Fury and the Graphics of AIDS Activism," *But is it Art? The Spirit of Art as Activism,* ed. Nina Felshin (Seattle: Bay Press, 1995): 51–83. For other discussions of "Kissing Doesn't Kill," see Paul Nonnekes, "Kiss-In at the Heterosexual Bar as Dialectical Image," *Dianoia* (Spring 1992), 76–78; Kevin Michael Deluca, "Unruly Arguments: The Body Rhetoric of Earth First!, ACT UP, and Queer Nation," *Argumentation and Advocacy* (1999): 9–21.

55. Bruni, "Culture Stays Screen-Shy," 328.

56. Meyer, "This Is to Enrage You," 66–69; Douglas Crimp and Adam Rolston, *AIDS Demo Graphics* (Seattle: Bay Press, 1990), 53–69.

57. Meyer, "This Is to Enrage You," 68.

58. Crimp and Rolston, AIDS *Demo Graphics,* 55. Insofar as we focus broadly on representation of queer kissing, the distinction between the image "Read My Lips" and a local, performative spectacle of the kiss-in is negligible here. However, we would argue for the necessity of discursive and visual, ideographic and performative, national and local, circulation of the queer kiss.

59. DeLuca, "Unruly Arguments," 18.

60. Lauren Berlant and Elizabeth Freeman, "Queer Nationality," in *Fear of a Queer Planet: Queer Politics and Social Theory,* ed. Michael Warner (Minneapolis, University of Minnesota Press, 1993), 195.

61. Berlant and Freeman, "Queer Nationality," 195.

62. Berlant and Warner, "Sex in Public," 326.

63. Weinraub and Rutenberg, "Gay-Themed TV," A1; Dennis Hensley, "Messiah Complex," *The Advocate* 16 September 2003, 50. *Queer as Folk* in Britain offers a worthy model of the queer worldmaking project we describe. See Precious Williams, "MUM, I'VE SOMETHING TO TELL YOU . . . " *The Independent* 23 January 2000, 4; Libby Brooks, "Without Prejudice," *The Guardian* 12 December 2003, 2. Whatever its shortcomings, the American version also fuses the cultural and political in largely unadulterated representation of non-normative sexuality. A key difference, of course, is that unlike with the British version, one must afford Showtime to encounter its man-on-man kissing. We also consider MTV noteworthy in this regard, invaluable in constituting queerness for a generation with its unflinching depictions of sexuality generally and kissing specifically. At the same time, we see it as reaching a limited audience, necessary but insufficient to achieve queer world making in its fullest sense.

64. Phillip Brian Harper, *Private Affairs: Critical Ventures in the Culture of Social Relations* (New York: New York University Press, 1999), 22.

65. Goran Therborn, *What Does the Ruling Class Do When It Rules?* (London: Verso, 1978), 174. We could of course discuss cultural discipline from a variety of perspectives. Utilizing the works of Michel Foucault or Judith Butler, for example, would have helped us provide a similar reading.

66. "Debate Over Gay Pride Event, Irvine Ordinance," *Los Angeles Times* 28 May 1989, A11.

67. "Debate" A11.

68. Lou Gelfand, "For Some, Story on TV Kissing Crossed the Line," *Star Tribune* 16 February 2003, 5A.

69. David Olson, "Read Their Lips," *The Village Voice* 24 July 1990, 14.

70. We want to highlight that amfAR wanted the text removed because, as worded, it would hurt

their corporate sponsorship. Hence, this very request was a form of "financial discipline." The text read: "Corporate Greed, Government Inaction, and Public Indifference Make AIDS a Political Crisis." Meyer, "This Is to Enrage You," 52–53.

71. Meyer, "This Is to Enrage You," 57.

72. Stuart, "No Tongues, Please," 90.

73. Gross, *Up From Visibility,* 91. Economic pressures have long worked against representations of same-sex kisses on television. CBS did not show a gay couple kissing at their wedding ceremony on *Northern Exposure* due to such pressures. HBO cut a kissing scene between Ian McKellan and B. D. Wong in *And the Band Played On.* McKellan was told by an executive that "he personally had no problem with the kiss, but it was his responsibility to see to it that viewers . . . not be grossed out." Craig Zadan has noted that "But today, you can't make a drama on ABC, NBC (or) CBS with a story about a gay character in a TV movie—they won't buy them." "Northern Exposure to Air a Wedding Without a Kiss," GLAAD, 29 April 1994, http://www.glaad.org/media/archive_detail.php?id=269& (accessed 9 June 2003). Gross, *Up From Visibility,* 192; Epstein, "Gay Themes in Television."

74. "Newspaper Refuses to Run Ad of Two Men Kissing," *The Advocate* 29 June 2004, http://www.advocate.com/new_news.asp?id=12930&sd=06/29/04 (accessed 15 July 2004).

75. Katherine Sender, "Sex Sells: Sex, Class, and Taste in Commercial Gay and Lesbian Media" *GLQ* 9.3 (2003): 355. Sender's notion of the "charmed circle" of sex is derived from Rubin: "According to this system, sexuality as 'good,' 'normal,' and 'natural' should ideally be heterosexual, marital, monogamous, reproductive, and non-commercial. It should be coupled, relational, within the same generation, and occur at home. It should not involve pornography, fetish objects, sex toys of any sort, or roles other than male or female. Any sex that violates these rules is 'bad,' 'abnormal,' or 'unnatural.'" Gayle Rubin, "Thinking Sex: Notes for a Radical Theory of the Politics of Sexuality," in *The Lesbian and Gay Studies Reader,* ed. Henry Abelove, Michèle Aina Barale, and David M. Halperin (New York: Routledge, 1993), 13–14.

76. Wilke and Applebaum, "Peering Out of the Closet."

77. Sender concludes, "The dominant voices of gay and lesbian media argue that the fundamental goals of the gay rights movement should be fought within Rubin's charmed circle. . . . Gay men and lesbians stepping outside that circle into the realm of dangerous, commercial, sleazy sexuality—whether in magazines, in stores, in theaters, or on the streets— are on their own, since the legitimate goals and principles of gay communities lie elsewhere." Sender, "Sex Sells," 359.

78. Jeffrey Epstein, "Review of Murder By Numbers," *Out,* http://www.out.com/filmreviews2.asp?ID=1192 (accessed 15 July 2004).

79. Peter Gehrke, "Physical Attraction," *OUT,* September 2002, 83.

80. Lynn Smith, "More Than Just a Kiss," E1.

81. Steve Hochman, "Peppers' Peck Stirs Bushels of Controversy," *Los Angeles Times* 7 September 1995, A1.

82. Hochman, "Peppers' Peck," A1.

83. Will O'Bryan, "The Plane Truth: Airlines Take Note of a Community," *The Washington Blade* 31 (2000): 59–60.

84. Barbara Dozetos, "Teacher Sues Over Censorship of Gay Image," *PlanetOut.Com* 10 July 2001, http://www.planetout.com/news/article.html?2001/07/10/3 (accessed 16 September 2003).

85. As in each episode during the first season, an opening death scene shapes a theme or plot line. Some are absurd, this one wrenching: twenty-something boyfriends stand at a Los Angeles ATM at night, playfully bantering; one boy clasps his arms around Marcus Foster's waist, sweetly kissing his neck. Loud music announces the arrival of car, out of which two similarly aged men leap and aggressively approach the couple. One of the men yells, "What the fuck is that shit?" The other screams, "Do you think you can do that kind of offensive shit like that in public?" Fearful apologies ensue, as does an attempt by the gay couple to escape the beating that has begun. Marcus Foster stumbles, falls, and is beaten to death in an empty lot. Throughout this and the following episode, Foster's violent death haunts (bodily, in some scenes) his parents and especially protagonist David, for whom the very legitimacy of his sexuality is shaken to its core. "A Private Life" (Episode 12, 2001), *Six Feet Under,* http://www.hbo.com/sixfeetunder/episode/season1/sea1_eps12.shtml (accessed 15 July 2004).

86. The caption under the photograph explained the context.

87. M. Eliza Harris, "Letter to the Editor," *St. Louis Post-Dispatch* 7 June 2000, B6.

88. Gene Carton, "Letter to the Editor," *St. Louis Post-Dispatch* 7 June 2000, B6.

89. Frank Baxendale, "Letter to the Editor," *St. Louis Post-Dispatch* 7 June 2000, B6.

90. Anthony Galuska, "Letter to the Editor," *St. Louis Post-Dispatch* 10 June 2000, B5.

91. Bob Hawkins, "Letter to the Editor," *St. Louis Post-Dispatch* 7 June 2000, B6.

92. Galuska, "Letter to the Editor," B5.

93. Thomas V. Wright, "Letter to the Editor," *St. Louis Post-Dispatch* 7 June 2000, B5.

94. Hawkins, "Letter to the Editor," B6.

95. Cited in Carolyn Kingcade, "The Complete Picture Sometimes Can Be More Than Readers Want," *St. Louis Post-Dispatch,* 11 June 2000, B4.

96. See, for example, Carole Blair, "Reflections on Criticism and Bodies: Parables from Public Places," *Western Journal of Communication* 65 (2001): 271–94; Gerard A. Hauser, "Body Rhetoric: Conflicted Reporting of Bodies in Pain," in *Deliberation, Democracy, and the Media,* ed. Simone Chambers and Anne Costain (New York: Rowman & Littlefield, 2000), 135–153; Raymie E. McKerrow, "Corporeality and Cultural Rhetoric: A Site for Rhetoric's Future," *Southern Communication Journal* 63 (1998): 315–29; Jack Selzer and Sharon Crowley, ed., *Rhetorical Bodies* (Madison: University of Wisconsin Press, 1999).

97. Hauser, "Body Rhetoric," 135.

98. Hauser, "Body Rhetoric," 135.

99. Berlant and Freeman, "Queer Nationality," 205.

100. Berlant and Warner, "Sex in Public," 325.

101. Berlant and Warner, "Sex in Public," 326.

102. Michel Foucault, "Nietzsche, Genealogy, History," in *The Foucault Reader,* ed. Paul Rabinow (New York: Pantheon, 1984), 88.

SECTION II

REMEMBERING AND MEMORIALIZING

Throughout U.S. history, Americans repeatedly have asked themselves, "What does it mean to be an American?" Answering this question often entails taking stock of the past. Historians argue that the United States is a "memory culture," meaning that we define ourselves in the present by how we understand our relationship to the past. As Michael Kammen (1993) observes, "For much of our history we have been present-minded; yet a usable past has been needed to give shape and substance to national identity" (p. 6). The creation of a "usable past," or what John Bodnar (1992) calls "a past worthy of public commemoration in the present" (p. 13), is always grounded in acts of communication. Rhetorical scholars have long recognized the important roles that remembering and memorializing play in political culture. Much work in visual rhetoric focuses explicitly on how art, visuality, and material culture participate in our conversations about the past. Each of the essays in this section recognizes that visual culture functions as an important site for remembering and memorializing.

By using the terms *remembering* and *memorializing,* we mean to focus attention on those public practices by which history is turned into memory. Though individuals can and do engage in remembering and memorializing in their private lives, here we emphasize remembering and memorializing as collective,

Figure 1   Washington, D.C., Inside the Lincoln Memorial. Photograph by Esther Bubley, 1943.

SOURCE: Farm Security Administration—Office of War Information Photograph Collection, Library of Congress.

cultural, and public processes. The term *public memory* is sometimes used to frame the rhetorical

99

actions of remembering and memorializing. Stephen H. Browne (1995) defines public memory as our "shared sense of the past, fashioned from the symbolic resources of community and subject to its particular history, hierarchies, and aspirations" (p. 243). For the scholars whose work is featured in this section, public memory is what is produced when members of a culture mobilize resources of symbolic action in the service of political and social aims. While remembering and memorializing are inevitably intertwined rhetorical actions, we may distinguish between them by noting that their relation is akin to that of genus to species. While rhetorics of remembering focus on the broader processes by which rhetors use symbolic resources in their attempts to make sense of the public past, rhetorics of memorializing describe the material products of the desire to remember and commemorate people, places, or events, such as memorials, museums, and the like.

When we remember or memorialize, we are embedded in an ongoing and ever-shifting dialogue about a number of important questions of interest to the student of visual rhetoric: What people, places, or events are deemed worthy of remembering or memorializing? What is ignored or deemed unworthy? What narratives about the past get told through our practices of remembering and memorializing? What narratives are left out? Whose voices or images are present or missing? Through what kinds of visual appeals do remembering and memorializing do their rhetorical work? Who has the power to authorize remembering and memorializing? How are viewers or spectators invited to participate in specific rhetorical acts of remembering or memorializing? What happens when a culture forgets what it should remember? How does visual rhetoric sometimes use memory to distort history? Questions such as these reveal that the stakes for remembering and memorializing are high and remind us that these rhetorical actions lie at the core of our public understandings of self and other.

Remembering and memorializing are material practices. That is, we remember and memorialize in and through the artifacts, images, and objects that we create, circulate, appropriate, or use. As the essays in this section illustrate, the rhetorical actions of remembering and memorializing may be located across a wide variety of visual artifacts, including memorials, editorial

cartoons, photographs, feature film, and television documentary. Despite the variety of the artifacts they examine and the diversity of methodological perspectives that the authors employ, however, the essays share a number of commitments. Collectively, they explore how visual rhetoric encourages viewers to read the present through the past. They illustrate the utility to rhetorical critics of concepts such as form, genre, icon, and ideograph. They attend to the ways that photographic, televisual, and cinematic techniques shape acts of remembering and memorializing. And they account for the multiple ways that images circulate in public and are appropriated for different purposes.

The first essay in this section explores the ways that visual rhetoric shapes audience expectations and public memories of historical events. In "The Rhetoric of the Frame: Revisioning Archival Photographs in *The Civil War*," Judith Lancioni argues that the popular television documentary *The Civil War* reframes historical photographs in ways that encourage the viewer to interpret the events of the Civil War through the lens of the present. Documentary practice is paradoxical, because while documentaries rely on the fiction that "seeing is believing," documentary filmmakers also employ rhetorical strategies in order to persuade their viewers to adopt a particular point of view. Lancioni describes two specific techniques employed in *The Civil War* to guide viewers' interpretations: *mobile framing* and *reframing*. These techniques allow filmmakers to concentrate viewers' attention on only one aspect of an image (for example, a slave in the background of a picture) or to put parts of an image in juxtaposition with other parts. Taken together, Lancioni argues, these techniques make available to audiences a revised public memory of the Civil War because they force viewers to focus on things typically left out of traditional histories, such as the African American experience.

Observing that the meaning of a visual artifact emerges in the interaction between an artifact and its audience, Lancioni shows how mobile framing and reframing encourage certain viewer responses to the film while discouraging others. The essay also introduces us to scholarly discussions about genre in that it considers how *The Civil War* relies on audience knowledge of the norms of documentary when it uses archival photographs to construct an aura of historical authenticity. In addition to being explored in light of the other essays in this section, Lancioni's essay might also productively be paired with Nathan Stormer's "Embodying Normal Miracles" (in Section I) in order to allow further exploration of the role of the photographic image in documentary film.

In "Representative Form and the Visual Ideograph: The Iwo Jima Image in Editorial Cartoons," Janis L. Edwards and Carol K. Winkler also consider uses of the past in the present as they explore the functions of *visual parody*. Edwards and Winkler study editorial cartoonists' appropriations of the famous photograph of U.S. Marines planting a flag on the island of Iwo Jima in 1945 and show how the Iwo Jima image serves as a frequent and potent visual *topos,* or commonplace reference. Examining editorial cartoons that comment on everything from gays in the military to gas prices and presidential politics, Edwards and Winkler argue (following Kenneth Burke) that the Iwo Jima image is both a *representative form* that illustrates political ideals and also functions as what Michael McGee (1980) has called an *ideograph,* a rhetorical fragment that implicitly references ideological beliefs. Edwards and Winkler thus designate the Iwo Jima image a *visual ideograph,* which they define as a visual representation that can be used in political discourse to emphasize collective commitment, ground claims of power, and frame cultural norms for behavior. Edwards and Winkler's essay demonstrates that concepts such as the ideograph and form offer much to scholars interested in the analysis of visual images. In addition, the authors' interest in the variety of appropriations of the Iwo Jima image reveals how visual images, especially those that circulate widely across time and space, gain power as cultural representations. Readers might also wish to pair Edwards and Winkler's essay with another essay in the volume that takes up the role of the *ideograph* in visual culture, Dana L. Cloud's essay, "'To Veil the Threat of Terror': Afghan Women and the <Clash of Civilizations> in the Imagery of the U.S. War on Terrorism" (in Section V).

Carole Blair and Neil Michel consider how events of the past are memorialized for the present in their examination of the Civil Rights Memorial in Montgomery, Alabama. Their essay, "Reproducing Civil Rights Tactics: The Rhetorical Performances of the Civil Rights Memorial," argues that the memorial actually enacts civil rights tactics rather than merely represents them. For example, the memorial's physical structure "troubles" the visitor by interrupting her or his passage along the public sidewalk. The memorial thus forces the visitor to confront the memorial directly, just as lunch counter sit-ins and other forms of nonviolent resistance forced Americans to confront the racist system of segregation during the civil rights movement. In addition, the authors note that the memorial sits in a commemorative landscape devoted to the Confederacy, disrupting the unified nature of that narrative just as the movement itself disrupted the white supremacy of Southern cities. These and other strategies, Blair and Michel explain, "rewrite" the civil rights movement in ways that comment not only on the past but also on the role of race in contemporary U.S. society.

Blair and Michel's study extends the insights of earlier scholarship on public commemorative memorials, including important studies of the Vietnam Veterans Memorial by Sonja Foss (1986) and Peter Ehrenhaus (1988). By studying not only the material and design features of the memorial but also the politics of its placement in the cityscape of Montgomery, Blair and Michel situate the Civil Rights Memorial within a broad commemorative landscape. In addition, Blair and Michel's emphasis on *performance* highlights the importance of viewer engagement with memorials. Like Lancioni, Blair and Michel argue that it is through interaction with a visual artifact that audiences make sense of it. Blair and Michel's essay might also be paired with Margaret L. LaWare's "Encountering Visions of Aztlán: Arguments for Ethnic Pride, Community Activism and Cultural Revitalization in Chicano Murals" (in Section III), which also explores how marginalized communities use memorializing to make arguments about community and civil rights.

Barbara Biesecker's essay, "Remembering World War II: The Rhetoric and Politics of National Commemoration at the Turn of the 21st Century," studies a variety of artifacts produced in the 1990s that constructed late-20th-century public memory about World War II: the building of the World War II Memorial on the National Mall in Washington, D.C., Steven Spielberg's film *Saving Private Ryan,* Tom Brokaw's best-selling book *The Greatest*

Generation, and the Women in Military Service for America Memorial. Biesecker interprets these different artifacts as rhetorical constructions of World War II memory designed to educate subsequent generations about the values they should hold as U.S. citizens. Biesecker finds these World War II "civics lessons" problematic, however, because they define citizenship in ways that ignore status and power differences in American society. Unlike other essays in this section, Biesecker's critical approach to World War II engages a variety of artifacts from multiple media. The essay thus serves as an excellent example of the ways that disparate kinds of rhetoric (e.g., film, book, memorial) may be studied together to uncover the broader cultural forces at work in the construction and circulation of public memory. For further exploration of the ways that history is often nostalgically memorialized and commodified, Biesecker's essay might also be paired with Ekaterina V. Haskins's essay, "'Put Your Stamp on History': The USPS Commemorative Program *Celebrate the Century* and Postmodern Collective Memory" (in Section IV).

In "Public Identity and Collective Memory in U.S. Iconic Photography: The Image of 'Accidental Napalm,'" Robert Hariman and John Louis Lucaites study how famous photographs sometimes become icons of public memory. As the authors define the term, an *iconic photograph* is a photograph that, over time, comes to function as a repository of complex and often conflicting beliefs and attitudes about American identity. Hariman and Lucaites engage in a close reading of an iconic photograph known as "Accidental Napalm," the famous Vietnam War-era image of a young, naked girl running down a road (and toward the viewer), escaping a Napalm attack. When this dramatic image of a child crying out in pain and fear circulated during the Vietnam period, it tapped into moral questions about war and violence. However, as the political questions of Vietnam receded into the past, the story of the photograph increasingly became the personal story of the girl in the image, Kim Phuc: her subsequent immigration to Canada, her friendship with the photographer, and her experience of motherhood. Hariman and Lucaites argue that such personal narratives removed the image from the realm of political

judgment and thus dampened its power to make a moral argument about war and violence.

Hariman and Lucaites's study of iconic photographs reveals that *circulation* is an important aspect of visual rhetoric. By studying the variety of ways that iconic photographs and their appropriations organize and frame public memory of important events, Hariman and Lucaites explore the rhetorical functions of photography in U.S. culture. Hariman and Lucaites's essay might also be paired with Lester C. Olson's "Benjamin Franklin's Pictorial Representations of the British Colonies in America: A Study in Rhetorical Iconology" (in Section V), which explores the appropriation of images produced by Franklin during the colonial period.

As you read the essays in this section, we invite you to consider the discussion questions below. We also encourage you to explore related scholarship in the references and in our suggestions for further reading. There is a substantive visual rhetoric literature on remembering and memorializing; these five essays are only a sample of the excellent work in this area. The suggestions for further reading highlight other scholarship on remembering and memorializing that you may wish to explore.

Discussion Questions

1. Coauthors Edwards and Winkler and coauthors Hariman and Lucaites address the circulation and appropriation of images, especially circulation over time. Consider how each essay explores these concepts. How do the critics account for circulation and appropriation in each instance? What does the fact of circulation and appropriation suggest about the rhetorical power of the "original" images themselves?

2. A dominant theme running through all of the essays is that remembering and memorializing are as much about the present (or, perhaps, even the future) as they are about the past. Select examples from the essays to illustrate this feature of remembering and memorializing.

3. Photographs seem to be particularly powerful sites of memory. Drawing on the work of Lancioni and coauthors Hariman and Lucaites, speculate about why this seems

to be the case. What makes photographic rhetoric a powerful mode for remembering and memorializing?

4. Consider the rhetoric of the public commemorative memorial as interpreted by Biesecker and coauthors Blair and Michel. What aspects of the built environment should the rhetorical critic of memorials examine? What might be some challenges of studying public commemorative space as visual rhetoric?

5. Considering the essays you read in this section, is it fair to suggest that sometimes visual rhetoric uses memory to distort or misrepresent the past? Do you think that the resources of visual rhetoric, as opposed to the resources of rhetoric more generally, are more likely to distort the past than other modes of remembering and memorializing? Why or why not?

REFERENCES

Bodnar, J. (1992). *Remaking America: Public memory, commemoration, and patriotism in twentieth-century America.* Princeton, NJ: Princeton University Press.

Browne, S. H. (1995). Reading, rhetoric, and the texture of public memory. *Quarterly Journal of Speech, 81*(2), 237–265.

Ehrenhaus, P. (1988). The Vietnam Veterans Memorial: An invitation to argument. *Argumentation and Advocacy, 25*(2), 54–64.

Foss, S. K. (1986). Ambiguity as persuasion: The Vietnam Veterans Memorial. *Communication Quarterly, 34*(3), 326–340.

Kammen, M. G. (1993). *The mystic chords of memory: The transformation of tradition in American culture.* New York: Vintage.

McGee, M. (1980). The ideograph: A link between rhetoric and ideology. *Quarterly Journal of Speech, 66*(1), 1–16.

SUGGESTIONS FOR FURTHER READING

Armada, B. J. (1998). Memorial agon: An interpretive tour of the National Civil Rights Museum. *Southern Communication Journal, 63*(3), 235–243.

Dickinson, G., Ott, B. L., & Aoki, E. (2006). Spaces of remembering and forgetting: The reverent eye/I at the Plains Indian Museum. *Communication and Critical/Cultural Studies, 3*(1), 27–47.

Gallagher, V. J. (1999). Memory and reconciliation in the Birmingham Civil Rights Institute. *Rhetoric & Public Affairs, 2*(3), 303–320.

Owen, A. S. (2002). Memory, war and American identity: *Saving Private Ryan* as cinematic jeremiad. *Critical Studies in Media Communication, 19*(3), 249–282.

Sturken, M. (1997). *Tangled memories: The Vietnam war, the AIDS epidemic, and the politics of remembering.* Berkeley: University of California Press.

Taylor, B. C. (2003). "Our bruised arms hung up as monuments": Nuclear iconography in post–Cold War culture. *Critical Studies in Media Communication, 20*(1), 1–34.

Zelizer, B. (1995). Reading the past against the grain: The shape of memory studies. *Critical Studies in Mass Communication, 12*(2), 214–239.

5

THE RHETORIC OF THE FRAME

Revisioning Archival Photographs in The Civil War

JUDITH LANCIONI

Thanks to *The Civil War*, first broadcast on PBS September 23–27, 1990, audiences have become accustomed to seeing the camera rove over or delve into the flat surface of a photograph as if that photograph were a three dimensional entity. This technique did not originate with the 11 hour Florentine Films production. It is standard Hollywood practice, as filmmaker Ken Burns was the first to acknowledge (Milius 43), but it certainly was made familiar by the documentary. Some joked about the frequency of slow and deliberate movement "up the legs, past the belt, now the chest" (Adler 59). Others credited the film's use of 3,000 archival stills (Milius 43) with creating an "unremittingly authentic record in black and white" (Broder D7) that contributed to the film's historical authenticity. This essay will argue that the archival photographs are appropriated in ways that go beyond exposition to constitute visual rhetoric.

Mobile framing and reframing, the two techniques on which this essay focuses, involve alterations to the frame and composition of archival photographs. Mobile framing is Bordwell and Thompson's term for camera work (specifically the pan, the tilt or the tracking shot) that gives viewers the illusion of movement, regardless of what actually took place in the profilmic event. In mobile framing, the camera treats the archival still as if it were a three-dimensional entity, endowing it with depth and motion. Mobile framing, especially the slow pans and tilt shots used so frequently in *The Civil War*, problematizes viewing by prolonging, beyond normal expectations, the time it takes viewers to decipher exactly what they are seeing. As Carole Berger explains, delayed recognition "highlights the sense-making activity itself and obliges us to reflect on it" (150). Thus mobile framing encourages viewer awareness of the linkage between seeing and knowing and the epistemological assumptions involved in that linkage. Reframing accomplishes the same goal, though more subtly.

In reframing, an archival still is dissected into several different shots, one of which

SOURCE: Lancioni, J. (1996). The rhetoric of the frame: Revisioning archival photographs in *The Civil War. Western Journal of Communication, 60*(4), 397–414. Reprinted with permission of Western States Communication Association.

shows the photograph in its original form and others which reframe portions of the original. Reframing is often used to provide close-ups of individuals barely noticeable in the original photograph, thus inviting viewers to question why this is so. Why does the original photograph relegate this particular person or detail to the background? Why does the film place them in the foreground? These questions highlight the rhetorical construction of the photographs, and, ultimately, of the film. That is, the photographs give witness to the past as viewed by a photographer influenced by the conventions and ideology (and of course the technology) of the nineteenth century. Reframing suggests other interpretations of the photographs and the past they represent, thereby providing the more complex analysis called for by visual historians like Robert Rosenstone, Joshua Brown, and Andrew Britton. Ultimately, reframing visually advances the argument that history is not a product, an absolute truth enshrined in libraries and archives, but rather an on-going critical encounter between the past and present. That encounter, moreover, is not passive or accidental; it is rhetorical.

This analysis of the rhetorical function of reframing and mobile framing in *The Civil War* begins with a brief review of the concept of visual rhetoric, establishes its relevance for documentary studies, then applies the concept to portions of the film series which best illustrate both the aesthetic operation of these techniques and their rhetorical implications. Special attention is paid to segments depicting the slave experience to demonstrate that reframing and mobile framing not only compensate for gaps in the visual record but also encourage viewers to question the reason for the gaps. Past and present ideologies are juxtaposed, inviting viewers to question the implications of their own ideological stance and to recognize that representation and ideology are inextricably linked (Minh-ha 97).

VISUAL RHETORIC

A wide range of visual forms have been the subject of rhetorical analysis, including the Vietnam Veterans Memorial (Foss), print advertisements (Scott), fiction films (Rushing and Frentz, Gronbeck), 1930s social documentary (Medhurst & Benson), newsreels and newscasts (Nichols), news documentary (Rosteck), and direct cinema (Benson; Nichols). Nevertheless, two similarities can be found amid this diversity: the concept of audience as actively engaged with the visual text and the linkage of aesthetic and rhetorical functions.

In "Respecting the Reader," Tom Benson points out that rhetorical analysis of visual texts must investigate "the ways the text positions the spectator as an active participant in the making of meaning" (197). Rhetorical critics, he argues in "The Rhetorical Structure of Frederick Wiseman's *Primate*," must go beyond "*what* meaning emerges from a text or artifact" to an explanation of "*how* it emerges" (204). Tackling the *how* means attending to the specific properties of visual images and their processing by viewers. The job of the rhetorical critic, Benson explains, is to locate those effects in the complicated interaction between text, context, and audience: "The text implies its audience and the interpretive actions of its audience" (204).

Sonja Foss agrees that meaning comes from interaction between the visual object and the viewer; indeed her definition of a rhetorical response is that a "viewer attributes meaning" (331) by engaging in "a critical, reflective analysis of the work or a cognitive apprehension of it" (329). The visual object invites certain responses and discourages others (Foss 329). This analysis, moreover, can lead viewers out of the self-contained, non-referential universe of the text, which Foss calls its aesthetic dimension, to the world beyond the text (329).

In *The Civil War,* the impetus to make this journey from aesthetic experience to rhetorical analysis is provided by mobile framing and reframing. Together these two techniques focus attention on the archival photographs as constructions that embody past ideologies open to reinterpretation (Trachtenberg 70; Levine 26). In deconstructing these photographs, the film invites viewers to question their own formulation of abstractions like individuality, community, family, and freedom. This deconstruction is crucial to the depiction of the slave experience because it can stimulate audience awareness that these concepts are absent from archival photographs of African Americans. Visual images of slave families, for example, must be wrenched from group photographs. Mobile framing and reframing demonstrate that the social relationships previously regarded as "real" and constant are, in fact, "rhetorically constituted" and susceptible to change (McKerrow 103).

Viewers' ability to analyze a visual text is grounded in their familiarity with generic conventions of production and reception (Gronbeck 140–41; Nichols 24). Ernst Gombrich, for example, has demonstrated that pictorial art forms are based on conventions common to artist and viewer. Alan Trachtenberg makes a similar argument with regard to documentary photographs. Likewise Scott argues that in decoding advertising images, "consumers draw on a learned vocabulary of pictorial symbols . . ." (264). Foss advances similar claims in her analysis of non-pictorial art forms (329–31). Rosteck, in his analysis of television news documentaries, and Benson, in his studies of Wiseman's films, discuss the generic conventions utilized by particular audiences. First among these is viewers' recognition of "conventional form," which Burke defines as "the appeal of form as *form*" (126), that is, the expectations and attitudes an audience brings to its initial encounter with a particular visual text.

Documentary Assumptions: Seeing Is Believing

Most viewers of historical documentary expect to see a faithful representation of the past. They bring with them to the viewing experience an "assumption that sounds and images stand as evidence . . . rather than as elements of a plot" (Nichols 20). Instead of the suspension of disbelief characteristic of fiction, documentary film invokes in many viewers an "activation of belief" that they are seeing evidence of the real world (Nichols 28). Viewers assume that documentaries are "transmitting" historical events rather than fictionally creating them (Guynn 223). Documentary "produces the referential illusion and in fact derives its prestige from that production" (Guynn 223). Instead of the power of the imaginary, documentary invokes belief in the real—whether it be the reality of the present or of the past.

The Civil War inspires belief in its ability to capture a past reality primarily through lavish use of archival materials. Over 160 archives were visited in gathering material for the film; 16,000 archival photographs were shot, 3,000 of which ultimately were used (Milius 43). The filmmakers treated these photographs as "evidence of the past" ("Civil War" 58) and tried to let them "speak for themselves, to convey meanings and emotions and stories on their own" (Ken and Ric Burns qtd. in Ward xvii).

Nevertheless, to transform these archival photographs into a meaningful film experience for modern audiences demanded considerable creativity. Mobile framing was used to create the illusion of three dimensionality and movement, while reframing provided the close-ups or mid-range shots that were beyond the technology of nineteenth century photographers. As theorists like John Berger, Ernst Gombrich, and Nelson Goodman have demonstrated, seeing is conventional. The postmodern era has been conditioned by snapshot photography and its "nonselective accuracy of detail" (Kouwenhoven 187) to value minutia which mid-nineteenth century viewers, who prized panoramic views, would have regarded as trivial.[1] Thus, in the film, an archival photograph of slaves gathered in front of a cabin is reframed to focus attention on one detail of the photograph, a detail that is much less noticeable in the original: a girl holding a book. Through mobile framing, a shot which begins with a distant view of pickets around a campfire in a field ends with a zoom into a close-up of hands extended over the embers. In both these instances, a small detail from the original photograph is singled out for special attention.

The panoramic and group shots, crammed with information viewers might not master in full, present the past as past, as strange and different. The close-ups achieved through mobile framing and reframing enable viewers to experience the past on the intimate terms they have been conditioned to regard as "reality" (Kouwenhoven 187; Snyder 20). The archival photographs retain their historical authenticity and thus contribute to viewer expectations about documentary form. Nevertheless, their mode of presentation goes beyond historical exposition to critique. Both mobile and reframed shots have rhetorical implications because they invite viewers to recognize that the photographs are versions of the past that can be evaluated for the ideological implications of their composition.

Trachtenberg, for example, points out that photographers of the Civil War era adopted many of the props and conventions of portrait painters. Social class, he argues, could be inferred from the pose the photographer employed for the subject and from the amount of retouching expended on the final product (21–28). Photographs of soldiers and camp life also were composed according to pictorial conventions (Trachtenberg 73–75). For example, seen in the film is a photograph of Custer sitting with a captured Confederate (actually his cousin), a young body-servant at their feet. This is a conventional pose (Trachtenberg 84). Nevertheless, this photograph, like the others used in the film, comes with no annotations regarding its embodiment of nineteenth century attitudes about class. Instead, camera work is used to lure viewers beyond consideration of the informational content of the photographs to the attitudes and values implied by the arrangement and selection of subjects. The photographs are authentic. The people and places they depict did in fact exist. But the film's manner of presentation calls attention to itself, encouraging viewers to pay attention to the construction of the photographs and to the ways construction and reconstruction affect meaning.

Even when the archival materials seem simply to serve the narrative, the way they are presented helps establish a viewing pattern which, in other segments, leads to critique. For example, to illustrate narrator David McCullough's account of preparations for the siege of Yorktown (II: 16),[2] viewers are shown a series of shots taken from portions of an archival photograph. The photograph itself is not remarkable. It shows fortifications, including a cannon with soldiers behind it and piles of cannon balls to the left front. But, as is typical in this film, segments of the photograph are shown separately before the camera pulls back to reveal the whole photograph. In this instance, the first shot shows soldiers grouped around the cannon. Then the camera moves up to reveal the earthworks with a line of soldiers atop it. Next comes a far shot in which viewers see the photograph in its entirety.

There is no ostensible reason to first present portions of the photograph as single shots, except that this manner of presentation conditions viewers to question the relationship between the parts of the photograph and the whole. The camera work encourages viewers to "join in the mental exercise of sifting historical evidence" and thus establishes a pattern in which viewing becomes an act of purposeful discovery (Hulser 23). As Hulser points out, when "the historical mode of representation itself attracts . . . critical attention," viewers will begin to question "how what they see is supposed to prove a point" (23).

For example, in the second episode, as viewers hear Lincoln's words urging McClellan to act, they see first a far shot of a clearing among trees where the General camped out, then a cut to a head shot of Lincoln. Next viewers hear McClellan's haughty rejoinder to the President. Simultaneously they see a photograph of McClellan and three staff members; the shot is framed so that McClellan is center screen. In the next shot, the photograph is reframed to provide a close-up of McClellan, similar to the previous head-shot of Lincoln. The combination of head shots (first Lincoln, then McClellan), invites viewers to compare these two men, to match up their characters much as the film has matched their close-ups. At this point in a traditional documentary, an omniscient narrator, "the textual dominant," would speak with unchallenged authority to draw conclusions for the audience and thus advance the film's argument (Nichols 35). McCullough, however, voices no overt judgment about McClellan's shortcomings. Instead archival materials are selected and edited to provide evidence and imply a judgment, while camera work encourages viewers to move from implication to conclusion.

That McClellan should be judged the loser in the visual match up with Lincoln is cued by pairing a quotation from an unidentified private with two shots of an archival photograph in which a lone figure sits in a chair atop a huge earth mound. To the left, below the mound, is a cannon. In the background is a harbor with boats barely visible. In the left foreground of the photograph is a man on a horse; three men occupy the right foreground. These are a part of the York River defenses abandoned by the Confederates (Ward 132), but the film provides no identification or explanation. Instead it cuts to a closer view of the seated figure perched incongruously and inexplicably atop the earth mound.

This close-up must activate, at least in some viewers, a common assumption: the soldier at the front knows more than the general back at camp because workers always know more than their bosses. That assumption gains further support from the quotation: "I don't see the sense of piling up earth to keep us apart. If we don't get at each other some time, when will the war end? My plan would be to quit ditching and go to fighting" (II: 16). If an audience, based on its "stock of opinion and knowledge," makes the assumption and draws the conclusion which follows from that assumption it, in essence, persuades itself (Bitzer 407). Examining the ways in which this film appropriates archival photographs can provide an explanation of how such self-persuasion is elicited and how it supports larger claims about the nature of history.

AUDIENCE COLLABORATION WITH DOCUMENTARY FORM

Audiences collaborate in assigning particular meanings to a visual text (Foss 330). In that collaboration they draw on their own life experiences as well as on prior aesthetic and rhetorical experiences (Thompson 10; Foss 330). However, viewer collaboration is circumscribed by the text, which "renders one rhetorical interpretation more likely than another" (Foss 330). Through their content selection, shot composition, camera work, and editing, filmmakers guide what is seen, for how long, and in what order (C. Berger 149). Viewers construct meaning from shot content and context, from the relationship of shot to shot, and from the "rhythm of the cutting," all of which contribute to a film's "visual rhythms" and constitute an important aspect of its rhetoric (Medhurst & Benson 58). The visual rhythms of *The City,* for example, reinforce the claim that suburban life is an attractive compromise midway between the hectic rush of city life and the soporific pace of the country (Medhurst & Benson 59).

The concept of visual rhythm is useful in explaining the ways in which *The Civil War* establishes patterns that guide viewer collaboration in the meaning-making process. The visual rhythms of *The Civil War* tend to be slow. Frequently the film uses a slow tilt shot that

ends with either a long take or a cut to a close-up. For example, a shot in which the viewer's line of vision, controlled by the camera, travels very slowly up the photographic subject's torso will end with a long take of the subject's face or else cut to a close-up of the subject's face or eyes. Long takes, slow pans, and tight close-ups invite viewers to explore images, reflect on their possible meaning (C. Berger 150), and wonder how that meaning is arrived at (Hulser 23).

In *The Civil War,* the visual rhythms are often so slow as to unnaturally delay recognition of what the image is. For example, in the sequence of shots that follows the opening credits, the camera moves very slowly up a black surface adorned with white spheres. The image is unidentifiable until the camera reaches the face of a Union soldier. It then becomes clear that the camera has been panning up the soldier's uniform, but at such close range as to disorient and confuse the viewer. The next shot also begins with a mystifying image which, as the camera pans slowly screen left, reveals itself to be a rifle butt lying near what turns out to be the corpse of another soldier. Again recognition of the total image has been delayed. Another segment begins with a slow tilt shot down a black surface, which eventually resolves itself into a tree trunk. But recognition of the tree is not complete until the camera zooms back to reveal women standing beside the huge tree trunk. The slow camera movement in these shots focuses attention on the act of cognition, alerting viewers to their own participation in the meaning-making process.

Slow panning and tilt shots frequently are used to build suspense, but filmmakers can also use them to create a pattern of audience expectation that differentiates itself from conventional viewing patterns (C. Berger 150). Viewing patterns contribute to the form of a text, which Burke defines as "the creation of an appetite in the mind of the auditor, and the adequate satisfying of that appetite" (31). Form is "a way of experiencing" (Burke 143). A text which satisfies pre-existing audience expectations is conventional in form (Burke 127); its emphasis is on the information conveyed (Burke 39). The conventional form of a historical documentary would be the delivery of authentic information in a straightforward manner, since this would fulfill audiences' prior expectations that such films "do not actively represent reality . . . but [instead] are identifiable with it" (Britton 27).

The Civil War, in part because it plays against these expectations, achieves what Burke calls "formal elegance or eloquence" (37). The eloquent text focuses audience attention on the presentation of information rather than on the information itself (Burke 37–39). This emphasis on presentation is also characteristic of parametric form in film; that is, form in which "artistic patterns compete for our attention with the narrative functions of devices" (Thompson 19). For example, the pattern of "seeing" by beginning at the bottom of a human form and moving very slowly up to the face, pausing there, at rest, is not necessary to visually identify who is being referenced; in fact, it delays recognition. In parametric form, "colors, camera movements, sonic motifs, will be repeated and varied across the entire work's form" in such a way as to call attention to themselves; means of presentation supersedes expository function (Thompson 20). Mobile framing and reframing are primary contributors to the eloquent, or parametric, form of this documentary.

THE MOVING FRAME

Besides the obvious function of animating still photographs, camera movement in *The Civil War* can expand the frame of the original photograph, thus giving it symbolic importance far beyond the specific scene photographed. Slowly panning the photograph of a line of corpses along a fence conveys the sense that the fence and the remnants of slaughter go on and on; the particular scene of slaughter becomes emblematic of all similar scenes. Slowly panning the photograph of slaves at work in the cotton fields creates the illusion that the line of slaves stretches on eternally; these slaves symbolize legions of slaves toiling endlessly in countless fields. When the camera pans a line of soldiers photographed at march through a street, viewers not only get a sense of movement, but also, because the camera defies the limits of the photographic frame, the impression that the line is endless.[3]

The slow camera movement also gives viewers time to contemplate the image and to question its significance. The more time viewers spend moving through the illusionary depths of the image,[4] the more significance that image takes on. Slow panning prolongs the point at which viewers can process what they see because as long as the camera keeps moving (within the shot), it is still providing information necessary to the assessment of the shot's total meaning. As Tom Daly, editor for *City of Gold*,[5] explains, "It's the mind that moves . . . your understanding takes a little journey through the movement inside the shot" (qtd. in "Still Photo" 1). In other words, prolonged pans and tilts encourage viewers to engage with visual images on both a cognitive and an emotional level.[6]

The rhetorical implications of this engagement are exemplified by a sequence of shots utilizing daguerreotypes of African-born slaves, stripped to the waist. The film provides no information about the origins of the daguerreotypes. Instead they are paired with McCullough's reading of historical quotations about the degradation of slave life.

> "No day ever dawns for the slave," a freed black man wrote, "nor is it looked for. For the slave it is all night—all night forever." One White Mississippian was more blunt: "I'd rather be dead," he said, "than be a nigger on one of these big plantations." (I:6a)

The words suggest the degradation. The images show it. The camera work intensifies it, making explicit the "aggression" Sontag suggests is "implicit in every use of the camera" and supporting her claim that photographs "turn people into objects that can be symbolically possessed" (14). Moreover, the camera, as it moves slowly upward, exploring every nuance of muscle and bone, intensifies that violation by prolonging it. The longer the camera explores the images, the longer viewers have to consider, not just the informational value of the photographs, but their manner of presentation. The camera is viewers' only means of sight; it controls what and how they see. Thus as viewers' eyes move slowly over the images, they symbolically participate in the violation.[7]

Most viewers will not know that J. T. Zealy photographed the slaves at the request of Harvard professor Louis Agassiz. They will not know that Agassiz used the daguerreotypes to identify African traits he then tried to trace in American-born slaves (Trachtenberg 53). But all viewers know that to be stripped naked and publicly perused is a gross violation of human dignity. This is the common knowledge, the *doxa,* that viewers can be counted on to bring to their interpretation of the photographic sequence.[8]

To link slavery, which some might regard as a dead issue, a historical abstraction, to such an elemental human experience can revitalize the issue for contemporary audiences. But the rhetorical effect is more subtle than that. The same camera work that discourages passive spectatorship encourages viewers to engage in the kind of self-confrontation that will enable them to experience "alternative subject positions" (Shohat and Stam 358). They are both the victims and the perpetrators of the cruel depersonalization represented by the photographs.

Mobile framing makes viewers symbolic enactors of the very act they would condemn as inhuman. Thus slavery becomes a personal issue as well as a contemporary one. To regard this inhumane act as both personal and present (i.e., viewers engage in it as they watch) is crucial to the film's overarching claim that history is about the confrontation of the present with the past. This short sequence in Episode I reverberates throughout the film (and in fact the daguerreotypes do appear more than once). Ultimately the mobile framing of the Zealy daguerreotypes in this sequence leads inexorably to Barbara Fields's statement in the final episode: "The Civil War is not over until we today have done our part in fighting it . . . " (IX: 30).

REFRAMING

Reframing, too, supports the film's claim that history is about the confrontation of the present with the past. It also enables filmmakers to raise issues for which there are no archival images, encouraging viewers to question why such gaps in the visual record exist (Hulser 20). Thus reframing is especially significant in the representation of African Americans. As Shohat and Stam explain, "The tension between presence and absence points to a possible reconceptualization" of texts that ignore anything that challenges the dominant ideology (220). Through reframing, subjects who are marginalized in the archival photographs can be made the center of the film frame, creating "a contrastive diaphony or counterpoint" (Shohat and Stam 239) which combats assumptions that archival photographs reveal the whole truth about the past.

In reframing, filmmakers show viewers part of a photograph and then the whole of it—or the whole and then particular parts. Creating several separate frames from a single photograph calls attention to a part of the whole photograph that might otherwise be missed ("Still Photo" 5). The filmmaker working with stills can choose to frame individually any segment of the original photograph. Each reframing produces a different emphasis; consequently, "images from the same photograph would have a different meaning" (Daly qtd. in "Still" 4).

For example, in "Gun Men" (I:9a), a segment about camp life, viewers see in succession three different shots of a single photograph. The original shows five men, three seated and two standing behind them. One of the men holds a pistol to the head of the man seated in front of him. One reframe focuses on the gun. Another focuses exclusively on two of the men, one of whom has his hand on the other's shoulder. These reframed shots call attention to the ambiguities of this photograph—the hand on the shoulder, the gun to the head—made during a bloody war in which guns brought death, not laughter. The multiple reframings of the archival photograph also imply that there are non-lethal aspects of gun play and of war. The hand on the shoulder might connote the camaraderie that developed on the battlefield, the gun to the head, a mock recklessness, perhaps. The war created "gun men" but did not obliterate their need for fun and friendship.

The reframing of this particular photograph of "Gun Men" at play is in itself playful. But that playfulness serves a purpose. As Trinh T. Minh-ha points out, "playing upon the illusion" that the camera can totally capture reality produces "one irreality on the other and the play of nonsense . . . upon meaning . . ." (107). The purpose, then, is to fracture meaning, total and indisputable, into meanings, relative and debatable. Just as the composition of the archival photograph plays with the meaning of war, the film, by reframing the photograph to foreground its playfulness, calls attention to its polysemy and relativizes the photograph's value as evidence. Reframing demonstrates that the same photograph can have several different meanings, depending on which aspects of it are foregrounded. This polysemy challenges the photograph's documentary purity, its factuality and total objectivity. Reframing encourages viewers to regard the photograph as one way of representing what was there, one interpretation of actuality. To reframe is to suggest alternative interpretations.

The effect of reframing is analogous to the operation of a very elemental perceptual gestalt, namely the figure/ground relationship. Figure and ground are relative, but exclusive, terms; in other words, what is conceived as background cannot be reconstituted as figure without a certain amount of conscious adjustment. When viewers see in close-up (i.e., as figure) an individual whom they have just seen as part of a group shot (i.e., as background), they must make perceptual readjustments that may make them more conscious of the epistemology of seeing. Those readjustments may lead viewers to question why some individuals (especially slaves) were backgrounded in archival photographs and why, through reframing, they are foregrounded in the film.

In the opening episodes, photographs of individual slaves are rare. In addition to the Zealy daguerreotypes, the film includes a photograph of an elderly slave with a white child on his lap (his formal dress suggests that he is a house servant) and a photograph of another older man, also formally dressed.[9] There are also several photographs of recaptured escapees whose punishment included having their heads encased in metal contraptions resembling dog collars. Following the Emancipation Proclamation, however, viewers are shown photographs of African American soldiers, many of whom had their portraits made, just as white soldiers did. Thus the film reflects the changing status of African Americans by its selection and arrangement of the archival photographs available.

Before Emancipation, viewers see the individual slave primarily through reframing of group photographs. For example, a group shot of slaves working with livestock in a field is reframed as a close-up of one male slave's head and upper torso. Through reframing, the individual slave is singled out from the group; his facial features are now clear. Without reframing he would have remained a featureless member of the group. The archival photograph shows one version of the slave experience; the reframe shows another. Both versions exist within the same photograph, just as both realities existed in the past. Slaves were individuals with dreams and desires, even though the dominant culture (instantiated in the photograph) tried to obliterate that individuality.

Singling out an individual by reframing a group shot as a close-up invites viewers to speculate on the diverse ways of seeing and thinking about the subjects of these photographs—as a mass of laborers almost indistinguishable from the fields they worked, or up close, as individuals important in themselves, apart from their labor. Consequently, when viewers realize that the primary way they see individual slaves is through reframing of group shots, they may come to question the ideology of the photographs.

That ideology not only denied the individuality of slaves, it also denied their right to live as a family. Rather than reframe photographs to create family groupings, however, the film reframes to foreground the tentative and temporary nature of slave families. Viewers see African American women and children together, but whether they comprise a family is left unclear. For example, as McCullough begins to describe slave life (I:6a), viewers see a group photograph of African American men and women, some holding babies, seated on the ground in front of a wooden structure. While McCullough reports that children were sent into the fields at the age of twelve, this group photograph is reframed as a close-up of a woman and three children. Singling out these four figures from the group suggests that they might have some special relationship, but the suggestion is never clarified; viewers are left wondering.

Soon afterwards, the camera focuses attention on three African American children seated with an African American woman in a field. She holds the head of the youngest. Once again, the composition of the shot suggests that this woman and children are related in some way. Then the film seems to contradict this suggestion by cutting to a wide range shot of the entire photograph, so that viewers see the woman and children as part of a larger group engaged in field work. In both these examples, the camera work contrasts close-ups suggesting a family relationship with far shots in which the women and children at first singled out recede into a larger group. Thus reframing calls attention to the ambiguity of family relationships in the archival photographs of African Americans.

A possible explanation for this ambiguity is provided by McCullough: "A slave could expect to be sold at least once in his lifetime, maybe two times, maybe more" (I:6a). Accompanying these words is a shot of an African American woman holding a child's hand, but the connection between the words and the visual image remains unexplained. Viewers may be tempted to see the two as mother and child, but their relationship is not clarified. As McCullough speaks of slaves struggling to maintain some semblance of family life, viewers see, excerpted from a larger photograph of field workers, a group of children seated in a circle in a field. Combining the words with the reframed image implies these children are related, but also can, on reflection, make viewers aware that family relationships are almost impossible to determine in these archival photographs, which depict slaves solely in amorphous groups.

The next shot further explores the nature of slaves' family life. While McCullough explains that "slave marriages had no legal status" (I:6a), viewers see a group of African American men and women, two of whom are dressed in white; one wears a white head-covering like a veil. The film cuts to another view of the same photograph, focusing on the group of onlookers seated in front of the women in white. The combination of words and visual images (especially the women in white) implies a wedding is taking place. But again that implication is left ambiguous.

In this sequence on slave life, the audience is made to work actively to construct notions of marriage, family, individuality. That is, viewers see through the eye of the camera and try to assign meaning to what they see based on "patterns of perception and valuation rooted in

the . . . American consciousness" (Gronbeck 143). But reframing thwarts this effort, implying one meaning in the reframes and yet suggesting another contradictory meaning in the composition of the archival photographs. While groping to fathom the relationships implied in various reframings of these group photographs, viewers experience slavery as the disruption or denial of those modes of being (marriage, family, individuality) that most would regard as natural and undeniable. The archival photographs record that denial and the ideology that sanctioned it. Reframing calls attention to that denial by challenging it with revisions of the visual record.

But this revision has other implications as well. First, reframing, by focusing on groups that might be families, implies that slave families did exist, despite the difficulties. Second, the fact that the slave families constituted through reframing do not resemble the nuclear family unit may lead some viewers to question their own ideological constructs of what constitutes a family or a marriage. Finally, reframing group photographs visually supports, in a way that simply displaying photographs of African American leaders would not, historian Barbara Fields' assertion that slaves took action on their own behalf (III:8). Reframing enables viewers to experience visually the slaves' struggle for freedom, even though almost no photographic record of that resistance exists.

For example, a photograph of African American men, women and children gathered in front of a cabin is reframed to show a girl seated with three children. Her head rests on her clasped hands, in what might be a gesture of defeat or futility. This interpretation is supported by the narrator's comments about the disease and early death of most slave children. However, the visual which accompanies McCullough's commentary challenges the hopelessness of his comments. Another portion of the same archival photograph (slaves in front of a cabin) is reframed as a close-up of a woman with her hand on her hip, her elbow jutting out. She looks proudly into the camera; her pose seems to signify defiance, not the degradation and early death McCullough speaks of. But when the camera zooms back to reveal the whole photograph, the woman fades away into the group, and so does the defiance. Should viewers, listening to McCullough's account of slaves' short life span, see this woman as one of a group of victims destined for an early death? Are they meant to respond to the defiance signified by the woman's posture, a defiance visually created by reframing? Both interpretations are possible because both are based on the same historically authentic photograph.

Reframing creates visual support for the claim that the spirit of rebellion lived, even amid the degradation of slavery. Helpless victimization and defiance existed as twin realities of slave life, and both are held in tension by the film text. The photograph, in fact, shows slaves who had fled their masters (Ward 13), but the film holds back this factual information; instead it creates visual images of two aspects of slavery within the same photograph. This is a complex, rather than a simplistic and patronizing account of slavery, one that makes the visual record itself the "site of interaction and struggle" (Shohat and Stam 347).

Thus through reframing, *The Civil War* avoids the "victimization model" which Lawrence Levine (16) denounces in documentary photography and which Brian Winston charges has existed in documentary film since its inception. Both critics assert that through selection and composition, photographers and documentarists bent on dramatizing one particular aspect of life may ignore contradictory aspects. Poverty, for example, is often pictured as unalloyed misery, thus denying the poor the power to rise, even momentarily, above their circumstances. But, as Levine points out, "Neither in photographs nor in life is reality composed of a series of either/or images" (21). Portraying the life of the poor or the life of the slave as unremitting misery and helpless victimization oversimplifies by ignoring the capacity of individuals to rise above their circumstances. It denies human complexity and therefore subverts historical understanding (Levine 22–23).

The Civil War avoids oversimplification by using reframing to make viewers aware that alternatives existed, even amid slavery. For example, as McCullough explains that the South could conceive of no alternative to slavery (I:8a), the film cuts to a group photograph of African American women and children standing in front of a log cabin. The next shot reframes an easily missed detail of the photograph: a girl holding an open book. In most areas of the South, it was illegal to teach slaves to read and write. Yet the film offers no explanation, providing instead McCullough's explanation of the impact of the cotton gin on the South's economic development and on the institution of slavery. The audience is left to ponder the significance of the girl with the book, which reframing has singled out as important but has left unexplained. Precisely because it remains unexplained, the reframe can be interpreted as an alternative to total subjugation. To reframe is to reveal the cultural hegemony that surrounds and informs the photograph, creating for the viewer a "clash of perspectives" in which that hegemony is made to confront marginalization (Shohat and Stam 357).

CONCLUSION

In "Knowledge and Time," Tom Farrell lists, as one of the requirements of rhetorical argument, that "the given be placed against a horizon of unrealized, unchosen alternatives" (128). Those who study historical documentary make a similar demand, complaining that filmmakers oversimplify and consequently distort history because they ignore the ideology and conventions embedded in visual artifacts (Walkowitz 57). Instead these critics call for films that construct a complex relationship of images, words, sounds, and music that encourages viewers to fill in gaps, confront discrepancies, and draw their own conclusions (Brown 122).

It is precisely this open acknowledgment of contradiction and inconclusiveness that viewers confront throughout *The Civil War.* Through mobile framing and reframing, this film series crafts a polysemic critique that discloses the alternative (and sometimes contradictory) meanings latent in the visual artifacts it explores. By playing the moving film frame against the still frame of the photograph, the documentary series creates a visual argument about the nature of history and its role in people's lives.

By accepting the photographs as polysemous, viewers enlarge their meaning (as mobile framing enlarges their visual content) and acknowledge (through reframing) that the historical meaning instantiated in the photographs is contingent. In so doing, viewers come to realize that meaning depends on their interaction with the text. The text provides the parameters of interpretation (Foss 329). The viewers provide the common knowledge needed to activate that potential (Farrell 128). Of course, ethnic, class, gender, and racial differences make it impossible to assume that all viewers interpret a text in exactly the same way. However, the open structure of the text not only tolerates diversity, it encourages it. Reframing, after all, foregrounds the disparity between past and present attitudes about race and human rights. By problematizing cognition, mobile framing and reframing elevate viewers' awareness of their role. This is especially evident in the segment on slavery, in which viewers are urged to contest that cooperation. Viewers are invited to become makers, rather than spectators, of history.

Ultimately the film confirms Farrell's statement that "history, whatever else it is, is an invention and revision of argument" (123). Invention, in the rhetorical sense, involves the filmmakers' selection of archival photographs and their pinpointing of those issues (embedded in those photographs) that have salience for modern audiences: the dignity of individuals, especially those whom the dominant culture marginalizes, and the contingent meaning of taken-for-granted concepts like freedom and family. Revision comes about through camera work that calls attention to itself by playing against viewers' conventional expectations about historical photographs and films. That camera work (the aesthetic dimension) invokes those salient issues and calls upon audiences to analyze and critique their preconceptions about the past and its relationship to the present (the rhetorical dimension). Thus in implementing Benson's dictum that critics of visual rhetoric must attend to *how* meaning emerges and is processed by viewers, this analysis of *The Civil War* also confirms Foss's contention that in visual argument, the aesthetic and the rhetorical are inseparably intertwined to create a text that can be acted upon as well as experienced.

History is thus presented as an on-going and ever changing process in which the present revisits the archives to question, reinterpret, rediscover. *The Civil War,* through mobile framing

and reframing of archival photographs, enables viewers to symbolically enact this vision of history, to examine "the past in order to make the present and the future richer" (Burns qtd. in Milius 1). Thus camera work visually advances the film's overall argument, voiced by Barbara Fields, that "the Civil War is still going on. It's still to be fought and regrettably it can still be lost" (IX:31). Mobile framing and reframing invite viewers to join the battle.

Notes

1. While Kouwenhoven argues that the development of dry plate technology and smaller, more mobile cameras is responsible for this change, Snyder insists that nineteenth century audiences prized panoramic shots because they thought the photograph should provide as much objective information as possible.

2. Quotations and paraphrases from the film were taken from a transcript obtained from Florentine Films. Since each of the nine episodes was separately paginated, roman numerals have been used to indicate episodes. Arabic numerals indicate page numbers within episodes. Letters *a* and *b* are used to distinguish between the two halves of episode one, which were also separately paginated. I:6a means page six of the first section of the first episode.

3. Recalling his work on *City of Gold,* Tom Daly suggests that avoiding the edges of photographs created "the illusion that the world went on in all directions beyond the camera frame. . . ." ("Still Photo" 3). In a personal interview (May 1995), as well as in several published interviews, Ken Burns identified this film as influential in his own work.

4. Hugo Munsterberg, in *The Photoplay* (NY: Appleton, 1916), was among the first to speculate on the viewer activity involved in completing and giving meaning to the incomplete perceptions supplied by a film, especially the mechanism by which viewers attribute depth to what they know to be a flat screen.

5. National Film Board of Canada, 1957. Directed by Colin Low and Wolf Koenig. Erik Barnouw, in *Documentary, A History of Non-Fiction Film* (rev. ed. Oxford UP, 1983: 200), credits the film with creating a new genre. See also John Tibbetts, "All That Glitters," (*Film Comment* March/April 1995: 52–55) on the film's use of archival stills.

6. Jim Wilson, a former chief of the National Film Board of Canada's Animation, Optical and Title

Photography Division, provides brief but interesting comments on the relationship between the pace of perceived camera movement and the mood of the film. See "Graphics" sidebar in "Still Photo" 6.

7. Similar camera work is used in the direct cinema film *No Lies* (Producer/Director Mitchell Block; distributor Phoenix Films, 1973). Vivian Sobchack, in "No Lies: Direct Cinema as Rape," *New Challenges for Documentary,* ed. Alan Rosenthal (University of California Press, 1988: 332–341), argues that this film uses camera movement as an instrument of symbolic enactment.

8. Farrell, in "Knowledge, Consensus, and Rhetorical Theory" (*Quarterly Journal of Speech* 62, 1976), explains that common, or social, knowledge "is a kind of general and symbolic relationship which acquires its rhetorical function when it is assumed to be shared by *knowers* in their unique capacity as audience" (4).

9. Beaumont Newhall (*The Daguerreotype in America,* New York: Graphic Society, 1961, plate #75) identifies the man as Caesar, the last slave owned in New York state.

References

Adler, Jerry, and others. "Revisiting the Civil War." *Newsweek* 8 Oct. 1990: 58–64.

Benson, Thomas J. "Respecting the Reader." Rev. of *A Certain Tendency of the Hollywood Cinema,* by Robert B. Ray; *Cinema and Sentiment* by Charles Affron; *Speaking of Soap Operas,* by Robert C. Allen. *Quarterly Journal of Speech* 72 (1986): 197–204.

———. "The Rhetorical Structure of Frederick Wiseman's *High School.*" *Communication Monographs* 47 (1980): 233–261.

———. "The Rhetorical Structure of Frederick Wiseman's *Primate.*" *Quarterly Journal of Speech* 71 (1985): 204–17.

Berger, Carole. "Viewing as Action: Film and Reader Response Criticism." *Literature Film Quarterly* 6 (1978): 144–51.

Berger, John. *Ways of Seeing.* London: BBC and Penguin Books, 1987.

Bitzer, Lloyd. "Aristotle's Enthymeme Revisited." *Quarterly Journal of Speech* 45 (1959): 399–408.

Bordwell, David, and Kristen Thompson. *Film Art.* 2nd ed. New York: Knopf, 1986.

Britton, Andrew. "Invisible Eye." *Sight and Sound,* Feb. 1992: 27–29.

Broder, David S. "A Lot to Learn from 'The Civil War.'" *Washington Post* 30 September 1990, D7, col. 1.

Brown, Joshua. "Visualizing the Nineteenth Century: Notes on Making a Social History Documentary Film." *Radical History Review* 38 (1987): 114–25.

Burke, Kenneth. *Counter-Statement.* 1931. Berkeley: U of California Press, 1968.

The Civil War. Prod. Ken Burns and Ric Burns. Written by Geoffrey Ward, Ric Burns, and Ken Burns. Eds. Paul Barnes, Bruce Shaw, and Tricia Reidy. Cinematography by Ken Burns, Allen Moore, and Buddy Squires. Florentine Films, 1990.

"The Civil War. Ken Burns Charts a Nation's Birth." *American Film* Sept. 1990: 58.

Farrell, Thomas B. "Knowledge in Time: Toward an Extension of Rhetorical Form." *Advances in Argumentation Theory and Research.* Eds. J. Robert Cox and Charles A. Willard. Carbondale: Southern Illinois U Press, 1982. 123–153.

Foss, Sonja K. "Ambiguity as Persuasion: The Vietnam Veterans Memorial." *Communication Quarterly* 34 (1986): 326–40.

Gombrich, Ernst H. *Art and Illusion: A Study in the Psychology of Pictorial Representation.* Princeton: Princeton U Press, [1960].

Goodman, Nelson. *Languages of Art. An Approach to a Theory of Symbols.* Indianapolis: Bobbs-Merrill, 1968.

Gronbeck, Bruce E. "Celluoid Rhetoric: On Genres of Documentary," *Form and Genre: Shaping Rhetorical Action.* Eds. Karlyn Kohrs Campbell and Kathleen Jamieson. Falls Church, VA: SCA, 1978. 139–164.

Guynn, William. *A Cinema of Nonfiction.* Rutherford, NJ: Fairleigh Dickinson U Press, 1990.

Hulser, Kathleen. "Clio Rides the Airwaves. History on Television." *The Independent* 12 (March 1989): 18–24.

Kouwenhoven, John A. *Half a Truth Is Better Than None.* Chicago: U of Chicago Press, 1982.

Levine, Lawrence W. "The Historian and the Icon: Photography and the History of the American People in the 1930s and 1940s." *Documenting America, 1935–43.* Eds. Carl Fleischhauer and Beverly W. Brannon. Berkeley: U of California Press, 1988. 15–42.

Mast, Gerald. "On Framing." *Critical Inquiry* 11 (Sept. 1984): 82–109.

McKerrow, Raymie. "Critical Rhetoric: Theory and Praxis." *Communication Monographs* 56 (1989): 97–102.

Medhurst, Martin J., and Thomas Benson. "*The City:* The Rhetoric of Rhythm." *Communication Monographs* 48 (1981): 54–72.

Milius, John. "Reliving the War Between Brothers." Interview with Ken Burns. *New York Times* 16 Sept. 1990, Sec. 2: H1+.

Minh-ha, Trinh T. "The Totalizing Quest of Meaning." *Theorizing Documentary.* Ed. Michael Renov. New York: Routledge, 1993. 90–107.

Nichols, Bill. *Representing Reality.* Bloomington: Indiana U Press, 1991.

Rosenstone, Robert A. "History in Images/History in Words: Reflections on the Possibility of Really Putting History onto Film." *American Historical Review* 93 (1988): 1173–1185.

Rosteck, Thomas. *"See It Now" Confronts McCarthyism.* Tuscaloosa: U of Alabama Press, 1994.

Rushing, Janice, and Thomas S. Frentz. "*The Deer Hunter:* Rhetoric of the Warrior." *Quarterly Journal of Speech* 66 (1980): 392–406.

Scott, Linda M. "Images in Advertising: The Need for a Theory of Visual Rhetoric." *Journal of Consumer Research* 21 (Sept. 1994): 252–273.

Shohat, Ella, and Robert Stam. *Unthinking Eurocentrism.* London: Routledge, 1994.

Snyder, Joel. "Photographers and Photographs of the Civil War." *The Documentary Photograph as a Work of Art: American Photographs, 1860–1876.* Organized by Joel Snyder and Doug Munson, The David and Alfred Smart Gallery. Chicago: U of Chicago Press, 1976. 17–22.

Sontag, Susan. *On Photography.* New York: Farrar, Straus, Giroux, 1977.

"The Still Photo in Cinema." Interviews with Tom Daly, Don Winkler, Veronica Soul, and Doug McDonald. *Pot Pourri (National Film Board of Canada Newsletter)* 22 (Summer 1977): 1–7.

Thompson, Kristin. *Breaking the Glass Armor.* Princeton: Princeton U Press, 1988.

Trachtenberg, Alan. *Reading American Photographs. Images as History. Mathew Brady to Walker Evans.* New York: Hill and Wang, 1989.

Walkowitz, Daniel J. "Visual History: The Craft of the Historian-Filmmaker." *Public Historian* 7 (1985): 53–64.

Ward, Geoffrey C., with Ric and Ken Burns. *The Civil War. An Illustrated History.* New York: Alfred A. Knopf, 1990.

Weisberger, Bernard A. "The Great Arrogance of the Present Is to Forget the Intelligence of the Past." An Interview with Ken Burns. *American Heritage* Sept./Oct. 1990: 97–192.

Winston, Brian. "The Tradition of the Victim in Griersonian Documentary." *New Challenges for Documentary.* Ed. Alan Rosenthal. Berkeley: U of California Press, 1988. 269–87.

6

Representative Form and the Visual Ideograph

The Iwo Jima Image in Editorial Cartoons

Janis L. Edwards and Carol K. Winkler

On February 23, 1945, Joe Rosenthal, a photographer working for the Associated Press, climbed a rough volcanic hill on the Pacific island of Iwo Jima. He hoped the view from the summit would allow for some good shots of the military activity in the area, and he got one. Along with three other photographers and a film cameraman, Rosenthal snapped a picture of a large American flag being hoisted into place, a picture that would become one of the most famous and controversial American photographs ever made. The story of this photograph has invited scholarly attention among those interested in the visual artifacts of American culture. Our interest in the image, however, is not in its historical context, but in its appropriation by editorial cartoonists in the present day. The image of those five Marines and one Navy Corpsman raising the flag has appeared in recent editorial cartoons[1] so frequently that it was derided as a visual cliché by David Astor (1993) in the magazine of the American Association of Editorial Cartoonists.

While the term "cliché" may be pejorative, the repetitive use of the Iwo Jima image is what initially inspires investigation into its rhetorical aspects, for rhetorical analyses often involve a search for recurrent patterns. The cultural salience of the image also compels attention. Images used strategically in the public sphere reflect not only beliefs, attitudes, and values of their creators, but those of the society at large. Cartoonists must use cultural references that readers can easily understand or, as Roger Fischer predicts, "risk almost certain failure, for obscurity and snob humor are fatal to the medium" (1996, p. 122).[2] Yet, our sample of cartoons shows that in more than fifty instances, cartoonists have reached back half a century to appropriate Rosenthal's patriotic cultural icon in service of an art directed at iconoclasm rather than sanctification.[3]

The assumptions common to research in iconology raise more questions than they resolve regarding the rhetorical experience provoked by the parodied Iwo Jima image. The

SOURCE: Edwards, J. L., & Winkler, C. K. (1997). Representative form and the visual ideograph: The Iwo Jima image in editorial cartoons. *Quarterly Journal of Speech, 83,* 289–310. © National Communication Association.

term "icon" proves problematic in this case because, despite its variant meanings and aspects,[4] the presumptive definition usually focuses on factors of representation by concrete resemblance. In describing visual studies as "iconology," Lester Olson (1987) defines icon as "a visual representation so as to designate a type of image that is palpable in manifest form and denotative in function" (p. 38). W.J.T. Mitchell (1986) and Ernst Gombrich (1996) similarly emphasize the quality of resemblance in iconographic study. Writings on the editorial cartoon, specifically those by Gombrich (1963) and Sol Worth (1981), call attention to the importance of denotation in establishing recognizability and subsequent interpretation of a caricature's meaning.

If representation proceeds from resemblance, the cartoon parodies of Iwo Jima should denote and represent the historical moment of February 23, 1945, as it occurred on Mt. Suribachi.[5] This denotative reading of the Iwo Jima image, however, is incongruent with the nature of political cartoons. Cartoonists concern themselves with contemporary subjects; the Iwo Jima flag-raising is a fixed moment in past history. The historical reference to Iwo Jima in editorial cartoons does not provide a theme, in the manner of a motif, but serves as a reference point for other themes. The image functions as visual topos, a visual reference point that forms the basis of arguments about a variety of themes and subjects.

The rhetorical experience of the parodied Iwo Jima image is not defined so much, then, by the denotative function of the iconic image, but by the abstracted qualities of the image as symbol. Paul Messaris (1994) notes the presence of ambivalence in parodied images, which he calls an ineffability that pushes an image beyond its concrete, motivated constraints, allowing for elasticity in application and interpretation. The visual image thus becomes more of an abstraction, an available site for the attachment of multiple connotations serviceable in multiple contexts. We contend that the Iwo Jima image, as appropriated and parodied in recent editorial cartoons, is a special type of symbolic form that represents an essence of cultural beliefs and ideals at a high level of abstraction. As such, we will argue, the parodied image constitutes an instance of depictive rhetoric that functions ideographically.

Our argument proceeds in three stages. First, we review literature on visual form and repetitive form that provides suggestive, but limited, explanations for the power and rhetorical function of this recurring visual image. Then, we consider the metaphoric properties of the image and argue that metaphor is not sufficient to explain the image's use in the parodied context. Instead, we articulate a concept of *representative form* to more fully account for the rhetorical experience and function of the parodied Iwo Jima image in cartoons. Third, we isolate the ways in which the parodied image functions as visual ideograph in editorial cartoons, thus challenging the assumption that only verbal expressions can fulfill such a rhetorical function. In the process, we expand Michael C. McGee's (1980) definition of the ideograph, posit potential differences between verbal and visual ideographs, and explore how the context of cultural parodies functions to express ideographic forms.

THE IWO JIMA IMAGE AS VISUAL FORM

The power of the Iwo Jima image in editorial cartoons necessarily draws from the visual and symbolic power of Joe Rosenthal's photograph, which depicts the raising of an 8′ by 4′8″ American flag by five Marines and a Navy corpsman to mark the successful capture of Mt. Suribachi, an early moment in a protracted battle for the strategically located Pacific island of Iwo Jima. This large flag replaced a smaller flag that had been planted earlier that day as Americans first reached the summit.[6] The second, more visible flag signaled the patriotic significance of the battle at this strategic place, an effort that would take weeks to complete and kill more than 20,000 Japanese and nearly 7,000 American soldiers, including three of the six men depicted in Rosenthal's picture and the Marine camera operator who made a motion picture record of the event.[7]

Previous scholars have identified meaningful compositional features of the photograph in an effort to account for its power and impact as a memorable image. Parker Albee and Keller Freeman (1995), Lance Bertelsen (1989), and Vicki Goldberg (1991) note the emphatic diagonal element of the flagpole and the vaulted perspective with the sky as backdrop as significant compositional elements. Kevin Leary and Carl Nolte (1995) suggest the strong, "sculptural" lighting makes some detail stand out in sharp relief, even as the men's faces are obscured in shadow. Following from Roland Barthes (1977) we might say the pose of the photograph connotes a sacred effort, as the bodies strain in unified action and the hands reach heavenward in lifting the flag, which is caught in a moment of unfurling. These interpretations of the image's visual form are consistent with theoretical propositions concerning a universal vocabulary of graphic or compositional features, summarized by Evelyn Hatcher (1974) and Paul Martin Lester (1995). They note that the elemental dynamic quality of the diagonal lines and the triangular form of the image are particularly vital, suggesting movement, energy, determination, virility, and strength. Directionality and placement are also significant, according to the grammar identified by Gunther Kress and Theo van Leeuwen (1996). The flag, symbolizing the American ideals of liberty, equality, and democracy, is moving toward the upper space in the frame—the space of the ideal, a place, as Goldberg (1991) suggests, that is "waiting to be filled" (p. 142).

Other compositional features signify more symbolic notions of communal effort, egalitarianism, and patriotism. Paul Fussell (1982) and George Roeder (1993) posit that the group effort and the obscured faces[8] speak to common cause and communal involvement. James Guimond (1991) asserts that photographs published in mass outlets at that time, as Rosenthal's was, function to embody common values and goals that would unite the public. The spontaneous photograph was embraced as an embodiment of a culturally preferred interpretation of war's heroism and valor.[9] Additional symbolic connotations derive from one feature of the image, the American flag. Bertelsen (1989) argues that military flag fetishism plays a role in the canonical reception of Rosenthal's photograph by inducing patriotic associations.

No doubt, the compositional and symbolic associations of Rosenthal's photograph contribute to its resonance with the American public. The flexibility of interpretation as cartoonists omit, distort, and add to the original composition

without losing its recognizability attests to the image's visual power. But any number of images display dramatic compositional elements or possess historical and symbolic significance, yet have not emerged as recurrent visual topoi to the extent we have seen with the Iwo Jima image in recent cartoons.

The Iwo Jima Image as Recurring Form

Unsatisfied that the account of Rosenthal's photograph as a distinctive image fully accounts for the rhetorical import of the image as visual topos in political cartoons, we examined literature on repetitive form to search for an explanation for the image's modern day resonance. Karlyn Campbell and Kathleen Jamieson's (1978) insights into form and genre appeared relevant, given that generic criticism "permit[s] the critic to generalize beyond the individual event which is constrained by time and place to affinities and traditions across time" (p. 27), and Fischer (1990, 1995) has previously recognized the generic features of political cartoons. But, as before, a generic interpretation of the Iwo Jima's recurrence in editorial cartoons was insufficient to explain the rhetorical application of the image. Unlike genre, which depends on recurrent situational elements that prompt recurrent substantive and stylistic elements, our sample displays the Iwo Jima image within a wide variety of contexts. While military settings predominate, more than a third of our sample uses the image in non-military references.

Beyond the lack of situational constraint, the lack of a constellation of recurrent stylistic and substantive elements renders any interpretation of the parodied image as genre suspect. Campbell and Jamieson insist that a constellation of elements should be present for an artifact to meet the audience's expectations associated with a specified genre. Our sample reveals that the formal elements of the Iwo Jima image are frequently omitted, distorted, or substituted during the parody operation. The cartoonists substitute elephants, rats, veterans in wheelchairs, etc., for the Marines; gas tanks, George Bush, eating utensils, a baseball bat, a Christmas tree, and alternative flags for the American flag; and pedestals, a trash can, and Bosnian quicksand for the rubbled peak of Mt. Suribachi. In one cartoon, the only remaining formal feature of Rosenthal's image is the summit's terrain which, like many of our examples, lacks the fusion of dynamic elements necessary for a successful application of genre, but appears to still have utility for the cartoonist in providing a resonant image for the audience.

While the concept of genre has limited applicability to the Iwo Jima image in editorial cartoons, the repeated presentation of the image, as well as its concrete nature, signal its categorization as depictive rhetoric. Michael Osborn (1986) defines depictive rhetoric as "strategic pictures, verbal or nonverbal visualizations, that linger in the collective memory of audiences as representative of their subjects when rhetoric has been successful" (p. 79). In the functions of depictive rhetoric (to present, intensify, facilitate identification, implement, and reaffirm identity), we discover a close correlation with the function of the Iwo Jima image as it appears in cartoons. Osborn (1986) declares that, through repeated presentations, depictive rhetoric generates "pictures for sharing that can be transmitted quickly and precisely by the mass media" (p. 89). The Iwo Jima image as rhetorical depiction would appear to be an instance where cartoonists use graphic lessons from the past to identify solutions for present decisions.

Osborn (1986) further defines the particular symbols of depiction as culturetypes which, grounded in cultural specificity, "authorize arguments and social practices" (p. 89) through their status as shared, communal symbols. The Iwo Jima photographic image as national icon is recalled in the depictive function of reaffirmation of identity, where symbols serve as "moral markers [that] fill our minds again with their radiance and power, and coronates them as basic premises that ought to govern moral reasoning" (Osborn, 1986, p. 95).

Among forms of figuration known as culturetypes, Osborn (1994) lists icons, which he defines as concrete embodiments of an abstraction, implying that this is a suitable label for nonverbal rhetorical depictions. According to Osborn (1986), icons also acquire a "secular sacredness" among the public (p. 82). Certainly, the original photographic image of Iwo Jima inspired a reverential attitude, demonstrated by its widespread popularity and achievement of the Pulitzer Prize in the months following initial publication. But the parodied use of the image in cartoons is distinctly irreverent. Furthermore, the decontextualization and elasticity that characterizes the parodied image suggests that its meaning is not grounded in what it concretely represents or denotes, but in its more general and abstract function.

THE IWO JIMA IMAGE AS REPRESENTATION

When conceived as an abstraction, the parodied Iwo Jima image moves into the representational realm. It functions symbolically to represent events and subjects that expand beyond the historical constraints of the original battle at Iwo Jima. Specifically, the role of metaphor and representative form appear relevant to this broader conceptualization of the image's resonance.

Metaphor

When a familiar figure is placed in a new, incongruent context, it is not uncommon to assume that metaphor is the functional rhetorical operation. Messaris (1997) makes this assumption about the Iwo Jima image as parodied in a motion picture advertisement, and similar conclusions could be drawn regarding Iwo Jima parodies in editorial cartoons. Recent research on political cartoons, although subject-centered,[10] strongly suggests the potentials of metaphor as an explanatory framework for the functions of symbolic imagery in cartoons.[11] Through the use of subversive mimicry, which often involves a metaphorical transformation, cartoonists offer debunking parodies of their subjects.

Carl Hausman (1989) notes that "one of the marks of a metaphor is that its particular conjoining of terms is integral to its significance. This indispensability of the expression as it is initially articulated must be sustained if the expression is to be regarded as a metaphor" (p. 14). However, in many of these cartoons, the Iwo Jima image is not indispensable to meaning, but is replaceable. Frequently, the Iwo Jima image is used as a sign for the military, rather than a metaphor that creates a new conception through a transforming mutual adjustment between tenor and vehicle. This use of sign, rather than metaphoric adjustment, is evident in a group of cartoons about gays in the military. Dennis Renault of the *Sacramento Bee,* for example, draws the group of Iwo Jima Marines as a sign for a generic military organization being reviewed by the military establishment for homosexual infiltration (see Figure 1). However, any relationship between yesterday's heroes and today's military policies and population is not metaphorically constructed as a matching and transformation process where qualities of one are mapped onto the other, and there is no specific and evident referral to the military of yesterday. The configuration of the soldiers into the familiar pose of the Iwo Jima image functions more as a sign, assisting the viewer in quickly identifying the military context.

Where Renault's soldiers in the Iwo Jima pose stand for the rank-and-file under review by the military establishment, Bill Schorr, in a 1993 cartoon, converts the flag-raising soldiers into representatives of the military establishment through their collective effort to keep the closet door closed on the gay issue (see Figure 2). Any reference to the original Iwo Jima image is an implicit and vague contrast between the heroic accomplishments of yesterday's military and today's concern with the sexual orientation of its members. This contrast reflects a common rhetorical strategy used by editorial cartoonists, identified by Denise Bostdorff (1987), where cartoonists provide perspective by incongruity. But incongruity as a factor is neither consistent nor explicit. A metaphor, to be clear, should function explicitly. The cartoon plays off the familiarity of the military context of the Iwo Jima configuration more than it alludes to the metaphorical meaning of that image in relationship to the cartoon's subject—gays in today's military.

In some other cartoons that refer to the military, the comparison with the heroes at Iwo Jima is a strictly ironic one, indicative of the perceived weaknesses of today's military "anti-heroes." For example, some of the more recently published cartoons in our study make reference to criminal sexual misconduct—the rape of an Okinawan girl by American soldiers or sexual harassment against female military members. In these cases, no indication exists that the group of soldiers patterned visually after the Iwo Jima Marines stands for anything other than themselves, but there is an implied contrast with the more

'Wait! Before we take the picture – Is anybody gay?'

Figure 1 "Wait!"

SOURCE: Dennis Renault, *Sacramento Bee.*

SCHORR/from the Kansas City Star

Figure 2 "THE CLOSET."

SOURCE: Bill Schorr reprinted by permission of United Feature Syndicate, Inc.

positive values exhibited by "yesterday's" military. Similarly, two cartoons in our sample depict today's military members as self-absorbed, media-oriented, and cynically shallow in contrast to the selfless, dedicated heroes represented in Rosenthal's 1945 photograph.

Some cartoons are structured more clearly as metaphors. If the heroism of Iwo Jima is only a dream, it is a daydream of Bill Clinton's, as envisioned by Wayne Stayskal (1995). In this cartoon, Clinton metaphorically transforms himself into the heroic World War II Marines who are raising a proud flag over Haiti. Several other cartoonists recall the heroism of the Iwo Jima soldiers as they convey laudatory comments about the U.S. military's role in providing famine relief to Somalia. While some parodied references to the Iwo Jima image are metaphoric, the relationship induced between the image and its referenced subjects is not consistent across our sample.

Representative Form

The limitations of compositional symbolism, visual metaphor, and genre theory in providing a comprehensive explanation for the Iwo Jima image's rhetorical significance in contemporary editorial cartoons and the suggestion that, as a clichéd image, its representative qualities have transcended the denotative, prompts us to consider the question of representation more directly. We propose that the Iwo Jima image is a special type of visual presentation that, through a combination of determined visual features and symbolic attributions, constitutes a representative form. A representative form transcends the specifics of its immediate visual references and, through a cumulative process of visual and symbolic meaning, rhetorically identifies and delineates the ideals of the body politic.

In proposing the idea of a representative form, we refer to two related constructs which inform the concept: Burke's "representative anecdote" (1969a) and S. Paige Baty's (1995) "representative character." Although an anecdote is a formal feature, the representative anecdote is not merely a reductive element featured in the text. Rather, as Barry Brummett (1984) notes, the representative anecdote may be a filter identified by the critic in the course of reconstructing discourse. In a sense, cartoonists function as cultural critics; some have chosen the Iwo Jima image, not because it is literally embedded in the discourse of the Gulf War, gays in the military, presidential campaigns, etc., but because it provides a perspective on the situation. Burke

considers the representative anecdote to demonstrate the aspects of representation and reduction by fulfilling the requirements of an explanatory language of human motives. It serves as a discussion point or frame offering a prototype that Burke (1969a) argues, "sums up action" (p. 61) in accounting for the varieties of human nature or envisioning future conditions. Representative stories outline strategies for human responses to situations, or "equipment for living" (Burke, 1957, p. 262). Because they aim at collective understanding they are "sufficiently generalized to extend far beyond the particular combination of events named by them in any one instance" (Burke, 1957, p. 260). Burke (1969a) notes, "a given calculus must be supple and complex enough to be representative of the subject matter it is designed to calculate. It must have scope. Yet it must also possess simplicity, in that it is broadly a reduction of the subject matter" (p. 60).

The Iwo Jima image functions similarly in editorial cartoons. Visually, its compositional power can be likened to a kind of simplicity, which allows for recognizability of the abstract symbolic allusions we bring to the photograph from our understanding or knowledge of World War II. Yet the image also possesses sufficient complexity to be applicable to a wide variety of military and non-military subjects and is supple enough to withstand and accommodate frequent visual distortions and alterations. The anecdotal nature of the Iwo Jima flag-raising is not predominantly represented in the cartoons. Even for those five in our sample that implicitly or directly recall the history of Iwo Jima, the formal image is paramount, for rather than depict a specific moment of heroic achievement, they coalesce a set of abstracted attitudes about communal effort, patriotism, and militarism that transcend the facts of the event. The Iwo Jima image functions representatively in cartoons, then, not as anecdote, but as visual form.

The transcendence of the particular to a representation of the general is also outlined in Baty's concept of the representative character, extended from work by Robert Bellah, Richard Madsen, William Sullivan, Ann Swidler, and Steven Tipton (1985). In their construct, a person (character) is abstracted and elevated to the status of a cultural figure, and becomes a surface for the articulation of the political character, embodying cultural ideals. As Bellah et al. (1985) have described the concept,

> a representative character is more than a collection of individual traits or personalities. It is rather a public image that helps define, for a given group of people, just what kinds of personality traits it is good and legitimate to develop. A representative character provides an ideal, a point of reference and focus, that gives living expression to a vision of life (p. 39).

Like the Iwo Jima image, a representative character originates in actuality and specificity, but is abstracted into a symbol or concentrated image, and provides an explanatory model for human motive.

Baty further charts the process for how such a cultural figure comes to represent and articulate the political character. Rather than characterize these figures as static representations, Baty posits that they are "reconstructions that reveal the nature of conversations about the present even as they draw on materials from the past. . . . [They point] to inclusions and exclusions made in the greater construction of a national identity" (p. 49). For Baty, the representative character is a featured element of mass-mediated modes of remembering that reconstitute the space of politics each time they are invoked. Such representations help articulate the fast-paced space of politics, and "allow for building and expressing forms of community" (Baty, p. 41). At the same time, each invocation of a representative character adds to the definition of the character.

In a similar way, we would argue that each use of the Iwo Jima image, as parodied in editorial cartoons, contributes to the meaning of the image and to the way in which the image defines and constructs a political and ideological reality. Although the U.S. government singled out the surviving men depicted in Rosenthal's photograph as embodiments of heroic ideals, the specific individuals do not give the image its rhetorical force. For one thing, the personal stories of the flagmen are characterized by death and self-destruction as well as heroism. Moreover, their individual identities are obscured in the photograph in the cartoons. Again, the symbolic import of the total

visual form is representative, not indicative of the individual characters who are present in the visual form. In this sense, the form becomes abstracted, creating a new perception or concept that is grounded in the original meaning, while transcending it.[12] As Chris Jenks (1995) describes the process, "To abstract implies a removal, a drawing out from an original location, and an enforced movement of elements from one level to another. Abstraction, then, involves the transposition of worlds. . . . The new world, the created level, the (re)presentation, provides the potential arena for the manipulation and control of images. Images become infinitely malleable once freed from their original context, whilst still retaining significations within that original context" (p. 9).

The abstraction that allows for the Iwo Jima image's flexibility and applicability to various contexts creates new worlds of signification in what the Iwo Jima image represents. It also recalls the original context in some indirect, referential, and continuously reifying way, suggesting that the Iwo Jima image functions rhetorically as an ideograph, rather than an icon.

THE IWO JIMA IMAGE AS VISUAL IDEOGRAPH

In 1980 Michael C. McGee formulated the concept of ideographs—culturally-grounded, summarizing, and authoritative terms that enact their meaning by expressing an association of cultural ideals and experiences in an ever-evolving and reifying form within the rhetorical environment. An ideograph's meaning develops through its usages and applications, operating as an abstraction and a fragment within the larger rhetorical environment. McGee identifies ideographs as a word or group of words, such as "liberty" or "patriotism," that serve to rhetorically create communities according to ideological constraints and beliefs.[13] By stressing the role of language, McGee specifically confines the notion of the ideograph to the linguistic realm.

McGee's assumption that ideographs must be "actual words or terms" lacks a clear rationale (p. 8). While maintaining that ideology by necessity is always false and thereby rhetorical, he insists that the "clearest access to persuasion (and hence to ideology) is through the discourse used to produce it" (p. 5). He presumes that the relevant discourse must be "political language preserved in rhetorical documents," (p. 5) never addressing the potential inclusion (or exclusion) of nondiscursive forms.[14] Further, he argues that ideographs should be restricted to words because he rejects propositional logic to explain incidents of "social conflict, commitment, and control" (p. 6). McGee distinguishes between the use of terms and the ideas that become clouded through the use of those terms. Defining the ideograph as "language imperatives which hinder and perhaps make impossible pure thought" (p. 9), he again disregards the rhetorical potential of visual images. In the process, he limits the ideograph to the verbal rather than the visual realm.

McGee outlines four characteristics that constitute his formal definition of an ideograph. Based on an application of these characteristics, we argue that the Iwo Jima image, originally disseminated by governmental sources, is a "non-ideographic use" (p. 15) of the image. A review of recent popular history as represented through editorial cartoon depictions, however, reveals modern day usages of the Iwo Jima image do fall within the definitional and functional boundaries of the ideograph, the "language term" requirement notwithstanding. The image has become a discourse fragment that multiple publics appropriate for diverse purposes.

Ordinary Term in Political Discourse

McGee contends that the ideograph must be "an ordinary language term found in political discourse" (p. 15). He argues that ideographs in their ordinary sense garner much of their power precisely because they are not reserved for the political elite. They are "transcendent, as much an influence on the belief and behavior of the ruler as on the ruled" (p. 5). The artifacts which expose ideographs are not limited to academic treatises and documents recording the words of the nation's leadership. McGee suggests that critics examining a particular ideograph look to "popular history" (p. 11), such as novels, films, plays, songs, and grammar school history to trace the chronological expansions and contractions of such terms.

On one level, the Iwo Jima image does appear to qualify as "an ordinary image" (McGee, p. 15). Rosenthal's photo was widely published within days of Suribachi's capture. Government officials subsequently used both the photographic image and the surviving men depicted in it to nurture Americans' personal involvement in the war effort. Although the Iwo Jima image's power arguably evokes a narrative about heroism, the rank and file Marines' obscured faces and diverse backgrounds form a representation of the common citizen/warrior, enhancing the "ordinary" quality of the image.

Unlike the present day usage of the Iwo Jima image, however, the first mass dissemination of Rosenthal's photograph was reserved for the nation's leadership. The original photograph was a product of a liberalized censorship policy ordered by Admiral Kelly Turner in response to a Washington directive that the Navy pursue a more aggressive policy of press coverage related to Pacific Ocean military activities. After negotiating with the Associated Press to use the photograph as the official image of the flag-raising without cost, the Marines subsequently used the visual symbol for war bond drives and Marine recruiting. The photograph appeared on 3,500,000 posters and 15,000 panels, as recorded by Joe Rosenthal and W.C. Heinz (1955). On July 11, 1945, the federal government issued an official postage stamp bearing the image of the Iwo Jima flag-raising. The flag itself was treated as a national relic during the Seventh War Loan Drive (Albee & Freeman, 1995). While the early uses of the photograph, and subsequent monument, undoubtedly qualify as ordinary visual images with high public recognizability, neither garnered the power commensurate with regular use in political discourse by both elite and non-elite sources.

The use of the Iwo Jima image as visual material within the context of editorial cartoons, however, disseminates the ordinary visual image into both elite and non-elite public discourse. With access to national audiences, editorial cartoonists arguably have "as much influence on the belief and behavior of the ruler as on the ruled" (McGee, p. 5). William Gamson and David Stuart (1992) propose that the wide syndication of cartoons provides their creators with a national forum for addressing the public, and a segment of scholarship argues that such a forum has public influence.[15]

All of the cartoons using the Iwo Jima image parody aspects of political decision-making to some degree. Nearly one-third (17 of 53) of the cartoons we surveyed directly address political campaigns or public opinion on political issues. In one, Mike Luckovich (1995) transforms the soldiers of Iwo Jima into the New Hampshire primary challengers for the 1996 Republican Presidential nomination to parody the lack of unity evident in the GOP leadership (see Figure 3). Each candidate has an independent concern: Arlen Spector advocating a more centrist position, Pat Buchanan proclaiming even right-wing talk show hosts as liberal, Phil Gramm worried about his war record, and Bob Dole concerned about distancing himself from his past. In other cartoons by Doug Mariette (1994) and Bill Schorr (1995), the focus shifts to questioning the day-to-day decisions of the nation's chief executive. In these parodies, the cartoonists remove some soldiers from the image to signify military budget cutbacks. As these illustrations suggest, the Iwo Jima image has been appropriated from the exclusive control of the ruling elite to those who would parody the nation's leadership.

Abstraction Representing Collective Commitment

McGee's second characteristic of an ideograph is that it must be a "high-order abstraction representing collective commitment to a particular but equivocal and ill-defined normative goal" (p. 15). The abstraction is necessary to distinguish between those publics that fall within the social control motivated by the term and those that fall outside those parameters. The equivocal normative goal is necessary to ensure that the ideograph could never be empirically verifiable; the ambiguity allows the ideograph to be more inclusive of groups that might otherwise feel excluded.

As already argued, the compositional and symbolic representations of Rosenthal's original photograph constitute a visual abstraction reminiscent of the national unity required for success in war efforts. The use of a large amount of empty space in the background, the anonymity of the soldiers' faces, and the reliance on the flag as an icon for patriotism, all contribute to the Iwo Jima image as a form representing collective commitment to shared ideals.

The appeal to collective commitment embodied in Rosenthal's photograph also serves as an

Figure 3 "New Hampshire."

SOURCE: Mike Luckovich, *Atlanta Journal-Constitution.*

abstraction to "a particular but equivocal and ill-defined normative goal" (McGee, p. 15). Initially, the government used the photograph to serve as a public relations vehicle for celebrating the capture of the Japanese stronghold, and as the official symbol of the Seventh War Loan Drive. However, the symbolic interpretations of the image, as noted earlier, tapped into broader, inchoate notions of heroism, honor, and patriotism which proved transcendent, and permitted its force to expand beyond its utility for a given war effort, resulting in a broader public subscription to cultural ideals.

Within the context of editorial cartoons, the use of the Iwo Jima image retains the representative quality of collective commitment, while focusing that commitment towards equivocal and ill-defined normative goals. The use of the Iwo Jima image across our sample of editorial cartoons demonstrates the elasticity and abstractness of this image in its application. When applied to military contexts in editorial cartoons, the Iwo Jima image functions to comment on collective commitment required for a wide range of modern usages of the nation's armed forces. Where referring to humanitarian relief efforts such as Somalia, the United States flag is transformed into a bag of grain, a sack of food, or a spoon. When coupled with protracted ethnic struggles such as Bosnia, the rocky terrain of Mt. Suribachi is replaced with a swampy quicksand. In proposed military interventions that lack the full support of foreign citizenries, such as Haiti, the soldiers prop up Aristide rather than the Stars and Stripes.

The cartoons analyzed in our sample suggest that the image of Iwo Jima has come to represent collective commitment to normative goals that transcend the military environment. In a 1989 cartoon published in the *Los Angeles Times,* Paul Conrad replaces the terrain of Mt. Suribachi with the pinnacle of the U.S. Supreme Court Building, the soldiers with five of the nation's Supreme Court justices, and the intact United States flag with a half-burned United States flag. The caption on the cartoon reads: "Monument to the First Amendment." Here, Conrad uses the visual image of Iwo Jima to expose the irony of those who support a flag-burning amendment for patriotic reasons.

While the Iwo Jima image accommodates application to a wide array of political contexts, the precise normative goal being represented defies an easy explanation. Democracy, freedom, liberty, patriotism, military preparedness, and equality of opportunity are all components of the representation, but no single language term sums up the interpretations of the image. The Iwo Jima image, like its verbal counterparts, "liberty" and "patriotism," functions as "a high-order abstraction representing collective commitment to particular but equivocal and ill-defined goal" (McGee, p. 15).

Warrants Power/Guides Behavior

McGee maintains that an ideograph also "warrants the use of power, excuses behavior and belief which might otherwise be perceived as eccentric or antisocial, and guides behavior and belief into channels easily recognized by a community as acceptable and laudable" (p. 15). He dispels the widely-held notion that ideology is discussed as propositional logic in the public arena.

Even when Rosenthal's famous photograph first appeared in public forums, the use of the image was an attempt to warrant behavior that could be deemed as antisocial. Without an alternative frame in which to interpret the event, the public might have considered the large number of casualties that the military leadership was willing to sacrifice in the capture of Iwo Jima (6,281 dead; 19,217 wounded) to be unacceptable. Placed within the frame of collective, heroic effort embodied in Rosenthal's photograph, however, the battle of Iwo Jima—expressed metonymically through the Mt. Suribachi flag-raising—comes to represent the success that is achievable through collective sacrifice. Viewed from this perspective, the cost of military engagement becomes an indicator, if not evidence, for the acceptability of U.S. risk-taking during wartime.

In the context of contemporary editorial cartoons, the Iwo Jima image is used to parody governmental actions for the purpose of highlighting whether they are acceptable or antisocial in nature. Instead of guiding "behavior and belief into channels easily recognized by a community as acceptable and laudable," the parodied image functions to expose the "eccentric or antisocial" (McGee, p. 15). It further highlights unwarranted attempts by the government to call for collective sacrifice. Richard Morin (1990) provides an illustration in one of his cartoons printed during the Persian Gulf War (see Figure 4). Rather than climb the hilly terrain of Mt. Suribachi, the soldiers struggle along the oil fields of Saudi Arabia, an ally of the United States. Raising an oversized gas pump in place of the Stars and Stripes, the cartoon belittles the motivation for U.S. involvement in the Gulf War to be one of economic self-interest.

Repeatedly, editorial cartoonists manipulate the flag in the Iwo Jima image to parody the less than noble motivations that govern American society. Our sample reveals that cartoonists transform the flag into a dollar sign to symbolize the greed of those in the drug trade, into a campaign banner to underscore the political agenda of Gulf War supporters, into a gas tank or gas gauge to reveal the oil interests motivating U.S. military defense of Saudi Arabia, into a

poll indicator to signify the political agenda behind the invasion of Haiti, and into the figure of Aristide to expose the political motivations behind U.S. military intervention in Haiti. Rather than function as a subject of parody itself, in these cartoons the Iwo Jima image serves as a point of comparison for determining what is an "acceptable and laudable" use of governmental power (McGee, p. 15).

Culture-bound

The final characteristic McGee identifies for the ideograph is that it must be culture-bound. He insists that society's interactions with ideographs work to define and exclude groupings of the public. He claims that members who do not "respond appropriately to claims on their behavior warranted through the agency of ideographs" will experience societal penalties (pp. 15–16).

From the initial release of Rosenthal's photograph for public consumption, the Iwo Jima image came to represent the ideals of American culture. Karal Ann Marling and John Wetenhall

Figure 4 "PREMIUM."

SOURCE: Richard Morin, 1990. Reprinted with special permission of King Features Syndicate.

(1991) describe how the soldiers themselves contribute to cultural definition embodied in the image: "That the group indeed included a son of immigrants, an Indian, boys from the Midwest, the plains, the East, only confirmed the representative character of the image" (p. 9). In addition to reinforcing the American heritage of a melting pot of diverse cultures, the image of Iwo Jima relies on the American flag, the cultural icon of patriotism.

The use of irony in editorial cartoons makes the medium particularly suited to society's infliction of penalties on individuals who might ignore or misuse the ideograph. The question of society's tolerance of cultural diversity serves as an example. Bill Schorr (1993) uses the Iwo Jima image to expose the military's own intolerance for gender diversity. Instead of raising the flag, the grouped Marines harass a female recruit by peering under her skirt (see Figure 6). Schorr juxtaposes the military's current intolerance for diversity with the celebrated ideal of cultural heterogeneity embodied in the Iwo Jima image.

Perhaps the most obvious linkage of the Iwo Jima image to American culture involves a cartoon by Steve Benson for the *Arizona Republic* (1995). Above the visual image of the cartoon, a caption reads, "As the nation reflects, memories return of the opening day, the struggle in the sand, the deafening roar—and Americans ponder the things that, to them, matter most" (see Figure 6). In this case, though, it isn't the sand and roar of the heroic battlefield, but the playing field that "matters most" as our soldiers join together to raise a dominant symbol of American culture—the baseball bat.[16]

CONCLUSIONS

As a representative form, the parodied Iwo Jima image transcends its historical referents, gains meaning from its subsequent symbolic associations, and helps create and reaffirm the identity of the body politic through its ideographic functions. Like representative anecdotes and representative characters, such forms provide instructive perspectives on varied, multiple situations by summing up the culturally-defined essences of human motivations.

This conceptualization of representative form extends conventional interpretations of how visual images function within societal contexts. Rather than serve in an iconic relationship to a verbal referent, representative forms perform as visual ideographs. While our review of related literature uncovers no specific discussion of ideographs relative to visual forms, we do find implicit assumptions about the nature of the relationship. Like McGee, Osborn (1986, 1994) emphasizes the implicit verbal features of the ideograph by setting it apart from its companion construction—the icon. Osborn implicitly assigns a verbal quality to ideographs when he contrasts them with the concrete qualities of icons; ideographs and icons are positioned as rival terms, a view consistent with the commonplace definition of icon as picture representation.[17] Even though both the icon and the ideograph are culturetypes in Osborn's view, the terms are not interchangeable. To consider the icon as an embodiment of the ideograph is to establish a hierarchical relationship whereby the icon primarily illustrates that which is already linguistically manifested in the ideograph. The ideograph is more authoritative because it expresses a concept that an icon can only reconstruct through illustration.[18] Following this line of thought, the icon's relationship to the ideograph is circumvented; it can only redescribe and imitate the meaning of the ideograph, which *stands for* something. The ideograph, as a verbal expression, is privileged because language is often considered paradigmatic for meaning. Maria Mayenova (1981) typifies this view in

Figure 5 [No title]

SOURCE: Bill Schorr reprinted by permission of United Feature Syndicate, Inc.

AS THE NATION REFLECTS, MEMORIES RETURN OF THE OPENING DAY, THE STRUGGLE IN THE SAND, THE DEAFENING ROAR — AND AMERICANS PONDER THE THINGS THAT, TO THEM, MATTER MOST.

Figure 6   [No title]

SOURCE: By permission of Steve Benson and Creators Syndicate, Inc.

saying, "I regard iconic signs in general as being of a derivative, lame character, requiring verbal intervention" (p. 134). In this view, the icon may refer to the ideograph, but ideographs do not refer to icons, and must be preceded by language to obtain meaning.[19]

Osborn may have foreseen a stronger symbolic potential for icons in asserting "the *combination* of ideograph and icon may be especially potent in popular discourse, because it offers the virtues of both abstract and concrete rhetorical expression" (1994, p. 93). In the cartooned Iwo Jima image, we find these virtues coexistent and transcendent. We do not deny the denotative aspects of these visual parodies. We do propose, however, that the function of denotative representation associated with icons is a secondary feature of the totalized rhetorical function of these images. More significantly, the images are symbols realized as representative forms that transcend univocal denotative reference. Similarly, metaphor may operate as a presentational mechanism in these cartoons, but it is transcended as the source of rhetorical invention by the more abstract symbolic aspect of representative form.

Confirmation that certain visual images can function as ideographs, rather than be confined to the more restricted representational territory of icons, emerges in light of previous scholarship on repetitive form. Unlike recurrent forms operative in rhetorical genres, representative forms such as the parodied image of the Iwo Jima flag-raising transcend particular groupings of symbolic or rhetorical contexts. The situations prompting the use of the parodied Iwo Jima image are not wholly recurrent; instead they vary from military to political to entertainment contexts. Even the military-related themes span domestic and international arenas with subjects ranging from motives for war to questions of military policy and from actions by individual soldiers to the conduct of the media. Like McGee's example of equality, the parodied Iwo Jima image is "paramorphic, for even when the [image] changes its signification in particular circumstances, it retains a formal, categorical meaning, a constant reference to its history as an ideograph" (p. 10).

Our examination of the Iwo Jima image would readily concede that, in many cases, visual images bear an iconic relationship to the ideas they represent. If either the elite or the non-elite are influenced by the image exclusively, or the purposes of the image are clearly defined and unequivocal, or the image lacks the elasticity to accommodate meanings beyond its contextual specifics, the image fails to meet the requirements of the ideograph. Only in its appropriation does the influence of the image transcend the domain of the political elite to affect both the nation's leadership and its citizenry.

Appropriation and recontextualization appear to be central features of the transformation of visual images into representative forms. By choosing the situational context for the use of the image, the editorial cartoonist identifies the times and places that warrant ideological judgement. Like McGee's verbal ideographs, representative forms garner their meaning through the description they provide to situations.[20] Editorial cartoons present politicized contexts that, through satire, irony, and parody, motivate differing senses of community. The cartoonist can elevate actions through complementary comparison to the visual ideographs, i.e., equating humanitarian relief in Somalia to the valor of World War II by transforming the flag into a spoon feeding the hungry. Or, the parody can denigrate actions that fail to meet the moral standards established by the ideology, i.e., underscoring the economic rather than the moral justification for entering the Persian Gulf conflict by transforming the flag into a gas pump or gas gauge. By replacing the heroic Marines at Iwo Jima with distinctly unheroic businessmen or political operatives, or with wheelchair-bound soldiers suffering from war's less glorious effects, cartoonists provide an ironic counter-perspective that questions the boundaries of ideological concern.

Not only does the parodied context of a representative form identify the specific circumstances which inspire the ideology's application, it also draws attention to key elements of the ideology at issue. Cartoonists direct the audience's attention by the addition, omission, substitution, and/or distortion of visual elements. Changes made to the flag within the image, for example, can applaud or denounce the motivations used by the nation's leadership to call for collective effort. Manipulation of the Iwo Jima

servicemen can focus attention on who constitutes (or does not constitute) the cultural membership of the ideology. Alterations in the terrain of the Iwo Jima image can prompt the audience to consider the degree of sacrifice called for in the ideological application.

The ability of cartoonists to alter visual images arguably distinguishes the verbal from the visual ideograph. Unlike the verbal version, visual ideographs can appear to members of the culture in a variety of forms through the addition, omission, and distortion of their component elements. For the audience to respond to an image manifested in an array of forms, they must have a prior memory or recognition of the original. By comparing the cartoonist's rendition of the image to the memory of the original form, the audience can participate in the reinforcement of the ideograph's categorical meaning, and the creation of the expansions and contractions that result from its parodied contexts. Since words have a limited capacity for manipulation before their recognizability is lost, the opportunity for potential audience participation in the linguistic realm is comparatively small.

The comparative potentials of visual and verbal ideographs also relate to the ability of the visual realm to embody iconic images. A single language term usually lacks an iconic relationship between the letters of its makeup and a situational referent. Visual ideographs like the Iwo Jima image can embody icons such as the American flag to bolster tenets of the ideology at work. The inclusion of these icons can both constrain and expand the meaning of representative forms. Representative forms in parodied contexts, then, would appear to have persuasive potentials unavailable to their linguistic counterparts.

At this point we are unprepared to identify definitively other visual images that function ideographically as representative forms. Messaris (1994) has identified a small number of widely parodied, resonant images (such as Grant Wood's *American Gothic* and Flagg's "I Want You" poster of Uncle Sam) that might serve as a basis for future study of images that serve as representative forms. To Messaris's list we might add Mt. Rushmore and specific photographic records of the Vietnam War.

Although we agree with Mitchell (1994) that "visual experience. . . . might not be fully explicable on the model of textuality" (p. 16) and that visual images and language resist conflation, this study illuminates the value of considering visual images in light of existing rhetorical constructs and emphasizes the importance of continued attention to visual forms of rhetorical experiences. Rather than marginalizing visual studies within the communication discipline, as Sonja Foss (1992) warns is inevitable when visual images are compared with the properties of discursive symbols, we believe the case for the visual ideograph affirms the value of multi-strategic inquiry into rhetorical acts and artifacts.

NOTES

1. In this study, we define an editorial cartoon as a graphic presentation typically designed in a one-panel, non-continuing format to make an independent statement or observation on political events or social policy (as opposed to illustrating a written editorial). Such cartoons are a type of graphic art which regularly appear on newspaper editorial and op-ed pages, and which are typically created by a person employed on a newspaper staff, but may be distributed through syndication. We located fifty-eight editorial cartoons published between 1988 and 1996 which used the Iwo Jima image in reference to a current event or concern. Our sample consisted of cartoons collected from newspapers, from periodical and book collections of cartoons, and, in two cases, directly from a syndicate source, but all meet the above definitional criteria. In this essay, we use the terms "political cartoon" and "editorial cartoon" interchangeably.

2. In making the same point about the necessity of recognizable reference points, Medhurst and DeSousa (1981) identify literary/cultural allusions, political commonplaces, recognizable character traits, and situational factors as the "inventional storehouse" of cartoonists.

3. Despite the fame of Rosenthal's photograph, its contemporary recognition value is unclear, as those who would personally remember the events of World War II are replaced by those familiar only with collective memory. Messaris (1994), for example, in an informal survey of 29 college students, found that not quite half could accurately place the image in historical context. Similar results occurred in our own survey of 78 students responding to a cartoon version of the image, although we speculate recognition might be greater among an audience more representative of the general population in age distribution.

4. See, for example, a discussion of verbal icons in Leff and Sachs (1990), "Words the most like things: Iconicity and the rhetorical text;" and J.A. Campbell (1990), "Between the fragment and the icon: Prospect for a rhetorical house of the middle way" in *Western Journal of Communication* 54. In calling Rosenthal's photograph an "icon" we refer to the definition of icon as a highly symbolic, canonical, emblematic figure or object of uncritical devotion.

5. For example, Olson's (1987, 1990, 1991) investigation of iconic images such as political cartoons focused on early visual representations of the American colonies in artifacts of the historical moment.

6. The effort to claim the summit took four days, but by the time Rosenthal took his picture, the fighting was in hiatus. That Rosenthal photographed the *second* flag-raising is the crucial factor in controversies about the authenticity of the photograph. The facts of the two flag-raisings, and their photographic record, are recounted in detail in Albee and Freeman (1995), *Shadow of Suribachi: Raising the Flags on Iwo Jima,* and Thomey (1996), *Immortal Images: A Personal History of Two Photographs and the Flag-Raising on Iwo Jima.* Additionally, we drew historical information from accounts in Bertelsen (1989), Dart (1995), Marling & Wetenhall (1991), Rosenthal (1995), Rosenthal & Heinz (1995), and Ross (1986).

7. At least eleven photographs taken by six photographers, in addition to film shot by Bill Genaust, captured the two flag-raisings and the subsequent scene at Suribachi from a variety of perspectives. Rosenthal himself took two additional pictures at the summit that day.

8. The exact identity of the men remained uncertain for some time after Rosenthal's picture was published.

9. See, for example, Gregory and Lewis (1988) and Bertelsen (1989).

10. These subject categories include presidential campaigns and candidates as in (Edwards, 1997, 1995; DeSousa & Medhurst, 1982; Hill, 1984; Kenner-Muir, 1986; Sewell, 1993); other political figures (Bostdorff, 1987; DeSousa, 1984; Templin,

1995); religion (Sewell, 1987; Edwards, 1988); and wartime enemies (Edwards, 1993).

11. See, for example, (Bostdorff, 1987; DeSousa, 1984; Edwards, 1993, 1995, 1997; Hill, 1984; Kenner-Muir, 1986; DeSousa & Medhurst, 1982; Medhurst & DeSousa, 1981; Sewell, 1993; and Worth, 1981).

12. Fischer's (1995) analysis of the use of the Lincoln Monument in editorial cartoons also reflects the idea of a representative form, yet the centrality of Lincoln as an American figure retains aspects of the representative character, which would seem to impede the abstraction of the Lincoln Monument. In other respects, cartoonists' visual exploitation of the monument, as argued by Fischer, is conducted to ends similar to their use of the Iwo Jima image—it is held up as ideal against which lesser men are measured.

13. In this sense, they are similar to Weaver's (1953) and Burke's (1969b) articulation of "ultimate terms" which embody propositions through their place in a constellation of terms that progress sequentially.

14. Burke (1969b) provides a rationale for the potential of the visual ideograph in suggesting that nonverbal meanings take on the nature of words.

15. See also Bohrmann, Koester, and Bennett (1978), Langeveld (1981), and Root (1996).

16. The linkage between militarism and masculine sport may itself be revelatory of currents in American culture that substantiate the Iwo Jima image as a meaningful ideograph. For discussions of the intersections of masculine culture and paramilitarism, especially during the time frame when our sampled cartoons were published, see L.E. Boose (1993) and J.W. Gibson (1994).

17. Argan (1980), J.A. Campbell (1990), Mitchell (1986), Olson (1983), and Steakley (1983) employ the term "icon" in this sense.

18. Gombrich (1963) echoes Osborn's interpretation of the relationship between language and image when he specifically says of cartoons that they are "merely [the tangible expression] of what language has prepared" (p. 128).

19. The view that pictures can only have meaning through their illustrations of words is common, particularly in the realm of photography theory, but it has been challenged by Barthes (1977), who maintained that an image may function as the principle message which is rationalized by words.

20. J.A. Campbell (1990) maintains that we come to understand the rhetorical function of ideographs through their performances, as they "enact what they mean" (p. 367).

REFERENCES

Albee, P.B., Jr. & Freeman, K.C. (1995). *Shadow of Suribachi: Raising the flags on Iwo Jima.* Westport, CT: Praeger.

Argan, G.C. (1980). Ideology and iconology (R. West, Trans.) In W.J.T. Mitchell (Ed.), *The language of images* (pp. 15–23). Chicago: University of Chicago Press.

Astor, D. (1993, Summer/Fall). Jack and Joel hack the hackneyed. *The Association of American Editorial Cartoonists Notebook,* 12–13.

Barthes, R. (1977). The photographic message. *Image—music—text* (S. Heath, Trans.). New York: Hill and Wang.

Baty, S.P. (1995). *American Monroe: The making of a body politic.* Berkeley, CA: University of California Press.

Bellah, R.N., Madsen, R., Sullivan, W.M., Swidler, A., & Tipton, S.M. (1985). *Habits of the heart: Individualism and commitment in American life.* Berkeley, CA: University of California Press.

Benson, S. (1995, February). [Cartoon]. *Arizona Republic.*

Bertelsen, L. (1989). Icons on Iwo. *Journal of Popular Culture, 2,* 79–95.

Bohrmann, E.G., Koester, J., & Bennett, J. (1978). Political cartoons and salient rhetorical fantasies: An empirical analysis of the '76 presidential campaign. *Communication Monographs, 45,* 317–329.

Boose, L.E. (1993). Techno-muscularity and the boy eternal. In M. Cooke & A. Woollacott (Eds.), *Gendering war talk* (pp. 67–106). Princeton, NJ: Princeton University Press.

Bostdorff, D.M. (1987). Making light of James Watt: A Burkean approach to the form and attitude of political cartoons. *Quarterly Journal of Speech, 73,* 43–59.

Brummett, B. (1984). Burke's representative anecdote as a method in media criticism. *Critical Studies in Mass Communication, 7,* 161–176.

Burke, K. (1969a). *A grammar of motives.* Berkeley, CA: University of California Press.

Burke, K. (1969b). *A rhetoric of motives.* Berkeley, CA: University of California Press.

Burke, K. (1957). *The philosophy of literary form: Studies in symbolic action.* (Revised Edition) New York: Vintage Books.

Campbell, J.A. (1990). Between the fragment and the icon: Prospect for a rhetorical house of the middle way. *Western Journal of Communication, 54,* 346–376.

Campbell, K.K. & Jamieson, K.H. (1978). *Form and genre: Shaping rhetorical action.* Falls Church, VA: Speech Communication Association.

Conrad, P. (1989 June). [Cartoon]. *Los Angeles Times,* p. B7.

Dart, B. (1995, February 20). "Grateful" nation thanks survivors of Iwo Jima. *Atlanta Journal-Constitution,* p. 16.

DeSousa, M.A. (1984). Symbolic action and pretended insight: The Ayatollah Khomeini in U.S. editorial cartoons. In M.J. Medhurst & T.W. Benson (Eds.), *Rhetorical dimensions in media: A critical casebook* (pp. 204–230). Dubuque, IA: Kendall/Hunt.

DeSousa, M.A. & Medhurst, M.J. (1982). Political cartoons and American culture: Significant symbols of campaign 1980. *Studies in Visual Communication, 8,* 84–97.

Edwards, J.L. (1988). Keepers of the flame: Rhetorical themes in recent editorial cartoons on religion. Paper presented at the Eastern Communication Association, Baltimore, MD.

Edwards, J.L. (1993). Metaphors of enmity in Gulf War political cartoons. *Ohio Speech Journal, 30,* 62–75.

Edwards, J.L. (May, 1995). Wee George and the seven dwarfs: Caricature and metaphor in campaign '88 cartoons. *INKS Cartoon and Comic Art Studies,* 26–34.

Edwards, J.L. (1997). *Political cartoons in the 1988 presidential campaign: Image, metaphor, and narrative.* New York: Garland.

Fischer, R.A. (1990). The Lucifer legacy: Boss Tweed and Richard Nixon as generic sleaze symbols in cartoon art. *Journal of American Culture, 13,* 1–19.

Fischer, R.A. (1995, February). The "monumental" Lincoln as an American cartoon convention. *INKS Cartoon and Comic Art Studies,* 12–25.

Fischer, R.A. (1996). *Them damned pictures: Explorations in American political cartoon art.* North Haven, CT: Archon Books.

Forceville, C. (1996). *Pictorial metaphor in advertising.* London: Routledge.

Foss, S. (1992). Visual imagery as communication. *Text and Performance Quarterly, 12,* 85–96.

Fussell, P. (1982). *The boy scout handbook and other observations.* New York: Oxford University Press.

Gamson, W.A. & Stuart, D. (1992, March). Media discourse as a symbolic contest: The bomb in political cartoons. *Sociological Forum,* 55–86.

Gibson, J.W. (1994). *Warrior dreams: Violence and manhood in post-Vietnam America.* New York: Hill & Wang.

Goldberg, V. (1991). *The power of photography.* New York: Abbeville Press.

Gombrich, E.H. (1963). *Meditations on a hobby-horse.* Chicago: University of Chicago Press.

Gombrich, E.H. (1996). Aims and limits of iconology. In R. Woodfield (Ed.), *The essential Gombrich* (pp. 457–484). London: Phaidon Press Limited.

Gregory, S.W., Jr. & Lewis, J.M. (1988, Fall). Symbols of collective memory: The social process of memorializing May 4, 1970, at Kent State University. *Symbolic Interaction,* 213–233.

Guimond, J. (1991). *American photography and the American dream.* Chapel Hill, NC: University of North Carolina Press.

Hatcher, E.P. (1974). *Visual metaphors: A methodological study in visual communication.* Albuquerque, NM: University of New Mexico Press.

Hausman, C.R. (1989). *Metaphor and art: Interactionism and reference in the verbal and nonverbal arts.* New York: Cambridge University Press.

Hill, A. (1984). The Carter campaign in retrospect: Decoding the cartoons. In M.J. Medhurst & T.W. Benson (Eds.), *Rhetorical dimensions in media: A critical casebook* (pp. 182–203). Dubuque, IA: Kendall/Hunt.

Jenks, C. (Ed.). (1995). *Visual Culture.* London: Routledge.

Kaplan, S.J. (1990). Visual metaphor in the representation of communication technology. *Critical Studies in Mass Communication, 7,* 37–47.

Kaplan, S.J. (1992). A conceptual analysis of form and content in visual metaphors. *Communication, 13,* 197–209.

Kenner-Muir, J. (1986). *Political cartoons and synecdoche: A rhetorical analysis of the 1984 Presidential campaign.* Unpublished doctoral dissertation, University of Massachusetts, Amherst.

Kress, G. and van Leeuwen, T. (1996). *Reading images: The grammar of visual design.* London: Routledge.

Langeveld, W. (1981). Political cartoons as a medium of political communication. *International Journal of Political Education, 4,* 343–371.

Leary, K. and Nolte, C. (1995, February 19). The shot of a lifetime. *San Francisco Chronicle,* Sunday section, p. 3.

Leff, M. and Sachs, A. (1990). Words the most like things: Iconicity and the rhetorical text. *Western Journal of Speech Communication, 54,* 252–273.

Lester, P.M. (1995). *Visual communication: Images with messages.* Belmont, CA: Wadsworth Publishing Company.

Luckovitch, M. (1995). [Cartoon]. *The Atlanta Constitution.*

Mariette, D. (1994, Winter). [Cartoon]. *Notebook of the AAEC, 25.*

Marling, K.A. & Wetenhall, J. (1991). *Iwo Jima: Monuments, memories, and the American hero.* Cambridge, MA: Harvard University Press.

Mayenova, M.R. (1981). Verbal texts and iconic-visual texts. In W. Steiner (Ed.), *Image and code* (pp. 133–137). University of Michigan.

McGee, M.C. (1980). The "ideograph": A link between rhetoric and ideology. *Quarterly Journal of Speech, 66,* 1–16.

Medhurst, M.J. and DeSousa, M.A. (1981). Political cartoons as rhetorical form: A taxonomy of graphic discourse. *Communication Monographs, 48,* 197–236.

Messaris, P. (1994). *Visual "literacy": Image, mind, and reality.* Boulder, CO: Westview Press.

Messaris, P. (1997). *Visual persuasion: The role of images in advertising.* Thousand Oaks: SAGE Publications.

Mitchell, W.J.T. (1986). *Iconology: Image, text, ideology.* Chicago: University of Chicago Press.

Mitchell, W.J.T. (1994). *Picture theory: Essays on verbal and visual representation.* Chicago: University of Chicago Press.

Morin, R. (1990, August 20). [Cartoon]. *Political Pix.*

Olson, L.C. (1983). Portraits in praise of a people: A rhetorical analysis of Norman Rockwell's icons in Franklin D. Roosevelt's "Four Freedoms" campaign. *Quarterly Journal of Speech, 69,* 15–24.

Olson, L.C. (1987). Benjamin Franklin's pictorial representations of the British colonies in America: A study in rhetorical iconology. *Quarterly Journal of Speech, 73,* 18–42.

Olson, L.C. (1990). Benjamin Franklin's commemorative medal, *Libertas Americana:* A study in rhetorical iconology. *Quarterly Journal of Speech, 76,* 23–45.

Olson, L.C. (1991). *Emblems of American community in the revolutionary era: A study in rhetorical iconology.* Washington, D.C.: Smithsonian Institute Press.

Osborn, M. (1986). Rhetorical depiction. In H.W. Simons & A.A. Aghazian (Eds.), *Form, genre, and the study of political discourse* (pp. 79–107). Columbia, SC: University of South Carolina Press.

Osborn, M. (1994). The invention of rhetorical criticism in my work. In W.L. Nothstine, C. Blair, & G.C. Copeland (Eds.), *Critical questions: Invention, creativity, and the criticism of discourse and media* (pp. 82–94). New York: St. Martin's Press.

Renault, D. (1993, January 27). [Cartoon]. *Sacramento Bee,* p. B6.

Roeder, G., Jr. (1993). *The censored war: American visual experience during World War Two.* New Haven, CT: Yale University Press.

Root, J.R. (1996). *Is a picture worth a thousand words? A methodological study of political cartoons.* Unpublished doctoral dissertation, University of Houston, Texas.

Rosenthal, J. (1995, May 31). [Telephone interview with author].

Rosenthal, J. & Heinz, W.C. (1955). The picture that will live forever. *Collier's Magazine.* 18 Feb, pp. 62–67.

Ross, B.D. (1986). *Iwo Jima: Legacy of Valor.* New York: Vintage Books, 1986.

Schorr, B. (1993, February 7). [Cartoon]. *The Sacramento Bee,* p. Forum 5.

Schorr, B. (1994). [Cartoon]. In C. Brooks (Ed.), *Best editorial cartoons of the year, 1994 edition,* (p. 8). Gretna, LA: Pelican Publishing Company.

Schorr, B. (1995, July 23). [Cartoon]. *San Francisco Examiner & Chronicle,* p. 8.

Sewell, E.H. (1987). Exorcism of fools: Images of the televangelist in editorial cartoons. In M. Fishwick & R.B. Brown (Eds.), *The God pumpers: Religion in the electronic age* (pp. 46–59). Bowling Green, OH: Bowling Green State University Popular Press.

Sewell, E.H. (1993). Editorial cartoon images of Bill Clinton in the 1992 Presidential campaign. Paper presented at the meeting of the Speech Communication Association, Miami, FL.

Stayskal. (1995, March). [Cartoon]. *Tampa Tribune.*

Steakley, J.D. (1983). Iconography of a scandal: Political cartoons and the Eulenburg affair. *Studies in Visual Communication, 9,* 20–51.

Templin, C. (1995). The political cartoon and the President's wife: Bashing Hillary. Paper presented at the meeting of the International

Society for Humor Studies, Birmingham, England.

Thomey, T. (1996). *Immortal images: A personal history of two photographers and the flag-raising on Iwo Jima.* Annapolis, MD.: Naval Institute Press.

Weaver, R. (1953). *The ethics of rhetoric.* Chicago: Henry Regency.

Worth, S. (1981). *Studying visual communication.* L. Gross (Ed.). Philadelphia: University of Pennsylvania Press.

7

REPRODUCING CIVIL RIGHTS TACTICS

The Rhetorical Performances of the Civil Rights Memorial

CAROLE BLAIR AND NEIL MICHEL

Perhaps the very first thing we need to do as a nation and as individual members of society is to confront our past and see it for what it is. It is a past that is filled with some of the ugliest possible examples of racial brutality and degradation in human history. We need to recognize it for what it was and is and not explain it away, excuse it, or justify it. Having done that, we should then make a good-faith effort to turn our history around so that we can see it in front of us, so that we can avoid doing what we have done for so long.

—Franklin 74

What seems called for now and what many contemporary artists wish to provide is a critical *public art that is frank about the contradictions and violence encoded in its own situation, one that dares to awaken a public sphere of resistance, struggle, and dialogue.*

—Mitchell 395

The Civil Rights Memorial, located in Montgomery, Alabama, and dedicated in 1989, enjoyed its tenth anniversary this past November. The Memorial was commissioned by, and composes the front entrance plaza of, the Southern Poverty Law Center (SPLC), a not-for-profit organization founded in 1971 by Morris Dees and Joe Levin.[1] The Memorial was designed by Maya Lin, the architect best known for her design of the Vietnam Veterans Memorial, in Washington, D.C.[2] Although the Civil Rights Memorial is located in Montgomery, and thus

SOURCE: Blair, C., & Michel, N. (2000). Reproducing civil rights tactics: The rhetorical performances of the Civil Rights Memorial. *Rhetoric Society Quarterly (RSQ), 30*(2), 31–55. Taylor & Francis.

removed from the most well-worn tourist trails of the nation, it has received considerable attention in the media, because of events that have been staged at its site, the fame of its designer, and the high public profile of the SPLC and Dees since the mid-1980s (*Southern Poverty Law Center*). It is an important cultural marker not only because of the attention it has received, but also because of its rhetoric—its representations and enactments of racial dynamics of the past, present, and future.

Our goal is to offer a reading of the Civil Rights Memorial as a rhetorical performance, or more precisely, as an ensemble of interrelated performances that rewrite the Civil Rights Movement of the 1950s and 1960s for the late twentieth-century U.S.[3] Specifically, we will suggest that the Memorial's rhetorical performances reproduce the tactics of Civil Rights activities of the mid-century, but that these re-productions work toward a commentary on race issues of the present and open up possibilities for politics, rather than advancing a summary or unitary stance. Our reading is based not only upon an interpretation of the Memorial's design (including its inscribed text) but also upon its contexts.[4]

Our focus here on the Civil Rights Memorial is motivated, in part, by Daniel Abramson's claim that Maya Lin's memorials (the Vietnam Veterans Memorial, the Women's Table at Yale University, and the Civil Rights Memorial) harbor fundamentally conservative political messages, largely as a result of what he sees as their shared central feature—inscribed timelines. Although allowing for the possibility of reading the Lin memorials as "potentially transformative," Abramson clearly favors a different interpretation. He suggests rather disparagingly that Maya Lin's memorials "repackage the difficult, the divisive, and the controversial into loci of popular satisfaction and conciliation" (705); represent a "conservative position" on 1960s political, social, and artistic movements; and "reestablish points of traditional authority" (707). Specifically with regard to the Civil Rights Memorial, he suggests that "the civil rights struggle is represented as being, in effect, about the authority and legitimacy of the American Constitution and its legal and political instruments (an appropriate program for a monument sponsored by a law firm)" (701).[5] However, we are convinced that a rhetorical reading—one

that attends not only to multiple design features of the Memorial, but also to its material performances and force within its context(s)—suggests a conclusion quite different than that rendered in Abramson's more formalist reading.

We believe it is important to heed and respond to Abramson's reading for three reasons. First, critical commentary is one means by which "the" meaning of a public artwork is established culturally (Foucault, "Discourse" 220–221). That is, interpretations like Abramson's (or our own) can be appropriated and used in more public, if often unofficial, interpretive operations. They seep into public discourse and become "correct" ways of reading cultural artifacts or sites. We believe it would be unfortunate if Abramson's rendering were taken as the final word on the Civil Rights Memorial.

Second, in considering what Abramson's reading overlooks—vital dimensions of the Civil Rights Memorial that participate in composing its political message—we can attend to issues of materiality in rhetoric that are becoming increasingly salient.[6] Abramson suggests, inexplicably in our view, that "the physical composition of the monument functions not so much to convey meaning in and of itself as to create a physical space of reading. . . . It is left to the text itself and its graphic arrangement to convey the specific message of the memorial" (692). By "text," Abramson clearly means the inscriptions on the stone of the Memorial, so his reading acknowledges but leaves uninterpreted the physical profile and spatial dimensions of the Memorial.

Abramson also neglects the specific operations of the geographical/cultural contexts of the Memorial. Left aside are the Memorial's physical locale, the historical events it marks, and its placement in a national culture saturated by racial anxiety. To read the Lin memorials "as a suite of work" (680) seems a worthy project, but that move necessarily shifts the critical stakes from the rhetorical work each monument does to Maya Lin's signature political aesthetic. In sum, to juxtapose Abramson's reading and the one we propose here is to call attention to issues of rhetorical materiality at two levels: (1) the material conditions, contexts, and other discourses that articulate with a given rhetorical artifact, and (2) the materiality of the rhetorical artifact itself (Blair 16). If we wish to understand the messages available in the Civil Rights Memorial, it surely is wise to heed Abramson's claims but also to add to them, for there is much more to attend and respond to in this important cultural site than a timeline that teaches a conservative lesson.

Third, we believe a closer look at the Memorial and ways of reading it are warranted because of the specifics of its response to one of the most profound rhetorical challenges faced in the design of any commemorative site: how to make an event of the past—what the memorial marks—relevant to the needs and desires of the memorial's own present. That is a profoundly rhetorical challenge, and an understanding of its dynamic is unavailable in a formalist reading that bases its claims exclusively on the engraved words on a memorial.[7] Abramson's claims about the Memorial participate in a larger discourse that questions whether public art—specifically public commemorative art—can ever perform a rhetorical function beyond stabilization and reinforcement of the status quo (Abramson 709).[8] If we answer with Abramson's (only delicately qualified) "no," then we are faced with a very serious rhetorical matter: a genre that offers no openings for difference or resistance. We find that not only unlikely but inaccurate in the case of public commemorative art.

We will begin with a brief discussion of the micropolitics of the Southern Civil Rights Movement, in order to highlight its tactical-level practices. Then we will turn to a descriptive "tour" of the Civil Rights Memorial site, followed by a discussion of its performative reproduction of the Movement's tactics. We will conclude with a reconsideration of the political messages harbored by the Memorial, suggesting that it enacts the kind of political stance suggested by Franklin and Mitchell in the passages that stand at the beginning of this essay.

Tactical Dimensions of Civil Rights Protest Actions

The sit-ins and protest marches of the 1950s and 1960s Civil Rights Movement surely were multidimensional in their rhetorical character and capacity, but the specifically tactical nature of

these actions carried particular messages that helped to compose the larger Civil Rights position. Our aim in describing them here is not encyclopedic but selective, not exhaustive but partial. Instead of focusing on what the protest rhetoric *meant,* we examine its material dimension—what it *did.* Specifically, these protest actions disrupted (peacefully) the ordinary activities of towns, businesses, and citizens. They also announced the resilience and determination of those pledged to civil rights. And they situated the individual observer as the agent of change, by placing their cause—and the often cruel counter-reaction—visually and materially in the space of the everyday.[9]

First, Civil Rights actions—sit-ins especially, but also boycotts and marches—infringed upon or inconvenienced the space of the everyday, of "business as usual," so as to call attention to the participants and their political and moral claims to justice. King described the tactical dimension explicitly in his "Letter from Birmingham City Jail," in 1963: "Nonviolent direct action seeks to create such a crisis and establish such creative tension that a community that has constantly refused to negotiate is forced to confront the issue" (40).[10] The point was to get in the way. As Chalmers suggests, "The later experiences of SNCC in Mississippi and in southwestern Georgia, where it was joined in Albany by King and the SCLC in 1962, strongly indicated that 'out of the streets' was 'out of mind'" (23). To counter that tendency, Civil Rights groups enacted a material politics, "the use of the 'black body' against prejudice" (Rustin 337).[11]

Second, the protests announced the determination of their participants, and they did that by persevering over time. This display of tenacity was vital, for as Chong argues, any breach in the visible exposition of resolve would send "an encouraging signal to the opposition and [harm] the interests of the group" (18). The activists' determination had to be overtly maintained, sometimes for weeks or months, often in the face of taunts, harassment, and beatings, as well as threats of arrest or even death. The performance of such resolute purpose served as a demonstrative proof that the activists would not be discouraged easily, that they and their cause would not just conveniently disappear. But their maintenance of the collective front in the face of brutal opposition reinforced that argument, serving notice that the demonstrators would not be intimidated, because their cause was so consequential.

Third, the Civil Rights Movement in the South sought change by moralizing the individual and positioning her/him as the agent of change. There is no doubt that the Movement sought governmental and legal remedy; Civil Rights leaders worked directly to persuade those in positions of institutional authority, e.g., presidents, congresspersons, governors, local officials, and so forth.[12] But the visible, public organizing was aimed at the quotidian, and the aim was not just to persuade voters to pressure officials, but also to change themselves. As James Lawson argued with regard to sit-ins,

> the issue is not integration. . . . [I]t would be extremely short-sighted to assume that integration is the problem or the word of the "sit-in." In the first instance, we who are demonstrators are trying to raise what we call the "moral issue." That is, we are pointing to the viciousness of racial segregation and prejudice and calling it evil or sin. The matter is not legal, sociological or racial, it is moral and spiritual. (312)

The sacrifice and suffering endured by the demonstrators were considered (and were, in some quarters) influential. As King argued, "Suffering . . . has tremendous educational and transforming possibilities" ("Pilgrimage" 110). Or, as Chong suggests in less manifestly moral terms, "From the protesters' perspective, it is obvious that their best outcome is realized when they choose nonviolence while the authorities use unjustified force. A nonviolent strategy works only if the protesters are seen as blameless victims" (22).

Each of these tactics worked by means of a visual performance or display. The material presence and visibility of the demonstrators, as well as of their opponents, was the crucial element. The Civil Rights Movement disrupted, displayed its own resolve, and moralized individuals as change agents by compelling shifts in attitudes based on the seen. For example, the neatly-dressed, polite African American demonstrators were visible, as were their often brutish, white supremacist opponents. The visual juxtaposition reversed historically accreted, stereotypical images of African and European Americans and their relative abilities to engage civilly. As Cmiel

argues, "the boycotts, sit-ins, and marches were strategic dramas outside the purview of daily decorum that inverted the social order. Whereas the caste system of the South had been built on the supposed superior 'civilization' of whites and the 'backwardness' of blacks, the [protest activities] turned this around" (267). While Movement leaders and lawyers argued the case, the demonstrations created scenes for performing it.

THE CIVIL RIGHTS MEMORIAL

Before turning to the Civil Rights Memorial's reproduction of these Movement tactics, a brief tour of the site is in order. The Memorial is located in downtown Montgomery, on the plaza fronting the SPLC office building, a modern white and mirrored glass structure. The Memorial and the SPLC are perched on the side of a hill. Occupying the hilltop behind them is an imposing, palatial structure—the Alabama Center for Commerce. It towers above the Law Center and dwarfs it and the much smaller Memorial. The relative sizes of the three structures are exaggerated by their occupancy of different elevations on the hillside (Figure 1).

The Memorial, the smallest and most proximate of the three, as one ascends the hill, is composed of two structures. The first is a peculiar black granite structure, an inverted, asymmetrical, conical pedestal, 31 inches in height and twelve feet in diameter (Figure 2). From a distance, this piece resembles a teacup minus a handle, but Lin and the SPLC refer to it as a "table" (see Abramson 689n; and *Southern Poverty Law Center*). While its structure is asymmetrical, its top surface is a perfect circle (Figure 3). From an off-center well on the tabletop flows water that spreads smoothly and evenly over the full surface, falls over its edge and disappears down a small drain at the bottom of the base. The water flows over inscriptions arranged in a circle around the circumference of the tabletop.

The 53 inscriptions mark events of the 1950s and 1960s, forming an annular timeline (see Figure 3). The majority (32) of the inscriptions name *forty individuals and the circumstances of their deaths*. Few of these individuals, with the exceptions of Medgar Evers and Martin Luther King, Jr., were public figures; most achieved public prominence only in death, if even then.[13]

Figure 1   Civil Rights Memorial, Montgomery, Alabama.

SOURCE: Neil Michel/Axiom.

Figure 2   Civil Rights Memorial, Montgomery, Alabama.

SOURCE: Neil Michel/Axiom.

Most were murdered in retaliation for their participation in nonviolent activism, or in attempts to obstruct advances of the Civil Rights Movement. Others' deaths energized further activism (Zinsser 28, 36). For example, included among the inscriptions are these:

28 AUG 1955 • EMMETT LOUIS TILL • YOUTH MURDERED FOR SPEAKING TO WHITE WOMAN • MONEY, MS.

25 SEP 1961 • HERBERT LEE • VOTER REGISTRATION WORKER KILLED BY WHITE LEGISLATOR • LIBERTY, MS

15 SEP 1963 • ADDIE MAE COLLINS • DENISE MCNAIR • CAROLE ROBERTSON

Figure 3   Civil Rights Memorial, Montgomery, Alabama.

SOURCE: Neil Michel/Axiom.

• CYNTHIA WESLEY • SCHOOLGIRLS KILLED IN BOMBING OF 16TH ST. BAPTIST CHURCH • BIRMINGHAM, AL

The remaining 21 inscriptions—irregularly and infrequently punctuating the murders—tell of various Civil Rights related events during the same period. Seven of these chronicle organizing activities of the Movement, for example:

5 DEC 1955 • MONTGOMERY BUS BOYCOTT BEGINS

1 FEB 1960 • BLACK STUDENTS STAGE SIT-IN AT "WHITES ONLY" LUNCH COUNTER • GREENSBORO, NC

Nine others report legal remedies or advances secured by the Movement, for example:

24 SEP 1957 • PRESIDENT EISENHOWER ORDERS FEDERAL TROOPS TO ENFORCE SCHOOL DESEGREGATION • LITTLE ROCK, AR

9 JUL 1965 • CONGRESS PASSES VOTING RIGHTS ACT OF 1965

And the remaining five tell of setbacks or obstructionist reactions, for instance:

14 MAY 1961 • FREEDOM RIDERS ATTACKED IN ALABAMA WHILE TESTING COMPLIANCE WITH BUS DESEGREGATION LAWS

3 MAY 1963 • BIRMINGHAM POLICE ATTACK MARCHING CHILDREN WITH DOGS AND FIRE HOSES

The chronology begins with the 1954 Brown v. Board of Education decision that mandated school desegregation. And it ends with Dr. Martin Luther King, Jr.'s assassination, in 1968. Between these first and last entries is a noticeable blank space (see Figure 3), that instructs visitors where to begin their reading. The second structure, but likely the first one that catches the view of the visitor, is a convex curved, black granite wall, approximately nine feet tall and forty feet long, with water rushing down its face at waterfall speed (Figure 4). It bears a single inscription: " . . . UNTIL JUSTICE ROLLS DOWN LIKE WATERS AND RIGHTEOUS-NESS LIKE A MIGHTY STREAM. —MARTIN LUTHER KING, JR." This wall forms a lower level façade for the SPLC office building, behind the table in the plaza area. To the side of the wall is an arced stairway up to the entrance of the SPLC. The stairway is roped off; only Center employees and others with business with the SPLC are allowed to ascend the stairs. Those few who are permitted up to the second level see a different view of the wall. Forming the area immediately above the wall is an absolutely still pool of water standing on uninscribed black granite (Figure 5). The Civil Rights Memorial is a remarkably complex commemorative rhetoric. Its design components, e.g., color, shape, size, and inscriptions, combine and recombine with its contexts to create a web of multiple performances, spectacles that both reproduce and transform historically the tactics of the Civil Rights movement. We turn our attention to those now.

Figure 4 Civil Rights Memorial, Montgomery, Alabama.

SOURCE: Neil Michel/Axiom.

Figure 5 Civil Rights Memorial, Montgomery, Alabama.

SOURCE: Neil Michel/Axiom.

A READING OF THE PERFORMATIVE RHETORIC OF THE CIVIL RIGHTS MEMORIAL

As with our discussion of the Civil Rights Movement, our focus on the Memorial attends less to issues of symbolism than to materialism. That is, we concentrate here on the performative dimension of the site, attending to what it does (Pollock 21).[14] We are more interested here in its enactments than its representations, for the Memorial seems a perfect exemplar of Della Pollock's suggestion that performance "discomposes history as myth, making of it a scene awaiting intervention by the performing subject" (27).

Like the Movement it commemorates, the Civil Rights Memorial disrupts and infringes on public space. The Memorial itself now is the "black body" positioned so as to create dislocation, tension, and (minor) inconvenience. The Memorial's table structure interrupts the sidewalk and the vector of pedestrian action along it (see Figure 2). To walk in a straight line is to run headlong into the table, so the pedestrian is confronted with the choice of attending to, even engaging with, the Memorial or to go out of her/his way to avoid doing so. To engage with it is to be drawn into its narrative, to touch its historical re-creation, and to be cooled by the feel of the water. It "troubles" the pedestrian just enough to command her/his attention and at least some degree of involvement.

The Memorial infringes in a less individuated way as well. Its location in downtown Montgomery places it in a position of overt challenge to most of the landmarks in the area.[15] Except for the King Memorial Baptist Church on Dexter Avenue and a few small signs, there are few prominent markers in the area of anything but the glories of the Confederacy and the more contemporary white establishment. Within easy walking distance are the beautifully preserved and lovingly tended first White House of the Confederacy, where Jefferson Davis resided for the first couple of months after secession; the Confederate Soldiers Monument, on the State Capitol grounds; the star embedded on the steps of the Capitol where Davis stood to deliver the declaration of secession; a historical marker at the end of Dexter Avenue commemorating the first rendition of "Dixie"; a statue of Jefferson Davis on the Capitol grounds; the preserved interior areas of the Capitol where the secession debates were held; and the state's Center for Commerce, best characterized, we believe, as a monument to the state's economic/political icons.

The Civil Rights Memorial disrupts this cityscape performatively, intruding upon the otherwise rather unitary character of Montgomery's other symbolic spaces (Carr, et al. 187–191, 294). It does so serenely and with dignity, but assertively; the Memorial calls attention to the cityscape it infringes by projecting images of the city in its refractive wall. This wall does not, like its famous predecessor in Washington, simply reflect the images of those present in the area that constitutes the Memorial's space. Although one might catch images of oneself, those images are vague. Much clearer are scenes from outside the plaza area. The convex curve of the wall bends light, poaching those scenes from outside and incorporating them. And it appropriates and involves those who take no action to attend to it and even those who go out of their way to avoid it.

The Civil Rights Memorial also reproduces the mid-century Civil Rights protests' announcement of resolve. It is small and appears even more diminutive against the backdrop of the gigantic Alabama Center for Commerce (see Figure 1). But it stands solidly, even determinedly, in the midst of what can be described only as an inhospitable symbolic context, "headlining" in its inscribed text the extraordinary efforts of ordinary people in securing the most basic of human rights. It displays their dedicated efforts as ongoing and resolute, even when attended by the risk of violent obstruction and murder. But the Memorial does more than represent those past actions; it reproduces them. The Memorial stands in the entrance plaza of its patron, the Southern Poverty Law Center, whose office building was constructed on this site in the aftermath of a firebombing of its previous office in 1983, by members of the Klan. The construction of the new SPLC office building itself served notice, but that announcement was invigorated by the appearance of the Memorial as part of its front façade. For this organization not only to recover, but to bring back with it a costly and prominent piece of public art, and one designed by the nation's most famous architect, was to post a clear message that it and the issues it raises are not going away.

The assertion of determination is bolstered by the overt and intrusive presence of uniformed security personnel at the Memorial site (Figure 6). They are stationed there principally to deter terrorist action against the SPLC, which is under seemingly perpetual threat from hate groups.[16] Although the security personnel make every effort to be "ambassadors for the Center" and to intrude as little as possible upon visitors' experience of the Memorial (Brinkman), their presence and activities simply do (and must) disrupt the serenity of the site. But the "disruption" reinforces the message of resolve. It asserts a strong determination to continue in the Center's work on race-related educational and legal programs. And the security presence reminds visitors by implication that there remains a forceful and dangerous opposition, willing to engage in violence to halt moves toward racial justice. The security force becomes a part of the Memorial's performative scene, "arguing" for the necessity of ongoing vigilance and social action.

The Memorial's reproduction of the third tactical dimension of Civil Rights protests—moralizing the individual as an agent of change—is also reproduced here and is in no way compromised by the prominence of the "institutional" presence, such as the SPLC or its security force. The Memorial, like the Movement, situates the visitor as agent. When the visitor engages the narrative inscribed in the tabletop, s/he literally towers over

Figure 6 Civil Rights Memorial, Montgomery, Alabama.

SOURCE: Neil Michel/Axiom.

history; the table is only 31 inches in height, and so visitors gaze down to read the inscriptions (Figure 7). Moreover, a gaze across the table encompasses the whole of the narrative, allowing the visitor a commanding viewpoint on the past.[17] His/her touch disturbs the flow of the water over the inscriptions, enabling a somatic, if symbolic, intervention in history. Because it is the ordinary person, the visitor to this public space, who is summoned as the audience, the issue posed is ethical and individual, rather than juridical or legislative. Such an audience has no standing to construct institutional edicts. And in any case, and as we will address further on, such institutional action is represented, in other rhetorical features of the Memorial, as having provided only partial remedy. Racial issues remain symbolically unresolved in the Memorial's rhetorical gestures.

Finally, just as the Civil Rights Movement worked its politics through a visual/material rhetoric, the Civil Rights Memorial's visual/material dimensions invite changed attitudes by compelling shifts of perspective. There are multiple examples of such shifts. But perhaps the

most important case is the Memorial's transmutation of attention from the past to the present and future. Although it does the work that any memorial must do—honoring the people or events it names—the Civil Rights Memorial also performs history in a conspicuously political fashion. As Abramson points out, the Civil Rights struggle is displayed in a realist mode, as the "neutral" disposition of a timeline engraved on the perimeter of the tabletop, with dates foregrounded and with no regular intervals among the events. However, in this timeline we see an interesting and politicized construal of history, one characterized by successes and accomplishments to be sure, but also one of suffering, capricious violence, and failure.

The timeline's chronicle cannot be described as a narrative of progress, as one might expect. The engraved successes are far fewer in number than the murders. Moreover, the accomplishments—legislation, judicial appointments, enforcement of desegregation laws, and so forth—are relentlessly succeeded on the timeline by additional murders or obstructionist actions. The initial inscription of the *Brown v. Board of Education*

Figure 7 Civil Rights Memorial, Montgomery, Alabama.

SOURCE: Neil Michel/Axiom.

decision represents a success for the Movement,[18] but the final one marks the tragedy of Martin Luther King, Jr.'s assassination. In fact, nine of the last ten entries in the timeline describe murders. The abbreviated [Biblical] quotation from King on the wall, like the unfinished timeline, suggests that the expressed goals of justice and righteousness have not been achieved. It seems fair to conclude that the representation of the past—the events of the Civil Rights Movement in the 1950s and 1960s—is unsatisfying and ambivalent.

But the temporal dimensions of the Memorial do not end with its words or even its borders. The Memorial transmutes attention from a display of the past to a rhetorical construction of the present, from "this happened," to this "is happening." There are any number of signals of temporal continuity in the Memorial, including the circularity of the table, the continuous flow of the water, and most directly, the space on the table after the final inscription, as well as the ellipses and beginning of the quotation on the wall: " . . . UNTIL. . . ." These two latter gestures of the memorial in particular shift our attention to the present and future, by posing questions about when we might expect justice to prevail, and what might come next on the timeline.

The shift in time to the present and its configuration of social justice is buttressed by another, physical feature of the Memorial as well, its refractive wall. By refracting the images of its surroundings, the Memorial implicates in its own design the scene of *contemporary* Montgomery and the city's residents and visitors. That scene is composed not just of the city's surrounding Confederate memory sites, but also of the profile of Montgomery as a city and seat of government. It is a divisive, tensive profile. The city and its environs remain heavily segregated, and the city "feels" as well as looks divided.[19] The wall, thus, references us to an imperfect and unresolved present, offering a visual image matching what Richard Gray describes: "[T]he old ways survive in however shadowy a disguise; the old racial prejudices are sustained in indirect, coded form" (224). The upper level of the Memorial and its still pool of water clearly seem to represent the future. Ironically, access to the second level is foreclosed for security reasons.[20] However, the view from the "future" is an interesting one. Not only

is the water still, a standard cultural marker of contemplation and peace (Moore 120–129), but the elevated area also offers a vantage point to view the lower plaza level scene. The face of the wall is no longer visible; the representation of the present disappears, collapsed into the representation of the past. As one gazes down at "the past" (the table), s/he is distanced from it, removed to a space where racial strife clearly is a remnant of the past. This time shifting by visual perspective seems to suggest above all that racial justice remains a future imaginary, that it was *not* realized in the Civil Rights Movement.

Another example of visual/material perspective shifting that seems important here has to do with the Memorial's color. Not all black granite is the same, and the stone used for this memorial is not at all like the uniformly black granite composing the Vietnam Veterans Memorial. The material of the Civil Rights Memorial is highly variegated in color, almost mosaic-like in its composition. That color variation is not visible from even a short distance or in most photographs, but the multiple colors are unmistakable in a close view of the Memorial. Thus, as a visitor approaches the Memorial, the stark black-white color double recedes, as if as a reminder that race cannot be rendered in binary form but must be recognized as diverse and multiple, but still suffused by common interest. When we focus on color, the table, which performs the Memorial's representation of the past, appears as a dark body inscribed with and indentured to white words. The representation of the future, however, remains uninscribed, free of any verbal coding and unencumbered of the white, discursive containment that characterizes the symbolic past.

Whiteness is displaced and subverted too by the character of many of the table's inscriptions marking death. The mostly African American murder victims are described in the timeline not only by name, but frequently in terms that point to their innocence and/or their civic status: "youth," "Rev." [Reverend], "students," "voter registration worker," "Cpl." [Corporal], "children," "Civil Rights leader," "schoolgirls," "witness to murder," "Civil Rights workers," "march volunteer," "seminary student," and "black community leader." Their murderers, by contrast, are described as "Nightriders," "white legislator," "police," "Klan," "state trooper," "deputy," and "highway patrolmen."

These nameless individuals are represented as authorized or at least protected by institutional authority or group solidarity. When the perpetrators are not identified explicitly, the context of the murder is: "killed for leading voter registration drive," "murdered for organizing black voters," "murdered for speaking to white woman," "killed protesting construction of segregated school," and "killed after promotion to 'white' job." Starkly represented here are mindless and ruthless bids to maintain power. Although the murderers are rarely identified as white, the implication is obvious. Read together, the identities named by the timeline point to a reversal of identification much like that advocated by Cornel West:

> To engage in a serious discussion of race in America, we must begin not with the problems of black people but with the flaws of American society—flaws rooted in historic inequalities and longstanding cultural stereotypes. How we set up the terms for discussing racial issues shapes our perception and response to these issues. As long as black people are viewed as "them," the burden falls on blacks to do the "cultural" and "moral" work necessary for healthy race relations. (3)

Rhetorically, the timeline seeks alignment of the visitor with those murdered (majority African Americans) and solicits division between the visitor and the murderers (presumably all European Americans).

But the timeline's representation of the murderers as so often those in positions of cultural authority and its named "reasons" for the murders signal an even stronger move than reassigning "us" and "them." Homi Bhabha could be describing the Memorial's critique of whiteness when he suggests that:

> The subversive move is to reveal within the very integuments of "whiteness" the agonistic elements that make it the unsettled, disturbed form of authority that it is—the incommensurable "differences" that it must surmount; the histories of trauma and terror that it must perpetuate and from which it must protect itself, the amnesia it imposes on itself; the violence it inflicts in the process of becoming a transparent and transcendent form of authority. (21)

The timeline performs the dynamics of whiteness as a form of authority that maintains itself through brutality and terror and only under the sign of rationalized insanity. Who but a terrorist or a lunatic, after all, would murder a minister, a schoolgirl, a military officer, or a community leader, or do so for the "reasons" named in the timeline? Whiteness is indeed displayed here as unsettled, disturbed, and violent in its struggle to preserve its dominance.

Conclusion: What Brand of Racial Politics?

What might we learn from the juxtaposition of these two readings of the Civil Rights Memorial—the one based on a critical posture that takes author, genre, and symbolism as the significant constellation of issues in its hermeneutic, and the other predicated on readings not only of symbolic but material considerations? We certainly agree with Abramson that the shape and substance of the Memorial's timeline are important components of its rhetoric. However, the critical moves he makes are to identify the characteristics (and political shortcomings) of the timeline as a standard historical regimen and then to assign those characteristics to the Civil Rights Memorial.

We believe that is a mistaken approach for two reasons. First, it overlooks the specific substance of the timeline's symbolic representations in the case of the Memorial. Even if we heeded only the symbolism of the timeline, in other words, we would be inclined to read the Memorial as more critical (in Mitchell's sense) than does Abramson. Second and more important, his reading abjures any attention to the material features of the Memorial or of its context. If we understand those material considerations as interacting with the symbolism of the Memorial, we read a much different message than Abramson does; the Memorial, in our view, encourages its visitors to reject the very position that Abramson argues the Memorial promulgates. Although we believe that studying symbolism alone and in the absence of materiality is inadequate to an understanding or critique of *any* rhetoric, it certainly is so in the case of public art. The discrepancies between our reading and Abramson's highlight the differential possibilities. So, as we pose this critical reading alongside Abramson's, what might we conclude about the Civil Rights Memorial's political rhetoric?

Abramson's reading of the Memorial confines its rhetoric to the inscriptions in the timeline, the Memorial's symbolic representation of the past. Abramson concludes that the Memorial approves a reliance on institutional authority as the appropriate agency of change, thereby reiterating the status quo and reducing the difficult issues of race to a non-controversial and too easy formulation. His critique apparently presumes that the Memorial affirms for the present the substantive politics of the past. Abramson's account of the Memorial's timeline is descriptively accurate, if incomplete. The Memorial *does* represent governmental action as the principal form of intervention in and redress of racial injustice. But the Memorial's timeline represents a past it makes every effort to displace rhetorically. If there is a politics that it preserves from the past, it is not the substantive authority of the law, but the tactical performance of resistance. What the Memorial *can* tell us is precisely the message Abramson reads. But if we read beyond the representations of the timeline to the Memorial's material performances, we see a more complex and more subversive rhetoric.

We understand the Civil Rights Memorial's rhetoric as assigning the events in the timeline to the past and declaring the actions of that finite past worthy of memory but inadequate to the goals of "justice" and "righteousness" articulated by King and quoted on the Memorial's wall. Nothing in the Memorial's timeline should lead to the conclusion that the past it inscribes is a past that we should "emulate" in the present and future. If anything, the highly unsatisfying and troubling end of the timeline seems to us to imply precisely the obverse, that this is a past we should remember but not repeat or continue. The clear separation of representations of past and present from that of the future appears (literally) to reinforce that reading.

That the Memorial shifts attention from the past and even seems to argue for a break with the past is not to suggest that it dishonors the Civil Rights Movement or its participants. Instead, its message about the past seems more akin to Dyson's assessment about the impact of King and the Civil Rights Movement:

despite the significant basic changes that King helped bring about, the present status of poor black Americans in particular presents little cause for celebration. Their situation does not mean that King's achievements were not substantial. Rather it reflects the deep structures of persistent racism and classism that have not yet yielded to sustained levels of protest and resistance. . . . In order to judge King's career, we must imagine what American society would be for blacks without his historic achievements. Without basic rights to vote, desegregated public transportation and accommodations, equal housing legislation, and the like, American society would more radically reflect what Gunnar Myrdal termed the American Dilemma. King and other participants in the civil rights movement wrought historic change, but that change was a partial movement toward real liberation. (235–236)

Indeed, what the Memorial does preserve from the past is not the Movement's reliance on institutions, but its tactical performances of protest and resistance. It imports into the present—the time of the visitor—the tactical rhetoric that draws attention, announces resolve, and enjoins the moral agency of the individual. It refuses the damage that arises from the pretense that racism ended with the Civil Rights Movement, by reenacting the Movement's *tactical* politics in the present. In other words, it creates a continuity with the past by importing into its own rhetoric the performances of the Civil Rights Movement's activist dimension. That appropriation seems to suggest that the continuity between past and present is racism. But the Memorial creates a clear discontinuity between past and present in terms of the "solutions" it symbolizes. The timeline tells the visitor that, despite the institutional changes, the goal of racial justice has not been achieved, that the methods of the past have succeeded only in part. It does not prescribe the precise means of achieving racial concord in the present and future, but it clearly argues that change is possible and desirable now, in its refracted projection of the ever changing and changeable scenes of Montgomery and in its elevated view of the future.[21]

The Memorial does offer, however, at least some cues for current resistance and protest. If we notice the multicolored granite of the Memorial, as we can at close range, it suggests an aesthetic of difference and a politics of coalition, a much different position than that represented in the timeline. That message is buttressed in the fact that the designer of the Memorial is of Asian, not European or African, descent. Moreover, if we attend to the representations of the murderers in the Memorial's inscriptions of the past, there is a devastating moral critique of whiteness to be read there. And by posing government institutions as the means of social change *and* as the legitimating cover for a number of the represented perpetrators of violence (e.g., legislator, police, state trooper), it reveals precisely the kinds of contradictions upon which whiteness sustains its control. The Memorial, in other words, harbors as part of its rhetoric moves toward a coalitional politics of diversity and what bell hooks has named a "deconstruction of the category 'whiteness'" (150). That hardly constitutes a continuity with remedies of the past, at least those represented by the Memorial.

In general, then, we would argue that the Civil Rights Memorial's rhetorical stance is not the preservative, conciliatory one that Abramson reads. Instead, we believe it participates in the kinds of memory and public art projects described at the beginning of our essay respectively by John Hope Franklin and W.J.T. Mitchell. It faces us with our own history for the purposes of change and efforts to avoid repeating the past. And it is a critical art project in every sense Mitchell describes, in its display of the violence from the Civil Rights era, its reenactments of the tactical moves of the Movement, and in its willingness to engage issues of the present and future in frank, if controversial, ways.

Acknowledgements

The authors would like to express their gratitude to the Southern Poverty Law Center, and particularly to Penny Weaver, the SPLC Communications Director. They would also like to thank Victoria Gallagher, North Carolina State University, for frequent and generous suggestions about the authors' larger project on the Civil Rights Memorial.

Notes

1. The SPLC reports on its website: "Most recently, the Center has become internationally known for its success in developing novel legal strategies to cripple extremist activities and to help victims of hate crimes win monetary damages against groups like the Klan." See *Southern Poverty Law Center* <http://www.splcenter.org>. The SPLC gained perhaps the most fame by virtually bankrupting some hate groups by filing and winning civil claims on behalf of families of murder victims. But it has a strong educational, as well as legal, mission. The Intelligence Project tracks and reports on hate group activities and hate crimes across the U.S. And Teaching Tolerance offers grants and curricula for innovative projects on tolerance in schools. For fascinating personal accounts of some of the Center's legal and watchdog work, see; Dees, *Season;* Dees, *Hate;* and Dees, *Gathering Storm.*

2. The Civil Rights Memorial has received less attention than its famous forerunner in Washington, but it has received some critical commentary, e.g., in Abramson; Blair; Senic 38–39; Symmes 132–133; and Zinsser. It is discussed also in the 1994 film, *Maya Lin: A Strong Clear Vision,* which won the 1995 Academy Award for best feature documentary.

3. We see the performative character of the Civil Rights Memorial as a fundamental part of its rhetoric. Our position is reliant on and works from the following sources that also treat public sites or public art as instances of (or somehow implicating) communication, rhetoric and/or performance: Armada; Blair; Blair, Jeppeson, and Pucci; Blair and Michel; Bowman; Carlson and Hocking; Dickinson; Ehrenhaus, "Silence"; Ehrenhaus, "Vietnam"; Foss; Gallagher, "Memory"; Gallagher, "Remembering"; Griswold; Haines; Hattenhauer; Jackson; Jorgensen-Earp and Lanzilotti; Katriel; Marback; Mechling and Mechling; Rosenfield; Stuart; Sturken; and Trujillo.

4. Our reading, like Abramson's, will be partial. That is the case not only because of the truism that all readings are partial, but also because we are focusing on some of the features Abramson did not. Even then, there are many other rhetorical features of the Memorial that will receive far less attention here than they merit, e.g., the water imagery in the Memorial, its religious overtones, the Memorial's place in the context of a late twentieth-century commemorative "boom," the Memorial in relation to other Civil Rights-related memory sites, its development and construction in an era of race-related setbacks and backlashes, and so forth. This essay represents only a small portion of our critical reading; we are working on a larger project on the Civil Rights Memorial as this essay goes to press.

For excellent treatments of other Civil Rights memory sites, see Armada (Civil Rights Museum, Memphis); Gallagher, "Remembering" (King Memorial, Atlanta); and Gallagher, "Memory" (Civil Rights Institute, Birmingham).

5. Abramson also complains that the Memorial makes "no reference to other aspects of the 1960s civil rights struggle, such as the separatist agenda of radical black nationalism propounded by the early Malcolm X, among others" (701). It should be noted that the Civil Rights Movement typically is not regarded as containing separatism or black nationalism as among its "aspects." If one honors the achievements of Civil Rights groups, separatist and radical groups of the mid-century would be definitionally excluded on almost any grounds. Nationalists and separatists did not seek equality of rights under the civil law of the United States; they sought, explicitly, a separate community affiliation. There certainly is every reason to honor those who have defended such separation, but to demand that a memorial to Civil Rights honor them is to make something of a category error. And it also treats separatism rather dismissively, reducing it to an "aspect" of another movement with which it was not typically even aligned.

6. The following collections directly address the question of a material rhetoric or have clear implications for it: the two-volume special issue of *Argumentation and Advocacy,* on "Body Argument," edited by Gerard A. Hauser; and Selzer and Crowley, eds. Also see: Charland; Cloud, "Materiality"; Cloud, "Null Persona"; Condit; Cox; Crowley; Greene; Krippendorff; McGee, "Ideograph"; McGee, "Materialist's Conception"; McGee, "Text"; McGuire; McKerrow, "Corporeality"; McKerrow, "Critical Rhetoric"; Railsback; Scholle; Stewart; Thomas; and Wood and Cox.

7. What we find most peculiar about Abramson's conclusion is that he does attend to some other features of the Civil Rights Memorial and the other memorials, but that he ultimately dismisses the other features in favor of focusing on the timeline.

8. See also, for example, Miles. He suggests that monuments and memorials stand "for a stability which conceals the internal contradictions of society . . ." (58).

9. Chong does a masterful job of describing the tactics of the Civil Rights Movement and in a far more thorough way than we will attempt here. Although his account suffers to some degree from the turgidity of game theory, and although Chong would

certainly not describe his work this way, his book represents an admirable account of the material dimension of the protest activity.

10. Also see Haiman; and Rustin 337.

11. Also see CORE 241. The point, as Hauser suggests, is to demonstrate the irrefutability of a movement's position: "Removal and control of the dissident's physical body . . . underscores the body's argumentative potency. Rebuking the dissident's self-sufficiency in this extra-symbolic fashion creates tension for the state's own self-sufficiency. Removing the opposition by forcibly controlling its body serves as an admission that dissident ideas cannot be refuted, thereby bestowing a hyper-rhetorical presence on the political prisoner's body" (6).

12. There are any number of genuinely fine accounts of the Civil Rights Movement. Certainly the most complete in detailing the activities of the Movement leadership is Taylor Branch's two-volume work: *Parting the Waters;* and *Pillar of Fire.* Weisbrot offers a much more condensed but still very useful history, and John Lewis's book, *Walking With the Wind,* is one of a number of excellent autobiographical chronicles.

13. Sara Bullard, the SPLC director of research, suggests that, "A big problem [in doing the research for the Memorial] was that newspapers in the South didn't cover these deaths" (quoted by Zinsser 36).

14. There is at least some precedent for understanding artworks as performative, given particular conditions. Discussing Henry Sayre's work, for example, Pollock argues that: "For Sayre, Fischl's paintings are performative. They require 'our collaboration, amplification, [and] embellishment.' By positioning audience members as agents in the production of cultural meanings, they also thus position audience members as social agents, who work out their relations with each other in and through the process of meaning making engendered by the artwork/event. The performative work thus fans outward. It makes of its own capacity for historicity an occasion for the articulation of difference and re-production of cultural authority, and so for contests over value, meaning, and power" (27).

15. There certainly are sites of interest to those more inclined to value the Civil Rights history of the city, but to suggest that they are prominent or easily accessible to a first-time visitor would be a gross overstatement. It took us two ten-day visits to Montgomery and repetitive, stubborn inquiries to learn that there was even a driving tour brochure of Civil Rights-related sites in Montgomery. It was unavailable at the

city's visitor center as well as at the state's Chamber of Commerce offices in the Center for Commerce building. We finally located one at another tourist site. And it is worth noting that, while most brochures for historical and tour sites in the city are free, this one is not. For another description of the tourist context, see Blair 42–44.

16. According to Tom Brinkman, the Chief of Security for the Southern Poverty Law Center, the Center receives an average of two-three threats per day, either by phone or by the appearance of known hate group members at the site.

17. Barthes discusses this kind of empowering view in his classic reading of the Eiffel Tower.

18. Whether *Brown v. Board of Education* was a real success, of course, has been called into question, particularly by critical race theorists. For a discussion of the issues, see Hasian and Delgado 251 ff.

19. Our own experiences have been of a divided, racially tense city. But we are "outsiders" and not as well situated to get or give a sense of the city as are its residents. However, some of them would agree with us. Joe Levin, co-founder with Morris Dees of the SPLC, asserted in an interview with us that he believed Montgomery is extremely racist. And an editorial in the local newspaper hints of a similar admission about the state: "Like it or not, fair or not, accurate or not, the simple fact is that many people who have never been to Alabama still look on it as a haven for redneckism. *There's enough kernel of truth in that image to make it hurt*" ("Pride." Emphasis added).

20. Although visitors are not allowed to climb the stairs, the second level is and was intended to be part of the Memorial. According to Morris Dees, Personal interview, the SPLC plans call for a new office space in the next few years and the conversion of the current office building to a visitor center. At that point, we presume, access to the upper level will be open.

21. As bell hooks argues so forcefully, "No responsibility need be taken for not changing something if it is perceived as immutable. To accept racism as a system of domination that can be changed would demand that everyone who sees him- or herself as embracing a vision of racial social equality would be required to assert anti-racist habits of being" (271).

REFERENCES

Abramson, Daniel. "Maya Lin and the 1960s: Monuments, Time Lines, and Minimalism." *Critical Inquiry* 22 (1996): 679–709.

Armada, Bernard J. "Memorial Agon: An Interpretive Tour of the National Civil Rights Museum." *Southern Communication Journal* 63 (1998): 235–243.

Barthes, Roland. "The Eiffel Tower." *A Barthes Reader.* Ed. Susan Sontag. New York: Hill and Wang, 1982. 236–50.

Bhabha, Homi K. "The White Stuff." *Artforum International,* May 1998. 21–24.

Blair, Carole. "Contemporary U.S. Memorial Sites as Exemplars of Rhetoric's Materiality." In Selzer and Crowley, eds. 16–57.

———, Marsha S. Jeppeson, and Enrico Pucci, Jr. "Public Memorializing in Postmodernity: The Vietnam Veterans Memorial as Prototype." *Quarterly Journal of Speech* 77 (1991): 263–88.

———, and Neil Michel. "Commemorating in the Theme Park Zone: Reading the Astronauts Memorial." *At the Intersection: Cultural Studies and Rhetorical Studies.* Ed. Thomas Rosteck. New York: Guilford, 1999. 29–83.

"Body Argument." Special Issue—Parts I and II. Ed. Gerard A. Hauser. *Argumentation and Advocacy* 36:1 and 2 (1999): 1–49; 51–100.

Bowman, Michael S. "Performing Southern History for the Tourist Gaze: Antebellum Home Tour Performances." Pollock, ed. 142–158.

Branch, Taylor. *Parting the Waters: America in the King Years, 1954–63.* New York: Simon and Schuster, 1989.

———, *Pillar of Fire: America in the King Years, 1963–65.* New York: Simon and Schuster, 1998.

Brinkman, Tom. Personal interview. Montgomery, AL. 30 March 1998.

Carlson, A. Cheree, and John E. Hocking. "Strategies of Redemption at the Vietnam Veterans' Memorial," *Western Journal of Speech Communication* 52 (1988): 203–215.

Carr, Stephen, Mark Francis, Leanne G. Rivlin, and Andrew M. Stone. *Public Space.* New York: Cambridge University Press, 1992.

Chalmers, David. *And the Crooked Places Made Straight: The Struggle for Social Change in the 1960s.* 2d ed. Baltimore: Johns Hopkins University Press, 1996.

Charland, Maurice. "Constitutive Rhetoric: The Case of the *Peuple Québeçois.*" *Quarterly Journal of Speech* 73 (1987): 133–150.

Chong, Dennis. *Collective Action and the Civil Rights Movement.* Chicago: University of Chicago Press, 1991.

Cloud, Dana L. "The Materiality of Discourse as Oxymoron: A Challenge to Critical Rhetoric." *Western Journal of Communication* 58 (1994): 141–163.

———, "The Null Persona: Race and the Rhetoric of Silence in the Uprising of '34." *Rhetoric and Public Affairs* 2 (1999): 177–209.

Cmiel, Kenneth. "The Politics of Civility." *The Sixties: From Memory to History*. Ed. David Farber. Chapel Hill: University of North Carolina Press, 1994. 263–290.

Condit, Celeste. "Clouding the Issues: The Ideal and the Material in Human Communication." *Critical Studies in Mass Communication* 14 (1997): 197–200.

CORE Action Discipline. Version Adopted by the National Convention of the Congress of Racial Equality, June 1945. Leaflet, 1945, CORE Archives, State Historical Society of Wisconsin. Rpt. in Meier, et al., eds. 240–243.

Cox, J. Robert. "On 'Interpreting' Public Discourse in Post-Modernity." *Western Journal of Speech Communication* 54 (1990): 317–329.

Crowley, Sharon. "Reflections on an Argument that Won't Go Away: Or, a Turn of the Ideological Screw." *Quarterly Journal of Speech* 78 (1992): 450–465.

Dees, Morris. Telephone interview. 27 March 1998.

———, with James Corcoran. *Gathering Storm: America's Militia Threat*. New York: HarperCollins, 1996.

———, with Steve Fiffer. *Hate on Trial: The Case Against America's Most Dangerous Neo-Nazi*. New York: Villard, 1993.

———, with Steve Fiffer. *A Season for Justice: The Life and Times of Civil Rights Lawyer Morris Dees*. New York: Charles Scribner's Sons, 1991.

Dickinson, Greg. "Memories for Sale: Nostalgia and the Construction of Identity in Old Pasadena." *Quarterly Journal of Speech* 83 (1997): 1–27.

Dyson, Michael Eric. *Reflecting Black: African-American Cultural Criticism*. Minneapolis: University of Minnesota Press, 1993.

Ehrenhaus, Peter. "Silence and Symbolic Expression." *Communication Monographs* 55 (1988): 41–57.

———, "The Vietnam Veterans Memorial: An Invitation to Argument." *Journal of the American Forensic Association* 25 (1988): 54–64.

Foss, Sonja K. "Ambiguity as Persuasion: The Vietnam Veterans Memorial." *Communication Quarterly* 34 (1986): 326–40.

Foucault, Michel. "The Discourse on Language." Trans. Rupert Swyer. Appendix to *The Archaeology of Knowledge*. Trans. A.M. Sheridan Smith. New York: Pantheon, 1972. 215–237.

Franklin, John Hope. *The Color Line: Legacy for the Twenty-First Century*. Columbia: University of Missouri Press, 1993.

Gallagher, Victoria J. "Memory and Reconciliation in the Birmingham Civil Rights Institute." *Rhetoric and Public Affairs* 2 (1999): 303–320.

———, "Remembering Together: Rhetorical Integration and the Case of the Martin Luther King, Jr. Memorial." *Southern Communication Journal* 60 (1995): 109–119.

Gray, Richard. "Negotiating Differences: Southern Culture(s) Now." *Dixie Debates: Perspectives on Southern Cultures*. Ed. Richard H. King and Helen Taylor. New York: New York University Press, 1996. 218–227.

Greene, Ronald Walter. "Another Materialist Rhetoric." *Critical Studies in Mass Communication* 15 (1998): 21–41.

Griswold, Charles L. "The Vietnam Veterans Memorial and the Washington Mall: Philosophical Thoughts on Political Iconography." *Critical Inquiry* 12 (1986): 688–719.

Haiman, Franklyn S. "The Rhetoric of the Streets: Some Legal and Ethical Considerations." *Quarterly Journal of Speech* 57 (1967): 99–114. Rpt. in *The Rhetoric of Our Times*. Ed. J. Jeffery Auer. New York: Appleton-Century-Crofts, 1969. 101–119.

Haines, Harry W. "'What Kind of War?': An Analysis of the Vietnam Veterans Memorial." *Critical Studies in Mass Communication* 3 (1986): 1–20.

Hasian, Marouf, Jr., and Fernando Delgado, "The Trials and Tribulations of Racialized Critical Rhetorical Theory: Understanding the Rhetorical Ambiguities of Proposition 187." *Communication Theory* 8 (1998): 245–270.

Hattenhauer, Darryl. "The Rhetoric of Architecture: A Semiotic Approach." *Communication Quarterly* 32 (1984): 71–7.

Hauser, Gerard A. "Incongruous Bodies: Arguments for Personal Sufficiency and Public Insufficiency." *Argumentation and Advocacy* 36 (1999): 1–8.

hooks, bell. *Killing Rage: Ending Racism*. New York: Henry Holt, 1995.

Jackson, Shannon. "Performance at Hull House: Museum, Microfiche, and Historiography." Pollock, ed. 261–293.

Jorgensen-Earp, Cheryl R., and Lori A. Lanzilotti. "Public Memory and Private Grief: The Construction of Shrines at the Sites of Public Tragedy." *Quarterly Journal of Speech* 84 (1998): 150–170.

Katriel, Tamar. "Sites of Memory: Discourses of the Past in Israeli Pioneering Settlement Museums." *Quarterly Journal of Speech* 80 (1994): 1–20.

King, Martin Luther, Jr. "Letter from Birmingham City Jail, April 16, 1963." *The Rhetoric of the Civil-Rights Movement.* Ed. Haig A. Bosmajian and Hamida Bosmajian. New York: Random House, 1969. 37–57.

———. "Pilgrimage to Nonviolence." *Stride Toward Freedom: The Montgomery Story.* New York: Harper and Row, 1958. 101–107. Rpt. in *The Sixties Papers: Documents of a Rebellious Decade.* Ed. Judith Clavir Albert and Stewart Edward Albert. New York: Praeger, 1984. 108–112.

Krippendorff, Klaus. "Undoing Power." *Critical Studies in Mass Communication* 12 (1995): 101–132.

Lawson, James W., Jr. "From a Lunch-Counter Stool." Address at SNCC conference. Raleigh, NC, April 1960. Rpt. as "We Are Trying To Raise the 'Moral Issue.'" Meier, et al., eds. 308–315.

Levin, Joe. Personal interview. Montgomery, AL. 2 April 1998.

Lewis, John, with Michael D'Orso. *Walking With the Wind: A Memoir of the Movement.* New York: Simon and Schuster, 1998.

Marback, Richard. "Detroit and the Closed Fist: Toward a Theory of Material Rhetoric." *Rhetoric Review* 17 (1998): 74–92.

Maya Lin: A Strong Clear Vision. Dir. Freida Lee Mock. Sanders & Mock. Productions/American Film Institute. 1994.

McGee, Michael Calvin. "The 'Ideograph': A Link Between Rhetoric and Ideology." *Quarterly Journal of Speech* 66 (1980): 1–16.

———. "A Materialist's Conception of Rhetoric." *Explorations in Rhetoric: Studies in Honor of Douglas Ehninger.* Ed. Ray E. McKerrow. Glenview, IL: Scott, Foresman, 1982. 23–48.

———. "Text, Context, and the Fragmentation of Contemporary Culture." *Western Journal of Speech Communication* 54 (1990): 274–89.

McGuire, Michael. "Materialism: Reductionist Dogma or Critical Rhetoric?" *Rhetoric and Philosophy.* Ed. Richard A. Cherwitz. Hillsdale, NJ: Lawrence Erlbaum Associates, 1990. 187–212.

McKerrow, Raymie E. "Corporeality and Rhetoric: A Site for Rhetoric's Future." *Southern Communication Journal* 63 (1998): 315–328.

———. "Critical Rhetoric: Theory and Praxis." *Communication Monographs* 56 (1989): 91–111.

Mechling, Elizabeth Walker, and Jay Mechling. "The Sale of Two Cities: A Semiotic Comparison of Disneyland with Marriott's Great America." *Journal of Popular Culture* 37 (1973): 253–63. Rpt. in *Rhetorical Dimensions in Media: A Critical Casebook.* Ed. Martin J. Medhurst and Thomas W. Benson, Dubuque, IA: Kendall/Hunt, 1984. 400–413.

Meier, August, Elliott Rudwick, and Francis L. Broderick, eds. *Black Protest Thought in the Twentieth Century,* 2d ed. New York: Macmillan, 1971.

Miles, Malcolm. *Space and the City: Public Art and Urban Futures.* London: Routledge, 1997.

Mitchell, W.J.T. "The Violence of Public Art: *Do The Right Thing." Picture Theory: Essays on Verbal and Visual Representation.* Chicago: University of Chicago Press, 1994. 371–396.

Moore, Charles W. *Water and Architecture.* New York: Harry N. Abrams, 1994.

Pollock, Della. "Making History Go." Pollock, ed. 1–45.

———, ed. *Exceptional Spaces: Essays in Performance and History.* Chapel Hill: University of North Carolina Press, 1998.

"Pride in the Past." Editorial. *The Montgomery Advertiser* 21 June 1989. 8A.

Railsback, Celeste Condit. "Beyond Rhetorical Relativism: A Structural-Material Model of Truth and Objective Reality." *Quarterly Journal of Speech* 69 (1983): 351–363.

Rosenfield, Lawrence W. "Central Park and the Celebration of Civic Virtue." *American Rhetoric: Context and Criticism.* Ed. Thomas W. Benson. Carbondale: Southern Illinois University Press, 1989. 221–265.

Rustin, Bayard. "The Meaning of Birmingham." Meier, et al. eds. 332–340.

Sayre, Henry M. *The Object of Performance: The American Avant-Garde Since 1970.* Chicago: University of Chicago Press, 1989.

Scholle, David J. "From the Theory of Ideology to Power/Knowledge." *Critical Studies in Mass Communication* 5 (1988): 16–41.

Selzer, Jack, and Sharon Crowley, eds. *Rhetorical Bodies.* Madison: University of Wisconsin Press, 1999.

Senie, Harriet F. *Contemporary Public Sculpture: Tradition, Transformation, and Controversy.* New York: Oxford University Press, 1992.

Southern Poverty Law Center. <http.//www.splcenter .org>. Accessed 26 September 1997.

Stewart, John R. *Language as Articulate Contact: Toward a Post-Semiotic Philosophy of Communication.* Albany: State University of New York Press, 1995.

Stuart, Charlotte L. "Architecture in Nazi Germany: A Rhetorical Perspective." *Western Speech* 37 (1973): 253–63.

Sturken, Marita. *Tangled Memories: The Vietnam War, The AIDS Epidemic, and the Politics of Remembering.* Berkeley: University of California Press, 1997.

Symmes, Marilyn. "Fountains as Commemoration." *Fountains: Splash and Spectacle: Water and Design From the Renaissance to the Present.* Ed. Marilyn Symmes. New York: Rizzoli, 1998. 123–135.

Thomas, Douglas. "It's Not What You Say, It's *That* You Say It: Speech, Performance, and Sense in Austin and Deleuze." *Philosophy and Rhetoric* 29 (1996): 359–368.

Trujillo, Nick. "Interpreting November 22: A Critical Ethnography of an Assassination Site." *Quarterly Journal of Speech* 79 (1993): 447–466.

Weisbrot, Robert. *Freedom Bound: A History of America's Civil Rights Movement.* New York: Penguin, 1991.

West, Cornel. *Race Matters.* Boston: Beacon Press, 1993.

Wood, Julia, and J. Robert Cox. "Rethinking Critical Voice: Materiality and Situated Knowledges." *Western Journal of Communication* 57 (1993): 278–287.

Zinsser, William. "I Realized Her Tears Were Becoming Part of the Memorial." *Smithsonian,* September 1991. 32–43.

8

REMEMBERING WORLD WAR II

The Rhetoric and Politics of National Commemoration at the Turn of the 21st Century

BARBARA A. BIESECKER

A significant event is taking place on the Washington Mall: the construction of the WWII Memorial on the sacred ground between the Washington Monument and the Lincoln Memorial. First proposed in December of 1987, signed into law by President Clinton on 25 May 1993, and promoted by former Senator and disabled veteran Bob Dole as well as the popular cultural icon Tom Hanks, the projected one hundred million dollar memorial is scheduled to open on Memorial Day 2003. As described on its fund-raising campaign's home page, the structure will at once pay just tribute to the sixteen million World War II veterans, do appropriate homage to all Americans who supported the war effort on the home front, and show respect to "its magnificent site on the National Mall."[1]

Although first proposed at a time when the Mall's "satisfying geometry," long "an analogue of our society," whose "orderly vistas" which "open receptive minds to the symmetry, balance, proportion and temperateness of our political institutions and the civil society that sustains our common purposes" were reputedly being endangered by over eighty "irritable factions" vying for national visibility and recognition,[2] approval of the World War II

Figure 1   World War II Memorial, Washington, DC.

SOURCE: Photograph by the author.

SOURCE: Biesecker, B. A. (2002). Remembering World War II: The rhetoric and politics of national commemoration at the turn of the 21st century. *Quarterly Journal of Speech, 88*(4): 393–409. © National Communication Association.

Memorial progressed swiftly and with relative ease. In this case, unlike so many others, there was no debate over whether "there are any other existing memorials that pay tribute to like or similar subjects" or doubt about its "preeminent historical and lasting significance to the nation."[3] Indeed, the only serious reservation aired was that its monumental significance to the nation would seem to necessitate the raising of an edifice whose proper magnitude threatened to overwhelm the democratically sublime symmetry of the Mall.[4] As John Graves, speaking on behalf of a minority of WWII veterans opposing the initiative, put it on the day the memorial won resounding approval from the Commission, "we want a memorial but not on that particular spot."[5] Given that six other sites had been considered for placement of the memorial (the Capitol Reflecting Pool area, the Tidal Basin, West Potomac Park, the Washington Monument grounds, Freedom Plaza, and Henderson Hall), it is no minor detail that nearly five years *previous to* final design selection, the Commission of Fine Arts, the National Capitol Planning Commission, and the National Park Service swiftly and unanimously settled on the east end of Constitution Gardens, between Constitution Avenue and the Rainbow Pool, calming opposition by stipulating only that the design "not interrupt the vista between the Capitol, the Washington Monument and the Lincoln Memorial."[6]

Why was priority granted to pride of place? The strong answer came from President Bill Clinton on Veterans Day 1995 in an oration that officially brought to a close the nation's 50th commemoration of World War II:

> [L]et me urge all of us to summon the spirit that joined that generation, that stood together and cared for one another. The ideas they fought for are now ours to sustain. The dreams they defended are now ours to guarantee. In war they crossed racial and religious, sectional and social divisions to become one force for freedom.
>
> Now, in a world where lives are literally being torn apart all over the globe by those very divisions, let us again lead by the power of example. Let us remember their example. Let us live our motto, *E pluribus Unum*—from many, one. Let us grow strong together, not be divided and weakened. Let us find that common ground for which so many have fought and died.[7]

Like the memorial's fund-raising campaign, the central theme of Clinton's panegyric to WWII is the urgent need for national reunification.[8] As he put it again later that afternoon during the site dedication ceremony, the memorial "will be a permanent reminder of just how much we Americans can do when we work together instead of fighting among ourselves." A prime piece of property was parceled out for the repair of a nation crippled by "division and resentment."[9]

Given the memorial's singular location on the Mall and the authorizing logic invoked on its behalf, there is more at stake than establishing an eternal repository of the heroic accomplishments of a generation past. Indeed, over the course of this essay I will suggest that the historic decision to place the WWII Memorial at the very center of the Capitol is symptomatic of the pivotal ideological role WWII has begun to play in U.S. public culture in the present. Specifically, I will argue that recent popular cultural representations of the "Good War," from blockbuster movies to cable television series, best selling books and museum displays, together constitute one of the primary means through which a renewed sense of national belonging is being persuasively packaged and delivered to U.S. audiences for whom the question what does it mean to be an American has, at least since the Civil War, never been more difficult to answer. Put differently, I will suggest that if, as scholars from both the left and the right have argued, "for the second time in the nation's history, there is a real question of how to maintain a stable and effective relationship between America's *unum* and *pluribus*,"[10] present recuperations of WWII may be understood as a decisive answer to it. Thus, following the lines drawn by the WWII Memorial's salient images and motifs, I first turn my attention in the essay to two of the most popular rehabilitations of WWII, Steven Spielberg's *Saving Private Ryan* and Tom Brokaw's *The Greatest Generation*. I then close the essay with a tour of the less familiar Women in Military Service for America Memorial. By examining these three representative "memory texts" and the discourses that circulated about them in the popular press and mass media,[11] I hope to show how these extraordinarily well-received reconstructions of the past function rhetorically as civics lessons for a generation beset by fractious disagreements about the viability of U.S. culture and identity.[12] By manufacturing and embracing a particular *kind* of American, a certain idea of what it means to be a "good citizen," these popular cultural texts, best understood as technologies of national cultural transformation, promote social cohesion by rhetorically inducing differently positioned audiences—by class, race, ethnicity, sexuality, and gender—to disregard rather than actively to seek to dismantle the inequitable power relations that continue to structure collective life in the United States.[13]

Late in the summer of 1998, as the English Only debates were raging in Los Angeles, the Christian Coalition and the Family Research Council were running national ads urging gay men and lesbian women to abandon homosexual activity, and the country was debating the likely impeachment of Bill Clinton, *Saving Private Ryan* opened in theaters across the country. Set against the backdrop of World War II and the epic invasion of Normandy and delivered from the point of view of the so-called grunts in the trenches, this celluloid fanfare for the common man tells the guardedly triumphant tale of the rescue of "one James Francis Ryan" who, dropped deep behind enemy lines, is discovered to be the last surviving son of a mother of four whose three older boys had recently been felled by enemy fire. Having only narrowly escaped the slaughter on the sands of Omaha Beach, Captain John Miller (played by Tom Hanks) receives new orders from no less a figure than George C. Marshall, the Army's Chief of Staff: Miller is to patch together a small Ranger unit and bring Ryan home to his mother, alive. For the remaining two-and-one-half hours of the film we watch a "public relations" mission for the home front morph into an eight-man moral pilgrimage that leads the 'multicultural' squad— Sergeant Horvath (Miller's right-hand man and confidant), Corporal Upham (the bookish, feminized translator), Wade (the merciful medic), Private Reiben (the Brooklyn bad boy), Private Jackson (the Scripture-citing sharpshooter), Private Caparzo (the Italian), and Private Mellish (the Jew)—into greater and greater peril. With them we set out on the journey asking, "Can [anyone] explain the math in this to me? Where's the sense to risk the eight of [them] to save one

guy?" At the end, like the young Ryan, we are left standing on an Allied-held bridge in the fictitious town of Romelle, with Miller's last, barely whispered, command echoing in our ears, "Earn this." Therein lie the simple contours of a story about doing the decent, patriotic thing even when "the whole world has taken a turn for the surreal," even when, on their face, the numbers just don't add up.

Of course, the numbers add up in *Saving Private Ryan* at an astonishing rate. Much of the enthusiasm for the movie is attributed to what is typically, albeit mistakenly, referred to by reviewers as its "opening scene," Spielberg's recreation of the U.S. invasion of Normandy. Again and again those twenty-five minutes of meticulously chronicled mass slaughter on Omaha Beach are credited with having set new standards for realistic film-making. In *Newsweek,* for example, Jon Meacham heralds *Saving Private Ryan* for being the first war film to represent "battle as it really was, in all its bloodshed and brutality, terror and tedium";[14] Jay Carr of *The Boston Globe* calls it "the war movie to end all war movies";[15] writing for *The New York Times,* Martin Arnold imputes the film with "introducing a whole new generation to the spilled-guts school of war storytelling."[16] What Norman Mailer's *Naked and the Dead* did for literature, he argues, Stephen Spielberg's *Saving Private Ryan* does for film: expose audiences to "the same brutal, sudden, absurd death—but in this case concentrated carnage—that is, the chaos and reality of combat."[17] However tempting it may be to see the film as, in James Wolcott's words, "an overture of pure cinema" that wholly rejects the "ideals of both patriotism and patriarchy" characteristic of nearly all previous Hollywood renditions of World War II,[18] I want to argue that *Saving Private Ryan* functions rhetorically less as a medium for the demystification of the so-called Good War than as a vehicle for the production of a new national sensibility that is predicated on retooling the category of citizenship.

The first thing that deserves critical attention is the particular manner in which the film deploys the white male body in pain. Almost from the start, Spielberg gives movie-goers what he calls an "unblinking look" at the chaos and carnage that is war.[19] As the Higgins landing craft, crowded with U.S. soldiers, approaches Omaha Beach, the ocean breaking over its sides, orders are issued and raw fear takes its most humble, human form: one GI's hand trembles as it reaches for a canteen and another's vacant eyes look toward the beach; two soldiers vomit and others are barely able to draw in what is certain to be their last breath. Within thirty seconds the ramp is released. Most of the GIs are cut down by merciless, rapid German gunfire before they even step off the craft. Those who manage to clamber over the sides of the vessel are plunged into a sea of streaming bullets. Some drown from the weight of their gear; others are struck down by what appears to be wandering gunshot. Blood billows. As scores of boys and men scramble to get out of the bloody surf, onto the beach and over to the seawall, bodies are blown in half, legs and arms are torn off, faces ripped away. Others die more slowly, clutching their wounds, crying out for their mothers, receiving their last rites as they look with horror at their own entrails pouring out on the sand.

What sets Spielberg's rendition of the carnage of war apart from all the others is neither the rate at which it confronts us with those pained male bodies nor that, for the first time, "we [get to] see, thanks to advances in technology, precisely what happens to the soft-shelled human body when it encounters explosives, projectiles, fuel, flame, and sword."[20] The real "sneak punch" of Spielberg's film, as Wolcott correctly points out, "is that it bypasses the usual introductions to its characters" and goes straight into war.[21] What difference does it make that our encounter with a battlefield soon to be littered with the pained bodies of war precedes our knowing anything about its many victims and few survivors other than that they are all American? There is more than a touch of artistry in Spielberg's inversion; there is rhetoric. In exposing us to countless trembling, perspiring, gagging, punctured, drowning and bleeding bodies, bodies with missing arms, legs, eyes, and faces, before informing us of their individual histories, Spielberg's Omaha Beach scene effectively promotes our patriotic identification with *all* of them while blocking our subjective identification with any *one* of them. In bombarding the audience with these not quite empty signifiers, we become witnesses to a mass execution in which the white pained male

body of war begins to function as a ground for the production of knowledge and judgment. In all its positivity, our collective, albeit mass mediated, experience of the mass slaughter of Americans is a great leveler of sorts; bearing witness to material, corporal, sensual pain stands in for the preideological, apolitical, universal and, thus, universalizing experience out of which truth ("what really counts") and prudential wisdom ("what should be done") may emerge.

That bearing witness to the sheer facticity of the U.S. GI in pain may be the foundation for a new rationality from which a vision of "the life worth living" can be derived is, of course, the story *Saving Private Ryan* finally tells. Having made the trek back to Normandy and standing over Captain John Miller's grave, the aged Ryan with generations in tow closes the film with the following words:

> Tell me I have lived a good life. . . . Tell me I'm a good man.

If Ryan is positioned *in* the film as someone scripted to gauge the value of his life in relation to those soldiers who, despite differences in age, education, class, religion, and ethnicity, collectively sacrificed their own to save it, we are positioned *by* the film to do so as well. Having come "as close to combat as most of us will ever get,"[22] those dead American men, to turn only slightly the well-known phrase from Protagoras, become for us the measure of all things. In this way the moral message of the film bleeds beyond its diegetic frame and is infused with modern rhetorical force: the white pained male body of World War II is made to serve as arbitrator of individual and collective national life.

The second thing to notice about *Saving Private Ryan* is its heavy reliance on verbal and visual paramnesias, images that, as Lauren Berlant has put it, "organize consciousness, not by way of explicit propaganda, but by replacing and simplifying memories people actually have with image traces of political experience about which people can have political feelings that link them to other citizens and to patriotism."[23] Without a doubt, the pained body of war is one such image; "home" is another. I think it is no accident that the two-and-a-half hour rescue of Ryan is punctuated by real as well as remembered scenes of home.

Indeed, when the men in Miller's ranger unit are not fighting desperately to survive the battles so as eventually to get home, they incessantly talk about it. With them we visit, visually or imaginatively, sanitized and sentimentalized images of "home," from the country kitchen and pristine porch of the Ryan family farm in Iowa to a dressing room in a small women's shop on a small street in Brooklyn to a young boy's bedroom visited by a mother who has just returned from the second shift and to the hammock and rose bushes in Miller's backyard. Decisively juxtaposed against the gritty chaos of war on foreign territory, "home" is transformed over the course of the movie into a fantastical space that is utterly bereft of the complexities, ambivalences, and incoherence of daily U.S. life both in those war-torn years and today. Such an idealized vision/version of "home" is represented in this film as the nation's humble, homely, utopian aspiration, its version of "the good life."[24]

Having attended critically to these two typically under-acknowledged elements of the film, it becomes possible to appreciate more fully the rhetorical import of another: the frame narrative. Contrary to what reviews in the popular press would lead us to believe, *Saving Private Ryan* begins and ends with a multigenerational journey to the gravesite of Captain John Miller in a U.S. cemetery in France, at which the now grayhaired and teary-eyed Ryan delivers his long awaited soliloquy:

> My family is with me today. They wanted to come with me. To be honest with you, I wasn't sure how I would feel coming back here. Every day I think about what you said to me that day on the bridge. I have tried to live my life the best I could. I hope that was enough. I hope at least in your eyes I have earned what all of you have done for me.

Claiming *Saving Private Ryan* as the progenitor to a new generation of U.S. realist cinema all but necessitates that critics not mention this highly sentimental, even saccharine, scene. Something else is at stake as well. In refusing to attend to the truncated narrative that frames the tale of the rescue of young Ryan, critics disavow what may be one of the film's most disturbing consequences for U.S. collective life today: its domestication of civic responsibility.[25]

The drama of the core narrative hinges to a significant degree on the anxiously anticipated encounter with the real James Francis Ryan. For Miller and his rangers, progress on this mission is neither steady nor swift. The journey to Ryan is interrupted by unexpected and costly encounters with hostile German forces, re-routed because of a mistaken middle name, and nearly aborted by a one-man mutiny. With each calamity and casualty, the investment in Ryan goes up, to the point at which even Miller, the Captain whose steadfast determination to find Ryan and thus "earn [him] the right to get back to [his] wife," is given pause to question the "mission [that] is a man": "This Ryan better be worth it. He better go home and cure some disease or invent the longer lasting light bulb or something." Of course, by its end, audiences know that Ryan went home, and they may reasonably surmise on the basis of his mild demeanor and modest dress that he neither developed a vaccine nor "brought new good things to life."

Here the motif of counting that played such a central role in the core narrative of the film makes itself felt in—and beyond—the frame. Did Ryan earn it? Is he a good man? The film ends with the assurance that its audience has learned to count the ways: a wife; a son and daughter-in-law; a grandson and granddaughters. A solid body count; a fruitful and productive life; a closing portrait of the multigenerational white iconic citizen subject who embodies the becoming-national of home and the becoming-private of citizenship. For all its blood and guts, *Saving Private Ryan* rhetorically expresses, justifies, and induces nostalgia for a national *future* in which each individual's debt to the republic may be paid in minor acts of "privatize[d] patriotism."[26]

Less than four months after the release of *Saving Private Ryan* and on the eve of the Jasper dragging-death trial, the Center for Individual Rights' anti-affirmative action lawsuit against the University of Washington Law School, and a landmark settlement of $3.1 million to underpaid female employees of the Texaco oil company, Tom Brokaw's *The Greatest Generation* appeared in bookstores across the nation. Within two months this collection of the life stories of forty-seven U.S. men and women whom Brokaw began interviewing on the fortieth anniversary of D-Day and who in one way or another played a part in the Allied war effort was number one on the *New York Times* non-fiction bestseller list. By mid-January of 1999, NBC's *Dateline* had aired its own prime-time documentary on Brokaw's book, and, owing to its remarkable popularity, *The Greatest Generation* was reissued in paperback, large print, and audio editions.[27] On the basis of the substantive and stylistic similarities between Spielberg's and Brokaw's odes to the Americans who came of age during the Great Depression and the WWII years, as well as U.S. audiences' obvious appetite for them, columnists proclaimed the emergence of "World War II chic" or "retro patriotism," a new popular culture form whose "purpose . . . is to represent a world where all the tensions of the present are subsumed by the mission and the men."[28]

To read *The Greatest Generation* as inducing readers to escape the social conflicts of the present by imaginatively transporting themselves into the past is to grossly oversimplify the rhetoricity of Brokaw's text. Not only does the book invoke explicitly the domestic social injustices that vexed the country during and immediately after the war as well as commemorate the individuals who overcame them, it also persistently calls up the disparities of social power which plague it today and lays all blame for any citizen's failure at her or his own feet. Indeed, by strategically juxtaposing an imperfect past and a troubled present, Brokaw's trip down memory lane doubles as a vicious attack on today's identity politics, using history as an alibi for a civics lesson that instructs its readership to turn a blind eye to the social differences that still make a difference.

Much like Spielberg's cinematic account, Brokaw's treatment of WWII delivers the World War II of "ordinary" Americans. In the main, it tells the story of the little people's war, of their heretofore unsung struggles and unacknowledged sacrifices: of Lloyd Kilmer who, after spending ten months in German prisoner camps, returned home to marry, raise a family, sell real estate, and serve as County Clerk; of Daphne Cavin, a near newlywed who, after learning her 22-year-old husband had been killed by enemy fire in France, made her way as a beautician in Lebanon, Indiana; of Martha Settle Putnea who, as a young black member of the Women's

Auxiliary Corps, contended daily with institutional racism but later earned her doctorate and became a professor of history; of Wesley Ko, who, upon his return to the States after serving in the 82nd Airborne, joined forces with a friend and opened a printing business, married, and raised a son and two daughters. As has already been hinted, for all their striking similarities there is something that sets *The Greatest Generation* apart from *Saving Private Ryan*. *The Greatest Generation* has as much to tell us about the lives of these Americans after the war as during it. Indeed, most of this book describes in meticulous detail the U.S. postwar era, those decades during which "more than twelve million men and women put their uniforms aside," "returned to civilian life,"[29] and, along with those who had worked on behalf of the allied victory on the home front, "immediately began the task of rebuilding their lives and the world they wanted" (xx).

What is the significance of Brokaw's treating our "rendezvous with destiny" as the point of departure for forty-seven tales of personal triumph that take place when all is again relatively quiet on the European and Pacific fronts? It facilitates the transmogrification of WWII from a sign that has the status of an event into what Michel Foucault has called a technology, what rhetoricians have long called *doxa,* and what I, following others, have termed a new *esprit de corps* that has the status of a structure. In *The Greatest Generation,* WWII shifts from being an event in the past about which we make sense to become a mode of sense-making in the present. Under Brokaw's pen, WWII becomes a shorthand for a retroactive common sense or "matrix of practical reason" through which we are able collectively to comprehend and negotiate the challenges of modern life,[30] not the least of which is the ideological unity of the U.S. polity itself. As Brokaw opines in the closing pages of the book:

There is no world war to fight today nor any prospect of one anytime soon, but racial discrimination remains an American cancer. There is no Great Depression, but economic opportunity is an unending challenge, especially in a high-tech world where education is more important than ever. Most of all, there is the need to reinstate the concept of common welfare in America, so that the nation doesn't squander the legacy of this remarkable generation by becoming a collection of well-defined, narrowly cast special-interest fiefdoms, each concerned only with its own place in the mosaic. (388–89)

As he reports over the course of his sympathetically spun stories, a citizenry that has become ever more heterogeneous and contentious has begun to leave its demoralizing and devastating mark on the nation. Here the anchorman joins with other like-minded statesmen and spokespersons in bemoaning the new "identity" or "victim" politics, holding it accountable for an impending crisis of national character and national culture. Whereas "the women and members of ethnic groups who were the objects of acute discrimination" during and immediately after the war "have not allowed it to cripple them, nor have they invoked it as a claim for special treatment now" (388), subsequent generations of socially injured Americans are, according to Brokaw, disproportionately invested in their own putative subjection. How, then, might we arrest this attitudinal erosion? How might we reverse the national course, "transcend partisan considerations," and cultivate a sense of oneness? By training, to use Brokaw's words, "a new kind of army" (xx) of citizen-subjects schooled in three classic American virtues— self-reliance, self-discipline, and self-sacrifice— that have been retooled to suit the demands of the multicultural state. Notably, *The Greatest Generation* is that new army's field handbook. Here, what Toby Miller has identified as the call for "the well-tempered self," which first rang out in mid-sixteenth-century Europe with the mass dissemination of Erasmus's *De civilitate morum puerilium (On civility in children),* reaches a new pitch.[31] To have read *The Greatest Generation* is to have completed a tutorial in the kind of radical subjective reformation requisite to national renewal.

It is hard to imagine a popular text more adroit at using history for the purpose of U.S. national (re)building. *The Greatest Generation's* success in doing so lies in the precise manner in which it strategically invokes and foregrounds the social and cultural differences of the past— economic, racial, gender, and ethnic—in order to prompt its readers to discount them in the present. That is, *The Greatest Generation* engineers a singular version of the "then" in order to induce its readers to disavow their own primary and political passionate attachments "now"; allegiance to the nation or interpellation into the national is to be secured by a willed disregard for certain particularities of self that readers, in their reading, will already have begun to enact.

By its end, readers will be well-versed and practiced in the art of personal abstraction that in this book is the *sine qua non* of national consubstantiality. Brokaw's assemblage of tales, both thematically and formally, is an exercise in disincorporation.[32] First, thematically. Again and again, readers encounter variations on the same basic theme: thanks to the qualities of character developed during the war—self-reliance, self-discipline, and self-sacrifice—scores of Americans were able to beat the incredible odds that mitigated against their success, be it physical disability, economic privation, gender oppression, or racial and ethnic discrimination. In each case, becoming part of "the greatest generation" is accomplished through the self-conscious dismissal of the particular and potentially disabling material attributes of the body. One representative example is the profile of Sergeant Johnnie Holmes. Indeed, the life story of this black American who served in the 761st Tank Battalion and later in life "specialized" in "low-income rental apartment in buildings in black neighborhoods" supplies Brokaw with an exemplary illustration of how the racially marked and stigmatized person can succeed by reimagining himself as unmarked:

For all of his combative ways, Johnnie decided he wouldn't personally bow to the inherent frustration of discrimination. As he puts it today, "If I let all of the negatives intervene, 1 would have never achieved anything. I kept focused on what I wanted to do, which was to make money, provide for my family. . . ." It was as a landlord and as a black man who had overcome so much on his own that he came to hate the welfare system that grew so fast in the fifties, sixties, and seventies. "It just killed ambition," according to Holmes. "I had all of these [black] tenants who in their late twenties had never worked a day in their life. They just waited around for that government check. No incentive." (200–01)

Obviously, this is the unabashed celebration of the individuated liberal subject as well as a bourgeois norm of relative material comfort, the discursive obliteration of the politics, as effects of power, of the asymmetrical distribution of opportunity and resources in the nation, and the privatization of civic responsibility and social virtue.[33] Notably, what underwrites all of the above in this vignette is the persistent self-repudiation of the particularities of embodiment. Requisite to success and, thus, national belonging, is what Sergeant Johnnie Holmes, in his "twilight years," calls keeping one's "focus on what one wants to do" (200).

Second, by virtue of the serial structure of the book, the social and cultural particularities of physical ability, class, gender, race, and ethnicity are rendered paratactic. That is, in this assemblage asymmetries of embodiment become differences to which readers learn to be indifferent, markings to which readers are taught to turn a blind eye. It is hardly fortuitous, then, that the first of the forty-seven vignettes recounts the travails and triumphs of Thomas Broderick, who lost his sight to a German bullet in the head. *"What's a handicap?"* asks Brokaw's blind bard in the epigraph that opens the book. *"I don't have a handicap"* (17). Here the pained male body of World War II, which, in *Saving Private Ryan,* was the preideological ground for prudential wisdom and judgment, reaches its apogee.

If *The Greatest Generation* is a pedagogy for citizenship in the multicultural age that induces readers to enact the fantasy of the undifferentiated "We" of "We the People," what are we to make of the photographs throughout of "those men and women who have given us the lives we have today" (xxx)? Might these visual displays of the particular block the reader's translation into disincorporated subjectivity? When, in his preface, Brokaw reflects on his book and declares that he does not understand it to be "the defining history of [the WWII] generation" but "instead, think[s] of [it] as like a family portrait" (xxx), he is not speaking only figuratively. Indeed, Brokaw, his research assistants, and his publishers have gone to considerable lengths to recover and reproduce some one hundred and thirty amateurish snapshots, stock family photos, and studio portraits that lend the volume the appearance and feel of a family photo album whose images visually relate a tale that has yet to be determined. As Annette Kuhn has written in *Family Secrets: Acts of Memory and Imagination,* in family photo albums,

> pictures get displayed one after another, their selection and ordering as meaningful as the pictures themselves. The whole, the series, constructs a family story in some respects like a classical narrative: linear, chronological; though its cyclical repetitions of climactic moments—births, christenings, weddings, holidays . . .—is more characteristic of the open-ended narrative form of the soap opera than of the closure of classical narrative. In the process of using—producing, selecting, ordering, displaying—photographs, the family is actually in the process of making itself.[34]

What sort of national family story, then, is being made as we read Brokaw's ensemble of inscriptions of shadow and light?

Significantly, like its verbal counterpart, Brokaw's collection of images is structured as a series of discrete but intimately related vignettes, each of which is composed of at least two photos, a "before the return from the war" shot followed by a "long after the return from the war" shot. Obviously, the strategic sequencing has one primary function, to visually authenticate the verbal text,[35] but if each pair of photos works alone to certify the verisimilitude of the verbal tale, taken together they produce a different truth effect. When viewed together, as an album or archive, serialization displaces sequence, and the negation of difference is effected through its pluralization. On the visual plane, then, a paratactical logic reduces the asymmetries of embodiment to equivalence, interchangeability, invisibility. Indeed, by the time readers near the end of Brokaw's tutorial, they will have been trained to disregard the otherwise noticeable fact that the concluding seventeen vignettes, notably entitled "Famous People" and "The Arena," feature the life stories of fourteen white men, two white women, and one "model minority," Daniel Inouye, whose closing words in this context encapsulate, to use Wendy Brown's terms, "liberalism's universal moment" for the multicultural state in late-capitalism:[36] "The one time the nation got together was World War II. We stood as one. We spoke as one. We clenched our fists as one, and that was a rare moment for all of us" (356). *The Greatest Generation* is a particularly insidious rhetoric, an anti-political political image-text that, in claiming merely to be representing what it is helping to produce and promote, advances a highly normative, indeed exclusionary, notion of the citizen-subject, of the *sensus communitatis,* of the national family.

With the opening of its doors to the general public in the fall of 1997, the Women in Military Service for America Memorial, a 33,000-square-foot structure situated at the ceremonial gateway to Arlington Cemetery, would appear to have dealt a decisive blow to (largely white) masculine presumption and male privilege on the Washington Mall and in the national symbolic. For the first time in our nation's history, the heretofore unacknowledged accomplishments of the more than two million U.S. women who had served in domestic and international crises since the Revolutionary War were understood to be worth their symbolic weight in granite, steel, and glass. Thus, on the eve of the new millennium and in the wake of the Tailhook, Aberdeen, and Citadel investigations, it seemed we were a nation finally prepared to get our history right. As Mary Rose Oakar, who while serving as a member of the House of Representatives introduced Resolution 36 to authorize the establishment of the Memorial, put it on dedication day: "This Memorial will change the teaching of American history. We will know that in every war, contrary to past popular belief, women have been killed, disabled and injured physically and psychologically. We will know of women's bravery, courage, their love, dedication and sacrifice for their country and their strong desire for world peace."[37] The Women's Memorial does much more than call attention to the systematic exclusion of women from the annals of U.S. military history and, thus, implicitly call for its revision. Rather than leave that job to posterity, the memorial takes on itself the compensatory task. "This memorial," as the mission statement on one of the central interior walls boldly declares, not only "honors the women who have served in and with the U.S. Armed Forces from the time of the American Revolution to the present. . . . The Education Center within this memorial tells the stories of these forerunners and then focuses on women of

the 20th century who have served both in and with the military in ever-expanding roles."

Because of its educative function, WIMS is more akin to a museum than a memorial or monument. To step into the Women's Memorial is to leave the minimalist rhetoric and aesthetic of national commemoration and to move into an elaborate system of representation in which a complex assemblage of image-texts is strategically engineered for particular pedagogical effect.[38] Upon crossing its threshold, patrons of the memorial find themselves in a centrally located exhibit gallery. There, various objects, from reproductions of photographs, paintings, drawings, and posters to flight log-books, dog tags, hand-made clothespins, undergarments, and uniforms, are consolidated within exhibit alcoves that track the numerous roles women have played in the nation's military history. With the assistance of explanatory plates and a guidebook as well as a thirteen-minute video presentation, "In Defense of a Nation: The History of Women in the Military," shown at regular intervals in the memorial's state-of-the-art theater, visitors become witnesses to an impressive collection of evidence that points toward one unambiguous and uncontestable truth, that from the beginning, women have been *agents* of U.S. history even if they have been excluded from its interested (re)telling.

The memorial's declared pedagogical purpose is advanced in other ways as well. From the renovated hemicycle wall "representing the barriers to greater opportunity and recognition that women have encountered in their efforts to serve our country" to the four new stairways "carved through the existing stone and concrete, symboliz[ing] women's efforts to break through these barriers,"[39] the memorial challenges conventional wisdom and makes visible a national past in which women are seen always to have been vital participants in rather than passive beneficiaries of military engagement, both at home and abroad. Indeed, nowhere is the memorial's repudiation of majoritarian male culture and its biased retelling of U.S. military history made more explicit than on its roof, a literalization, indeed materialization, of the "glass ceiling," this one constructed out of 138 rectangular transparent glass tablets, on eleven of which are etched words such as the following:

From the storm-lashed decks of the Mayflower . . . to the present hour, woman has stood like a rock for the welfare of the history of the country, and one might well add . . . unwritten, unrewarded, and almost unrecognized (Clara Barton, Founder of the American Red Cross, 1911); Let the generations know that women in uniform also guaranteed their freedom. That our resolve was just as great as the brave men who stood among us and with victory our hearts were just as full and beat just as fast—that the tears fell just as hard for those we left behind (Unknown U.S. Army Nurse, WWII); The ground they broke was hard soil indeed. But with great heart and true grit, they plowed right through the prejudice and presumption, cutting a path for their daughters and granddaughters to serve their country in uniform (Secretary of Defense William J. Perry, Groundbreaking, June 22, 1995).

An unguarded, dare we say militant, feminist stance against the received history?

For the rhetorical critic of U.S. culture poised to appreciate the memorial's contestatory force, a seemingly abstract lesson of so-called elite or high theory, that a discontinuous relation always already obtains between origins and ends, may make itself felt as a productive practical caution, that is, to refuse the presumption that, as Peggy Phelan has put it, "increased visibility equals increased power."[40] Not necessarily, not always, not only, because at this particular conjuncture, it may not.[41] In this instance, as Lacan once put it, visibility may be a trap.[42] Indeed, a critical analysis of the memorial makes it possible to discern the way in which this lesson in revisionary history may be pressed into the service of another ideological agenda.

As noted, the heart or center of the memorial is an exhibit gallery housing sixteen alcoves that, by virtue of running the length of the renovated hemicycle, may be accessed from double doors on either end. Upon entering, visitors to the memorial inescapably happen upon seven glass-enclosed display cases, four of which house exhibits devoted to women's role in World War II, the other three home to displays documenting women's service in the 18th and 19th centuries, between 1901–1945, and since 1946. Although all of these exhibits visually document the always crucial but expanding role of women in the armed

forces through the deployment of reproductions of photographs, drawings, and paintings, the veracity and impact of the former are enhanced considerably by the incorporation of a massive collection of the paraphernalia of women and war. Indeed, these World War II displays are loaded from floor to ceiling with an array of objects that, notably, do not record the fantastic feats of singular individuals but, instead, metonymically mark the regular rhythms and daily practices of our nation's service women. Among scores of others are a pair of mosquito boots that protected one Army nurse in Africa from contracting malaria, a sample identification card issued to all WAC recruits, one of the hundreds of summer uniforms issued to WAVES inductees, the helmet and calculation instruments used by an unidentified Air Force Service Pilot, one anonymous student's handwritten notes on how to repair guns and pack parachutes, and another's Army-issued underwear and pajamas. From the first installment to the last, what the World War II collection features are ordinary, commonplace objects; typicality rather than rarity subtends the order of things here. The principle of typicality also underwrites the photographs that have been incorporated into the permanent exhibits. Instead of bearing witness to striking moments of uncommon valor, these archived images make visible the collective or cooperative, anonymous, even monotonous or generic character of servicewomen's daily life: here a sea of telephone operators, there a secretarial pool, here the U.S. Cadet Nurse Corps in formation, there a mass of women working on a factory line so as to "free our men to fight." Although rare, when they do appear, formal portraits and snapshots of individual women in particular situations are reconfigured into a collage, thereby reconstituting them as members of some larger whole and those events as part of a broader-based effort. When amassed, arranged, and placed under or behind glass, then, the artifacts presented in the exhibit alcoves are invested with new significance, are infused with new force, with "representativeness." In this way, a seemingly complete, unabridged history of women in the U.S. armed services begins metonymically to be made visible and present.

As noted, all of the objects brought together at WIMS are placed in individual exhibit alcoves that have been clearly labeled and chronologically arranged: "Serving with the Military: 18th and 19th Centuries," "Serving in the Military: 1901–1945," "Women Go to War: World War II," "Servicewomen in World War II: Recruiting, Training and On the Job," "Volunteering On the Homefront: World War II," "Overseas With the Military: World War II," and "Serving In The Military Since 1946." Thus, although each individual window onto the past is made to represent a distinct period of U.S. military history and women's place in it, the passage from the first to the last reveals, step-by-step, women's *ever-evolving* role in the armed services, their *natural* ascension over time from handmaiden to helicopter pilot, from battlefield nurse to Brigadier General. The sequential display of periodized artifacts has been supplemented by two complementary narratives, a relatively elaborate *Self Guided Tour* manual that visitors may pick up at the entrance to the memorial and a much abbreviated version that appears in installments over the course of the exhibit.[43]

The hand-held script is a mechanism to normalize and naturalize women's integration into the Armed Services by making it appear as the always already determined outcome of a process whose reasonableness has been made legible over time. First of all, the repeated deployment of the constative utterance helps to conceal the discursive status of the display, thereby leaving patrons with the impression that, rather than having been authored by someone, the written supplement has been dictated by the objects and movement of U.S. history itself.[44] The impact of this "exhibition rhetoric," which accentuates the objects as it effaces itself, is augmented by two strategic silences that conceal the artistry at work.[45] Not once does the name of a photographer appear on the legend that accompanies each display case (in every case, however, the collection or archive from which the object has been extracted or donated is clearly identified), and nowhere in the memorial or in any of its public relations literature are the curators of the exhibits acknowledged. Second, the script's adroit inclusion of directives to patrons on how they are to read crucial elements of the visual text controls to a considerable degree the images' signifying effects. Indeed, when pictures alone may fail, words appear: "The individuals pictured here are representative rather than famous"; "Again, the majority of photos are not of famous women but show the variety of ways in which women have served with the military since WWII"; "The increased number of photographs in this panel reflects the increasing numbers of women in the services during peacetime and times of conflict. . . ." (*Tour*). Third, the thoroughgoing exclusion from the script of any reference to the asymmetrical social relations, material circumstances, and hierarchical logics that have structured and continue to structure the recruitment and incorporation of women into the Armed Services, makes these processes appear to be the inevitable outcome of women's ever-evolving place in the military establishment, which belies the historicity of women's enfranchisement. Indeed, this is sensationally demonstrated in the decision to mark and mark off the Women's Armed Services Integration Act of 1948.[46] Presented as a singular, even watershed, moment in the exhibit gallery, the memorialization of the Integration Act neatly buries gender inequality within U.S. military history as a *fait accompli,* thereby constituting the present as postfeminist, postpolitical.

Figure 2 Women in Military Services of America Memorial.

SOURCE: Photograph by the author.

Often, to represent history in evolutionary terms is to privilege a conservative model of social transformation, one that promotes a general tolerance of the status quo predicated on the understanding or belief that change is the consequence of some greater force—capital H History or biology, for example. Nonetheless, the exhibit gallery can be seen to make a call for a certain kind of collective action, one that is given palpable expression through the memorial's computerized registry and receives dramatic reinforcement from its engraved glass ceiling. Adjacent to the exhibit hall but visible from it is a room that houses twelve individual computer keyboards and screens through which visitors may access "the photographs, military histories and memorable experiences" of "women veterans, active duty, reserve, and guard women, and women who have served in direct support of the military throughout history" (*Tour*). Additionally, three larger-than-life screens have been placed above the entrance to the registry; there the name, record of service, and photographic image of every registered service-woman serially appears by way of a computer-generated around-the-clock roll call. Operating in tandem with the exhibit gallery, the computerized registry deftly deploys the new information technologies, linking the abstract national to the situated local; in their engagement with the official image archive, visitors literally perform acts of identification that provide them with embodied models of normative national character. Finally, the pilgrimage to the upper terrace caps off the "self-guided tour" of WIMS. For patrons already party to the complex rationalization displayed below, the words etched on the roof not only grant official public voice to the women who have served, but they also function rhetorically as injunctions to serve the national cause:

You have a debt and a date. A debt to democracy, a date with destiny (Oveta Culp Hobby, Colonel, Director of the Women's Army Corps, World War II); All of us must work at patriotism, not just believe in it. For only by our young women offering their services to our country as working patriots in the armed forces can our defense be adequate (Helen Hayes, Defense Advisory Committee on Women in the Services, 1951); The qualities that are most important in all military jobs—things like integrity, moral courage, and

determination—have nothing to do with gender (Rhonda Cornum, Major, U.S. Army Medical Corps, Operation Desert Storm).

Hence, in addition to advancing an account of U.S. military history that, for the first time, duly acknowledges women's role in it, the Women's Memorial scripts a version of normative U.S. identity in which service to the nation is the *arche* and *telos* of what it means for any American—man or woman—in the words of the *Self Guided Tour,* to "exercise full citizenship." Thus, out of a memorial "dedicated to the women who have served" emerges an abstract category of civic agency that folds feminine subjectivity into universal (masculine) virtues. As Major Marie Rossi, killed in a helicopter crash the day following the close of the Gulf War, stoically noted in a nationally televised interview, a portion of which is woven into the Memorial's own video presentation: "It's our jobs. There was nothing peculiar about our being women. We were just the people called upon to do it."

Between the release of *Tora! Tora! Tora!* in 1970 and the premier of *Saving Private Ryan* in 1998, WWII virtually disappeared from U.S. popular culture. Today it is a cottage industry. Thus, this essay asks and offers one answer to the question why and how, exactly, is the "Good War" being given back to us today, and to what effect? Like other analyses of collective memory's relationship with nation (re)building, this study is underwritten by the more or less explicit assumption that what we remember and how we remember it can tell us something significant about who we are as a people now, about the contemporary social and political issues that divide us, and about who we may become. As Michael Kammen put it in the introduction to his classic study of the connection between collective memory and U.S. identity from the antebellum period to the mid-1980s, "societies . . . reconstruct their pasts rather than faithfully record them, and . . . they do so with needs of contemporary culture clearly in mind—manipulating the past in order to mold the present" and, I would add, the future.[47] Hence, with others, I have assumed that claiming and representing the past is far from being an innocent affair. In fact, the stakes could not be higher because, in the words of Michel Foucault, "if one controls people's memory, one controls their dynamism."[48]

Just as important as recognizing that collective memory is rhetorical is recognizing that the kind of rhetorical work particular memory texts do is not determined in advance. Collective memory *per se* is neither necessarily conservative nor innovative in force. Instead, the political entailments of collective memory are an effect of what and how we remember, and the uses to which those memories are put. Thus, prompted by the unprecedented decision to break ground between the Washington Monument and the Lincoln Memorial for a structure commemorating not just the veterans of WWII but also an exemplary era of "American national unity," this examination of several contemporary WWII texts argues that the return of WWII may be understood as a more or less thinly veiled conservative response to the contemporary crisis of national identity, to our failing sense of what it means to be an American and to do things the so-called American way. Indeed, I have tried to demonstrate how *Saving Private Ryan* and *The Greatest Generation* redefine in highly restrictive and distinctively centrist terms what it means to be a "good American." Although both the film and book advocate the domestication and privatization of civic responsibility, the latter heightens the effect by coaching readers to an individualist sense of civic self predicated on the imaginative discounting of the marks of structurally and institutionally supported social inequalities that are recoded in these popular culture texts as *mere* cultural difference. I have also tried to show how the potentially innovative or progressive political force of the Women in Military Service for America Memorial is colonized by its articulation into this broader popular culture frame or formation. Taken together, then, these memory texts assist in the reconsolidation and naturalization of traditional logics and matrices of privilege that today traverse the various arenas of collective life, from the political to juridical, the economic to the social. By inflecting the constitutive and not merely reflexive role of these popular culture memory texts, this essay also argues implicitly that it is possible to remember otherwise, that not only what we remember but how we remember it could be different, and that collective memory could be pressed into the service of a very different politics. Finally, then, this essay urges rhetorical critics and theorists and teachers to critically engage these extraordinarily popular and rapidly multiplying commemorative rhetorics in whose renovated narratives of national belonging our future may (not) lie.

NOTES

1. "The design concept for the memorial is an ensemble of a lowered plaza surrounding the Rainbow Pool, parapet walls surmounted by transparent architectural arms of stone and metal and two monumental memorial arches. The memorial will include iconography, inscriptions, and sculpture as part of the final design. . . . Bronze laurel wreaths are suspended from the oculus of each arch . . . [which] overlook the memorial plaza and Rainbow Pool. . . . The floor of the memorial plaza is an orchestrated blend of green spaces and paved surfaces surrounding the Rainbow Pool. A central ceremonial area is placed at the western apex of the memorial plaza. A curvilinear granite wall is embedded into the waterfalls that navigate the vertical transition between the Reflecting Pool and the Rainbow Pool. Inscriptions honoring the fallen and all who served and a flame of freedom will be incorporated into the ceremonial area. . . . In the center of the plaza, the fountains of the reconstructed Rainbow Pool will be restored to their former splendor as part of the memorial." "About the Memorial: World War II Memorial Homepage" at http://www.wwiimemorial .com, 3 September 1999.

2. George F. Will, "The Statue Sweepstakes," *Newsweek*, 26 August 1991, 64.

3. Subcommittee on Libraries and Memorials of the Committee on House Administration, *Guidelines for the Consideration of Memorials Under the Commemorative Works Act,* 103rd Cong., 2nd sess., 1994, 2.

4. Substantively and stylistically, public debate or lack thereof over the World War II Memorial differs markedly from the lengthy and often heated political struggles that emerged over other proposals to recognize the nation's fallen heroes by raising a structure on their behalf on the Mall, e.g., the Vietnam Veteran's Memorial, the Vietnam Women's Memorial, and the Women in Military Services for America Memorial. An interesting exception in the case of the WWII Memorial was delivered by Judy Scott Feldman, chairwoman of the National Coalition to Save Our Mall, during her testimony before the Commission of Fine Arts. She objected vigorously to the proposed memorial's "imperial and triumphal design," which was "unacceptably reminiscent of

Fascist and Nazi regimes." Cited in Irvin Molotsky, "Panel Backs World War II Memorial on Mall in Washington," *New York Times,* 21 July 2000, Al.

5. Molotsky, I. Across the country, 43 newspapers, including *The New York Times, The Washington Post,* and *USA Today,* printed at least one article or editorial opposing the site, many of them reprints.

6. Rolland Kidder, "War Memorial Will Be In Its Proper Setting," *Buffalo News,* 6 June 1997, 3C.

7. "Remarks by President Clinton at the Tomb of the Unknown Soldier, Arlington National Cemetery," *Federal News Service,* 11 November 1995. Online. Lexis. 22 July 2000.

8. The memorial's statement of purpose reads: "The World War II Memorial will be the first national memorial dedicated to all who served in the armed forces and Merchant Marine of the United States during World War II and acknowledging the commitment and achievement of the entire nation. All military veterans of the war, the citizens on the home front, the nation at large, and the high moral purpose and idealism that motivated the nation's call to arms will be honored. Symbolic of the defining event of the 20th century in American history, the memorial will be a monument to the spirit, sacrifice, and commitment of the American people, to the common defense of the nation and to the broader causes of peace and freedom from tyranny throughout the world. It will inspire future generations of Americans, deepening their appreciation of what the World War II generation accomplished in securing freedom and democracy. Above all, the memorial will stand for all time as an important symbol of American national unity, a timeless reminder of the moral strength and awesome power that can flow when a free people are at once united and bonded together in a common and just cause." "About the Memorial: WWII Memorial Homepage" at http://www.wwiimemorial.com, 3 September 1999.

9. "Clinton Salutes Veterans, Dedicates Memorial Site," *Los Angeles Times,* 12 November 1995, 4A.

10. Stanley A. Renshon, ed., *One America: Political Leadership, National Identity, and the Dilemmas of Diversity* (Washington, D.C.: Georgetown University Press, 2001), 3. On the contemporary crisis of national identity in the U.S., see also, for example, Peter Brimelow, *Alien Nation: Common Sense about America's Immigration Disaster* (New York: Random House, 1995); Todd Gitlin, *The Twilight of Common Dreams: Why America is Wracked by Culture Wars* (New York: Henry Holt & Company, 1995); Gertrude Himmelfarb, *One Nation, Two Cultures* (New York: Knopf, 1999); John J. Miller, *The Unmaking of Americans: How Multiculturalism Has Undermined America's Assimilation Ethic* (New York: The Free Press, 1998); Susan Moller Okin, ed., *Is Multiculturalism Bad for Women?* (Princeton, New Jersey: Princeton University Press, 1999); Robert Reich, *The Work of Nations: Preparing Ourselves for 21st Century Capitalism* (New York: Vintage Books, 1992); Richard Rorty, *Achieving Our Country* (Cambridge, Mass.: Harvard University Press, 1998); Arthur A. Schlesinger, Jr., *The Disuniting of America: Reflections on a Multicultural Society* (New York: Norton, 1992); and Ronald Takaki, *A Different Mirror: A History of Multicultural America* (Boston: Little, Brown & Company, 1993).

11. I borrow this terminology from Marita Sturken's *Tangled Memories: The Vietnam War, the AIDS Epidemic, and the Politics of Remembering* (Berkeley and Los Angeles: University of California Press, 1997).

12. Another way to describe my analysis is that it seeks to extend Michael McGee's 1975 call for the rhetorical accounting of the discursive production of a <people> by attending not only to the "material forces, events, and themes in history *only as they have already been mediated or filtered by the Leader whose words [we have typically] studied*" (249) but also to those other enunciative sites through which national affiliation is today being produced. Michael McGee, "In Search of 'The People': A Rhetorical Alternative," *Quarterly Journal of Speech* 61 (1975): 235–49.

13. There is a growing theoretical and critical literature on the relationship between the nation, the media, and the discursive production of the citizen-subject in the late twentieth century. This analysis takes several of its cues from Lauren Berlant's analysis of infantile citizenship in *The Queen of America Goes to Washington City: Essays on Sex and Citizenship* (Durham and London: Duke University Press. 1997), Lawrence Grossberg's account of the politically disaffected citizen in *We Gotta Get Out of this Place: Popular Conservatism and Postmodern Culture* (New York: Routledge, 1992), and Toby Miller's treatment of the cultural citizen in *Technologies of Truth: Cultural Citizenship and the Popular Media* (Minneapolis: University of Minnesota Press, 1998).

14. Jon Meacham, "Caught in the Line of Fire," *Newsweek,* 13 July 1998, 50.

15. Christopher Caldwell, "Spielberg at War," *Commentary* 106 (October 1998): 48.

16. Martin Arnold, "'Private Ryan' Revives a Genre," *New York Times,* 30 July 1998, E3.

17. Arnold, E3.

18. James Wolcott, "Tanks for the Memories," *Vanity Fair* 456 (August 1998): 73.

19. Henrick Hertzberg, "Theatre of War," *New Yorker,* 27 July 1998, 31.

20. Jean Bethke Elshtain, "Spielberg's America," *Tikkun* 13 (Nov/Dec 1998): 73.

21. Wolcott, 75.

22. Meacham, 50.

23. Berlant, 57.

24. In a book-length analysis of the return of WWII now in progress, I attend at length to the question of the representation of women and its political entailments. I note here the sexism and, at times, unabashed misogyny at work throughout the film but most visible in scenes during which combat abates and members of the ranger unit engage in "intimate" conversation. Consider, for example, the Brooklyn bad boy's recounting of Mrs. Rachel Cherbowitz's advice from the dressing room of his mother's shop that "if [he's] ever scared" he "close [his] eyes and remember these" "44EEs" or "massive things"; and Ryan's jovial recollection of "the last night the four [Ryan brothers] were together," memorable for the brothers' thwarted rape of Alice Jardine, "a girl who just took a nose dive from the ugly tree and hit every branch coming down." Furthermore, although there are no fantasy rape scenarios in *The Greatest Generation,* I will argue that certain women fare no better there. I will suggest that the subtle but crucial shift from a neo-conservative rhetoric of "family values" to a rhetoric of the "national family" that I analyze in this essay is effected in part by the strategic re-membering and repositioning of female bodies and desire. Out of this re-membering emerges a newly-determined abject feminine, the "feminist," who refuses to submit her agency to the will of the national family.

25. *Saving Private Ryan* structurally elides the sixties and seventies, those socially and politically tumultuous decades in U.S. history during which citizens literally took to the streets.

26. Edward Rothstein, "Rescuing the War Hero from 1990's Skepticism," *New York Times,* 3 August 1998, E2.

27. Brokaw since has edited and published several other best-selling books for which World War II is a central reference, organizing theme, or point of departure. See, for example, *An Album of Memories: Personal Histories from the Greatest Generation* (New York: Random House, 2001) and *The Greatest Generation Speaks: Letters and Reflections* (New York: Random House, 1999), both reissued in audio format.

28. Richard Goldstein, "World War II Chic," *Village Voice,* 19 January 1999, 47.

29. Torn Brokaw, *The Greatest Generation* (New York: Random House, 1998), 15. All subsequent references to this text will be indicated parenthetically in the essay.

30. Michel Foucault, "Technologies of the Self," in *Technologies of the Self: A Seminar with Michel Foucault,* ed. Luther H. Martin, Huck Gutman, and Patrick H. Hutton (London: Tavistock Publications, 1988), 18.

31. Toby Miller, *The Well-Tempered Self: Citizenship, Culture, and the Postmodern Subject* (Baltimore and London: The Johns Hopkins University Press, 1993).

32. My discussion of disincorporation is indebted to Michael Warner's theorizing in "The Mass Public and the Mass Subject," in *The Phantom Public Sphere,* ed. Bruce Robbins (Minneapolis: University of Minnesota Press, 1993), 234–56.

33. The dismantling of the welfare state and privitization of social responsibility is sometimes boldly, sometimes subtly, but always anecdotally encouraged. See, for example, the story of James and Dorothy Dowling, in the midst of which Brokaw writes: "James Dowling was orphaned soon after he was born. His mother died when he was only six months old and his father was unable to care for this baby and his four brothers and sisters. *In those simpler times, when much of social welfare was a matter of good-hearted people,* the plight of James and his siblings was made known in the church. The minister announced that someone had to take in these children. James and two of his brothers were taken home by the Conklins, Clarence and Anna . . ." (46, emphasis added). Or Brokaw's closing words to "The Dumbos," a vignette recounting the postwar trials and tribulations of four couples "in the small South Dakota city of Yankton": "Outside of our own families, to those of us growing up in Yankton at the time, these World War II couples were emblematic of the values that shaped our

lives. In many respects, *their marriages and the way they conducted them were a form of community service*" (249, emphasis added).

34. Annette Kuhn, *Family Secrets: Acts of Memory and Imagination* (London and New York: Verso, 1995), 17.

35. The literature on the relation of the visual image or the photograph and the verbal text is extensive. Some key works are: Roland Barthes, *Mythologies* (London: Cape, 1972); Roland Barthes, "The Rhetoric of the Image," *Image—Music—Text* (New York: Noonday, 1977), 32–37; John Berger, *Ways of Seeing* (New York: Viking Penguin Inc., 1977); W.J.T. Mitchell, *Picture Theory: Essays on Verbal and Visual Representation* (Chicago: University of Chicago Press, 1994); Susan Sontag, *On Photography* (New York: Doubleday, 1977); and John Tagg, *The Burden of Representation: Essays on Photographies and Histories* (Minneapolis: University of Minnesota Press, 1993).

36. Wendy Brown, *States of Injury: Power and Freedom in Late Modernity* (Princeton, New Jersey: Princeton University Press, 1995), 57.

37. Linda Witt, ed., *The Day the Nation Said "Thanks!" A History and Dedication of the Women In Military Service For America Memorial* (Washington, D.C.: Military Women's Press, 1999), 96.

38. On the minimalist aesthetic and the rhetoric of monumental material culture see, for example, Carole Blair, Marsha S. Jeppeson, and Enrico Pucci, Jr., "Public Memorializing in Postmodernity: The Vietnam Veterans Memorial as Prototype," *Quarterly Journal of Speech* 77 (1991): 263–88; John Bodnar, *Remaking America: Public Memory, Commemoration, and Patriotism in the Twentieth Century* (Princeton, New Jersey: Princeton University Press, 1992); John R. Gillis, ed., *Commemorations: The Politics of National Identity* (Princeton, New Jersey: Princeton University Press, 1994); Kirk Savage, *Standing Soldiers, Kneeling Slaves: Race, War, and Monument in Nineteenth-Century America* (Princeton, New Jersey: Princeton University Press, 1997); and Marita Sturken, *Tangled Memories: The Vietnam War, the AIDS Epidemic, and the Politics of Remembering* (Berkeley and Los Angeles: University of California Press, 1997).

39. Witt, 94.

40. Peggy Phelan, *Unmarked: The Politics of Performance* (London and New York: Routledge, 1993), 7.

41. I am not arguing that WIMS never could perform a radical, interruptive politics. I am claiming that at this particular time and place, in the context of the cultural formation of which it is a part, it is not doing so now. One implication of this analysis for thinking about rhetoric generally is that the popular "polysemy thesis" often begs rather than answers the question, what rhetorical work is being done by or through this text? Although grasping the polysemic nature of all discourse and practice is an important first step, a rigorous rhetorical analysis proceeds to discern those forces that operate provisionally to secure, through processes of articulation, disarticulation, and rearticulation, the effectivity of the text, utterance, or practice. For a cogent review of the conversation in the field that stops short of addressing the question of effectivity, see Leah Ceccarelli, "Polysemy: Multiple Meanings in Rhetorical Criticism," *Quarterly Journal of Speech* 84 (1998): 395–415.

42. "In this matter of the visible, everything is a trap." Jacques Lacan, *Four Fundamental Concepts of Psychoanalysis,* ed. Jacques-Allain Miller, trans. Alan Sheridan (New York: Norton, 1978), 93.

43. *Self Guided Tour: Women in Military Service for America Memorial* (Washington, D.C.: Women in Military Service for America Memorial Foundation, Inc.). All subsequent references in the essay to the *Self Guided Tour* will be indicated by *Tour.* The booklet is not paginated.

44. The exhibit's hand-held script is replete with various gestures of pointing: "See the uniform of Navy nurse Doris Yetter"; "Notice the hand-made clothespin used by Madeline Ullom"; "Also in the exhibit is a pair of custom-made mosquito boots, worn by Army nurses in Africa"; "Notice the photograph of a woman packing a parachute"; etc. For an analysis of the deployment of the constative utterance in museums of natural history and fine art, see Mieke Bal, *Double Exposures: The Subject of Cultural Analysis* (New York and London: Routledge, 1996).

45. I borrow the term "exhibition rhetoric" from Bruce Ferguson's "Exhibition Rhetorics: Material Speech and Utter Sense," in *Thinking About Exhibitions,* ed. Reesa Greenberg, Bruce W. Ferguson, and Sandy Nairne (London and New York: Routledge, 1996), 175–90. There he links Enzensberger's expanded concept of the "cultural industries," which includes "advertising, education, and any institutional use of media techniques intended for vast audiences or what is now often referred to cynically as

'infotainment'" (176) and a classical conception of rhetoric as "a strategic system of representation" (176) in order to argue that "[t]he will to influence is at the core of any exhibition" (179).

46. The Integration Act exhibit, originally placed next to a separate exhibit documenting the history of the memorial's emergence, is soon to be moved to a display case situated between the WWII and new Korean War exhibits. Brigadier General Wilma L. Vaught, Ret. (President, Women in Military Service for America Memorial Foundation, Inc.), interview by author, Washington, D.C., 6 June 2000.

47. Michael Kammen, *Mystic Chords of Memory: The Transformation of Tradition in American Culture* (New York: Vintage Books, 1991), 3.

48. Michel Foucault, "Film and Popular Memory: An Interview with Michel Foucault," trans. Martin Jordan, *Radical Philosophy* (1975): 25.

9

PUBLIC IDENTITY AND COLLECTIVE MEMORY IN U.S. ICONIC PHOTOGRAPHY

The Image of "Accidental Napalm"

ROBERT HARIMAN AND JOHN LOUIS LUCAITES

The growing scholarly attention to visual culture has special significance for those who study mass media, which now are using ever more sophisticated technologies of visual imaging. For the most part, however, the analysis of visual media has been guided by a hermeneutics of suspicion (Jay, 1993; Postman, 1985; Peters, 1997). From this perspective, it is unlikely that a visual practice could ever be equal or superior to discursive media for enacting public reason or democratic deliberation, or that the constitution of identity through the continual reproduction of conventional images could be emancipatory. Indeed, this skepticism imbues the two most important theoretical perspectives on the relationship between discourse and society: ideology critique and the theory of the public sphere.

Although Jürgen Habermas's account of the rise and fall of an ideal public culture has many critics, few have challenged his assumption that

deliberative rationality is subverted by visual display. For Habermas, the verdict is clear: when the public assumed its specific form, "it was the bourgeois reading public . . . rooted in the world of letters" (1989, p. 85), and the subsequent disintegration of that culture was accomplished in part through the rise of the electronic mass media and its displacement of public debate by political spectacles. That said, there is also a strategy of reformulation, employed most recently in the pages of *Critical Studies in Media Communication* by Kevin DeLuca and Jennifer Peeples (2002), which grants the necessity of a public sphere and considers how such a culture could work if it were freed of the constraints of this or that assumption in the classical model. Thus, DeLuca and Peeples argue that in a televisual public sphere, corporate image making is balanced at times by a subaltern staging of image events which demonstrate "[c]ritique through spectacle, not critique versus spectacle" (2002,

SOURCE: Hariman, R., & Lucaites, J. L. (2003). Public identity and collective memory in U.S. iconic photography: The image of "accidental napalm." *Critical Studies in Media Communication, 20*(1), 35–66.

p. 134; see also DeLuca, 1999). We want to go a step further to suggest that the public sphere depends on visual rhetorics to maintain not only its play of deliberative "voices," but also its more fundamental constitution of public identity. Because the public is a discursively organized body of strangers constituted solely by the acts of being addressed and paying attention (Warner, 2002, pp. 65–124), it can only acquire self-awareness and historical agency if individual auditors "see themselves" in the collective representations that are the materials of public culture. Visual practices in the public media play an important role at precisely this point. The daily stream of photojournalistic images, while merely supplemental to the task of reporting the news, defines the public through an act of common spectatorship. When the event shown is itself a part of national life, the public seems to see itself, and to see itself in terms of a particular conception of civic identity.

No one basis for identification can dominate, however, or the public devolves into a specific social group that necessarily excludes others and therefore would no longer be a public. As Habermas notes, "The public sphere of civil society stood or fell with the principle of universal access. A public sphere from which specific groups could be excluded was less than merely incomplete; it was not a public sphere at all" (Habermas, 1989, p. 85). The strategic value of Habermas's grounding of the public in reading is thus apparent, as the positive content of *who* is reading *what* remains tacit. Picture-viewing is another form of tacit experience that can be used to connect people: all *seem* to see the same thing, yet the full meaning of the image remains unarticulated. Most important, visual images also are particularly well suited to constituting the "stranger relationality" that is endemic to the distinctive norms of public address (Warner, 2002, pp. 74–76). The public must include strangers; it "addresses people who are identified primarily through their participation in discourse and who therefore cannot be known in advance" (Warner, 2002, p. 74). Basic principles of the Habermasian public sphere—public use of reason, the bracketing of status, topical openness, and in-principle inclusiveness—have a fundamental orientation toward interaction with strangers. One need not follow any of these

norms to interact with, persuade, be persuaded by, and otherwise live amiably among those one knows; families, for example, typically require these norms to be checked at the door. If photojournalistic images can maintain a vital relationship among strangers, they will provide an essential resource for constituting a mass media audience as a public.

Even if one grants that public deliberation can be mediated visually, the question remains of the extent to which visual practices are subject to ideological control. The belief that a photograph is a clear window on reality is itself an example of the natural attitude of ideology; by contrast, it becomes important to show how a photographic image fails to achieve a transparent representation of its perceptual object. As Victor Burgin notes, all representation is structured, for at "the very moment of their being perceived, objects are *placed* within an intelligible system of relationships. . . . They take their position, that is to say, within an *ideology*" (Burgin, 1992a, pp. 45–46, emphasis in original). Photography, it seems, is no exception. "Photographs are *texts* inscribed in terms of what we may call 'photographic discourse,'" (Burgin, 1992b, p. 144, emphasis in original) and photographic realism is the outcome of an "elaborate constitutive process" (Tagg, 1992, p. 111). From there it's all downhill: once thought to be windows to the real, photographic images become the ideal medium for naturalizing a repressive structure of signs. And there is no doubt that they can function that way, as both prized shots and millions of banal, anonymous images reproduce normative conceptions of gender, race, class, and other forms of social identity.

This critique relies on a pervasive structuralism—and an accompanying logocentricism—that begs the question before us. There is a reading strategy available for working beyond such structural models, however, which is to emphasize the interaction of the several layers of signification that comprise photographic practices. Roland Barthes, despite his strong use of semiotics, acknowledged that the photographic image does have some degree of representational autonomy, and his critical studies focused on the ability of the image to puncture conventional beliefs (1981). Umberto Eco resolved this tension between the individual image and the social repertoire of interpretive codes by recognizing the ways in which every image operates in the context of "successive transcriptions" (1992, p. 3). Such transcriptions negotiate both the general shift between visual and verbal semiotics, and the more specific shifts in meaning that occur as the viewer is cued to specific narratives or interpretive terms by different patterns in and extending beyond the composition. The question, then, is not the autonomy of the visual or the dominance of the system of signs, but how interpretation necessarily moves across different strata of representation, each of which is incomplete yet partially closed off from the others. The full implication of this idea is stated by W.J.T. Mitchell: "The interaction of pictures and text is constitutive of representation as such: All media are mixed media, and all representations are heterogeneous; there are no 'purely' visual or verbal arts, though the impulse to purify media is one of the central utopian gestures of modernism" (1994, p. 5). Following the textual metaphor embedded in most critical discourse about visual practices, this correction applies not only to captions and other verbal materials that frame an image, but to all of the codes of the social text as well. No one code controls all signs, and any sign can shift across multiple codes.

To take this idea a step further, we need to recognize the sense in which visual images are complex and unstable articulations, particularly as they circulate across topics, media, and texts, and thus are open to successive reconstitution by and on behalf of varied political interests, including a public interest. The photographic image coordinates a number of different patterns of identification from within the social life of the audience, each of which would suffice to direct audience response, and which together provide a public audience with sufficient means for comprehending potentially unmanageable events. Because the camera records the decor of everyday life, the photographic image is capable of directing attention across a field of gestures, interaction rituals, social types, political styles, artistic motifs, cultural norms, and other signs as they intersect in any event. As a result, photographs are capable of aesthetic mediations of

political identity that include but also exceed ideological control.

The ambiguous potentiality of photojournalism is particularly evident with those images that become iconic (Goldberg, 1991, pp. 135–62; Hariman and Lucaites, 2001, 2002). On the one hand, these images are moments of visual eloquence that acquire exceptional importance within public life. They are believed to provide definitive representations of political crises and to motivate public action on behalf of democratic values. On the other hand, they are created and kept in circulation by media elites (Perlmutter, 1998), they are used in conjunction with the grand narratives of official history, and they are nothing if not conventional. Most important, perhaps, is the fact that this tension between the performative embodiment of a public interest and the ideological reconstitution of that interest is played out in the process by which collective memory is created through the extended circulation and appropriation of images over time. Even though iconic images usually are recognized as such immediately, and even if they are capable of doing the heavy lifting required to change public opinion and motivate action on behalf of a public interest, their meaning and effects are likely to be established slowly, shift with changes in context and use, and be fully evident only in a history of both official and vernacular appropriations.

The iconic photograph of an injured girl running from a napalm attack provides a complex construction of viewer response that was uniquely suited to the conditions of representation in the Vietnam era, while it also embodies conventions of liberal individualism such as personal autonomy and human rights that have become increasingly dominant within U.S. public culture since then. This ongoing mediation of public life can be explicated both by examining how the photograph's artistry shapes moral judgment and by tracking subsequent narrative reconstructions and visual appropriations of the image in the public media. In what follows, we show how this photograph managed a rhetorical culture of moral and aesthetic fragmentation to construct public judgment of the war, and how it embodies a continuing tension within public memory between a liberal-individualist narrative of denial and compensation and a mode of democratic dissent that involves both historical accountability and continuing trauma. In turn, we believe, this tension reflects and reproduces essential features of the public itself, a social relationship that, because it has to be among strangers, is ever in need of images.

CIVILIANS IN PAIN

The naked little girl is running down a road in Vietnam toward the camera, screaming from the napalm burns on her back and arm. Other Vietnamese children are moving in front of and behind her, and one boy's face is a mask of terror, but the naked girl is the focal point of the picture. Stripped of her clothes, her arms held out from her sides, she looks almost as if she has been flayed alive. Behind her walk soldiers, somewhat casually. Behind them, the roiling dark smoke from the napalm drop consumes the background of the scene.

The photo (Figure 1) was taken by AP photographer Nick Ut on June 8, 1972, released after an editorial debate about whether to print a photo involving nudity, and published all over the world the next day. It then appeared in *Newsweek* ("Pacification's Deadly Price," 1972) and *Life* ("Beat of life," 1972) and subsequently received the Pulitzer Prize. Today it is regarded

as "a defining photographic icon; it remains a symbol of the horror of war in general, and of the war in Vietnam in particular" (Buell, 1999, p. 102; see also Goldberg, 1991, pp. 241–245). Amid many other exceptional photographs and a long stream of video coverage, the photo has come to be regarded as one of the most famous photographs of the Vietnam War and among the most widely recognized images in American photojournalism (Kinney, 2000, p. 187; Sturken, 1997, pp. 89–94). Its stature is believed to reflect its influence on public attitudes toward the war, an influence achieved by confronting U.S. citizens with the immorality of their actions (Sturken, 1997, p. 90; for a more skeptical perspective see Perlmutter, 1998, p. 9).

These claims are true enough, but they don't explain much. By 1972 there had been many, many press reports and a number of striking photos that would suffice as evidence for any claim that the U.S. was fighting an immoral war. Indeed, by 1972 the public had seen burned skin hanging in shreds from Vietnamese babies, a bound Vietnamese prisoner of war being shot in cold blood, and similar pictures of the horror of war (see, e.g., Buell, 1999, pp. 62–67, 78–81; Griffiths, 1971; and Faas and Page, 1997). The photograph could not have been effective solely because of its news value, nor does it appear to be especially horrific. In addition, the captioning and other information about the causes of the event and its aftermath would seem to limit its documentary value. The story is one of "accidental napalm" (as the photo was captioned in some reports, e.g., "Accidental Napalm Attack," 1972, 1A; see also Lester, 1991, pp. 51–52); the strike was by South Vietnamese forces (not U.S. troops); the girl was immediately tended to and taken to a hospital. As an indictment, there isn't much that would stand out after cross-examination. And why would a still image come to dominate collective memory of what is now called the first television war, a war the public experienced via kinetic images of firefights, strafing runs, and helicopters landing and taking

Figure 1 "Accidental Napalm," Nick Ut, 1972.

SOURCE: Reprinted by permission of AP/Worldwide.

off in swirls of dust and action (Franklin, 1994; Hallin, 1986; Sturken, 1997, p. 89)?

An image of suffering can be highly persuasive, but not because of either the realism ascribed to the photo or its relationship to a single set of moral precepts (Burgin, 1996; Griffin, 1999; Tagg, 1988). A logic of public moral response has to be constructed, it has to be one that is adapted to the deep problems in the public culture at the time, and it has to be consistent with the strengths and weakness of the medium of articulation. This iconic photo was capable of activating public conscience at the time because it provided an embodied transcription of important features of moral life, including pain, fragmentation, modal relationships among strangers, betrayal, and trauma. These features are strengthened by photographic representation, particularly as they reinforce one another, and their embodiment in a single image demonstrates how photojournalism can do important work within public discourse, work that may not be done as well in verbal texts adhering to the norms of discursive rationality.

The little girl is naked, running right toward you, looking right at you, crying out. The burns themselves are not visible, and it is her pain—more precisely, her communicating the pain she feels—that is the central feature of the picture. Pain is the primary fact of her experience, just as she is the central figure in the composition. As she runs away from the cause of her burns, she also projects the pain forward, toward the viewer, and it is amplified further by the boy in front of her (his face resembles Edvard Munch's famous drawing of "The Scream"). This direct address defines her relationship to the viewer: she faces the lens, which activates the demanding reciprocity of direct, face-to-face interaction, and she is aligned with the frontal angle of the viewer's perspective, which "says, as it were: 'what you see here is part of our world, something we are involved with'" (Kress and van Leeuwen, 1996, pp. 121–130, 143). The photograph projects her pain into our world.

This confrontation of the viewer cuts deeper still. Her pain, like all great pain, disrupts and breaks up the social world's pattern of assurances. Just as she has stripped off her clothes to escape the burning napalm, she tears the conventions of social life.

Thus, her pain is further amplified because she violates the news media's norms of propriety. Public representation is always constituted by norms of decorum; without them, the public itself no longer exists (see Hariman, 1995). Yet war by its nature is a violation of civility, normalcy, civic order. Thus, a visual record of war will have to negotiate an internal tension between propriety and transgression (on photojournalistic norms governing the portrayal of bodily harm see Moeller, 1989; Robins, 1996; and Taylor, 1998). So it is that lesser forms of transgression can play an important role in the representation of war. The non-prurient nudity of the napalm photo doesn't just slip past the censor's rule, for the seeming transgression of her nakedness reveals another, deeper form of concealment. The image shows what is hidden by what is being said in print—the damaged bodies behind the U.S. military's daily "body counts," "free fire zones," and other euphemisms. The photo violates one set of norms in order to activate another; propriety is set aside for a moral purpose.

Girls should not be shown stripped bare in public; civilians should not be bombed. Likewise, U.S. soldiers (and many viewers mistakenly assume the soldiers are U.S. troops) are supposed to be handing out candy to the children in occupied lands, and the United States is supposed to be fighting just wars for noble causes. Just as the photograph violates one form of propriety to represent a greater form of misconduct, that breach of public decorum also disrupts larger frameworks for the moral justification of violence. Like the explosion still reverberating in the background, the photograph is a rupture, a tearing open of established narratives of justified military action, moral constraint, and national purpose. It is a picture that shouldn't be shown of an event that shouldn't have happened, and it projects a leveling of social structure and chaotic dispersion of social energies. The picture creates a searing eventfulness that breaks away from any official narrative justifying the war.

The photograph appeared during a period when the public was recognizing that their government was waging war without purpose, without legitimacy, without end. The illusion of strategic control had been shattered by the 1968

Tet offensive, all pretense of consensus had been killed in the 1970 shootings at Kent State, and by 1972 even those prolonging the war were relying on a rhetoric of disengagement. To those living amidst the public controversy about the war, it seemed as if the war made no sense and U.S. society was coming apart at the seams.

This sense of fragmentation was amplified by the media practices defining the Vietnam War. Day after day the public saw a jumble of scenes—bombings, firefights, helicopter evacuations, patrols moving out, villages being searched, troops wading across rivers—that could seemingly be rearranged in any order. If there was any organizational principle to this flow of images, it was that of collage: a seemingly shapeless accumulation of images that contained moments of strong association, or of irony, or of unexpected allure, but that lacked any governing idea. This continual stream of images reflecting a war without clear battle lines dovetailed perfectly with the government's lack of either a plausible rationale or coherent strategy. In addition, the reproduction of the details of everyday decor and ordinary behavior underscored the general substitution of scene for purpose. Try as the proponents of the war in Vietnam might to resurrect the idea of a theater of war with clear battle lines and victories, all on behalf of a justifiable political objective, such ideas were at odds not only with the nature of that war, but also, and perhaps more important for their persuasive objectives, with the visual media that were shaping public knowledge of the war.

In short, what was a sorry truth about the war became a dominant feature of its coverage. The daily visual record of activities was likely to make the war seem to have no purpose. Although this media environment was primarily televisual, it reinforced the most significant effect that photography can have on the understanding of war. As Alan Trachtenberg has observed of Civil War photography, the "portrayal of war as an event in real space and time," rather than "the mythic or fictional time of a theater," was accompanied "by a loss of clarity about both the overall form of battles and the unfolding war as such and the political meaning of events" (1989, pp. 74–75). In other words, the photographic medium is inherently paratactic: because photographic images operate meaningfully without a connecting syntax (Barthes, 1977, pp. 37–46), these images denote only fragments of any coordinated action. They give specific events a singular significance, but they leave larger articulations of purpose outside the frame.

The accidental napalm photograph is a model fragment. Featuring anonymous figures in a featureless scene that could be occurring anywhere in Vietnam, lacking any strategic orientation or collective symbol, confounding any official rhetoric of the war's purpose or of our commitment to the Vietnamese people, devoid of any element of heroism, and clearly recording an unintended consequence, it would not seem to qualify as an event at all. But it does qualify, because the photo's fragmentation carries with it a shift in the basic definition of an event. An event is no longer an action that comes at a dramatic moment in a sequence of purposive actions; instead, it is an experiential moment having heightened intensity independent of any larger plot.

The photo's embodiment of an aesthetic of fragmentation not only captured the character of a purposeless war, it also provided a means for resolving the moral predicament the war presented to the American public. How can any idea of right conduct be established within a condition of political and representational incoherence? It is within this context that the girl's nakedness acquires additional meaning. As Michael Walzer observes, even hardened soldiers are averse to killing an out of uniform— unmarked—enemy (1977, pp. 138–143). Simple vulnerability, particularly as it is symbolized by nakedness, puts us in an elemental moral situation. More to the point, nakedness in war foregrounds the moral relationships that still bind strangers to one another. The uniformed soldier has an identity; the naked body has been stripped of conventional patterns of recognition, deference, and dismissal. Like the parable of the Good Samaritan, which featured a naked man discovered along a road, the girl's naked vulnerability is a call to obligation, and, as in the parable, one that has occurred unexpectedly. In the words of John Caputo, "Obligation happens" (1993, p. 6). Obligation can appear out of nowhere, without regard to one's social position, directly encumbering one in ways that are decidedly inconvenient and, worse, that may disrupt deep assumptions regarding how one's life is patterned and what the future should hold. Thus, the photo abruptly calls the viewer to a moral awareness that cannot be limited to roles, contracts, or laws; neither is it buffered by distance. A fragmented world is still a world of moral demands, only now they may be most pressing when least expected, and the demand itself can shatter conventional wisdom.

This identification with the stranger has both a modern face and the structure of classical tragedy. The girl's nakedness provides a performative embodiment of the modern conception of universal humanity. She could be a poster child for the Universal Declaration of Human Rights (and as an adult she has both served as a good will ambassador for the United Nations and founded an international organization to aid children harmed by war). The dramatic charge of the photo comes from its evocation of pity and terror: we see a pathetic sight—the child crying in pain—and as we enter into her experience we feel both pity for her (or compassion toward her) and the looming sense of terror that lies behind her injuries. The terror (or fear or horror) that tragedy evokes comes not from the physical injury itself but from the social rupture behind it, which is why Aristotle noted that the most effective tragedies involved harms done off stage and within the family (*Poetics*, 1453b). The picture reproduces this design. First, despite its patently visual nature, the napalm attack is already over and the girl's burns are not visible—most are on her back, and the photograph's low resolution minimizes the others. Second, she is a child—a member of a family— and familial relationships are either modeled (between the children) or broken (between parents and children, as the biological parents are absent and the other adults are indifferent soldiers). The pity for the child is compounded by this sense of social breakdown—again, the horror of war is the destruction of social order and of meaning itself. Her pain activates the terror of tragedy, which comes from the realization that humans can be abandoned to a world no longer capable of sympathy, a world of beasts and gods, of destructive powers and impersonal forces, of pain without end.

This tragic structure is filled out by the relationships between the children and the soldiers. The crucial fact is that the soldiers are walking along slowly, almost nonchalantly, as if this were an everyday experience. Their attitude of business as usual contrasts vividly with the girl's sudden, unexpected, excessive experience of pain and terror. The message is clear: what seems, from looking at the girl, to be a rare experience sure to evoke a compassionate response, is in fact, as evidenced by the soldiers, something that happens again and again, so much so that the adults involved (whether soldiers there or civilians in the U.S.) can become indifferent, morally diminished, capable of routinely doing awful things to other people. Precisely because the photo is operating as a mode of performance, its formal implication is that what is shown is repeated, and repeatable, behavior (Schechner, 1985, pp. 35–116; States, 1996, p. 20). The photo that will be reproduced many times is itself not the record of a unique set of circumstances, but rather a dramatic depiction of those features of the war that are recurring over and over again past the point of caring. As the girl screams and other human beings walk along devoid of sympathy, the photo depicts a world of pain that reverberates off the hard surfaces of moral indifference. This is why knowledge of the circumstantial events (such as the girl receiving treatment immediately) rightly provides no qualification to the moral force of the photograph. The knowledge that would matter would be a demonstration that this was a rare use of napalm, or that U.S. forces and their Vietnamese allies almost never harmed civilians in the war zone. But, of course, by 1972 the truth of the brutality of the war had breached the surface of national consciousness.

The photo is not about informing the public at all; rather, it offers a performance of social relationships that provide a basis for moral comprehension and response (cf., Sontag, 1973, pp. 17–19). These modal relationships in turn can exemplify morally significant actions such as self-sacrifice or betrayal. The full significance of the photo's depiction of their relationship becomes clear when one recognizes how it also reflects the dilemma of democratic accountability in modern war. On the one hand, the citizen-soldier is both agent and representative of the public; on the other hand, the public has authority for but no direct control over their troops. When those troops are projecting power far away, yet reported on daily in the national media, the situation gets even worse. It is easy for the public to find itself guilty for actions it did not sanction, and for soldiers to be blamed for events no one anticipated. Soldiers and civilians alike can feel betrayed.

The napalm photo features two betrayals. Whether American or Vietnamese, the soldiers are agents of the United States who are supposed to be protecting the girl, yet they appear content merely to herd her and the other children down the road. The soldiers are not helping, they even seem to be treating the children like prisoners of war (for guns are still drawn), and they are indifferent to the suffering before them. Thus, while a little girl seems to appeal directly to the public for help, it can do nothing while its representative in the picture adds insult to injury. As the girl is betrayed by the institutional figures who are supposed to protect her, so is the public betrayed by the same institution.[1]

Although the activity within the frame directs action, the fact that this is a photograph—a "static" image—means that time has been stopped. The picture holds its experience of terror and uncompleted action for all time, while having the activity within the frame eternally repeat itself (for that is what it is, performatively-restored repetitive behavior). This mythic sense of eternal recurrence, and its "vertigo of time defeated" (Barthes, 1981, p. 97), corresponds perfectly to the phenomenological structure of trauma: one simultaneously feels stopped in time (or thrown outside of time, temporal movement, history, change) while constantly repeating the actions within that isolated moment (Herman, 1992; for a selected bibliography on posttraumatic stress disorder with special reference to Vietnam see "Vietnam Yesterday," 2001). The normal flow of time has been fragmented into shards of isolated events, while the traumatized subject remains trapped in the continually recurring scene, unable to break out of the ever-recurring pain. Although this phenomenological state is commonly thought to result from exposure to carnage, Jonathan Shay has pointed out how the deeper cause is a sense of betrayal (Shay, 1994, pp. 3–22). Likewise, an iconic photo that is said to capture the horror of war is not gruesome, but it does freeze the spectator in a tableau of moral failure. Betrayal short-circuits the power of institutional narratives to sublimate disturbing incidents, and the

photograph perpetuates this sense of rupture. One is helpless, unable to change a thing about what happened and yet is still before one's eyes. This sense of powerlessness extends to control of the memory itself, as the image circulates through the media, recurring again and again unbidden.

Thus, the photograph came to provide symbolic representation of the U.S. public's experience of the Vietnam War. Somehow, it seems, the United States got caught in a situation not of its own making, a morally incoherent situation in which we knew we did terrible things to other people—things we still can't face and can never set right. Against processes of denial, the photograph provides at least an image of our condition: having already done the wrong thing, wanting to do the right thing, yet frozen, incapable of acting in that place at all. Nor will history oblige by allowing us to start over or restore a sense of innocence. The basic conditions of modern U.S. warfare are all there: imperial action in a distant, third world country far from the public's direct control; massive, technologically intensive firepower being used to spare our soldiers' lives at enormous rates of "collateral damage"; mass media coverage sure to confront us with our guilt while apparently providing no means for action. The moral danger of this world is captured tonally in the picture's composition of light and darkness: as the dark smoke blots out the sky and while the girl bathed in light has in fact been seared with liquid fire, the elements of the sublime are present but out of order, gone demonic. Light hurts, darkness towers over all, awe is induced by destruction, terror is not sublimated to a transcendent order. The image calls a public to moral awareness, but its rhetorical power is traumatic.

THE LIBERAL ANTIDOTE

The photograph's activation of the structure of trauma is evident as well in its subsequent history of interpretation. According to Shay, the crucial step towards healing from a traumatic experience is to construct a narrative of one's life that can contextualize the traumatic moment (1994, pp. 181–193). The narrative does more than soothe, for it addresses the crucial characteristic of trauma, which is being bracketed from any sense of temporal continuity. The traumatic moment is stopped in time, and narrative gets time moving again so that the moment may eventually recede, dissipate, or become complicated by other elements of larger stories.

This photo has produced several narratives. The most frequently told of these is the story of the relationship between the girl in the photo and the photographer (see, e.g., Buell, 1999, pp. 102–103). Both of Vietnamese ethnicity, they became lifelong friends as he helped her relocate to Canada. The story functions as a convenient displacement of responsibilities while breaking out of the traumatic moment: both Vietnamese-American and Canadian identities provide an easy surrogacy that allows a happy ending without either involving the U.S. public directly or leaving them completely out of the story. This easy resolution validates a significant change, however, for the anonymous girl has become an individual person. She has a name (Kim Phuc), and the story is now *her* story, a unique personal history that may or may not be publicized.

A recent variant of this story is Denise Chong's *The Girl in the Picture,* which chronicles Kim Phuc's personal odyssey of recovery while trying to free herself from the publicity generated by the photo. "She felt as though the journalistic hounds would make her into a victim all over again. 'The action of those two women [journalists, one with a camera] on the sidewalk,' she lamented to Toan, 'was like a bomb falling out of the sky'" (1999, p. 6). Note how this narrative replays the performance of the iconic photograph: allied technology continues to harm an innocent Vietnamese civilian, while the public again is drawn into an act of inflicting pain it did not authorize, an act that can only be redeemed through empathic identification with her suffering. The traumatic "scars [that] war leaves on all of us" (Chong, 1999, bookjacket flap) are then ameliorated by a narrative of her life after the war.

This relationship between the physical wound and a rhetoric of healing that can displace concerns about justice is most evident in the picture of Kim with her infant child (Figure 2) taken by photographer Joe McNally in 1995 ("Portrait," 1995; Sixtieth Anniversary, 1996,

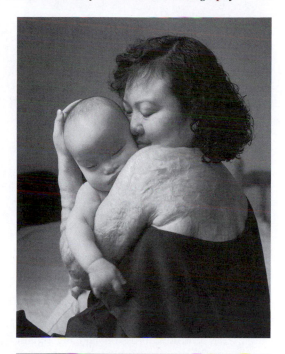

Figure 2   Kim Phuc and child.

SOURCE: Reprinted by permission of *LIFE*/Joe McNally.

p. 102; Chong, 1999, p. 191).[2] This picture may also be an attempt at something like a visual sequel to the iconic photo, and one that supplies a Hollywood ending for the story. The continuities and discontinuities between this photo and the icon establish the key differences in effect.

Her nakedness is still there, but it has been carefully controlled by changes in posture and camera angle to maintain the modesty expected of a grown woman and a tranquil public culture. Her injury is still there, of course, but now the effects of the war are to be dealt with on an individual basis, and those who created them are no longer in the picture, no longer capable of being interrogated or condemned.

Perhaps the soldiers have been replaced by the scars on her skin. The display of the scars also reveals the relationship between the physical and symbolic dimensions of the two images. In the iconic photo, her physical wounds were not visible; they were communicated by her expression and the other child's cry of terror. Thus, the physical harm that was the most basic consequence and moral fault of American military actions was depicted indirectly. In the sequel, the physical harm is revealed, but given its relationship to the other features of the picture, it acquires a different significance. Now the wounds are superficial, for they appear to have no effect on the woman's internal health. Inside, she is capable of bearing a "normal," healthy baby. And what a baby it is: unblemished, its new, smooth skin a striking contrast to her mature scars. Now the physical damage to Kim is merely the background for a tableau of regeneration. Although she is not doing that well in one sense, for she is still scarred, she obviously has achieved one of the great milestones of personal happiness by giving birth to a beautiful child. While the past is still present, it is inert—no more than ugly tissue that has no power to prevent a new beginning and personal happiness. In the United States, history lasts only one generation.

The sunny optimism of this story of war's aftermath is validated by the rest of the composition. Her beatific expression and the figural enactment of Madonna and child portraiture suggest a serenity in which traumatic memory or persistent conflict has no place. Likewise, in place of the dark smoke from the napalm blast, the background of this photo is a darkened blank wall. This gentle décor and her carefully draped clothing invoke the conventions of retail studio photography, which in turn anchor her happiness within a familiar scene of private life: the framed portrait that is displayed proudly by the child's grandparents.

All of these changes occur within a thoroughly traditional transcription of gender roles. The muted sexuality of her late girlhood has been channeled into the conventional role of motherhood. Men clearly maintain their monopoly on violence (Ehrenreich, 1997, p. 125), while a woman embodies the virtues of nurturing; Vietnam and peace itself remain feminized while war and the American military establishment retain their masculine identity. The scene defines private life as a place centered on women and children, where mothers are devoted to and fulfilled by caring for their families.

The shift from public to private virtues has been encoded by taking a second photo for public dissemination in a manner similar to taking a photo for distribution within one's family. The substitution of photos provides a double compensation: Kim has been given a beautiful child to replace her own damaged childhood, and the second image is given to the public in recompense for its past discomfort. The baby also replaces the other children in the original scene—those running down the road and those who didn't make it. The war is over, and children who could be running in terror for their small, vulnerable lives are now sleeping quietly in their mothers' arms. Moreover, where the earlier children were Kim's siblings, and so the sign of collective identity, this child is her child, her most dear possession and a sign of the proprietary relationships essential to liberal individualism. The transformation is complete: from past trauma to present joy, and from the terrors of collective history to the quiet individualism of private life.

Thus, this sequel to the iconic photo inculcates a way of seeing the original image and the history to which it bore witness. A record of immoral state action has become a history of private lives. Questions of collective responsibility—and of justice—have been displaced by questions of individual healing. The wisdom that recognizes the likelihood of war's eternal recurrence has been displaced by a narrative of personal happiness and of a new, unblemished, innocent generation.

What is important to note here is that the reinscription of the iconic photograph by the second image is neither unique nor inappropriate. Indeed, it invokes a therapeutic discourse that has become a symptomatic and powerful form of social control in liberal-democratic, capitalist societies (see Cloud, 1998; Ehrenhaus, 1993). Two dimensions of such discourse are directly relevant to the case at hand. First, as Ehrenhaus observes, the therapeutic motif "voyeuristically dwells on intimacy and poignancy while never violating the illusion of privacy" (pp. 93–94). And second, as the emphasis shifts attention from public to private trauma, it invokes a discourse of "individual and family responsibility" that contains dissent directed towards the social and political order (Cloud, 1998, p. xv; Ehrenhaus, 1993). In the second photograph, then, Kim Phuc's "private" recovery and maternity substitute for the napalm girl's "public" cry of pain; the effect is to foreclose on acts of dissent that would question state accountability.

This narrative containment of the original image is not a wholly unwarranted imposition, however, for that image draws upon conceptions of personal autonomy and human rights that are foundational in a liberal-individualist society, it features a wounded individual crying out for help, and it produces a traumatic effect. The second photo's visual reinterpretation of the war is achieved not by distorting the iconic photo but rather by extending designs in the original that were essential for its moral significance and rhetorical appeal. In short, as the second photograph imitates aesthetic elements of the iconic image, it enhances an ideological transcription that was already available within the scene. Indeed, the "second" inflection helps to define the original image, as when the icon is celebrated in an exhibition because it is "a symbol that has helped lead toward reconciliation" (Exhibit Recalls German Destruction, 2000).

So it is that this iconic photo can be both unusually striking and unavoidably ambivalent. On the one hand, a partial record of a supposedly incidental moment became a defining event of the war, one capable of negating the moral certainty and aesthetic unity of the U.S. culture that had coalesced during World War II. On the other hand, the photograph is not only a transgression, but also the enactment of another model of political identity always available within U.S. public life and ascendant amidst the prosperity and contradictions of the post-war era. Rather than simply tear down one set of ideals, it also advances the habits of another way of life.

In this liberal sensibility, actions are meaningful because they are symptomatic of internal conditions rather than because they adhere to proven models of character. The individual's experience is the primary locus of meaning, and conflict resolution may be as much psychological as political. The individual's autonomy and human rights supercede any political identity, and obligations are encountered along the road rather than due to any sense of tradition or collective enterprise. Collective action is essentially moral and humanitarian rather than defined by national interests, but it also is *ad hoc,* not directed by long-term objectives and analysis. The fundamental tension in political life is between the individual and society; once the individual is protected, other political possibilities

are likely to be deferred to the more immediate engagements of private life. And when private life is synonymous with national healing, public life becomes a dead zone: a place, as we shall see, that is inhabited by ghosts and where images become specters of reanimation.

DISSENT AND THE HAUNTING OF PUBLIC CULTURE

Barthes asks, "Mad or tame? Photography can be one or the other" (1981, p. 119). The photograph of "accidental napalm" is repeatedly tamed and in a multiplicity of ways: by the banality of its circulation, by personalizing the girl in the picture, by drawing out a liberal narrative of healing, by the segue into the celebrity photo of Kim's regeneration, and more. But it also remains mad: an indelible image of terror that obsessively repeats itself, that keeps the public audience interned in the real time of fatality rather than fantasies of renewal, staring at screams that cannot be heard and haunted by ghosts that will not speak. This madness is something that need not be far from the anger fueling political dissent, and, although grounded in the image, it does not happen by itself; rather, like taming, it is something that results from continued use of the image. Thus, the history of the iconic photograph demonstrates how a visual practice can be a site of struggle.

As images become disseminated they also become resources for public argument, particularly as advocates themselves are skilled in using visual materials. A strong example of artistic accomplishment in grass-roots public discourse is provided on a web page titled "Veritatis Vietnam," designed by Ed Chilton, a Vietnam veteran and anti-Vietnam War advocate (Chilton, 2000). The first image we find on that web page digitally superimposes the napalm photograph over the U.S. flag and the face of Cardinal Spellman (Figure 3). The explicit intention is to excoriate Spellman for his support of the war in Vietnam. Although the verbal text following the image may seem too much of a harangue, the visual collage is hard to get out of one's mind. It achieves this effect by reproducing key features of the original photograph's rhetorical power, but now through a seemingly

Figure 3 "Veritatis Vietnam."

SOURCE: Reprinted by permission of Edward Chilton.

supernatural projection of that image into the present. The composition is haunting, and for good reason: the girl is now a ghost, a fragment of the past that will not be assimilated into the amnesia of the present.

Once again, the photograph breaks into official representations of U.S. institutional legitimacy. Once again, it is aesthetically and morally disruptive: it should not be inserted into the image of the flag, just as the naked, terrified girl should not have been on everyone's breakfast table, and it tells the audience that things that should not happen did happen. In the composite image, the photograph's role in a struggle over the meaning of the war is heightened: by intruding into images of the flag and the two crosses on the Cardinal's shoulders, the scene becomes a battle between the icons themselves. The war is brought home, as actions over there are shown in direct clash with symbols of legitimacy here, and the dominant symbols of collective organization (religion and the state) are confronted with their complicity in the war's destruction of innocent children.

As before, the napalm image is a fragmentary scene, one obviously located in the specific historical event of the war, yet not enfolded into any sense of a progressive historical narrative or sound military strategy. Indeed, the children's screams of terror tear apart the official narratives of American political and moral superiority. This attack on institutional authority is strengthened by the image of Cardinal Spellman. His position at the front of the composition parallels the position of the soldiers in the rear as they are roughly equidistant from the children. His crosses are placed as if they were military insignia (Cardinal or General, did it matter?), and his expression can be read as either implicitly predatory (the large round head, raised eyebrows, and intently focused eyes are owl-like) or morally hardened (the facial mask is uniformly controlled and blank while his mouth is pursed as if to make a dismissive remark). Once again, the public sees its representatives—now those who promoted the war along with the soldiers who fought it—acting as if they were habituated to the suffering they imposed on others.

The fact that it is *once again* is no accident. As before, the image captures the trauma victim's sense of being stuck in time. In direct contrast to the narratives of compensation and healing used in the mainstream media to neutralize the iconic photograph's sense of guilt, this image reinserts the past into the present to immobilize those attempting to "move beyond" past conflicts and historical responsibility. The superimposition of images does not just compare the past with the present, it fuses them: the image of terror and guilt now is always within the flag, an ineradicable part of the United States's legacy. Likewise, the flag and institutional religion are exposed as covering devices, symbols and discourses (such as the Cardinal's public speeches on the war) that are used to hide moral truth and public guilt. Like the icon within it, the composition evokes a psychology of eternal recurrence and denial. Although this structure of feeling can be dismissed as yet another example of Vietnam syndrome, it also is another instance of the tragic dimension of war's pathos: Why will more continue to be sacrificed? Because the knowledge gained of suffering will be lost, or denied, to those who remain.

All the advocate wants to do is blast Cardinal Spellman, and he does a pretty good job of that, at least visually. His most important accomplishment, however, is restoring the iconic photograph to its rightful place in public discourse. As any icon floats through media space across subsequent generations, and particularly as it gets rewritten into liberal narratives of individual healing, it can lose too much of the political history and emotional intensity that are essential for participation in democratic debate. By placing the icon against the symbols of the flag and the cross, this appropriation restores the conflict, hypocrisy, complicity, confusion, and intensity that fuels debate about the war. Above all, it restores a sense of public life. The girl is no longer a single individual, and the question is not whether she is happy today. Once again it is a picture of the victims of American military action and those who marshaled their destruction, of the public's lack of control over a war fought in its name, of the questionable moral and political legitimacy of U.S. institutions. By restoring the public context that in turn allows the iconic photo to challenge authority, the composite image demonstrates that perhaps not everything is lost after all.

This call to public conscience is evident in another remediation of the photo, this time by transposing the girl into an illustration that accompanies a *Boston Globe* review of a book on the Vietnam Veterans' Movement. The story is entitled "Soldiers of Misfortune," and the visual composition (Figure 4) is a stunning depiction of the multiple layers of suffering that characterized the Vietnam War (DeCoster, 2001, D3). The girl is running forward, her arms stretched out, as she always is running, but now she is passing through a sprinkler on a suburban lawn. She still is screaming, but now she is wearing a bright polka-dot bikini. Behind her smoke still billows upward, although now it comes from

Figure 4 "Soldiers of Misfortune."

SOURCE: Reprinted by permission of Jeffrey DeCoster.

the chimney of a suburban house, over which a military helicopter hovers against a pastel blue sky. Beside the girl, a U.S. veteran sits in a wheelchair. It is as if he had been parked there to watch her, but his dark glasses, blank face, and slack limbs suggest some awful combination of social isolation and internal preoccupation. He and the girl form the two rear points of a triangle; at the third point equidistant between them and at the front of the picture, there is a child's plastic ball. It is red, white, and blue.

We doubt anyone could draw a more disturbing image of the war at home, or one that better confronts the liberal-individualist narrative with democratic responsibility, or one that so vividly captures the traumatic sense of continued suffering and unresolved guilt evoked by the original photograph. The girl's magical appearance in the most characteristic contemporary U.S. setting is profoundly unsettling. She won't go away, she has even turned up here. But that is only half of it: her transposition into the suburban scene doesn't just bring the war home, it erases the ethnic difference undergirding the moral indifference to Vietnamese suffering. As with any strong appropriation, the later image amplifies key features of the original design: in this case, by (re)clothing the girl the illustrator has completed the work begun by her originally being naked. While the first image made her less Vietnamese, because universally human, this image takes the next step by placing her in the United States's most familiar sense of humanity— our own culture. To spell it out even further, it becomes even easier to recognize that it was wrong to inflict pain on girls in Vietnam, because it would be just like bombing our kids while they were playing in our backyards. Perhaps this act of imagination is made easier as immigrant Vietnamese have become ever more assimilated into U.S. public culture, but the illustration makes it clear enough: she could have been one of ours.

If left there, the picture would have been a dated and heavy-handed condemnation of Vietnam veterans. The juxtaposition of the disabled veteran changes all that. Someone incapable of walking is not going to harm civilians now, and even if he did before he has paid for it. The picture's balanced positioning of the two representative figures makes it clear that both were harmed by the war, both scarred for life. They both are victims, but that victimage is no longer the liberal pathos of individuated harm and therapeutic recovery. Instead, the picture restores the iconic photograph's depiction of types—Vietnamese civilians, not Kim Phuc— and it positions the seemingly different figures (young, female, Vietnamese civilian; adult, male, U.S. soldier) in equivalent categories of continued trauma. It is the visual equivalent of President Clinton's verbal evocation of two nations united by "shared suffering" (2000).

The two figures share another similarity. The girl's emergence in the suburban scene many years after the end of the war is supernatural—a haunt- ing of the American imagination. This return might be indicative of society's continued trauma- tization by the war, or it might symbolize the fail- ure to confront historical responsibility, but it is a haunting nonetheless. The veteran has a similar nature, for he is a ghostly figure, so transparent that you can see the outline of a tricycle behind him showing through his body. The difference between them is that she is vivid and active while he barely has strength of presence, much less a capacity to act. The contrast could be (and probably is) an argument that the public has been more fixated on one set of victims than another for which it has equal or greater responsibility. But it seems more complicated than that. She shouldn't be there but is there; he should be there but is disappearing. Neither one belongs in the scene, because both are aesthetic disruptions of the Happyville template that provides the background for the picture. The key to understanding their mutual estrangement is the two small details of the smoke and the ball. The smoke is the thick, oily product of bombing taken from the original napalm drop, but now it is coming from the furnace of the house. (Why the heat is on in the summer appears to be artistic license.) The dirty pollution of war is also the byproduct of U.S. affluence, because both imper- ial power and domestic tranquility are fueled by the same dark processes. The moral buffering pro- duced by the United States's distance and wealth, and the dirty truth that we waste lives needlessly, are shown to be deeply linked and largely hidden. The picture exposes eloquently the complicity between the good life at home and criminal behav- ior in the third world.

But who then is responsible? The ball pro- vides part of the answer. Both a perfect prop

within the scene and a reference to the nation- state, it is positioned to mediate the relationship between the two figures. Together the three form a closed, harmonious form. But the red, white, and blue ball is not "Old Glory." Instead, it signifies an ersatz patriotism, the broad dis- semination of national symbols that character- izes mainstream popular culture. There is only the barest trace of any sense of collective responsibility, while the object typifies the easy activities of kids' games and backyard leisure, or at most the fireworks on the fourth of July. This reduction of political identity and collec- tive responsibility to a small, soft plastic toy is what is necessary to represent its place within the suburban scene. It is there, but ironically so and easily kicked aside.

This projection of responsibility to the front of the pictorial frame follows directly from the composition of the iconic photo. Both victims are still in need of help, and both are not likely to be helped by what little sense of collective responsibility is available in the contemporary U.S. scene. As before, the picture hails the viewer. As before, the viewer is positioned aside from the state that is the agency of harm (it has harmed the girl, brought the soldiers to harm, and is not caring adequately for those soldiers today). As before, the picture can be a sweeping denunciation of moral indifference, although now the accusation is given an additional, sharper edge: the problem is not a runaway state or uninformed public, but a nation lulled to irre- sponsibility by its pursuit of domestic happiness. This irresponsibility includes not listening to the Vietnamese civilians and U.S. soldiers who have had direct experience of the war, but who have been silenced subsequently. As before, the pic- ture fragments consensus through embarrassing depictions of suffering; by placing that suffering within a context of unthinking routine it both identifies a collective responsibility and locks the experience of guilt into a haunting, eternal recurrence of traumatic memory.

THE ICON, THE STRANGER, AND AMERICAN COLLECTIVE MEMORY

The multiple transcriptions and deep ambiva- lences of visual eloquence allow skilled advo- cates a rich repertoire for democratic deliberation.

Iconic photographs are calls to civic action, sites of controversy, vehicles for ideological control, and sources of rhetorical invention. Although the appropriation of such icons has to be consistent with the original photograph's basic designs, and although they typically extend its strongest tendencies, they are also a source of new and at times remarkably sophisticated appeals. Most important, perhaps, they can articulate patterns of moral intelligence that run deeper than pragmatic deliberation about matters of policy and that disrupt conventional discourses of institutional legitimacy. That is not the end of the story, however.

Vietnam veteran William Adams has remarked, "What 'really' happened is now so thoroughly mixed up in my mind with what has been said about what happened that the pure experience is no longer there. . . . The Vietnam War is no longer a definite event so much as it is a collective and mobile script in which we continue to scrawl, erase, rewrite our conflicting and changing view of ourselves" (quoted in Sturken, 1997, p. 86). The situation is even more fluid for the public audience that never experienced the war directly. Amidst a "torrent" of books, movies, articles, memorials, web sites, and more, U.S. public life continues to be defined by its conduct and loss of the war in Vietnam (Perlmutter, 1998, p. 52). Explanations for this lack of closure range from the critique of the mass media's overexposure of the war, to the war's "resistance to standard narratives of technology, masculinity, and U.S. nationalism" (Sturken, 1997, p. 87). We believe that iconic photographs emerge and acquire considerable influence because of their capacity for dealing with the dual problems of overexposure and ideological rupture.

The Vietnam War has the distinction of being a rich lode of iconic photographs. Four in particular receive the widest circulation: the burning monk, the execution of a bound prisoner of war, the napalm girl, and the girl screaming over the dead student at Kent State. By explicating several relationships within this set of images, the additional functions of the napalm photograph, its genre, and photojournalism generally can be highlighted. As Marita Sturken has noted, the common features of this set of images include their depictions of horror, their challenge to ideological narratives, and the fact that they have acquired far greater currency than any

video images of the war, including identical footage of two of the events (the execution and the napalm attack). Sturken's account of this last difference is telling: the photographs highlight facial expressions, connote a sufficient sense of the past, circulate more easily, and are "emblems of rupture" demanding narration; in addition, the filmed events are actually more chaotic or horrific (1997, p. 87).

These observations are accurate, although also at odds with the general assessment that the iconic image is the best representation of the horror of war. Our close reading of the napalm photograph suggests how that idea needs to be refined. The iconic image of the Vietnam era becomes the telling representation because of its fragmentary character. It represents not so much physical harm as the loss of meaning, the futility of representation itself in a condition "when words lose their meaning" (White, 1984). A visual medium becomes the better vehicle for representing this slippage or incapacity. The image implies that another medium (words) has already proved incapable of full representation of the war, and, because the image can show but not tell, it automatically represents both the event and the gap between the event and any pattern of interpretation. The still image performs this dual sense of representation and absence most effectively: it frames the event for close, careful examination, while also providing nothing outside the frame and interrupting any sense of continuity. The result is not blankness, however, but an "optical unconscious" (Benjamin, 1980, p. 203) that can supply both exact knowledge of the morally decisive moment and the "lacerating emphasis" of fatality as it incorporates past and future alike in the eternal present of the image (Barthes, 1981, p. 96). As we have also noted, this epistemological condition is deeply resonant with the psychological structure of trauma.

There is a three-way relationship between loss of meaning, traumatic injury, and moral response that characterizes the deep lack of resolution regarding the Vietnam War, and that also is a key feature of the iconic photographs. The photos are indeed less horrific than they could be; they show little physical damage, while pictures taken seconds later in every case show more blood or burned flesh. The performative key is not physical damage, however, but the expression or conspicuous absence of an expression of pain. This distinction between physical gore and pain is crucial, for several reasons (see also Robins, 1996; Taylor, 1998; Zelizer, in press). Bodily disruption does not automatically call for a moral response, as it always is subject to interpretation (think of surgery). Pain, however, by its very nature cuts through and destroys patterns of meaningfulness, while its expression is evidence of an internal world—the world within the body that Elaine Scarry (1985, p. 63) defines as the "interior content of war"—and so a basis for connection with others without regard to external circumstances. Moral response requires not evidence of harm, but a sympathetic connection that is most directly evoked by pain. For the same reason, justifications of violence always have to minimize the pain it produces.

The four icons of the Vietnam War exemplify the dialectic between displays of pain and indifference to pain. The napalm and Kent State photos are the most powerful registers of moral outrage precisely because they are performances of the pain experienced by an innocent victim of U.S. military action. "The image of the burned girl made Americans see the pain the war inflicted," and it also used that pain to bond the girl and the public emotionally (Kinney, 2000, p. 187). The girl at Kent State acts as a ventriloquist for the murdered body on the pavement in front of her, while also directly venting the pain experienced sympathetically (and, therefore, modeling sympathetic response to the dead and wounded as the appropriate form of citizenship in respect to that event) (Hariman and Lucaites, 2001). Each performance also is gendered, as a girl crying represents the "victimized, feminized" country of Vietnam and the peace movement at home (Sturken, 1997, p. 93).

The logic of conventional gender typing also structures the other two icons, each of which is notable for its repression of emotion. The expression of the man being shot is sometimes described as a searing expression, but not often; it could double as an expression one might see in a dentist's office. What is most significant is the executioner's lack of emotion. The photo's moral punch comes from its documentation of how the state can kill with such complete lack of regard for the pain it is causing. As with the laconic soldiers in the napalm photo, the officer's businesslike manner is a cue to the fact that this situation is routine, something that those in the picture see every day. The lack of empathy becomes the sign of immoral conduct, a sign that can't be erased by circumstantial knowledge about the soldiers involved. The burning monk follows a similar logic that operates in the reverse direction. The salient fact in the photo is that someone's resolve to resist the government could be so great that he would not only commit self-immolation, but be able to do so without showing pain. The Saigon government was shown to be not only illegitimate, but so powerless that it could not conquer the body as it burned. Male suppression of pain thus becomes the vector for projecting a power that can be used either to extend or resist state control, while female expression of pain becomes the vehicle for public response to the abuse of power by the state that, unlike the male acts, can be imitated by anyone who is looking at the picture.

One conclusion to be drawn at this point is that the iconic images from the Vietnam War—along with the subsequent images of Kim Phuc that are used to put the war to rest—also create a fragmented regendering of the public sphere. The public is feminized in a manner that has both positive and negative consequences. On one hand, set against a masculine monopoly on violence and state action that is increasingly irrational, the feminized public reinstates the essential features of the classical model. In addition, this gendering corrects for various faults in that model, not least its inattention to emotion, norms of reciprocity and care, divisions between public and private life, and the need for openness in actual practice. On the other hand, such gendering hardens a number of dangerous alignments among power, violence, and masculinity, and against discourse, deliberation, and social reciprocity. Worse yet, as women only cry out and scream while remaining helpless, public speech becomes hysterical and without agency, and as their meaning is transferred to the visual medium that is featuring a woman's body, the public becomes subject to the male gaze while being reduced to the politics of spectacle. Such logics produce both more war and further constriction of public culture.

These transcriptions of gender are as important as they are obvious, but they are not the only means by which iconic photos can embody essential features of the public sphere. Michael Warner (2002) has identified, among others, two features of public culture that are especially pertinent to the case at hand: "the public is a social space created by the reflexive circulation of discourse" (p. 90), and it is a "relation among strangers" (p. 75, 74). The still photo acquires greater mnemonic capacity due to its ease of wide and continuous circulation. Even in digital environments, video clips are more time and skill intensive, whereas still photos circulate easily and also can be reproduced across posters, editorial cartoons, book covers, t-shirts, and an astonishing range of other items (e.g., see Franklin, 2000, pp. 1–24; Hariman and Lucaites, 2002). As the public is constituted in the dissemination and circulation of texts that compete for attentiveness (and verbal "uptake") within audiences, the images that circulate best have a natural tendency to become the carriers of public consciousness (Warner, 2002, p. 87). The iconic images then stand out further because their conjunction of aesthetic form and political function allows for a reflexive representation of not only the particular event, but also the conditions of public representation most crucial to understanding the event. No one text or image can do this, but those that can capture the tensions within the discursive field will be more likely to become the markers of the field.

Because a public is always, by definition, a group whose membership cannot be known in advance, public discourse is addressed to strangers. A public "might be said to be stranger-relationality in a pure form, because other ways of organizing strangers—nations, religions, races, guilds, etc.—have manifest positive content." Perhaps most important, "We've become capable of recognizing ourselves as strangers even when we know each other" (Warner, 2002, p. 75, 74). If the public audience is to be capable of response and action, however, those within it cannot be operating in a realm of pure relationality, not least because there is no such language available. The discourses of public address must be inflected, embodied, and otherwise provide real bases for identification through aesthetic performance,

and they have to do this in a manner that also maintains the reflexive openness of public identity. Warner's own language seems to be a description of the iconic photograph:

> The development of forms that mediate the intimate theater of stranger relationality must surely be one of the most significant dimensions of modern history, though the story of this transformation in the meaning for strangers has been told only in fragments. It is hard to imagine such abstract modes of being as rights-bearing personhood, species being, and sexuality, for example, without forms that give concrete shape to the interactivity of those who have no idea with whom they interact. (2002, p. 76)

The iconic photograph is one such form for mediating stranger relationality. A relationship that is hard to imagine is in need of images, and the iconic image acquires public appeal and normative power as it provides embodied depictions of important abstractions (such as "human rights") operative within the public discourse of an historical period. In addition, the photograph becomes a condensation of public consciousness to the extent that, while it provides figural embodiment of abstractions, it also keeps the lines of response and action directed through relationships among strangers rather than specific individuals or groups. Thus, the photo of the napalmed little girl provides figural embodiment of the concepts of political innocence, human rights, third world vulnerability and victimage, mechanized destructiveness, criminal state action, and moral callousness. As it does so, it also puts the girl in the place of the stranger within the public. Her relationship with the viewer is an embodied case of stranger relationality. Set amidst characteristic features of public life (e.g., civil infrastructure, state action, press coverage) and appealing directly to the public audience (e.g., created through circulation, contrasted to the family and state in the picture, identified by no ethnic or other localized identity, not known in advance) the girl and the audience alike are anonymous, essentially strangers to each other.

Because the girl is distinguished by her pain, her strongest positive content is the internal content of the war; because the war also is conducted among strangers, it becomes a perverse form of stranger relationality. Because the girl's pain is presented directly to the viewer, she embodies the stranger we can recognize within ourselves, and so her world and ours are drawn together into a single public realm. It is at precisely this point that her Vietnamese identity is significant. As Warner notes, the stranger of modern public life is not exotic or inherently disturbing (2002, p. 75); we would add that it is different from the Other that is articulated through every form of social exclusion (i.e., all forms of nonpublic identity). One consequence is that, by coupling the two forms together, an image can bestow public identity. The girl's appeal for help would be subverted by her being perceived as one of the Other, a small, marginal figure within a minor, distant, marginalized group. Her moral force comes from being perceived as a stranger in pain, which not only activates the transcription of Biblically directed compassion, but also makes her someone who is numbered among the public and so has the right to hold the state accountable.

The iconic photograph's fragmentary framing of the girl's combination of naked expressiveness and personal anonymity also keys subsequent narratives about "the girl in the picture." As Kim Phuc becomes clothed, and then partially, modestly unclothed to reveal her scars while holding her baby, she becomes a symbol for the restoration of domestic tranquility. As she forgives those who bombed her, she becomes a symbol of political reconciliation and also a means for forgetting the obligations of political history ("Pilot Finds Forgiveness," 1997). As she becomes a celebrity promoting universal human rights, she personalizes the stranger identity that is an essential element of moral judgment in public discourse.

The other Vietnam photos offer similar mediations of public life, just as they also are subject to a range of appropriations that comprise a continuing negotiation of American political identity. Franklin's study of how the execution photo was reworked in popular films and comics to become a conservative icon provides the most dramatic example of how icons figure prominently in the continuing struggle over the meaning of the Vietnam War (2000, pp. 1–24), but all four of the images are at issue (see Hariman and

Lucaites, 2001; Skow and Dionisopoulos, 1997). The napalm girl's reappearances within the mainstream public media provide a varied range of examples.[3] Such appropriations are inevitable in public discourse due to a corollary of stranger relationality: the condition of topical openness (see Habermas, 1989, p. 36). Thus, the napalm icon has been taken beyond the Vietnam War to condemn other forms of betrayal or injustice. In a cartoon protesting the Disney theme park that would have been located near the Manassas battlefield, Goofy is running down the road beside the crying girl (Toles, 1994). In a more recent cartoon protesting Nike labor practices, the girl reappears, wraith-like, as a poster on the wall of a factory in Vietnam (Danziger, 1997, A-10). As Vietnamese girls (or women) work at the assembly line, the cry of pain speaks for them, its anguish amplified further by the Nike slogan at the top of the poster: Just Do It. Their only choice is to keep working at "starvation wages," while U.S. mechanization operated by Vietnamese proxies continues to harm the Vietnamese people. The photo can operate as a rhetorical figure within the picture and as a linking device that activates historical memory and obligation (Vietnam then and now; U.S. immorality then and now; public indifference then and now) to motivate public intervention. The device works because the cartoonist has drawn on essential features of the icon in order to recreate its original effect of activating moral judgment within a supposedly amoral scene (war then and the free-market economy now). The transfer of moral response is possible because Vietnam continues to be feminized while the girl has been restored to her original anonymity and pain. These devices combine to constitute a public culture known to itself by the continued circulation of iconic images.

As appropriations of the napalm photo accumulate, and as the photo slides back and forth along a continuum from public anonymity to personal celebrity, an additional dimension of public culture emerges. Stranger relationality is constituted in a field of visual representation defined by the presence of celebrities and ghosts. Both are exceptional forms of individual presence, known through their circulation, and simultaneously familiar and strange. (Icons have the same features as well.) No reader of this essay is likely to have ever met Kim Phuc in person, much less spent any time with her, but most will have known who she is. Like any icon, the celebrity is self-constitutive of public culture: created by dissemination and evidence of a broad field of attention. So it is that celebrity developed in conjunction with the ascendancy of the mass media, and the category has been a commonplace in photojournalism at least since *Life* magazine in the 1940s. The celebrity is the widely recognized stranger, that is, a stranger whose image is in wide circulation. More to the point, celebrity is a compensatory mechanism within the media to mask its strangeness. The celebrity image dresses the impersonal process of circulation in signs of private, personal expressiveness. Thus, the redefinition of the napalm girl as Kim Phuc accomplishes a powerful shift in public consciousness. The direct engagement with the stranger on the road is attenuated into a much more familiar world of everyday sociality where one lives among specific individuals who have more or less intimate relationships with one another.

The circulation of images doesn't stop there, however. Despite the many iterations of Kim Phuc and her message of forgiveness, her past life as the napalm girl won't go away. That image of trauma continues to appear, ghost-like, in tableaus of the American flag, suburban lawns, economic expansion, and so forth. A ghost is an after-image, a specter that should disappear but refuses to go away, and whose very presence troubles the modern present and its logic of linear time. Photojournalism disseminates images, mechanically reproducing them by the millions and spreading them without control over their destination or use. Dissemination always has been accompanied by mythologies of haunting, including photography's early association with spirit worlds, and death remains a preoccupation in photography theory (Barthes, 1981; Peters, 1999). Ghosts are, like signs, bodies without material agency, and re-animation is itself a metaphor for the circulation and uptake constituting public culture. The ghost also embodies stranger relationality, an unbidden presence who functions as a witness to other relationships and who makes the familiar strange. More significantly, ghosts also are a reminder of unfinished business. Thus, the ghost of the napalm girl triggers

another strong shift in public consciousness: the familiar social world becomes unsettled, the ghostly figure presents a call for justice, for redress, and time begins flowing backward. This powerful undertow can pull one into a world of signs, swirling images, and the eternal recurrence of traumatic memory, but it can also provide an escape from the amnesia of the present. A sense of strangeness is necessary for reflection on the limits of one's moral awareness, not least as that is produced by the mass media, and it also may be necessary for deliberation.

The celebrity is one extreme of the field of stranger relationality, and its covering device; the ghost is the other extreme, and perhaps an essential means for re-animating public consciousness amidst other forms of social reality. Both the celebrity and the ghost exemplify essential features of the modern stranger: they are within but not fully of the social group, they are in intermediate positions between the viewer and larger sources of power, they are related to the viewer abstractly rather than through more organic ties, and they are at once both far and near (Simmel, 1950). This last characteristic is especially important, as it is perfectly coordinate with the phenomenology of photographic experience: the content of the photograph is always both far and near, whether a distant scene brought into one's reading space, or a loved one placed within an impersonal medium of paper and ink. This may be why emotional response is so crucial to whether a photograph is appealing. The emotional identification temporarily overcomes any sense of artificiality or awkwardness that comes from seeing the image as an image. Likewise, in a world lived among strangers, emotional resonance becomes an important measure of connection. So it is that both incarnations of the napalm girl succeed, as both the celebrity Kim Phuc and the traumatized little girl on the road activate strong emotional responses. More generally, this iconic image, like all iconic images, marks out a particular kind of public culture. In this culture, a strong form of stranger relationality underwrites heightened moral awareness, rational-critical deliberation about state action, and continued accountability. Even so, historical events are constituted as moments of emotional intensity rather than as decisive actions, and there may remain a permanent lack of connection between moral sentiment and any specific model of action. Neither ghosts nor celebrities do much other than circulate and watch the rest of the world. That, of course, is essentially what publics do, but they are valued because of the belief in a sense of agency. The test of that belief may lie in how the public image can influence political cognition and collective memory.

A common feature of deliberation and memory is a sense of time. We will close by considering how the iconic photo can delay or stop time. The traumatic structure of the napalm photo freezes an action that is happening quickly and would be quickly forgotten. This strong temporal delay is the visual equivalent of the extended duration of verbal deliberation, and it is a contribution to restoring meaningfulness. In addition, extended attention to the image in the present can activate a stronger connection between past and future, and one that is directed by the image and not just by larger narratives: one can see the past moment still recorded in the photograph beheld in the present, while the image projects a future which also has been fulfilled in time before the present and may be still unfolding. The iconic photo can operate in a postliterate society as a democratic moment, one that slows down the public audience to ponder both what has been lost in the rush of visual images and what is still unrealized in what has been seen. As Paul Virilio and Sylvere Lotringer have observed, "Democracy, consultation, the basis of politics, requires time," while the fundamental dynamic of modern society is the *acceleration* of all modes of exchange (1983, p. 28). This acceleration is driven by the combination of technological development and logistical mobilization that occurred as the economy was oriented toward a permanent condition of military preparedness. It has produced a war culture that permeates modern life while disabling democratic practices. Visual media are highly complicit in this process of social reorganization. The cinema is Virilo and Lotringer's primary example, although video and digital technologies have become the primary media and employ stronger techniques for both fragmenting and accelerating representation (Der Derian, 1992, 2000; Gray, 1997).

In respect to the mediation of public life, we might say that the problem is not the presence of a political spectacle, but the kinetic quality of that spectacle. Amidst this torrent of sights and sounds, the iconic photograph can induce a consciousness that is almost a form of slow motion. As Lester has remarked of iconic images, "Interestingly, moving films shown to television audiences were made at the same time . . . but it is the powerful stillness of the frozen, decisive moment that lives in the consciousness of all who have seen the photographs. The pictures are testaments to the power and the sanctity of the still, visual image" (1991, p. 120). This is a common sentiment in the print media (see, e.g., Eicher, 2001), but it should not be seen as mere special pleading. "The electronic image flickers and is gone. Not so with the frozen moment. It remains. It can haunt. It can hurt and hurt again. It can also leave an indelible message about the betterment of society, the end of war, the elimination of hunger, the alleviation of human misery" (Mallette, 1978, 120).

If a still photo can slow down the viewer, it might nurture a more reflective, more deliberative mentality. That deliberative moment is not a pure space, however, but one already inflected by the photo's embodiment of public discourse and its performance of public identity as stranger relationality. Photojournalism provides such resources on a daily basis that are necessary for maintaining public life, while the iconic photo then becomes a condensation of events and public culture alike that has the artistic richness necessary for continued circulation. The icon is a *lieu de mémoire:* a site where collective memory crystallizes once organic sociality has been swept away amidst the "acceleration of history" produced by modern civilization (Nora, 1989, p. 7). "Simple and ambiguous, natural and artificial, at once immediately available in concrete sensual experience and susceptible to the most abstract elaboration," iconic photographs operate in a dialectic of loss and recovery, official codification and vernacular disruption, verbal context and visual immediacy (Nora, 1989, p. 18). "In this sense the *lieu de mémoire* is double: a site of excess closed upon itself, concentrated in its own name, but also forever open to the full range of its possible significations" (Nora, 1989, p. 24). The photo of the napalm girl is not a figure of nostalgia amidst modernity's inevitable sense of alienation, however, but rather a symbolic form suited to the stranger relationality that constitutes, extends, and empowers public life. Thus, it provides the means through which moral capability can be retained by a public that has no common place, social structure, or agency. Both as a singular composition and as a figure in circulation, the icon provides a rhetorical structure for remembering and judging what otherwise would be consigned to the past.

The image of the little girl running from her pain became a moment when the Vietnam War crystallized in U.S. public consciousness. The photo could become such a "flashbulb memory" of the era not only because it represented the moral error at the heart of the U.S. war effort, but also because it embodied a process of cultural fragmentation that was accelerated by the war and its coverage. The features of that composition then became a template for remaking the public world through its continued circulation in the public media. Or worlds: the audience can choose one world where resilient individuals get on with their lives, where history has the inert presence of a scar, and moral response to others culminates in personal reconciliation. Or the audience can choose another world in which the past haunts the present as a traumatic memory, one that continues to demand public accountability for those who would betray the public by harming fellow strangers exposed to the relentless operations of imperial power. So it is that a democratic public will work out its capacity for thought and action in a discursive field where striking images can shape both moral judgment and collective memory.

NOTES

1. On the other side, some soldiers feel as though they have been betrayed by the picture (Timberlake, 1997). Their argument is strengthened when one sees how the photograph typically has been cropped: left out are soldiers whose stance suggests that all could be in danger and a photographer who is at least as professionally preoccupied as the soldiers on the road. The last omission is the most significant: it erases any sense of journalistic complicity in the war, while it also reduces the photo's reflexivity. We are to reflect on the war, but not on how it is photographed. Another photo that was taken a few moments later as the kids ran past a gaggle of video cameramen and still photographers is even more damning in this regard (Leuhusen, 2000).

2. Another, almost identical photo is also in circulation. Taken by Anne Bayin, it, too, looks over Kim's bare, scared shoulder as she holds her smooth-skinned baby. As reported in a "Ms. Moment" sidebar, the photograph "is part of a nationwide exhibit entitled 'Moments of Intimacy, Laughter, and Kinship.'" Its placement in *Ms.* magazine is equally clear: "If there is a picture that captures the madness of war, it is the one of nine-year-old Kim Phuc running naked, burned by the napalm that U.S. troops dropped on her Vietnamese village on June 8, 1972. And if there is a picture that captures the power of hope and the joys of renewal, it is the one above . . ." ("From Hell to Hope," 2001).

3. The photo's prominent place in public memory of the Vietnam War is likely to continue. It is continually reproduced in volumes on famous and noteworthy photographs (e.g., Buell, 1999, pp. 102–103; Goldberg, 1991, p. 244; Robin, 1999, p. 59; Stepan, 2000, pp. 134–135) and it is one of two photos (the other is the execution shot) on the war in an award winning historical text for "young people" (Harkin, 2001, p. 132). Additionally, it continues to be used to join private recollection and public memory in short stories (Lam, 1998, pp. 111–121) and poetry (Durazzi, 2001a, 2001b; Vo, 2001). Other appropriations appear in Milos Forman's *The People vs. Larry Flynt* (1996) and Jon Haddock's *Screenshots* (Haddock, 2000). The photo also is used as a means for photojournalistic contextualization across the political spectrum. For example, it has been paired by an Israeli newspaper with the photo of a Palestinian father and son in the midst of a gunfight, in order to highlight the "excessive" emotional impact of the latter photo (Burger, 2000, p. 2b). More appreciatively, it was the one photograph selected for a commemorative art exhibit at the Guernica Culture House in Guernica, Spain to commemorate the 63rd anniversary of the German bombing of that town during the Spanish Civil War (Exhibit Recalls German Destruction, 2000). In addition, we are indebted to Nancy Miller for bringing to our attention a number of important appropriations of the napalm image by contemporary artists; her work on artistic remediation of the image as a form of personal testimony is an important complement to our analysis (in press).

REFERENCES

Accidental napalm attack. (1972, June 9). *New York Times,* pp. 1A, 9.

Aristotle. (1973). The poetics (W. H. Fyfe, Trans.). In *Aristotle: Volume 23. Loeb Classical Library.* Cambridge: Harvard University.

Barthes, R. (1977). The rhetoric of the image (Stephen Heath, Trans.). In *Image—Music—Text* (pp. 32–52). New York: Hill and Wang.

Barthes, R. (1981). *Camera lucida: Reflections on photography* (R. Howard, Trans.). New York: Noonday Press.

The beat of life. (1972, June 23). *Life, 72,* pp. 4–5.

Benjamin, W. (1980). A short history of photography. In A. Trachtenberg (Ed.), *Classic essays on photography* (199–216). New Haven, CT: Leete's Island Books. (Original work published 1931)

Buell, H. (1999). *Moments: The Pulitzer prize photographs, a visual chronicle of our times.* New York: Black Dog and Leventhal.

Burger, J. (2000, October 5). The influence of fear in the eyes of the child. *Ha'aretz,* p. 2B.

Burgin, V. (1992a). Photographic practice and art theory. In V. Burgin (Ed.), *Thinking photography* (pp. 39–84). London: MacMillan.

Burgin, V. (1992b). Looking at photographs. In V. Burgin (Ed.), *Thinking photography* (pp. 142–153). London: MacMillan.

Burgin, V. (1996). *In/Different spaces: Place and memory in visual culture.* Berkeley: University of California.

Caputo, J. (1993). *Against ethics: Contributions to a poetics of obligation with constant reference to deconstruction.* Bloomington: Indiana University.

Chilton, E. (2000). Veritatis Vietnam, dormant website currently unavailable. Accessed January 15, 2000.

Chong, D. (1999). *The girl in the picture: The story of Kim Phuc, the photograph, and the Vietnam, war.* New York: Viking.

Clinton, W. J. (2000, November 17). Remarks at Vietnam national university in Hanoi, Vietnam, *Weekly compilation of presidential documents, Vol. 46, no. 36.* Washington, D.C.: Government Printing Office.

Cloud, D. (1998). *Control and consolation in American culture and politics: Rhetorics of therapy.* Thousand Oaks, CA: Sage.

Danziger, J. (1997, April 5). *The Press Enterprise,* p. A10.

DeCoster, J. (2001, May 20). Soldiers of misfortune. *Boston Globe,* p. D3.

DeLuca, K. M. (1999). *Image politics: The new rhetoric of environmental activism.* New York: Guilford Press.

DeLuca, K. M. & Peeples, J. (2002). From public sphere to public screen: Democracy, activism, and the violence of Seattle. *Critical Studies in Media Communication, 19,* 125–151.

Der Derian, J. (1992). *Antidiplomacy: Spies, terror, speed, and war.* Oxford: Blackwell.

Der Derian, J. (April 3, 2000). War games: The pentagon wants what Hollywood's got. *The Nation,* pp. 41–43.

Durazzi, A. (2001a, January 22). Phan Thi Kim Phuc at the Vietnam memorial, Veterans Day, 1996. Retrieved February 21, 2002 from http://www.deimel.org/poetry/vietnam.htm.

Durazzi, A. (2001b, July 2). Kim Phuc, found poem, veterans day, 1996. Word's Worth Poetry Readings, Seattle City Council. Retrieved February 21, 2002 from http://www.ci.seattle.wa.us/ council/licata/p_0007a_ad/htm.

Eco, U. (1992). The currency of the photograph. In V. Burgin (Ed.), *Thinking photography* (pp. 32–39). London: MacMillan.

Ehrenhaus, P. (1993). Cultural narratives and the therapeutic motif: the political containment of Vietnam veterans. In D. Mumby (Ed.), *Narrative and social control: Critical perspectives* (pp. 77–96). Newbury Park, CA: Sage.

Ehrenrich, B. (1997). *Blood rites: Origins and history of the passions of war.* New York: Henry Holt.

Eicher, D. (2001, September 23). Images: Despite the barrage of video footage, it's still photos that haunt us. Retrieved February 23, 2002 from www.denverpost.com/stories/0,1002,1078%1007E153737,153700.html.

Exhibit recalls German destruction of Spanish town of Guernica. (2000, April 25). Retrieved February 21, 2002 from http://www.cnn.com/2000/Style/arts/2004/2025/guernica.anniversary.ap.

Faas, H. & Page, T. (Eds.). (1997). *Requiem: By the photographers who died in Vietnam and Indochina.* New York: Random House.

Franklin, H. B. (1994). From realism to virtual reality: Images of America's war. In S. Jeffords & L. Rabinovitz (Eds.), *Seeing through the media: The Persian Gulf war* (pp. 25–44). New Brunswick, NJ: Rutgers University Press.

Franklin, H. B. (2000). *Vietnam & other American fantasies.* Amherst, MA: University of Massachusetts.

From hell to hope. (October/November 2001). *Ms.,* p. 20.

Goldberg, V. (1991). *The power of photography: How photographs changed our lives.* New York: Abbeville.

Gray, C. H. (1997). *Post-modern war: The new politics of conflict.* New York: Guilford.

Griffin, M. (1999). The great war photographs: Constructing myths of history and photojournalism. In B. Brennan & H. Hardt (Eds.), *Picturing the past: Media, history, and photography* (pp. 122–157). Urbana: University of Illinois Press.

Griffiths, P. J. (1971). *Vietnam Inc.* New York: MacMillan.

Habermas, J. (1989). *The structural transformation of the public sphere: An inquiry into a category of bourgeois society* (T. Burger, Trans.). Cambridge, MA: MIT Press.

Haddock, J. (2000). Children fleeing, Screenshot Series. Retrieved July 18, 2002 from http:// www.whitelead.com/jrh/screenshots/children_ fleeing.jpg.

Hallin, D. C. (1986). *The "uncensored war": The media and Vietnam.* New York: Oxford University.

Hariman, R. (1995). *Political style: The artistry of power.* Chicago: University of Chicago.

Hariman, R. & Lucaites, J. L. (2001). Dissent and emotional management in a liberal-democratic society: The Kent State iconic photograph. *Rhetoric Society Quarterly, 31,* 5–32.

Hariman, R. & Lucaites, J. L. (2002). Performing civic identity: The iconic photograph of the flag raising on Iwo Jima. *Quarterly Journal of Speech, 88,* 363–392.

Harkin, J. (Ed.). (2001). *All of the people, 1945–1998* (Vol. 10). New York: Oxford University.

Herman, J. L. (1992). *Trauma and recovery: The aftermath of violence from domestic abuse to political terror.* New York: Basic.

Jay, M. (1993). *Downcast eyes: The denigration of vision in twentieth-century French thought.* Berkeley: University of California.

Kinney, K. (2000). *Friendly fire, American images of the Vietnam war.* New York: Oxford University.

Kress, G. & van Leeuwen, T. (1996). *Reading images: The grammar of visual design.* New York: Routledge.

Lam, A. (1998). Show and tell. In B. Tran, M. T. D. Truong & L. T. Khoi (Eds.), *Watermark: Vietnamese-American poetry and prose* (pp. 111–121). New York: Asian American Writer's Workshop.

Lester, P. (1991). *Photojournalism: An ethical approach.* Hillsdale, NJ: Lawrence Erlbaum.

Leuhusen, P. (2000). "Under fire" at *The Vietnam war website.* Retrieved March 12, 2001 from http:// www.vietnampix.com/fire9a2.htm.

Mallette, M. F. (1978, March). Should these news pictures have been printed? *Popular Photography, 83,* 120.

Miller, N.K. (2004). The girl in the photograph: The Vietnam War and the making of national memory. *JAC, 24,* 261–290. (Also presented as the Addison Locke Roach Memorial Lecture, Bloomington, Indiana, October 24, 2002.)

Mitchell, W. J. T. (1994). *Picture theory.* Chicago: University of Chicago.

Moeller, S. D. (1989). *Shooting war: Photography and the American experience of combat.* New York: Basic Books.

Nora, P. (1989). Between memory and history. *Representations, 26,* 7–25.

Pacification's deadly price. (1972, June 19). *Newsweek, 79,* p. 42.

The people vs. Larry Flynt. (1996). M. Forman (Dir.). United States: Columbia Pictures.

Perlmutter, D. D. (1998). *Photojournalism and foreign policy: Icons of outrage in international crises.* Westport, CT: Praeger.

Peters, J. (1997). Beauty's veils: The ambivalent iconoclasm of Kierkegaard and Benjamin. In D. Andrew (Ed.), *The image in dispute: Art and cinema in the age of photography* (pp. 9–32). Austin, TX: University of Texas.

Peters. J. (1999). *Speaking into the air: A history of the idea of communication.* Chicago: University of Chicago.

Pilot finds forgiveness—24 years after attack. (1997, April 13). *Indianapolis Star and News,* pp. 1, 2.

Portrait of Kim Phuc, the "napalm girl," 23 years later. (1995), at the *Life* magazine website. Retrieved September 15, 2002 from http://www.lifemag .com/Ldfe/pictday/wppa04.html.

Postman, N. (1985). *Amusing ourselves to death: Public discourse in the age of show business.* New York: Penguin.

Robin, M.M. (Ed.). (1999). *The photos of the century: 100 historic moments.* Koln: Evergreen.

Robins, K. (1996). *Into the image: Culture and politics in the field of vision.* New York: Routledge.

Scarry, E. (1985). *The body in pain.* New York: Oxford University.

Schechner, R. (1985). *Between theater and anthropology.* Philadelphia: University of Pennsylvania.

Shay, J. (1994). *Achilles in Vietnam: Combat trauma and the undoing of character.* New York: Simon and Schuster Touchstone.

Simmel, G. (1950). The stranger. In K. Wolff (Ed. and Trans.), *The sociology of Georg Simmel.* New York: Free Press.

Sixtieth anniversary of *Life,* (1996, May), *Life, 18,* p. 102.

Skow, L., & Dionisopoulos, G. (1997). A struggle to contextualize photographic images: American print media and the "burning monk." *Communication Quarterly, 45,* 393–409.

Sontag, S. (1973). *On photography.* New York: Dell.

States, B. (1996). Performance as metaphor. *Theatre Journal, 48,* 1–26.

Stepan, P. (Ed.). (2000). *Photos that changed the world: The 20th century.* Munich: Prestel.

Sturken, M. (1997). *Tangled memories: The Vietnam war, the AIDS epidemic, and the politics of remembering.* Berkeley: University of California.

Tagg, J. (1988). *The burden of representation: Essays on photographies and histories.* Amherst, MA: University of Massachusetts.

Tagg, J. (1992). The currency of the photograph. In V. Burgin (Ed.), *Thinking photography* (pp. 110–141). London: MacMillan.

Taylor, J. (1998). *Body horror: Photojournalism, catastrophe, and war.* New York: New York University.

Timberlake, R. (1997, November). The myth of the girl in the photo. Retrieved August 18, 2001 from http://www.vietquoc.com/ju124-98.htm.

Toles, T. (1994, September 2). *The Buffalo News.*

Trachtenberg, A. (1989). *Reading American photographs.* New York: Hill and Wang.

Vietnam yesterday and today: Post-traumatic stress disorder (PTSD) a selected bibliography. (2001, January 22). Retrieved November 21, 2002 from http://servercc.oakton.edu/ ~ wittman/ptsd.htm.

Virilio, P. & Lotringer, S. (1983). *Pure war* (M. Polizzotti, Trans.). New York: Semiotext(e).

Vo, L. D. (2001, December 14). The girl in the photograph. Retrieved July 18, 2002 from http://grunt.space.swri.edu/lvopoems.htm.

Walzer, M. (1977). *Just and unjust wars.* New York: Basic.

Warner, M. (2002). *Publics and counterpublics.* New York: Zone Books.

White, J. B. (1984). *When words lose their meaning: Constitutions and reconstitutions of language, character, and community.* Chicago: University of Chicago.

Zelizer, B. (2004). The voice of the visual in memory. In K. R. Phillips (Ed.), *Framing public memory.* Tuscaloosa, AL: University of Alabama Press.

SECTION III

CONFRONTING AND RESISTING

Symbolic acts of confronting and resisting seek to disrupt the façade of civic consensus by overt and ostentatious displays that occur in public spaces—in the street, the square, on buildings, in the public commons, on the body, on screen, wherever they can be seen. Rhetorical scholars have variously termed such actions protest rhetoric, movement rhetoric, rhetoric of the streets, body rhetoric, image events, rhetoric of resistance, and rhetoric of confrontation (Morris & Browne, 2006). We pair the actions of *confronting* and *resisting* in order to highlight the relationship between visual rhetoric and those symbolic actions developed by rhetors who confront authorizing institutions and resist the established order through their use of visual images, artifacts, symbols, bodies, and performances.

Visible performances of activism disrupt the presumption that citizens should always acquiesce to authoritative policies. They confront the established order with accusations of immorality and hypocrisy and thus alter the shape of public discourse. By interrupting and disturbing the flow of authorized and commercial images, activists attempt to redefine and restructure the public face of morality and justice. In doing so, they enact what Kevin DeLuca (1999) terms "image politics." Frequently, such actions involve the physical and symbolic use of bodies to defy the social order. Often, such challenges evoke repressive and sometimes violent responses from authorities. Some critics of such tactics argue that image politics are "irrational," and therefore

Figure 1   "Pittsburgh, 1916," Robert Minor.

SOURCE: *The Masses* magazine, Library of Congress.

inappropriate, because they do not appear to be deliberative in the traditional sense of enabling "civil," "rational" argument. However, as the essays in this section reveal, visual rhetorics of confrontation and resistance are highly deliberative and often necessary modes of rhetorical engagement, particularly when other strategies are unavailable or ineffective. As Scott and Smith (1969) argue, such confrontational acts explicitly enact "the charge that civility and decorum serve as masks for the preservation of injustice" (p. 8).

Visuality plays an important part in acts of confrontation and resistance. Visual rhetoric enables citizens to reveal deep divisions in social and civic hierarchies of power, illuminate instances of perceived injustice, and persuade diverse publics of the necessity for social change. For example, during the middle of the 20th century, civil rights activists sought equality in suffrage, education, and access to public spaces by confronting prevailing policies and traditions. They made their strategies of confrontation public and highly visible by engaging in sit-ins, marches, and freedom rides. By occupying places where segregationist laws forbade them to be and refusing to move unless dragged away, demonstrators disrupted routines of commerce and social interaction and created visual dramas that brought the attention of the media. Another rhetorical strategy used by civil rights activists was to circulate photographs that depicted the injustices of racist practices. For instance, sanctions against the social "mixing" of the races were upheld by laws against miscegenation and enforced by violent punishment of suspected infractions of interracial intimacy (Hope, 1985). In a few famous cases, including the Emmett Till case explored by Christine Harold and Kevin DeLuca in an essay in this section, activists appealed to media organizations that agreed to circulate photographs that called international attention and condemnation to racial hypocrisy in the United States (Tyson, 1999).

Visual rhetoric predominates in mass demonstrations, marches, flag burnings, and the distribution of photographs and videos by those opposing war and oppression and advocating for social justice. Antiwar demonstrators protesting the Vietnam War and later the U.S. occupation of Iraq, for instance, used multiple modes of visual rhetoric to expose what they believed were nefarious U.S. policies. In the late 1990s, global demonstrations against the World Trade Organization (WTO) sought to direct attention to the devastating effects of "free trade" on the poor and working classes and to expose the simultaneous increase of wealth generated by and for the richest corporations. Activists organized mass demonstrations, costumed parades, street theater, and rallies (DeLuca & Peeples, 2002). Beginning in the 1990s, activists used the World Wide Web to circulate images and calls for action with greater speed and effectiveness.

The essays in this section illustrate that visual rhetorics of confrontation and resistance are often rhetorics of the body. The strategy of passive resistance espoused by civil rights leaders such as Martin Luther King Jr. and the Student Non-Violent Coordinating Committee (SNCC), for example, involved the direct use of the body to oppose, confront, and resist authority. These strategies were adapted by a variety of groups, including environmental activists who have chained themselves to trees, buried themselves in roads, and lived in trees as acts of resistance to deforestation practices (DeLuca, 1999). Resistance also occurs more symbolically when groups enact "visibility politics" by performing in public, painting murals, or marking their bodies to publicly announce their refusal to be invisible.

Another form of resistance is the act of rhetorical criticism itself. Some scholars of visual rhetoric believe that the critic should use criticism not just to describe or interpret the world but to "participat[e] in a critical project" that evaluates and judges with an eye toward social change (DeLuca, 1999, p. 148). But even criticism itself may not be enough when rhetoric has real, material consequences in the world. Dana L. Cloud (2006) argues that approaches to rhetoric that focus "nearly exclusively on symbolic commitments" may "give away the ground for political instrumentality" necessary for real social change (p. 331). In other words, Cloud is concerned that an exclusive focus on the symbolic may lull us into the false thinking that merely "doing criticism" is enough to accomplish change in the world. Cloud makes similar arguments in her essay, which appears in this book, "'To Veil the Threat of Terror'" Afghan Women and the <Clash of Civilizations> in the Imagery of the U.S. War on Terrorism" (in Section V). The work of scholars such as Cloud reminds us that scholarly insight into rhetorics of confrontation and resistance can and, according to some, should lead to more direct social and political activism on the part of the critic.

Students and scholars who wish to investigate the symbolic acts of confronting and resisting in relation to visual rhetoric may want to explore these questions: How are visualized forms of confrontation open to "reasonable" and "ethical" analysis as arguments? How do visual actions exemplify resistance? How do actions of resistance incorporate visual rhetoric? How are power relations negotiated by marginalized groups when institutional access is limited to those in power? Do some visual technologies alter the relationship between power hierarchies? How do we name rhetorical strategies that vilify the norms of "reasoned" public debate as ineffectual—or worse—as part of the condition of oppressive power hierarchies? How do we understand violence within the frame of visual discourse? How do we understand and theorize the rhetoric of dissent and resistance when it is collectively enacted *by* and *on* individual bodies? And finally, what is the role of the rhetorical critic regarding dissent and resistance to instances of injustice?

The first essay in this section is Dan Brouwer's "The Precarious Visibility Politics of Self-Stigmatization: The Case of HIV/AIDS Tattoos." Brouwer argues that groups marginalized by media invisibility and stigma, or demeaned in portrayals of "otherness," sometimes seek visibility as a means to announce legitimate identity and assert a place of power that needs to be recognized. But visibility is often a risky confrontational strategy. Brouwer's essay theorizes visibility politics by exploring the practice of "self-stigmatization" in people who choose to disclose publicly their serostatus—HIV antibody positive—with tattoos of self-stigmatization even though they could choose to keep their status private. Tracing the meaning of "stigma" through the work of Erving Goffman and others, Brouwer notes that tattoos historically have been associated with marking certain bodies as "spoiled" or undesirable. The display of tattoos is thus an act of self-stigmatization by asymptomatic individuals who choose not to "pass" as "healthy." Brouwer's essay traces the rationale and justification for self-stigmatization in three men who voice their reasons for moving their HIV-positive status from the private to the public stage and argues that the tattoos are both liberating and "precarious" acts of resistance. In addition to being considered with the other essays in this section, Brouwer's essay might also be read alongside Morris and Sloop's essay, "'What Lips These Lips Have Kissed': Refiguring the Politics of Queer Public Kissing" (in Section I), in that they both explore facets of queer public visibility.

Margaret R. LaWare's essay, "Encountering Visions of Aztlán: Arguments for Ethnic Pride,

Community Activism and Cultural Revitalization in Chicano Murals," explores the role of mural art in shaping community development and community identity for traditionally marginalized groups. LaWare observes that murals constitute one way that minority communities in the 20th century resisted racist representations of themselves, representations that often led to discrimination. For LaWare, murals and other visual images are important because they "may advocate a fairly specific concept of community development and community identity . . . in ways that make them distinct from discursive arguments" (p. 228). Examining murals that explore the history of Mexico and Mexican American people, whose cultural background is blended and who thus have a history different from other immigrant groups, LaWare shows how the very public form of the mural reinforces the bonds of community and fosters cultural pride. The essay details how the celebration of specific symbols (e.g., the Virgin of Guadalupe), leaders (e.g., César Chávez, Reies Tijerina, Rodolfo Gonzalez, and José Angel Gutiérrez), and organizational emblems (e.g., the United Farm Workers) portrayed a widely shared heritage, promoted identifications within community, and created a symbolic space for revitalizing the community. LaWare's discussion of the relationship between public images and ethnic pride serves as a provocative contrast to Ekaterina V. Haskins's essay, "'Put Your Stamp on History': The USPS Commemorative Program *Celebrate the Century* and Postmodern Collective Memory" (in Section IV); it may be useful to compare LaWare's analysis to Haskins's examination of how visual imagery reinforces a hegemonic story of American history rather than a culturally distinct one.

Anne Teresa Demo's essay, "The Guerrilla Girls' Comic Politics of Subversion," uses Kenneth Burke's concepts of the *comic frame* and *perspective by incongruity* to analyze the visual rhetoric of the feminist art activists who call themselves the "Guerrilla Girls." Demo finds Burke's comic frame to be a humanistic alternative to rhetorics of confrontation. She argues that the posters and theater of the Guerrilla Girls work through strategies of "demystification rather than revolution" as the activists challenge the male-dominated art world. Demo begins by tracing how women's participation in the arts historically has been marginalized. She then chronicles the emergence of resistance to that marginalization and exclusion by the Guerrilla Girls, an anonymous group of artists, critics, art institution staff, educators, and art lovers who hide their individual identities and emphasize their collectivity by wearing gorilla masks. In interviews and performances, the anonymous women assume the names and personae of "underacknowledged" women artists. In this way, Demo argues, public attention is focused on the issues the Guerrilla Girls want to raise, rather than on individual activists; this diffuses the risk of retribution inherent in visibility politics.

Demo analyzes three "strategies of incongruity" present in the Guerrilla Girls' rhetoric: mimicry, historical revision, and strategic juxtaposition. For example, both terms, *guerrilla* and *girls*, mimic meaning from oppositional contexts and are transformed into visual displays in images as well as in live performances. The comic, visual punning of the word *guerrilla* with the ferocious masks of gorilla heads is featured in the group's posters, books, Web site, and performances. The use of *girls* rather than *women*, as feminist dogma would prefer, is visually reinforced by the use of the color pink in posters and in the ultra-feminine attire worn by the gorilla-headed activists: fishnet stockings, ultra high heels, and short skirts. Demo reads these visual displays of incongruously costumed bodies as a rhetorical strategy that uses mimicry to challenge traditional definitions of femininity. Demo's essay might be read productively alongside Edwards and Winkler's essay, "Representative Form and the Visual Ideograph: The Iwo Jima Image in Editorial Cartoons" (in Section II), because both explore the rhetoric of visual parody.

In "Behold the Corpse: Violent Images and the Case of Emmett Till," Christine Harold and Kevin Michael DeLuca contribute to rhetorical analysis of the civil rights movement by exploring the significance of one photograph as central to the solidarity of civil rights activists. Harold and DeLuca argue that the brutal murder of the young Emmett Till might have become another footnote in the long and continuing struggle against racism were it not for a crucial decision made by Till's mother. Mamie Till Mobley courageously chose to open the coffin of her son and, in an act of confrontation, allow the black community of Chicago to witness the mutilated body. Photographs of the brutalized remains of the young man's face were circulated widely in juxtaposition with a family photograph of a smiling Emmett Till and published in *Jet* magazine. Harold and DeLuca read the juxtaposed photos as "amplifying calls for justice" in the black community. Citing a host of Americans, including Muhammad Ali, Johnny Cochran, Julian Bond, Charlayne Hunter-Gault, and black studies communication scholar Molefi Asante, who recall the images as a turning point in their lives and as an inspiration for resistance, Harold and DeLuca argue that the power of the images redefined the meaning of racial violence. Tracing the photographic history of violence against African Americans, especially in images of lynchings that depicted crowds of white citizens participating in the spectacle of death as entertainment, the essay argues that circulated images of Emmett Till's mutilated body constituted "an event—a rhetorical event that require[d] a response" (p. 268). Harold and DeLuca thus read the civil rights movement as a response of resistance: In addition to the speeches that have garnered so much attention from rhetorical critics, the image of an "abject body" also moved the nation to action. This essay could productively be read alongside Blair and Michel's essay, "Reproducing Civil Rights Tactics: The Rhetorical Performances of the Civil Rights Memorial" (in Section II), for exploration of the relationship of civil rights–era rhetoric to contemporary memorialization.

We invite you to examine further the wide range of visual rhetoric scholarship related to the rhetorical actions of confronting and resisting by exploring the discussion questions below as well as the suggestions for further reading.

Discussion Questions

1. In the essays gathered in this section, a number of concepts recur. For example, the strategy of appropriation is documented and analyzed by critics studying the meanings of visual rhetoric in actions of resistance. Compare the essays' approach to appropriation and detail the ways in which

appropriation emerges as a viable strategy for those engaging in confrontation and resistance.

2. "The rhetoric of the body" is one of the oldest concepts in scholarly debate about movements, resistance, and confrontation. All of the essays here explore meanings of the body: Brouwer and Demo discuss inscribed, marked, and costumed bodies; LaWare analyzes representations of bodies appearing in murals; and Harold and DeLuca explore the rhetoric of the photographed body of Emmett Till's corpse. Based on what you find in these essays, explain the various ways that bodies can be used rhetorically in actions of confrontation and resistance.

3. Some of the essays here focus on *performances* of resistance; others focus on *images*. What are the connections between rhetorics of performance and images? Compare and contrast them as examples of confrontation and resistance in visual rhetoric.

4. The rhetorical critics represented in this section investigate actions of resistance and confrontation in instances that span nearly half a century. In doing so, their work reveals the extent to which troubling events and ideologies in American history and culture have produced bias and discrimination toward specific groups. How have such events and ideologies been made manifest in visual rhetorics?

REFERENCES

Cloud, D. L. (2006). *The Matrix* and critical theory's desertion of the real. *Communication and Critical/Cultural Studies, 3*(4), 329–354.

DeLuca, K. M. (1999). *Image politics: The new rhetoric of environmental activism.* New York: Guilford.

DeLuca, K. M., & Peeples, J. (2002). From public sphere to public screen: Democracy, activism and the "violence" of Seattle. *Critical Studies in Media Communication, 19*(2), 125–151.

Hope, D. S. (1985). Communication and human rights: The symbolic structures of racism and sexism. In T. W. Benson (Ed.), *Communication in the twentieth century* (pp. 63–89). Carbondale: Southern Illinois University Press.

Morris, C. E., III, & Browne, S. H. (2006). *Readings on the rhetoric of social protest* (2nd ed.). State College, PA: Strata Publishing, Inc.

Scott, R. L., & Smith, D. K. (1969). The rhetoric of confrontation. *Quarterly Journal of Speech, 55*(1), 1–8.

Tyson, T. B. (1999). *Radio free dixie: Robert F. Williams and the roots of black power.* Chapel Hill: University of North Carolina Press.

SUGGESTIONS FOR FURTHER READING

Ehrenhaus, P., & Owen, A. S. (2004). Race lynching and Christian evangelicalism: Performances of faith. *Text and Performance Quarterly, 24* (3–4), 276–301.

Enck-Wanzer, D. (2006). Trashing the system: Social movement, intersectional rhetoric, and collective agency in the Young Lords organization's garbage offensive. *Quarterly Journal of Speech, 92*(2), 174–201.

Owens, L., & Palmer, L. K. (2003). Making the news: Anarchist counter-public relations on the World-Wide Web. *Critical Studies in Media Communication, 20*(4), 335–361.

Pezzullo, P. C. (2003a). Resisting "National Breast Cancer Awareness Month": The rhetoric of counterpublics and their cultural performances. *Quarterly Journal of Speech, 89*(4), 345–365.

Pezzullo, P. C. (2003b). Touring "cancer alley" Louisiana: Performances of community and memory for environmental justice. *Text and Performance Quarterly, 23*(3), 226–252.

Shugart, H. A. (2005). On misfits and margins: Narrative, resistance, and the poster child politics of Rosie O'Donnell. *Communication and Critical/Cultural Studies, 2*(1), 52–76.

Squires, C. R., & Brouwer, D. (2002). In/Discernible bodies: The politics of passing in dominant and marginal media. *Critical Studies in Media Communication, 19*(3), 283–310.

10

THE PRECARIOUS VISIBILITY POLITICS OF SELF-STIGMATIZATION

The Case of HIV/AIDS Tattoos

DAN BROUWER

On the editorial page of the *New York Times* of March 18, 1986, conservative political commentator William F. Buckley, Jr. argued for the following HIV/AIDS public health policy: first, all people in the United States were to be tested for HIV; second, all those who were diagnosed with AIDS were to be "tattooed on the upper forearm, to warn common needle users, and on the buttocks, to prevent the victimization of other homosexuals" (A27). Apparently, Buckley's proposal exemplified what a significant number of Americans considered to be sound AIDS public health policy, for in a 1988 *New England Journal of Medicine* review of fifty surveys in the U.S. between 1983 and 1988, "twenty-nine percent [of Americans surveyed] said they favored requiring a tattoo for anyone with a positive blood test" (Okie A7).[1]

Six years after Buckley's proposal, the June/July 1994 issue of *POZ* magazine (a glossy, high-distribution magazine for people with HIV and those impacted by HIV)[2] included a two-photo layout of HIV "body art." In each of the photos, a man with HIV or AIDS shows the viewer the tattoo that he has acquired. On one man's shoulder is inked "Action=Life," an affirmative revision of the by-now popular ACT-UP (AIDS Coalition to Unleash Power) slogan "Silence=Death." On the shoulder of another man is a large, black "+" (positive) sign, with "HIV" written across the horizontal transverse.

The next issue of *POZ* (August/September 1994) included two more pictures of people with HIV or AIDS displaying the tattoos that they have acquired. The man shows us his shoulder, upon which he has had inked the international symbol for biohazardous waste. The woman shows her arm upon which has been tattooed "Silence=Death." The photos are accompanied by a short essay by Matt Fuller who, although he is not pictured, tells the reader that he acquired a tattoo on his right arm with the words "HIV positive" next to a pink triangle, the Nazi's marker for gay men during the Holocaust. Fuller reveals that he acquired a

SOURCE: Brouwer, D. (1998). The precarious visibility politics of self-stigmatization: The case of HIV/AIDS tattoos. *Text and Performance Quarterly, 18,* 114–136. © National Communication Association.

tattoo so that he might be "visible, not invisible" (Fuller 34).

There is something similar between William F. Buckley's proposal and the actions that the people in *POZ* magazine have taken: it is that they all view marking the body—inscribing the skin—as a potentially beneficial way of dealing with the HIV/AIDS crisis in the United States. The dissimilarities between Buckley and the others are more obvious, however: the same result—tattooed bodies—is rendered from vastly different motivations. On the one hand, Buckley and his ilk want to prevent further HIV infections by warning non-infected people of their risk of infection if they engage in certain behaviors with a seropositive[3] other. That Buckley's tattoos would be mandatory (though they are private) would reduce the ability of their wearers to control disclosure of their serostatus.[4] On the other hand, the people profiled in *POZ* choose to tattoo themselves and publicize their infection, thus presenting curious communicative and performative conundra.

In this essay, I wish to examine the phenomenon of self-stigmatization—or the conscious and willful marking of oneself as "tainted"—as a particular communicative and performative strategy grounded in visibility politics and practiced in the context of AIDS activism. On one level, the tattoos act to convey basic, technical information about the presence of Human Immunodeficiency Virus in the wearer's body, thus functioning communicatively, but certain qualities of the act of wearing these tattoos make them performative.[5] The display of an HIV/AIDS tattoo is a qualitatively different act from the staging of a theatrical performance about HIV and AIDS, not only because the "stages" upon which the tattoo wearer performs her or his enunciation include the everyday settings of work, play, and home, but also because for the tattoo wearer the body announces the invisible even when the wearer remains vocally silent. Tattoo wearers textualize the surface of the body, and the body becomes "a surface on which various productions take place" (Reinelt 99),[6] including the staging of a commitment to "safer sex" practices, a refusal to internalize the "shame" of HIV infection, and an intervention against the functioning of normative expectations about the appearance of "health."[7]

Toward the end of better understanding the phenomenon of self-stigmatization, I explore in this essay the relationship between stigma and tattoos, first outlining "stigma" as a sociological category that can be mobilized to either uphold or criticize community norms and then noting ways in which tattoos have been used in history as a negative stigma mark. Second, I provide a general outline of the assumptions that motivate visibility politics before noting specific ways in which visibility politics have informed AIDS activism. Understanding HIV/AIDS tattoos as self-imposed stigmata which continue the project of visibility in AIDS activism, I then outline claims made in defense of the tattoos as symbols of personal and political expression, and I excavate the assumptions about visibility and visibility politics that motivate such claims. Finally, I pose specific questions concerning the communicative and performative efficacy of the tattoos.

The wearing of an HIV/AIDS tattoo is a precarious act, one that simultaneously disrupts expectations of the appearance of health and challenges norms of 'patient' behavior, yet one that also invites surveillance (which can be oppressive, punitive, or physically painful) and runs the risk of reducing the wearer's identity to "disease carrier." On the one hand, the visible tattoo participates in a critical performativity that "enable[s] a powerful appreciation of the ways that identities are constructed iteratively through complex citational processes" (Parker and Sedgwick 2) by reminding its seer that boundaries between the "healthy" and the "ill" are unstable, at least to the extent that the "ill" are not always visibly recognizable as such. Furthermore, the asymptomatic person with HIV/AIDS who gets an "HIV positive" tattoo moves himself from the realm of the "discreditable" (where the dilemma is the management of information; that is, 'when, how, and to whom do I disclose my hidden stigma?') into the realm of the visibly "discredited" (where the dilemma becomes the management of tension; that is, 'how do I go about assuaging the discomfort that my visible stigma compels in others?'). Erving Goffman (1963) notes that societies typically assign the visibly stigmatized individual full responsibility for assuaging the social discomfort. Here, social disruption must be returned to balance, or homeostasis, and it is the responsibility of the stigmatized individual to reestablish that balance. The asymptomatic individual with the tattoo rejects this model of normative behavior by making the disruption intentional and unrepentant.

On the other hand, making one's HIV status visible through the medium of a tattoo can invite oppressive surveillance, invite verbal or physical harassment, or lead that person to be defined primarily on the basis of that foregrounded identity marker. Furthermore, wearing an HIV/AIDS tattoo might be considered an act of privilege in terms of the social support system that is necessary for such visibility and in terms of the assumption that such visibility is an act of freedom.[8] Concerning the relationship between visibility and surveillance, Peggy Phelan warns: "visibility is a trap . . . ; it summons surveillance and the law" (6). Whereas much of the original HIV/AIDS legislation in the United States secured protections of confidentiality for people who were infected, those protections of confidentiality are eschewed in part by the wearer of the tattoo who, whether or not she or he intends to, invites surveillance by institutions and individuals. Indeed, the visibility of the AIDS tattoo creates the possibility for verbal or physical harassment from those who recognize it. In addition, the AIDS tattoo runs the risk of serving as an abridging symbol, a symbol that reduces the complexities of a phenomenon into a simple image or gesture. In the case of the AIDS tattoo, the identity of the wearer runs the risk of being condensed or reduced to "person with AIDS." In his short essay in *POZ,* after he explains that "visibility" is the reason that he has acquired a tattoo, Matt Fuller states:

> If people choose to label me when they see my tattoo and see me only as a person living with AIDS, that's fine with me. I know that there is no label that could encompass all that I am . . . (34).

Here, while Fuller affirms the complexity of his life, he is also cognizant of the reductive readings that viewers of the tattoo might engage in. Thus, the wearing of an AIDS tattoo confers both possibilities and risks.

In the remainder of this essay, I will outline the meanings of "stigma" and the relationship of tattoos to stigmatization. Then, I will outline some of the key assumptions about visibility politics as well as show how visibility politics have undergirded AIDS activism. Next, I will examine the claims made in support of the tattoos, including the wearers' beliefs about how they function for themselves, for other seropositive people, for the AIDS community, and for the larger "general population."[9] This will be followed by an analysis of the communicative and performative possibilities and limitations of the tattoos.

Stigma and Tattoos

In his 1963 book, *Stigma: Notes on the Management of Spoiled Identity,* Erving Goffman begins with the etymological and cultural origins of that titular word. To the ancient Greeks, "stigma" meant a mark upon the body, but stigma referred to a mark placed upon the body (of a slave, for example) rather than one that was naturally occurring. Thus, a stigma was placed upon the body to indicate that the bearer was somehow inferior, polluted, or corrupt. The stigma warned others to avoid contact or communion with the bearer. Stigma has since come to refer not only to marks placed upon the body by others but also to naturally occurring physical characteristics (such as a cleft palate); as well, stigma has come to refer to the social conditions that impact and are impacted by personal characteristics (physically visible or not) that are non-normative.[10] The literature review in Angelo Alonzo's and Nancy Reynolds's recent (1995) article, "Stigma, HIV and AIDS: An Exploration and Elaboration of a Stigma Trajectory," demonstrates that theorists are largely in consensus with the idea that "stigma represents a construction of deviation from some ideal or expectation, whether the ideal is for 'correct' sexual orientation or to be free of a disfiguring or fatal infectious disease" (304). Katz, for example, suggests that stigma "encompasses a perception of a negative characteristic and a global devaluation of the possessor of the characteristic" (in Alonzo & Reynolds 304). As noted above, this negative characteristic can be perceived through a physical manifestation (such as a cleft palate or, in the case of HIV/AIDS, wasting syndrome or a tattoo) or through deductive interpretation (of homosexuality, for example, where a number of clues are used to interpret someone as lesbian or gay in the absence of explicit evidence). While the 'negative characteristic' is an individual attribute, the 'global devaluation' points to the social nature of stigma, or what Goffman calls a "language of relationships" (in Alonzo & Reynolds 304). Collectives of all shapes and sizes determine what is normative and non-normative, assign meanings to non-normative practices and characteristics, accord punishments for non-normativity (even if it is psychical or social punishment rather than physical), and negotiate exceptions to the social rules. And stigmatized people go through a variety of different experiences with stigma, including rejection of the stigma, alienation, internalization, or active resistance.

Although its current usage refers to the "disgrace" of corruption whether or not that disgrace is visible upon the body, the example of tattooing people with HIV/AIDS returns us to the origins of "stigma"'s meaning. In the history of tattoos, the use of tattoos to symbolize negative stigma is not without precedent.[11] Clinton Sanders (1989) notes how in thirteenth century Japan, for example, the practice of tattooing was revived as a method of "marking criminals and other social undesirables" (11–12); the tattoos inked upon a criminal would often indicate the type as well as location of the crime. In *The Decorated Body,* Robert Brain recounts the late nineteenth century practice of the British Army wherein men of "bad character" were marked with a "BC," and deserters of the army were marked with a "D" (160). Even more currently, in the early twentieth century in Europe and the U.S., tattoos were viewed as crude or spectacular stigmata of the lower classes. Thus, HIV/AIDS tattoos continue one particular symbolic trajectory in which a permanent mark placed upon the surface of the body signifies what some would consider to be negative or "tainted" characteristics about its wearer. What HIV/AIDS tattoos also do, however, is continue in a long line of efforts by AIDS educators and activists to 'make AIDS visible.' Later in this essay, I will examine the claims that wearers make about the increased visibility that their tattoos give them, and I will explicate the assumptions about visibility that undergird the wearers'

claims. Before examining those claims, however, a brief discussion of visibility politics—and the specific case of visibility politics and AIDS—is warranted.

Visibility Politics

For the purposes of this essay, visibility is defined as presenting oneself, in mediated or unmediated form, in public forums.[12] Visibility politics, then, might be defined as theory and practice which assume that "being seen" and "being heard" are beneficial and often crucial for individuals or a group to gain greater social, political, cultural or economic legitimacy, power, authority, or access to resources. With this understanding, individuals and collectives which call for their greater visibility might create or demand more (or different) fictive or non-fictive texts about themselves, more (or better) visual images of themselves in public media, or more (and better) physical presence in public spaces. Visibility politics move individuals and collectives out and away from the shadows and margins (whether they have been forced there, have placed themselves there, or have been ignored) into the light of public spaces. In her insightful and provocative book on the politics of performance, *Unmarked,* Peggy Phelan (1993) outlines four basic assumptions about visibility that seem common across social movements and activist groups:

1. Identities are visibly marked. . . . Reading physical resemblance is a way of identifying community.

2. The relationship between representation and identity is linear and smoothly mimetic. What one sees is who one is.

3. If one's mimetic-likeness is not represented, one is not addressed.

4. Increased visibility equals increased power (7).[13]

Notably, visibility is strongly linked to identity in Phelan's summary; "reading" facial characteristics, skin colors and tones, clothing styles, gaits, etc. can enable an observer to identify that individual's "membership" in one or a number of different social groupings. Thus, lesbians and gays read rainbow flag bumper stickers as emblematic of the owner's membership in a lesbian and gay community, or members of youth gangs read the color of clothing and the position of a baseball cap as emblematic of membership in an affiliated or rival gang.[14] Most notable in Phelan's summary, however, are the assumptions that the lack or absence of media representations of a social group precludes participation in relevant discussion and that visibility necessarily garners greater power for those who practice it. Visibility politics (as well as multiculturalism, identity politics, and liberal democracy) sometimes assume (rather problematically) that to give or take voice, or to make oneself visible as a willing and perhaps necessary participant in civic discussion and decision-making, is an inherently liberating act. Thus, for example, AIDS awareness campaigns that portray people with AIDS as vibrant, active, and/or erotic, efforts by underrepresented groups to produce grassroots documentary films, mass media efforts to portray Arabs and Arab-Americans as something other than terrorists—these efforts manifest at least a desire to displace dominant mimetic likenesses with more diverse or more "realistic" mimetic likenesses of the group. Furthermore, the promises of reward for such visibility are numerous: greater social acceptance, reduced cultural stereotypes, greater access to resources, or passage of policies that benefit the group. Visibility, whether physical presence in public places or media representations, is appealing, Phelan agrees, but while "underrepresented communities can be empowered by an enhanced visibility" (7), she argues that this visibility can in fact thwart a community's efforts to ameliorate itself. Through co-optation,[15] enforced hyper-visibility,[16] or the greater surveillance capabilities that visibility enables, collectives might find their efforts attenuated or deflected.

Throughout this essay, I will attempt to clarify the differing politics of visibility that motivate HIV/AIDS tattoo wearing practices. In this section, I have attempted to outline some assumptions about the benefits of visibility politics as well as some of the risks or disadvantages of visibility politics. With this framework in place, the task that remains is to connect tattoo-wearing to other visibility practices in AIDS activism: the next section should accomplish that task.

Visibility in AIDS Activism

> All vision doubts and hopes for a response. . . . To see is nothing if it is not replied to, confirmed by recourse to another image, and/or another's eye (Phelan 18).

To discuss visibility politics and AIDS together requires keen attention to the subjects, objects, means, and motivations of AIDS visibility. Jan Zita Grover (1992) provides a chronology of AIDS visibility practices in U.S. mass media: prior to 1983, images of AIDS in medical journals and in mainstream media were mostly scientific, including microscopic views of the virus and the virus's effects on bodily tissues and organs. After 1983, she observes, more images of people who were sufferers of the syndrome emerged. Unfortunately, the conditions of that visibility were such that distinctions between "guilty" and "innocent" victims of AIDS were upheld visually: while "innocent victims" such as hemophiliacs and babies were depicted in communal and sometimes public settings, "guilty victims" such as IV drug users and gay men were typically depicted as alone, in isolated settings, sometimes abject. Even through the early years of the epidemic, however, lesbians, gays, and others inordinately affected by the epidemic produced and disseminated visual texts designed to counter mainstream visual practices; these counter-texts emphasized the vitality, the communion (sometimes erotic or sexual), and the publicness of people with HIV/AIDS. However, it was not until around 1988, according to Grover, that mass media in the U.S. attempted to portray people with HIV/AIDS in a sympathetic light. People in the AIDS service industry initiated campaigns to "Give a Face to AIDS" designed to dispel fear and hostility through personalizing the syndrome, and liberals in the media began to respond.

Unlike the mandatory visibility practices of tattoos or quarantine camps (which emphasized imposition and isolation), visibility practices advocated by people in the AIDS industry emphasized choice and sympathy. "Giving a Face to AIDS" campaigns were joined by safer sex campaigns which sometimes showed condoms, explicit sexuality, or emphasized the difficulty of being able to see HIV or AIDS signifying on the surface of another's body. In addition, efforts were made to make AIDS visible as a *public* issue, rather than solely a (regrettable and unfortunate, but ultimately) *private* affliction; by making AIDS a *public* issue, elected or appointed officials, institutions, and social prejudices became targets of criticism and judgment.[17] Notable amidst radical activist efforts to make AIDS visible is the example of AIDS Coalition to Unleash Power (ACT UP). ACT UP combines a thorough knowledge of medicine and law with an often intentionally disruptive performativity; in their demonstrations, they attempt to publicize perceived injustices that individuals, officials, institutions, and social stereotypes commit upon people with HIV/AIDS.

Thus, HIV/AIDS tattoos follow in a long line of strategies and methods by people with AIDS and AIDS activists to make AIDS and people with AIDS more visible. By signifying their infection on the surface of the skin, they publicize what would otherwise remain hidden or unknown. Certainly, tattoo wearers assume that certain benefits will be derived—for themselves, for other people with HIV/AIDS, and for society at large—as a result of their visibility; the next section will explore the wide range of justifications that tattoo wearers offer, many of them echoing the assumptions about visibility politics that Phelan and others define.

Stigmatization to Self-Stigmatization

> Who might have predicted that Mr. Buckley's suggestion would be taken up by AIDS activists? (Stryker 8).

In the next two sections of this essay, I will be interested in the tattoo-wearer who is asymptomatic—that is, infected but neither experiencing HIV-related illnesses nor visibly manifesting immune suppression on the surface of the body.[18] Anyone in the U.S. who has encountered any kind of media in the last decade should be familiar with the ubiquitous images of people with HIV/AIDS afflicted with wasting syndrome or marked by the tell-tale cancerous lesions of Kaposi's sarcoma (KS).[19] Along with swollen lymph nodes in the neck, wasting syndrome and KS are the dominant stigmata for symptomatic people with HIV/AIDS. However,

it is the infected yet *asymptomatic* individual who remains unmarked as a "person with HIV (or AIDS)," a condition that challenges the assumption of visibility politics that "identities are visibly marked" (Phelan 7). Asymptomatic seropositives have the "privilege" of "passing" as "normal" or "healthy" (seronegative), but the asymptomatic seropositives who acquire tattoos clearly reject the privilege of passing.[20]

The reasons, justifications, and arguments for wearing an HIV/AIDS tattoo that I will examine come primarily from three individuals: John Baldetta as reported in *The Recorder* (15 Feb. 1995), Andrew Coats as reported in *POZ* magazine (Feb./Mar. 1996), and Gregg Cadieux as shared during an interview with this author (28 July 1997). Baldetta's, Coats's, and Cadieux's claims are supplemented with statements by other tattoo wearers, statements made by writers and cultural commentators, and by reference to (and comparison to) other ways of publicizing one's seropositivity. To preview, I would note that a diverse range of reasons and functions are attributed to the wearing of an HIV/AIDS tattoo, from personal or individual expressiveness to social expression, whether that social expression is oriented toward potential sexual or needle-sharing partners, to others in the "AIDS community,"[21] or to the "general public."[22] Furthermore, it will become apparent that distinct motives or reasons for wearing the tattoos are connected to distinct spheres of communication; whereas Buckley's imposition of tattoos upon infected individuals was meant to "protect common needle users" and "to prevent the victimization of other homosexuals" in *private* settings, seropositives who choose to wear a tattoo do so not only to communicate in private, intimate settings but also in larger, *public* settings (such as place of employment, or in the street). The "meanings" and motives for wearing HIV/AIDS tattoos will now be explored.

The practice of people with HIV/AIDS and AIDS activists choosing to wear AIDS tattoos began receiving notable national publicity in the United States in 1994.[23] During that year, for example, two issues of *POZ* magazine included photographs of people with HIV or AIDS displaying their tattoos—"Silence=Death," "Action=Life," "HIV +," and the international symbol for biohazardous waste. The few sentences of script in the first issue proclaim that these men are two of a number of people who have chosen to use body art for "social and political commentary." Neither the specific nature of the social and political commentary nor the questions of to whom and how the tattoos function as commentary are addressed. The next issue of *POZ* included images of PWAs with tattoos as well as a brief essay by Matt Fuller which outlines his reasons for recently acquiring an "HIV positive" tattoo. In general, Fuller hopes to become "visible, not invisible" (34) as a person with HIV, yet this visibility has certain qualities: it is a different sort of visibility than the ubiquitous red ribbon unveiled by the Visual AIDS project in 1991 which, according to Fuller, "has lost its impact." Instead, his tattoo is meant to "remind *everyone*" (my emphasis) that its wearer is indeed HIV positive and *not just* AIDS-aware, AIDS sympathetic, or fashionably political. Fuller conjures a scene of everyday social interaction in which people who sit next to him in a restaurant or swim in the same pool as he are made aware that their "everyday social interactions" might, or probably, include interaction with someone who is HIV positive. Thus, for Fuller, the tattoo functions as an assertive reminder, rather than a strident warning.

John Baldetta

Not only are HIV/AIDS tattoos intended to remind others of the everyday circulation of seropositive people in society, they are also accorded more active roles of dispelling myths about what it means to be seropositive and encouraging discussion about HIV/AIDS. For example, John Baldetta, who had inch-high red letters spelling "HIV POSITIVE" tattooed onto his inner left forearm in December of 1992, hopes that with his tattoo he will "dispel myths that all people with HIV are too sick to carry on with their lives, . . . dispel the sense of shame . . . [in having to] . . . hide . . . [one's] . . . HIV status, . . . gain a sense of control over . . . life with HIV[, . . .] and . . . encourage discussion of issues related to HIV" (in Stryker 8). For Baldetta, each of these functions has been manifested, albeit amidst controversy that cost him his job as a nurse's aide at a medical center. After acquiring his tattoo, Baldetta continued

to work as an aide, but he was fired from his job after refusing to conceal the tattoo because of concerns that the tattoo would have negative psychological and/or physical effects on the health of the medical center's patients. The discussion of HIV-related issues that Baldetta wished to press went beyond the interactions between Baldetta, his superiors, and the patients that he worked with; eventually, Baldetta filed a law suit against the medical center, leading to greater publicity.[24] The local *Seattle Times,* in addition, published an editorial that supported the hospital's decision to terminate Baldetta's employment.

Besides promoting discussion, Baldetta's tattoo affirms his acceptance of his infection. In Baldetta's self-understanding, his visibility actively and publicly resists the internalization of shame and guilt that people with HIV/AIDS have often been made to feel in the aftermath of their diagnosis. Angelo Alonzo and Nancy Reynolds (1995) note that among the other negative consequences of an individual's failure to disclose his or her serostatus—deprivation of social support, risk of future breaches of trust, delay of needed activities (such as medical attention), and the continuation of risky behaviors in order to maintain a façade of seronegative "health"—the seropositive individual who fails to disclose his or her diagnosis also risks a sort of emotional exhaustion from leading a "double life" (309). Those like Baldetta who publicize their seropositive status do so at least in part to resist the emotional exhaustion that guilt and shame work upon an individual.

Another personal function that Baldetta accords to his tattoo is the function of "gain[ing] a sense of control over . . . life with HIV" (in Stryker 8). At first consideration, it seems rather paradoxical to state that a prominent, indelible statement that publicizes one's serostatus all of the time, indiscriminately, *empowers* its wearer to gain a sense of control of his life: certainly, in one sense, the wearer of the tattoo *loses* some control over when, where, how, and to whom his or her serostatus is made known.[25] The anxiety that can result from one's inability to control disclosure of his or her serostatus—whether because of HIV/AIDS symptoms that are visible on the surface of the skin, or because of breaches of confidentiality—sometimes causes individuals to regret, and sometimes avoid, public appearances. As Alonzo and Reynolds note, given the possibility of future breaches of confidentiality, the submission to various forms of institution surveillance, and the potentially damaging uses or effects of such information (such as in employment), one might be better served through silence about, or at least tight control over, one's serostatus (Alonzo & Reynolds 309) and the avoidance of public appearances.[26] The control that Baldetta claims to gain from his tattoo, however, is not control over disclosure of his serostatus but rather control over his life. Admitting to himself and publicizing to others the fact that he is infected empowers Baldetta to live his life honestly and without the damaging specter of a "personal secret" looming in his psychological background.

The personal nature of Baldetta's tattoo is further underscored by its function as an "indelible declaration" (Stryker 8) of his commitment to safer sexual practices.[27] Quite unable to hide the inch-high red letters of his "HIV POSITIVE" tattoo in most potentially sexual situations, Baldetta uses the tattoo to clarify to others what is undetectable through vision (undetectable because of his lack of visible symptomologies), and he reduces the need for the sometimes awkward, sometimes non-existent pre-sex discussions about serostatus, sexual histories, and sexual practices.[28] Baldetta's tattoo is an eerily accurate manifestation of Buckley's proposal for tattooing; however, Baldetta's appropriation of the HIV tattoo is more expressive than punitive. Besides the obvious difference of *choice* between Buckley's proposal and Baldetta's decision to acquire an HIV tattoo, there is an important difference in the cultural milieu from which Baldetta's tattoo wearing emerges, an AIDS activist cultural milieu in which, as Cindy Patton notes, "safe sex was viewed . . . not as a practice to be imposed on the reluctant, but as a form of political resistance and community building that achieves both sexual liberation and sexual health" (1990, 42). Hence, while this paragraph introduces the tattoo's function of signifying his commitment to safer sex practices as being of a "personal nature," Baldetta's self-identification as an AIDS activist suggests that his tattoo signifies to an audience larger than the person or people that he might have sex with; it signifies also to

(and from) a larger community of people with HIV/AIDS and people impacted by HIV/AIDS.

In summary, John Baldetta accords both personal and social functions to the "HIV POSITIVE" tattoo that he wears: personally, the tattoo signifies his refusal to internalization shame, his effort to gain control over his life, and his commitment to safer sex practices; to wider audiences, his tattoo is meant to challenge stereotypes about weak, passive, and inactive "AIDS victims" and to encourage discussion among its viewers. The next section introduces Andrew Coats, a Dallas chiropractor and gay man with AIDS who offers mostly similar, sometimes slightly different, reasons for acquiring his "HIV+" tattoo.

Andrew Coats

Coats sees his tattoo signifying to four rather distinct audiences: himself, other gay men who might find him physically attractive and/or appealing as a sexual partner, other people with HIV or AIDS, and what he calls the "straight world" (roughly akin to "the general population"). Like many contemporary wearers of any kind of tattoo, Coats ascribes an expressive function to it. "There's no damn reason to be ashamed," (in Trejo 46) he asserts, and the publication of his serostatus works in explicit contrast to the secretive, private world of HIV shame.[29] "Coming out" about his seropositive status has helped Coats to cope with the depression that his diagnosis has incurred, he claims. In addition, as his chronicler notes, Coats is "determined not to remain anonymous" as one of thousands of "the faces of AIDS" in the United States, one of a multitude of people who "have AIDS" or are "living with AIDS."[30] In this sense, Coats and others like him who have chosen to publicize their medical diagnosis for expressive and political purposes construct AIDS as a "morbid" disease, rather than a "macabre" disease (to borrow Foucault's distinction in *The Birth of the Clinic*).[31] Macabre diseases like leprosy and cancer are undifferentiated, mass, impersonal. Morbid diseases, like tuberculosis or now, perhaps, HIV/AIDS, are rarefied, individual, distinct, characterizing, and expressive. Rejecting the anonymity that secrecy secures and the non-specificity that liberal "faces of AIDS" media campaigns offer, Coats manifests a creative, expressive response to his disease.

Coats, whom the writer describes as quite attractive, speaks frankly about the effect that he would like his tattoo to have on men who find him attractive: "I do want guys who might look at me to say 'Boy, I'd sure like to fuck him or have him fuck me.' And then I want them to look at this [his tattoo]" (in Trejo 46). Although he does not specify what the tattoo is meant to communicate to his potential sexual partners, he does imply that he wants to challenge the assumptions, still circulating within the gay community, that "you can tell if someone is positive by looking" and that seropositive people are not sexy or sexual. "I want people *who would have gone to bed with me to see* this" (my italics 46), he continues, suggesting that his inscription is meant to linger in the eyes and minds of men who, for whatever reasons (but including fear of intimacy and/or sex with someone who is positive), decided not to pursue sex with Coats once they discovered his "HIV+" tattoo.

In addition to his potential paramours, Coats also hopes to signify to other people with HIV/AIDS. What he is signaling to other seropositives is a sense of solidarity, perhaps an alliance with symptomatic seropositives or those in late stages of AIDS. Stating that he owes it to other seropositives to be visible (either through mentioning his serostatus or being seen with his tattoo), Coats foregoes the privilege of passing that he, as an asymptomatic person with HIV, has access to. Other men, Coats tells the reporter, thanked him for his courage (Trejo 46).[32]

Finally, Coats indicates that he has a message for what he calls the "straight world." His seropositive visibility, whether through verbal or symbolic disclosure, is meant to let mainstream society know that HIV does "touch" their lives. Coats argues that "for mainstream middle America, HIV is kind of like starvation in Ethiopia: you see some pictures, you hear about it, have a little fundraiser here and there, but it doesn't really touch their lives" (in Trejo 81). To contravene the abstract or distant encounters with HIV/AIDS that he views as typical for most Americans, Coats moves about in public space with a material body that is marked as infected, a body that through its self-stigmatization

challenges assumptions about the appearance of health as well as the nature of stigmatization itself.

Gregg Cadieux

"First you have to figure out how you're going to live in your own skin." Gregg Cadieux (personal interview, 28 July 1997).

Thus far, the individuals whom I have had speak on these pages have come from secondary sources; that is, I have cited and paraphrased the already-edited words of HIV/AIDS tattoo-wearers from other sources. In this section, however, I share and present claims that emerged from an hour-and-a-half interview I conducted with Gregg Cadieux, a gay white male "POZ" tattoo-wearer who is a resident of Chicago.[33] A self-described "circuit party" boy, Gregg registers physically as tall (over 6'), handsome, and strappingly muscular. The letters "P O Z," in red ink about an inch high and encircled, are positioned on his left deltoid.[34]

Like Baldetta and Coats, Cadieux imagines his tattoo signifying to a diverse audience of people; however, he is strikingly clear about whom he perceives as his target audience of readers.

Dan: Is there a specific or perhaps a primary audience to whom your tattoo is is. . . .

Gregg: Gay men.

Dan: Okay that's who . . . you primarily want

Gregg: Gay men in 60657 [the zip code that encompasses much of Boystown, the predominantly gay neighborhood in Chicago]. . . . Gay men who are in the bars, in . . . the circuit party world, . . . in the gym not the whole. . . .

Dan: Okay, if you happen to display your tattoo in what you call "the real world" or quote "the general population" or whatever. . . . is that incidental or . . . something that you're less conscious about or less concerned about?

Gregg: Yah, the political statement is not for. . . . They can read it that way if they want to. [But] it's for the audience of gay men.

While it also happens that in his gay neighborhood, non-gays observe the tattoo, and while he moves about in non-gay spaces where non-gays will observe his tattoo, Cadieux is not as concerned with these peoples' witnessing. Rather, it is on the specific stages and scenes of his everyday life in Boystown—at the gym, on the streets, in bars, at (circuit) parties—that Cadieux performatively announces his seropositivity.

Upon my initial inquiry as to what he wanted the tattoo to do—that is, how he meant for it to function for his intended, primary audience of gay men in Boystown, Chicago—Gregg hesitated for a long while, seemingly unsure as to what the question meant or perhaps wondering where to start. In short time, however, he was able to articulate a cogent list of intentions, including giving other seropositives hope for a healthy, happy life and facilitating discussion between seropositives and seronegatives. Cadieux also claims to have acquired the tattoo in order to reduce the stress of the double life that the "discreditable" leads and to bring friends and family earlier into the process of managing his precarious health (two of the beneficial effects of serostatus disclosure that Alonzo & Reynolds note). And, like Andrew Coats, Cadieux views his tattoo as an index of his desire to live life honestly.

Gregg: My brother was . . . incredibly, you know, honest and direct and good about so many things, and that [being seropositive] was one of them. And you know, after . . . after I lost him, I started try'n' I thought it was somewhat of a disservice . . . for me not to be a little more forthright about it, especially having lost him and yet having been so very lucky myself. . . . I was diagnosed in '89, and . . . [am] . . . probably in the best shape of my life right now . . . a long time later and . . . was fortunate to have jobs and insurance and, and, access, you know, to good medical treatment. And . . . I . . . did, like, really well with the drugs and so forth, so you know kind of my thinking is if . . . if someone like me who has absolutely nothing—really, nothing—to complain about isn't willing to like kinda come forward and try to put a face on this for people then, then who is? . . . It's honesty. I mean it is what it is.

In addition, Gregg has used the tattoo to make sure that men he meets and is intimate or sexual with are aware of his seropositive status. Gregg reiterated his statement that the tattoo is "a great form of shorthand to help you facilitate full disclosure before a roll-roll-roll-in-za-hay" (no page), published in the June 18, 1997, edition of *gab,* in our July 28 interview.

Gregg: I would tell someone—well say I'm going home with someone from a bar or whatever. . . . : I'd tell them that I'm HIV positive, and this was before the tattoo and even now I forget—like I'm, "you do remember that I'm HIV positive?," and then they like point and [say] "well I think I can remember . . . [because of] the tattoo." . . .

Dan: Once you get home . . . do you let the tattoo speak for itself?

Gregg: No.

Dan: Okay.

Gregg: I verbalize at that point as difficult as it still is . . .

Gregg remarked twice during our interview that while he felt his tattoo was legible enough to potential sexual partners, it was his personal policy to confirm the tattoo's visual legibility with verbal confirmation.

Clearly, Gregg envisions his tattoo as functioning communicatively and performatively in both sexual settings that are typically construed as "private" and social settings that are typically construed as "public." In both private and public settings, Gregg imagines his tattoo functioning as a political statement.

Dan: Do you think that your tattoo makes a political statement?

Gregg: Absolutely.

Dan: Okay.

Gregg: Absolutely.

Dan: . . . Then, what kind of statement?

Gregg: (long pause) I'm not sure. I know it is. . . . Like we've said, you know how big is Chicago? And I'm the only person I think who has one. So to come up with that kind of, you know, for this . . . Wichita, Kansas, boy . . . who's an attorney and so forth to kind of . . . jump in with both feet with this thing. . . . I think that that's part of what is political for groups who are—who have not been seen before: it's just the fact of being seen . . . and therefore having people get comfortable with it. . . . If you've never been around a person in a wheelchair, it's going to scare you to death until there's a person around you in a wheelchair. . . .

I asked Gregg if he thought that the displaying of his tattoo participated in a larger political project of AIDS visibility. His eloquent, if self-deprecating, response was:

Gregg: . . . This is like my very pathetic version of Rosa Parks sitting at the . . . front of the bus. And that's the way that change happens: it's someone doing something however small it may be.

Thus, to summarize, Cadieux understands his tattoo wearing to be political because it is unique (at least in Chicago), because it places a "backwoods" boy into the public eye, because in wearing the tattoo he takes a risk as a professional in the public sector, because it participates in the larger project of AIDS visibility, and because (as he succinctly stated), "it's someone doing something however small it may be." Like Andrew Coats, Gregg Cadieux hopes to target a broader public of gay men, both seropositive and seronegative, with his tattoo, conveying to the former messages of hope, dignity, and playfulness while conveying to the latter messages about pride and presence. Yet like John Baldetta, Cadieux also intends for his tattoo to function in more private, sexual or intimate settings—that is, as an announcement that equips its reader with important information for "safe" decision-making. When Baldetta, Coats, and Cadieux display their tattoos, they are consciously contesting an operative assumption of visibility politics that "identities are visibly marked" (Phelan 7). And when Andrew Coats imagines his would-be sexual partners doing a double-take at his "HIV+," and when Gregg Cadieux witnesses men at his gym realizing what "POZ" stands for, they are both celebrating the possibility that "sometimes visibility or marking makes ideology conscious . . .

[perhaps] . . . as an alienation technique" (Reinelt 104). Two primary ideologies that the tattoos promise to bring to consciousness in their viewers are 1) an ideology dependent upon a rather facile linking of HIV-AIDS-illness-diminished capacity-physical manifestations, and 2) an ideology that bifurcates "public" and "private" spheres and relegates issues of personal health to the private sphere.[35]

DISCUSSION

In this section, I will address certain questions about the communicative potential of the HIV/AIDS tattoos, questions that emerge from the claims that wearers make about the tattoos. First, we might ask: are HIV/AIDS tattoos critically communicative? This question necessitates a more nuanced response than a simple, unqualified "yes" or "no." Most importantly, the question of how the tattoos might be subversive *for whom* must be addressed. In Buckley's proposal, the tattoo was meant to communicate a private warning to "common needle users" or "other homosexuals."[36] Tattoo wearers affirm the communicative value of the tattoo but twist its meaning, turning it from a private phenomenon (in Buckley's configuration) into a public one, and shifting the wearer's psychological valence from humiliating retreat and censure to one of openness and proclamation. I argue that tattoo wearers participate in a "true political project" of "performing . . . acts and gestures which contest boundaries, displace norms, disrupt regulatory and normalizing practices" (Reinelt 100).[37]

We might further inquire: do the tattoos function in a critically communicative way for others? AIDS tattoos follow in a long line of methods and strategies that AIDS activists and people with AIDS have employed to make HIV, AIDS, and HIV/AIDS issues visible. While in the early years of the U.S. epidemic, activism for and by people with HIV/AIDS was intended to protect the choice of "invisibility" or secrecy for seropositive people (through, for example, confidentiality policies and protections from discrimination), activist efforts were also mobilized around the perceived social and political benefits of making AIDS visible early in the epidemic. The HIV/AIDS tattoo is a recent addition to the numerous strategies that AIDS activists have employed to make HIV/AIDS and people with HIV/AIDS visible. In fact, like the NAMES Project AIDS Memorial Quilt and the numerous candlelight vigils that are held to honor those passed and those still fighting the battle, the HIV/AIDS tattoo mobilizes aesthetic and ritualistic practices for explicitly political goals. Those who wear the tattoos argue that through the tattoo, seropositive visibility is achieved, and that visibility is said to enable not only individual expressiveness but also a disruption of social habits of perception and a critique upon power and the conditions of silence that homophobia and AIDS-phobia promote. Thus, for example, the "healthy-looking," asymptomatic seropositive tattoo-wearer disrupts social expectations about what "healthy" people and "sick" (here, read "HIV-positive") people look like; furthermore, the tattoo functions as a symbol of rejection of "good AIDS victim" role expectations wherein the seropositive person is expected to reduce social discomfort for those around him or her.

To continue our inquiry, we might ask: how does an HIV/AIDS tattoo participate in the construction of an AIDS or seropositive "community"? While Baldetta and Coats both intend the tattoo to function as a personal, ritualistic refusal to internalize the "shame" of infection, both also emphasize that the tattoo is intended to address a larger audience of other people with HIV or AIDS. Thus, while the wearing of a tattoo is an individual gesture that is not dependent on a group performance, wearing the tattoo does necessitate some basic sense of security and support from others. The tattoo signifies "membership" in a collective of people much like Greek fraternity or sorority letters, clothing with labor union insignia, or rainbow flags for lesbians and gays. Like members of any sort of collective, people with HIV/AIDS tattoos often share common rituals—discovery of their diagnosis, visits to physicians or hospitals, participation in demonstrations, the mourning of friends and loved ones, or perhaps more formal rituals like those performed at the NAMES Project AIDS Memorial Quilt ceremonies. Thus, HIV/AIDS tattoos participate in the construction of an AIDS community by publicizing an individual's otherwise hidden condition which

in turn implies the force of a collective large enough or strong enough to support such an act.

Finally, we might ask: what limitations or disadvantages does tattoo-wearing entail? First and most obvious is the exemption from privacy and security that "invisibility" often affords. Seropositive visibility invites seropositive surveillance, whether that surveillance is carried out by agencies or institutions, by neighbors, or, in a worst case scenario, by AIDS-phobes who might commit verbal or physical harassment upon the wearer.

In addition, the tattoos run the risk of being reductive in that they signify a "mere" biological (sero)status and cannot convey, in and of themselves, a fuller idea about the individual who wears it. Matt Fuller is aware of the potentially reductive readings that viewers of his "HIV positive" tattoo might engage in:

> If people choose to label me only as a person living with AIDS, that's fine with me. I know that there is no label that could encompass all that I am and all that I have become since the diagnosis of my illness. And even if there were, it certainly would not fit on my arm. (34)

One of the limitations of visual signification is acknowledged here—visual images do not necessarily clarify themselves and their "intended" meanings; they are ambiguous (or ambivalent) *statements,* not *discussions.* Thus, for the viewer who only glimpses the tattoo without asking or hearing Fuller elucidate his intentions for it, the tattoo may reduce, synecdochically, the richness and complexities of Fuller's life to a mere medical condition.[38] John Baldetta, too, laments that the hospital that fired him "viewed him as a disease, not a person" (in Stryker 8); in other words, Baldetta suggests that to his superiors at the hospital, his tattoo functioned as a reductive symbol that rendered him "a carrier of an infective virus" rather than "an employee with HIV." Baldetta's and Fuller's concerns that the "linear . . . relationship between representation and identity" (Phelan 7) can be reductive confirm the negative valence that certain practices of visibility politics can take. This conundrum is not the fault of the wearers, of course, but of the general tendency to define individuals in terms of prominent characteristics, such as disease.

A final limitation to the AIDS tattoos should be addressed here. Ironically, like the privilege of passing that the tattoos dispermit, the wearing of an HIV/AIDS tattoo is itself an act of privilege. Peggy Phelan notes that "some bodies are always more secure than others. The institutionalized forces of misogyny, racism, and economic injustice (to rehearse just the short list) register real effects across different bodies" (173). It is significant that of the nine seropositive tattoo wearers that I encountered in my research, none are identified or identifiable as people of color, and only one is a woman. It is also significant that except for Scott O'Hara (see footnote 28), all of the wearers are described as, describe themselves as, or appear to be asymptomatic. While it certainly takes real courage for the seven white, asymptomatic men to wear their tattoos, the ability of these men to experience tattoo wearing as a critical, political act of visibility is contingent to a large degree upon privileges conferred by maleness, whiteness, and asymptomaticity. Cindy Patton (1996) describes the social conditions that enable certain people in the People Living With AIDS (PLWA) movement to experience AIDS visibility as liberating: in the PLWA movement,

> the "coming out" experience of gay liberation is mobilized as a model for people with AIDS, who, it is believed, can create an identity and group unity by claiming the common experience of living with AIDS. . . . [Yet,] [d]ifferences in class, race, gender, and sexuality, in drug use, in diagnostic protocols, and in the concentration of cases across regions produce divergent models of identity (or non-identity); thus many people diagnosed with AIDS do not immediately relate to "coming out" about their diagnosis, since they may never enjoy the benefit of freedom from "hiding" or repression which is the implicit reward for openness in the coming out model (9).

While the tattoos do mark their wearers as members of a relatively cohesive group of "people with HIV/AIDS" and/or "AIDS activists," the tattoos might also mark their wearers as "inhabitants" of more "secure" bodies.[39]

In summary, then, while we can view HIV/AIDS tattoos as performative and as communicatively subversive, we must also recognize that the surveillance which they invite has the potential for being repressive or violent, that the tattoos can be reductive, and that they are able to be worn with a certain kind of privilege.

CONCLUSION

At the beginning of this essay, I noted the conundrum that communication scholars are presented with when considering the phenomenon of self-stigmatization among people with HIV/AIDS—Buckley's earnest, public health policy proposal *mandating private* visibility for seropositives is eerily replicated in seropositives' *choosing public* visibility of their serostatus. I have examined specific ways in which bodies (more specifically, the surfaces of the skin) are mobilized in the context of AIDS visibility and AIDS activism,[40] and I have noted the ways in which HIV/AIDS tattoos encapsulate, in a contemporary setting, the traditionally ambivalent and multiple "meanings" of tattoos—aesthetic or expressive symbols, public markers of (sero)status, ritual functions (becoming an AIDS activist), and "stigmata" that separate marked individuals from others.

The limitations of my study should be obvious. First and foremost, my textual analysis relies heavily upon the already-edited statements of a small number of people: I have interviewed only one tattoo wearer myself. Secondly, I have not researched (through interviews, surveys, or focus groups) peoples' perceptions of the tattoos and of tattoo wearers. Finally, I have not studied ethnographically the movement of tattoo wearers in public spaces and between public and private spaces. Each of these limitations results in certain shortcomings in this essay, most notably the lack of a concrete portrayal of the dramaturgy of the tattoos as actually enacted and performed in public settings.[41] Nevertheless and despite these limitations, this essay does offer some insight into contemporary communication practices.

The goal of my analysis has *not* been to determine the meaning of these tattoos, but rather to catalogue the claims made about them by their wearers, then to explicate the assumptions about visibility that these claims entail. These two activities, in turn, have hopefully resulted in a more sensitive understanding of the communication practices of marginal or stigmatized social groups. For example, while it is oft-noted that marginal and dominant groups appropriate themes and strategies from each other for different effects, what this study presents is a case in which a marginal group appropriates a mainstream strategy (tattooing) for the same, originally intended effect—greater visibility of people with HIV/AIDS. Similarly, I have attempted to show how performative communication is used to comment upon the relationship between the margins and centers of power. The same effect—visibility through tattoos—has its "meanings" twisted by those who *choose* to tattoo themselves; rather than punitive or worn to warn others, the tattoos are worn with pride and a bit of mischief.

In addition, I hope to have illustrated how individual acts contest not only out-group practices (mainstream media, the government, politicians, mainstream society and its stereotypes) but also how they contest in-group practices (assumptions that a healthy, attractive physical appearance denotes seronegativity, anti-sexual prejudice against seropositives within the gay community). Andrew Coats and Gregg Cadieux, especially, comment upon the audiences of "potential sexual partners" and "other people with HIV" that they are trying to communicate to through their tattoos. Finally, I have tried to clarify the conditions of security and stability under which the tattoo can be considered a liberating, empowering gesture by someone who is positive. In this light, the tattoo should be viewed both as a mark of courage and a mark of privilege.

NOTES

1. (Mock) debate over the efficacy of such a proposal reemerged recently at the 11th Annual YMCA Model United Nations in Baton Rouge, LA. One of the mock bills put forth for consideration before the youth delegates was a bill requiring HIV-infected individuals to be tattooed. A reporter for the Baton Rouge-based *The Advocate* noted that "delegates heatedly discussed the bill, even to the point of deciding the tattoos should be placed in the thigh area. Several students attacked the bill as unfair. 'I'm against it because it would be against people's human rights if forced on them,' said Sally Richardson, a sophomore at University Laboratory School. Other delegates said the measure

was necessary to help stop the spread of AIDS and make it less likely for people to have sex with someone who is infected" (Warren 8E).

2. Founded in 1994, *POZ* includes the following in its Mission Statement: "*POZ* was founded primarily to get information to HIV positive persons for whom it could extend or improve the quality of their lives . . . We also want to create a common media context between fulltime treatment activists—the extraordinarily empowered patient—and those impacted by HIV who are not going to read the technical newsletters and attend meetings—*POZ* brings a much larger HIV-impacted community into a common conversational ballpark" (available via *POZ* website: http://www.poz.com)

3. In this essay, "seropositive" functions as both an adjective (indicating the condition of having tested positive to HIV antibodies) and a noun, indicating the individual who has tested positive for HIV antibodies.

4. Buckley is vigilant against accusations that his proposal is reminiscent of Hester Prynne's scarlet letter "A." Anticipating this accusation in his 1986 editorial, Buckley writes: "for Hester Prynne, the letter functioned as public castigation; the HIV tattoos on the other hand, function to warn people in private settings" (A7). Thus for Buckley, the tattoo provides only a limited (though mandatory) visibility for seropositive individuals, and he purports to respect the mobility and confidentiality of seropositives in public places.

5. A number of scholars, critics, and performers have explored the often complex relationship between performance(s) and HIV/AIDS. Recent publications addressing representations of AIDS in staged theater productions include: Alberto Sandoval, "Staging AIDS: What's Latinos Got to Do With It?" in Diana Taylor and Juan Villegas (Eds.), *Negotiating Performance,* 1994; David Román, "Performing all Our Lives: AIDS, Performance, Community" in Eds. Janelle Reinelt and Joseph Roach, *Critical Theory and Performance,* 1992; and David Román, "'It's My Party and I'll Die if I Want To,'" in *Theatre Journal,* 1992. Other scholarly publications exploring performative and performance dimensions of HIV/AIDS include the proceedings from the 1993 Arizona State University conference, *HIV Education: Performing Personal Narratives* (edited by Frederick Corey), and Cindy Patton's chapter, "Performativity and Spatial Distinction: The End of AIDS Epidemiology," in Eds. Andrew Parker's and Eve Sedgwick's *Performativity and Performance,* 1995.

6. Janelle Reinelt discusses the possibilities for political resistance that performances of race, gender, and sexuality might have in theatrical stage productions in her theoretical article, "Staging the Invisible: The Crisis of Visibility in Theatrical Representation," in *Text and Performance Quarterly,* 1994. In this quotation, Reinelt eloquently paraphrases theorist Judith Butler's assumption about bodies' signification processes in Butler's *Gender Trouble.*

7. HIV or AIDS tattoos take a variety of forms: "HIV+," "HIV positive," "POZ," "Silence=Death," "Action=Life," "ACT-UP," or the international symbol for biohazardous waste. Certainly, each of these tattoos signifies slightly different meanings; in addition, not all of the tattoos listed are infallible indicators of the wearer's serostatus: the "Silence=Death," "Action=Life," and "ACT-UP" tattoos, for example, might indicate the wearers' status as AIDS activists, but they do not guarantee that their wearers are seropositive. Because of this ambiguity, I focus on wearers of "HIV+," "HIV positive," or "POZ" tattoos. I would also note at this point that in addition to signifying slightly different meanings, the tattoo types listed above have different levels of "legibility," or degrees to which they are clearly and accurately read and understood by an interpretive community. "HIV+" and "HIV positive," for example, are lucid announcements of serostatus (although *what else* these tattoos are meant to announce—such as whether or not the wearer is an activist or is only romantically and/or sexually interested in other seropositive individuals—is not immediately clear). The biohazardous waste symbol, on the other hand, is less precisely identifiable as an index of HIV infection. "POZ" tattoo wearer Gregg Cadieux (whose comments will appear in fuller detail later in this essay) offers the following account of the "illegibility" of the biohazardous waste symbol in this explanation of his tattoo choice:

Gregg: [T]he biohazard thing—I don't know if I would know what that meant . . . even if I saw it today. I'm not sure if I would recognize it or what it was, and I think you either got to be in the medical profession to know what that is or have seen so many of those little red containers at . . . clinics that . . . you might know what it is. So that's . . . like way too obscure . . . That's kind of like a secret code among people who would know what that meant. That wasn't what—I was looking for something a lot more . . . controversial, I guess, than that (personal interview, 28 July 1997).

Cadieux suggests that even in queer and HIV/AIDS communities, the biohazardous symbol is not commonly recognized or recognizable as an index of infection.

8. Cindy Patton (1995) warns that while people with HIV or AIDS diagnoses might as a group be considered marginal to a non-infected, "healthy" social center, to assume that marginality registers uniformly across seropositive bodies regardless of biological sex, sexual orientation, or race/ethnicity is to assume incorrectly. "If it is relatively easy," Patton explains, "through concepts like stigma, to correlate a range of marginalized others in similarly antipodal positions to the idea of a codifying center . . . , this does not mean they are in the same *place,* subjected to the same discursive and institutional tyrannies" (179). I will revisit this problematic later in this essay.

9. I use the term "general population" self-consciously. Many critics, especially Jan Zita Grover (1988/1991, 23–24), have noted the insidious usages of the term "general population"—as a term of contrast to homosexuals, prostitutes, intravenous drug users, and hemophiliacs, the term serves to separate "us" (non drug-using heterosexuals) from "them" (those at-risk of infection); furthermore, the term gained currency as an impetus for medical and political representatives to more actively promote AIDS awareness and education, as when AIDS began moving from the "risk groups" (itself a problematic term) to "the general population." My usage of the term here is meant to designate those individuals who have little or no direct experience with people with AIDS, AIDS treatment, AIDS politics, or AIDS activism.

10. In this essay, I shall utilize three distinct yet corollary meanings of "stigma"—stigma as a mark or inscription upon the skin, stigma as an individual attribute, and stigma as a "language of relationships." As a note to the reader, my meaning of "stigma" should be clarified by the context of the sentence such that the reader should easily interpret when I mean "stigma" to refer to the HIV/AIDS tattoo or scar, or to the seropositive's act of making his or her serostatus visible, or to the social and cultural milieu in which the tattoo and the wearing of the tattoo by an infected person are made to mean.

11. British colonialist explorer James Cook introduced the term "tattoo" into the English language in 1769. In his published travel journals, he notes that the Tahitian practice of body painting was

self-understood as "ta tu" (or "tattou," "tatau," and "tattaw" in other Polynesian cultures). Of course, the practice of permanently marking the skin occurred much earlier than Cook's observations: evidence points to the practice in Europe beginning in 6000 B.C., in Egypt from 4000 B.C., and among the Aztec, Incas, and Mayans by the first century A.D. (Sanders 9–10). Anthropologists state that there are several functions that tattoos, or permanent body markings, serve that are common to many cultures worldwide: these include aesthetic, decorative, and ritualistic functions as well as function of marking social status. While tattoos have been used to signify positive qualities in individuals (the wisdom of an elder, the fertility of a woman, the bravery of a soldier, the health of a child), tattoos have also been used to signify an individual's negative qualities (as noted above). The 1960's saw a "renaissance" of legitimate tattoo-wearing in the United States. Middle-and upper-class individuals began wearing tattoos for decorative purposes, and as Deborah Irmas argues, contemporary tattoo-wearing in the U.S. is viewed as aesthetic and expressive; the "personal relationship between the tattoo and the person on which it has been drawn" (62) is the defining quality of contemporary tattooing. Later in this essay, I will examine the personal relationship between seropositive individuals and the tattoos that they have chosen to publicize their infection.

12. A few clarifications are in order here. First of all, "mediated" forms of visibility involve publication in print media, discussion or appearance on television, on radio, or in film, or participation in any of the numerous forms of computer-mediated communication. By "unmediated" forms of visibility, I mean the physical presence of the body as when individuals or collectives take to the streets or engage in demonstrations. Secondly, I wish to note that there are definitions of visibility politics other than "self-presentation in public forums." Visibility politics are not always directed from the margins toward the center; sometimes, words and images are directed from one "subculture" within a marginal group to other members of that group. One might call this *intra*-group visibility. Transgendered people, for example, have called for and practiced greater visibility *within* the "gay and lesbian" or "queer" communities as well as to wider publics.

13. It is crucial to note that in offering this summary of the assumptions of visibility politics, Phelan is not endorsing them; rather, the bulk of her book is a critique of these assumptions.

14. See Dwight Conquergood (in press), "Street Literacy and Performative Writing," where he documents and explains the complex signifying and reading practices among youth gang members in Chicago.

15. Phelan spells out the link between visibility and co-optation: "The risk of visibility then is the risk of any translation—a weaker version of the original script, the appropriation by (economically and artistically) powerful 'others.' The payoff of translation (and visibility) is more people will begin to speak in your tongue" (97).

16. In the context of AIDS in the U.S., enforced hyper-visibility refers to the recurrent images of AIDS and people with AIDS that render them a spectacle to be consumed with both fascination and distance. Thus, for example, through the 1980's, representations of gay sexuality as promiscuous, anonymous, and filthy and representations of gay men with AIDS as "patients" or "victims," wasting and deteriorating, were the recurrent images in mainstream media. As a result (gay men's) sexuality and (gay male) people with AIDS were rendered "hypervisible" in particular (and in particularly limited) ways.

17. Douglas Crimp (1992, 120) notes the ways in which mainstream media representations of AIDS and people with AIDS serve to maintain AIDS as a private affliction.

18. For some individuals, disclosure of their HIV positive serostatus occurs only when they become symptomatic—when their bodies "betray" their internal condition through physical manifestations on the surface. "POZ" tattoo wearer Gregg Cadieux expresses his frustration with individuals who wait until they are symptomatic to disclose their seropositive status:

Gregg: What was bugging me was that I saw a lot of cases where no one would tell anyone until, until they became ill, and even people who are . . . AIDS and HIV activists . . .—the people who should be most out about their status— were not willing to do that until such time as . . .—it's the "Oops, I Got Caught" syndrome. . . .

Dan: Hospital, hospitalization. . . .

Gregg: Yah, you know, it's like—"Well, you know, I guess I finally have to . . . come clean with things given that I, you know, I've got a catheter in my arm while I'm on life-support here . . . ". (personal interview, 28 July 1997)

19. Alonzo and Reynolds note that Kaposi's sarcoma is "most typically manifested as nodules that are usually pigmented and violaceous (red to blue) and difficult to conceal. Distinct patch-stage lesions appear quite early in some individuals and may be initially mistaken for bruises, but the patches then form into plaques and eventually form into nodular tumors that may appear at any time, characteristically on the tip of the nose, eyelid, hard palate, posterior glans penis, thigh and sole of the foot" (310). It is true that for Caucasians and people with light skin tone, Kaposi's sarcoma lesions appear in a violaceous color; however, for people of color, these lesions often appear as dark brown patches. The universalization of the "purplish lesion" description for Kaposi's prompted non-diagnoses of the cancer among people of color earlier in the epidemic.

20. "Passing" can be defined as the practice or performance of normative, or homeostatic, qualities or identities. Goffman's (1963) discussion of passing is still instructive today (see 73–91).

21. The "AIDS community" is alternately a real entity, a contested term, and a useful fiction. If "we are all affected by AIDS" as some informational campaigns impress, then everyone in the nation (and the world) would conceivably be a member of the AIDS community. Less broadly but still generally, we might define those people who are seropositive, who are partners, spouses, friends, or family members of people with HIV/AIDS, people who work in the AIDS service industry, activists, and physicians who study and treat AIDS-related illnesses as members in the AIDS community. My usage of the term in this essay is intended to include individuals who feel the impact of HIV/AIDS on a consistent basis and who commit themselves to learning and/or doing something to ameliorate problems that AIDS has occasioned.

22. Grover (1988/1991) wonderfully deconstructs this problematic term. See footnote 9.

23. Debate over the phenomenon of HIV/AIDS in the United States was catalyzed to a large degree by William F. Buckley, Jr. in 1986. Fundamentally, the call for mandatory tattooing expresses an imperative to make the (potentially deadly) "invisibility" of infection visible as a warning to others to avoid infective contact with the stigmatized. For Buckley, the tattoo functions as a very private scarlet letter, warning others who encounter the infected in private settings about the risk of "contamination" by the infected. The laudable goal of reducing the number of HIV transmissions was rendered problematic, however, by precedents for a seropositive's rights of confidentiality, privacy, and choice, as well as concerns over the efficacy of such a proposal. Except for the agitation of a few extremists who pushed the mandatory tattoo idea, the controversy subsided until a shocking new ad campaign by the clothing distributor Benetton in 1993 invigorated debate between people with HIV/AIDS, AIDS activists, and Benetton advertising designers over the use of tattoos to stigmatize people with HIV/AIDS. The controversial images of the ad campaign were three body parts—an arm, a lower abdomen, and a backside—upon which the words "HIV positive" had been superimposed. Amidst charges by several French AIDS agencies that the campaign "created in the public an emotional shock by reawakening the memory of past methods of racial stigmatization" thereby "adding humiliation to the stigma," (Agence Française de Lutte contre le Sida [French Agency in the Struggle against AIDS], reported in *Women's Wear Daily* 10) the campaign's originator, Oliviero Toscani, defended it as educationally efficacious and socially responsible: not only does the ad indicate the primary means of HIV transmission—sharing intravenous needles, vaginal intercourse, and anal intercourse—but it also exemplifies a company's duty to "take a position on the larger issues" (*Women's Wear Daily* 10), he states. While this ad campaign is only one of several controversial campaigns that Benetton has launched, it is notable in this essay for the negative ways in which people with HIV/AIDS and people in the AIDS service industry reacted to it.

24. Both the 31 July 1997 issue of *Disability Compliance Bulletin* and the September 1997 edition of *Managing Risk* report that subsequent to his firing, Baldetta filed a discrimination suit against Harborview Medical Center, a suit which he ultimately lost. Baldetta and his lawyers argued that his termination violated provisions of the Americans with Disabilities Act, the Rehabilitation Act, and First Amendment rights of free speech, but both a district court and a circuit appeals court concurred with the defense which argued that Baldetta was justifiably fired for insubordination (for his refusal to conceal the tattoo) and not fired because he had HIV.

25. It would be a mistake, I believe, to assume that wearers of HIV/AIDS tattoos display them to all people, at all times, and in all places, thus losing total control over disclosure. Instead, I speculate that wearers make strategic choices about when to reveal and when to conceal the tattoo, or that on occasion they might "take a break" from visually announcing their serostatus. In my interview with Gregg Cadieux, Gregg expressed a fairly undiscriminating approach to revealing his tattoo, yet he invoked a notion of propriety to explain that he might conceal his tattoo if he thought that he would be in a public place in Chicago where he might encounter coworkers, most of whom do not know about his serostatus. Rather than fearing their finding out about his serostatus, Gregg felt that perhaps their finding out *in this way*—via the tattoo—would be insensitive and inappropriate.

26. Tom Stoddard, an AIDS activist, prominent lawyer, former head of the Lambda Legal Defense and Education Fund, and New York University professor, communicated this anxiety about appearing in public with visible stigmata of AIDS. With a number of tell-tale Kaposi's sarcoma lesions evident on his face just weeks before a number of public speaking appearances, Stoddard told a friend: "I really resent having my illness speak to everyone I meet through my skin" (in Murphy 38). Stoddard died of AIDS-related complications on February 12, 1997.

27. Amidst the publicity that his lawsuit garnered, Baldetta added "commitment to safer sex" to his list of reasons for acquiring and displaying the tattoo ("HIV tattoo flaunted by health care worker" 9).

28. Scott O'Hara, a writer, advocate for anonymous, public or semi-public sex and former gay porn star, echoes this reason for his own "HIV+" tattoo: "It makes it easier for me that my partner knows" (in Provenzano 41).

29. Although Coats equates "seropositive visibility" with "rejection of shame," he does not articulate the antithetical equation that unwillingness to publicize one's serostatus is evidence of that individual's shame regarding his or her status. Many people who argue that increased visibility brings increased benefits are also sensitive to the particularities of an individual's situation which may prevent her or him to participate in visibility politics.

30. While "faces of AIDS" campaigns were intended to personalize the syndrome thus countering stereotypes and irrational fears and anxieties and promoting sympathy or compassion, and while these campaigns were effective to some degree, they run the risk, as Cindy Patton (1990) argues, of collapsing individual specificities into a mass grouping. Commenting on the August 10, 1987 cover story of *Newsweek*, "The Face of AIDS" (which featured photographs of 302 men, women, and children who had recently died from AIDS-related complications), Patton argues: "Although the relentless march of faces was moving, even to the most bitter activist, the faces were, finally, a parade. The compression into the phrase 'The Face of AIDS' of the lives, hopes, foibles, and, yes, faces of the many, many people infected with HIV or diagnosed with AIDS did the opposite of personalizing the tragedy: it collapsed a disease into substitutable bodies. . . ." (85).

31. See Foucault (1973/1994), page 171.

32. The stigma that Coats has inscribed upon his skin has "negatively" affected his interactions with others. With other gay men, for example, he jokingly notes that he has become less attractive as a candidate for dating: "In the meat market I'm not as hot a piece of merchandise; I've been demoted to grade B" (in Trejo 46).

33. "Gregg Cadieux" is the *nom de plume* for a Chicago-based state employee who occasionally contributes articles for *gab* magazine, a queer, "predictably unsavory" Chicago weekly. Aware that I was interested in the phenomenon of HIV/AIDS tattoo-wearing, a friend drew my attention to a June 18, 1997, article in *gab* wherein Cadieux briefly explained the procedure and some reasons for acquiring his "POZ" tattoo: "As promised in February, I headed to my local tattoo parlor for a delightful "POZ" tattoo, given that the biohazard symbol is now perhaps a bit passé. . . . As for branding myself "POZ," I couldn't be happier. It's a great form of shorthand to help you facilitate full disclosure before a roll-roll-roll-in-za-hay, not to mention seeing the lightbulbs dawning on my fellow gymboyz faces as they finally understand what POZ really means" (no page). I contacted him via email in early July, and we eventually arranged for a late July interview in his Boystown neighborhood of Chicago. A thirty minute phatic conversation at a cozy but loud bar preceded our hour-and-a-half recorded interview at a cozy and not-so-loud coffeeshop. Two previous efforts to locate Chicago-area individuals with HIV/AIDS tattoos—asking case manager friends if they knew of any tattooed individuals, and scouting the June 1997 Gay Pride Parade (with its high quotient of exposed skin)—proved fruitless. If Gregg is to be believed when he claims to be the only individual in Chicago

that he knows of with a legible HIV/AIDS tattoo (and I have no evidence at this time to contradict this claim), then it is not for wont of trying that I have been unable to locate more Chicago-area individuals with the tattoos. The phenomenon of HIV/AIDS tattoo-wearing does not seem to have been energetically taken up in the urban center of the Midwest.

34. When I asked Gregg to explain why he chose a tattoo over other means of disclosure or visibility and why he chose the specific location of his tattoo, he replied rather humorously, as if he were incredulous toward my naïveté.

> Gregg: Well, let's see. I'm a gay boy living in Boystown. I go to circuit parties, you know. A tattoo on your left deltoid is what you're supposed to have these days, and I figure why not . . . join the club and . . . give it a little boost or something. . . .

Gregg's good-humored response at this juncture—"I got the tattoo in order to be trendy"—should not be construed as the entirety of his justification. As will soon become apparent, Gregg eloquently articulates a wider range of reasons and intentions for his "POZ" tattoo.

35. Perhaps I should not be surprised to discover that there is at least one reported case where an individual who has acquired an HIV/AIDS tattoo has not, in fact, tested positive for HIV antibodies. These are, after all, postmodern times when appropriation is both a conscientious objective as well as a habit of everyday life and when the expectation that surface manifestations/postures/signs will correspond to a more "essential" nature or condition of things has been rendered asunder. Yet I must confess that I was surprised to read in the June 1997 issue of *Interview* magazine about Jonathan Davis, the lead singer of the popular industrial-metal band, Korn, who has an "HIV" tattoo but does not claim to be HIV positive. In his interview with Davis, reporter Ray Rogers inquires about the origin of Davis's "HIV" tattoo.

> RR: Tell me why you have a tattoo that says "HIV."
>
> JD: That nickname was dumped on me by the band because they thought I was gay, and I was so thin they'd call me "HIV."

> RR: That, to me, is a sick joke.
>
> JD: It is a sick joke.
>
> RR: Has the tattoo given you a deeper understanding of what people who really have the disease [*sic*] go through?
>
> JD: Yeah—because everyone thinks I have AIDS, I know what it might feel like when everyone trips out and treats you weird. I'm not going to take the tattoo off—it's become a part of my life.

Strikingly, although he claims not to have tested positive for HIV antibodies, Davis announces "HIV" on his skin, perhaps exemplifying Judith Butler's description of the "performative" as that which reveals identities and essences as "*fabrications* manufactured and sustained through corporeal and linguistic signs" (Reinelt 99). Readers might scrutinize the ethical propriety of Davis's appropriation of the tattoo as well as the "authenticity" of Davis's empathy for seropositives based on his wearing and getting reactions to the tattoo. [The interpretive link between "gay" and "thin" as a reliable indicator of HIV infection or an AIDS diagnosis should not go unnoticed here as it illustrates a still common way in which individuals try to read HIV/AIDS.]

36. Buckley's proposal elides, of course, the fact that even in 1986, people who were neither intravenous needle sharers nor homosexuals were being diagnosed with HIV and AIDS.

37. Here, Reinelt is paraphrasing one of Judith Butler's claims.

38. In this essay, I do not examine peoples' reactions to the tattoos except in an indirect and cursory way. Although the tattoos are indelible, announcing the same words regardless of setting or the viewer(s), it should be understood that they are subject to multiple meanings and interpretations. Gregg's experiences bear out this fact. Friends and acquaintances reacted to his "POZ" tattoo with a wide range of interpretations, ranging from a misreading of the tattoo as "pose" (as in flexing and posing) to a reading of it as an indicator that Gregg was only interested in meeting and dating other seropositive men.

39. I asked Gregg about issues of safety and privilege, and he seemed quite conscious of the ways in which his economic status and the current quality of his health played an important part in the ways in which he was able to experience his tattoo.

Dan: What makes you feel safe that you can wear this [tattoo]?

Gregg: . . . Other people don't have all—haven't had the good fortune to have had all the things that I've had in terms of . . . good looks, and health, and work and smarts and education. And so you start taking away those things and when—and people who are HIV negative are more likely to to pull away from those people because they just don't have this, you know, incredibly full package to offer.

Dan: Which would enable them to sort of look through . . .

Gregg: Yah.

Dan: a positive status?

Gregg also responded earnestly to a question that I posed about the differences between symptomatic and asymptomatic tattoo wearing.

Dan: Do you think it's a difference for someone who is asymptomatic like you to wear the tattoo versus someone who is symptomatic to wear the tattoo?

Gregg: Yah, it probably is.

Dan: Do you want to go more with that? Sort of, what do you think?

Gregg: That scares me. I mean . . . that's definitely the frightening thing because I've—like I said, I've been so lucky, and I have never had any symptoms. Would I have done it . . . if. . . .

Dan:.   . . . If you were symptomatic?

Gregg: I were symptomatic? [long pause] It would probably be a—probably not, because it's nice to get—what I like is . . . having the luxury of doing it while I was asymptomatic.

Dan: Because it's your choice?

Gregg: Because it's my choice. Yah, exactly because it's my choice and because it's not a, you know, well, "duh."

Dan: Okay. Are you speaking to . . . a redundancy . . . ?

Gregg: Yah.

Dan: Someone who is symptomatic . . .

Gregg: Yah, I mean . . . [you] . . . state the obvious, and . . . it's more fun to be a little strident as an asymptomatic person to me than it would be as, as a symptomatic person.

40.   There are so many things about AIDS that make the body an especially fertile site of signification. Although some would deny it, talking about AIDS necessitates talking about sex and death, of bodies in engagement and bodily fluids in exchange; needles piercing skin and veins; bodies emaciated from wasting syndrome; the charge of blood, its mythical status, its life-giving, but now also "deathly" iconicity; the fear of bodies in public discourse; and de-eroticization and re-eroticization.

41.   In her article "Performativity and Spatial Distinction," Cindy Patton (1995) laments the "relative lack of consideration of the stage or context or field of the performance or performative act" (181), and she calls for more and better studies that examine the movement of bodies within and between spaces. Clearly, an ethnographic component of this study that sought to observe and move with tattoo wearers in and in-between various settings and contexts would contribute to the kind of scholarship that Patton is calling for.

REFERENCES

Alonzo, Angelo A. & Reynolds, Nancy R. "Stigma, HIV and AIDS: An Exploration and Elaboration of a Stigma Trajectory." *Social Science & Medicine* 41 (1995): 303–315.

"Benetton's New Shocker: AIDS-Related Ad Campaign." *Women's Wear Daily* 17 Sept. 1993: 10.

Brain, Robert, "The Tattooed Body." *The Decorated Body.* New York, NY: Harper & Row, Publishers, 1979. 48–67.

Buckley, William F. "Identify All Carriers." *New York Times* 18 Mar. 1986: A27.

Cadieux, Gregg. "Lint." *gab* 18–24 June 1997: no pages.

Cadieux, Gregg. Personal interview. 28 July 1997.

Conquergood, Dwight. "Handbook of Research on Teaching Literacy Through the Communicative and Visual Arts." *Handbook for Literacy*

Educators. Eds. James Flood and Shirley Brice Heath. New York, NY: Macmillan Press, 1997.

Corey, Frederick C., Ed. *HIV Education: Performing Personal Narratives.* Tempe, AZ: Arizona State University, 1993.

Crimp, Douglas. "Portraits of People With AIDS." *Cultural Studies.* Eds. Lawrence Grossberg, Cary Nelson and Paula Treichler. New York, NY: Routledge, 1992. 117–133.

Foucault, Michel. *The Birth of the Clinic: An Archaeology of Medical Perception.* 1973. Trans. A.M. Sheridan Smith. New York: Vintage Books, 1994.

Fuller, Matt. "Trends." *POZ* Aug./Sept. 1994: 34.

Goffman, Erving. *Stigma: Notes on the Management of Spoiled Identity.* New York, NY: Simon & Schuster, Inc., 1963.

Grover, Jan Zita. "AIDS: Keywords." *AIDS: Cultural Analysis, Cultural Activism.* Ed. Douglas Crimp. 1988. Cambridge, MA: The MIT Press, 1991. 17–30.

Grover, Jan Zita. "Visible Lesions: Images of the PWA in America." *Fluid Exchanges.* Ed. James Miller. Toronto: University of Toronto Press, 1992. 23–52.

"HIV Tattoo Flaunted by Health Care Worker." *Managing Risk* Sept. 1997: 9.

Irmas, Deborah. "Drawn and Colored." *Artforum* Dec. 1992: 62–64.

Murphy, Robert. "Fear of Disclosure." *POZ* Oct/Nov. 1995: 36–39, 59.

Okie, Susan. "Much Hostility Seen Toward AIDS Carriers." *Washington Post* 13 Oct. 1988: A7.

Patton, Cindy. *Fatal Advice: How Safe-Sex Education Went Wrong.* Durham, NC: Duke University Press, 1996.

Patton, Cindy. "Performativity and Spatial Distinction: The End of AIDS Epidemiology." *Performativity and Performance,* Eds. Andrew Parker and Eve Kosofsky Sedgwick. New York, NY: Routledge, 1995. 175–196.

Patton, Cindy. *Inventing AIDS.* New York, NY: Routledge, 1990.

Phelan, Peggy. *Unmarked: The Politics of Performance.* New York, NY: Routledge, 1993.

Provenzano, Jim. "Sex Positive." *POZ* June/July 1995: 41.

Reinelt, Janelle. "Staging the Invisible: The Crisis of Visibility in Theatrical Representation." *Text and Performance Quarterly* 14 (1994): 97–107.

Rogers, Ray. "Get an Earthful of Korn: A Band That's Ripe for the Picking." *Interview* June 1997: 96.

Román, David. "'It's My Party and I'll Die if I Want To!': Gay Men, AIDS, and the Circulation of Camp in U.S. Theatre." *Theatre Journal* 44 (1992): 305–327.

Román, David. "Performing All Our Lives: AIDS, Performance, Community." *Critical Theory and Performance.* Eds. Janelle Reinelt and Joseph Roach. Ann Arbor, MI: The University of Michigan Press, 1992. 208–221.

Sanders, Clinton R. *Customizing the Body: The Art and Culture of Tattooing.* Philadelphia, PA: Temple University Press, 1989.

Sandoval, Alberto. "Staging AIDS: What's Latinos Got To Do With It?" *Negotiating Performance: Gender, Sexuality, and Theatricality in Latin/o America.* Eds. Diana Taylor and Juan Villegas. Durham, NC: Duke University Press, 1994. 49–66.

Stryker, Jeff. "Disability, Dread & Discrimination: HIV+ Tattoos in the Hospital." *The Recorder* 15 Feb. 1995: 8.

Trejo, Frank. "Well Adjusted." *POZ* Feb./Mar. 1996: 46, 81.

Warren, Chante Dionne. "Model U.N.: Local Teens Weigh World Problems." *The Advocate* [Baton Rouge, LA] 11 Jan. 1997: 8E.

"Worker's Refusal to Conceal HIV Tattoo Amounts to Misconduct." *Disability Compliance Bulletin* 31 July 1997: 3.

11

ENCOUNTERING VISIONS OF AZTLÁN

Arguments for Ethnic Pride, Community Activism and Cultural Revitalization in Chicano Murals

MARGARET R. LAWARE

Recent essays have shown that arguments can include propositions that are visual as well as discursive (Birdsell and Groarke, 1996; Blair, 1996). Given the visual orientation of contemporary society and the richness and complexity of visual images, visual propositions may, in certain contexts, be more effective in conveying messages to particular audiences (Foss, 1993). Reasoning takes various forms, and pictures may be instrumental in facilitating types of reasoning that cannot be accomplished discursively. For example, in order for a minority community to argue that its culture has distinct properties that set it apart from the dominant culture, it needs to show those distinctions within cultural artifacts, including visual artifacts. In the late 1960s and 70s, minority communities in the United States deployed visual images to resist racism, discrimination

and social injustices. Walls within urban neighborhoods became a medium for expressing arguments for solidarity, for ethnic pride and for political activism. One of the first "people's" murals painted during this period was the "Wall of Respect," a mural celebrating African-American heroes. Painted in 1967 on an abandoned building in an area targeted for urban renewal on the South Side of Chicago, the "Wall of Respect" became not only an argument for Black pride, but also a reason for the community to resist outside control of its neighborhood (Cockcroft, Weber and Cockcroft, 1977). The mural transformed an abandoned space into a community space, a space for rallying together as a community against the city bureaucracy.

Visual images, therefore, can serve an argumentative function for a community. Contrary to Blair's (1996) assertions that "visual arguments

SOURCE: LaWare, M. R. (1998). Encountering visions of Aztlán: Arguments for ethnic pride, community activism and cultural revitalization in Chicano murals. *Argumentation and Advocacy, 34*(3), 140–153.

are not distinct in essence from verbal arguments" and that the "power" and "suggestiveness" of visual arguments is gained at the "cost of a loss of clarity and precision" (39), this essay argues that visual images may advocate a fairly specific concept of community development and community identity. Within particular cultural contexts, visual images make tangible abstract possibilities and clarify connections in ways that make them distinct from discursive arguments. For example, while Mexican Americans "do not form a homogeneous group politically, socially or racially" (Meier & Ribera, 1993, p. 6), certain images may remind them of a shared cultural heritage and shared experiences. For example, the Virgin of Guadalupe, the patroness of Mexico, has become a symbol of liberation and social justice for Chicanos/as. Placed within a visual context of historical images of the struggle for Mexican independence, the Virgin of Guadalupe becomes part of an argument for defining Mexican American or Chicano/a culture as distinct from "Anglo" culture. As pictures have been used by scientists to demonstrate the evolutionary "progress" of human beings from apes to modern humans by demonstrating a process of mental inference and reasoning (Shelley, 1996), pictures can make an argument for community development, calling attention to unique cultural characteristics and historical events that have shaped a community's progress.

In order to better understand how visual arguments can serve an argumentative function for a community, this essay focuses on a community for whom visual images have played an important role in creating an empowering identity. Many of the "people's" murals of the late 1960s and early 1970s were painted in Mexican American communities. These murals helped to achieve the goals of "El Movimiento," the Chicano civil rights movement, that emerged during the 1960s and extended into the late 1970s and beyond. One of the principal goals of the Movement was to reconnect Mexican American communities with their shared cultural roots by building "greater awareness of and pride in Mexican American cultural uniqueness" (Meier and Ribera, 1993, p. 235). Supporters of the Movement resisted assimilation into the dominant culture, arguing for the recognition of a distinct cultural identity, a Chicano/a identity.

For Mexican Americans or Chicanas/os,[1] many of whom live "with the unique experience of being a border culture between Mexico and the Southwest part of the United States," negotiating a space of identity and community is a challenging and sometimes emotionally wrenching process (Flores, 1996, p. 142). Because of this experience of both literally and figuratively living within a borderland, Chicanas/os may feel isolated, feeling neither Mexican nor American. As Flores demonstrates in her analysis of Chicana writers, locating a self-affirming identity requires symbolically constructing a "homeland."

Visual images, particularly mural images, have played an important role in participating in the construction of a "homeland," in defining a cultural and communal identity in Chicana/o neighborhoods, particularly in urban areas. When the artist Judy Baca turned to mural painting in Los Angeles in the late 1960s, she recognized that young Chicanas/os in Los Angeles needed spaces where they saw themselves reflected back; the existing built environment did not provide any validation of their own experiences. She explains:

> The group of people I was working with was very connected to and influenced by visual symbols—in tattoos, in the kind of writing that went on in the street—but there was no visible reflection of themselves in the larger community. Nothing of the architecture or visual symbols reflected the presence of the people—other than the graffiti. First it was a Jewish community, then Mexican people moved in. What I could see was that any population could move through the place without being reflected in it. Symbols already had significance in this community, and it made sense to create another set of symbols acknowledging the people's commonality. (qtd. in Neumaier, 1990, p. 261)

Baca and other Chicana/o muralists turned to symbols that represented the traditions of Chicanos/as, traditions that distinguished them from mainstream American culture.

The murals discussed in this essay reference the history of Mexico and the Mexican American peoples whose Mestizo culture is defined by a blending of Spanish and Indian cultures and who are distinguished from most other immigrant groups to the United States by the experience of being "descendents of a twice-conquered people" (Meier and Ribera, 1993, p. 5). These murals provide a visible reminder of the cultural connections between Mexican Americans, who are one of the most diverse ethnic groups in the United States,[2] by highlighting, through representative images, the notion of Aztlán, a concept which links the pre-Conquest past and post-colonial future, expressing Chicano pride and nationalism.[3] Further, the murals contain portraits that resemble community members, and which consequently make particular arguments about what deeds and which people are memorable. Finally as Tomás Ybarra-Frausto (1993) explains, Chicano/a art reflects a "continual effort toward developing an enhanced art of resistance—an art which is not a resistance to the materials and forms of art, but rather a resistance to entrenched social systems of power, exclusion and negation" (p. 67). The Chicano/a murals constitute an argument by providing an alternative vision, by making visible what institutions of power (political, cultural, economic) have rendered invisible—a self-defining Chicano/a identity.

This essay recognizes the importance of analyzing visual arguments in context, particularly when pictures serve geographically localized and culturally specific concerns and needs. Therefore, the essay begins with a discussion of "people's art," which is also referred to as the "community-based mural movement." In this section, I consider the unique aesthetic characteristics that shape the rhetorical impact of the community-based mural, particularly its use of scale, stylistic innovation and themes and images familiar to the local audience. The essay then turns to the particular context of Chicano murals, focusing first on the historical experience of Mexican Americans in the United States and their ethnic origins and then addressing the particular situation of the Chicago neighborhood where the murals analyzed in this essay are located. Finally, the essay provides an analysis of the murals. This particular grouping of Chicano murals, located on the interior and exterior of a community center, Casa Aztlán, in the Pilsen neighborhood of Chicago, was chosen for several reasons. First, Chicago has been an important location for community-based murals. The Public Art Workshop and the Chicago Mural Group, an artist collective, were organized in Chicago in the early 1970s to facilitate interactions between mural artists working in different communities around the city and to support their activities. Raymond Patlán, the artist who both painted and directed the painting of the original murals at Casa Aztlán belonged to the Chicago Mural Group. In addition, these murals at Casa Aztlán present an interesting case study since they are the product of several different periods of work and several different artists, from the early 1970s to the present. In addition, the Pilsen neighborhood where the murals are located is populated by one of the largest communities of Mexican Americans outside of the Southwest (Barnett, p. 68). Finally, understanding the murals on the interior and exterior of the Community Center, as functioning together to construct an argument for a unique cultural identity, responds to theorists who have focused on pictures as isolated, individual expressions (see Fleming, 1996).

PEOPLE'S ART AS ARGUMENTS FOR COMMUNITY DEVELOPMENT

Contemporary public spaces are literally filled with a profusion of visual images competing for attention. Many of these images are alienating and dehumanizing; they deny the real experiences of people, particularly people with little economic or political power. Given this situation, artists engaged in "people's art" understand their role to be one of enabling disenfranchised communities to locate a symbolic space that reflects their own needs, history and lived experience. According to Cockcroft, Weber and Cockcroft (1977), "people's art" portrays the story of the people it addresses; "their history and struggles, their dignity and hopes" (p. xxii). As Kenneth Burke explains, the artistic symbol appeals to its audience by both interpreting a situation and offering correctives (Burke, 1968, pp. 154–55). From a Burkean perspective then, people's art provides strategies for living and coping within a social environment that subjects minority communities to racism and social injustices such as substandard housing and limited job opportunities. Alan W. Barnett, a chronicler of the Community Mural Movement, notes that "Graffiti and murals are types of struggle art by which people seek to survive as human in an increasingly dehumanized world" (1984, p. 38).

In their *Mural Manual*, mural artists Mark Rogovin, Marie Burton and Holly Highfill explain that they create murals for "their own communities, working people of all ethnic backgrounds" (1975, p. ix). The artists have chosen mural painting as an exemplary people's art because of its accessibility to the community. Artists paint murals on the walls of community centers, churches and commercial buildings, on benches at bus stops as well as on bridges and freeway supports, on a variety of publicly accessible surfaces that constitute the built environment of a community. Artists choose to paint community-based murals in order to "educate and inspire" (Rogovin, Burton and Highfill, 1975, p. vii) as well as to affirm the "identity of [a] people" (Barnett, 1984, p, 38).

The size and scale of wall murals, and their location within public spaces, enhance their ability to make visible and relevant concepts and historical events and to link them to present struggles in the community. As Foss (1993) indicates in her hypothesis of visual appeal, visual images "arouse interest in," and emotionally involve viewers through the use of technical novelty (such as scale in the case of wall murals), decontextualizing the image so that it is viewed with new insight and new meaning (p. 215). For example, as Baca observes, the history of the deportation of Mexican Americans from Los Angeles during the 1930s may have a more profound impact on an individual if she or he is confronted with a large scale image depicting the suffering of individuals torn from their families and homes. The image makes the historical event relevant for the present community by calling attention to the deleterious effect of anti-immigration movements.

Further, as Foss (1993) suggests, visual images that succeed in persuading individuals to come to some new understanding or shift in perspective provide viewers with references to the familiar, and thereby alleviate the tension generated by the technical novelty. She explains that "[i]mages that appeal . . . help viewers comprehend the image by clearly referencing associations that point to contexts with positive connotations for them. These associations may be generated by the form of the image, the content of the image, or both" (p. 216). By choosing images that have positive connotations for a community, but which

are removed from their normal associations through technical novelty, the artist presents a different perspective on cultural identity and can ideally transform it from a marginalized, alienating identity, to one that is a source of pride and solidarity. As Flores (1996) concludes in her discussion of Chicana feminist writers, constructing one's own symbolic space means creating one's own center and refusing "to accept a marginal identity" (p. 146).

The size and location of community murals functions to insert local communities into public space, into the center of their own communities, making visible sources of cultural pride that may have been previously invisible or inaccessible. Further, the mural can also prolong moments of community solidarity and political action and as a consequence, prolong the feelings of pride attached to them as well as the belief that social change is possible. For example, many Chicano murals incorporate images of community demonstrations, including the murals painted in the interior of Casa Aztlán. According to Barnett (1984), the process of creating community-based murals itself can be understood as a form of demonstration, as a way of "enacting community" (p. 42).

Given its ability to move the community from the margin into its own center, a community-based mural can also be understood as a visual form similar in quality to epideictic rhetoric. Lawrence Rosenfield (1980) points out that epideictic brings together a community to witness the present, illuminating the community's inherent reality—its humanity and its relationship to a particular place, making visible the previously invisible. In response to those theorists who would deny epideictic any significant rhetorical functions, Rosenfield argues that epideictic rhetoric appeals not through well-reasoned arguments, but through the charm of the rhetor and the poetic appeal of the discourse which invokes a radiance, replacing the urgency for action with the urgency of recognition and the need to acknowledge what exists, who is present, and perhaps even what is possible.

In terms of understanding visual epideictic's relationship to standard arguments, visual epideictic presents particular claims about the community it addresses, about how it should view itself, but the reasons do not have to be overtly expressed. The audience understands the reasons almost intuitively, because it understands its own experience, especially when it can literally see itself reflected back in the faces of the images populating a mural. Visual epideictic therefore plays a significant role for "minority" communities denied access to their own realities through prejudice and oppression. Visual epideictic can create a space for what Flores (1996) refers to as a "rhetoric of difference," enabling individuals to feel connected to and empowered by an ethnically and politically defined community.

Consequently, community-based murals can present an argument about community development by combining an epideictic, or celebratory function, with the technical novelty of the mural form itself and its position within the public spaces of the community. Through representations of a shared cultural heritage in the form of familiar symbols and familiar figures in the history of a particular ethnic group, community-based murals present an image of community that resists marginalization and reverses internalized prejudices. According to Barnett (1984), community-based murals are "freeing ordinary people from ways of seeing that are not their own and helping them to take control of their perceptions, which," he explains, "is necessary to taking charge of their own lives" (p. 15).

Yearning for Aztlán: The Experiences of a Twice-Conquered People

In order to understand how images can argue for a notion of community development that leads to Chicano/a mobilization for social change, it is important to understand the historical experience of Chicanas/os, an experience that has been rendered invisible by institutional discourses in the United States. As Mexican American communication scholars have pointed out, although Mexican Americans have become the second largest immigrant group in the United States and the most "rapidly growing minority," they remain relatively invisible in the mainstream mass media (Gonzalez & Flores, 1994; Rios, 1994). Chicano murals can therefore serve to literally make visible a suppressed heritage, and many of the images chosen for the murals result from a "revaluation of history" (Cockcroft, Weber, & Cockcroft, 1977, p. 73).

As indicated in the introduction, Mexican Americans are a diverse ethnic group genetically, socially and in terms of the amount of time people have lived in the United States. However, as an ethnic group, they are united by a "bedrock of cultural identity," which includes the Spanish language (Meier and Ribera, 1993, p. 6). The cultural identity of Mexican Americans is shaped by the cultures of Spain and the cultures of the people native to Mesoamerica-particularly the Toltecs, Aztecs and Mayans, who were colonized by the Spanish people beginning in the 1500s. This blending of European and Indian cultures to create a "Mestizo" culture is an important aspect of the uniqueness of Mexican culture. The Mexican people experienced colonization yet again when their extended settlements in North America came under the control of the United States, as part of the Treaty of Guadalupe Hidalgo in the mid 1800s after the Mexican American War. While the Treaty guaranteed land titles, many Mexicans lost their lands due to prejudice and the pressures of a growing Anglo population. Stereotypes of Mexican Americans as "dirty, lazy, drunken, cruel, violent, treacherous, fanatical, priest-ridden, ignorant, and superstitious," which were formed in early interactions between Anglos and Mexicans, helped to foster exploitative practices which continue today (see Meier and Ribera, 1993, pp. 46–47).

In the 1960s, a number of Chicano leaders, including César Chávez, Reies Tijerina, Rodolfo Gonzalez and José Angel Gutiérrez, gained national visibility as they organized and mobilized their communities around civil rights for Mexican Americans including economic justice, political recognition and regaining land rights lost after the Treaty of Guadalupe Hidalgo (see Hammerback and Jensen 1980, 1980a). In order to unite Mexican Americans, these leaders employed rhetorical terms that reminded Mexican Americans of their unity and common history. An important rhetorical term used to create a sense of symbolic cohesiveness was La Raza, which literally means "the Race," and refers to the people of mixed heritage, Mestizos, including Mexicans and other Latino peoples. La Raza also suggests a sense of "spiritual unity" with the pre-conquest Indian civilization (Powers, 1973, p. 343). "Huelga," another key term, literally means strike, but has a much more powerful community resonance. As Powers explains, "it also became a symbol of successful protest against the Anglo establishment" (p. 344). During the 1960s, César Chávez and the United Farm workers succeeded in improving conditions for farm workers in California (of all nationalities, not just Chicanos) through the use of strikes.

Aztlán also came into use at this time as a key political term, by not only expressing this notion of Mexican Americans as a unique race set apart from others, but also by incorporating feelings of oppression and the sense of having been robbed of land through U.S. colonization. In referencing the ancient Aztec nation which originated in the lands between the southwestern United States and northwestern Mexico, Aztlán provides a link to the past and the future, restoring a sense of nationalism and pride in Chicano identity. As Hammerback and Jensen explain, "To many, Aztlán was an ideal, to others a physical reality in the future. In either case Aztlán was a powerful image for building solidarity in the community" (1980a, p. 196).

In the Chicano murals that appeared in California, the Southwest and in the Midwest, these terms—La Raza, Huelga and Aztlán—gained visual expression, as Chicano artists sought to define a contemporary Chicano identity. To achieve an understanding of a contemporary identity, the artists turned to history. Marcos Raya (1994), who has painted a number of murals in Chicago, explains, "Gringos don't have the urge to look back, Mexicans have to look back and see what is happening" (n.p.). The Chicano muralists sought to paint the history they knew, a history often based on "oral traditions, legends and myths" (Romo, 1994, p. 136). Chicano artists rejected "American interpretations that either omitted ethnic people or placed them in negative roles" (p. 136).

CHICANO MURALS AT
CASA AZTLÁN, CHICAGO

During the 1950s and 1960s, the Pilsen neighborhood in Chicago was transformed from a predominantly Polish neighborhood, to a largely Mexican American one, becoming in the process the "largest Chicano area outside of the Southwest" (Barnett, 1984, p. 68). In the 1960s, Pilsen was also one of the poorest neighborhoods in Chicago with high unemployment, substandard housing, inadequate health care and low levels of education amongst the population. However, in the late 1960s, the neighborhood took charge of its own redevelopment and murals were a part of this redevelopment process (Barnett, 1984, p. 68). During this time, the old settlement house, founded by Jane Addams in 1905, became Casa Aztlán, serving the local Mexican American population by providing a variety of social services including health care, citizenship classes, parent support programs and youth programs. In 1970, a local artist, Raymond Patlán, who was studying at the Art Institute of Chicago, began painting the main room in the interior. Borrowing stylistic components, images and techniques from the Mexican muralists Siqueiros and Orozco, Patlán painted a visual history of La Raza on the interior panels of Casa Aztlán, which not only included Chicano leaders of the past, but also images of Chávez, Tijerina and Gonzalez. In conjunction with local students, who Patlán introduced to the design motifs and images of pre-Columbian art, the exterior of the building was also painted with a mural titled, *"Hay Cultura en Nuestra Communidad"* (there is culture in our community). In 1974, a fire in Casa Aztlán destroyed some of the panels painted by Patlán. Between 1975 and 1978, Marcos Raya and other artists including Aurelio Díaz touched up and replaced some of the panels Patlán painted (Barnett, 1984, p. 329). The front exterior of Casa Aztlán [was] painted by Raya, Salvador Vega and Carlos (Moth) Barrera. During the spring and summer of 1994, the murals on Casa Aztlán were repainted by the artist Marcos Raya, who saw the importance of using the images to re-emphasize the need for Chicanos to continue to work together to fight oppression and exploitation even as members of the community were leaving the neighborhood for the middle class suburbs.

As Alberto Gonzalez (1990) indicates in his discussion of Mexican "otherness," a theme which he argues runs through both Mexican and Mexican American literature, many of the symbols used in Mexican American rhetoric can be "both mysterious and perplexing to Anglo American audiences" (p. 276). Through the following analysis of the murals at Casa Aztlán, I will show that the symbols used in the murals relate to particular historical themes and stories understood by the local Mexican American community. Further, these images serve to make visible and therefore accessible key rhetorical concepts that served to motivate Mexican American audiences to engage in political organizing around their distinct identity as La Raza, as Chicanos/as, distinguishing their needs, values and aspirations from the surrounding Anglo culture.

VISUAL ARGUMENTS IN THE MURALS OF CASA AZTLÁN

The mural painted on the front of the Casa Aztlán, a mural which reaches two stories high, contains images that are familiar and inviting to its local Chicano/a audience. It attracts attention through the use of vibrant colors and engaging design elements and through the use of symbols and images that represent the goals of the Movement—the goals of social justice, independence and a celebration of Chicano/a culture. Above the portal appears a young Mexican American family who look out over the community. The family indicates the typical residents of the community served by Casa Aztlán—young couples and their children. As mentioned earlier, some of the murals on Casa Aztlán, which had faded over time, have been repainted in recent years, and consequently the colors are brilliant. An Aztec pattern painted with green, yellow and black fills the bottom portion, while painted bright orange banners unfurl against a blue sky in the upper portion. The colors used on Casa Aztlán reference the rich colors of a tropical region, the rich colors of the traditional arts of Mexico. Together these colors and design patterns, a repeated pattern of skulls, a mythical beast with its tongue lolling out of its mouth, a pink rose representing the Virgin of Guadalupe, make distinct cultural references with celebratory overtones.

The mural itself fits into a long tradition of mural painting in Mexico which dates back to the Aztecs and which reached its height of artistic excellence through the great Mexican muralists of the 1920s and 30s, whose murals depicting traditional and historical themes decorated public buildings and celebrated Mexico's transition from a dictatorship to a democracy. Mexican Americans are also familiar with the folk tradition of mural painting because mural paintings, referred to as *pulquería* painting, are part of the architectural landscape of towns in Mexico and the southwestern United States. Colorful, decorative paintings appear on the exteriors of shops, restaurants and other businesses, including the taverns that lent them their name (they serve a liquor called *pulque*).

While making references to *pulquería* painting, the mural on the front of Casa Aztlán goes beyond mere decorative intent (Figure 1). The mural visually calls the community together to bear witness to its historical legacy as well as its present. The family above the portal is joined by the images of other "average" community members on the mural. Two enlarged figures, a man and a woman dressed in jeans, appear on either side of the mural and seem to have climbed up the building to help hold the painted banners unfurled over the front windows. Others gather in small groupings at the outer edges of the bottom of the mural. What the community is being asked to witness is the historical struggle of the Mexican American people for liberation from imperialism. The mural on the exterior and those inside argue that the community is part of that history and therefore must continue to move this particular historical narrative forward and promote the independence and the unique cultural heritage of Mexican Americans.

The argument for continuing the liberation struggle is manifested in the images that appear on either side of the front door, images of prominent figures in the history of the struggle for liberation by the people of Mexico and Latin America. On one side appears Emiliano Zapata, the "brilliant peasant leader" who fought against the Hacienda system during the Mexican revolution of the early 1900s. Below him, on a red background, appears the recognizable image of Che Guevara, the Argentinean who fought in the Cuban war of independence and who has become a symbol for liberationist struggle in the Americas. On the bottom of this trio appears Frida Kahlo, the artist and wife of Diego Rivera who, through her autobiographical art and self-presentation, celebrated the native cultures of

Figure 1　Street view of Casa Aztlán.

SOURCE: Margaret R. LaWare.

Mexico. To the right side of the door appears Francisco "Pancho" Villa, the famed leader of Los Dorados who managed to evade United States forces sent into Mexico to capture him. Above Villa appears Father Miguel Hidalgo, whose organized resistance to Spanish rule in the early 1800s led to Mexico's revolution for independence. Below Villa appears an Aztec warrior. All six painted busts greet visitors like the painted images of saints and holy figures who greet the visitor when entering a Byzantine church. They say to the visitor, here are individuals who have shaped the history of Mexican Americans; their deeds and lives should be remembered.

In addition to the six individuals surrounding the door, two additional busts appear, which connect the historical images more directly to the local community. At the top of the mural, above two sets of windows, one on either side of the main entrance, appear two orange and gold banners set against the sky-blue background of the mural. On one banner is the portrait of César Chávez, the leader of the United Farm Workers, who died in 1994. On the other banner appears the portrait of a local community leader, Rudy Lozano, who was assassinated in the early 1970s.[4] The images pay tribute to the memory of these two men.

The central focus of the mural is a symbol that ties the argument of the mural together, and which offers the conclusion that social organizing is the only effective way to ensure equal fights and freedom from injustice and exploitation for Mexican Americans (Figure 2). This symbol, the geometrical black eagle (an Aztec symbol) in a white circle on a red background, is the symbol of the United Farm Workers. The symbol is readily understood by its audience. In Mexico, the red and black stand for the Huelga, thus the choice by the UFW to place the black eagle against the red field. As Ricardo Romo (1992–1996) points out, the black eagle is an important and prevalent symbol that appears in many Chicano murals, because it "represents the earliest organizing that Chicanos had for economic change" (p. 139). Since the eagle appears on the front door, the visitor must walk through the center of the eagle to gain access to the community center. By requiring the visitor to walk through the symbol of the UFW, a symbol that signifies an organized commitment to improving the conditions of "working-class people" and the poor, the artists symbolically request visitors to recognize and agree to these goals. The front mural therefore uses color and design elements to engage the viewer's feelings of joy and pride and to locate the viewer within a particular social and political history that emphasizes not only identification with the traditional (as opposed to European) cultures of Mexico, but also with the movement against imperialism and economic exploitation. Finally, through the location of the symbol of the UFW at the center of the mural, on the door providing entrance to the community center, the viewer is asked to recognize that the only way to counter exploitative practices that target Mexican Americans is through social organizing.

The murals painted in the interior of Casa Aztlán, in the main meeting room or *sala*, further the argument expressed in the front mural by providing illustrated scenes of Mexican history that emphasize the theme of the liberation struggle. One panel portrays Father Hidalgo's confrontation with Spanish soldiers, and an image of him hanging at the end of a noose. Overlaid on this scene of struggle, a Mexican man holds a rifle vertically in his enlarged hand, a long-white banner with the word, *independencia* (independence) unfurled behind his head. On another panel, Emiliano Zapata, holding a rifle in one hand and brandishing a sword above his head with the other hand, leads a group of *campesinos* forward, the ranks behind

Figure 2 Close-up of mural front of Casa Aztlán.

SOURCE: Margaret R. LaWare.

him indicated by their broad brimmed sombrero hats. On another panel, in front of the red flag of the Huelga emblazoned with the black eagle of the UFW, workers harvest grapes. As Romo (1992–96) writes, "Although historical images in murals are from battles that people fought in other times and places, the battles are as specific and as socially legitimate as those the communities struggle with today" (p. 140).

Through the use of modern stylistic devices and color, the murals portray energy and determination, making the viewer feel that the liberation struggle is moving forward and will succeed. The murals call the local audience into the struggle through the use of resemblance. Community members can literally see themselves in the murals.

In one mural, a large group of people engaged in a demonstration appear to be marching out of the panel (Figure 3). One of the three front people is a revolutionary woman soldier, known as "La Adelita," reminding the viewer of the important work performed by women in the struggle by Mexicans and Chicanos/as against oppression, her face and the faces of the people marching beside and behind her are the faces of community members, including the artist of the mural, Marcos Raya. She and the man on the opposite end of the triumvirate hold large red flags of the Huelga. One man even wears a red shirt with the face of Che stenciled on it. The artist has used this panel to link the past and the present, showing that contemporary demonstrations such as this one protesting the lack of hiring of Latinos in Chicago, can be linked to the liberationist activities of people such as Hidalgo, Zapata and Guevara.[5] On another panel, painted in a similar style, young people are gathered together, pulling on a set of three ropes, which could be raising a banner, or pulling the covering off of a mural. A man behind these young people waves the red flag of the Huelga, while another holds a sign which reads, "*La juventud no es la edad del placer, sino la edad del heroismo*" (youth is not the age of pleasure, it's the age of heroism). The conclusion to be drawn from this series of murals is undeniable: the local community, young people and adults are located within the history of La Raza, invited to see themselves as carrying on the battle against the exploitative practices of the dominant culture. The prevalent image of

Figure 3 "La marcha" (The march) 1976, painted by Marcos Raya. Interior mural, Casa Aztlán.

SOURCE: Margaret R. LaWare.

the red flag of the Hidalgo and the eagle symbol of the United Farm Workers, two symbols familiar to Chicano/a audiences, and the two images of community people demonstrating in the streets, suggest that successful resistance to exploitative practices can be achieved only when the community joins together and recognizes their power to bring about change.

The argument for a unified community sharing a unique Chicano/a cultural identity is furthered by two additional murals painted in the interior sala. One mural portrays the mythic Aztlán, the homeland of the native Mexican people. A golden Aztec city with tall, geometrical pyramids backed by snowcapped mountains, serves as a visible reminder of the location and the population of one of the first civilizations in North America. The final mural, originally painted by Patlán and containing the most stylistically interesting elements, offers a critique of the notion of progress. Located next to the mural of grape harvesters, this painting, which is one of the largest murals in the room, connects the agricultural workers to the industrial workers. In an early version of the work, the bust of a young César Chávez is contained in an egg-shaped frame which is held up by a tall pedestal and which seems to be both pushed forward and pulled back by two naked figures who emerge from the bottom left corner of the mural. There is a tension between the two naked figures, perhaps representing ancestors, and a young woman on the right-hand side of the pedestal who holds the pedestal as she marches forward behind three, muscular bare-chested industrial workers. The three workers, in turn, appear to be entering the encapsulating teeth of a machine. The image indicates that progress in the dominant culture, the move from an agricultural to an industrial economy, is not progress for the Chicano community. Industrial labor becomes another type of bondage. In addition, the tension between the figures on the left and right suggests that moving forward means not leaving the past behind. The future of the Chicano/a community, the "homeland," Aztlán, emerges out of struggle, the struggle to realize a unique culture that looks both to the past and to the future. Since the original painting, the central bust of Chávez has been replaced by a more generic, unisex image, a Chicano/a or Mexican with long dark braids who wears crisscrossing straps of ammunition and a bandana with the insignia, Aztlán.

CONCLUSION

In my discussion, I have shown how the murals of Casa Aztlán provide a symbolic space for reconstituting the local community. These murals provide a critique of dominant cultural practices and re-contextualize Mexican Americans, as Chicanos/as, as people who can act to liberate themselves from the jaws of the oppressor. Through technical novelty, including the large scale of the mural images and the artists' use of modernist stylistic features and ancient patterns, the murals demonstrate the tension created by the "border" experience and resolve the tension through representations of moments of community progress, of successful demonstrations. Understood together, the murals argue that Mexican American people need not assimilate or give up their culture to survive in an urban center that is both geographically and socially distant from Mexico and from the Southwest. On the contrary, for a community that has experienced living on the borders between cultures, survival requires opening a space where it is possible to construct one's own identity, drawing upon empowering experiences in both cultures.

As Flores (1996) points out, after opening a space where marginalized communities can create their own definitions of self and reject those imposed from the outside, the next step in locating an empowering identity is transforming that space into a homeland. A "homeland" defines a space where an individual can see him or herself reflected and his or her own identity affirmed. For Chicanos/as, the idea of Aztlán has served the function of reminding Chicanos/as of their shared beginnings, as a people whose traditions combine Amerindian culture with European culture. In addition, Aztlán has also symbolized a promise for a future in which Chicanos/as gain visibility and power. The identity created by the murals at Casa Aztlán resists the positioning of Chicanos/as as "other." The Chicano murals make the concept of Aztlán visually tangible and emotionally palpable to its local audience. Incorporated into the built environment, the murals transform a generic urban space into one that illuminates and affirms the history, traditions and aspirations of the Chicano/a people who live there.

While the murals at Casa Aztlán have undergone changes over time, the themes expressed in these have remained unchanged. In 1994, the artist Marcos Raya clearly understood that repainting the murals created an argument against apathy, an argument for the community to do something to confront the new problems facing Pilsen. Raya's implicit message was not unwarranted. In 1997, the Pilsen neighborhood faced significant pressures from gentrification and an expanding University of Illinois campus. Casa Aztlán, as a representative organization of the community, has led the fight to maintain the community's coherence, protecting the interests of the local people (Arango, 1997).

By focusing on a localized and culturally specific group of visual images, the essay has emphasized the importance of considering historical and cultural contexts for analyzing the function of visual arguments. The analysis demonstrates that visual images can make a particular argument about a community, about its origins, its sources of power and its collective identity. There are undoubtedly other ways that visual images can serve a community function, by defining its spatial boundaries for instance, or by envisioning resolutions to communal conflicts. Clearly, people's art, or the community-based mural movement, which references the lives of a localized group of people at a particular time and place, offers rich possibilities for extending our understanding of the varied possibilities of visual argument.

NOTES

1. The terms Chicano and Mexican American will be used interchangeably in this essay. While in use since the turn of the century, as a means for Mexican Americans to name themselves, Chicano gained popularity during the movement of the 1960s and consequently has "overtones of ethnic nationalism and activism" (see Meier and Ribera, 280).

2. Hammerback and Jensen (1982) quote Joan W. Moore, who argues that Mexican Americans are probably, "more diverse in social composition than any immigrant minority group in American history" (p. 72).

3. The term "people's art" is perhaps most appropriate for the works analyzed in this essay. However,

murals painted in ethnic neighborhoods for social and political purposes were made possible by the community-based mural movement, which has also been referred to as the public art movement, the contemporary mural renaissance and street art. See the preface of Cockcroft, Weber and Cockcroft (1977).

4. My understanding that Lozano was assassinated came from two places: Victor Sorrell's (1987) discussion of the mural and from the artist, Marcos Raya.

5. This information was gathered in an interview with Gregg Mann, Arts and Culture Chairman of Casa Aztlán's Board of Directors on June 10th, 1993, Casa Aztlán, Chicago.

REFERENCES

Arango, Carlos (1997, February 17). Phone interview with the director of Casa Aztlán.

Barnett, A. W. (1984). *Community murals: The people's art*. New York: Cornwall Books.

Birdsell, D. S. & Groarke, L. (1996). Toward a theory of visual argument. *Argumentation and Advocacy, 33*, 1–10.

Blair, J. A. (1996). The possibility and actuality of visual argument. *Argumentation and Advocacy, 33*, 23–39.

Burke, K. (1968). *Counter-statement*. 2nd ed. Berkeley: University of California Press.

Cockcroft, E., Weber, J., & Cockcroft, J. (1977). *Toward a people's art: The contemporary mural movement*. New York: E.P. Dutton &Co.

Edwards, E. (1966). *Painted walls of Mexico, from prehistoric times until today*. Austin: University of Texas Press.

Fleming, D. (1996). Can pictures be arguments? *Argumentation and Advocacy, 33*, 11–22.

Flores, L. A. (1996). Creating discursive space through a rhetoric of difference: Chicana feminists craft a homeland, *Quarterly Journal of Speech, 82*, 142–156.

Foss, S. K. (1994). A rhetorical schema for the evaluation of visual imagery. *Communication Studies, 45*, 213–224.

Foss, S. K. (1993). The construction of appeal in visual images: A hypothesis. In D. Zarefsky (Ed.), *Rhetorical Movement: Essays in Honor of Leland M. Griffin* (pp. 211–225). Evanston: Northwestern University Press.

Gonzalez, A. & Flores, G. (1994) Tejana music and cultural identification. In A. Gonzalez, M. Houston & V. Chen (Eds.), *Our Voices: Essays in culture, ethnicity, and communication: an intercultural anthology*. Los Angeles, CA: Roxbury Publishing.

Gonzalez, A. (1990). Mexican 'Otherness' in the rhetoric of Mexican Americans. *Southern Communication Journal, 55*, 276–291.

Hammerback, J. C. & Jensen, R. J. (1980). I. The rhetorical worlds of César Chávez and Reies Tijerina. *Western Journal of Speech Communication, 44*, 166–176.

Hammerback, J. C. & Jensen, R. J. (1980a). II. Radical nationalism among Chicanos: The rhetoric of Jose Angel Gutierrez. *Western Journal of Speech Communication, 44*, 191–202.

Jensen, R. J. & Hammerback, J. C. (1982). No revolutions without poets: The rhetoric of Rudolfo "Corky" Gonzalez. *Western Journal of Speech Communication, 46*, 72–91.

Meier, M. S. & Ribera, F. (1993). *Mexican Americans/ American Mexicans: From Conquistadors to Chicanos*. New York: Hill and Wang.

Neumaier, D. (1990). Judy Baca: Our People are the internal exiles. In G. Anzaldúa (Ed.), *Making face, making soul: Haciendo Caras: Creative and critical perspectives by women of color*. San Francisco: Amt Urk Books.

Powers, L. D. (1973). Chicano rhetoric: Some basic concepts. *Southern Speech Communication Journal, 38*, 340–346.

Raya, M. (11 June 1994). Interview with artist. Chicago, Illinois.

Rios, D. (1994). Mexican American cultural experiences with mass-mediated communication. In A. Gonzalez, M. Houston & V. Chen (Eds.). *Our Voices: Essays in culture, ethnicity, and communication*. Los Angeles: Roxbury Publishing.

Rodriguez, A. (1969). *A history of Mexican mural painting*. New York: GP Putnam's Sons.

Rogovin, M., Burton, M. & Highfill, H. (1975). *Mural manual*. T. Drescher (Ed.), (2nd ed.). Boston: Beacon Press.

Romo, R. (1992–1996). Borderland murals: Chicano artifacts in transition. *Aztlán 21*(1,2), 125–154.

Rosenfield, L. W. (1980). The practical celebration of epideictic. In E. E. White (Ed.), *Rhetoric in transition: Studies in the nature and uses of rhetoric*. University Park, PA: Pennsylvania State University Press.

Shelley, C. (1996). Rhetorical and demonstrative modes of visual argument: Looking at images of human evolution. *Argumentation and Advocacy, 33*, 53–68.

Sorell, V. (1987). The enduring presence of the Chicano-Mexicano mural in Chicago. In Arceo, R. H., Sorell, V. A., & Rogovin, M. (1987). *The Barrio murals = Murales del Barrio,* July 21-September 1, 1987 (pp. 5–9). Chicago: The Mexican Fine Arts Center.

Spero, J. (Ed.). (1990). *Mexican mural postcards by Rivera, Orozco and Siqueiros.* New York, Dover Publications.

Trejo, A. D. (Ed.). (1979). *The Chicanos as we see ourselves.* University of Arizona Press.

Ybarra-Frausto, T. (1993). Arte Chicano: Images of a community. In E. S. Cockcroft & H. B. Sanchez (Eds.), *Signs from the heart: California Chicano murals.* Albuquerque: University of New Mexico Press.

12

THE GUERRILLA GIRLS' COMIC POLITICS OF SUBVERSION

ANNE TERESA DEMO

THE ADVANTAGES OF BEING A WOMAN ARTIST

Working without the pressure of success.
Not having to be in shows with men.
Having an escape from the art world in your 4 free-lance jobs.
Knowing your career might pick up after you're eighty.
Being reassured that whatever kind of art you make it will be labeled feminine.
Not being stuck in a tenured teaching position.
Seeing your ideas live on in the work of others.
Having the opportunity to choose between career and motherhood. . . .
Getting your picture in art magazines wearing a gorilla suit.

The preceding excerpt, taken from a 1988 poster plastered throughout the streets of lower Manhattan, satirically encouraged passers-by to consider the so-called "sunny side" of institutionalized sexism (Guerrilla Girls, 1995, p. 53). Created by the Guerrilla Girls—a feminist collective of women artists and art world professionals—this sardonic chronicle of art world double standards has been translated into more than eight languages and immortalized in feminist literature and pop-culture post-cards. The poster's litany of contradictions illustrates both the spectrum of sexism that women artists face and a principal strategy of the Guerrilla Girls' rhetoric: perspective by incongruity.

The growing literature on Kenneth Burke and dramatic frames well establishes the potential for perspective by incongruity to function as a discursive tool for enacting social change (Allen & Faigley, 1995; Carlson, 1986, 1988, 1992; Christiansen & Hanson, 1996; Dow, 1994; Powell, 1995). According to Burke, perspective by incongruity works by "a constant juxtaposing of incongruous words, attaching to some name a qualifying epithet which had heretofore gone

SOURCE: Demo, A. T. (2000). The Guerrilla Girls' comic politics of subversion. *Women's Studies in Communication, 23*(2), 133–157. Used with permission of the Organization for Research on Women and Communication.

with a different order of names" (Burke, 1954, p. 90). The use of terms, images or ideologies that are incongruous reorders—even remoralizes—a situation or orientation in a process akin to consciousness-raising (Dow, 1994). This essay is indebted to much of the literature on dramatic frames and seeks to further contribute to the study of marginalized (specifically feminist) discourse by examining how strategies of incongruity engender a comic politics of subversion. My analysis focuses on three strategies found in the rhetoric of the Guerrilla Girls: (1) mimicry, (2) an inventive re-vision of history, and (3) strategic juxtaposition. I argue that the organizing logic for these strategies in particular, and Guerrilla Girls' rhetoric in general, is the technique that Burke labels perspective by incongruity. I foreground strategies of incongruity because of their potential to both denaturalize and restructure a particular context, ideology, or sedimented meaning through "comparison, reclassification, and re-naming" (Dow, 1994, p. 229). Even though perspective by incongruity structures the Guerrilla Girls' rhetoric, its more general function is to create a comic politics of subversion and is, therefore, closely linked to Burke's discussion of the comic frame. The Guerrilla Girls' rhetoric, then, demonstrates how planned incongruity not only pokes fun at the failures of the social structure but also offers a comic corrective to such failings.

Many critics have recognized the symbiotic relationship between perspective by incongruity and the comic frame in Burke's work (Christiansen & Hanson, 1996; Dow, 1994; Gusfield, 1989). Described as a frame of acceptance, the comic frame hinges on the ambivalence engendered by incongruities. The comic frame privileges audiences by providing a unique vantage point from which to see the inaccuracies of a situation—creating what Burke labels "maximum consciousness" (1937/1984, p. 171). Likening the process to a play, Burke explains, "The audience, from its vantage point, sees the operation of errors that the characters of the play cannot see; thus seeing from two angles at once, it is chastened by dramatic irony" (1954, p. 41). For Burke, the comic frame functions as a middle ground: "It is neither wholly euphemistic, nor wholly debunking— hence it provides the *charitable* attitude toward

people that is required for purposes of persuasion and cooperation" (1937/1984, p. 166). As William Rueckert maintains, the comic frame "does not believe in absolutes, in categorical Nos" (1990, p. 11). This outlook is key to the Guerrilla Girls' rhetorical approach, as one member explained it in a 1991 interview; "Making demands are the tactics of the 70s and let's face it, they didn't really work very well. So we decided to try another way: humor, irony, intimidation, and poking fun" (Lederer, 1991, n.p.). The machinery of perspective by incongruity and the comic frame, then, engenders a form of social criticism that seeks to correct the inadequacies of the present social order through demystification rather than revolution (Burke, 1937/1984, p. 167).

The line of inquiry pursued throughout my analysis responds to recent calls for increased critical attention to nontraditional forms of feminist rhetoric (Carlson, 1992; Dow, 1997) and for critiques engaging the activist potential of specific comic strategies (Carlson, 1988; Christiansen & Hanson, 1996). Despite the Guerrilla Girls' visibility and longevity, they have received limited interdisciplinary attention (Loughery, 1987; Schor, 1990; Withers, 1988). This academic silence stands in stark contrast to the group's stature as a model for grassroots activists. Gloria Steinem even cited the Guerrilla Girls as a "group that symbolized the best of feminism in this country. . . . Smart, radical, funny, creative, uncompromising, and (I assume) diverse under those inspired gorilla masks, they force us to rethink everything from art to zaniness" (Guerrilla Girls, 1995, back cover). In addition, the aesthetic style of the group's posters has been widely recognized by their inclusion in museum and gallery exhibitions. As a group who communicates its message through primarily visual forms and in unconventional public fora, the Guerrilla Girls demonstrate how comic strategies function within a visual idiom.

This essay unfolds in four sections. I begin with a brief overview of feminist art activism as it bears most directly on the Guerrilla Girls' rhetoric, while highlighting feminist antecedents and the cultural pretext for the group's formation. The second section examines the conceptual linkages between feminist rhetoric, perspective by incongruity, and the comic frame. The analysis that follows features three strategies of incongruity; the role of mimicry in the group's performances and formation of their public personae; the Guerrilla Girls' inventive approach to the history of women artists; and strategic juxtapositions in two broadsides created by the Guerrilla Girls. I conclude by discussing the potential for unconventional forms and fora of persuasion to enact social change.

FEMINIST CONSCIOUSNESS RAISING IN THE VISUAL ARTS: PRECEDENTS AND PRETEXT

The history of women's exclusion and marginalization within the arts is well documented (Nochlin, 1988; Chadwick, 1990). More than twenty years after American women were granted suffrage, formal and informal obstacles to art world institutions remained intact. The birth of the Abstract Expressionist movement in the 1950s, however, appeared to usher in a new sensibility regarding what was considered art and who could create it. Artists like Lee Krasner, Dorothy Dehner, Joan Mitchell, and Elaine de Kooning (all members of the New York School of Art) began exhibiting alongside male contemporaries like Willem de Kooning, Jackson Pollock, and Andrew Gottlieb. Even as these and other women artists gained some visibility, however, their careers remained at the periphery, tethered by an art establishment doctrine that "only men had the wings for art" (Chadwick, 1990, p. 302).

The convergence of the modern feminist movement and art activism opened gallery doors that had long been closed to women artists. In the late 1960s, the sinking arm of the Women's Liberation Organization, the Women's International Terrorist Conspiracy from Hell (WITCH), began masquerading as crones during protests over women's subordination. Their demonstrations consisted primarily of theatrical events such as showering the "Sociology Department at the University of Chicago with hair cuttings and nail clippings after the firing of a radical feminist woman professor" (Morgan, 1970, p. 538). Both the group's appropriation of a "patriarchally designated" archetype and tactical

management of dominant symbols established a rhetorical precedent for future feminist guerrilla groups like the Guerrilla Girls (Radner & Lanser, 1993, p. 10). Art historian Whitney Chadwick credits the pressure from groups like WITCH, the Guerrilla Art Action Group (GAAG), Women Artists in Resistance (WAR), Women Students and Artists for Black Art Liberation (WSABAL), and the Art Workers Coalition (AWC) with inducing museums like the Whitney to "exhibit a larger percentage of women and minority artists" and producing an "explosion of work that reinserted women's personal experiences into art practices" (Chadwick, 1990, p. 321).

Even as such actions radicalized women artists, their personal empowerment did not translate into lasting systemic changes. Liz Moore, an exhibiting artist at the first "Women's Liberation Art Group," expressed the exhilaration felt by many women artists during the period. "Women artists are making contact with each other, coming out of their isolation. We are beginning to acknowledge the validity of our own and of each other's work; to learn to do without male approval, to be proud to show in the company of each other. We are learning to provide each other with the confidence to explore and develop our own vision of a new consciousness" (1972, p. 1). Although the convergence between art activism and feminism lingered, a backslide was palpable by the late 1970s. Henry Sayre documents the dismal statistics:

By 1976, things had barely improved: only 15% of the one-person shows in New York's prestige galleries were devoted to work by women. . . . A poll of ten leading New York galleries conducted in 1975 by WiA [Women in Art] indicated that some represented no women, others a few, but none more than three. In 1977, in a follow-up survey, women had not gained at all. By 1979, another survey of eighteen leading New York galleries revealed that, of all the artists these galleries represented, still only 20.8% were women. (1989, pp. 86–87)

Even in the context of this backslide, the 1985 "International Survey of Painting and Sculpture" at the Museum of Modern Art proved to be a breaking point. With an estimated two to three dozen members, the Guerrilla Girls organized their first action in response to the exhibition. According to Guerrilla Girl Meta Fuller, "We began to ask ourselves some questions. Why did women and artists of color do better in the 1970s than in the '80s? Was there a backlash in the art world? Who was responsible? What could be done about it?" (1995, p. 13). As was the case with many feminist agitators, their answers prompted a move to the streets (Chadwick, 1995, p. 11).

The entangled web of art world politics dictated the "means of persuasion" used in taking to the streets (broadsides) and the Guerrilla Girls' anonymity as they plastered their message on the construction fences, gallery doors and kiosks of SoHo. The first battery in the poster assault addressed the "pass the buck" mentality of the art world establishment by making the dismal records of galleries, critics, and museums public with posters that put names with statistics. Poster headings varied in form from bold statements—"THESE GALLERIES SHOW NO MORE THAN 10% WOMEN ARTISTS OR NONE AT ALL" and "THESE CRITICS DON'T WRITE ENOUGH ABOUT WOMEN ARTISTS"—to a question/answer format: "WHAT DO THESE ARTISTS HAVE IN COMMON? THEY ALLOW THEIR WORK TO BE SHOWN IN GALLERIES THAT SHOW NO MORE THAN 10% WOMEN ARTISTS OR NONE AT ALL." Most important, however, the posters singled-out over forty-two well-known male artists (e.g., Chuck Close, Keith Haring, Claes Oldenburg, and Julian Schnabel), along with twenty prominent galleries (e.g., Mary Boone, Leo Castelli, Blum Helman, and the Dia Art Foundation), all the major New York Museums (e.g., Guggenheim, Metropolitan, Modern, and Whitney) and twenty-two art critics (e.g., Hilton Kramer, Gary Indiana, Roberta Smith and Calvin Tomkins).

By attempting to embarrass galleries, critics, and museums into recognizing the institutionalized nature of art world sexism and racism, members put their own careers at risk. "The art world is a very small place," Guerrilla Girl GG1 explains, "we were afraid that if we blew the whistle on some of the most powerful people, we could kiss off our own art careers" (1995, p. 14). Although the identities of the Guerrilla Girls remain masked by a mix of bohemian black and gorilla drag, members of the group work in every facet of the art world. According to one Guerrilla Girl, members "may be working as secretaries at the Museum of Modern Art, they may be Hilton Kramer's proctologist" (Feldstein, 1994). The member's individual anonymity provides protection from retribution even as the group creates a readable collective identity through the gorilla mask. The ambiguity over membership further works to create a sense of omnipresence in the art community. Even more important to the Guerrilla Girls, however, anonymity keeps attention focused on issues rather than individuals.

Since the group's inception in 1985 the Guerrilla Girls have produced over 80 posters, graphic works, and guerrilla actions targeting sexism and racism both in and outside of the art world. Their books, *Confessions of the Guerrilla Girls* and *The Guerrilla Girls Bedside Companion to the History of Western Art,* each exhausted their first-run printings of 20,000. Despite the varied forms of media used by the Guerrilla Girls, the group's rhetoric coheres into a meaningful message because each poster, action, or book project confronts sexism and racism by revealing the incongruity between social ideals and practices. The group thus couples a sarcastic wit with hard facts. Indeed, many of the Guerrilla Girls' early posters used statistics either from the very galleries and museums the group was targeting or established sources such as the *Art in America Annual.* This approach seeks to embarrass and intimidate—but not overturn—the current social order through a process that I label feminist "atom-cracking."

FEMINIST "ATOM-CRACKING": PERSPECTIVE BY INCONGRUITY AND THE COMIC FRAME

In *Attitudes Toward History,* Kenneth Burke equates perspective by incongruity with "verbal 'atom cracking'" (1937/1984, p. 308; also see Burke, 1954, pp. 90, 119). The metaphor suggests the highly charged nature of the symbolic alchemy produced when differing rhetorical/ideological orientations mix. The juxtaposition of incongruous words, ideographs, and even arguments has the effect of shattering "pieties," which, according to Thomas Rosteck and Michael Leff, function as "the stable frames of reference which direct human perception and determine our judgements about what is proper in a given circumstance" (1989, p. 329). The fracturing process engendered by planned incongruity is "at once subversive and constructive: old pieties must fall to provide space for new ones" (Rosteck & Leff, 1989, p. 330). It is this rhetorical quality that makes perspective by incongruity an effective strategy for inducing social change. Indeed, the metaphor of "atom cracking" in many ways symbolizes what Karlyn Kohrs Campbell argues is "the principle of rhetorical invention" for women and marginalized rhetors. According to Campbell, the "key element in the erosion of the myths that justify women's subordination and the ideological barriers that retard social change" is subversion, or "using the master's tools to undermine, even sabotage, the master's house" (1998, p. 112). The tactics that Campbell highlights, such as "inventive uses of the past," "symbolic reversal," and the creation of a "speaking self" through "persona or role," challenge institutionalized sexism by denaturalizing the formulation of patriarchy (1998). In short, these tactics function through a process of feminist "atom cracking," or the strategic juxtaposition of incongruent ideals, values, practices, and symbols that not only call into question gender ideologies but also remoralize them.

Burke's comic frame sparks feminist "atom cracking" by introducing the "everyday" as a site of scrutiny. In making people both students of themselves and of their social structure, the comic frame casts a communal failing or censurable act in a comedic light. As a result, the comic frame "treats this misbehaving individual [or institution] as mistaken, and embarrasses him or her by revealing the error of the action to all" (Brummett, 1994, p. 134). The comic frame thus offers a corrective to the inequities of the present system while working within the existing social structure. Burke's "comic corrective," Hugh Duncan explains, "seeks to unmask vices by confronting ends or ideals with means or practice. The final transcendence in comedy is society itself, people who in hate and love try to resolve differences" (1962, p. 390). For feminists, a primary means

for reaching such transcendence is the appropriation and ironic repositioning of conventional patriarchal symbolic codes.

The growing literature on Burke's dramatic frames demonstrates that many comic strategies used by marginalized groups recast dominant tropes or archetypes as a mean of "engineering a shift" in the social order (1937/1984, p. 173). Spirituality, ironic or playful word play, and the exaggeration and concealment of identity markers are among the strategies previously isolated by rhetorical critics (Carlson, 1986, 1988; Christiansen & Hanson, 1996; Powell, 1995). By borrowing "forms or materials" normally associated with dominant culture, marginalized rhetors create a perspective by incongruity that draws attention to social inequities (Radner & Lanser, 1993, p. 10). This is not to suggest that appropriation is a subset of comic strategies of incongruity. Rather, the point is that dominant symbolic codes—when opened up to what they exclude through planned incongruity—constitute a powerful inventional resource within a feminist comic corrective (Campbell, 1998, p. 123; Radner & Lanser, 1993, p. 11).

The strategies of incongruity used by the Guerrilla Girls foreground the very myths that seek to keep women in their place as muses, not creators of art, and as objects rather than agents of history. Indeed, the group's mission since forming in 1985 has been to fight sexism and racism by demonstrating the incongruity of conventional definitions of artists, femininity, and feminist activism. Their rhetoric subverts traditional definitions of the artist as an individual genius (read male) producing "seminal" and "potent" works by exposing the networks of power (past and present) that put women artists at a professional disadvantage—such as being prohibited from attending art academies until the mid-nineteenth century. In addition, an exaggeration and playfulness with norms of femininity, which defines the Guerrilla Girls' rhetoric, connects feminism and femininity in ways that deconstruct dominant understandings of both terms. Finally, the group draws attention to the gap between formal rights and actual practices with statistics and "believe it or not" quotations that make denial and indifference an unfitting response to gender inequality.

STRATEGIES OF INCONGRUITY:
MIMICRY, HISTORICAL RE-VISION,
AND STRATEGIC JUXTAPOSITIONS

My analysis is organized around the three strategies that most define the group's rhetorical style: mimicry, a feminist re-vision of history, and strategic juxtapositions. In the first section, I address how the group's use of mimicry, or the exaggeration of a "patriarchally designated position," calls into question conventional notions of femininity and sexuality that maintain the male/female, artist/muse dichotomies (Radner & Lanser, 1993, p. 10). From the group's name and dress to their use of sexual innuendo, the Guerrilla Girls transform what it means to be a "girl" producing art. The second strategy of incongruity addressed is the group's inventive approach to history. By assuming the names of under-acknowledged female artists during interviews and performances, the Guerrilla Girls draw attention to the number of forgotten women artists who have produced art throughout history. This tactic is further realized in the group's book project, *The Guerrilla Girls Bedside Companion to the History of Western Art,* which recasts the history of art as a "history of discrimination" (1998, p. 7). Finally, I examine how strategic juxtapositions in the Guerrilla Girls' broadsides illuminate the incongruity of American claims to equal opportunity. These strategies displace the pieties that define artistic genius as a singularly male trait and sexism as an issue of the past. Ultimately, this displacement constructs a new piety based on inclusiveness, diversity, and equality.

Mimicry

In a 1975 interview published in *Dialectiques,* Luce Irigaray delineates the subversive potential of mimicry as an avenue for disrupting the phallocentric order. By self-consciously adopting an exaggerated version of traditional femininity, feminists "convert a form of subordination into an affirmation, and thus begin to thwart it" (Irigaray, 1977/1985, p. 76). Mimicry works by demonstrating the impropriety of "a masculine logic" that defines women in univocal terms (Irigaray, 1977/1985, p. 76). The challenge involved

in mimicry, then, is to expose the incongruity of a normative standard without being "reduced to it" (Irigaray, 1977/1985, p. 76). The Guerrilla Girls' name, appearance, and visual style all illustrate how feminists can subvert a static definition of femininity through mimicry. Their comic transgression of the binaries that sustain such a standard places femininity within the lens of a fun-house mirror, as Burke would say—at the "reverse end" of one's glass (1954, p. 120). The perspective by incongruity engendered by such a view fractures associations between the feminine, passivity, and subordination that maintain patriarchy.

Like other marginalized groups that reclaim the names and epithets used against them, the Guerrilla Girls' reclamation of the term "girl," as well as all things girlish, demonstrates how mimicry functions as a strategy of incongruity (Allen & Faigley, 1995, pp. 152–153). When asked if labeling themselves "girls" stands in contradiction to their feminist politics, Guerrilla Girl Frida Kahlo explained, "Calling a grown woman a girl can imply she's not complete, mature, or grown up. But we decided to reclaim the word 'girl,' so it couldn't be used against us" (1995, p. 14). This process of reclamation is not limited to the group's name, however. The Guerrilla Girls' signature color is pink and is featured in their posters, postcards, and fliers. For example, the Guerrilla Girls combined a pink background with a decorative script, deferential language, and even a dainty (albeit frowning) flower sketched at the top of their 1986 poster that targeted art collectors; the poster's text read, "Dearest Art Collector, It has come to our attention that your collection, like most, does not contain enough art by women. We know you feel terrible about this and will rectify the situation immediately. All our love, Guerrilla Girls." The Guerrilla Girls' compliant tone and curlicue script mocked the equivalence between femininity and passivity while concomitantly violating that very association. The posters, even sugarcoated in pink, were part of a guerrilla assault on a system that long encouraged women artists to conceal any references to their history and experiences as a woman (Chadwick, 1990). The Guerrilla Girls wield femininity as a weapon, and in so doing, not only make "'assets' out of 'liabilities'" but also mock the contradictions inherent in a logic that dismisses women's contributions to art (Burke, 1937/1984, p. 171).

A natural extension of the Guerrilla Girls' strategic playfulness with norms of femininity is their use of sexually charged language and innuendo. For instance, many Guerrilla Girl performances begin with an audiotape. The voice, which mimics Marilyn Monroe's breathiness, advises the "boys" in the audience to protest the "drastic NEA cuts" by sending their "schlongs," wrapped up "real pretty," to the office of Senator Jesse Helms—a popular target for the group. As the men in the audience squirm, the Monroesque voice purrs, "We know it makes you uncomfortable. It's not easy handing your reproductive organ over to the federal government. But take it from us girls, you'll get used to it" (Guerrilla Girls, 1995, p. 27). By attempting to seduce male listeners to symbolically identify against themselves, the Guerrilla Girls recontextualize the reproductive rights afforded to women and men. Moreover, the contrast of ribald expressions with the subversive citation of Monroe's voice works to simultaneously entice and unsettle audiences. The Guerrilla Girls further challenge a static, essentializing vision of femininity with their playful blurring of binaries. Systems of representation regarding gender, race, sexuality, even human dominance over animals, are interrupted, resignified, and turned upside down by the group's jungle drag. According to Guerrilla lore, the decision to use the mask as a disguise came only after a Guerrilla Girl misspelled "guerrilla" as "gorilla." Viewed as an "enlightened mistake," Guerrilla Girl Käthe Kollwitz recast the spelling error as an opportunity to challenge the male/female binary by deeming the misspelling the source of the group's "mask-ulinity" (1995, p. 15). The group's masks, like its members, are diverse. Some are ferocious, fangs exposed, while others appear to be smiling, almost mocking. The diversity of masks used by members also underscores the group's commitment to a multicultural membership. Some gorillas are albino, whereas others have facial features ranging in color from mahogany to sable. The aggressiveness suggested by the gorilla/guerrilla association and the mask's beastly countenance stands in direct contrast to the exaggerated femininity embodied in the group's press photos and

performances. Although some Guerrilla Girls make appearances in the art-world uniform of "nondescript, bohemian black clothes," others don fishnets and stilettoes. One Guerrilla Girl explains, "Wearing these clothes [short skirts and high heels] with a gorilla mask confounds the stereotype of female sexiness" (1995, p. 15). At a Guerrilla Girl performance, then, one may find the "girls" in everything from micro minies and stilettoes to a maternity dress. Recent press photos feature an even newer look for the Guerrilla Girls—non-western attire such as serapes (Goldstein, 1998, p. 47). The mix of masks and jungle drag allows the Guerrilla Girls to go wild with the strictures that have defined women in direct relation to their bodies and "natural instincts." In so doing, the goal is not simply reinterpreting the feminine but "jamming the theoretical machinery itself, of suspending its pretension to the production of truth and of a meaning that are excessively univocal" (Irigaray, 1977/1985, p. 78). This process creates a perspective by incongruity that not only apes feminine conventions but also, as I will demonstrate in the next section, recasts women's place within art history.

Historical Revision

When art historian Linda Nochlin posed the now infamous question, "Why have there been no great women artists?" in her 1971 *Art News* essay, there was, in Nochlin's words, "no such thing as a feminist art history" (Nochlin, 1988, p. xi). The accomplishments of women artists appeared, if anywhere, in the footnotes of the artistic canon. Since Nochlin's essay, a number of inroads have been made. The recovery and revaluation of women artists from the past is just one example of the effect of feminist art history on the study of art. The question that now drives feminist art activists, particularly the Guerrilla Girls, is "Why haven't more women been considered great artists throughout Western history?" (1998, p. 7). Indeed, this question functions as the focal point for the 1998 book *The Guerrilla Girls Bedside Companion to the History of Art,* which surveys women artists from ancient Greece forward. The rhetorical style of the book, like the group's poster assault on sexism and racism, mixes humor with historical fact. The history by incongruity engendered by the group's re-vision violates the conventions (pieties) that have made the term "woman artist" an oxymoron within the history of art.

From their beginnings in 1985, the Guerrilla Girls have understood the power of history. Karlyn Kohrs Campbell's words provide a fitting description of the group's attitude toward history when she writes that "women's history is a profound resource: similarly, ignorance of such history confounds interpretations of discourse by and about women of the past" (Campbell, 1998, p. 115). In the years since their inception, the group has tried to avenge the omission of women artists from art history textbooks and museum exhibitions by both reintroducing women artists (past and present) into the public view and exposing the legacy of art world discrimination. One of the group's earliest attempts to subvert the canon of Western art history was to reintroduce the names of dead, under-acknowledged women artists as a way to distinguish between Guerrilla Girls. For example, Guerrilla Girl Rosie Camera took on the name of an underappreciated 17th-century Venetian court artist listed in a footnote in Rainer Maria Rilke's *Letters to Cézanne.* By adopting the names of under-acknowledged women, the group draws attention to the historical and creative contributions often unrecognized by canonical surveys such as Janson's *History of Art* and Gardner's *Art Through the Ages.* Ultimately, this process of planned incongruity through naming reclaims women's history as an inventive resource while debunking the justifying myth that women lack the sensibilities and skills necessary to be "great artists."

The Guerrilla Girls Bedside Companion to the History of Art also serves as a recovery project, albeit with a twist. The book juxtaposes short biographical sketches of artists overlooked in the canonical surveys of art history with cartoons, top-ten lists, and "believe it or not" quotations that dramatize the formal and informal barriers women artists have faced throughout time (Guerrilla Girls, 1998, back cover). As a rhetorical work, the book is structured to disrupt "our sense of what properly goes with what" (Burke, 1954, p. 74). By attaching irreverent titles to "serious subjects" and a sarcastically whimsical tone to the history of art, the Guerrilla Girls mock the artistic canon and "provide

ammunition for all the women who are—or will become—artists" (1998, p. 9). The perspective by incongruity offered throughout prompts new answers to old questions regarding the history of women artists.

Feminist arguments that the personal is political radicalized the women's liberation movement during the 1960s. The Guerrilla Girls' use of fictionalized narratives in their 1998 book has a similar effect on the history of art. From imagined conversations with twentieth-century African-American artist Augusta Savage to a posthumous letter addressed to the Guerrilla Girls by eighteenth century artist Élisabeth Vigée-Lebrun, fictive exchanges within the book dramatize the struggles faced by women artists because of their gender and race. The intimate tone used in "correspondences" between artists and readers evokes identification across time. For example, the two-page conversation between the Guerrilla Girls and Augusta Savage fictionalizes some of the artist's most painful memories about being an African-American artist during the days of Jim Crow:

[No gallery] would show the work of living black artists for fear that the artists and their friends would hang around the gallery and no white folks would come. Under pressure, some caved in and proposed special evening hours for "colored people." How insulting. You had to have a lot of courage as a black woman to set foot in museums, too. At the State Fair in New Jersey, black artists were shown in the same section as the mentally impaired. The Museum of Modern Art always showed lots of African art because it made the modern white boys look good, but show African-American artists? It was out of the question. (Guerrilla Girls, 1998, p. 76)

In addition to being historically accurate, this imagined recollection not only publicizes but also personalizes the history of discrimination absent from most surveys of art. The implied message suggested by such remembrances is that the history of art has been, for the most part, a rigged game. This perspective challenges conventional criteria for gauging who is included and omitted from the history books by reminding readers that making art "is not a free autonomous activity of a super-endowed individual" (Nochlin, 1988, p. 158).

Indeed, one aim of the book is to enact an understanding of

> the total situation of art making, both in terms of the development of the art maker and in the nature and quality of the work itself . . . [that] are mediated and determined by specific and definable social institutions, be they art academic, systems of patronage, mythologics of the divine creator, artist as he-man, or social outcast. (Nochlin, 1988, p. 158)

If such imagined conversations provide a glimpse at the "personal," then snapshots of how custom, laws, and culture shaped women's lives offer insight into how the "political" has restricted art-making. By situating women's accomplishments in relation to their historical context, the Guerrilla Girls foreground the institutional barriers that legislated women's artistic silence. Such an approach, as Nochlin suggested in her classic 1971 essay, exposes "the entire romantic, elitist, individual-glorifying, and monograph-producing substructure upon which the profession of art history is based" (p. 153). In contrast, the history by incongruity fashioned by the Guerrilla Girls' irreverent and personal approach to history challenges both the evidence and organizing logic of the question, "Why have there been no great women artists?" Their personification of under-acknowledged women artists not only serves as a tribute to the artists' achievements, but also contradicts the myth that women lack artistic genius. Even more importantly, however, the group's emphasis on social and institutional conditions for producing great art confounds the very notion of artistic genius that structures the canonical approach to art history. The group's reliance on perspective by incongruity to dramatize social conditions is not limited to their critique of art history, however. As the following section reveals, the Guerrilla Girls also employ perspective by incongruity to redress contemporary forms of institutionalized inequality both inside and outside the art world.

Strategic Juxtaposition

Strategic juxtaposition constitutes a mainstay of both Burke's comic corrective and feminist rhetoric (Christiansen & Hanson, 1996; Powell, 1995). Characterized as a strategy for social change, juxtaposition "brings together in a state of tension the discourses of two or more status groups" (Allen & Faigley, 1995, p. 159). The strategy of juxtaposition works on a number of levels within the Guerrilla Girls' visual rhetoric. As Kimberly Powell notes, groups use juxtaposition to remoralize the social order by "placing conflicting commitments of the system side by side" (Powell, 1995, p. 94). The Guerrilla Girls accomplish this goal by employing three forms of juxtaposition. First, the group juxtaposes quotations from individuals and institutions with ironic headers that underscore the incongruity of conservative positions on rape, abortion, as well as gay and lesbian rights. For example, the Guerrilla Girls' 1992 poster, "SUPREME COURT JUSTICE SUPPORTS RIGHT TO PRIVACY FOR GAYS AND LESBIANS," pairs an image of Justice Thomas at his 1991 hearings with an excerpt from his testimony:

> I'm not going to engage in discussions of what goes on in the most intimate parts of my private life or the sanctity of my bedroom. They are the most intimate parts of my privacy and will remain just that.

Unwilling to leave the implications of such a juxtaposition up for grabs, the Guerrilla Girls offer their own conclusion: "Clarence Thomas claims that a person's sex life is none of the government's business." Second, the group juxtaposes images with rhetorical questions to denaturalize conventional frames of reference. For example, one of the 1991 posters produced by the group to oppose the Gulf War juxtaposed an image of a female solider with the question: "DID SHE RISK HER LIFE FOR GOVERNMENTS THAT ENSLAVE WOMEN?" The text/image juxtaposition recontextualizes the propriety of the U.S. military commitment to countries who deny women basic rights. Finally, by mixing dominant cultural symbols such as the *Mona Lisa* and Jean Auguste Dominique Ingres's *Grande Odalisque* with the Guerrilla Girls' unique brand of feminist aesthetics, the group exposes the hypocrisies of the art world and social politics. Although these varied forms of juxtaposition appear in much of the group's visual rhetoric, two broadsides in particular showcase how juxtaposition functions as a strategy of incongruity: the Guerrilla Girls' 1989 critique of the Metropolitan Museum's exhibition record and the group's 1991 anti-Gulf War poster.

During the fall of 1989, the Guerrilla Girls asked museum-goers a question they would not soon forget: "Do women have to be naked to get into the Met. Museum?" In so doing, the group concomitantly created an image that would become one of its most lasting icons—the gorilla-masked odalisque (Figure 1). The odalisque figure, appropriated from Jean Auguste Dominique Ingres's 1814 painting of the *Grand Odalisque,* anchors the poster and is positioned in opposition to the bold-face punch-line that reads: "Less than 3% of the artists in the Modern Art Sections are women, but 83% of the nudes are female." Unlike the figure in Ingres's painting, this odalisque dons a gorilla mask. The text/image juxtaposition and implied contrast between the Ingres and Guerrilla Girl odalisque create an argument by incongruity that challenges art world claims of gender equality.

Historically, the image of Ingres's odalisque, like its twentieth-century twin, created controversy. Although Ingres was called "the conservator of good and true art" from the mid-1820s forward, upon completion of the painting in 1814, he was highly criticized for creating a painting deemed "primitive" (Croix & Turner, 1986, p. 824). The reclining nude, a common *topos* for painters from Titian forward, was made exotic by Ingres when he depicted the figure as an inhabitant of a Turkish harem. The artist's reliance on a cool palette for this languid figure makes the deadened stare of his kept woman even more vulnerable. With her back to the viewer, breast partially revealed, the odalisque waits, submissive and indifferent.

In stark comparison, the Guerrilla Girls' odalisque rests on a bed of cranberry colored sheets and dons a gorilla mask. The dark background of the painting, which frames the odalisque, is now recast in the shade of banana yellow. The fan that Ingres's odalisque once held now appears strikingly similar to an erect penis. A sack-like shape, moreover, is attached to the handle of the fan. Indeed, the Guerrilla Girls transformed Ingres's vision of "idealized female beauty" into an "exotic" nude with a dangerous bite. The teeth on the gorilla mask are outlined, making them more noticeable and ferocious. By appropriating Ingres's odalisque, the Guerrilla Girls illustrate how history can be re-presented. Yet in order to represent their vision of idealized female beauty, the Guerrilla Girls must not only appropriate the odalisque image but also mark it. Ingres's odalisque is a classic symbol of patriarchal art; by defacing it, the Guerrilla Girls use the odalisque to critique the very institutions that canonize such images. Their juxtaposition of symbols produced by the dominant (male) culture with feminist imagery calls into question the ideological construction of idealized femininity as submissive.

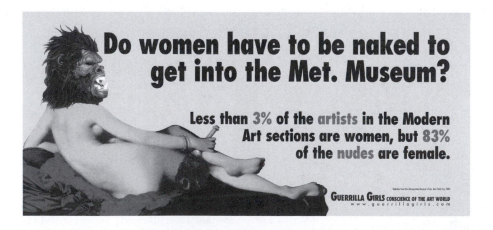

Figure 1   "Do women have to be naked to get into the Met. Museum?" (1989).

SOURCE: Reprinted with permission of the Guerrilla Girls (www.guerrillagirls.com).

After leading viewers on, or rather toward, one way of conceptualizing how women artists "get into" the Met, the group abruptly shifts the frame. The dramatic margin of difference between the percentage of women artists exhibited and the number of nude female figures displayed foregrounds the legacy of objectification within the artistic canon. Historically, women have been limited to three roles: muse, model, or object. The suggestion that, even in 1989, a woman has better chances of appearing on gallery walls as a nude model rather than an artist dramatizes the art world entailments of institutionalized sexism. The group's tactical use of color further emphasizes the point. By juxtaposing the submissive figure with the gorilla's growling countenance, the group highlights the disparity revealed in the hot pink punchline accents—3% artists, 83% nudes. In addition, the banana-yellow backdrop attracts the viewer even from a distance. The tactical use of the cranberry color for the "fan" and sheets may even suggest that the odalisque holds a severed penis, since from a distance the "fan" seems to bleed into a larger pool of burgundy.

Does this image suggest a castrating, gorilla-masked odalisque? Such an interpretation would certainly reframe—if not completely subvert—the art world's conception of the submissive muse.

In addition to targeting individuals and institutions within the art community, the Guerrilla Girls made an initial foray into the political arena with a 1989 poster addressed to Senator Jesse Helms. By 1991, the Guerrilla Girls began to aim their attacks at the nation's political leader—President George Bush (Figure 2). Like many of their more political posters, the Bush broadside is structured by two title/image juxtapositions. First, the poster contrasts the bold-face heading, "George Bush, 'The Education President,'" with an image of countless military graves crowned with commencement caps to dramatize the contradictions of Bush's education policy. This somewhat atypical graduation portrait implies that during Bush's tenure as the "education president," students will bear a heavy cross—their lives. The cruciform markers imbue the image with patriotic and religious weight and undermine Bush's campaign emphasis on education.

Figure 2 "George Bush, 'The Education President'" (1991).

SOURCE: Reprinted with permission of the Guerrilla Girls (www.guerrillagirls.com).

A second juxtaposition further questions the motives behind military recruitment efforts that targeted poor Americans. The incongruity engendered by the contrast of the graveyard backdrop and caption, "Many poor Americans join the Army to get an education and a better life," puts an insidious spin on military recruiting rhetoric used since World War II (Boyd, 1998, p. 128). Even as the broadside emphasizes the opportunities that military service offers to "disadvantage" Americans, the poster's backdrop engenders a uniquely unpatriotic point of view—a view further punctuated by the concluding question, "If Bush had a *real* policy for public education, who would fight his wars?" When the poster first appeared in public, favorable media coverage of the Gulf War was flooding airwaves. Within this context, the conflicting image created by the Guerrilla Girls denaturalized the patriotic slant so often attached to military service. More specifically, the poster's image/text juxtapositions underscored the government's vested interest in maintaining a subordinate class. Having "shattered" the piety attached to military service (as an answer to the war on poverty), the group suggested another solution—a *real* policy for public education. Although the Bush broadside represents a broadening of targets beyond art, the group's continued reliance on strategic juxtaposition attests to its potential as an effective tool for social critique.

The three strategies discussed in this section enable the Guerrilla Girls to dramatize the patterns and conventions that sustain a culture of denial regarding gender inequality (see Rhode, 1997). As my analysis illustrates, the Guerrilla Girls' use of mimicry unhinges the social equivalence between femininity and passivity. Their playfully ironic brand of femininity redefines popular images of feminism. One important element in this redefinition, moreover, is the Guerrilla Girls' re-vision of art history. This re-vision not only functions as a recovery process bul also exposes the contradictions traditionally glossed in the making of art history. Finally, the Guerrilla Girls employ strategic juxtapositions to denaturalize the patterns of discrimination institutionalized in both the artistic community as well as political and popular culture. Taken together, these three strategies create a perspective by incongruity that exposes the difference between equality in the abstract and inequality in practice.

CONCLUSION: A COMIC POLITICS OF SUBVERSION

Perspective by incongruity engenders social change by highlighting contradictions in the social order. For the Guerrilla Girls, perspective by incongruity is the most agile rhetorical strategy for confronting the myths and denials of institutionalized sexism. Even as the group shatters one system of pieties, or frame of reference, they ready audiences/viewers for another.

At the most basic level, all of the group's strategies of incongruity (mimicry, re-vision of history, and strategic juxtaposition) undermine the assumption of achieved equality, or as the Guerrilla Girls put it: "Today women are equal, right?" (1998, p. 90). Not quite. In dramatizing different forms of gender and racial inequality, the group enacts alternative visions based on diversity and social justice. Mimicry exaggerates norms of femininity to the point of rupturing the very logic that naturalizes the association between femininity, passivity, and objectification. This exaggeration also functions as a reappropriation of sorts by creating a new empowered frame of reference that fuses feminism with femininity. In addition, the group's irreverent and inventive approach to history demystifies the masculinized mythology of artist-genius. In so doing, the group not only advances a definition of art that is sensitive to the conditions productive of great art but also enacts a world-view best reflected in one of the group's 1989 posters, which read "YOU'RE SEEING LESS THAN HALF THE PICTURE without the vision of women artists and artists of color." Finally, strategic juxtaposition dramatizes the incongruity of assumed equality in the face of institutionalized inequalities. As examples of feminist "atom-cracking," each strategy subjects the language and ideology of patriarchy to a "'cracking' process" that wrenches apart the language and mythologies of institutionalized sexism so as to enable a "fresh point of view, the heuristic or perspective value of a planned incongruity" (Burke, 1954, pp. 119, 121).

When framed comically, perspective by incongruity establishes a frame of acceptance that remoralizes a situation through "charitable debunking" rather than revolution (Burke, 1937/1984, p. 166; Carlson, 1988, p. 310). Although their appropriation of the "guerrilla" namesake may suggest otherwise, my analysis demonstrates that the Guerrilla Girls seek to gain equal access into the system, not to overturn it altogether. In an interview published in *Art in America,* the group argues that to

> actually change the system is so unbelievably complex that at this point, our interest, as we have already said, is in getting women more access to it. So that's our attitude about change, as opposed to breaking down the system. (Gablik, 1994, p. 47)

This attitude is evident throughout the Guerrilla Girls' rhetoric, which casts censurable acts as entailments of human fallibility rather than evil. Their posters and performances operate as public scoldings that seek to embarrass rather than scapegoat or spark violence. By casting the failure to live up to communal ideals in a comic light, the Guerrilla Girls are able to restructure the master's house without leveling it first. The end goal, as Barry Brummett notes, is "awareness of these contradictions and of the harm to society that they cause" (1984, p. 220). This objective motivates all of the group's projects, explains one Guerrilla Girl in her 1999 web page travel diary: "Our M.O. has always been to upset people a bit, then get them to listen and change their minds. It worked!" (1999).

Although the Guerrilla Girls' success is impossible to quantify, their longevity and visibility do indicate that the group has made an impact. Their online site and 1995 book, *Confessions of the Guerrilla Girls,* include letters and emails from both fans and foes—testaments to the group's influence and capacity to spark dialogue. Feminists such as Susan Faludi, Robin Morgan, and Lucy Lippard cite the group as a model. bell hooks, for example, writes that "the work of the Guerrilla Girls represents a most powerful political union between theory and practice. They set an example for feminists everywhere" (Guerrilla Girls, 1999). Another compelling testament comes from the numerous art world targets who, like Museum of Modern Art Director of Paintings and Sculpture Kirk Varnedoe, assert that the Guerrilla Girls are "are prime consciousness raisers and they do it in a way that's effective, with wit in all senses of the word" (Guerrilla Girls, 1995, p. 99). Since the group's inception in 1985, "jungle fever" has spread across the globe with the emergence of Guerrilla Girls West in San Francisco, Guerrilla Girls MA & PA in Boston and Paris, Las Chicas Guerrilleras in Barcelona and Palme Girls in Stockholm (Guerrilla Girls, 1995, p. 94).

An important key to the group's influence in the art community as well as for feminist politics is the Guerrilla Girls' visual format. Despite the growing literature on comic strategies of social change, few have considered how such strategies work in visual forms (Christiansen & Hanson, 1996). My analysis contributes to this line of inquiry by demonstrating how the Guerrilla Girls' visual rhetoric facilitates a comic perspective. First, the broadside format is non-threatening yet emphatic. Second, the mix of outlandish imagery and statistics forms a credible hyperbole that raises consciousness about the inadequacies of the social order without scapegoating. Finally, the group's visual style maximizes the resources of popular culture—specifically an advertising aesthetic—in order to foster identification with those who would typically reject or ignore feminist rhetoric. "We have fun playing around with our image," one Guerrilla Girls explains, "We are aware that there are people who have a very negative take on the word 'feminist,' but we're not about to do away with the word . . . We are trying to get across a certain amount of humor—that's one way in which you engage people" (O'Neil, 1990, p. 11). In sum, the coupling of comic subversion and visual rhetoric opens up both how and where feminist resistance happens.

Since the 1848 Seneca Falls women's rights convention, activists advocating for gender equality have often been denied conventional forums for bringing their message to the people. As a result, feminist rhetoric frequently occurs away from the platforms and statehouses of government. Feminist scholarship in rhetorical studies, as Bonnie Dow reminds us, "must turn its attention to the variety of contexts in which feminist struggle occurs" (Dow, 1997, p. 104). This study reveals how one group of feminist art activists, the Guerrilla Girls, responded to their institutional constraints by making the streets of New York their canvas. Even the group's most recent action—a sticker produced prior to the Academy Awards that scolds Hollywood for its record for nominating women directors by asking "AS GOOD AS IT GETS?"—advocates transforming movie theater bathroom stalls into sites of feminist consciousness-raising. Although unconventional and decidedly impious, the Guerrilla Girls' comic politics of subversion demonstrates the interplay between visual rhetoric, feminist resistance and social change. Further exploration of the capabilities and constraints of visual strategies of incongruity are needed, however. Be it at the podium, on the streets, even in fake fur, the rhetoric of feminist resistance, while not always recognized, lurks throughout the jungle of cultural politics.

NOTES

1. Although appropriation functions as both a related process to strategies of incongruity and implied element within particular manifestations of the Guerrilla Girls' rhetoric, the unifying strategy that runs throughout the group's work as a whole is more aptly described by the entailments of perspective by incongruity. For an excellent discussion of appropriation as a feminist rhetorical tool see Radner & Lanser (1993) and Shugart (1997).

2. This free play with symbolic codes, however has its costs. Responding to the charge that the masks reproduce racist constructions, the group maintains that in using the gorilla mask, they are "exploding stereotypes" (Guerrilla Girls, 1995, p. 23). Guerrilla Girl Mela Tuller even makes the argument that, "There is nothing second rate or inferior about the gorilla and to think so is Homo-sapiens-centric" (1995, p. 23).

REFERENCES

Allen, J., & Faigley, L. (1995). Discursive strategies for social change: An alternative rhetoric for argument. *Rhetoric Review, 14,* 142–172.

Boyd. C. (1998, February). Careers in the military *Black Collegian, 28,* 128, 166.

Brummett, B. (1984). Burkean comedy and tragedy, illustrated in reactions to the arrest of John De Lorean. *Central States Speech Journal, 35,* 217–227.

Brummett, B. (1994). *Rhetoric in popular culture.* New York: St. Martin's Press.

Burke, K. (1954). *Permanence and change: An anatomy of purpose.* Los Altos. CA: Hermes Publication.

Burke, K. (1984/1937). *Attitudes toward history (3rd ed.).* Berkeley: University of California Press. (Original work published in 1937).

Campbell, K. K. (1998). Inventing women: From Amaterasu to Virginia Woolf. *Women's Studies in Communication, 21,* 111–126.

Carlson, A. C. (1986). Gandhi and the comic frame: "Ad bellum purificandum." *The Quarterly Journal of Speech, 72,* 446–455.

Carlson, A. C. (1988). Limitations on the comic frame: Sonic witty American women of the nineteenth century. *The Quarterly Journal of Speech, 74,* 310–322.

Carlson, A. C. (1992). Creative casuistry and feminist consciousness: The rhetoric of moral reform. *The Quarterly Journal of Speech, 78,* 16–32.

Chadwick, W. (1995). Women who run with the brushes and glue. In *Confessions of the guerrilla girls* (pp. 7–11). New York: Harper Perennial.

Chadwick, C. (1990). *Women, art, and society.* London: Thames and Hudson.

Christiansen, A., & Hanson, J. (1996). Comedy as cure for tragedy: ACT UP and the rhetoric of AIDS. *The Quarterly Journal of Speech, 82,* 157–170.

Croix, H., & Tansey, R. (1986). *Gardner's art through the ages (8th ed.).* New York: Harcourt Brace Jovanovich Publishers.

Dow, B. (1994) AIDS, perspective by incongruity, and gay identity in Larry Kramer's "1,112 and Counting." *Communication Studies, 45,* 225–240.

Dow, B. (1997). Feminism, cultural studies and rhetorical studies. *The Quarterly Journal of Speech, 83,* 90–131.

Duncan, H. D. (1962). *Communication and social order.* London: Oxford University Press.

Feldstein, M. (1994, February 20). *Gender wars: Part two.* Atlanta: CNN.

Gablik. S. (1994). 'We spell it like the freedom fighters': A conversation with the guerrilla girls. *Art in America, 82,* 43–47.

Goldstein. R. (1998. February 24). Aping power. *The Village Voice, 43,* 47–48.

Guerrilla Girls. (1999). Dear diary: Travels with the Guerrilla Girls. Guerrilla Girls: Facts, humor and fake fur [web page] Available: http://www.guerrillagirls.com/travels/diary_index.html.

Guerrilla Girls. (1998). *The guerrilla girls' bedside companion to the history of western art.* New York: Penguin Books.

Guerrilla Girls. (1995). *Confessions of the guerrilla girls.* New York: Harper Perennial.

Gusfield. J. (Ed.). (1989). *Kenneth Burke: On symbols and society.* Chicago: University of Chicago Press.

Ingres, J. A. D. (1814). *Grand odalisque.* Louvre, Paris.

Irigaray, L. (1985). The power of discourse and the subordination of the feminine. In *This sex which is not one* (Catherine Porter, trans.) (pp. 68–85). Ithaca: Cornell University Press. (Original work published in 1977).

Lederer, C. (1991). *Guerrilla girls talk back: The first five years.* Falkirk, CA: Falkirk Cultural Center.

Loughery, J. (1987). Mrs. Holladay and the guerrilla girls. *Arts Magazine, 62,* 61–65.

Moore, L. (1972). Statement for the first women's liberation show at the Woodstock Gallery, March 1–13, 1972. *Towards a Revolutionary Feminist Art, 1,* 1.

Morgan, R. (1970). *Sisterhood is powerful: An anthology of writing from the women's liberation movement.* New York: Random House.

Nochlin, L. (1988). Why have there been no great women artists. In Linda Nochlin (Ed.), *Women, art, and power and other essays* (145–178). New York: Harper & Row.

O'Neil, K. (1990. December 17). Striking at sexism in the art world. *Christian Science Monitor,* p. 10–11.

Powell, K. (1995). The association of southern women for the prevention of lynching: Strategies of a movement in the comic frame. *Communication Quarterly, 43,* 86–99.

Radner, J., & Lanser, S. (1993). Strategies of coding. In J. Radner (Ed.), *Feminist messages: Coding in women's folk culture* (pp. 1–29). Urbana: University of Illinois Press.

Rhode, D. (1997). *Speaking of sex: The denial of gender inequality.* Cambridge, MA: Harvard University Press.

Rosteck, T., & Leff, M. (1989). Piety, propriety, and perspective: An interpretation and application of key terms in Kenneth Burke's Permanence and Change. *Western Journal of Speech Communication, 53,* 327–341.

Rueckert, W. H. (1990). Criticism as a way of life or criticism as equipment for living. *Kenneth Burke Society Newsletter, 6.2,* 7–15.

Sayre, H. (1989). A New Person(a). In *The object of performance: The American avant-garde since 1970* (66–100). Chicago: University of Chicago Press.

Schor, M. (1990). Just the facts ma'am. *Artforum, 29,* 124–127.

Shugart, H. (1997). Counterhegemonic acts: Appropriation as a feminist rhetorical strategy. *The Quarterly Journal of Speech, 83,* 210–229.

Withers, J. (1988). The guerrilla girls. *Feminist Studies, 14,* 284–291.

13

BEHOLD THE CORPSE

Violent Images and the Case of Emmett Till

CHRISTINE HAROLD AND KEVIN MICHAEL DELUCA

We do not know what the body can do.

Spinoza

Society is concerned to tame the Photograph, to temper the madness which keeps threatening to explode in the face of whoever looks at it.

Roland Barthes

If the men who killed Emmett Till had known his body would free a people, they would have let him live.

Reverend Jesse Jackson Sr.

"I had to get through this. There would be no second chance to get through this. I noticed that none of Emmett's body was scarred. It was bloated, the skin was loose, but there were no scars, no signs of violence anywhere. Until I got to his chin.

When I got to his chin, I saw his tongue resting there. It was huge. I never imagined that a human tongue could be that big. Maybe it was the effect of the water, since he had been in the river for several days, or maybe the heat. But as I gazed at the tongue, I couldn't help but think that it had been choked out of his mouth. I forced myself to move on, to keep going one small section at a time, as if taking this gruesome task in small doses could somehow make it less excruciating. . . . From the chin I moved up to his right cheek. There was an eyeball

SOURCE: Harold, C., & DeLuca, K. M. (2005). Behold the corpse: Violent images and the case of Emmett Till. *Rhetoric & Public Affairs, 8*(2), 263–286, published by Michigan State University Press.

hanging down, resting on that cheek. . . . It was that light hazel brown everyone always thought was so pretty. Right away, I looked to the other eye. But it wasn't there. It seemed like someone had taken a nut picker and plucked that one out. . . . [His nose] had been chopped, maybe with a meat cleaver. It looked as if someone had tenderized his nose."[1]

When Mamie Till Bradley entered Chicago's A. A. Rayner and Sons funeral home in 1955 to identify the mutilated corpse of her 14-year-old son, Emmett, she could not have prepared herself for what she would see. Less than two weeks earlier, she had put her son on a train to begin a journey that would take him from Chicago to Money, Mississippi, where he was to spend two weeks of his summer vacation visiting his relatives. As they said their goodbyes, she gave the precocious teenager a quick lesson in how to behave as a young black man in the South: "'[do] not hesitate to humble yourself,' she advised the boy, '[even] if you [have] to get down on your knees.'"[2]

The facts remain hopelessly inconsistent as to whether or not Emmett took his mother's advice when he bought a pack of bubblegum from Carolyn Bryant, the 21-year-old wife of a Money shopkeeper, on the evening of August 24, 1955. While most descriptions of the event agree that Till wanted to impress his new Mississippi friends by taking their dare to flirt with Bryant, they differ over the degree to which he made good on the wager. By some accounts, he "made advances [and] tried to block her path" and even "put his hands on her waist, and in a lewd manner propositioned her."[3] Another account suggests that Till merely said, "Gee. You look like a movie star."[4] Bryant herself testified that Till "called her 'baby' and another unsavory name, and 'wolf whistled' at her.[5] Till's friends recall that he simply said 'bye, baby' as he exited the store."[6] Despite the disparate versions of the exchange between Emmett Till and Carolyn Bryant, one fact is indisputable: the events of that evening led to one of the most brutal and most publicized race murders in American history.[7]

Although there is increasing evidence the killers did not act alone, most people familiar with the Till case believe that the boy was slain by the two men charged with his murder: Roy Bryant and J. W. Milam, Carolyn Bryant's husband and his half-brother. Even the jurors "later confessed that not a single member of the panel doubted the defendants were guilty of murder."[8] However, the all-white, all-male jury found the two brothers not guilty after little more than an hour of deliberations. *Emerge* magazine reports that they would have rendered an innocent verdict even sooner, but the town's sheriff-elect sent a message to jurors telling them "that they should wait a while before announcing their verdicts to make it 'look good.'"[9] Amazingly, Bryant and Milam later confessed to the murder to a journalist for *Look* magazine in exchange for $4,000.[10]

In 1955, the photographic image of Emmett Till's corpse put a shocking and monstrous face on the most brutal extremes of American racial injustice. The grainy image was widely circulated in the black press, and thousands of mourners viewed his body directly at the funeral home. The imagery of the Till case—the grisly image of his corpse, but also the image of a happy Emmett in his Christmas suit, the image of his mother's anguished face as she watched his casket lowered into the ground, the image of Till's elderly uncle publicly identifying one of the murderers in the courtroom, bravely declaring "dar he," and images of the segregated Mississippi courtroom in which African American community members, journalists, and a congressman were herded into an unventilated corner in the sweltering summer heat—became a crucial visual *vocabulary* that articulated the ineffable qualities of American racism in ways words simply could not do. As we will suggest, the imagery of the case, and that of Till's corpse specifically, served as a political catalyst for black Americans in the then-fledgling civil rights movement.

The visceral imagery of the Till murder refuses to be filed away in a dusty archive of American civil rights history. In 2004, nearly 50 years after the original trial, the Justice Department reopened the Till murder case. U.S. senator from New York Charles Schumer, a champion of the reinvestigation, has said, "The murder of Emmett Till was one of the seminal moments in our nation's civil-rights movement and the failure to bring his murderers to justice remains a stain on America's record of reconciliation," and hence he and others called on U.S. Attorney General John Ashcroft to "fulfill the promise he made at his confirmation hearings to fully enforce America's civil-rights laws. In this rare instance, justice delayed may not be justice denied."[11] The case of Emmett Till continues to demand justice, largely because his killers were never punished for the crime, despite their post-trial confession. As we will suggest, however, the haunting images surrounding the case should not be overlooked as a crucial component of its continued rhetorical force. As Schumer suggests, they continue to "stain" America's dream of itself.

Renewed interest in the case has been sparked, in part, by the investigative work of documentary filmmaker Keith Beauchamp, who spent most of the 1990s researching the case for his film *The Untold Story of Emmett Louis Till.* Beauchamp interviewed a number of eyewitnesses who claim that as many as ten people may have been involved in the Till murder, some of whom are still alive.[12] In 2003, PBS aired another documentary, *The Murder of Emmett Till,* as part of its *American Experience* series, and Random House published Mamie Till-Mobley's *Death of Innocence: The Story of the Hate Crime That Changed America.* Mrs. Till-Mobley passed away while touring in promotion of the book, less than a year before her dream of the case's being reopened was realized.

These projects came on the heels of the powerful book *Without Sanctuary: Lynching Photography in America,* a collection of photographs that continues to tour U.S. museums and galleries. The *New York Times* review of the book rightly describes the timelessness of such graphic images:

> These images make the past present. They refute the notion that photographs of charged historical subjects lose their power, softening and becoming increasingly aesthetic with time. These images are not going softly into any artistic realm. Instead they send shock waves through the brain, implicating ever larger chunks of American society and in many ways reaching up to the present. They give one a deeper and far sadder understanding of what it has meant to be white and to be black in America. And what it still means.[13]

In other words, lynching images, such as those of Emmett Till, are too visually provocative, too viscerally challenging, to be contained by time or distance.

In this essay, we explore the role of a particular image that has had an electrifying effect on many Americans. The "shock waves" produced by the corpse of Emmett Till in the mid-1950s continue to reverberate powerfully in the memory of those exposed to it. We suggest that they do so, in large part, because of the forcefulness of the image of the human body in peril. The dissemination and reception of this image—of the severely mutilated face of a child—illustrates the rhetorical and political force of images in general and of the body specifically. In what follows, we will first describe the rhetorical function of this image by exploring the dissemination of the photograph of Emmett Till within the context of the racial lynching tradition in the United States. We will then discuss the ways in which the images of the case served as a call to action for many of the African Americans who visually "consumed" them. Finally, we will explore the ways in which the African American community reinterpreted the horrible imagery of this brutalized black body. Whereas the black body in pain had traditionally served as a symbol of unmitigated white power, the corpse of Emmett Till became a visual trope illustrating the ugliness of racial violence and the aggregate power of the black community. We suggest that this reconfiguration was, in part, an effect of the black community's embracing and foregrounding Till's abject body rather than allowing it to be safely exiled from communal life.

THE BLACK BODY AT RISK: IMAGE RHETORIC AND RACE

> It would not be going too far to say that [Mrs. Till Bradley] ... invented the strategy that later became the [Southern Christian Leadership Council]'s signature gesture: literally *illustrating* southern atrocity with graphic images of black physical suffering, and disseminating those images nationally.
>
> Sasha Torres, *Black, White, and In Color*

The received rhetorical history of the civil rights movement has largely been a story of a people mobilized by the great speeches of charismatic leaders, most famously Martin Luther King Jr., but also Malcolm X, Stokely

Carmichael, Fannie Lou Hamer,[14] and others. In addition to this traditional story, we want to suggest that bodies, perhaps more than eloquence, moved a nation. Black bodies were at stake—their meaning, their treatment, their possibilities. Black bodies at risk were a crucial rhetorical resource for transforming the meaning and treatment of black bodies at large. Young African Americans in Birmingham, for example, being mercilessly battered by high-pressure fire hoses and attacked by police dogs, put on display the lengths to which institutionalized racism would go to maintain its dominance as well as the risks black citizens were willing to take to challenge it. Further, in an age when the "public screen" was emerging as a dominant venue for political action, American audiences were forced to confront the visual tropes of racial strife as never before.[15]

It is tempting to say that bodies at risk call out to an innate human empathy, but even the most cursory review of the historical record belies any such comforting notion. The record of atrocities in the twentieth century suggests that bodies at risk—even mutilated and tortured bodies—can inspire even greater barbarity. Although bodies at risk can have multiple meanings, they are undoubtedly a potent source of rhetorical power. That is, competing social groups will contend over the meanings of bodies. The witnessing of bodies retains a privileged authority, but the meaning of those bodies, what mute bodies say, is a site of political struggle. In the twentieth-century United States, black bodies comprised the bloodiest battleground.

Arguably, the regime of Jim Crow was the second act of the Civil War, a war over the meaning of black bodies continued by other means. Blacks were now "free," which, for many whites, made them all the more necessary to control and subordinate. Lynching was the most violent instrument of control. In her analysis of torture, Elaine Scarry argues that regimes create bodies in pain to make real their power and to anchor their ideological belief systems: "The physical pain is so incontestably real that it seems to confer its quality of 'incontestable reality' on that power that has brought it into being. It is, of course, precisely because the reality of that power is so highly contestable, the regime so unstable, that torture is being used."[16] As in torture, violence against black bodies materializes ideological beliefs. The incontestable reality of black bodies in pain was used to confer the status of incontestable reality onto the belief in white supremacy.

Under Jim Crow, lynched black bodies were offered as evidence of white supremacy. They were the "strange fruit" swinging in the Southern wind of racial hatred; their "bulging eyes and twisted mouths" mutely testifying to the horrible extremes of white power.[17] As the images in *Without Sanctuary* make clear, however, lynched and mutilated black bodies, far from inspiring sympathy, primarily inspired revelry and celebration among participating whites. Lynchings were public spectacles, carnivals of atrocity, so-called "Negro Barbecues," attended by prominent citizens, business leaders, elected officials, church members, judges, rednecks, peckerwoods, women, and children. Kodaks clicked as whites sought to preserve the moment and share it with others in the form of postcards. As the back of one such postcard reads, "This is the barbeque [*sic*] we had last night. My picture is to the left with a cross over it. Your son, Joe."[18] Another reads, "This was made in the court yard in Center Texas he is a 16 year old black boy. He killed Earl's Grandma. She was Florence's mother. Give this to Bud. From Aunt Myrtle."[19] In these lynching pictures, crowds of whites pose with the mutilated bodies. The crowd is often dressed in their Sunday best. Many smile for the camera. Women and children are present. Lynching was an *event,* an occasion to see, to be seen, and to memorialize for others.

Whites also clambered for keepsakes more grisly than the pictures. Before the Holbert couple was burned to death in Mississippi in 1904, for example, "The blacks were forced to hold out their hands while one finger at a time was chopped off. The fingers were distributed as souvenirs."[20] Two thousand white Georgians watched an equally gruesome scene, the lynching of Sam Hose: "before saturating Hose with oil and applying the torch, they cut off his ears, fingers, and genitals, and skinned his face. . . . Before Hose's body had even cooled, his heart and liver were removed and cut into several pieces and his bones were crushed into small particles. The crowd fought over these souvenirs."[21] The mobs turned victims' body parts into horrible mementos of the event, corporeal relics intended to preserve, to *re-present* what might otherwise have forever slipped into the past.

Lynched black bodies were spectacles of white supremacy that helped forge white community. They were also messages of warning and terror for black communities. Lynchings were violent acts with an explicitly rhetorical agenda: "The idea, after all, as one black observer noted, was to make an example, *'knowing full well that one Negro swinging from a tree will serve as well as another to terrorize the community.'*"[22] Lynchings served as a kind of racial terrorism, anchoring white supremacy in a mutilated black body. Often any black body would do. Indeed, family members of an accused black person were sometimes lynched alongside or in lieu of the accused person. When a white mob near Columbus, Mississippi, was frustrated in its efforts to find and lynch Cordelia Stevenson's son, for example, they "settled on his mother, seized and tortured her, and left her naked body hanging from the limb of a tree for public viewing."[23] Often, the pretext of an accusation was not even necessary. When a likely lynch mob participant was asked why a black man had been killed, he replied, "Oh, because he was a nigger. And he was the best nigger in town. Why, he would even take off his hat to me."[24] Apparently, one's blackness, even when humbly performed in line with rigid social codes, was the only necessary provocation for violence.

By the time of Emmett Till's murder, lynching was no longer an acceptable public spectacle, though it was still an acceptable community practice. That is, by 1955, lynching had become an invisible public event: everyone in town would know what had happened, to whom, and "why," but it was no longer performed before a large crowd in the public square. Racial violence had gone more "underground"; however, within the context of a long tradition of lynching, even the inexplicable disappearance of a black body made a perverse kind of sense. History had taught both blacks and whites how to fill in the blanks, how to create a narrative around the missing body. Rumor and speculation now performed the rhetorical violence formerly exacted by the public lynching.

The tortured black body nonetheless was still designed to bear witness to white supremacy and black subordination. However, increasingly, this witness was silent or, in the case of Emmett Till, intended to be *absent*. The belated admission of Till's murderers attests to this intention. Kirk W. Fuoss, in his excellent study "Lynching Performances, Theatres of Violence," reminds us that visuality was a crucial component of the power of lynching.[25] Indeed, traditional lynchings were spectacles or, as Fuoss suggests, *theatrical events* performed before an audience. Although, as we will discuss, Emmett Till's killers did not intend for his body to be found (to wit: they tied a 75-pound gin fan to his body before throwing it in the river, and, in court, their lawyers argued that the body found was not that of Emmett Till, the boy they admitted only to kidnapping), they did participate in what Fuoss describes as "performance chaining": "I use the term 'performance chaining' to refer to the ways in which one type of performance led to another. The oral recitations of narrative recounting details of the alleged precipitating crime, for example, not only functioned as performances in their own right, they also fomented future performances."[26] The power of lynchings continued to be performed rhetorically through gruesome stories told and retold in both white and black communities.

In the year after their acquittal, Roy Bryant and J. W. Milam told their story to William Bradford Huie in a piece for *Look* magazine. According to Huie, the two admitted to killing the teenager. Upon abducting Till at the home of his great-uncle Mose Wright, Milam recalled asking him: "You the nigger who did the talking?" "Yeah," Till answered. "Don't say 'Yeah' to me: I'll blow your head off."[27] In his account, Milam continued to characterize the incident as a legitimate effort to maintain white-black social hierarchy. Blaming an unrepentant Till for his own murder, Milam explained, "He was hopeless. I'm no bully; I never hurt a nigger in my life. I like niggers in their place. I know how to work 'em. But I just decided it was time to put a few people on notice. As long as I live and can do anything about it, niggers are going to stay in their place."[28] So, when the brutalized body of Emmett Till became dislodged and resurfaced on the banks of the Tallahatchie River, Milam and Bryant were forced to defend themselves against a murder charge. Only after their acquittal could they weave the body back into a familiar and violent story, one meant to remind blacks that "niggers are going to stay in their place."

Milam's account also suggests the difficulty in maintaining a social order anchored in subservient black bodies when interrupted by defiant Northerners unschooled in the intricate social orders tied to race. The gap between Chicago, Illinois, and Money, Mississippi, was untranslatable, a difficult hermeneutic problem for young Emmett. Mamie Till Bradley's instructions to her son on how to act in the South anticipated the interpretive challenges he would face. Allen describes how many African Americans met those challenges: "Within rigidly prescribed boundaries, black men and women . . . improvised strategies for dealing with whites. The choices were never easy; the risks were always great. To survive was to make what a Louisiana black man called a *'pragmatic resignation'* to reality, to watch every word and action in the presence of whites, to veil their inner feelings, to wear the mask."[29] As a means of survival, Southern blacks had perfected a complex rhetorical masquerade. They codified a careful way of being among whites that at least provisionally protected them from harm. Milam's rage at Till points to a conflict between seemingly incommensurate codes. Milam claims to have told Till, before shooting him, "Chicago boy, I'm tired of 'em sending your kind down here to stir up trouble. Goddamn you, I'm going to make an example of you—just so everybody can know how me and my folks stand."[30]

As he stood naked on the banks of the Tallahatchie, Till's last word apparently triggered Milam's wrath: "You still as good as I am? 'Yeah,' Till answered."[31] That "Yeah" presented, in a word, a remote world obdurate to the regime of Jim Crow, a world increasingly deaf to the cultural tones of the South. That a young black man dared reject the "yes, Sir" deference expected of him—be it from obstinacy or ignorance—was apparently enough to inspire murderous rage. Till's body became, in the hands of Milam and Bryant, a rhetorical text, one more installment in the brutal, yet thoroughly American, story of racial violence. Significantly, this specific instance of violence was, for its perpetrators, "caused" by Till's failure to keep his *body* in line. That is, he supposedly committed (again, the facts remain hopelessly disputed) the worst crime a young black man could: being sexually suggestive toward a white woman. As Milam told Huie in *Look,* "when a nigger gets close to mentioning sex with a white woman, he's tired o' livin.' I'm likely to kill him." Indeed, Milam and his brother-in-law decided to erase Till's body—as a warning to others that miscegenation, the racial "mixing" of bodies, could be a capital offense. Like all rhetorical texts, however, Milam and Bryant's horrible message, inscribed on the body of young Emmett Till, could not be made to signify obediently what its authors demanded. Mamie Till Bradley and her growing network of supporters refused to put Emmett's body "in its place." Instead, as Till's corpse (both his physical body and pictures of it) began to circulate among the national black community, it came to signify much more than his murderers could have expected.

Mamie Till Bradley's decision to display Emmett's body in Chicago challenged the dominant meaning of lynched bodies in general. Bryant and Milam would, after their trial, try to interpret Till's murder as another "uppity nigger" put in his place by justified violence. Mrs. Till Bradley preemptively contested that meaning by exposing her son's mutilated corpse to thousands of mourners in Chicago and the glare of national media attention. In displaying her son's body, she challenged the meaning of lynched black bodies, thus challenging the validity of a Southern white supremacist social order buttressed by these bodies. By moving Emmett Till's corpse from a muddy river bottom in the Mississippi Delta to a public exhibition in urban Chicago, Mamie Till Bradley transformed her son from a victim of white racism to an unforgettable symbol that mobilized a generation of activists.

BEHOLD THE CORPSE: THE EFFECTS OF "WITNESSING" EMMETT TILL

People had to face my son and realize just how twisted, how distorted, how terrifying race hatred could be. People had to consider all of that as they viewed Emmett's body. The whole nation had to bear witness to this.

Mamie Till Bradley[32]

In his autobiography *The Greatest,* Muhammad Ali describes standing on the corner with friends as a teenager looking at newspaper pictures of

Emmett Till in the black newspapers: "In one he was laughing and happy. In the other his head was swollen and bashed in, his eyes bulging out of their sockets and his mouth twisted and broken."[33] Ali was haunted by the images and says that he "felt a deep kinship" with Till after learning that the two were born on the same day and year. The murder became for Ali a turning point in his consciousness as a young black man living in a racist society: "I couldn't get Emmett out of my mind until one evening I thought of a way to get back at white people for his death. I remember a poster of a thin white man in striped pants and a top hat who pointed at us above the words Uncle Sam wants you. We stopped and hurled stones at it."[34] Ali and his friends then placed two iron shoe rests, stolen from an unattended shoeshine stand, on the nearby train tracks, creating extensive damage when a train came shortly after:

> I remember the loud sound of the ties ripping up. I broke out running . . . and then I looked back. I'll never forget the eyes of the man in the poster, staring at us. Uncle Sam wants you. It took two days to get up enough nerve to go back [to the tracks]. A work crew was still cleaning up the debris. And the man in the poster was still pointing. I always knew that sooner or later he would confront me, and I would confront him.[35]

Although we hesitate to construct an uncomplicated, sutured cause-effect relationship between the image of Till's corpse and the civil rights movement, the former clearly played a significant role in spurring the momentum of the latter. For Ali, for example, the image of a glowering Uncle Sam became twisted when juxtaposed with the image of a battered Emmett Till. Rather than a familiar patriarch calling young men to battle, Uncle Sam's "I want you!" was symbolically recoded as a sinister "You're next!" As such, the young Cassius Clay began to see American "values" quite differently. Seeming to anticipate the effect the atrocity would have, Mamie Till Bradley declined the funeral director's offer to retouch Emmett, insisting that her son's corpse be displayed just as it was found:

> I knew that I could talk for the rest of my life about what had happened to my baby, I could explain it in great detail, I could describe what I saw laid out there on that slab at A. A. Rayner's, one piece, one inch, one body part, at a time. I could do all of that and people still would not get the full impact. They would not be able to visualize what had happened, unless they were allowed to see the results of what had happened. They had to see what I had seen. The whole nation had to bear witness to this.[36]

As she recalls telling the funeral director, "Let the world see what I've seen."

And the world did see—at least the world that mattered most, the expanding network of African Americans who knew all too well the dangers they faced and yet were beginning to exercise their collective power and do something about it on a national scale. Pictures of Emmett before and after the murder were circulated in *Jet,* the *Chicago Defender,* the *Pittsburgh Courier,* the *New York Amsterdam News,* and *Crisis.*[37] In addition to the readers of these mainly black press publications, many others viewed the corpse directly at an open-casket memorial that was, again, insisted upon by Mamie Till Bradley. The most conservative estimates put attendance that day at around 10,000.[38] But most assessed a turnout of more like 100,000, and "some estimates say as many as 600,000" mourners walked in a steady procession to view the body.[39] Christmas photos of a smiling and robust Emmett were attached to the casket, making the corpse all the more horrible in contrast.

Muhammad Ali was not alone in responding to the image as a call to action. The famous trial attorney Johnny Cochran has said that Till's murder was the main cause for his career choice.[40] Molefi Asante, founder of the first Ph.D. program in African American studies, writes that "My life's pilgrimage, in many respects, has been to seek liberation from the moment of Till's death."[41] Former NAACP chairman and SNCC communications director Julian Bond has said, "My memories are exact—and parallel those of many others my age—I felt vulnerable for the first time in my life—Till was a year younger—and recall believing that this could easily happen to me—for no reason at all. I lived in Pennsylvania at the time."[42] Audre Lorde, Bebe Moore Campbell, Toni Morrison, and Gwendolyn Brooks have all written poems or whole novels based on the story. Bob Dylan expressed the feelings of many whites of his generation in his song "The Death of Emmett Till": "If you can't speak out against this kind of thing / a crime that's so unjust / Your eyes are filled with dead men's dirt / your mind is filled with dust."[43]

Martin Luther King Jr. was known on many occasions to use Till's murder as an example of the effects of racial hatred in the South. Clenora Hudson-Weems, author of *Emmett Till: The Sacrificial Lamb of the Civil Rights Movement,* argues that Till's murder was "the epitome of the ugliness and hatred of racism. It made people uncomfortable, but it made people act. If you want to move a people, kill their children. . . . I believe that Emmett Till was the straw that broke the camel's back, that his death sparked the flame."[44] Robin D. G. Kelley, chair of the History Department at New York University, echoes:

> The Emmett Till case was a spark for a new generation to commit their lives to social change, you know. They said, 'We're not gonna die like this. Instead, we're gonna live and transform the South so people won't have to die like this.' And if anything, if any event of the 1950s inspired young people to be committed to that kind of change, it was the lynching of Emmett Till.[45]

This position abounds in most of the literature on Till. But what exactly is it about this case that evoked such a dramatic response? We suggest that, in addition to the cultural and political milieu at the time (that is, the so-called "camel's back" was already severely weakened by centuries of abuse and injustice forced on African American people), the *image* of Emmett Till's monstrous and grisly body could not be ignored. It served as graphic testimony to the brutal race hatred in the 1950s South in a way that written text could never have done. It allowed viewers to become witnesses to what for many had existed only as rumor and legend. Anne Moody writes in *Coming of Age in Mississippi* that before the Emmett Till murder, "I had heard of Negroes found floating in a river or dead somewhere with their bodies riddled with bullets. But I didn't know the mystery behind these killings then. I remember once when I was only seven I heard Mama and one of my aunts talking about some Negro who had

been beaten to death. 'Just like them low-down skunks killed him they will do the same to us.'"[46] As we will discuss shortly, the graphic image of Till's corpse linked up with these tales in a way that produced tangible social and political effects.

As many have noted, a photograph is often seen as a slice of the real, a trace of that which was. As Roland Barthes argues, "in Photography I can never deny that *the thing has been there.* . . . Every photograph is a certificate of presence. . . . An emanation of *past reality.* . . . That-has-been."[47] The power of Till's body is intensified not because it is a photo of a corpse, but a photo of the face of a corpse or, *what was a face.* In encountering this face, we are reminded of philosopher Alphonso Lingus's observation that "In the face of another, the question of truth is put on each proposition of which my discourse is made, the question of justice put on each move and gesture of my exposed life."[48] Till's face-that-was haunted the nation individually and collectively, amplifying calls for justice. But even before the haunting, this face-that-was momentarily impedes thought, confuses, belies detachment, interrupts civilization, and kicks us in the gut.

This kick in the gut, and our reflexive shudder, is intensified by the dialogue between photos. Emmett Till before encountering Mississippi and Jim Crow justice gazes with confident eyes and the serene smile of a young man looking forward to his future. The close shot depicts a sharply dressed Till on the cusp of manhood—white dress shirt, tie, jauntily placed hat. But Till does not become a man, does not see a future. The photo of the bloated face-that-was Emmett Till after Mississippi and after Jim Crow justice is monstrous and incomplete, violating the norms of civilized society. Missing an eye, an ear, and most of his teeth, and bloated beyond recognition, Till's disfigured face calls the viewer to ask: What happened? Where is justice?

As many have attested, it provokes a physical response that temporarily precedes and exceeds "sense"—a reflexive shudder, an involuntary retching. The basketball star Kareem Abdul Jabbar recalls his visceral reaction thus: "I was 8 years old when I saw a photo of Emmett Till's body in *Jet* magazine. It made me sick."[49] The writer James Baldwin admitted, "I do not know why the case pressed on my mind so hard—but it would not let me go."[50] As Reverend Jesse Jackson puts it, "when Emmett Till was killed, unlike with *Brown* [*v. the Board of Education*] there was no need for definition. It shook the consciousness of a nation. It touched our bone marrow, the DNA of our dignity."[51] Christopher Benson, who co-wrote Mrs. Till Bradley's 2003 account of the case, suggests that Till's "is a story that clawed at our conscience like fingernails on a blackboard. It challenged a nation in the most fundamental way. We looked at the tortured face of Emmett Till and saw what a nightmare the American dream had become for so many of us."[52] As then, now. Still. The photo of Till's monstrous face-that-was continues to haunt the American imagination like a ghost that refuses to be exorcised. Its dissonance still disturbs, "like fingernails on a blackboard." Perhaps this is why so many have demanded that the case be reopened, that Emmett Till have another chance at justice.

In the most mundane sense, then, seeing is believing. As Mamie Till Bradley decreed, "let the people see what I've seen." Indeed, John Hartley in *The Politics of Pictures* points out that "The classic *OED* general definition of 'truth'—'that which exists in fact'—is commonly verified by taking it to refer to 'that which can be seen.'"[53] The image of Till's corpse documented a tradition of racial terrorism in the most graphic and shocking way. Clearly, the corpse of a martyr serving as an impetus to political action for its witnesses is a well-known narrative to anyone familiar with world history. In the Catholic tradition, to cite the most obvious example, it is precisely the body of Christ—wounded and emaciated—featured as a spectacle for public consumption that grounds followers' faith. To this day, images of the abject Jesus icon continue to be an indispensable focal point for Catholics. This corporeal spectacle serves as a testimony of an injustice ("look at what they've done to our Lord"), a warning of the risk of discipleship, and an ennobling of the martyr who sacrificed his or her life for others.

Similarly, Till's corpse testified to the outrage, the risks, and ultimately the veneration of those who fell victim to racial violence in the United States. Martin Luther King Jr., in a 1958 speech, solidified Till's role as a "sacred martyr" of the struggle for freedom: "Emmett Till, a mere boy, unqualified to vote, but seemingly used as a victim to terrorize Negro citizens and keep them from the polls."[54] Whether or not Till's murderers meant to deter the black vote, miscegenation, or something less specific is irrelevant. What concerns us here is the multiplicity of meanings his body was made to convey. As Susan Bordo rightly suggests, "bodies *speak* to us."[55] In different contexts, Till's body spoke to different audiences in different ways. In the context of the African American community, the proliferation of the mortician's photograph and the open-casket memorial allowed witnesses, in a kind of visual communion, to *consume* the body of Emmett Till and be transformed by doing so. Reverend Jesse Jackson Jr. puts it thus: "Mamie [Till Bradley] turned a crucifixion into a resurrection," and tells her, "you turned death into living. . . . You awakened the world. . . . You gave your son so a nation might be saved."[56]

The transformation Jackson describes seems at least two-part. In one way, particularly for African Americans in the North, the image galvanized a transformation from cautious ambivalence into outright fear. In the 1950s, many Northern blacks were new transplants from the South, recent immigrants looking for work in Northern cities such as Chicago. Although the racial climate of the North was not as explicitly violent as it was in the South, African Americans were surely aware of the dangers inherent in white society. For many, Till's story both reminded Northern blacks of those southerly dangers and blurred any protective divide offered by the Mason-Dixon line. As Till's body was displayed before thousands of Chicago mourners, any comforting geographical boundaries were forever punctured.[57]

Shelby Steele recalls, for example, that Till was "the quintessential embodiment of black innocence, brought down by a white evil so portentous and apocalyptical, so gnarled and hideous, that it left us with a feeling not far from awe. By telling his story and others like it, we came to *feel* the immutability of our victimization, its utter indigenousness, as a thing on this earth like dirt or sand or water."[58] Similarly, Charlayne Hunter-Gault remembers that "From time to time, things happened that intruded on our protected reality. The murder of Emmett Till was one such instance . . . pictures of his limp, water-soaked body in the newspapers . . . were worse than any image we had ever seen outside of a horror movie."[59] The Till narrative, made all the more real by its images, provided a grounds for what Elizabeth Alexander calls a "collective identification with trauma." African American communities have added the story to their folklore tradition in order to pass along an important lesson: "never forget what can happen to a black person in America." Overwhelmingly, Emmett Till's story was told less by narratives than by images, images that produced an unforgettable visceral response. The image of Emmett Till helped people to transform the horrible event into a souvenir, a memento to be shared and disseminated rather than stashed away. As we will argue shortly, this memento does not strike us as an effort to *dissociate* from Till ("I am not that"), but to *remember* and to *embrace* Till. Whereas racist whites increasingly preferred lynching to be practiced as a hidden, underground activity, blacks used Till as a focal point, as an image to foreground in their public memory.

A second transformation that seems to occur from the consumption of this image is, for many, a reconfiguration of that fear into some kind of action. That action may simply be a telling and retelling of Till's story in the hopes of warning future generations of the potential dangers they face. For others, like Muhammad Ali, it was first an adolescent rage followed by a deeper conviction to fight racism on multiple levels. See, for example, Ali's involvement in the civil rights movement, which included his eschewing the white Christian tradition and joining Malcom X and the Black Muslims, and his famous refusal to fight in Vietnam, claiming, "no VietCong ever called me nigger." Or, for Molefi Asante, Robin D. G. Kelley, and countless others, action came in the form of a life devoted to the study and education of black people.

So, does all this imply that the image of Emmett Till garners its rhetorical power simply from its ability to accurately document reality—that his story "speaks the truth" of racial violence? As Jacqueline Goldsby contends, the notion that seeing is believing is certainly one with much cultural currency: "The murder of Emmett Till and the visual codings of it detail the shape public literacy took at this time, and the use of and belief in photography's discursive capacities to represent the 'real' thus becomes one way to explain the power of his death in the public's imagination."[60] Goldsby argues, however, that the discourse surrounding Till's death was not due to its unquestioned verification through pictures: "On the contrary, the effort to represent the murder demonstrated the limits of tele-photo realism, revealing to the public the anxiety that underlies the genre's appeal: namely, that the 'real' is not spontaneously formed; that the 'real' is a social construction; that, in other words, reality is fiction."[61]

We disagree with the assumptions inherent in Goldsby's argument—that the photograph constructs a reality that always fails to reproduce real-world events. Of course images always produce a fragmented reality, but this is only a problem if we expect them to do otherwise, if we assume that we can *ever* experience unmediated reality. All the pictures in the world, shot from every possible angle, will not sufficiently reconstruct the events that led to the death of Emmett Till. We are more interested, here, in what kind of reality was produced by the image of Till's corpse than in how accurately it was able to serve as evidence of a violence that is forever irretrievable. This image did not construct a makeshift reality, or a "fiction," as Goldsby suggests, that merely poses as a reality to which we can never have access. Rather it produced *real* sensations and *real* social relations; it materially produced a new way of being for the African Americans we have discussed in this essay. The image, like the open casket in Chicago, became a gathering place, a temporary nexus around which people could link themselves to each other in a new network, thus reconfiguring their agency in powerful ways.

Goldsby also wants to suggest that the Till images contribute to what she calls a "high-tech" lynching; not a lynching that depended upon "the coarse end of a rope, the flaming end of a torch, and a crowd of thousands" for its violence, but one that manifested itself on the pages of newspapers and in the ether of television broadcasts. There is a distinct and important difference, however, between the lynch mob witnessing its own barbarous handiwork and a black community passing around magazines featuring Emmett Till's maimed body—that difference is the witnesses themselves. As we have argued, the African American community's encounter with the Till image contributed to a powerful political response. The African Americans who consumed the image confronted face-to-face what for many had long been mired in legend. For those who engaged in its visual consumption, the abject body of Emmett Till had significant transformative effects.

IMPLICATIONS AND CONCLUSIONS OR, WHAT CAN WE LEARN FROM ABJECT BODIES?

Till's body was ruined but nonetheless a body, with outlines that mean it can be imagined as kin to, but nonetheless distinct from, our own.

Elizabeth Alexander

Mamie Till Bradley reports that when Emmett's body arrived in Chicago from Mississippi it came securely padlocked in a nondescript casket. A State of Mississippi seal had been placed across the lid. The funeral director, the undertaker, and Mrs. Till Bradley's Mississippi relatives had signed papers agreeing not to break the seal just to get the body out of Mississippi. "Somebody in the state of Mississippi wanted to make sure we didn't see what was inside that box," Mrs. Till Bradley recalled. The grieving mother, however, was determined to see her child's body and would not be deterred. When the concerned funeral directors hesitated to open the casket, she told them, "if I ha[ve] to take a hammer and open that box myself, it [is] going to be opened."[62] In the years before Till's death, lynching had gone "underground" as a public spectacle in the South, no longer acceptable as a community event celebrated by cheering audiences. Of course, it was still an all-too-common practice, but most whites preferred it be confined, like young Emmett's corpse, to darkness and secrecy. For whites, the lynched body was no longer a souvenir to display, but a rumor to be whispered, an absence to be filled with a knowing glance. In the hands of Mamie Till Bradley,

however, her son's lifeless body would indeed become a souvenir of sorts. It became a horrible keepsake for a community whose survival depended on remembering that danger was everpresent, no matter how invisible. Mrs. Till Bradley demanded that Emmett's body, in all its grotesque abjection, be revealed and circulated among her community. As we have seen, it was an act that would have tremendous and longlasting effect.

The *Oxford English Dictionary* defines "abject" as "a state of misery or degradation." Discourses about abjection, most notably those engaging the work of sociologist Mary Douglas and feminist psychoanalyst Julia Kristeva, have done much to illuminate the ways in which humans come to self-consciousness through a process of distinguishing themselves from others. Kristeva, for example, argues that the significance of "the abject" lies in its role as something against which we compare ourselves favorably as individuals. She describes the abject as "a jettisoned object," which is "opposed to *I*," and is "radically excluded." For example, an image of the emaciated body of a person living with AIDS may evoke sympathy or, in some cases, fear, but it also fulfills the role of an abject, infected "other" that enables healthy Americans to feel clean, vital, even morally superior. Similarly, the starving bodies of developing countries in ways serve as boundaries or limits that contribute to this country's sense of self as a nation. American identity depends, in part, precisely upon what America is not.

Kristeva, however, indicates that such distinctions and the identities that depend on them are never final. She argues that the self, or "I," depends on the abject to constitute its border, to be that which "lies outside, beyond the set." She notes that from its "place of banishment," the abject "does not cease challenging its master."[63] In this sense, the abject other never remains subserviently at the margins; it never remains stagnant, creating stable boundaries for the self. Hence, Kristeva introduces a *dynamism* to the concept of identity that gets articulated and rearticulated through the self's dialectical interaction with the abject.[64]

Judith Butler follows Kristeva, granting the abject the important ontological role of establishing the external conditions of subjectivity. She writes that "the subject is constructed through acts of differentiation that distinguish the subject from its constitutive outside, a domain of abjected alterity conventionally associated with the feminine, but clearly not exclusively. Subjects are constructed through exclusion, that is, through the creation of a domain of deauthorized subjects, presubjects, figures of abjection, populations erased from view."[65] In other words, subjects, for Butler, can only exist by differentiating themselves from non-subjects—those who are denied entry into a particular public sphere. For centuries, blacks served as the abject "deauthorized" subjects that justified white supremacy.

Although Butler proposes a notion of subjectivity that is necessarily dependent on others, it is still, as with Kristeva, through a process of *repudiation,* an often unconscious negation of the other in order to establish the self. Near the time of Till's death, for example, white America, or even Northern blacks, albeit to a lesser extent, could define themselves through their relationship to the abject other that was the Southern black subject. As Till shows, though, the norms, or lines of understanding, created through abjection are not stable. To use Kristeva's words, Till did "not cease challenging [his] master," serving the docile role as abject outsider. As the examples of Muhammad Ali and others illustrate, Till's body forced a reconfiguration of the self along different lines. The utter horror of his death for some who witnessed his corpse surely punctured a sense of a safe, complete self. For others, it simply intensified a vulnerability of which they were already well aware. Either way, the boundaries of the witnessing subject were, in some sense, transformed.

Christopher Benson, Mamie Till Bradley's co-writer on her memoir, notes, "We looked at the tortured face of Emmett Till and saw what a nightmare the American dream had become for so many of us. One newspaper headline got it exactly right when it noted quite simply that [Mamie Till Bradley] had opened a casket and opened our eyes."[66] The shortcomings of the nation's promises were made conspicuous by the corporeal testimony of a murdered teenager. Goldsby writes:

The mutilation of Emmett Till's body—a child's body—demonstrated to us how uncivil we could be to one another, and it impressed upon us the social cost of systematically denying the political rights of the least amongst us. In that sense, this lynching commands such a prominent place in our collective memory because it performs the function of political myth as described by Roland Barthes.[67]

In a sense, the mythical "selfness" of African American people changed as they *embraced* and centralized Emmett. They refused to see his body as one more threatening message from racist white America. Many embraced, rather than feared (or, perhaps, more precisely *through the fear*), Emmett in all his abjection and made his body *mean* differently. Emmett Till illustrated that their very *bodies* were at stake. Alexander writes in *Black Male* that "Till's body was ruined but nonetheless a body, with outlines that mean it can be imagined as kin to, but nonetheless distinct from, our own."[68] Similarly, we would not suggest that the experience of viewing this body is easily described as an unproblematic *recognition* of one's self (and hence, one's vulnerability) in the corpse, but more of an inability to ignore the witnessing as an event—a rhetorical event that requires a response. Gilles Deleuze argues that thought, in this sense, is always a response to violence. He writes:

Do not count upon thought to ensure the relative necessity of what it thinks. Rather, count upon the contingency of an encounter with that which forces thought to raise up and educate the absolute necessity of an act of thought or a passion to think. . . . Something in the world forces us to think. This something is an object not of recognition but of a fundamental *encounter.*[69]

Although, as this quotation suggests, the encounter may not have been one of a recognition of self in other, we argue that an engagement, such as that with Emmett Till, provoked both affect and action because it demonstrated that conventional boundaries—between self and others, North and South, life and death—are irrevocably blurred. This blurring is not necessarily the result of a detached reflection, or contemplation of the viewer, for the force of the image is too strong. Till's head was swollen to three times its normal size, his individual features were indistinguishable, and he was missing an eye, an ear, and most of his teeth. All this was in the frame of a silk-lined casket in a funeral home, a context in which if bodies are shown at all they are almost without exception displayed in a state of tranquility and peace—the body *at rest,* not *at risk.* This visual encounter and the visceral reaction it demands force a reckoning, an active redistribution of knowledge that is different from what had sufficed before.

We contend that the example of Emmett Till shows us that the abject serves a larger function than the "outside" that provides us with a coherent "inside." As Butler rightly notes, the abject is necessarily *within* each subject. But does its force lie only in its role as that thing (within us) that we perpetually repudiate in order to try and preserve ourselves as pure, unadulterated subjects? At the risk of constructing too neat a narrative on this point, we think we can say that before the death of Emmett Till, Southern racism served as an abject constitutive border for the comparatively safe community Northern blacks enjoyed. When the images of Till's lifeless body made their way into the homes of people across the country, the limits of that constitutive border were pressed upon and demanded a response.

We began this discussion by asking what, if anything, we can learn from abject, violent images. Specifically, why does the horrible image of Emmett Till's corpse continue to compel and horrify us, when the names of so many other lynching victims are long forgotten? At least one response may be that, rather than relegating the abject body of Emmett Till to the borders of their community (as if his fate was an anomaly to black life), African Americans *transformed the abject into a souvenir* of what was an all-too-common consequence of blackness. The white racist community attempted to symbolically solidify its own supremacy by circulating "Negro barbecue" postcards and victims' body parts. Black bodies were forced to play the role of abject "other" to white bodies through the most violent means. In contrast, the African American community refused to relegate

the grotesque image of Emmett Till to its borders. Lerone Bennett, formerly of *Jet* magazine, the first to publish the image, told National Public Radio's Noah Adams that "as soon as [the issue containing pictures of Till] hit the streets, people started lining up at newsstands. Word spread from Chicago to Atlanta."[70] The abject—as it was passed from hand to hand, from neighbor to neighbor, from parent to child—became not something for the community to repudiate, but to embrace. As Robin D. G. Kelley puts it, the "sacrifice" of Emmett Till helped to transform a movement initiated by anger and repudiation into one propelled by love and communion. In his words:

> [W]hat I mean by that is into love for the people who they're trying to defend and love for a nation that had for so long oppressed them, but they felt was transformable. They felt that as black people involved in the movement, that Emmett Till's body was sacrificed in some ways . . . that many of the activists who were murdered were sacrificed for the sake of saving the country, redeeming this nation. And I think that's why, you think of something like the nonviolence philosophy of the civil rights movement as directly related to the violence meted out on people like Emmett Till.[71]

As it did for so many others, the picture became, for Charles Cobb, a Washington, D.C., journalist, a call to action: "Mississippi was kind of a vague part of our family's conversation as kind of like the most dangerous place for black people in the world. That's how it existed. But we had no concrete fix on what that meant until the Till photograph."[72] As Bennett puts it, "People in the black community have said for years, there's a motto: 'If it wasn't in *Jet,* it didn't happen.'" Barthes's notion that a picture reminds us that "that-has-been" transformed what had been, for many blacks, an unspeakable evil into a tangible reality—verified by the body of a Northern boy. The image of Till's body became a rallying point for a nascent civil rights movement; in effect, *it lynched lynching.* It made explicit that what "polite society" no longer acknowledged was still occurring. It once again made public spectacle of the abused black body, but transformed its meaning by doing so.

One component of the encounter with Till must certainly have been a kind of "Oh, save [by] the grace of God, go I" response that reestablishes for oneself the knowledge that "I am not *that*." However, the potential that it *could be,* and that it happened to anyone at all, linked together those folklore tales of white-hooded Klansmen and "Negroes found floating in a river" with an actual face looking back from the pages of a magazine. The image of Emmett Till did not represent or bring into being all of those other lynched men and women and their stories that so troubled the minds of black people, but it did serve as a connecting point, or a hinge, around which centuries of fear and anger converged. Unfortunately, it did so not by contradicting America's racial legacy, but by embodying its excess, testifying to its logical and potentially deadly conclusions. The pictures of Emmett Till's body foregrounded the body at risk; they reconfigured the abjection of white-black race relations by giving it a new visual vocabulary. The abject, black body at risk was transformed, from the dialectical "other" defining and bolstering white power to the grotesque product of that power. A large African American community rallied around Emmett Till's corpse; they visually consumed it, disseminated it, and preserved it as a horrible but precious relic of what must never be forgotten. The brutalized, fragmented body of a teenage boy visually testified not to the absoluteness of white supremacy but to its fraudulence. The victimized black body, which had once been a celebrated spectacle of white hatred, either through public lynchings or, later, portentous "disappearances," was now a powerful symbol of resistance and community. By embracing, consuming, and disseminating the abject body of Emmett Till, the African American community began a public discourse in which *white racism* became the ugly other.

NOTES

1. Mamie Till-Mobley and Christopher Benson, *Death of Innocence: The Story of the Hate Crime That Changed America* (New York: Random House, 2003), 135–36.

2. Jacqueline Goldsby, "The High and Low Tech of It: The Meaning of Lynching and the Death of Emmett Till," *Yale Journal of Criticism* 9 (1996): 249.

3. Hugh Murray, "False Martyr," *American Scholar* 60 (Winter 1991): 455.

4. George E. Curry, "Killed for Whistling at a White Woman," *Emerge,* July–August 1995, 27.

5. Consequently, the case became known as the "wolf-whistle murder." Mamie Till contends that the wolf whistle was likely Emmett's attempt to get over a severe speech impediment: "I taught Bo when you get hooked on a word, just whistle . . . and say it." Quoted in Curry, "Killed for Whistling," 28.

6. Goldsby, "The High and Low Tech of It," 245–82.

7. We have chosen primarily to describe the incident as a "murder" rather than a lynching. Although the Till murder certainly bears some traditional hallmarks of a lynching, it seems to have lacked the *spectacular* and public quality of lynchings. However, as we will argue, the murder can best be understood within a historical context in which lynching had very recently been prevalent. Although his reasoning is not completely clear, it is interesting to note that Hugh White, governor of Mississippi in 1955, said of the case: "This is not a lynching. It is straight out murder." Mamie Till Bradley disagrees, writing in her memoir that Bryant and Milam's post-trial boasting made clear their intent to send a message to other African Americans, "and sending a message to black folks is one of the key factors that distinguishes a lynching from a murder." Till-Mobley and Benson, *Death of Innocence,* 215.

8. Curry, "Killed for Whistling," 32.

9. Curry, "Killed for Whistling," 32.

10. Henry Hampton, *Eyes on the Prize: Awakenings (1954–1956).* Public Broadcasting System, 1987, videocassette.

11. Amita Nerurkar, "Lawmakers Want 1955 Mississippi Murder Case Reopened," *CNN Lawcenter,* CNN, April 13, 2004, *http://www.cnn.com/2004/LAW/04/13/till.murder.case/* (cited August 2004).

12. Laura Parker, "Justice Pursued for Emmett Till," *USA Today,* March 11, 2004, 3A.

13. *New York Times Book Review,* January 13, 2000, *http://www.amazon.com/gp/product/ product-description/0944092691/103–7861795–3019038?_encoding=UTF8&n=283155&s=books.*

14. It is important to note, however, that much of the power of Hamer's speeches came from her detailed depictions of the beatings she suffered as a civil rights activist. The body featured prominently, for example, in her account of a 1963 detainment in a Montgomery County jail: "They beat me until I was

hard, 'til I couldn't bend my fingers or get up when they told me to. That's how I got this blood clot in my eye—the sight's nearly gone now. My kidney was injured from the blows they gave me on the back." *"Who is Fannie Lou Hamer?" Pagewise* history pages, *http://nd.essortment.com/fannielouhamer_rgrh.htm* (cited February 2005). As Hamer's famous claim "I'm sick and tired of being sick and tired" makes clear, the fight for civil rights cannot be separated from the physical pain and exhaustion African Americans were forced to endure under white supremacy.

15. The concept of the "public screen" is taken from Kevin DeLuca and Jennifer Peeples, "From Public Sphere to Public Screen: Democracy, Activism, and the 'Violence' of Seattle," *Critical Studies in Media Communication* 19 (2002): 125–51.

16. Elaine Scarry, *The Body in Pain: The Making and Remaking of the World* (Oxford, UK: Oxford University Press, 1985), 27.

17. We cite, here, Billie Holliday's haunting and daring "Strange Fruit" (1939), largely recognized as the first significant song of the civil rights movement. See, for more information, David Margolick's *Strange Fruit: The Biography of a Song* (New York: Harper Collins, 2001).

18. James Allen et al., *Without Sanctuary: Lynching Photography in America* (San Francisco: Twin Palms Publishers, 2000), plate 26.

19. Allen et al., *Without Sanctuary,* plate 55.

20. Allen et al., *Without Sanctuary,* 15.

21. Allen et al., *Without Sanctuary,* 9.

22. Allen et al., *Without Sanctuary,* 16.

23. Allen et al., *Without Sanctuary,* 16.

24. Quoted in Allen et al., *Without Sanctuary,* 26.

25. Kirk W. Fuoss, "Lynching Performances, Theatres of Violence," *Text and Performance Quarterly* 19 (1999): 1–27.

26. Fuoss, "Lynching Performances," 25.

27. Quoted in Halberstam, *The Fifties* (New York: Villord Books, 1993), 435.

28. Halberstam, *The Fifties,* 435.

29. Quoted in Allen et al., *Without Sanctuary,* 31.

30. Quoted in William Bradford Huie, "The Shocking Story of Approved Killing in Mississippi," *Look,* January 24, 1956, 46–48.

31. Quoted in Huie, "Shocking Story," 46–48.

32. In unpaginated picture page (corpse in coffin), Till-Mobley and Benson, *Death of Innocence.*

33. Quoted in Elizabeth Alexander, *Black Male: Representations of Masculinity in Contemporary American Art* (New York: Whitney Museum of American Art, 1994), 104.

34. Quoted in Alexander, *Black Male,* 104.

35. Quoted in Alexander, *Black Male,* 104–5.

36. Mrs. Till notes that Mr. Rayner touched up the body despite her objections: "looking back on it now, I think he probably felt he had to do something. Emmett was in such bad shape when we got him back. Monstrous condition. But Mr. Rayner did what he could. That tongue had been removed, I guess, and put somewhere. The mouth was closed now. And you could see on the side of Emmett's head that some coarse thread had been used to sew the pieces back together. . . . The eye that had been dangling, that was removed, too, and the eyelid closed, like on the other side, where no eye was left. I told Mr. Rayner he had done a beautiful job." Till-Mobley and Benson, *Death of Innocence,* 140.

37. Goldsby, "The High and Low Tech of It," 250.

38. Goldsby, "The High and Low Tech of It," 250.

39. Curry, "Killed for Whistling," 30.

40. Clenora Hudson-Weems, "Resurrecting Emmett Till: The Catalyst of the Modern Civil Rights Movement," *Journal of Black Studies* 29 (1998): 187.

41. Hudson-Weems, "Resurrecting Emmett Till," 185.

42. Public Broadcasting Corporation, *American Experience* home page, "The Murder of Emmett Till," *http://www.pbs.org/wgbh/amex/till/sfeature/sf_remember.html* (cited February 2, 2005).

43. Bob Dylan, "The Death of Emmett Till," Columbia (1963).

44. Quoted in Hudson-Weems, "Resurrecting Emmett Till," 184.

45. Public Broadcasting Corporation, *American Experience* home page, "The Murder of Emmett Till, Interview with Robin Kelley: Spark for a New Generation," *http://www.pbs.org/wgbh/amex/till/sfeature/sf_kdhy_01.html* (cited February 2, 2005).

46. Anne Moody, *Coming of Age in Mississippi* (New York: Dell Publishing, 1968), 121.

47. Roland Barthes, *Camera Lucida* (New York: Noonday Press, 1981), 76, 87, 88, 78.

48. Alphonso Lingus, *Foreign Bodies* (New York: Routledge, 1994), 173.

49. Quoted in Thomas Doherty, "The Ghosts of Emmett Till," *Chronicle of Higher Education,* January 17, 2003, B12.

50. Quoted in Doherty, "The Ghosts of Emmett Till," B11.

51. Reverend Jesse L. Jackson Sr., foreword to Till-Mobley and Benson, *Death of Innocence,* xii.

52. Christopher Benson, afterword to Till-Mobley and Benson, *Death of Innocence,* 286.

53. John Hartley, *The Politics of Pictures: The Creation of the Public in the Age of Popular Media* (New York: Routledge, 1992), 140.

54. Martin Luther King Jr., "Address Delivered at the Launching of the SCLC Crusade for Citizenship at Greater Bethel AME Church," from "The Papers of Martin Luther King, Jr.," The King Center at Stanford University home page, *http://www.stanford.edu/group/King/publications/papers/v014/580212-002-Crusade_Launch.htm* (cited February 2, 2005).

55. Susan Bordo, *Unbearable Weight: Feminism, Western Culture, and the Body* (Berkeley: University of California Press, 1992), 124.

56. Jackson, foreword to Till-Mobley and Benson, *Death of Innocence,* xiii.

57. Rhetorical scholar William Lewis, in his analysis of the Till case, interprets the regional dynamic quite differently, arguing that the media characterizations of the case problematically focused too much on the South as the abject racist other to the North. Lewis suggests that the traditional story of Emmett Till's murder—the horrifying picture that sparked a movement—is too romantic and, as such, costs us much in the way of acknowledging more nuanced and enduring forms of racism. He writes that the case "was offered as a demonstration of the horrors of racism, but the simple romantic form of the story as we know it best reassures us too firmly of our own innocence, ascribes guilt too firmly and easily to other people at other times in other places, and fixes the standards of race relations too narrowly within an ambiguously defined context of legal standards and procedures." We agree that the story's "romanticism" may too narrowly define racism by its most extreme manifestation, possibly overshadowing other, more prevalent forms. Lewis's insights are incredibly valuable for understanding the full scope of the impact of the case. Our goal here, however, is to examine the role the image played in motivating activism among African Americans. That is, we are concerned with what effects the imagery surrounding the case *were* (restricted as they may have been) rather than what they *could* or *should* have been. See William Lewis, "1955/1995: Emmett Till and the Rhetoric of Racial Injustice," *Argumentation and Values: Proceedings of the Ninth Biennial Conference on Argumentation,* ed. Sally Jackson (Annandale, VA: SCA, 1996).

58. Quoted in Alexander, *Black Male,* 102.

59. Quoted in Alexander, *Black Male,* 103.

60. Goldsby, "The High and Low Tech of It," 273.

61. Goldsby, "The High and Low Tech of It," 273–74.

62. According to Till, the Mississippi officials had even packed the body in lime, "to make the body deteriorate faster, to make it even harder to identify. I guess those officials down in Mississippi felt a need to do that just in case the seal and lock didn't scare me off." Till-Mobley and Benson, *Death of Innocence,* 133.

63. Julia Kristeva. *Powers of Horror: An Essay on Abjection* (New York: Columbia University Press, 1982), 2.

64. For two lengthier discussions of the rhetoric of abject bodies, see Christine L. Harold, "The Rhetorical Function of the Abject Body: Transgressive Corporeality in *Trainspotting,*" *JAC: Journal of Advanced Composition* 20 (2000): 865–81; and Christine L. Harold, "Tracking Heroin Chic: The Abject Body Reconfigures the Rational Argument," *Argumentation and Advocacy* 36 (1999): 65–76.

65. Judith Butler, "How Bodies Come to Matter: An Interview with Judith Butler," *Signs* 23 (1998): 12.

66. Christopher Benson, afterword to Till-Mobley and Benson, *Death of Innocence,* 286.

67. Goldsby, "The High and Low Tech of It," 247.

68. Alexander, *Black Male,* 105.

69. Gilles Deleuze, *Difference and Repetition,* trans. Paul Patton (New York: Columbia University Press, 1994), 139.

70. Bennett, Lerone. 2004. Emmett Till and the Impact of Images: Photos of Murdered Youth Spurred Civil Rights Activism. Interview by Noah Adams. Morning Edition. National Public Radio, 23 June. *http://www.npr.org/templates/story/story.php?storyId=1969702/.*

71. Public Broadcasting Corporation, *American Experience* home page, "The Murder of Emmett Till, Interview with Robin Kelley: Spark for a New Generation," *http://www.pbs.org/wgbh/amex/till/sfeature/sf_kelley_02.html* (cited February 2, 2005)

72. Charles Cobb, 2004. "Emmett Till and the Impact of Images: Photos of Murdered Youth Spurred Civil Rights Activism. Interview by Noah Adams." Morning Edition. National Public Radio, 23 June. *http://www.npr.org/templates/story/story.php?storyId=1969702/.*

SECTION IV

COMMODIFYING AND CONSUMING

Two overlapping terms, *commodity culture* and *consumer culture,* name the political economy in which the mass consumption of goods, services, and information emerged as the dominant narrative in social and cultural relations. Although the terms *commodity culture* and *consumer culture* are sometimes used interchangeably, there are differences of focus in the rhetorical actions that construct and layer their meanings. "To commodify" and "to consume" name two different, albeit related, actions; the first transforms experience and events into "products," and the second describes how such "products" are used. Visual rhetoric lies at the center of each in the practices of public persuasion. Rhetorics of *commodification* focus on the symbolic processes by which the motives of commercial exchange are integrated into social, political, and cultural relations. By this move, virtually any thing and any experience can be commodified. Rhetorical acts of *consumption* focus on those symbolic practices that invite the use of such commodities for the expression of social status or individual and collective identity.

Take, for example, the visual rhetoric surrounding the international diamond trade. For years, diamonds have been marketed in ways that promote both commodification and consumption as symbolic actions. Traditional diamond advertising rhetoric *commodified* the most intimate of relationships through the creation and manipulation of visual symbols associating "love," sexual attraction, and "commitment" with gifts of gemstones, especially diamonds.

Figure 1   "Lasso Yourself a Western Vacation!"

SOURCE: Railroad Museum of Pennsylvania, with permission of American Premier Underwriters, courtesy of Special Collections, Wallace Library, Rochester Institute of Technology.

Visual symbols associated the cost, size, cut, and quality of diamonds with social status, the "quality" of romance, or the "worth" of a beloved individual. Thus, the visual rhetoric of diamond consumption invited consumers to picture themselves as traditional actors in the "good" story of romantic love and relational commitment. After U.S. media began to pay attention to the conditions and consequences of diamond mining and trade, marketers of diamonds intensified their traditional advertising campaigns and designed new visual appeals to distinguish "blood diamonds" from "legitimate" diamonds. Yet the circulation of photojournalistic images documented the human cost of diamond mining in funding war throughout Africa and the exploitation of children as miners. In this constructed narrative, consumers of diamonds became actors in villainous practices. Since the Kimberly Agreement, which seeks to regulate legitimate diamond trade, marketers have continued to use visual rhetoric to persuade buyers of diamonds that they can still participate in the "romantic" consumption of diamonds by making "good" purchasing choices. Thus, new rhetorics of consumption allow the continued commodification of relationships through the acquisition of diamonds. Visual rhetoric, in the form of advertising and marketing campaigns, was central to this persuasive campaign.

This section features three essays that focus on different forms of marketing rhetoric as prototypes of commodifying and consuming: a commercial campaign for Apple computers, a U.S. Postal Service campaign to promote itself through the creation of commemorative postage stamps, and a large Kodak display promoting the use of color film for family snapshots.

Rhetorical strategies developed in consumer advertising have entered the public sphere as legitimate frames for constructing contemporary identities, both intimate and private as well as public and collective. The escalation of consumerism as the dominant cultural ideology in the United States during the last half of the 20th century has been vigorously celebrated, critiqued, and resisted, even as the politics of globalization intensify the commodification of culture throughout the globe. Economies of advanced capitalism, global markets (and debt), and a renewed cultivation of "conspicuous consumption" produce a seemingly limitless display of commodities in the ubiquitous images of visual media. At the same time, proliferations of consumption sites from shopping malls to Web pages structure the rituals of social exchange. Rhetorical scholars recognize the influence of advertising strategies in cultural and civic life. For instance, Robert Hariman (2002) sees the cultural accumulation of advertising "devices" as "activating a mode of consciousness that is at once artificial and comprehensive" (pp. 283–284). Such pervasive rhetorics infiltrate private and public life by offering consumption as the means to acquire new identities and to influence power relations in the public sphere. In these rhetorical actions, consumption practices merge the personal and political in the construction of the consumer-citizen.

Marketers, corporate leaders, politicians, and their audiences frame commodity choice and consumption practices as evidence of "freedom" and promote material abundance as part of the "American Dream." Although such logic is widely contested, the rhetorical ambiguity embedded in the slippage between the civic and the commercial reveals a persistent tension between conceptions of publics as citizens and/or consumers. Lizabeth Cohen (2003) traces the historic growth of this tension and comments, "Rather than isolated ideal types citizen and consumer were ever-shifting categories that sometimes overlapped, often were in tension, but always reflected the permeability of the political and economic spheres" (p. 8). In the first decade of the 21st century, the roles of citizen and consumer have merged to such an extent that, even when warranted, distinctions are difficult to maintain. As Lawrence W. Rosenfield (2006) remarks, "In such an age, rhetoric transforms into marketing, the artful display of objects in order to tantalize and arouse the consumer's appetites" (p. 197). Thus, fashions, homes, cars, food, vacations, education, information, holidays, historical commemorations, art, and entertainments are commodified and consumed to appease desires constructed by advertising rhetoric.

Advertising campaigns visualize experiences of every kind in order to target audiences with appeals based on demographic studies of what specific consumers *wish to look like,* and what they want to *look at,* but rarely what they *actually look like.* Paul Messaris (1997) argues that viewers of ads do not expect advertising images to conform to reality; viewers understand advertising images are "idealizations not documentary reports" (p. 268). Yet other scholars argue that advertising's distorted images of human appearances and relationships contribute adversely to self-image, especially among young women (Jordan, 2003). Advertising's persistent promotion of overconsumption has also generated a body of work from rhetoric scholars who study the relationship between consumer culture and the environment (Waddell, 1998).

When advertising's techniques are appropriated in political image making, photojournalism, military displays, and ritual performances of national identity, scholars argue that the blurring of civic and consumer appeals can generate cynical disengagement among viewers. The most obvious merging of advertising and politics has been the use of advertising techniques in political campaigns and elections. Since the rise of television (and, later, the Internet) as the major source of news and political discourse, the visual "packaging" of candidates occurs in presentations designed, scripted, and edited for media consumption by professional image makers, who in turn buy airtime and space to "sell" their candidates (Jamieson, 1996). Public relations firms create and place images promoting events, products, locations, and people as "news" to be consumed by the public. Photojournalist and visual communication researcher Julianne H. Newton (2001) worries of such strategies, "The result is a delegitimization of reportage and an increased legitimization of advertising. And the ultimate result is a general distrust of images" (p. 90).

In sites of consumption—mediated, material, and virtual—publics are transformed into products deliverable to advertisers and institutions through actions of visual rhetoric. Consumers invent and reinvent themselves as commodities whose shifting identities are maintained, bought, and sold (and sometimes stolen) through the technologies of visual media and consumption performances. Thus, as commercial media strategize in order to "deliver" specific demographic groups to the advertisers who support them, political image makers promise delivery of "voter blocks" to politicians, and university students are identified as "consumers" of education

before they become "products" delivered to the information marketplace. In the "information age," knowledge, the production of knowledge, and the ways to access knowledge are commodified and consumed through rhetorical actions. Publics are informed about news, history, culture, environment, and health by media displays of images, events, and products offered for consumption and juxtaposed in a pastiche of visuals. Furthermore, the logic of consumption is legitimated and reinforced as a frame for citizens engaged with their governments and communities. People consume political spectacles, historical commemorations, and organizational memberships as ways to make visible their standing as citizens and participants in social exchange. In these practices, instances of visual rhetoric provide consumer-citizens with ways to negotiate through the commodity culture by framing, modifying, and defining consumption practices as indices of democracy, identity, and status.

The predominance of the rhetorical actions of commodifying and consuming in the public sphere generates a number of questions for the student of visual rhetoric: By what strategies do the producers of consumption rhetorics seek viewer identification with a visual commodity? Through what visual appeals do instances of commodification invite the blurring of civic action and consumption practices? How are visual narratives structured to invite viewer participation in consumption practices? Who invents and produces the rhetoric of consumption? What kinds of audiences are "produced" by the constant stream of visual rhetorics devoted to consumption? How do specific instances of commodification employ familiar visual icons? Are there recurring patterns of appropriation in rhetorics of consumption? What ethical issues arise in visual portrayals of consumption as identity? How do viewers find genuine identities in the midst of ubiquitous displays of consumption?

Scholars of advertising and visual persuasion have identified common strategies in visual persuasion and argument, including use of the *enthymeme* (an incomplete argument requiring the audience to fill in the missing pieces) and the appropriation of symbolic forms associated with religious iconography, historical events, patriotism, art, celebrity, and archetypal myths.

Scholars have also explored how various editing, photographic, and filmic techniques create visual narratives steeped in signs of nostalgia, sexual desire, and status displays. Juxtaposition, hyperrealism, parody, and reflexivity are but some of the rhetorical strategies employed by advertising professionals in order to sell goods by redefining consumers' desires, human frailties, and social status as problems easily resolved by consumption of the right brand-name commodities.

Some "target audiences" do resist such narratives, however. Visual rhetoric is often used in countercampaigns conducted by activists who are opposed to the dominance of consumerism. These activists deplore the ubiquity of visual marketing strategies throughout cultural, social, and civic life and have generated a critique of the ways that consumer culture discourse may reinforce (or abet) divisions among class, race, gender, sexuality, and ethnicity. In practices such as "culture jamming," for example, activists creatively employ the same kinds of rhetorical strategies common in advertising, but they use those strategies in a way that resists such discourse (Harold, 2004).

In the decade before and after the turn of the 21st century, increasing numbers of rhetorical scholars focused on the actions of commodification and consuming as constructions of public identity and culture. The essays featured in this section help us recognize how rhetorics of commodification and consumption are a collective occupation organized around nostalgia, myth, and fantasies of desire.

The first essay in this section, Ronald Shields's "The Force of Callas' Kiss: The 1997 Apple Advertising Campaign, 'Think Different,'" focuses on marketing appeals as indices of cultural performance. Shields uses Michel Foucault's concept of the *mirrored heterotopian site*—the idea that one can experience oneself to be in a cultural space that feels simultaneously both "real" and imagined—to explore how Apple juxtaposes images of celebrities to create a mythic narrative about creativity. For example, through editing techniques, Maria Callas throws a kiss to Mahatma Gandhi, and Muhammad Ali and Ted Turner share a salute. Shields names these displays *postmodern parody* and argues that the Apple campaign uses a nonsensical

perspective on images to serve corporate interests. Ultimately, the juxtaposition of diverse celebrity images *seems* to say something about cultural innovation, yet upon reflection, the connections are meaningless and arbitrary. Shields argues that the association of innovation and creativity with Apple is an instance of "branding the consumer," an advertising strategy developed in response to increased viewer sophistication. Although the Apple campaign is clearly a commercial enterprise, a comparison with the news practices outlined in Shawn J. Parry-Giles's essay, "Mediating Hillary Rodham Clinton: Television News Practices and Image-Making in the Postmodern Age" (in Section V), illustrates the use of similar strategies in news media and offers further evidence of the blurring of information, politics, and entertainment.

Ekaterina V. Haskins's essay, "'Put Your Stamp on History': The USPS Commemorative Program *Celebrate the Century* and Postmodern Collective Memory," critiques the production and circulation of stamps in the commemorative program as a pastiche of images whose juxtaposition produced a rhetoric of cultural commodification as much as commemoration. Haskins argues that *Celebrate the Century* provides a case study of how hegemonic narratives of technological progress are produced in postmodern discourse. The U.S. Postal Service invited the public to help select images used to commemorate the century's decades in a series of stamps. The project's resulting imagery, Haskins finds, privileges technological progress and valorizes consumer products along with historical and popular culture figures. Thus, the prevailing mythology erases social controversy with images of consumer democracy. Haskins argues for a reading of the stamp project that avoids the extremes of either uncritical approval or rejection. She concludes that we should attend instead to how the contributions of participants were used by the U.S. Postal Service to make its narrative of history seem more authentic. The essay raises important questions about how visual rhetorics create collective memory among diverse members of the consuming public. Students interested in collective memory might wish to compare this essay with Hariman and Lucaites's essay, "Public Identity and Collective

Memory in U.S. Iconic Photography: The Image of 'Accidental Napalm'" (in Section II), and ask whether the iconic images selected by the public for the commemorative stamp project work to erase the memory of the Vietnam War photograph that Lucaites and Hariman analyze.

The final essay in this section, Diane S. Hope's "Memorializing Affluence in the Postwar Family: Kodak's Colorama in Grand Central Terminal (1950–1990)," focuses on the first 20 years of Kodak images displayed in the giant Colorama in Grand Central Terminal. Hope argues that the huge family portraits displayed in the architectural space of Grand Central Terminal during the postwar years memorialized the family as a consuming unit, telling colorful stories of families that invoked ideas of consumerism. Kodak marketed color film by presenting the affluent nuclear family as a consumer enterprise surrounded by the icons of middle-class domestic virtue: material acquisitions. Vast numbers of consumers circulated through the terminal each day, passing and viewing Kodak's giant screen and the visual images of families it presented. Hope explores the connections among technology, mythology, family, nostalgia, and color photography presented in the display and argues that this heavily gendered rhetoric was also a rhetoric that memorialized consumption. Importantly, Hope emphasizes how the introduction of color photography enshrined it as a persistent sign of consumerism in American culture. Kodak's Colorama images of mythic white families were displayed during the same postwar years that the photograph of Emmett Till's murdered black body was circulated in national newspapers. For this reason, Hope's essay may be read alongside Harold and DeLuca's "Behold the Corpse: Violent Images and the Case of Emmett Till" (in Section III), to explore the confounding and contradictory uses of images of race in the postwar years.

Consider the following discussion questions as you read these essays. The three essays are but samples of the breadth of scholarly work on the visual rhetorics of commodification and consumption. At the end of this section, we have provided a list of additional readings that supplement our selections and open additional ways of thinking about the role of visual rhetoric in actions of commodification and consumption.

Discussion Questions

1. As we saw in a previous section of this volume, *memory* is of special significance in studies of visual rhetoric focused on the act of commemoration. Likewise, memory is often at the center of rhetorical actions of commodification and consumption. The three essays in this section all share a focus on the intersections among memory, identity, and rhetorics of commodifying and consuming. Compare the commodification of memory as it is presented in each of these essays. How do narratives of remembrance differ in these diverse sites of consumption? In each instance presented in the essays, who benefits from framing memory as nostalgia?

2. Shields, Haskins, and Hope each examine a series of images in their studies. In each campaign, the authors comment on audiences' reactions to the image displays and highlight those viewers who responded negatively to the meanings perceived in the images. Compare viewers' reactions to the Apple campaign, the *Celebrate the Century* stamps, and the Kodak Colorama. What attitudes are revealed in the actions of spectators? How do audiences experience visual rhetoric in which experience itself becomes a commodity available for consumption?

3. The essays selected here may open visual rhetoric scholarship to charges of selective interpretation of images. For example, Shields reads the image of diva Maria Callas as an icon in gay culture, and the positioning of her image in Apple Computer's advertising campaign as evidence of Apple's "continued courting of the gay market." Haskins argues that the *Celebrate the Century* project produces a culture in "which everyone is a tourist" of history. Hope concludes that the imaginary families in Kodak's Colorama reflected racial, class, and gender biases. Are these the only possible interpretations of these instances of visual rhetoric? Do you agree with these interpretations? How should such questions of interpretation be resolved in studies of visual rhetoric? Does visual rhetoric demand more or different kinds of interpretation than verbal rhetoric?

REFERENCES

Cohen, L. (2003). *A consumers' republic: The politics of mass consumption in postwar America.* New York: Knopf.

Hariman, R. (2002). Allegory and democratic public culture in the postmodern era. *Philosophy and Rhetoric, 35*(4), 267–296.

Harold, C. (2004). Pranking rhetoric: 'Culture jamming' as media activism. *Critical Studies in Media Communication, 21*(3), 189–211.

Jamieson, K. H. (1996). *Packaging the presidency: A history and criticism of presidential campaign advertising* (3rd ed.). New York: Oxford University Press.

Jordan, J. W. (2003). (Ad)Dressing the body in online shopping sites. *Critical studies in Media Communication, 20*(3), 248–268.

Messaris, P. (1997). *Visual persuasion: The role of images in advertising.* Thousand Oaks, CA: Sage.

Newton, J. H. (2001). *The burden of visual truth.* Mahwah, NJ: Lawrence Erlbaum.

Rosenfield, L. W. (2006). After Walter Benjamin. In L. Prelli (Ed.), *Rhetorics of display* (pp. 197–203). Columbia: University of South Carolina Press.

Waddell, C. (Ed.). (1998). *Landmark essays on rhetoric and the environment.* Mahwah, NJ: Lawrence Erlbaum.

SUGGESTIONS FOR FURTHER READING

Dickinson, G. (1997). Memories for sale: Nostalgia and the construction of identity in Old Pasadena. *Quarterly Journal of Speech, 83*(1), 1–27.

Goffman, E. (1979). *Gender advertisements.* New York: Harper & Row.

Kotchemidova, C. (2005). Why we say "Cheese": Producing the smile in snapshot photography. *Critical Studies in Media Communication, 22*(1), 2–25.

Marchand, R. (1985). *Advertising the American dream: Making way for modernity 1920–1940.* Berkeley: University of California Press.

McAllister, M. P. (1996). *The commercialization of American culture.* Thousand Oaks, CA: Sage.

Meister, M., & Japp, P. (2002). *Enviropop: Studies in environmental rhetoric and popular culture.* Westport, CT: Praeger.

Ono, K. A., & Buescher, D. T. (2001). Deciphering Pocahontas: Unpackaging the commodification of a Native American woman. *Critical Studies in Media Communication, 18*(1), 23–43.

Stabile, C. A. (2000). Nike, social responsibility, and the hidden abode of production. *Critical Studies in Media Communication, 17*(2), 186–204.

14

THE FORCE OF CALLAS' KISS

The 1997 Apple Advertising Campaign, "Think Different"

RONALD E. SHIELDS

The Apple campaign is pitched perfectly to match the fin de siècle *mood. Whenever the end of an era approaches and people feel the future pressing in upon them, culture tends to take a necrophilic turn. In our case, fascination with the past is a little more hysterical, thanks to the coming millennium, and a lot more hallucinatory, thanks to proliferating media that will rob any grave to feed their hunger for content.*

Debra Goldman, "Day of the Dead" 60

Far from creating ideas or meanings, advertisements actually remove *all meaning from objects and events in terms of material* context *and* content, *thus leaving gaps which can be filled by the product.*

Judith Williamson, *Decoding Advertisements* 166

All too rare is the pleasure of reading, hearing or watching something that doesn't seem to have an agenda.

Janet Maslin, "Creative Cannibalism" E1

Apple Computers ignited the personal computer revolution during the 1970s with the Apple II and reinvented the personal computer in the 1980s with the Macintosh. After the enormous success following the now legendary "1984" television ad during that year's Super Bowl game, the fame and fortune of the Apple corporation surprised many. During

SOURCE: Shields, R. E. (2001). The force of Callas' kiss: The 1997 Apple advertising campaign, "Think Different." *Text and Performance Quarterly, 21*(3), 202–219. © National Communication Association.

the "1984" ad campaign a clear sense of corporate identity emerged along with an innovative product designed to secure new markets. A combination of winning technological advances and mythic posturing dominated the images created to introduce Apple's logo. Apple's mythic posturing linked images of Adam's banishment from the Garden of Eden and David's triumph over Goliath with Apple's struggle against IBM. The "1984" ad campaign also introduced the theme of individual freedom promised Apple consumers (Berger 119). Toward the end of the decade, however, Apple's fortunes began to rot as the company lost ground to competing machines powered by Microsoft and Intel processors. Apple's losses in 1996 and 1997 totaled $1.85 billion, and market share fell to just 3% in 1997 from a high of nearly 10% in 1991 (Burrows 144; Williams C8). Clearly, things had to change for Apple to survive.

In 1997, Steve Jobs, an Apple cofounder who had been fired twelve years earlier, returned to slim down, revise, and turn around the ailing company. Working in conjunction with Lee Clow of the advertising agency TBWA Chiat/Day, Apple launched a major advertising campaign. The campaign began on September 28, 1997, with a 60-second television commercial that aired twice during the network premier of *Toy Story* on ABC's *Wonderful World of Disney.*[1] The massive "Think Different" campaign featured television spots, web-based events, striking print ads, and large outdoor ads on buses and buildings.[2] Collapsing "high" and "low" cultural appeals in a questionable utopian vision, the documentary style black-and-white television ad and photo print ads recycled images of twentieth-century innovators.

This analysis of the mythic strategies featured in the "Think Different" campaign links the theoretical concerns of media and performance studies scholars who investigate image and myth by focusing more specifically on the intersection of marketing appeals as cultural indices and performance as cultural text. Recent scholarship provides historical and theoretical links between mediated and live performance. John Tulloch reminds us that it is in the area of spectatorship that contemporary scholars of ritual and performance have "drawn most on media and cultural studies," working within a conceptual framework

of "agency, locality, strategy and skilled daily practice" (8). These concerns are rewriting the history of live performance. In *The Making of American Audiences: From Stage to Television, 1750–1990,* Richard Butsch traces the historical and cultural forces that shape audiences' responses to performances and develops an approach to theatre history that focuses on the evolution of audiences within the nexus of performance, performer, audience, media and market (1–19). Butsch's work provides historical background for Philip Auslander's theoretical work on the status of live performance in contemporary life, particularly his critical reflections on "liveness" and the tangled relationship between live and "mediatized" performance forms. Auslander draws attention to performance scholars' ongoing practice of "plac[ing] live performance and mediatized or technologized forms in direct opposition to one another" and urges performance studies scholars to learn from their media studies counterparts (41). Rejecting assumed distinctions between live and mediatized performance, Auslander writes:

> The qualities performance theorists frequently cite to demonstrate that live performance forms are ontologically different from mediatized forms turn out, upon close examination, to provide little basis for convincing distinctions. Mediatized forms like film and video can be shown to have the same ontological characteristics as live performance, and live performance can be used in ways indistinguishable from the uses generally associated with mediatized forms. (159)

Indeed, Auslander maintains that "scholars working in mass media studies, particularly those interested in television or popular music, have dealt more directly and fruitfully with the question of liveness than most scholars in theatre or performance studies" (3).

While Butsch and Auslander overtly investigate the relationship between live and mediatized performance forms, other scholars pursue this relationship more indirectly, focusing instead on appropriation and other modes of cultural circulation that reveal the porousness of the boundaries that ostensibly separate text from text, genre from genre, medium from medium, even culture from culture. Patrice Pavis, for example, reads Eugenio Barba's practice of intercultural performance as a site of cultural critique as well as textual analysis, construing performance as a series of "transforming and rewriting" acts of appropriation (37). And Nancy Robichaud and Ronald E. Shields critique Peter Sellars' recent operatic productions as the theatrical manifestation and circulation of attitudes and imagery dominant in popular culture, specifically television images concerning race, class, gender, and celebrity.

Taken together, these scholars foreground spectatorship and interrogate performance as negotiated translation, the articulation and circulation of appropriated meanings in various forms and cultural contexts. All pursue the intersection of spectatorship and cultural context without positing ontological differences between live and mediatized performance forms. All assume that live and mediatized performances circulate, mirror, and intersect in the same cultural economy. It is this theoretical orientation that informs my analysis of Apple's "Think Different" campaign. How do the mediatized performances staged in and around "Think Different" spin celebrity images into cultural circulation through mythic posturing? What cultural forces and spectator preoccupations contribute to this circulation? Theorizing "Think Different" as an example of Michel Foucault's mirrored heteropian site for the negotiation of cultural shifts, I argue that the ad campaign is structured to create an amphigorical perspective, a ubiquitous form of postmodern parody. Following a theoretical reading of how the ad uses an amphigorical perspective to discipline historical images and empower corporate myth, I turn my attention to how subsequent responses to the ad sustained its amphigorical perspective but shifted its status from marketing technique to cultural critique. "Think Different" was a highly successful campaign that refined and expanded Apple's corporate identity. It also sold a lot of product. By evoking and exploiting cultural myths associated with the Garden of Eden and reinscribing Apple's reputation as the computer of choice for creative young professionals, "Think Different" illustrates current media advertising's proclivity to manipulate *fin de siècle* preoccupations with memory, fame, and cultural status.

CREATING "THINK DIFFERENT"

Jeremy Miller, spokesperson for the advertising firm that created "Think Different," characterizes the campaign as a quest for market appeal and product identity. According to Miller, the ads presented a "change the world" kind of challenge "that Apple has always been part of." The ads worked, he reasons, by presenting an award-winning tribute to several creative innovators in order to evoke the "love of exploration and innovation that people have associated with Apple from the beginning." The campaign's appeal also emanated from its implicit promise to empower, via the use of Apple technology, "those of us in the creative fields today to move forward and do the same" sorts of work as the featured innovators. Stressing the current significance of the "Think Different" campaign, Miller maintains that the ad serves as "a reminder that the Apple Computer Company is still very relevant to those who not only think differently but those who choose to change the whole body of what they think about."

Obviously, "Think Different" is not grammatically correct. When challenged to change the phrase to the correct form ("think differently"), a spokesperson for Apple explained that the word "think" is used as a noun (telling people what to think about) and "different" is misinterpreted if viewed as a directive (Ono C2). Barbara Lippert, a media critic, simply labeled the phrase "brand-speak" (28). Grammatically correct or not, the campaign was effective. An *Ad Track* poll of consumers, conducted during the closing weeks of 1998, noted the overall effectiveness of the campaign. Based on a nationwide poll of 303 adults who had seen the ads, more than a quarter liked them, but only 17% said they were effective; however, 38% of the target group of 25–29 year olds rated the ads effective (Enrico 12B). Ultimately, the "Think Different" television advertisement won Emmy and Obie awards, among others (Elliot "TBWA Chiat/Day Wins").

In *The Making of "Think Different,"* a video produced for the Macworld Expo in January 1998, the creators of the campaign describe how the process of creating the ad demonstrates Apple technology's utility and potential. Indeed, the advertising firm's art directors used Macintosh systems for every aspect of the design process. With less than seventeen days from approval to air time, the creative team used Mac-powered editing machines to view and edit archival footage as it arrived from all over the world, and Apple's QuickTime technology played an important role in this process. Images from graphics stations were imported into the ever-changing rough-cuts, an advantage that allowed the agency's editorial department to complete the editing without leaving the office. In the words of Jennifer Golub, executive producer of the advertisement:

> With our schedule, it would have been impossible to have executed this campaign prior to having a nonlinear editing system. Producing the Think Different campaign was a very live situation, where new material was arriving each day. I was constantly changing the material and also changing the cut based on the copy and the text. What had to be infused was an emotional resonance to the spot. My researcher actually found Maria Callas' home movies. They came in from Greece in a can covered with dust. When we found that one moment when she blew a kiss and then put in the footage of Gandhi, there's incredible power and feeling in that moment. I couldn't have articulated what I needed there, but when I could see it, in front of me, I knew it was exactly what I was looking for. (qtd. in "Here's to the Crazy Ones" 3)

Golub's response while editing the Callas footage underscores the capacity of images to trigger emotions prior to cognitive processing. The meaning of the Callas image is associative and holistic, so that the image not only presents itself as literal but also speaks to the emotions, bypassing logic and working through the power of allegory.

Lee Clow of Chiat/Day boasts that the media technology used to create the ad actually expanded the possibility for innovation. By focusing on the manipulation of visual images through computer editing, the creators of the ad argue that the actual process of meaning-making shifts from the mind to the computer screen where the image can be viewed, responded to, and edited. Ultimately,

this shift from an embodied to a mediated experience becomes, for Clow, an "evolutionary" event connecting man and machine: "When Apple comes into play is when people are reaching a little bit higher for their human potential. That means that computers will become even more accessible, whether that's by price or by the design of the products. It's always an evolution and a pushing. It's all about how much further you can take what you've always done" (qtd. in "Here's to the Crazy Ones" 4).

Clow's linking of consumer needs, technology, and human potential corresponds to the multifaceted nature of visual perception. "The logic of perception," argues media critic Ann Marie Seward Barry, "moves in ever-widening metaphors, stretching the boundaries of linear logic through analogy, expanding understanding through symbols, and arriving at places where neither experience nor imagination has ever before traveled" (83). Similarly, Nicholas Mirzoeff writes, "Visual culture used to be seen as a distraction from the serious business of text and history; it is now the locus of cultural and historical change" (31).

Given Jobs' connections with computer animation as CEO of Pixar, given Apple's recent innovations in computer graphic and editing equipment, and given that Apple's "Think Different" campaign opened during the network debut of *Toy Story*, one might expect the "Think Different" ad to pitch the company's expanding multimedia and graphics applications. What Apple presented, however, appealed to something quite different. Not an advertisement about product, the commercial instead was something far more fundamental—Apple's restatement to the world and to themselves of corporate identity and mission.[3] The ad, a video montage of black-and-white moving images, connects the creative and bold accomplishments of individuals from all walks of life. Most of the featured innovators achieved fame before 1970. Most are dead.[4] As Richard Dreyfuss narrates a text celebrating originality, greatness, ambition, and absolute self-belief, visual images of famous individuals dissolve one into another:

IMAGES	TEXT
Albert Einstein	Here's to the crazy ones.
Bob Dylan	The misfits. The rebels.
Martin Luther King, Jr.	The trouble makers.
Richard Branson	The round pegs in the square holes. The ones who see things differently.
John Lennon and Yoko Ono	They're not fond of rules.
Buckminster Fuller	And they have no respect for status quo.
Thomas Alva Edison	You can quote them,
Muhammad Ali	disagree with them, glorify
Ted Turner	or vilify them.
Maria Callas	About the only thing you can't do is ignore them.
Mahatma Gandhi	Because they change things.
Amelia Earhart	They push the human race forward.
Alfred Hitchcock	And while some may see them
Martha Graham	as the crazy ones,
Jim Henson	we see genius.
Frank Lloyd Wright	Because the people who are crazy enough
Pablo Picasso	to think they can change the world,
Unidentified young girl	are the ones who do.
Apple Logo	"Think Different"[5]

WHO SHOULD "THINK DIFFERENT"?

The makers of the ad clearly targeted particular audiences. According to one anonymous Apple executive, the ad was not targeted to the general public: "The smart ones will be able to figure it out. The ones who aren't smart enough [. . .] will probably not be able to think different anyway" (qtd. in Grossman 18). Describing why the ad won an Emmy award, Maria Matzer argued that it continued Apple's focus on "creative professionals" as a niche market but moved away from appeals directed toward "business and mass consumer markets."[6]

The "Think Different" campaign targeted computer users who identified with the corporation's status as an outsider. In fact, one reporter attributed Apple's amazing rebound after the launching of "Think Different" to the corporation's forward-thinking youth culture and its corporate identity based on "rebellion (a skull-and-crossbones flag flew over the building in which the Mac was developed), jeans in the workplace, full benefits for unmarried, gay or lesbian partners, great company t-shirts, and sushi in the cafeteria" ("Rebound"). Apple's outsider image emerged in its earlier "1984" advertising campaign, a campaign that stood in sharp contrast to the flood of patriotic and family-value ads popular during the Reagan presidency. While Kodak's highly successful "Because Time Goes By" series, produced in 1984 and 1985, presented images of an "American Eden" (Himmelstein 224), Apple's "1984" series, which introduced the apple-with-a-bite-out-of-it corporate logo, mined the same mythic terrain toward quite different ends. According to Arthur Asa Berger, the blonde woman with the sledgehammer in the "1984" ad functions as an "Eve figure who leads humans to knowledge of good and evil, though she is functioning in a dystopian institution, just the opposite of the Garden of Eden" (119). Apple's 1997 "Think Different" campaign built on the outsider appeal established by the earlier campaign, providing spectators a complex restatement of Eden's mythological appeal that I explore in detail later. No celebration of the status quo, "Think Different" challenged spectators to "change the world" and celebrated those persons who "artistically or imaginatively did creative things" (Clow qtd. in "Here's to the Crazy Ones" 4).

The diverse images used in the "Think Different" campaign appealed to Apple's established markets while simultaneously tapping into new and expanding ones in gay and ethnic communities (Bhat, Leigh, and Wardlow 162). Apple's courting of the gay market began prior to the "Think Different" campaign. Apple sponsored the 1994 Gay Games, and its corporate policies supported nontraditional couples (Freitas, Kaiser, and Hammidi 90). The inclusion of the Callas footage in the "Think Different" gallery of innovators continued this courtship. To be sure, Callas' inclusion was intended as an appeal to the followers of elite art forms, but it can also be read as an appeal to the gay community. According to Wayne Koestenbaum, for many in the gay community, Callas serves as an uncontested cultural icon (134–153). Indeed, Koestenbaum maintains that the star persona embodied in Callas provides insight into "the typical biography of a gay person in the 20th century," those individuals who have "to fight against invisibility and silence" (qtd. in Grossberg 10C). Dave Mulryan, a partner at Mulryan/Nash Communications, notes that in addition to assuming an activist stance toward gay issues, Apple may also have been responding to market realities. The gay demographic is an affluent one that marketers increasingly choose not to ignore,[7] and, interestingly, the spoken text that accompanies Callas' image in the

television spot proclaims that "about the only thing you can't do is ignore them."

In addition to targeting the gay community, "Think Different" also targeted minorities, particularly African Americans. The early 1990s witnessed a dramatic rise in the overall purchasing power of ethnic minorities in the United States, with potential revenues increasing 47% between 1990 and 1996 to $447 billion. According to marketing critic John Templeton, the African-American market for computers expanded with the continual drop in prices for technology. Most computer ads directed to this market "stress consumer utility versus highlighting functions and features" (42). Apple took a different approach. Jessica Shulman, who selected the African-American images used in the campaign, states: "We wanted to show that creativity and creative people are very diverse—it's not just a middle-aged white male in a tower somewhere [who uses a Mac]" (qtd. in Templeton 43). The images she selected—Muhammad Ali and Martin Luther King, Jr., for the television ad and eventually Rosa Parks for photo ads on buses—feature African-American icons associated with a variety of public institutions, including sports, religion, and politics. While Shulman wanted the ad to "pay tribute to those who changed the world," she also hoped her selection of images would "empower the rest of us to do the same thing." To assess this, she visited one of the city buses where Rosa Parks's image was displayed.[8] The African-American driver told Shulman that, although she had been driving a bus for twenty years, she did not anticipate the response to the ad. Shulman reports that the woman told her that "the whole time people were talking about civil rights on the bus instead of the normal conversation" (qtd. in Templeton 44). Whether the ad prompted computer sales among African-Americans is unknown; however, in this instance at least, it clearly struck a deeply resonant chord.

"THINK DIFFERENT" AS MIRRORED HETEROTOPIAN SITE

Michel Foucault argues that sites of institutional power are contested through contrasting sites, "which are something like counter-sites, a kind of effectively enacted utopia in which the real sites, all the other real sites that can be found in the culture, are simultaneously represented, contested and inverted" (24). Identified by Foucault as "heterotopias," these sites serve as liminal spaces of possibility and revision connected with and in resistance to existing institutions of power and authority within the culture (22–25). Foucault also argues that the mirror, existing in a real space and time, can be used to discover the "absence from the place where I am since I see myself over there" (24). A transforming space of possibilities, a mirrored heterotopian site can be constructed "between utopias and these other quite other sites, these heterotopias." To do so would create "a sort of mixed joint experience, which would be the mirror" (24). Foucault's mirrored heteropian sites are conceptual spaces opened between imagined utopias and real heterotopian sites (e.g., museums, nineteenth-century boarding schools, the honeymoon trip) where time is altered and new social and personal relationships are negotiated. Foucault writes:

> Starting from this gaze that is, as it were, directed toward me, from the ground of this virtual space that is on the other side of the glass, I come back toward myself; I begin again to direct my eyes toward myself and to reconstitute myself there where I am. The mirror functions as a heterotopia in this respect: it makes this place that I occupy at the moment when I look into the glass at once absolutely real, connected with all the space that surrounds it, and absolutely unreal, since in order to be perceived it has to pass through this virtual point which is over there. (24)

For Foucault, then, the process of viewing the mirrored heterotopian site is neither passive nor ineffectual.

The visual rhetoric and mythic appeals of "Think Different" can be theorized as a mirrored heterotopian site in which the images serve as a mirror, reflecting and shaping the aspirations of the target audience. A close reading of the images mirrored in "Think Different" underscores the gaps between history and utopian projections, memory and reality, revealing the power of the mediated image to persuade. Most of the images in the ad contain little internal movement connecting

one image to another; however, two edits exploit what little internal movement is featured. The shadow boxing of Muhammad Ali visually mirrors and connects with Ted Turner's triumphant salute, and Maria Callas' kiss to her adoring public, through quick editing, is caught on the cheek of Mahatma Gandhi. The images of Ali and Turner connect the televised worlds of sport, news, and media, flattening the elements of race, class, and economic power referenced in the lives of Ali and Turner. The triumph of a defiant African-American-Muslim athlete is copied and co-opted by a white team owner and media magnate, and the shared gesture eases the slippage beyond critical awareness of economic status and race. In another moment of hallucinatory enactment, the edited images of Callas and Gandhi blur the boundaries between artistic triumph and national politics, personal satisfaction and social well-being. Responding to Callas' kiss, Gandhi connects political struggle with prima donna politics.[9] Similarly, other images in the ad flatten the boundaries between high and low cultural reference, linking Jim Henson and Martha Graham, Bob Dylan and Pablo Picasso. Although the many linkages contained in the ad may, upon critical reflection, appear strained, even ridiculous, the sequence of visual quotations and spoken text together create a compelling allegory that ultimately opens a mirrored heterotopian site useful to the promotion of Apple's stated corporate values. In the words of media critic Peter Diekmeyer, the "ads become the product" (D2).

The final image of the ad features a young girl slowly opening her eyes. The final line of spoken text states: "Because the people who are crazy enough to think they can change the world are the ones who do." The images of Frank Lloyd Wright and Pablo Picasso featured in the first part of the sentence give way to the image of a young non-Caucasian girl chosen to illustrate "the ones who do." Apparently, Wright's and Picasso's objectification of women was not seen as contradictory to the ideal of emancipation. Presenting the future through the embodiment of the exotic other, the final image paradoxically projects a utopian future through gendered and racial imagery. In this instance, global politics speaks through disciplined history as corporate myth. Blurring the boundaries of gender, race, class and cultural appeals—and empowered by Apple Computers—the image of the unknown, non-Caucasian girl is the image of the future opened within this mirrored heterotopian site.

"THINK DIFFERENT" AS INTELLECTUAL MONTAGE AND AMPHIGORICAL PERSPECTIVE

Film pioneer and theorist Sergei Eisenstein developed a theory for making images function rhetorically by deploying colliding images to create deliberate perceptual dissonance. According to Eisenstein, a dialectical collision of images forces the viewer to resolve the conflict and to derive a meaning not implicit in any of the individual frames, a gestalt in the mind of the viewer: "The projection of the dialectic system of things into the brain, into creating abstractly, into the process of thinking, yields: dialectic methods of thinking; dialectical materialism—Philosophy" (45). In Eisenstein's view, "intellectual montage" results in the creation of a forceful rhetorical and ideological argument, thus engaging viewers' perception and directing their thought. Film theorist Paul Messaris identifies this as "propositional editing" (107).

The march of images in the Apple ad plays out the rhetorical and aesthetic strategy of propositional editing. In media advertising, Messaris contends, propositional editing links the subject image to the object image by presenting conceptual similarity or difference rather than visual repetition, and this challenges the audience to accept the implied analogy and make meaningful connections between the images. The implied analogy in "Think Different," however, is a problematic one. What does it mean to connect Maria Callas and Mahatma Gandhi in an ad to sell computers? What is the force of Callas' kiss?

The mythic associations of the "Think Different" campaign echo the already described allusions to Eden introduced in their "1984" ad campaign. "Think Different," too, presents an Eve figure and celebrates those who leave the Garden, who creatively pursue a dream, who take a chance. An explication of the ad's use of Maria Callas and Gandhi illustrates this claim. Callas fans would immediately read the concert footage of Callas as coming from her late concert performances in the 1950s, a time when the recently beautifully slim Callas reigned on the operatic scene. Callas fans might also reflect on the image of a kissing Callas and associate that gesture with the only opera she ever sang that featured a dramatically significant kiss, Richard Wagner's *Parsifal*. While writing the libretto, Wagner struggled to build the mythic connections between the biblical Eve and his Kundry. Responding to Ludwig, his patron, about the significance of Kundry's kiss, Wagner wrote:

> Adam and Eve become "knowing." They become "conscious of sin." Because of this consciousness the human race had to do penance in shame and misery until it was redeemed by Christ, who took upon Himself the sin of man. My dear, can I speak about such profound matters other than in metaphor, through comparison? But only the clear-sighted person can inform himself of the inner meaning. Adam-Eve: Christ. What if we added to them: "Amfortas-Kundry: Parsifal"? (qtd. in Groos, 31)

Kundry embodies the nineteenth-century trope of woman as temptress and virgin, a combination of the themes of temptation and redemption that Wagner, in his earlier *Tannhäuser,* split between the female characters Elizabeth and Venus (Plaut 183; see also Poizat 194). Callas sang Kundry early in her career before her rise at La Scala in 1951. At that time she was a large, dramatic woman with a powerful voice (Galatopoulos 89–90). Kundry, a suffering woman in need of redemption, has been cursed to live forever because she dared to laugh at the suffering Christ on the cross. When she meets the innocent Parsifal—the "perfect fool"—she turns temptress and tries to seduce him with a kiss. At the turning point in his quest to serve the Holy Grail, Parsifal—unlike Adam in the Garden—rejects her kiss and flees. Years later, as an ordained Knight of the Holy Grail and transformed as a Christ-figure in the opera, Parsifal baptizes Kundry and announces her redemption.

The image of Callas as Kundry/Eve and Gandhi as Parsifal/Adam in the "Think Different" ad campaign extends the mythical associations with the Garden of Eden promoted in the earlier

"1984" ad campaign. "Think Different" catches the kiss of Callas/Kundry/Eve just at the moment of Parsifal's/Gandhi's/Adam's temptation. Catherine Clément, in *Syncope: The Philosophy of Rapture,* describes Gandhi's embodiment of syncopic strategies in the political arena, specifically Gandhi's life of nonviolence and chastity. Clément, in an image that resonates with the legend of Parsifal, calls the reformer Gandhi "a knight" who openly professed suffering from his asceticism, the pains of "a renouncer's chastity." For Gandhi, as well as for Parsifal as a follower of the Holy Grail, "fasting was his main syncope," the source of his personal and political power (Clément 243–245). Interestingly, Callas also endured much to achieve a body image equal to her musical talent, an act of personal discipline that dramatically altered her career, her personal life, and ultimately became a part of the Callas legend (Tommasini B4). Midway through the "Think Different" television ad, Callas/Kundry/Eve tempts Gandhi/Parsifal/Adam, a subtle reminder of the moment of choice for all that leave the Garden, for all who take a bite of the Apple.

In addition to reinscribing corporate and cultural myths, the "Think Different" campaign also exploits necrophilic preoccupations associated with end-of-century aesthetics (Goldman 60). In our millennium moment, the proliferation of visual imagery that saturate our media reflects our culture's preoccupation with reflexive rhetorical and aesthetic strategies. Critical response to the first broadcast of the ad focused on these strategies. For example, James Martin, a media critic, noted that the ad was "amusing rather than offensive (it's too ridiculous to be offensive)." Characterizing Apple customers as "lemming-like consumers," he read the intended response to the ad as follows: "Gee, if I buy an Apple computer, I'll be just as smart as Albert Einstein and discover a new theory of relativity and get to grow my hair long …" (22). Asked if it was overreaching to involve Einstein, Gandhi and Picasso in pitching their product, representatives from Apple declared that homage, not exploitation, was the goal: "We would never associate these people with any product; it's Apple celebrating them versus Apple using them. To say that Albert Einstein would have

used a computer would cross the line. Why would he need one? But it's different to say he looked at the work differently" (qtd. in Elliott, "The Media Business" 1D).

Through the use of documentary-style images, the video ad creates an amphigorical perspective—a kind of burlesque, nonsense writing or parody—and it is this amphigorical perspective that both troubles and appeals. As Paul Edwards argues, "It is impossible to draw the line between earnest, unhappy parody and more amphigorical attitudes: happily smart-ass mimicry, selfish appropriation, or sheer irresponsible unresponsiveness" (296). Given the artful black-and-white images and the lofty delivery of the spoken text, the amphigorical attitude emerges only upon critical reflection. Indeed, the formal visual structures of the ad carefully and tellingly harmonize with the rhythms and nuances of the spoken narration. One particular moment in the ad clearly reveals the attention to verbal syntax and underscores the playful tone of the amphigorical perspective within this mirrored heterotopian site: the image of Jim Henson manipulating Kermit the frog appears while Dreyfuss deftly notes "we see genius." By placing the emphasis on individual perspective rather than product, the ad effectively connects with the shifting cultural attitudes towards technology in our time. In the words of media critic Kathy Tyler: "Despite some of the criticism that the campaign is not 'different' enough, Apple's idea of branding the consumer who uses the computer instead of the computer itself is timely today. It may have been ahead of its time more than a decade ago, but the changing definition of computing makes Apple's message on target. Computing today has much more to do with people and communication than 13 years ago, when it represented a tool to run a business" (6).

WE ALL WANT TO "THINK DIFFERENT"

What does "Think Different" tell us about spectatorship in a world dominated by mediatized visual images? "Think Different" works to capitalize on visual appeals in terms of memory, fame, and cultural status. Counterposing corporate culture and the specific cultural moment reveals the complex layering of contradictory dualities that constitute the visual grammar of this ad. James Martin, a media critic, refers to the contradictory forces in contemporary advertising as "content dissonance," noting that it "occurs when an advertisement that follows (or precedes) an article is so at odds with the content of the article that it renders the advertisement either offensive or absurd, like insipid ads placed in the middle of serious stories or a silly television commercial that follows news of a tragedy. It is easy to spot; and once you've got the hang of it, you'll see it everywhere" (23). "Think Different" exploits the power of content dissonance as a means of cultural circulation and identification. Read only as documentary footage, as vestiges of real people in real places, the particulars of historical fact negate the rhetorical argument of "Think Different"—namely, that all of these individuals contributed in equal ways to the betterment of all by thinking differently. The visual juxtaposition and voice-over narration used throughout the ad, however, move the ad beyond mere reportage or quotation. The boldness of reference and audacity of association within the ad, through the techniques of intellectual montage, open a mirrored heterotopian site of renewal and possibility.

Audiences can read the visual icons of "Think Different" in a multiplicity of ways, sometimes consuming the text within the dominant ideology, sometimes recoding the text entirely, sometimes mixing elements of dominant or emerging ideologies. As S. Paige Baty reminds us: "Iconic remembering is fundamental to mass-mediated circulation. Icons are culturally resonant units that convey a familiar set of 'original' meanings and images. Because they represent content as form [. . .] they also provide a surface on which struggles over meanings can be waged" (59). These struggles are shaped, in part, by the audience's willingness and ability to identify and make associations between and beyond the specific images.

The design and reception of "Think Different" reveal how cultural forces and media content are mutually self-referential and reinforcing. Indeed, Apple's use of images of twentieth-century innovators—ranging from Bob Dylan to Maria Callas, Einstein to Gandhi—speaks to corporate image processes designed to exploit the collapse of high and low culture and the globalization of

cultural referent. Paul Messaris acknowledges that "some degree of specific experience with prepositional editing may be required for a viewer to be able to recognize its characteristic patterns of juxtaposition and iteration as frameworks for the conceptual integration of images" (111). Given the popularity and critical acclaim surrounding "Think Different," it can be assumed that most viewers got the point.

Advertising, Williamson argues, possesses the power to serve both specific ideological forces and individual desire:

> Ideology is the meaning made necessary by the conditions of society while helping to perpetuate those conditions. We feel a need to belong, to have a social "place"; it can be hard to find. Instead we may be given an imaginary one. All of us have a genuine need for a social being, a common culture. The mass media provide this to some extent and can (potentially) fulfill a positive function in our lives. (13)

Ultimately the marketing strategy in "Think Different" was, paradoxically, at once self-serving and visionary. Operating in a materialist and ahistorical culture, Apple extolled the virtue of rebelliousness to creative young professionals and marketed itself as the rebellious computer company. By doing so, it attempted to sell product through consumer identification with corporate myth. "Mythical thought," Lévi-Strauss contends, "builds ideological castles out of the debris of what was once social discourse" (qtd. in Williamson, 97). The surprising and contrasting celebrity-images appropriated in the ad create an amphigorical perspective framed as tribute, structured as polemic, and sold as advertisement, and this works for those consumers who want and expect an edge, a spin (both visual and conceptual), history and common sense be damned.

Visual rhetoric assumes particular force as a means of evoking cultural myths in marketing, particularly in an age preoccupied with the reframing and recirculation of individual lives as iconic images. The corresponding impulse to read these images as mythic narrative powers "Think Different." A string of documentary images become hallucinatory history/memory, blending the "high" with the "low" and leveling out class, bleaching out race, and erasing time. "Think Different" evokes the cultural myth of renewal and rebirth, a universal faith in the power of technology, progress, and the human potential. The ad functions as a postmodern media Eucharist, feeding the living images of the dead and evoking a desire for the bread and the body, the wine and the blood, a truth and a vision, a salvation myth and a constructed future. The final image of the young girl opening her eyes presents the imagined ideal world citizen (as a person waking from sleep? a person moving from darkness into light? Eve after taking a bite out of the Apple?). The future is here for all who think Apple.

THINKING ABOUT "THINK DIFFERENT"

In true postmodern fashion, the slogan, visual rhetoric and amphigorical tone of "Think Different" have been quoted and recirculated in a variety of venues as a form of product, media, and cultural critique. Steven Levy, for example, turns the ad campaign's slogan against Apple in his review of the company's 2000 product line, suggesting that it might be time to "stop Thinking Different" ("Should I Stay or Should I Go?" 45; "Apple's iBook" 54–56). Visual artist Alex Tehrani, in his 1998 series of photographs of people in Times Square, captured the massive "Think Different" image of opera diva Callas on the side of a building staring down over the shoulder of an unidentified black man next to a designated "hard hat area." With the photographs in the Times Square Project, Tehrani "provided an inversion of spectator and spectacle, audience and performer in a neighborhood in which the mongrel theater of the street competes with the legitimate theatre indoors" (Frailey 88). And, in another cycle of circulation testifying to the relevance of the amphigorical perspective in contemporary marketing, this particular image from the Times Square Project was featured on the cover of the July/August 1998 issue of *Print,* a graphic design magazine.[10]

More aggressive appropriations soon followed. In late 1998 and early 1999, Hocus Focus, a guerrilla art group, reacted to Apple's use of counter culture figures in the campaign.

According to its website, Hocus Focus is comprised of artists dedicated to "conducting rituals to reanimate the archetypes whose images have been rendered lifeless on billboards, city buildings, and magazine covers in the service of Apple Computer Corporation's international 'Think Different' marketing campaign."[11] In an effort to turn back the "mass cynicism" perpetuated by ads such as "Think Different," the members of Hocus Focus carefully orchestrated a series of midnight alterations, adding text to Apple's billboard images in San Francisco, Los Angeles, and New York. To an Apple billboard featuring the image of Gandhi, Hocus Focus activists added the phrase "corporate colonization of the unconscious" as well as a question mark after "Think Different." To a "Think Different" image of Callas, they added "prefer a pitch more sublime." According to Judith Coburn, a performance critic for *The Village Voice,* although Hocus Focus respects Apple's savvy in selecting culturally resonant figures, they resist and condemn the facile commodification of the dead:

> Using these heroes as "savage appliance hucksters" strips them of their cultural potency. They aren't simply co-opted, but become dead for us. "We are in a constant exchange with archetypal figures like these with whom we engage to orient ourselves psychologically. The morphing of these figures into retail salespeople creates direct psychic disorientation within us," argues one of the group's mission statements, in their heady brew of Jung, Marcuse, and Debord. (47)

Hocus Focus' acts of artistic protest (or vandalism) speak directly to the viewer and indirectly to the Apple Corporation. By drawing attention to how advertising works, Hocus Focus aims to empower consumers to resist the rhetorical and mythic appeal of the ad. Their midnight revisions of Apple's "Think Different" billboards construct "meanings that challenge people to think (if not differently)" (Coburn 47).

Additional reactions to "Think Different" continued to circulate, evidence of the pervasiveness and, for some, potential perverseness of the ad's amphigorical perspective. Consider, for example, the front and back covers of the April 20, 1998, issue of *New York.* The back cover featured the image of Maria Callas in a "Think Different" print ad, and the front cover featured an image of gutter-TV host Jerry Springer assuming a similar pose. Commenting on the visual parody, Steven Heller dismissed the cover image as evidence of a striking lack of originality in contemporary periodical publishing (10). However, the fact that the juxtaposed images were used at all assumes that the general reader would make the connection and get the joke. Another example of the recirculation of "Think Different" appears in a personal website established in 1998. The website underscores the dark side of "Think Different" with a group of images entitled "Ads that Apple Didn't Release." This gallery of images features the likes of mass murderers, including Adolf Hitler, as those who also "Think Different" (Bernard). A final example of the recirculation of "Think Different" appeared in a more traditional venue, the *New York Times*. In a series of full-page ads, the organizers of the Turning Point Project warned readers of the danger of megatechnology. Their third installment, "The Internet and the Illusion of Empowerment" challenged readers with the following: "Think Different. (Think differently, actually). Start asking questions about how this revolution is going. For inspiration you might check the work of, well, Gandhi, who actually spent his life working against the kind of centralizing technology that global computer systems represent" (A13).

"Think Different" entered American cultural life through a carefully orchestrated synergistic campaign. Given the number of texts that revise, recycle, and recirculate "Think Different," perhaps in this instance the synergy built message resistance and fatigue, as well as product recognition. Taken together, the many responses provoked by "Think Different" underscore the extent to which the advertising campaign spoke to the cultural forces that animate the contemporary moment. "Think Different" problematically and creatively mixed high and low cultural appeals, reached out to specific demographics, reinscribed corporate and cultural myths, and ultimately constructed the "ideal audience/consumer" for the computer product. Walter Benjamin predicted that with the rise of visual images in our culture (specifically, the use of photography in advertising), the caption would become the "most important component of the shot" (25).[12] In "Think Different," Richard Dreyfuss' narration and the carefully edited images plead the amphigorical logic of this mirrored heterotopian site. An act of cultural narration and utopian projection, the television, billboard and print ads of the "Think Different" campaign synergistically construct a vision of an Apple-dominated world filled with consumers who, paradoxically, all "think different."

Responses to that mediated construction, the image from the mirror, varied. In a critique of the synergistic marketing strategies used to promote popular films such as *The Blair Witch Project,* Janet Maslin warns of the corroding effects of aggressive marketing. She argues that the "accumulated impact of this much stealth marketing, and of the cultural cross-pollination that synergy entails, is to foster an atmosphere of deep mistrust" (Maslin E1). Perhaps Apple's "Think Different" created such feelings. No doubt, although many in the audience accepted the surface idealism of "Think Different," others rejected the deeper amphigorical logic of the ad and the saturation of the campaign. Nevertheless, as media theorist Mark Poster reminds us in his discussion of Foucault and cultural power: "Anything can be associated with anything else for a viewing subject who is structured by the rhetoric of the commercial" (120). And for Apple consumers during the closing months of the last century, most seemed ready to buy it: Callas' kiss awaits those who leave the Garden.

NOTES

1. Stuart Elliot, a *New York Times* reporter, quickly drew connections between Disney and the marketing appeal of Apple's "Think Different" ("New Apple Ad").

2. A variety of Apple press releases related to the campaign, including "Apple Launches Brand Advertising Campaign, September 29, 1997," are archived on the Apple website at (http://www.apple.co/pr/photos/ads/adphotos.html). Photos of a "Think Different" billboard and store display campaign can be found at (http://product.info.apple.com/pr/photos/ads/adphotos.html) and (http://www.expectingrain.com/ads/thinkdifferent.html). In Boston, the South Train

Station served as a site for saturation display of the ads. According to a *Boston Globe* reporter, during early 1998 "Think Different" posters used most of the available advertising space, usually shared by forty different companies (Reidy). CNN broadcast reports describing the origins, goals and success of "Think Different" ("Apple CEO Announcement"; "Award Winning Ads").

3. For a summary of the impact of management tactics, advertising, and product innovation on Apple's changing financial fortunes, see Bartholomew. For an example of critical response to the "Think Different" campaign a year after it began, see Alonso.

4. Debra Goldman explains this necrophilic turn: "In the '90s, we extol thinking different, but we reward people who think the same. If you don't believe me, try playing a game I suspect devotees of this campaign are already playing: Choose three candidates fit for a place on the 'Think Different' honor roll. They have to meet three criteria: They must have a high-enough celebrity quotient to be recognized by Apple's target market. They have to be real innovators. And to make it challenging, they can't be businesspeople. Where will you find them, among the quick or the dead? My three picks would be George Balanchine, Coco Chanel and Charlie Parker: May they rest in peace" (61). To promote interest in the campaign and to teach history and computer literacy, Apple urged the public to participate in a "Think Different Quiz" established on the corporation website.

5. Readers are encouraged to download the advertisement from the Apple Website. To view the video, access (http://www.thinkdifferent.nu/td/video.html).

6. Matzer conducted a survey of *Los Angeles Times* readers to determine which of that year's Emmy nominated ads the readers considered most creative and emotionally effective. Results revealed that e-mail response to the survey favored the Apple commercial. Noting that several of the e-mail votes for the Apple ad originated from persons on the e-mail system of TBWA Chiat/Day, the advertising firm that created the spot, Matzer dryly concluded: "Guess they don't 'think different'" (6).

7. For a discussion of contemporary marketing appeals to the gay community, see "Gay Advertising Examined."

8. A photo of a bus bearing the image of Rosa Parks can be found at (http://product.info.apple.com/pr/photos/ads/adphotos.html).

9. I am indebted to Susan J. Leonardi and Rebecca A. Pope for the phrase and concept "prima donna politics." In *The Diva's Mouth: Body, Voice, Prima Donna Politics,* they explore the place of the female voice in cultural life, providing a detailed feminist explication of the image of the prima donna in contemporary life and literature. They argue that "opera seems these days to cross boundaries between elite and popular entertainment in a way that calls these categories into question, so too do divas" (22). As I argue in this essay, the iconic images in "Think Different" function as cultural prima donnas, collapsing the categories of high and low culture.

10. The *Print* cover image appears in conjunction with Frailey's essay on Tehrani's Times Square Project. Only one photo in Tehrani's series featured the Callas image as backdrop/context.

11. Hocus Focus' website (http://www.Hocus Focus.org) contains information about the group and their performances, as well a gallery of images designed to subvert the Apple campaign. For information concerning the defacement of the Apple billboard near highway 101 in San Carlos, California, in April 1998, access (http://www.zdnet.com/zdnn/content/zdnn/0428/311073.html). According to Lisa M. Bowman (on the website), the words "Think Dissillusioned" replaced "Think Different." As a sign of not being willing to think too differently (and not willing to offend the Chinese government), the incident occurred shortly after Apple announced that the corporation would not use the image of the Tibetan leader in Hong Kong.

12. Mark Roskill and David Carrier provide a convincing example of the power of Walter Benjamin's "caption" to guide viewer response in their explication of a recent Chanel #5 ad featuring Catherine Deneuve (37–39).

REFERENCES

Alonso, Marie Ranoia. "An Apple Talk: On Thinking Different." *Business and Management Practices* 41.8 (January 1999): 42–43.

"Apple Billboard Defaced." (http://www.zdnet.com/zdnn/content/zdnn/0428/311073.hlml).

"Apple CEO Announcement." Cable News Network Transcript #97111012FN-L05. Broadcast 10 November 1997, 2:15 p.m. Eastern Time.

"Apple Launches Brand Advertising Campaign." (http://www.apple.com/pr/library).

Auslander, Philip. *Liveness: Performance in a Mediatized Culture.* New York: Routledge, 1999.

"Award Winning Ads." Cable News Network Transcript #98043005FN-L09. Broadcast 30 April 1998, 6:31 p.m. Eastern Time.

Barry, Ann Marie Seward. *Visual Intelligence: Perception, Image, and Manipulation in Visual Communication.* Albany: State UP of New York, 1997.

Bartholomew, Doug. "What's Really Driving Apple's Recovery?" *Industry Week* 248.6 (15 March 1999): 34–40.

Baty, S. Paige. *American Monroe: The Making of a Body Politic.* Berkeley: U of California P, 1995.

Benjamin, Walter. "A Short History of Photography." *Screen* 13.1 (1972): 5–26.

Bhat, Sudodh, Thomsa W. Leigh, and Daniel L. Wardlow. "The Effect of Homosexual Imagery in Advertising on Attitude Toward the Ad." *Gays, Lesbians, and Consumer Behavior.* Ed. Daniel L. Wardlow. New York: Harrington Park, 1996. 161–176.

Berger, Arthur Asa. *Narratives in Popular Culture, Media, and Everyday Life.* Thousand Oaks, CA: SAGE Publications, 1997.

Bernard, Ethan. Personal website featuring "Ads Apple Didn't Release." (http://ucs.orst.edu~bernarde/appleads/appleads.html).

"Bob Dylan Apple Think Different Poster." (http://www.apple.com/pr/library).

Burrows, Peter. "A Peek at Steve Jobs's Plan." *Business Week* 17 November 1997: 144.

Butsch, Richard. *The Making of American Audiences: From Stage to Television, 1750–1990.* Cambridge: Cambridge UP, 2000.

Clément, Catherine. *Syncope: The Philosophy of Rapture.* Trans. Sally O'Driscoll and Deirdre M. Mahoney. Minneapolis: U of Minnesota P, 1994.

Coburn, Judith, "Up Against the Wall: Hocus Focus Rewrites Apple's Ad Campaign," *Village Voice* 8 December 1998: 47.

Diekmeyer, Peter. "Ads Become the Products." *The Gazette* (Montreal). 12 January 1999: D2.

Edwards, Paul. "Neuschwanstein or The Sorrows of Priapus." *Text and Performance Quarterly* 19 (1999): 271–306.

Eisenstein, Sergei. "A Dialectic Approach to Film Form," *Film Form: Essays in Film Theory.* Trans. and ed. Jay Leyda. New York: Harcourt Brace Jovanovich, 1949. 45–48.

Elliot, Stuart. "New Apple Ad Lifts Off From Disney's Land." *New York Times* 29 September 1997: 13D.

——. "TBWA Chiat/Day Wins Top Obie Award." *New York Times* 25 September 1998: 2C.

——. "The Media Business: Apple Endorses Some Achievers Who 'Think Different.'" *New York Times* 3 August 1998: 1D.

Enrico, Dottie. "Experts Doubt Effectiveness of Apple's Star-Studded Ads." *USA TODAY* 5 January 1998: 12B.

Foucault, Michel. "Of Other Places." Trans. Jay Miskowiec. *Diacritics* 16.1 (1986): 22–27.

Frailey, Stephen. "Prime Times Square." *Print* 50.4 (1998): 82–89.

Freitas, Anthony, Susan Kaiser, and Tania Hammidi. "Communities, Commodities, Cultural Space, and Style." *Gays, Lesbians, and Consumer Behavior.* Ed. Daniel L. Wardlow. New York: Harrington Park, 1996. 83–108.

Galatopoulos, Stelios. *Maria Callas: Sacred Monster.* New York: Simon and Schuster, 1998.

"Gay Advertising Examined." Cable News Network Transcript #97122607FN-109, Broadcast 26 December 1997, 6:30 p.m. Eastern Time.

Goldman, Debra. "Day of the Dead." *Adweek* (New York) 38.48 (1 December 1997): 60.

Groos, Arthur. "Appropriation in Wagner's Tristan Libretto." *Reading Opera.* Eds. Arthur Groos and Roger Parker. Princeton: Princeton UP, 1988. 12–33.

Grossberg, Michael. "McNally Puts Gay Stereotype to Sound Dramatic Use." *Columbus Dispatch* 10 January 1995: 10C.

Grossman, Aaron. "Thinking Different is OK." *Brandweek* (New York) 39.16 (20 April 1998): 18.

Heller, Steven. "Separated at Birth." *Print 52.4* (1998): 10.

"Here's to the Crazy Ones." (http://www.apple.com/pr/library).

Heywood, Ian, and Barry Sandywell. "Introduction: Explorations in the Hermeneutics of Vision." *Interpreting Visual Culture.* Eds. Ian Heywood and Barry Sandywell. London: Routledge, 1999.

Himmelstein, Hal. "Kodak's 'America': Images from the American Eden." *Television: The Critical View.* Ed. Horace Newcomb. New York: Oxford U Press, 1994. 224–248.

Hocus Focus Website. (http://www.HocusFocus.org).

Koestenbaum, Wayne. *The Queen's Throat: Opera, Homosexuality, and the Mystery of Desire.* New York: Vintage, 1993.

Leonardi, Susan J., and Rebecca A. Pope. *The Diva's Mouth: Body, Voice, Prima Donna Politics.* New Brunswick, NJ: Rutgers UP, 1996.

Levy, Stephen. "Apple's iBook: A Mac to Go." *Newsweek* 2 August 1999: 54–56.

——. "Should I Stay or Should I Go?" *Newsweek* 15 May 2000: 45.

Li, Kenneth. "Past Programs the Future: Rethinking at Core of Campaign." *Daily News* (New York) 14 August 1997: 36.

Lippert, Barbara. "Think Ironic." *Adweek* (New York) 39.36 (7 September 1998): 28.

Martin, James. "Thinking Differently." *America* 3 January 1998: 22.

Maslin, Janet. "Critic's Notebook: Creative Cannibalism Nibbles at the Audience's Trust?" *New York Times* 26 August 1999: E1.

Matzer, Marla. "A 'Different' Stroke of Genius Earns an Emmy." *Los Angeles Times* 3 September 1998: 6.

McGinn, Daniel. "Chiat's New Day." *Newsweek* 3 August 1998: 40–41.

Meehan, Eileen R. "Conceptualizing Culture as Commodity: The Problem of Television." *Television: The Critical View.* Ed. Horace Newcomb. New York: Oxford UP, 1994.

Messaris, Paul. *Visual Literacy: Image, Mind, and Reality.* Boulder, CO: Westview, 1994.

Miller, Jeremy. "Concerning Apple Ads." E-mail to the author. 19 August 1999.

Mirzoeff, Nicholas. *An Introduction to Visual Culture.* London: Routledge, 1999.

Morgan, Adam. *Eating the Big Fish: How Challenger Brands Can Compete Against Brand Leaders.* New York: John Wiley and Sons, 1999.

Ono, Yumiko. "Apple Tries to 'Think Different.'" *Ottawa Citizen* 13 October 1997: C2.

Pavis, Patrice. "Dancing with Faust: A Semiotician's Reflections on Barba's Intercultural Mise-en scène." *TDR* 33.3 (1989): 37–57.

Plaut, Eric A. *Grand Opera: Mirror of the Western Mind.* Chicago: Ivan R. Dee, 1993.

Poizat, Michel. *The Angel's Cry: Beyond the Pleasure Principle in Opera.* Trans. Arthur Denner. Ithaca: Cornell UP, 1992.

Poster, Mark. "Foucault, the Present and History." *Cultural Critique* 8 (Winter 1987–88): 105–21.

Reidy, Chris. "The One, the Only." *Boston Globe* 16 July 1999: D1.

"Rebound Due to Readiness to Take Harsh Decisions." *Irish Times* 5 February 5, 1999, city edition: 54.

Robichaud, Nancy, and Ronald E. Shields. *"Pelleas et Melisande* through the Filter of American Experience: Comparing Notes with Peter Sellars." *Theatre Annual* 53 (2000): 37–68.

Roskill, Mark, and David Carrier. *Truth and Falsehood in Visual Images.* Amherst: U of Massachusetts P, 1983.

Templeton, John. "Ignoring a $447 Billion Market: African-Americans." *Business and Management Practices* 18.2 (1998): 42–45.

"Think Different" television ad. (http://www.apple .com/pr/library).

"Think Different Photography." (http://www.apple .com/pr/library).

"Think Different Quiz." (http://www.eworld.com/ education/k12/teachlearn/tdquest.html).

Tommasini, Anthony, "Callas: A Voice that Still Fascinates." *New York Times* 15 September 1997: B1.

Tulloch, John. *Performing Culture: Stories of Expertise and the Everyday.* London: Sage, 1999.

Turning Point Project. "The Internet and the Illusion of Empowerment." *New York Times* 10 July 2000: A13.

Tyler, Kathy. "Apple Tries to Bite Back." *Marketing Magazine* 12 January 1998: 6.

Williams, Molly. "Apple Computer Climbs Back." *San Diego Union-Tribune* 4 September 1999: C8.

Williamson, Judith. *Decoding Advertisements: Ideology and Meaning in Advertising. London:* Marion Boyars, 1978.

15

"PUT YOUR STAMP ON HISTORY"

The USPS Commemorative Program Celebrate the Century *and Postmodern Collective Memory*

EKATERINA V. HASKINS

Against the backdrop of the global fear of electrical blackout and prophesies of the end of the world, the end of the millennium occasioned retrospection, including recollections of famed individuals, museum exhibits, anthologies of photographs, and even comic strips. The United States Postal Service's *Celebrate the Century* promised to become "one of the nation's largest and most inclusive commemorations of the 20th century."[1] The program's scope—150 stamps were issued over a two-year period to honor the most significant people, events, and trends of each decade of the century—was matched by unprecedented public involvement and an array of promotional activities. The stamps representing the first five decades were chosen by members of the Citizens' Stamp Advisory Committee appointed by the Postmaster General; the public selected the images representing the second half of the century. Ballots were available at post offices

nationwide. In the balloting for *Celebrate the Century* all those interested, including schoolchildren, could vote an unlimited number of times provided proper postage was affixed to each ballot.

Much financial and organizational effort was exerted to excite and sustain public interest in this commemoration. Post offices across the nation were transformed into mini-museums featuring electronic panels that counted days, hours, and seconds remaining until the year 2000. On their way to the clerk's window visitors were greeted by colorful panes of stamps issued under the aegis of *Celebrate the Century*. In February 1998, as the ballots for the 1950s arrived, the USPS issued commemorative sheets for the decades of 1900 and 1910 and sponsored a series of unveiling ceremonies across the country, dubbed "thirty stamps in thirty days." Schoolchildren in some 300,000 classrooms were encouraged to "stamp history" as they learned

SOURCE: Haskins, E. V. (2003). "Put your stamp on history": The USPS Commemorative Program *Celebrate the Century* and postmodern collective memory. *Quarterly Journal of Speech, 89,* 1–18. © National Communication Association.

about earlier decades from the "Celebrate the Century Kit." Before the series of ten panels was completed, stamps issued to date were integrated into a train exhibit, "Celebrate the Century Express," a four-car museum that traversed the country from coast to coast, inviting visitors to "experience a century's worth of achievement and tragedy, entertainment and innovation, grit and greatness."[2]

Celebrate the Century was as much about remembering and celebrating as it was about reminding adults and children about what to remember. Commemorative postal stamps, like other artifacts of memory, have a problematic relationship with history because they identify and amplify certain people and events and consign others to oblivion.[3] Stamps, however, always speak on behalf of the entire nation and as such claim to represent crucial aspects of national identity to citizens and outsiders alike.[4] Stamp subjects and designs, therefore, are a matter of cultural politics.

Celebrate the Century is particularly illuminating as a case study of the production of collective memory in postmodernity. *Celebrate the Century* manifests a postmodern shift in the aesthetics and the politics of commemoration in several ways. The program's most conspicuous feature is a lack of discrimination between representations of historical events or persons and pop culture. Thus, the series is a mnemonic device in a cultural situation in which saturation by images or simulacra, to use Baudrillard's term, threatens a stable sense of history and identity.[5]

By the same token, the program relies on this volatility and fragmentation of the image to promote itself as a novel way to commemorate. That half of the icons were chosen by popular vote emphasizes popularity as the mark of their historical significance and political legitimacy. Despite *Celebrate the Century's* success as a popular program, however, its professed inclusiveness veils the process through which the public's political agency as co-creators of history is manipulated to benefit private, corporate interests. Although it was promoted as the result of a popular and open selection process, *Celebrate the Century* uses that process as a strategy to authenticate a hegemonic narrative.

Accordingly, the politics of inclusion became a strategy to assimilate "vernacular" interests into "official" ones.

To show how *Celebrate the Century* exemplifies a postmodern shift in the aesthetics of commemoration, I first trace thematic and stylistic transformations in commemorative postal iconography and its relation to postmodern simulacra. Because contemporary icons serve an important emotional and political function in an ever-accelerating culture of obsolescence, they constitute a visual lexicon out of which hegemonic and counterhegemonic interpretations of history may emerge. Next, I depict the politics of stamp selection as a struggle between official and vernacular interests to suggest that the public's participation in the process, although potentially disruptive of official culture's hegemony, ultimately was appropriated by official and corporate interests. Finally, I focus on several display mechanisms that helped to frame the collection as a commodity, the public as tourists, and history as progress toward consumer democracy.

From "Civil Religion" to Consumer Society: the Evolution of Commemorative Iconography

The evolution of commemorative aesthetics in general and postal iconography in particular forms the backdrop against which *Celebrate the Century* stands as an example of postmodern collective memory-in-the-making. Some observers have frowned on the "pop" character of the series in which somber photographs of child laborers and the "Migrant Mother" share iconic status with neon-bright images of consumer products from crayons to Barbie dolls.[6] That a collective memory project should be so closely entwined with popular culture is not simply a matter of taste.

The current postal iconography can be seen as one of many manifestations of a transformation in individual and collective experience of history in the West. Whether described as postmodernism, postnationalism, or post-Fordism, this change has affected the way citizens in liberal-democratic societies relate to past, present, and future.[7] In the United States, this shift was felt, in part, as a disenchantment with the legitimizing myth of "civil religion," itself a blend of religious faith in the nation as a chosen people and a civic republican ideal of the state as social covenant. Robert Bellah coined the term in 1967 in the midst of social upheavals of the Vietnam War era, when the symbolic fabric signified by the term already had begun to unravel.[8] Bellah defined civil religion as "the myths that have developed to help us interpret who and what we are in America."[9]

For over a century, U.S. postal iconography dramatized the dialectic of self-determination and destiny, stewardship and conquest.[10] Stamps promulgated the heroic imperative of leadership: presidents, statesmen, military leaders, and explorers remained the dominant themes of celebration well into the 1950s.[11] The style of depiction contributed to the sublime aura of the images. Statesmen often were shown in profile in the manner of Roman busts. Heroes of the American Revolution were leading their troops to victory. Explorers were landing triumphantly on the shores of new territories or ascending mountain peaks. Thus, whether the subject is the landing of Columbus, Marquette's crossing of the Mississippi, or Fremont's scaling of the Rocky Mountains, the composition of the images and the postures of those featured convey the momentousness of the event and the superhuman status of the central character, thereby establishing a kinship between the legendary conqueror of the New World and nineteenth-century pioneers.

In the meantime, stamps bearing icons of the industrial age carried the story of progress. The locomotive, the steamship, the automobile, and the bridge—the images marking the Pan-American Exposition issue of 1901—assume a sublimity unrivaled by human beings. Representation of these technological wonders in the commemorative context acquires the aura of a national myth. A particularly vivid example is the stamp, "Landing of Cadillac in Detroit 1701–1951," in which the image is formed by the juxtaposition of a familiar iconic scene of a hero's "landing" with Detroit's modern skyscrapers lurking in the background. Thus, the center of the U.S. automobile industry and the

birthplace of the assembly line is mythologized by its retroactive inclusion into the pantheon of the nation's civil religion.

From the mid-nineteenth century until the 1960s, the subjects and iconography of postal stamps replicate other commemorative practices of the era of nationalism. As John Gillis observes, "on both sides of the Atlantic, national commemorations were largely the preserve of elite males, the designated carriers of progress"; by contrast, "the role of women was largely allegorical," and workers, minorities and younger people "gained admission to national memories at an even slower pace than they were admitted to national representative and educational institutions."[12]

By most accounts, the sixties were a watershed decade that transformed memory practices throughout the world. After the establishment of the Citizens' Stamp Advisory Committee in 1957, postal commemoration entered a new era, as official memory became more open to influences from ordinary people. Although the final word still belonged to the Postmaster General, all citizens could now suggest postal themes and designs.[13] Official anniversaries continued to provide commemorative themes, but their representation no longer uniformly followed the heroic aesthetic of the nationalist era. For instance, a laconic image of a broken chain—black links against a navy blue background—hails the centennial of the Emancipation Proclamation. The abstract character of the image connotes a non-hierarchical value system without leaders or followers, wherein all are equally liberated via the freeing of an oppressed group. In the commemoration of the American Revolution's bicentennial, populist motifs mingle with the official icons of the Founding Fathers. Issued over a six-year period, four stamp series—"Colonial Craftsmen," "Colonial Communications," "Contributors to the Cause," and "The Spirit of '76"—exemplify a shift toward reconsidering crucial events of U.S. history from the perspective of a common citizen.[14]

The popular turn also is signaled by the inclusion of mundane subjects expressing the seemingly apolitical interests of regular Americans. Alongside space exploration, achievements in electronics, the Civil War centennial, and the

U.S. bicentennial, stamps of the sixties and the seventies salute amateur radio, professional baseball, and college football. In the post-bicentennial period, stamp subjects draw on popular culture more than on the patriotic lore of the nationalist era. In the eighties and nineties especially, commemoration runs the gamut from Will Rogers to Elvis to Comic Strip Classics to Classic Movie Monsters. Not only were women and minorities admitted to the national tableau, but a whole range of places, objects, holidays, and pastimes also acquired iconic status. This proliferation of icons is a symptom of the increasing speed of obsolescence and of the increasingly sophisticated capacity to preserve the past. As Gillis remarks, "On one hand, the past has become so distant and the future so uncertain that we can no longer be sure what to save, so we save everything. . . . On the other hand, never has the past been so accessible on film, on tape, and in mass-produced images."[15] Reproduction of mass-produced images on commemorative stamps captures the paradox of preservation and forgetting that is the mark of contemporary historical sensibility.

According to Aaron Betsky, "part of our twentieth-century loss of faith has been a loss of the kinds of icons that are unapproachable, semi-divine apparitions."[16] Nowadays, as Betsky puts it, "icons are all around us": "some of the most normal, run-of-the-mill objects we use in the United States have become iconic."[17] Ubiquity and ordinariness entail a corresponding aesthetic. In place of polychromatic and multi-layered compositions reminiscent of nineteenth-century painting and neo-classical sculpture, today's postal iconography favors the bright, glossy look of a color photograph. Images are supposed to convey the feeling of three-dimensional verisimilitude. This insistence on "hyperreality," as Umberto Eco notes, "suggests that there is a constant in the average American imagination and taste, for which the past must be preserved and celebrated in full-scale authentic copy."[18] If technology saves fragments of material culture from oblivion, their commemoration as fetishistic objects saves them from trivialization.

In *Celebrate the Century,* for example, pop icons have the same ontological status as representations of significant past events. Showcasing the preceding decades from the perspective of the present, the series highlights the popular and mundane along with major events and outstanding individuals. All ten panels contain the same five categories of subject matter: people and events, arts and entertainment, science and technology, sports, and lifestyle. Thus, even the earlier decades include a gallery of artifacts and pastimes supposedly accessible to all Americans at the time. On the 1900s panel, for example, a still from the movie *The Great Train Robbery* is sandwiched between President Teddy Roosevelt and a box of Crayola crayons, and W.E.B. Du Bois is next to the "Teddy Bear" stamp.

The principle of photographic verisimilitude is evident as well, although a number of stamps preserve the "authentic" look of original posters, sketches, and cartoons. Americans are introduced to the fashion world of the 1900s through an original sketch of a "Gibson Girl," to U.S. involvement in World War II through the "I Want You" poster of Uncle Sam, to the jazz era of the 1920s through a cartoon "Flappers do the Charleston," and to women's contribution to the war effort through the poster of "Rosie the Riveter." Such stamps invoke an aura of the period "through stylistic connotation, conveying 'pastness' by the glossy qualities of the image."[19] Other stamps present a faithful copy of a person, artifact, event, or trend. Images of presidents Teddy Roosevelt, Woodrow Wilson, and Harry Truman depart from the iconography that once presented U.S. leaders as static profiles or larger-than-life heroes. Roosevelt resembles a businessman at a board meeting, Wilson is holding on to his top hat at an outdoor rally, a grinning Truman is lifting up the *Chicago Daily Tribune* with a headline "Dewey Defeats Truman." A Model T Ford on the 1900s panel is authentic red. The image of Jackson Pollock, symbolizing the emergence of abstract expressionism in the 1940s, is based on a 1949 photograph of Pollock at work on one of his drip paintings.

The icons assembled under the aegis of the "American century" do not privilege a particular event as constitutive or a particular person as more important than others. There does not seem to be a grand narrative of origin, but rather a host of random historical snapshots, in which all images appear to be of equal significance. A collage such as this, in which small-scale and large-scale history mingle and dissolve into one another, fits Fredric Jameson's description of the postmodern historical project as a "vast collection of images, a multitudinous photographic simulacrum."[20]

The prospect of authenticity is not doomed simply because the manufactured "past" of mass culture substitutes a "simulacrum" for a real experience of history. Against the Platonic condemnation of images as false reality and Marxist critiques of "society of the spectacle" as a negation of history and fabrication of "present frozen time,"[21] I maintain that icons constitute a visual "vocabulary" whose meaning is continuously negotiated and adjusted. Because certain images become icons as a result of circulation and "condensation," icons act as "magnets of meaning": they "change appearance depending on how you look at them, from what angle, in what context, or what you bring to your looking."[22]

THE POLITICS OF INCLUSION: AT THE INTERSECTION OF OFFICIAL AND VERNACULAR INTERESTS

Until the late 1960s the selection of persons and events to be honored on postal stamps had been the privilege of the political and intellectual elites. Postal commemorations, like other official memory practices, "were largely for, but not of, the people."[23] *Celebrate the Century* appears, by contrast, to be an expression of popular will. To quote Postmaster General Marvin Runyon,

> Through *Celebrate the Century,* Americans can save the past as they look toward the future. U.S. postage stamps have been integral to the fabric of American life since the founding of our great country, and they continue to be a source of learning and pride for all Americans. Capturing history on stamps is a part of the Postal Service's proud heritage. What makes *Celebrate the Century* such a unique continuation of this heritage is that for the first time, the public will play a major role in determining the stamp subjects that will become a permanent record of the passing millennium.[24]

This amalgamation of personal remembrance and collective history-making confirms what social historians have been observing about

commemoration in postmodernity. Gillis points out that memory work has become open to many and has shifted from national centers to local communities and living rooms: "Every attic is an archive, every living room a museum."[25] Although this "democratization of the past causes some anxiety among professionals," and "conservatives decry Americans' lack of factual knowledge about their national history," argues Gillis, "there is good evidence to show that ordinary people are more interested in and know more about their pasts than ever before, though their knowledge is no longer confined to compulsory time frames and space of the old national historiography."[26]

The proliferation of sites of memory work and corresponding identities does not, in and of itself, bring an end to official commemoration. Rather, as analysis of the *Celebrate the Century* program reveals, official commemoration has found it vital to reinvent itself as part of the trend Gillis terms "democratization of the past," to craft an appearance of consensus, or at least of compromise, among historical and political interests of diverse publics. Accordingly, commemorations should be viewed as "official and vernacular expressions." According to John Bodnar, official culture articulates the views of "leaders or authorities at all levels of society," whose primary interest is promoting "social unity, the continuity of existing traditions, and loyalty to the status quo," and "relies on 'dogmatic formalism' and the restatement of reality in ideal rather than complex or ambiguous terms"; vernacular culture, on the other hand, "represents an array of specialized interests" of diverse and shifting groups, and conveys "what social reality feels like rather than what it should be like."[27] These definitions underscore the traditional aesthetic contrast between the "high" culture of political and intellectual elites and the "popular" culture of ordinary people. As some critics have argued, however, commemorations in postmodernity have become struggles over the meaning of the *same* artifacts. The vernacular character of commemorations, then, depends not so much on a particular aesthetic standard, but on the degree to which a sign from any level of culture is appropriated to meet the idiosyncratic needs of the user.[28]

Nowhere has the meeting (or the clash) of official and vernacular interests been more pronounced than in the case of the Vietnam Veterans Memorial in Washington, D.C. Although the Vietnam Veterans Memorial has been analyzed through a variety of critical lenses, most scholars regard it as a symptom of a break with the era of "dogmatic formalism" and as a symbol of a new political aesthetic that is more accommodating to small-scale, idiosyncratic memories, while retaining the capacity to symbolize large-scale patriotic abstractions.[29] If the Vietnam Veterans Memorial functions as a mnemonic magnet open to multiple interpretations, then the sheer cornucopia of images of *Celebrate the Century* should be an even greater opportunity for the expression of both official and vernacular interpretations of the past. Although *Celebrate the Century* was designed and promoted as a product of a pluralistic selection process, *Celebrate the Century* uses this process as a strategy to authenticate a hegemonic narrative of the American century. The politics of inclusion becomes a strategy to assimilate "vernacular" interests into "official" ones.

From the beginning the selection process was marked by a division of labor between representatives of the official culture and the "general public." The Citizens' Stamp Advisory Committee (CSAC), composed of professional historians, business leaders, marketing specialists, and celebrities, selected subjects to represent the first five decades and suggested a list of designs out of which the public chose the icons capturing the 1950s through the 1990s. This division between the elites and the masses was justified by "extensive market research" that "showed the public was more familiar with events from the latter part of the century."[30] Presumably, through education and ease of access to archives, the elites could reconstruct the decades that the majority of the population did not experience firsthand; personal recollections would add an authentic touch to the mosaic of national icons from the remaining fifty years of the century.

As ballots for the last five decades began to appear in post offices, people realized that they could stuff the ballot box in support of their favorite icons, provided that they paid the postage to mail in their votes. Although the menu of images (thirty for each decade) consisted of nationally recognizable persons, events, and trends, some images became the focus of enthusiastic grassroots campaigns. Residents of Brockton, Massachusetts, fought to commemorate their local hero Rocky Marciano, an undefeated boxing champion.[31] Marciano was one of five sports figures and events listed in the stamp selection ballot for the 1950s; however, for the people of Brockton, he is an example of a successful tough guy who always remembered his blue-collar roots. At George's Café, a family restaurant owned by Marciano's boyhood friend, walls are covered with black-and-white photographs of his famous fights and of his frequent visits to his hometown. A framed first-day cancellation of the Rocky Marciano stamp occupies a place of pride, yet it is one among many images of the boxing legend.[32] Marciano is now part of official national history, but here he lives in local memory.

Postal customers could choose only from subjects recommended by the Citizens' Stamp Advisory Committee. Because records of the CSAC deliberations were sealed from the public, the extent of outside lobbying to put particular subjects on the ballot is uncertain.[33] A notable exception is the National Council on Disability's effort to urge the Postal Service to issue a stamp commemorating the tenth anniversary of the Americans with Disabilities Act as part of the *Celebrate the Century* series. Posted on the NCD website, a letter to the CSAC Chairperson Virginia Nolke outlines the reasons for turning ADA into a national icon: "ADA is also distinctively American. It embraces several archetypal American themes such as self-determination, self-reliance, and individual achievement. ADA is about enabling people with disabilities to take charge of their lives and join the American mainstream."[34] Although such a stamp would have celebrated a crucial milestone in civil rights legislation for 54 million people, it was not considered for inclusion. Under the "people and events" rubric, the 1990s ballot offered "Improving Education," "Cultural Diversity," "Sustained Economic Growth," "Gulf War," "Recovering Species," and "Active Older Americans."

What, then, was the official intent behind the series? Government leaders, historians, and educators saw *Celebrate the Century* as an educational program to involve teachers, schoolchildren, and parents in a conversation about the nation's past and present. In its official press releases, the USPS stressed its alliance with the Department of Education's *America Goes Back to School* program, "a coalition of more than four thousand business, community, religious and educational organizations nationwide," and promised to give teachers "the opportunity to take their students on a fun and interesting field trip through the twentieth century."[35] Not coincidentally, perhaps, "Improving Education" was one of the finalists for the 1990s, although it signified a collective commitment rather than an achievement. Then Secretary of Education Richard W. Riley summed up the lofty aspiration of the program's government sponsors: "Exposure to the people and events of the twentieth century that will be honored on this series of stamps will give a dose of inspiration to the children who will some day perform great deeds of the twenty-first century."[36] The patriotic and practical aspects of *Celebrate the Century* reflected an official concern about how to teach young Americans "not to forget something they had neither known nor remembered in the first place."[37]

The program's goal of promoting a positive image of U.S. history to the younger audience can be gleaned from commentaries in the national press that followed *Celebrate the Century* for almost three years. Critical coverage highlighted two troublesome aspects of the collection: exclusion of some traumatic episodes of the century and positive modification of serious events that made the final cut. Commenting on the 1950s ballot, a *Boston Globe* writer noted with some sarcasm: "We can't choose stamps commemorating nuclear testing in Nevada, or the executions of Julius and Ethel Rosenberg, or the McCarthy hearings, or any of the more memorably awful events of the decade."[38] Reporters also were quick to point out that the Postal Service had put "a positive spin on some bad events: the Iran hostage crisis becomes 'American Hostages Freed,' the Depression becomes 'America Survives the Depression.'"[39]

What the critics found most disturbing, however, was the manipulation of a Jackson Pollock photograph in order to match the atmosphere of the "smoke-free, drug-free, 98 percent fat-free, child-friendly 1990s."[40] The image chosen to represent abstract expressionism on the 1940s collage, an original *Life* magazine picture of Pollock working on his "Number 1, 1949," was subjected to a series of alterations, including the removal of a cigarette from Pollock's mouth, before it became the picture on the stamp. CSAC chair Virginia Nolke, a history professor at Angelo State University in Texas, reasoned that the smokeless version was inoffensive historically and politically: "I think only a small percentage of the American public is going to be aware of that photograph—they're not going to realize there is even an issue here. If you leave the cigarette out, you're not giving a public message one way or another. If you leave it in, you are."[41] This compromise arguably sums up the motivation behind the entire series: a desire to preserve the historical verisimilitude of images without losing control over their potentially unruly significations.

If the inclusion of a cigarette constitutes an implicit endorsement of tobacco, what can be made of the many images of commercial Americana? Acknowledging that the program included a great many commercial products, Professor Nolke suggested that public participation, rather than corporate lobbying, was responsible for this decision: "When you open things up for a public vote," she said in a telephone interview, "you end up with what is popular, not necessarily with what is important."[42] To be sure, today popularity is often synonymous with commercial success. The Postal Service apparently agrees because *Celebrate the Century* broke one of its rules for subject selection by commemorating a host of commercial subjects, ranging from Barbie dolls and automobiles to electronics and computer technology. Once the precedent was set, however, the rule was amended to permit commemoration of "commercial products or enterprises . . . to illustrate more general concepts linked to American culture."[43]

Private business interests stood to gain from the series through implicit image politics; however, the deployment of *Celebrate the Century* as an educational program depended on the active involvement of corporations. In particular, Microsoft and its search engine "msn.com" were integral to developing the "Celebrate the Century Education Kit" for teachers of grades three to six. The purpose of the kit, besides motivating children to explore contemporary

U.S. history by searching *Encarta* encyclopedia for background information on each stamp, was to encourage stamp collecting. The Postal Service's educational plan was a clever marketing strategy; because the program was to be implemented in some 300,000 classrooms nationwide, revenue prospects for both Microsoft and the USPS were significant.

The key to the marketing success of *Celebrate the Century* was a belief that stamp collectors, as non-professional "history buffs," would cherish a chance to decide which stamps would become the permanent record of the passing era. Because schoolchildren could vote on stamp subjects along with the general public—student ballots were included in the educational kit—they were more likely to join the ranks of collectors. As *Promomagazine* commented on the "pop-culture-tinged lunge after young collectors," the Postal Service had become a "competitor in the $4 billion collectibles market, doing battle not with Federal Express and Airborne, but with Beanie Babies and baseball cards."[44]

Pop culture icons had been recognized on postal stamps even before millennial nostalgia set the stage for their commemoration en masse, yet soliciting the public's mandate for doing so is a recent marketing invention. The precedent was set by the popular vote for the Elvis stamp in 1993; given the choice between a "young, studly King" and "the older, rhinestone-studded version," millions of Americans cast their ballots in favor of the young Elvis.[45] Nostalgia drew masses of non-collectors to post offices to buy stamps, and the USPS apparently drew its own conclusions about personal remembrance and commodification. Rather than calling on abstract patriotic values, *Celebrate the Century* elicited sentimental identification with material signs of popular culture. This identification, whose perceived authenticity marked the program as a genuinely collective commemoration, validated the process by which commodities are mythologized and history commodified. *Celebrate the Century,* on its face, is a commemoration by the people for the people, but on closer inspection the professed inclusiveness turns out to be a shrewd cashing-in on the public's desire to make history.

Yet some citizens refused identification, thereby proving that commemorative images also are politically charged representations of who we are as a people in the present. One case that attracted the attention of the national press was the protest against the proposed "Godfather" stamp, meant to honor one of the most popular film epics of the seventies. The Sons of Italy, a group representing the interests of Italian Americans, launched a "national-get-out-the-vote campaign" to oppose the stamp on the grounds that the portrayal of Italian Americans as Mafia killers would be unfair and inaccurate. Arlington lawyer Joseph Scafetta, Jr., chairman of the Sons of Italy's stamp committee, told the *Washington Post* that he organized "a national campaign to get the fraternal organization's 450,000 members to vote for any proposed design other than 'The Godfather.'"[46] Notably, this fraternal organization consistently has protested popular culture's depictions of Italian Americans while investing effort and money in support of positive national commemorations such as the World War II Memorial in Washington, D.C. The success of the Italian American protest against "defamatory" portrayals suggests that oppositional interpretations of mass culture's messages are more likely when message "receivers" are a relatively advantaged group with greater "access to oppositional codes."[47] To re-politicize a seemingly innocuous memento of pop culture requires effort and political visibility. By contrast, no organized protests were mounted against the stamp representing the popular nineties sitcom *Seinfeld* despite its many jokes at the expense of less advantaged ethnic minorities.

DISPLAYING THE CENTURY: ICONS "IN CONTEXT" AND "IN SITU"

The public could accept or reject individual images, thereby exercising a degree of control over the visual vocabulary of the series. The rhetoric of the series, however, was shaped through various strategies of display and promotion. Hence, it would be a mistake to focus on the semantics of individual images in isolation. The critic's task, as Roland Barthes points out, is "rather of a syntactical order": one needs to go beyond the mythological lexicon to decipher "which articulations, which displacements constitute the mythic fabric of a mass-consumption society."[48] It is the "syntax" of the collection as a whole, not the specific images of pop culture and commercial Americana that punctuate it, that shapes the reader's relationship to these icons.

The different strategies of exhibition of the *Celebrate the Century* program fall between two approaches, known to critical ethnographers as "in context" and "in situ." The "in context" approach is traditionally used by museums: "Objects are set in context by means of long labels, charts, diagrams, commentary delivered by earphones. . . . Objects are often set in context by means of other objects, often in relation to a classification or schematic arrangement of some kind, based on typologies of form or proposed historical relationships."[49] Ten collectible panels of stamps of *Celebrate the Century* in which images are ordered thematically and chronologically through visual and verbal means are an instance of "in context" display. "In situ" installations, on the other hand, recreate an environment in which the object is only a part. They "privilege 'experience' and tend to thematize rather than set their subject forth."[50] Unveiling ceremonies for individual stamps were executed in this mode. The two modes are not mutually exclusive; the traveling exhibit "Celebrate the Century Express" incorporates both.

The narrative structure of *Celebrate the Century* is formed by the chronological progression of panels from the 1900s through the 1990s and by the interaction of visual and discursive components constituting each of the ten commemorative panels. The stamps, each bearing an identifying title, are arranged diagonally in several rows against a background image. With the exception of the 1990s pane (where stamps are superimposed on a collage featuring U.S. currency and the steep graph symbolizing economic boom), all background images are decade-specific photographs. Each stamp sheet also features a title caption, a short description of the key events and trends of a given decade, and a list of new words that appeared during the period. According to Barthes, verbal elements perform two functions, "anchoring" and "relaying." Anchoring occurs when the linguistic message (such as the title of each stamp) "fixes the floating chain of signifieds" by directing the reader "among the various signifieds of the image . . . ; through an often subtle dispatching,

it teleguides him [*sic*] toward a meaning selected in advance."[51] Relaying refers to a complementary relation between language and image: "the words are then fragments of a more general syntagm, as are the images, and the message's unity occurs on a higher level: that of a story, the anecdote, the diegesis."[52]

The background images for each panel also can direct the reader by suggesting the "title" moment of each decade. Thus, the first decade is summed up by the photograph of *Kitty Hawk,* the first of the Wright brothers' planes. Besides visually amplifying the image of the plane in flight, the photographic image anchors the meaning of other stamps on the 1900s sheet, from the debut of the Model T Ford to the architecture of Frank Lloyd Wright. The first decade of the century is about progress in diverse areas of U.S. experience. Although one might perceive ideological tensions among the individual icons, say between the Ford and new immigrants (expensive commodity versus cheap labor), or between the Ford and John Muir's advocacy of preservationism (technological progress versus the environment), these contradictions are palliated by the unifying aura of the background image.

The ambiguity of the collage is further reduced by the panel's discursive components, the caption and the short narrative. The 1900s are called "the Dawn of the Twentieth Century," and the story of the first ten years is punctuated by achievements signaling the beginning of a more technologically developed, more just, and more prosperous society. Among the stated achievements are President Roosevelt's protection of national forests, the Pure Food and Drug Act, the exposure of corruption in industry by muckrakers Ida Tarbell and Upton Sinclair, and the beginning of the NAACP's struggle for equal rights for African Americans. Even the description of Ford's contribution to the decade—he "made automobiles more affordable with the Model T"—sounds unequivocally laudatory.

Importantly, the first installment of the collection is set up as the beginning of a series of transformations leading to the technological and social state of grace at the century's end. This pattern is distinct from the old national mythology of civil religion that seeks to relate the present to a constitutive moment in the past, be it the landing of Columbus or the Revolutionary War.

Instead of a historical and mythical beginning, the progression of the narrative is dictated by its end.

The final decade establishes the narrative teleology, thereby authorizing the mythical trajectory of the century. Images in the nineties collage connote the material and social success of the national experience at the end of the century. The stamps are set against the backdrop of a pile of cash and a soaring graph of the stock market, and the caption reads: "In final decade, Cold War ends, economy booms." The stamp subjects resonate with the theme of post-Cold War U.S. lifestyle. Curiously, many of them are not uniquely American: the World Wide Web, cellular phones, and sport utility vehicles are tokens of affluence around the globe. Blockbusters *Titanic* and *Jurassic Park,* although bearing a distinct imprint of Hollywood, were distributed worldwide. Even baseball, an all-American pastime, is now a global phenomenon. The narrative role of these signifiers of prosperity and leisure becomes clearer in their articulation with images denoting social, environmental, and military concerns in the last decade. The domestic issues chosen for the collection—the threat of extinction of certain species of raptors and the decline in education—appear as positive strides thanks to upbeat captions "Recovering Species" and "Improving Education." Together with the stamp honoring the anniversary of the Special Olympics, these icons depict the nation's domestic concerns as a matter of protecting its nature and its future (children being the conventional symbol of the future). From the paucity of contemporary domestic issues one might surmise that social and economic disparities at home have been resolved and that Americans have achieved a state of contentment and abundance. Not incidentally, the "Cellular Phones" stamp depicts the user of the technology as an African American male in a business suit, thereby connoting the overcoming of racial inequality. The Gulf War stamp, on the other hand, suggests that the causes of our discontent lie elsewhere, which occasionally call for U.S. involvement in military conflicts overseas.

This inference is reinforced by the accompanying verbal description, which buttresses the link between national domestic progress and international leadership: "The Soviet Union collapsed, effectively ending the Cold War. Troops were deployed by the United States in the Persian Gulf, in Somalia and in the Balkans." At home, too, the nation was becoming more democratic: "In 1992—often called the Year of the Woman—a record number of women were elected to political office." Women also approached parity with men in athletics: "The U.S. women's softball, soccer and basketball teams proved themselves the best in the world." This narrative complements and augments the cumulative message of the stamps, that material prosperity and democracy go hand-in-hand. It also reassures Americans that they deserve their abundance and that their way of life is an example to other, less fortunate and less democratic countries.

If the nineties represent a historical and narrative climax, the preceding decades build toward it. The eighties highlight the space shuttle, the fall of the Berlin Wall, which "presaged the end of the Cold War," and the increasing closure of the gender gap in the workplace. Along with these momentous events, the stamps salute cable TV, video-games, personal computers, compact discs, cabbage patch dolls, and entertainment hits. On the seventies panel, the U.S. bicentennial (The Statue of Liberty), Earth Day, and the Women's Rights Movement icon mingle with "Smiley Face," "70s Fashions," "Monday Night Football," "Jumbo Jets," and VCRs. The "rebellious sixties" is announced as the "decade of extremes," which signals that it was an aberration, a ripple in an otherwise steady flow of history. The panel elaborates the theme of "extremes" by juxtaposing the icons of rebellion and its chief source ("Woodstock" and "Peace Symbol" versus "The Vietnam War") with those connoting positive and unifying achievements ("Martin Luther King, Jr.," "Man on the Moon," and "The Peace Corps"). Considered from the vantage point of the nineties, however, even the rebellious counterculture of the sixties appears as one among many stylistic options, evidenced by the transformation of the peace symbol into jewelry and the staged spectacle of Woodstock's twenty-fifth and thirtieth anniversaries. Nostalgia-laden pop icons—the Beatles, *Star Trek,* the Ford Mustang, the Barbie doll—contribute to the toy-box aesthetic. The fifties, the first decade for which the public selected the representative images, recreates the atmosphere of the pax Americana era of Eisenhower with its stereotypical ideals of suburban housing, nuclear families, and the living room TV set. Many of the fifties images—tail fins and chrome cars, teen fashions, drive-in movies, and rock-n-roll—seem to have sprung directly from George Lucas's nostalgic film *American Graffiti.*

The collage of the last five decades presents a chronological arrangement of images whose historical value has been transformed by multiple repetition and commercial usage. One might argue that they are an elaboration on the same theme that "culminates" in the nineties, but a similar modification of the past is evident in the "historical" reconstruction of the first five decades by the Citizens' Stamp Advisory Committee.

I began my account of the syntax of *Celebrate the Century* with the 1900s, noting that most achievements presented therein foreshadow the resolution of social problems and the triumph of technology at the end of the millennium. The next four decades follow the same narrative dynamic. In addition to icons of social progress (the regulation of child labor, the League of Nations, the ratification of women's right to vote and so on), signifiers of enriched leisure, whether or not they were iconic at the time, provide a thematic leitmotif that climaxes in the post-WWII era. The collage anticipates the postmodern collapse of the line between "high culture" and "mass entertainment." The 1900s display Crayola crayons, motion pictures, ice-cream-eating children at the St. Louis World Fair, the teddy bear, and "Gibson Girl" style. The teens feature Charlie Chaplin's "Little Tramp," avant-garde art at the Armory Show, the first crossword puzzle, and construction toys. The "jazz age" is represented by the stamps "Gatsby style," "Flappers do the Charleston," the "Jazz Club" musicians, radio, American realistic painting, and electric toy trains, while the verbal description mentions the first talkies and the first Academy Awards. During the Depression years, icons of entertainment abound: Monopoly board games, the movies *Gone With the Wind* and *Snow White and the Seven Dwarfs,* comic book hero Superman, and the photojournalism of *Life* magazine. The WWII decade also accommodates the abstract expressionism of Jackson Pollock, Orson Welles's *Citizen Kane,* the Broadway play based on Tennessee Williams's *Streetcar Named Desire,* jitterbug dancing, the Big Band sound, the "Slinky" craze, and the emergence of TV as the nation's entertainer.

To sum up, the serious and light subjects of the first five decades set in motion a progression towards a greater society and more democratized leisure, to be followed by a similarly optimistic trajectory from the fifties through the nineties. This popular history lesson, however benign its overall purpose, modifies the account of the passing century to fit the dominant ideological message, in which social controversy is effaced in favor of a consensual consumer democracy.

The chronological arrangement of *Celebrate the Century* narrows the signification of icons to a distinct teleology. In the case of unveiling rituals and the traveling exhibit, one might argue that the hegemonic totality of the collection would dissolve into fragments, as the cognitive control of the narrative is replaced by more environmental and supposedly less constraining experiences. Even if these experiences seem more interactive and spontaneous, however, they are by no means neutral because the environments in which they occur convert visitors into tourists in search of collectible heritage. In other words, "in context" and "in situ" displays of *Celebrate the Century* are complementary discursive strategies for positioning audiences as tourists and consumers.[53]

Because a particular place confers depth and an aura of authenticity on what appears to be a mere succession of glossy surfaces, the collection's stamps were unveiled separately in a variety of symbolically significant locations. The unveiling rituals reenacted constitutive images of the century by making present a particular association or memory in a charismatic scene. In the words of Greg Dickinson, these sites "suggest the ways the spatial mnemonic triggers memories that come with a whole host of associations (this indeed is their rhetorical power), and the ways the mnemonics serve to cover over other absences."[54] Or, to use Kenneth Burke's terminology, each of these locations is a symbolic container that conditions, if not dictates, an appropriate response.[55]

The stamp "Immigrants Arriving" from the 1900s set, for instance, was uncovered at Ellis Island, New York, concurrently with a naturalization ceremony, thereby renewing the "land of opportunity" message in the present along with the message of inclusiveness extended to new immigrants. Rebuilt thanks to corporate philanthropy and now a museum, Ellis Island signifies a friendly passage point into the "new world," rather than a vigilant border post. The site's narrative, however, excludes immigrants who bypassed the island, and those who are still barred from entering the United States by current immigration laws.[56] In this sense, the location's "spatial mnemonic" both reveals and conceals. Although the hostility and suspicion toward new waves of immigrants was as serious at the turn of the twentieth century as it is today, Ellis Island's inclusion in the tableau of all-American icons is secure and uncontroversial, as opposed to locations along the U.S.-Mexico border.

Unveiling rituals were "containers" in yet another sense; they simultaneously invoked and contained identities of the diverse publics commemorated by the stamps. Consider two occasions: the unveiling of the peace symbol at a famous 1960s nightclub in West Hollywood and of the Gulf War stamp at MacDill Air Force Base. Admittedly, these two events drew on incompatible political allegiances. The ceremony at the counter-culture haunt Whisky A Go-Go conjured the oppositional identity of anti-Vietnam protesters, while the honoring of Gulf War veterans celebrated the sacrifices and patriotic commitment of military personnel who fought to protect what former President George Bush called "our American way of life." Each occasion and place constituted a rhetorical situation, an epideictic moment of affirmation of a distinct group identity and political values.

It is tempting to hail this diversity of rhetorical enactments of identity as a welcome symptom of postmodern fragmentation of a unified national past, but we can do so only if we bracket the unifying mythology of the *present,* the mythology of U.S. consumerism. The epideictic context of unveiling framed these stamps and assured each audience of its historical agency and political legitimacy within the larger historical context, but it also foreclosed questioning the temporal and mythical logic of commemoration. The peace symbol ceremony is particularly instructive in this regard: while acknowledging a representation of "the voice of a generation who spoke out for peace and humanity during a decade of social unrest," speeches by postal officials referred to the stamp as a "wonderful example of the diversity

and richness of our *Celebrate the Century* stamp and education program" and described the purpose of the program as paying tribute "to the colorful events that have touched all of our lives in the history of this great nation."[57] By locating the peace movement and its political exigencies safely in the past, this framing neutralizes its political legacy. At the same time, in place of political radicalism, the commemoration substitutes a desire to possess the radical past in the present through "colorful" souvenirs—clothing, jewelry, and musical recordings. Similar to the commodification of other historical figures and social movements, the act of nostalgic consumption of counter-culture insignia "plays its proper role as a legitimating citation for the commodity system as a whole."[58]

Not all unveilings succeeded in fixing the political in the past, however. At the uncovering of a stamp featuring Martin Luther King, Jr., Atlanta Mayor Bill Campbell stressed the continuity between Dr. King's civil rights crusade in the sixties and current struggles of African Americans and other minorities. At the moment when Atlanta's affirmative action program was threatened by a civil suit from the Southeastern Legal Foundation, the Mayor chose the ceremony to call attention to unresolved social and economic injustices: "Let us not let anyone, any organization or any movement stop our struggle for justice. We will continue to fight like Dr. King. Affirmative action is our Selma. It's our Edmund Pettus Bridge."[59] The *Atlanta Journal and Constitution* labeled Campbell's intervention "Mayor gets political at MLK stamp event" as if to emphasize its incongruity with the pathos appropriate to such an occasion: "The imagery Campbell used in his brief comments contrasted sharply with the scene in the hall at Atlanta's Martin Luther King, Jr. Historic Site. King's widow, Coretta Scott King, and a member of the Postal Service's Board of Governors released a royal blue banner to uncover the first-class stamp as a recording echoed the final words of King's 'I Have a Dream' speech: 'Free at last. Free at last. Thank God Almighty, I'm free at last.'"[60]

Whereas rituals of unveiling helped to authenticate the icons by their association with particular locales and people, "Celebrate the Century Express" combined "in context" and "in situ" modes of display. The traveling museum capitalized on its symbolic association with "whistle stop" tours of political leaders of the past, reinforced by the inclusion of President Harry S. Truman's 1948 car in the four-car Amtrak train. With its restored vintage Railway Post Office car and an exhibition car housing the interactive displays of stamps, the museum exuded historical authenticity. The *St. Louis Dispatch* described visitors' reaction to the exhibit: "Fran and Bob Watson . . . liked the one of a laughing Truman holding aloft the *Chicago Tribune* front page announcing 'Dewey Defeats Truman,' and were thrilled to learn the original scene actually took place in the St. Louis station just two cars down."[61] Because Railway Post Office cars were discontinued in 1977, visitors were invited to experience what was no more: the working conditions of postal clerks as they sorted, processed, and delivered the mail. The exhibit did not offer technological and economic reasons for their discontinuance; the car was fashioned into an attraction to be marveled at, not a lesson in the politics of obsolescence.

A museum excursion typically culminates in a trip to a museum shop. Through various forms of display and promotion *Celebrate the Century* created an appetite, in a Burkean sense, to complete the "museum" pattern by purchasing a souvenir.[62] Even before the last commemorative pane was issued, the public was urged to take advantage of this "once-in-a-century" opportunity. Collectors and non-collectors could purchase the entire series as a deluxe coffee-table display— "the special heirloom book," as the *Postal Service Guide to U.S. Stamps* called it. *Celebrate the Century,* thus, would make its way into a family archive as a collection with instant heritage and into the family room as a ready-made conversation piece. The direct-mail offering pictured an older man contemplating stamp sheets with his grandson, an image linking stamp collecting with memory passed from generation to generation, a nostalgic trope conjuring good "old times" when collectors hunted for rare stamps and when children received history lessons from their grandparents rather than from commercial television and the Internet. The agency of the popular vote was to be consummated and immortalized by acquiring a pre-packaged visual relic.

POSTMODERN COLLECTIVE MEMORY: POLITICAL AGENCY AND POLITICAL AMNESIA

In reading the *Celebrate the Century* program, I have avoided the extremes of unqualified approval and pessimistic rejection that seem to accompany discussions of postmodern cultural practices. As an example of postmodern commemoration, *Celebrate the Century* contains both the centrifugal possibilities of a non-hierarchical image culture and the centripetal tendencies of the culture of marketing. The culture of simulacra generates opportunities for political subjects to enter the discourse of national memory through symbolic portals of their choice and to multiply narrative trajectories in a collective "language game" of history making. In the context of national commemoration, however, memory practices can be subjected to the funneling process of selection-through-elimination as well as a host of display mechanisms. In consequence, what begins as an open museum of a postmodern life world in which "everyone is a curator of sorts"[63] ends as a historical amusement park where everyone is a tourist.

As citizens in a republic of signs, Americans could draw on a stock of images that not only appealed to them but also represented some aspect of their identity. In this way the thematic scope and eclecticism of *Celebrate the Century* responded to the fragmented need to remember "serious" historical events and civic achievements as well as nostalgic objects and lifestyles. Yet even if individual and group identities had been fragmented, they were woven into a unified narrative, which was not the old national mythology of civil religion. In the present, Americans could see themselves as world leaders, free from social and political controversies that had divided them in the past, free to enjoy the material rewards of their membership in the consumer culture. Instead of Robert Bellah's 1967 futuristic vision of "a new civil religion of the world,"[64] which would grow with "the emergence of a genuine transnational sovereignty," we have "the consumer's sublime," an omnivorous ideology of the marketing culture that encourages fantasy, escapism, and a "rush of simulations."[65]

At first glance, this conclusion seems to offer a counter example to Lyotard's thesis about the end of grand narratives in postmodernity. In Lyotard's thinking, postmodernity is signaled by the decline of putatively universal narratives of science, Marxism, and the modern nation-state,[66] but this "incredulity toward metanarratives" does not preclude the formation of new forms of legitimation of social bonds, accomplished through different kinds of language games. I suggest that commemorative activity in postmodernity may be one of those games. *Celebrate the Century* exemplifies a multidimensional process by which a new cultural mythology can be constructed in place of an old one. Thus, the narrative of U.S. civil religion is replaced by the transnational mythology of the consumer's sublime. In this process, participants' agency as citizens is invoked to authenticate the narrative, although citizens ultimately are transformed into consumers. The apparent triumph of consumer culture may not have destroyed the postmodern subject's potential to resist imposition of some sort of teleology on lived experience, even if this experience is already mediated via a variety of representational mechanisms. Commodification does not automatically engender political amnesia. There is still much to be learned from the ways in which private and group memories can challenge quasi-consensual public commemorations, but it is just as important to attend to those commemorative practices that absorb and neutralize the political force of vernacular voices.

NOTES

1. United States Postal Service, *Postal Bulletin,* 6 November 1997, 50.

2. United States Postal Service, *Celebrate the Century Express* (http://www.usps.gov/ctc/train/what.htm).

3. On the tension between history and memory in commemorative activity, see Pierre Nora, "Between History and Memory: *Les Lieux de Memoire,*" *Representations* 26 (Spring 1989): 7–25, and Tamar Katriel, "Sites of Memory: Discourses of the Past in Israeli Pioneering Settlement Museums," *Quarterly Journal of Speech* 80 (Winter 1994): 1–20.

4. See David Scott, *European Stamp Design: A Semiotic Approach to Designing Messages* (London: Academy Editions, 1995).

5. On the disappearance of once "sovereign difference" between representations and referents, see Jean Baudrillard's *Simulations,* trans. Paul Foss, Paul Patton, and Philip Beitchman (New York: Semiotext[e], 1983). Baudrillard claims that Marxist assessment of capitalism as production of commodities is obsolete because capitalist production now revolves around the manufacture of signs, images, and sign systems rather than commodities. See Jean Baudrillard, *Pour une Critique de L'Economie Politique du Signe* (Paris: Gallimard, 1990).

6. See, for example, Stephan Kanfer, "The Post Office Stamps Out the 1980s," *Manhattan Institute City Journal* 10 (2000): 11.

7. Jean-François Lyotard gives a classic if limited definition of postmodernity as "incredulity toward metanarratives" in *The Postmodern Condition: A Report on Knowledge,* trans. Geoff Bennington and Brian Massumi (Minneapolis: University of Minnesota Press, 1984), xxiv. David Harvey traces a series of cultural transformations associated with postmodernity, especially those linked to post-Fordist economy of flexible accumulation and technologies that increase the turnover of production and consumption, in *The Condition of Postmodernity: An Enquiry into the Origins of Cultural Change* (Cambridge, MA: Blackwell, 1990).

8. Robert N. Bellah, "Civil Religion in America," *Daedalus* 96 (1967): 1–21.

9. Robert N. Bellah, *The Broken Covenant: American Civil Religion in Time of Trial* (Chicago: University of Chicago Press, 1992), 2.

10. I construct this account with the aid of *The Postal Service Guide to U.S. Postal Stamps,* 27th edition (New York: Harper Resource, 2000). This philatelist's manual contains photographs of all United States postal stamps issued between 1847 and 2000. The first commemorative collection was issued in 1893 in celebration of the 400th anniversary of Columbus's landing.

11. According to Donald J. Lehnus, "Government and Politics" and "Military" are the groups most often featured on postal stamps between 1847 and 1980; two-thirds of all commemorated individuals lived between 1700 and 1899. See *From Angels to Zeppelins: A Guide to Persons, Objects, Topics, and Themes on United States Postage Stamps 1847–1980* (Westport, CT: Greenwood Press, 1982).

12. John R. Gillis, "Memory and Identity: A History of a Relationship," in *Commemorations: The Politics of National Identity,* ed. John R. Gillis (Princeton: Princeton University Press, 1994), 20.

13. United States Postal Service, *The Citizens' Stamp Advisory Committee* (http://www.usps.com).

14. On the change in the iconography of the stamps depicting the American Revolution, see David Curtis Skaggs, "Postage Stamps as Icons," in *Icons of America,* ed. Ray B. Browne and Marshall Fishwick (Bowling Green: Popular Press, 1978), 198–208.

15. Gillis, 15.

16. Aaron Betsky, "The Enigma of the Thigh Cho: Icons as Magnets of Meaning," in *Icons: Magnets of Meaning,* ed. Aaron Betsky (San Francisco: San Francisco Museum of Modern Art, 1997), 22.

17. Betsky, 22.

18. Umberto Eco, *Travels in Hyperreality,* trans. William Weaver (New York: Harcourt Brace Jovanovich, 1990), 6.

19. Fredric Jameson, *Postmodernism, or, the Cultural Logic of Late Capitalism* (Durham: Duke University Press, 1990), 19.

20. Jameson, 18.

21. See Guy Debord, *Society of the Spectacle* (Detroit: Black and Red, 1983).

22. Betsky, 31. On the audience's role in decoding the meaning of popular texts, see John Fiske, "Television: Polysemy and Popularity," *Critical Studies in Mass Communication* 4 (1986): 391–408. Like Fredric Jameson, I believe that popular culture contains longings that are subversive of the status quo. See Fredric Jameson, "Reification and Utopia in Mass Culture," *Social Text* 1 (Winter 1979): 130–149.

23. Gillis, 9.

24. United States Postal Service, "Postal Service Announces Celebrate the Century Program." Release no. 97–095, November 5, 1997.

25. Gillis, 14.

26. Gillis, 17. Also see David Thelen, "History-Making in America," *The Historian* 53 (1991): 631–48.

27. John Bodnar, *Remaking America: Public Memory, Commemoration, and Patriotism in the Twentieth Century* (Princeton: Princeton University Press, 1992), 13–14.

28. The term "vernacular" has been employed by scholars in many disciplines, and has become a magnet for different meanings. Bodnar, for example, follows Susan G. Davis, who used the label "vernacular culture" to characterize street parades in antebellum Philadelphia. Davis contrasts vernacular communication with "industrial, commercial, and official modes of communication and media" in *Parades and Power: Street Theatre in Nineteenth-Century Philadelphia* (Philadelphia: Temple University Press, 1986), 15. Today, the boundary between "popular" and "commercial" is difficult to sustain or even detect: "there is no pure space outside of commodity culture," as Andreas Huyssen argues in "Present Pasts: Media, Politics, Amnesia," *Public Culture* 12 (2000): 29. Rather than focus on the aesthetics and politics of production, scholars in architecture and critical ethnography have moved to the aesthetics of reception. On this view, "vernacular" can be applied to the reception or appropriation of existing artifacts. See, for example, essays in *Perspectives in Vernacular Architecture, III,* ed. Thomas Carter and Bernard L. Herman (Columbia: University of Missouri Press, 1989). Barbara Kirshenblatt-Gimblett talks of "vernacular practices of connoisseurship" in *Destination Culture: Tourism, Museums, and Heritage* (Berkeley: University of California Press, 1998), 259–281. For rhetorical theorists the notion of vernacular rhetoric holds the promise of recovering voices of "publics" that may have been muted by the technocratic discourse of poll-driven "public opinion." See especially Gerard A. Hauser, *Vernacular Voices: The Rhetoric of Publics and Public Spheres* (Columbia, SC: University of South Carolina Press, 1999).

29. Sonja Foss was one of the first critics to address the persuasive power of the Vietnam Veterans Memorial in "Ambiguity as Persuasion: the Vietnam Veterans Memorial," *Communication Quarterly* 34 (1986): 326–40. Blair, Jeppeson, and Pucci discuss it as a postmodern "text" that defies a univocal reading and suggest that it "may have altered the public commemorative norm for the foreseeable future" (282). Peter S. Hawkins sees such self-consciously postmodern "monuments" as the NAMES Project AIDS Memorial Quilt as successors to "the intimate tableaux that mourners continue to create within the interstices of VVM" in "Naming Names: The Art of Memory and the NAMES Project AIDS Quilt," in *Thinking About Exhibitions,* ed. Reesa Greenburg, Bruce Ferguson, and Sandy Nairne (London: Routledge, 1996), 135. Gillis remarks that "the Vietnam Memorial, with its wall of names, is generally agreed to represent a turning point in the history of public memory, a decisive departure from the anonymity of the Tomb of the

Unknown Soldier and a growing acknowledgement that everyone now deserves equal recognition at all times in wholly accessible places" (13). Boime contrasts the VVM with the Marine Corps Memorial "whose unity of purpose and single-minded perspective represented a nation undivided on the question of war." The VVM, as "an anti-heroic monument dedicated to a war in which there could be no heroes," was "inscribed from the outset by ordinary people capable of reinterpreting the dominant ideological discourse for their own purposes." See *The Unveiling of the National Icons: A Plea for Patriotic Iconoclasm in a Nationalist Era* (Cambridge: Cambridge University Press, 1998), 308–309.

30. United States Postal Service, *Postal Bulletin,* 6 November 1997, 53.

31. See Bill McAllister, "Marciano's Postal Punch," *Washington Post* 6 March 1998, N70; Jeff McLaughlin, "Late Rounds for a Stamp of 'Rocky,'" *Boston Globe,* 22 February 1998, 1.

32. The author visited George's Café in Brockton in January 2002.

33. The Government Relations review of the operations of the Citizens' Stamp Advisory Committee states that although "confidential minutes of each of Committee's meetings are maintained," they "summarize the individual stamp proposals discussed and their current status," but not "strategic policy decisions arrived at by the Committee." The report noted that "Committee members and Postal Service management officials present at the meetings tried to recall past events and decisions without the benefit of any written documentation. Although officials usually agreed, their individual interpretation of past decisions sometimes differed, which sparked debate as to what had previously been decided." Among the "significant issues that were impacted by previous policy decisions" was the issue of "recognition of specific interests, sub-groups, and units." See Deborah K. Willwhite, "Review of the Operations of the Citizens' Stamp Advisory Committee-Management Advisory Report RG-MA-99–005," 27 July 1999.

34. "Letter to Dr. Virginia Nolke, Chairperson, The Citizens' Stamp Advisory Committee," 8 April 1999. (http://www.ncd.gov/newsroom/correspondence/ usps_4–8-99.html). In a telephone interview on September 18, 2001, Dr. Nolke denied knowledge of this petition.

35. United States Postal Service, "Postal Service Partners with the Department of Education's 'America Goes Back to School' Program." Release no. 98–106, 24 September 1998.

36. "Postal Service Partners."

37. Stephen H. Browne, "Remembering Crispus Attucks: Race, Rhetoric, and the Politics of Commemoration," *Quarterly Journal of Speech* 85 (1999): 176.

38. Diane White, "The Sticky Side of Stamp Choices," *Boston Globe,* 19 February 1998, C1.

39. Rainbow Powell, "'90s Stamps Take Licking," *Omaha World-Herald,* 16 June 1999, 19.

40. Arthur Hirsch, "Stamp Out Smoking," *Baltimore Sun,* 20 February 1999, 1E.

41. Quoted in David Brown, "Stamped Out," *Washington Post,* 7 March 1999, B1.

42. Virginia Nolke, Telephone Interview, 18 September 2001.

43. United States Postal Service. *Criteria. Stamp Subject Selection. (Updated 8/01).* (http://www.new .usps.com/cgi-bin/ uspsbv)

44. Al Urbanski, "Don't Mail It In," *Promomagazine,* 1999.

45. Urbanski.

46. Bill McAlister, "The Power of the Ballot," *Washington Post,* 13 November 1998, 72.

47. Celeste Michelle Condit, "The Rhetorical Limits of Polysemy," *Critical Studies in Mass Communication* 6 (1989): 111.

48. Roland Barthes, *The Responsibility of Forms: Critical Essays on Music, Art, and Representation* (New York: Hall and Wang, 1985), 67.

49. Kirshenblatt-Gimblett, 21.

50. Kirshenblatt-Gimblett, 3.

51. Barthes, 28–29.

52. Barthes, 30.

53. The concept of subject positioning (or interpellation) is explored in Louis Althusser, "Ideology and Ideological State Apparatuses," in *Lenin and Philosophy and Other Essays,* trans. Ben Brewster (New York: Monthly Review Press, 1971), 127–185.

54. Greg Dickinson, "Memories for Sale: Nostalgia and Construction of Identity in Old Pasadena," *Quarterly Journal of Speech* 83 (1997): 18.

55. Kenneth Burke, *A Grammar of Motives* (Berkeley: University of California Press, 1969), 3–20.

56. For a provocative critique of the Ellis Island Museum, see Kishenblatt-Gimblett, 177–187.

57. United States Postal Service, "Nancy Sinatra Joins U.S. Postal Service for Unveiling of Peace Symbol Stamp." Release no. 99–086, July 30, 1999.

58. Kent A. Ono and Derek T. Buescher, "Deciphering Pocahontas: Unpacking the Commodification of a Native American Woman," *Critical Studies in Mass Communication* 18 (2001): 28.

59. Quoted in Rhonda Cook, "Affirmative Action Lawsuit: Mayor Gets Political at MLK Stamp Event," *Atlanta Journal and Constitution,* 29 August 1999, 2C.

60. Cook, 2C.

61. Victor Volland, "Stamp Unveiling Pales Next to Snazzy Train Exhibit," *St. Louis Post-Dispatch,* 16 May 1999, D3.

62. I have in mind Kenneth Burke's famous definition of form as "an arousing and fulfillment of desires": "a work has form in so far as one part of it leads a reader to anticipate another part, to be gratified by the sequence." See Kenneth Burke, *Counter-Statement* (Berkeley: University of California Press, 1968), 124.

63. Kirshenblatt-Gimblett, 259.

64. Robert N. Bellah, "Civil Religion in America," 18.

65. David E. Nye, *American Technological Sublime* (Cambridge: MIT Press, 1994), 295–296.

66. Lyotard ponders what new language games can secure legitimacy after the erosion of metanarratives. He points out that narrative ("the little narrative") "remains the quintessential form of imaginative invention." See *The Postmodern Condition,* xxiv–xxv, 60.

16

MEMORIALIZING AFFLUENCE IN THE POSTWAR FAMILY

Kodak's Colorama in Grand Central Terminal (1950–1990)

DIANE S. HOPE

Beginning in 1950 and lasting until 1990, Eastman Kodak Company promoted itself and color photography through a changing display of 565 giant images installed in Grand Central Terminal in the center of New York City. The imposing exhibit, measuring 18 feet by 60 feet, was the largest advertisement ever seen. Promoted as "the world's largest photographs," the images exemplified the wonders of color photography made available by Eastman Kodak (Kerr, 1998a; Nordstrom & Roalf, 2004). In intense color pictures, the Colorama combined the most common expressions of image consumption existent in the popular culture: advertising and snapshots.

Color images were appearing in movies, advertising, and magazines by the 1940s, yet color print film was undependable, and equipment and reproduction processes were expensive. In 1949, only 2% of Kodak's market was in color film (Roalf, 2004). Although Kodachrome processing, introduced 10 years earlier, produced brilliant, long-lasting transparencies (Rijper, 2002), color print photography was not ready for the mass consumer market (Czech, 1996; Roalf, 2004). Family snapshots, newsprint images, and everyday uses of photography were produced and circulated primarily in monochromatic shades of black, white, and gray. Although color images were made to record and document World War II, images that circulated in newspapers, magazines, newsreel film, and personal snapshots memorialized the war in black and white (Coleman, 2002). But the shades of everyday photographic memory were about to change.

Postwar affluence and the abundant mass production of consumer goods solidified Kodak's determination to become the leader of color film photography in the mass market. The seizure

SOURCE: Hope, D. S. (2006). Memorializing affluence in the postwar family: Kodak's Colorama in Grand Central Terminal (1950–1990). In D. S. Hope (Ed.), *Visual communication: Perception, rhetoric, and technology* (pp. 91–110). Cresskill, NJ: Hampton Press/Rochester Institute of Technology Cary Graphic Arts Press.

and worldwide distribution of the trade secrets of Germany's Agfa Company[1] intensified competition for the mass marketing of color film and bolstered Kodak's own ongoing research for the "Ektacolor family of products" (Roalf, 2004, p. 77). In 1950, when Kodak displayed the first Colorama image, the advertising campaign launched color into the market for snapshot photography and became one of the most successful campaigns in corporate history (Kerr, 1998a).

This chapter focuses on the advertising rhetoric of the Colorama as a major expression of postwar memorializing. With the technologies of color film processing ready for mass consumption, Kodak intensified the established strategy of memorializing the family in snapshots by promoting the value of color photography as a celebration of postwar affluence. The Kodak images pictured the nuclear family as a consumer unit; Kodak marketed the affluent nuclear family as a collective consumer enterprise, engaged in the production and consumption of color images as commodities. Consumer goods were a perfect showcase for the bright hues of Ektacolor, and each image featured commodities as signs of ritualized family life.

In color-saturated pictures, Kodak advertised a fantasy world in which the ritual of making color photographs coincidentally highlighted material consumption as a domestic value. The Colorama punctuated the national ethic with images that valorized and conjoined affluence and the nuclear family as twin standards for a new U.S. culture. From 1950 through the middle years of 1970, the visual narratives in Kodak's images were remarkably consistent. No indication of the sociocultural changes occurring through those decades found reflection in Kodak portrayals. Targeting the young family as the most important market for postwar consumption of film and cameras, the Kodak Colorama froze the happy family and its possessions in an array of staged color photographs displayed in the "busiest intersection in the world."

Each day half a million people, mostly New York commuters, moved past the Colorama display, and every 3 weeks the picture changed (Roalf, 2004). (See Figure 1.) Located in the vaulted space of what had been designed in 1913 as the gateway to the continent, the stationary Colorama became an icon of commercial sentimentality. Although the images did not circulate, New York was the center of advertising, publishing, and, in the early days, TV. The cultural production at work in New York set the standard for the nation's popular cultural agenda. Located in the rapidly deteriorating terminal building, the snapshot advertisements presented New Yorkers with a mythical vision

Figure 1 Colorama in Grand Central Terminal.

SOURCE: Eastman Kodak Company.

of life in suburban small towns and rural settings. A full account of the parallel story of Grand Central Station's fall and rebirth is not possible here, but the intertwined history of Grand Central and the Colorama informs the chapter. Framed by the grand architectural space of the east balcony, the space occupied by the Colorama had figured prominently in the history of the landmark building during World War II.

During the war, the terminal was especially important as a hub of the rail system. In 1941, the Farm Security Administration (FSA) used the east balcony space to exhibit 22 photographs (enlarged by Kodak) in a montage 118 feet wide and almost 100 feet high as part of the war bond drive, that served to black out the east windows of the terminal for the duration of the war (Kerr, 1998a). In 1943, the east wall of the balcony housed a 75-foot high, 30-feet wide patriotic mural depicting flags, bombs, and soldiers to raise money for a second U.S. Defense Bonds campaign. Below the balcony, soldiers waiting for trains gathered in the Service Men's Lounge (Belle & Leighton, 2000). From 1944 to 1947, an average of 520 trains were accommodated every weekday. The peak of terminal use occurred in 1947; 65 million passengers, or over 40% of the U.S. population, were served by the station (Nevins, 1982).

Yet by 1949, New York Central Railroad, the operator of the terminal, was losing money; air travel, bus travel, and private automobiles had diminished the use of rail as the primary transportation system of the country. Government subsidies for airports and highways, corrupt and inefficient rail management, and the popular love of automobiles combined to drain railroad finances (Belle & Leighton, 2000). The rail company was eager to find revenue, and Kodak was eager to advertise color photography. Paying over $300,000 per year to rent the space in Grand Central Terminal, Kodak installed the Colorama in 1950 (Kerr, 1998a).

With few exceptions, two types of color images were displayed in the 40-year period of the Colorama display.[2] The first type, snapshot advertising, the primary focus of this chapter, depicted middle-class families in the act of making snapshots together. Attractive models depicted picture-takers and their families staged

in moments from affluent lives, at play, on holidays, on vacation, or as tourists. In nearly every image displayed from 1950 to the mid-1970s, the family—making pictures—was the subject. The second type of Coloramas were color spectacles that professionally reflected the travel slide shows amateurs produced as family entertainment. Exhibited from the mid-1970s until the final image of 1990,[3] the spectacle images celebrated Kodak color photography in panoramas of national rituals, nature, exotic locales, theme parks, sentimental subjects, sports scenes, and Kodak sponsored events.[4] The picture-making family was no longer in the frame.

By the mid-1970s, it was no longer necessary to sell color photography to families; the nearly total success of Kodak's campaign was complete. American families remembered themselves in color and identified themselves as a collective of consumers.

Image-based advertising exhibits a particular form of visual rhetoric. The critic, seeking to answer the basic question "What's going on here?" can consider the rhetoric of advertising from a variety of standpoints, including target audience, circulation, visual arguments and claims, aesthetics, semiotics, themes, effectiveness, and technology of production and reproduction. Scholars from communication, sociology, and marketing contribute to our understanding of advertising as a ubiquitous form of visual communication. Yet advertising's explicit persuasive goal—to market and sell goods, services, or brands—determines that the central set of questions must involve the rhetorical critic in direct consideration of a commercial enterprise intended to create profit through the circulation of representations (Goldman & Papson, 1996). Thus, the rhetoric of pictorial images in advertising cannot be separated realistically from its ideological roots. This approach to advertising's rhetoric follows the tradition of the early Marshall McLuhan (1951), Stuart Ewen (1976), Erving Goffman (1976), Roland Marchand (1985), and most important, Nancy Martha West (2000) for her detailed examination of Kodak's early advertising history.

Marchand borrowed the phrase "Capitalist Realism"[5] to describe some of the "serious distortions in advertising's mirror" as "inherent in the nature of advertising" (p. xviii). Like

Socialist Realism, emergent in the cultures of socialism, the images of Capitalist Realism at work in advertising depict "the ideals and aspirations" of capitalism more "accurately" than does the reality of U.S. culture (p. xvii). Goffman (1976) used a similar term, *commercial realism,* to describe "the standard transformation employed in contemporary ads, in which the scene is conceivable in all detail as one that could *in theory* have occurred as pictured" (p. 15; italics added). It is this theoretical picturing that dominates the snapshot advertising of the Colorama. Further complicating our analysis of the rhetoric is that the advertised product in the Colorama was color photography. In the case of the Colorama, photography advertised itself by promoting the making of color snapshots as a postwar ritual of family cohesion. As Norman Kerr (1998a), Kodak's Colorama historian, wrote, "One dramatic photograph could capture attention and communicate values to even the most diverse of audiences" (p. 1). Cultural values in use of snapshots become part of the frame for understanding Colorama advertising. Technology is another aspect of the Colorama advertising considered in this analysis. The size and place of the installation, and the mechanics of changing the image every 3 weeks for 40 years, influenced the content and presentation of the representations.

The practice of translating experience into instant memories was enhanced by snapshot photography as an amateur pastime. As West (2000) documented in her detailed examination of Eastman Kodak's advertising history from 1888 to 1932, Kodak was especially influential in promoting snapshots as nostalgia. Yet Kodak's advertising strategies reflected a crucial shift in focus during the early 40-year span: "Snapshot photography was transformed from a leisure activity—which like all forms of play, celebrates freedom, spontaneity, and the pleasures of the present—to an obligatory act of preserving memories as defense against the future and as assurance of the past" (p. 13). The turning point in Kodak's advertising, West argued, was World War I, "when Americans . . . desperately needed photographs to perform as confirmations of family unity" (p. 13). Like snapshots, advertising images were effective at "assuaging the anxieties of consumers about losses of community and individual control" brought on by

modernity (Marchand, 1985, p. xxi). Some 40 years later, after the end of World War II, Kodak revitalized its early advertising strategy in the promotion of color photography as the means to preserve family memory as a defense for future unknowns—in the "age of affluence," the vehicle for making reassuring memories was color. For Kodak, the Colorama "depicted the rebirth of human spirit after World War II, with the emphasis on expanding lifestyles, enticing destinations for jet age travel, triumphs in space exploration and momentous special events" (Kerr, 1998a, p. 1).

Kodak had always sought a mass market for its cameras and films, and the triumph of Kodak's earliest advertising campaigns is legendary. "Eastman's genius lay less in invention than in marketing" (Nickel, 1998, p. 9). Kodak's advertising campaigns rarely faltered from the strategy developed by George Eastman at the turn of the century—an appeal that combined the technical ease of producing a photograph with nostalgic portrayals of middle-class life, "for the easy availability of snapshots allowed people for the first time in history to arrange their lives in such a way that painful or unpleasant aspects were systematically erased" (West, 2000, p. 1). When Eastman patented his simple box camera in 1888, he immediately began to market photography as a pleasurable activity, a hobby available to all. Largely credited with making photography available to "ordinary people . . . to make pictures of themselves as they pleased" (Nickel, 1998, pp. 9–11), Kodak's focus on the amateur in its early mass advertising campaigns featured children making photographs as play or, in the case of the longrunning *Kodak Girl* campaign, on the new independent and adventurous woman.[6] Kodak's advertising strategy emphasized photography as a leisure activity—a way for amateurs to play with the camera, "the sheer pleasure and adventure of taking photographs are the main subject" (West, 2000, p. 13).

Kodak's early marketing goals were in sharp contrast to the practices of established photographers who sought to define photography as a profession. The success of Kodak's famous slogan, "You press the button, we do the rest," dismayed Alfred Stieglitz, who wrote in 1899, "It is due to this fatal facility that photography as a picture-making medium has fallen into disrepute" (cited in Nickel, 1998, p. 11). Nickel argued that Stieglitz and others were able to establish photography as an art form, in part by redefining the snapshot as something other. "Art photography defined itself against the example of the snapshot by asserting a new, symbolic, essentially public function for the medium" (Nickel, 1998, p. 11). As an artistic medium circulated in galleries, museums, and specialized publications, photography focused on the artist and on the aesthetics of the image for anonymous viewers. With the marketing of the Brownie cameras, Kodak's definition of photography as a leisure time performance defined the makers, subjects, and viewers of images as private consumers with individual, spontaneous desires.

West argued convincingly that Kodak's advertising themes shifted from play to memory, to emerge during World War I as a ritualized performance of domestic nostalgia residing in the family. Kodak advertisements were moral lessons about creating authentic memories for the family's future cohesiveness. The successful slogan, "Let Kodak Keep the Story," lasted over 20 years and reinforced ad copy and images that seemed to suggest to consumers that, "the horrors of war could be balanced and neutralized, even forgotten, through reassuring narratives implicit in photographs of home and family" (West, 2000, p. 167). Decades later, after the end of World War II, Kodak was to carry its marketing strategy of family nostalgia to new intensity in the Colorama program. In addition to family unity, themes in the Colorama display emphasized consumer goods as necessary props for middle-class family narratives. The maker, subject, and viewers of snapshots were pictured as the same people, telling stories of themselves as families and consumers.

STRATEGY AND TECHNOLOGY OF COLOR MARKETING

Kodak correctly identified a ready mass market for color photography after World War II in the growing affluence of the middle class. The *Cavalcade of Color,* a Kodachrome slide exhibit by Kodak at the World's Fair in 1939, had been a popular attraction, and Kodak was eager to repeat the success of the monumental installation to promote color film for the consuming public (Kerr, 1998a; Nordstrom, 2004). Although Walker Evans and other professionals initially disdained color photography as corrupt and vulgar (Eauclaire, 1984; Eklund, 2000),[7] Kodak reasoned that the amateur photographer—the taker of snapshots—was ready to embrace color photography as the perfect means to document the experience of postwar security and to subjugate the gray memories of the decade with visions of domestic affluence. To this end, Kodak seized the opportunity to install the Colorama in Grand Central Station.

Kodak applied the marketing conventions of mass advertising to the selling of color photography primarily and to its film and cameras secondarily. Adolph Stuber, vice president of sales and advertising, sharply instructed the staff of the Colorama information booth, "I want it made clear that you are here to promote photography—talk photography first—Kodak next" (Kerr, 1998b, p. 6). Rarely including any text but a title caption, the Colorama's snapshot advertising was an ostensive demonstration of what the amateur could do with a camera and color film. The images "were not billboard advertisements in the ordinary sense . . . seldom imposing a blatant sales pitch"; instead "photographic vision was the message" (Kerr, 1998a, p. 1). Kodak's vision of its target market was racially and sexually biased. Families were white and young, headed by men, depicted as groups of attractive heterosexual couples, babies, children, teenagers, and grandparents, and staged in scenes where "nothing but blue skies" provided locations for "dreaming in color" (Nordstrom & Roalf, 2004, p. 5).[8] For approximately 25 years of the 40-year span, the Colorama vision of the postwar family embodied an ordered hierarchy in which "men photograph women, women photograph children, children photograph other children, and everybody photographs a scenic view" while other family members "eagerly look on" as an appreciative audience for the picture-taking session (Nordstrom, 2004, p. 7).

At the heart of the Colorama project was Eastman Kodak's central marketing ploy voiced by Stuber: "Everyone who sees the Colorama should be able to visualize themselves [*sic*] as being able to make the same wonderful photo" (cited in Nordstrom, 2004, p. 5). The visual strategy was simple: Each image pictured someone in the frame taking a picture with a camera that was large enough to be identified as a Kodak. The picture-taker, looking through the lens at family members or a spectacular scene, was the focal point of every image, a management decision that irked many photographers, including Ansel Adams.[9] In an information center, Kodak staff offered help and instructions to consumers for making the best pictures, reinforcing the pretense that anyone armed with a simple Kodak camera and color film could produce images similar to those displayed in the Colorama. This despite the fact that all 565 Coloramas were taken by professional photographers, including Adams, Ernst Haas, Eliot Porter, Gordon Parks, Jon Abbot, Valentino Serra, and Ozzie Sweet (Handy, 2004; Kerr, 1998a; Nordstrom, 2004). Kodak professionals, including photographers and technical staff, produced most of the images, inventing technique as they went along.

The technology of producing and assembling the colorful images was a professional challenge. The original plan of duplicating the projection techniques used for the 1939 World's Fair *Cavalcade of Color* was abandoned because of the ambient light in Grand Central. Kodak's installation blocked natural light from reaching the Grand Concourse, negating one of the most remarkable features of the building's Beaux Arts design (Nevins, 1982), a fact that would later figure prominently in the effort to restore the terminal.[10] To overcome the lighting problem, the images were backlit, producing the effect of giant transparencies. The panoramic layout of most of the images was impossible to achieve with available snapshot technologies, and the size of the negatives mandated special equipment, including a custom-designed enlarger that had to be set up in Kodak's recreational building in Rochester. Kodak technicians wallpapered the images together, splicing negatives in rolls 20 feet long, weighing hundreds of pounds. The images were trucked from Rochester to Manhattan about every 3 weeks (Kerr, 1998a).

The disparity between Stuber's insistence on the illusion of the amateur snapshot and the actual production of the image was frequently ludicrous. Producing uniform color mandated lighting techniques that were a recurring challenge, even for Kodak professionals (see Figure 2). The technique used to light this image of Christmas Carolers, made by Kodak photographer Neil Montanus, is described and commented on by Norman Kerr (1999):

> Two-thirds of this Colorama's display area was devoted to a complex set erected in Kodak's photo illustration studio (the side panel showed the newest snapshot camera). The set was lit "outside" with blue-filtered electronic flash to simulate moonlight. This illusion was reinforced by Neil's clever application of urea and alcohol to create frosted windows, and by artificial snow on potted nursery plants. Neil's meticulous attention to lighting his exuberant cast, including his young son, conveys a convincing sense of reality. Management's insistence on including a snapshot camera seen being used from inside wasn't challenged, though it's doubtful that taking a flash picture through a window would have worked. (p. 31)

It is clear from the many references to management decisions in Kerr's history of the

Figure 2   Christmas Carolers Colorama.

SOURCE: Neil Montanus/Eastman Kodak Company 1961.

Colorama that the illusion implicit in the advertising campaign took precedence over fidelity to amateur possibilities.

Considerations of "how the ideology of the family and the technology of photography support and reinforce each other" permeate theoretical explorations of the snapshot (M. Hirsch, 1997, p. 48). More significant than amateur cameras in determining the subject and framing of images were the size, shape, and color saturation of the negatives demanded for the Colorama installation. The shape of the Colorama frame encouraged horizontal lines in landscapes, and rows of things as subjects: babies, surfboards, kittens, and hot-air balloons were popular Colorama images.[11] Before the development of techniques to make one long negative, the horizontal rectangle made proportions a problem that was solved by dividing the screen into a central frame with two sidebar images. This device allowed Kodak to picture the same family and the same event in different shots. Sidebars showed pictures that might have been taken by the picture-taker in the center (see Figure 3).

Collective memory of the 1950s family is largely a mediated creation in which the photo technologies of advertising performed an important role. The Colorama not only displayed images of what the proper family should look like, but the images instructed families in how to produce their own mediated memories *in color.* As Coleman (2002) pointed out, "Whenever the technology and economics of color photography have come abreast of monochrome closely enough to be competitive with it, color is automatically preferred. . . . Especially via the applied and vernacular usages and forms of color photography, the primacy of color in photography has been established by democratic vote" (p. 10). The circulation of color images in movies, fashion ads, and celebrity shots, popular in the 1940s and 1950s, stimulated the consumer demand for color in their own snapshots.

Sontag (1973) remarked on another dimension of photography's relationship to family especially pertinent to reading the interwoven demands of technology and ideology presented in *Farm Scene* (see Figure 3): "As that claustrophobic unit, the nuclear family, was being carved out of a much larger family aggregate, photography came along to memorialize, to restate symbolically, the imperiled continuity and vanishing extendedness of family life" (p. 9). After the war, the extended family was fractured further, and Kodak was ready to market color photography in sentimental appeals to traditional family mythologies. Although popular culture was rife with performances counter to the claustrophobic family, no trace of rebelliousness appeared in the Colorama images.[12] The farm scene in this image reflects the divided screen technique in a typically nostalgic image: a family farm in rural New York State. The red barn, dirt road, wooden fence, and horse and buggy reference a backward glance to a mythical past. Three generations of a family—cute kids, animals, a hint of some ritual in the corsage pinned on the mother's blouse, and especially, the picture-taking man—mark the photo as a Kodak ad.

As a collective unit, the family was producer, subject, and audience for memorials to itself and to the affluence of its domesticity. The collectiveness of the endeavor establishes the photographic act as an event whose significance equals

Figure 3   Farm Scene and Family Snapshots Colorama.

SOURCE: Hank Mayer/Eastman Kodak Company 1950.

or surpasses the subject of the snapshot. "Through photographs, each family constructs a portrait-chronicle of itself—a portable kit of images that bears witness to its connectedness. . . . It hardly matters what activities are photographed so long as photographs get taken and are cherished" (Sontag, 1973, p. 8).

Postwar advertising for family snapshots added another layer to the production and consumption of family images. The staging of family rituals, celebrations, and holidays in the advertisements tortured family memories into standardized commercial visions. The Colorama illuminated the postwar nuclear family as an intimate collective of consumers. No matter who was taking the photograph, family occasions were portrayed as celebrations of consumption.[13] Some images were subtle in the promotion of consumption, whereas others were not. In Colorama #155, made in 1959, *Camping at Lake Placid, New York,* photographed by Herb Archer (see Figure 4), the mother is photographing the children who sit in a fishing boat, framed by the Adirondack Mountains in the background. Framing the family in the foreground is a wealth of camping equipment. Tents, bikes, stoves, a cooler, sleeping bags, and assorted utensils compete with the family as the object of our gaze.

Norman Rockwell directed another Colorama, *Closing up a Summer Cottage,* photographed by Ralph Amdursky and Charles Baker, in which a family attempts to load a station wagon with a surplus of possessions that includes garden equipment, toys, boats, suitcases, and golf clubs (Nordstrom, 2004). In a nostalgic image, a young boy photographs the neighborhood children.[14] This focus on affluence merged family sentimentality with commodities and paved the way for advertising's accepted presence in American life. Technically, the ideal snapshot promoted in the Colorama mimicked advertising images in production value and pictorial quality; each image had to be "perfectly" framed, lit, and staged (Kerr, 1999, p. 1)—a model that reinforced the dominance of consumerism as a primary frame for domestic meaning. Colorama images stressed the features that distinguished the family of the 1950s from previous generations: a calcification of gender roles, a focus on the child, and an emphasis on material goods (Coontz, 1992).

In Memory of the Family

Family snapshots have engendered theoretical speculation as authentic artifacts of record. Yet as J. Hirsch (1981) concluded, conventional family photographs reference myths about families: "Pleasure has replaced stability as the most important family goal. And yet we still treasure paintings and create photographs which relate, no matter how tenuously, to ancient metaphors of family unity and cohesion: we still seem to acknowledge the values we have shed" (p. 32). The mythology of families may explain the interest in family snapshots as found objects. A scattering of museum exhibits, catalogues, and essays attends to anonymous snapshots as discoveries with "a license to circulate . . . at a flea market, photographic fair, or historical society" (Nickel, 1998, p. 13). Yet the separation of the family photo from the specific family of its making shifts the contextual relationship

Figure 4   Lake Placid Colorama.

SOURCE: Herb Archer/Eastman Kodak Company 1959.

away from a focus on the collectivity of image makers, subjects, and viewers, the defining characteristic of family snapshots. Snapshots as found objects highlight the relationship between the image and a curious viewer uninvolved with the subject as a known person. For example, Graves and Payne (1977) collected and published anonymous photographs, " . . . which were complete visual statements, needing neither explanation nor rationalization" (p. 9), effectively making the family photo a work of art—however unintended by the maker.

Roland Barthes' (1981) famous remarks emanating from his consideration of a single photograph of his mother as a child offer a stark contrast to the conventions of found snapshots and the staged images of the Colorama. In his *Camera Lucida,* Barthes discussed his mother's childhood image, made in 1898. The photograph touched the grown man after his mother's death. He wrote, "And no more than I would reduce my family to the Family, would I reduce my mother to the Mother" (p. 74). For Barthes, "what founds the nature of Photography is the knowledge that a living being for an instant was caught motionless in front of the lens" (p. 78). This sense of singularity is in exact opposition to the use of photography in advertising, and especially to the family scenes promoted by the Colorama. Goffman (1976) focused on the "pictured scenes" of advertising images as stand-ins for real situations and concluded: "Presumably what the advertisement is concerned to depict is not particular individuals. . . . Pictured scenes show examples of categories of persons, not particular persons" (p. 19). Just so, the rhetoric of the Colorama invites the production of interchangeable family images, using the specific conventions of consumerism: a display of goods and the identification of self with commodities.

In advertising images, American families are identified and reduced to the same events, the same poses. The whole family is implicated in the manufacturing of the myth. Commenting on the inadequacy of Barthes' musings as a way to understand snapshots, Nickel (1998) protested: "Barthes sought the essence of photography, its unique and inimitable feature (its *noeme,* as he calls it) in its capacity to ratify the existence of a particular moment in the past, something the snapshot often does well. But simple logic rules

here—while all snapshots may be photographs, not all photographs are snapshots" (p. 9). Colorama advertisements for the color snapshot presented yet another kind of family photograph, the staged dramatization of a happy family inexorably embedded in consumer ideologies, a performance picture-takers were invited to mimic.

In Colorama images, real lives often merged with mediated fictions. Perhaps nothing demonstrates more the eerie quality of the Colorama images than those featuring the family of Ozzie, Harriet, David, and Ricky Nelson. Kodak sponsored *The Adventures of Ozzie and Harriet* TV show, and the Nelson family appeared in four Colorama images. As the Nelsons did on TV (in black and white), they did in full color for Kodak. The Nelsons merged their real family life with that staged by media promoters. By presenting themselves as staged representations of themselves, the fictional Nelsons became emblematic commercials for real families. The last Colorama Nelson family image, made in 1960, captures Harriet doing a hula dance on Waikiki beach while Ricky plays the guitar, David gazes fondly, and Ozzie films them all for a home movie with a Kodak camera (Nordstrom, 2004). The melding of reality with representation is of course the seduction of photography in general and advertising in particular. Bruce Handy (2004), writing from a contemporary look backward, compared the Colorama with Roman inscriptions and medieval churches: "The Colorama was arguably the closest midcentury America came to narrating its own stories and celebrating its own secular myths in a similar epic, inspiring, and sometimes bludgeoning fashion" (p. 331) (see Figure 5).

At just about the same time the Colorama went up in Grand Central Terminal, Marshall McLuhan (1951) published *The Mechanical Bride,* his early examination of popular media at work in the culture of postwar America. McLuhan's probes into the "folklore of industrial man" identified the consistent links among technology, consumerism, and sex in the visual artifacts of advertising as "some sort of collective dream" (p. v). He described his method of inquiry as "providing typical visual imagery of our environment and dislocating it into meaning by inspection" (p. vi):

Figure 5 Monument Valley Arizona Colorama.

SOURCE: Peter Gales/Eastman Kodak Company 1962.

Where visual symbols have been employed in an effort to paralyze the mind, they are here used as a means of energizing it. It is observable that the more illusion and falsehood needed to maintain any given state of affairs, the more tyranny is needed to maintain the illusion and falsehood. Today the tyrant rules not by club or fist, but, disguised as a market researcher, he shepherds his flocks in the ways of utility and comfort. (McLuhan, 1951, p. vi)

From the vantage point of the 21st century, some of McLuhan's observations seem both naive and obvious, yet it may be that the marriage of photography to advertising, so ubiquitous a stream of our collective consciousness, forecast the victory of consumerism as the tyranny McLuhan feared.

The perfected family snapshot exemplified in the Colorama underscores the production of the image as a collective project necessary to the commercialization of family life. Family members, mimicking advertising images, do more than agree to be photographed: They participate by arranging themselves, posing and smiling, dressing in appropriate costume, and displaying the props of consumer life. The collective effort provides further evidence of domestic cooperation in the creation of memory. In the final decades of the Colorama, the families disappeared from the display, replaced by lush panoramas of exotic locales or beautiful scenes of nature, absent the mandatory picture-taker. Although slide shows declined as a family activity,[15] the family photograph had become, by then, a firmly ritualized performance of memorializing.

When the New York community learned that the Colorama would be removed, commentary reflected a love-hate relationship with the advertising monument. "Love it (as a spectacular display) or spurn it (as an aesthetic intrusion), there is one thing you cannot do in the presence of the Kodak Colorama in Grand Central Terminal: miss it. That may change in coming months" (Anderson & Dunlap, 1985, p. 5). Sadness, relief, anger, and approval were linked to the tragic condition of Grand Central Terminal in the 1970s and 1980s. The bitter letter of Joel Sachs, writing to the *New York Times* in 1989, is worth quoting for its passion:

> For almost 40 years, jaded New Yorkers, harried commuters and gawking tourists walking through the terminal have paused to observe the ever vibrant, ever colorful, ever changing Colorama. Oftentimes, it brightened up the gloomy stroll through an otherwise cold and impersonal space.
>
> Now with the demise of the Colorama those passing through Grand Central will have to be content with watching the somewhat less colorful and less exciting visual display of winos, panhandlers, and the homeless who have taken over the terminal, not to mention its ever-expanding array of gritty, fast-food establishments and downscale shops. Hats off to Metro-North. You've done it again.
>
> Joel H. Sachs

Other writers and commentators were sad, but resigned: "It's the first thing I look for when I come here . . . it's a changing picture postcard of the world." The missed "pictures of China at sunrise, the Taj Mahal at dawn, and pandas at the Bronx Zoo" (cited in Kendel, 1990, p. 8) reference the last 15 years of spectacle images that dominated the Colorama. Less frequently missed were the family snapshots, perhaps because they were least remembered, having ended 15 years earlier. Yet the family images were ambivalent constructs in the public mind. Grundberg's (1989) remarks on the images may reflect a common sentiment: "My least favorites were idealized pseudo-snapshots of happy families doing happy-family things. Scenes like these might be perfectly natural in Rochester, Kodak's home, but they were out of place in the context of Grand Central Terminal with its sorry population of homeless men and women and its wonderful diversity of races, creeds, and lifestyles" (p. 94).

Acknowledging the ambivalence of public sentiment, Grand Central's restoration committee removed the Colorama as a rhetorical act designed to influence public opinion of the project:

> We concluded that with one preemptive strike, it would be relatively simple and inexpensive to show the public something of the real Grand Central by dismantling the Kodak sign. . . . As the sunshine burst through three windows that had not been seen since 1950, it was as if life were being breathed back into the building. Many commuters stopped in their tracks, speechless and amazed at the change that had so instantly bought back the majesty of the space. (Belle & Leighton, 2000, p. 133)

PUBLIC SUPPORT OF THE RESTORATION PROJECT SOLIDIFIED

Narratives of wars, racial unrest, poverty, violence, and the continual challenge of modern and postmodern urban existence have no life in advertising or family photographs. Amateur family photographers have been taught to use photography as a talisman—a magical tool that denies family disruption and ultimately denies death itself. "Recently, photography has become almost as widely practiced an amusement as sex and dancing—which means that, like every mass art form, photography is not practiced by most people as an art. It is mainly a social rite, a defense against anxiety, and a tool of power" (Sontag, 1973, p. 8). The Colorama was a historic milestone in presenting Americans a vision of themselves as Kodak thought they wanted to be in the postwar years

of affluence. Although snapshot photography and especially digital technology may once again encourage amateurs to play with images, the ritual family photo persists to document and mythologize ritualized consumerism. The Colorama images, with their colorful narratives of happiness, affluence, and material comfort, produced the pictures that pointed the way to the commodity future of families.

NOTES

1. The American military seized the Agfa plant in Wolfen and "claimed the company's trade secrets for Agfacolor negative film as 'war indemnity'" and distributed the information (Roalf, 2004, p. 77).

2. Notable exceptions include the 1967 image of Earthrise from the moon, photographed by NASA's Lunar Orbiter I on Kodak film, and in 1969, the Apollo 11 moon landing, a Colorama displayed a day before the images were seen in weekly news magazines (Roalf, 2004). "During each of the final four years of the Colorama's lease, Grand Central's owner, the Metropolitan Transportation Authority, required that one subject be of their choosing" (Kodak e-Magazine). For example, the choice for 1986 was a photograph of the Metro-North commuter train traveling along the Hudson River, made by Kodak photographer Bob Clemens.

3. Roalf (2004) wrote, "The very last Colorama, which was displayed from November 1989 to February 1990, is now steeped in a nostalgia that has altered the photograph's original meaning since the events of September 11, 2001. In this picture, a glittering nighttime view of the New York City skyline features the Twin Towers of the World Trade Center, with the only digital enhancement ever created for the Colorama program—an oversize red apple nestled among the buildings to the towers' left. The copy that ran with the photograph reads: 'Kodak thanks the Big Apple for 40 years of friendship in Grand Central'" (p. 77).

4. In addition to TV shows (e.g., *The Adventures of Ozzie and Harriet* and *The Ed Sullivan Show*), Kodak-sponsored events included America's Junior Miss Pageant, various world Olympic meetings, world's fairs, and theme park exhibits.

5. The term was coined by Michael Schudson (1984) in his book, *Advertising, the Uneasy Persuasion: Its Dubious Impact on American Society* (pp. 214–218).

6. The fashionable *Kodak Girl* was interested more in the camera as an accessory to her ensemble, rather than in its technical properties, and was used to market Vanity Kodak cameras (available in five colors), as well as other products. For an extended discussion of Kodak's use of women in its ads, see West (2000), chapter 4, "Proudly Displayed by Wearers of Chic Ensembles: Vanity Cameras, Kodak Girls, and the Culture of Female Fashion." Marchand (1985) discussed Kodak ads for the Vanity Kodak as part of the "Mystique of the Ensemble" and as "the crowning achievement of advertising's emphasis on color, beauty, and style" in the 1920s (pp. 132–140).

7. Evans might have been describing the Colorama when he wrote that they "blow you down with screeching hues alone . . . a bebop of electric blues, furious reds, and poison greens" (cited in Eauclaire, 1984, p. 40). Evans eventually produced some color images, but preferred muted colors: "If you tone it all down it's just about bearable, and that's the only thing to do with it, make it as monotonous as possible" (cited in Eklund, 2000, p. 124).

8. Coleman (2002) reported the technical relationship of imaging whiteness to color processing: "The entire tonal palette of Kodachrome was premised on the necessity of rendering in a pleasing manner the skin tones of those who would be its principal consumers: Caucasians" (p. 10, f2).

9. Adams made six pictures for the Colorama. The first in May/June 1951, *Yosemite Valley in Snapshots,* featured two families taking pictures of the scenery and each other. Adams' objections to the selection of the photo with "the most prominent placement of the camera-user in the scene" were overruled. "Management's response was that the Colorama should not be ambiguous in promoting the excitement of color photography." A year later in July/August 1952, Adams made *Grand Canyon, Arizona,* the first Colorama "where strong emphasis was placed on the view itself, not the obligatory Kodak camera being used," in defiance of company policy. "However, Adams' contradictory and more pictorial choice was accepted—probably after some internal management debate" (Kodak e-magazine).

10. Removal of the Colorama was an event designed to impact public opinion: "The morning after the dismantling was finished and the protective curtain was taken down, the architects stood quietly watching the first commuters stream into the Main Concourse from the train platforms" (Belle & Leighton, 2000, p. 133). As the natural light came in, commuters were treated to a sight that had been blocked for 40 years, and public support for the project was enthusiastic.

11. *15 Babies* was one of the most popular of Kodak's images and was duplicated twice as the babies became toddlers and school children. When the Colorama came down, a number of New Yorkers isolated the Kodak Babies as something they would miss (Grundberg, 1989; Handy, 2004).

12. *Rebel Without A Cause,* the James Dean cult film of 1955, is a classic example. Filmed in color, the movie depicted a smothering family and adolescent rebellion.

13. By the end of World War II, the ensuing affluence of the middle class and the enactment of the G.I. Bill enabled thousands of veteran-headed families the means of home ownership. "Eighty-five percent of the new homes were built in the suburbs, where the nuclear family found new possibilities for privacy and togetherness" (Coontz, 1992, p. 24). The push by industry and government to encourage women to leave jobs created by the absence of men during the war was framed as a desire for a traditional family life that had rarely existed outside the network of extended families and communities. In fact the family of the 1950s reflected a reversal of trends: "For the first time in more than 100 years, the age for marriage and motherhood fell, fertility increased, divorce rates declined, and women's degree of educational parity with men dropped sharply" (Coontz, 1992, p. 25).

14. Although predating them by nearly 40 years, these images look like and connect the anticonsumer visual arguments made by Peter Menzel (1994) in his photographic collection of global families and their possessions, *Material World: A Global Family Portrait.*

15. The last slide projectors came off Kodak's assembly lines on October 22, 2004. The company made 35 million slide projectors in seven decades—the single most successful piece of equipment in Kodak's 125-year history (Rand, 2004).

REFERENCES

Anderson, S. H., & Dunlap, D. (1985, November 26). New York day by day: At Grand Central, Kodak could lose its beam. *New York Times,* p. B5.

Barthes, R. (1981). *Camera lucida* (R. Howard, Trans.). New York: Hill & Wang.

Belle, J., & Leighton, M. R. (2000). *Grand Central.* New York: Norton.

Coleman, A.D. (2002). Mama, don't take our Kodachrome away. In E. Rijper (Ed.), *Kodachrome: The American invention of our world* (pp. 1939–1959). New York: Delano Greenidge Editions.

Coontz, S. (1992). *The way we never were: American families and the nostalgia trap.* New York: Basic Books, HarperCollins.

Czech, K. P. (1996). *Snapshot: America discovers the camera.* Minneapolis: Lerner.

Eauclaire, S. (1994). *New color/new work: Eighteen photographic essays.* New York: Abbeville.

Eklund, D. (2000). The harassed man's haven of detachment: Walker Evans and the Fortune portfolio. In M. M. Morris Hambourg, J. L. Rosenheim, D. Eklund, & M. Fineman (Eds.), *Walker Evans* (pp. 121–129). New York: The Metropolitan Museum of Art, in Association with Princeton University Press.

Ewen, S. (1976). *Captains of consciousness.* New York: McGraw-Hill.

Goffman, E. (1976). Picture frames. In *Gender advertisements* (pp. 10–23). New York: Harper & Row.

Goldman, R., & Papson, S. (1996). *Sign wars: The cluttered landscape of advertising.* New York: Guilford.

Graves, K., & Payne M. (1977). *American snapshots.* Oakland, CA: Scrimshaw.

Grundberg, A. (1989, December 3). Camera; One of the city's most spectacular traditions will cease to exist at the end of the month. *New York Times,* Section 1, p. 94

Handy, B. (2004, September). Call of the wide. *Vanity Fair,* pp. 321–325.

Hirch, J. (1981). *Family photographs: Content, meaning and effect.* New York: Oxford University Press.

Hirsch, M. (1997). *Family frames: Photography, narrative and postmemory.* Cambridge, MA: Harvard University Press.

Kendel, B. (1990, February 22). Grand Central's facelift takes it back to the future. *USA Today,* p. 8A.

Kerr, N. (1998a). A capsule history. *A history of Kodak's Colorama.* Rochester, NY: George Eastman House Archive.

Kerr, N. (1998b). The Kodak Colorama display and information center site. *A history of Kodak's Colorama.* Rochester, NY: George Eastman House Archive.

Kerr, N. (1999, May/June). The Kodak Colorama: Lighting on a grand scale. *Photo Techniques Magazine, 20*(3), 31–35.

Kodak, e-magazine: The Kodak Colorama http://www.kodak.com/US/en/corp/features/coloramas/colorama.html.

Marchand, R. (1985). *Advertising the American dream.* Berkeley: University of California Press.

McLuhan, M. (1951). *The mechanical bride.* New York: Vanguard.

Menzel, P. (1994). *Material world: A global family portrait.* San Francisco, CA: Sierra Club Books.

Nevins, D. (Ed.). (1992). *Grand Central terminal: City within the city.* New York: The Municipal Art Society of New York.

Nickel, D. R. (1998). *Snapshots: The photography of everyday life.* San Francisco: San Francisco Museum of Modern Art.

Nordstrom, A. (2004). Dreaming in color. In A. Nordsrom & P. Roalf (Eds.), *Colorama: The world's largest photographs* (pp. 5–11). New York: Aperture Foundation.

Nordstrom, A., & Roalf, P. (Eds.) (2004). *Colorama: The world's largest photographs.* New York: Aperture Foundation.

Rand, B. (2004, November 19). Kodak projector, 67, slides into history. *Rochester Democrat & Chronicle,* pp. 1A–2A.

Rijper, E. (Ed.). (2002). *Kodachrome: The American invention of our world: 1939–1959.* New York: Delano Greenidge Editions.

Roalf, P. (2004). Picture perfect. In A. Nordstrom & P. Roalf (Eds.), *Colorama: The world's largest photographs* (pp. 77–79). New York: Aperture Foundation.

Sachs, J. H. (1989, August 13). Colorama [Letter to the editor]. *New York Times,* Section 10, p. 10.

Schudson, M. (1984). *Advertising, the uneasy persuasion: Its dubious impact on American society.* New York: Basic Books.

Sontag, S. (1973). *On photography.* New York: Picador, Farrar, Straus & Giroux.

West, N. M. (2000). *Kodak and the lens of nostalgia.* Charlotteville, VA: University Press of Virginia.

PART V

GOVERNING AND AUTHORIZING

The essays in this section each concentrate on visual rhetoric with an emphasis on governing and authorizing through such symbolic activities as agenda setting, campaigning for public office, or influencing constituencies. Governing authorities project a public image regarding leadership abilities, matters of social justice, and engagement with issues of the moment through the use of visual strategies and media. Such visual rhetoric scholarship tends to focus on the communicative practices of the politically powerful, economically resourceful, and socially privileged in U.S. culture, as well as the mainstream media that report on them. The visual rhetoric featured in this section con-

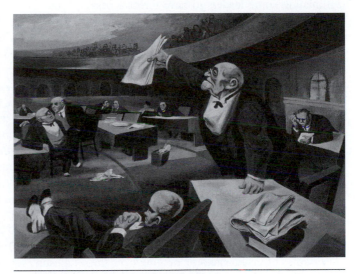

Figure 1 "The Opposition," William Gropper, 1942.

SOURCE: Courtesy of ACA Galleries, New York and UR Rochester Memorial Art Gallery.

centrates on high-profile institutions and civic forums for exercising power and privilege such as the federal, state, and local legislatures; the courts at all levels of government; and executive offices of the president and first lady. In addition, these essays feature media accounts of leaders and issues, underscoring how media construct visual rhetoric through such practices as selection, framing and reframing, recycling footage, voiceover, and, on occasion, overt distortion and manipulation.

By *governing,* we refer to leading or ruling through symbolic actions by right (as in the case of a sovereign) or by delegated authority (as in the case of elected or appointed leaders). More generally, governing encompasses campaigning, enacting leadership, or exercising a directing or restraining influence over public policy, judicial verdicts, or groups of people. By *authorizing,* we refer to delegating, the giving of authority or official power to another or others, and the symbolic activity of warranting, justifying, or otherwise sanctioning leaders' symbolic actions. This may be done either passively by condoning, permitting, or acquiescing to leaders' deeds or actively by affirming, supporting, electing, endorsing, and otherwise approving of them. In visual rhetoric scholarship, studies of governing and authorizing tend to focus on deliberate uses of visual symbolism for shaping beliefs concerning the strengths and weaknesses of candidates for public offices, the public image or persona of leaders, the formation and advocacy of public policy, the promotion of judgments concerning matters of morality or justice, and, above all, agenda setting.

327

Students of visual rhetoric may wish to ask certain questions concerning governing and authorizing as communication practices: Who has been authorized by what means to perform the symbolic actions in ways that others ordinarily recognize as legitimate or authoritative? With regard to public roles and offices, what are the symbolic processes and rituals by which their inhabitants come to occupy them? How do leaders enact and use their authority in endeavors to shape attitudes and beliefs of others? What underlying sociological, political, and economic factors have contributed to empowering and legitimating some leaders to have direct access to participation within certain public forums and offices, while most people do not? In what ways do underlying institutions, organizations, and forums enable these varieties of leadership, while also conditioning and influencing audiences' expectations of public leaders? What are the rhetorical possibilities and limitations for leaders who seek to influence audiences through mainstream forums, such as the legislatures, courts, and executive offices? In what ways do public rituals and ceremonies authorize and consecrate political, legal, religious, educational, and civic leaders to exercise leadership in their communities?

The essays in this section offer a broad range of examples of visual rhetoric, ranging from the 18th century to the last half of the 20th century in both colonial and contemporary U.S. culture. They encompass a broad range of media, including woodcut and engraved political prints, photojournalism in newspapers and television news, video footage, and stills. And they concentrate on elected officials and high-profile politicians: Benjamin Franklin as an 18th-century assemblyman and, later, as a lobbyist to Parliament; presidents from both of the major political parties throughout the last half of the 20th century; and a recent first lady in the United States. While visual rhetoric scholarship concerned with governing and authorizing has tended to concentrate on key leaders in public life, scholarship has also focused generally on how underlying ideologies "authorize" or "warrant" U.S. interventions abroad.

One dominant theme in the essays in this section underscores how audiences and media outlets interact with and sometimes deliberately reshape the public performances of leaders, which are sometimes staged in photo opportunities, photojournalism, and on television news. While public officials endeavor to shape their constituencies' beliefs and attitudes, their audiences are seldom passive in acquiescing to leaders' self-representations or policy positions. Audiences do not necessarily accept precisely what image makers promote; in fact, audiences can become quite active in deliberately reshaping public officials' messages, sometimes to those officials' detriment.

The section opens with 18th-century woodcuts and engravings employed by Benjamin Franklin for deliberative and apologetic functions in Britain and colonial America. Lester C. Olson's essay, "Benjamin Franklin's Pictorial Representations of the British Colonies in America: A Study in Rhetorical Iconology," focuses on two pictorial images Franklin produced and designed a decade apart, initially during a period when he was an elected office holder in the Pennsylvania Assembly in 1754 and, subsequently, when he was a lobbyist to Parliament representing Pennsylvania's government in London. Even though both "JOIN, or DIE" and "MAGNA Britannia: her colonies REDUC'D" were designed by Franklin to represent the British colonies in colonial America, Olson suggests that fundamental differences between the pictorial messages can be ascribed to the rhetorical functions of the messages for different audiences at the moment of their initial circulation. Olson contends that the latter of the two images was both deliberative, in that it was directed to the British Parliament to influence policy, and apologetic, in that it was calculated to counter criticisms from a moderate segment of the colonial public. Olson situates the pictorial images designating the British American colonies within the prevailing political and economic concerns during issues of the moment, noticing how radicals' appropriation of his earlier image, "JOIN, or DIE," fundamentally altered Franklin's original usages of that pictorial design. Indeed, Franklin's "JOIN, or DIE" image of a segmented snake was appropriated for rhetorical uses very different from what he himself had undertaken with the design a decade earlier in 1754, during the French and Indian war. Because Olson illustrates how the practices of appropriation and resistance might have caused rhetorical problems for Franklin in his roles as postmaster general for British America and lobbyist, he illustrates how appropriation of visual images can be a powerful rhetorical tool. In addition, Olson's essay highlights how diverse constituencies may interpret visual rhetoric differently when he explores how identical features in the design of "MAGNA Britannia" probably had different meanings for contemporaneous viewers in Britain and colonial America. As a result of its emphasis on image circulation and appropriation, Olson's essay could be productively paired with Robert Hariman and John Louis Lucaites's essay, "Public Identity and Collective Memory in U.S. Iconic Photography: The Image of 'Accidental Napalm'" (in Section II), to explore how icons may undergo changes in meanings across time and place.

While Olson's essay provides a glimpse into 18th-century political culture in British America, the next two essays in this section both concentrate on 20th-century political life and the high-profile institutions of the presidency and the powerful, though unelected, office of the first lady. Keith V. Erickson's essay, "Presidential Rhetoric's Visual Turn: Performance Fragments and the Politics of Illusionism," focuses on presidential leadership enacted at "photo opportunity performances." In Erickson's view, presidential photo opportunities are primarily useful for agenda setting because they stimulate political interest and create social awareness by reaching mass audiences. Erickson recognizes that the predominantly visual character of communication in the United States during the 20th century has fundamentally transformed how audiences access and understand political institutions. The century has witnessed a remarkable change in visual representations of presidents and their public deeds, moreover, because of the hidden role of White House operatives who carefully plan each president's photo opportunities. Erickson underscores that the presidents are actors in a public drama with highly theatrical qualities who use photo opportunities to legitimate their claims, to authenticate their role, and to enthrall their audiences. Photo opportunities project a persona for each of the presidents, even as their staged dramas tend consistently—regardless of political affiliation— to reduce citizens to the role of spectators.

Erickson suggests that photo opportunities are useful to presidents because their audiences are much more likely to see or view them than to listen to presidential remarks or read public statements. Photo opportunities can be deceptive, however, because in their theatricality, they may blur distinctions between fiction and reality. Furthermore, photo opportunities lend themselves to reiterating and re-presenting only dominant perspectives and ideologies in ways that undermine rationality and minimize thoughtful public engagement. Erickson argues that in place of public argument and deliberation, then, audiences often receive persona, image management, and dubious associations among images; in place of reason, there is affective, emotional response. In Erickson's view, photo opportunities lend themselves to concealing actual political objectives, and they tend to mystify the various presidents' positions on substantive issues of the moment.

Rich with numerous examples from several administrations, the essay ranges across illustrations from the Kennedy, Johnson, and Nixon administrations to Carter's and onward through the more recent Reagan, Clinton, and Bush presidencies. Drawing on the theoretical writings of Michael McGee and Raymie McKerrow, Erickson features the idea of "performance fragments," narrative representations that recount, portray, or depict events in ways that reshape a culture's understanding of political realities. Erickson's essay could be provocatively contrasted with the essay by Charles E. Morris III and John M. Sloop, "'What Lips These Lips Have Kissed': Refiguring the Politics of Queer Public Kissing" (in Section I), to examine how power and privilege impinge on the diverse ways in which photo opportunities and "performance fragments" function in public life.

Whereas Erickson's essay concentrates on how presidents have used photo opportunities for what is called "agenda setting," Shawn J. Parry-Giles's essay, "Mediating Hillary Rodham Clinton: Television News Practices and Image-Making in the Postmodern Age," emphasizes how media production practices in television news have affected one prominent political leader's public persona. Parry-Giles argues that even though Hillary Clinton and her staff deliberately sought to stage public appearances and events that would project a favorable image of the first lady's leadership abilities, the media's production practices often undercut those attempts at image building. Through specific techniques ranging from selection of footage and careful use of close-up images to voiceovers, image repetition, and overt manipulation, media organizations constructed their own, much different picture of Clinton. Parry-Giles details one instance when visual footage for an NBC newscast was "recycled" from an event different from the featured news story, creating what amounted to a fictional account of Hillary Clinton's public conduct. The story portrayed Clinton weeping, as though in reaction to her husband's alleged unfaithfulness, when the video footage actually was taken from the memorial service for Americans who had been killed in the Tanzania and Kenya Embassy bombings. As a result of their power to shape the news via production techniques, Parry-Giles concludes that media ultimately held more power to shape Clinton's image than did she or her staff.

Parry-Giles's essay contributes to visual rhetoric scholarship pertaining to governing and authorizing, moreover, in that it vividly explores and documents the significance of sex and gender stereotypes concerning women in powerful political offices. In this regard, her essay could be paired with Anne Teresa Demo's essay, "The Guerrilla Girls' Comic Politics of Subversion" (in Section III), because that essay offers a lesson in how some groups employ techniques for self-presentation through media in order to counter stereotypes of women.

In another essay examining stereotypic images of women, Dana L. Cloud's "'To Veil the Threat of Terror': Afghan Women and the <Clash of Civilizations> in the Imagery of the U.S. War on Terrorism" examines photographs of women from Afghanistan that circulated in the United States during the 2001–2002 "War on Terror." Cloud's essay illustrates how visual rhetoric scholarship concerning governing and authorizing may help us to recognize, and thus serve to demystify, ideologies that "authorize" or warrant a government's deeds. Cloud explores a series of photographs of women displayed during the U.S. war with Afghanistan and argues that they project an image of "foreign" women as vulnerable and the United States as heroic

rescuers. Cloud argues that such depictions of women were paternalistic in that they sought to warrant U.S. interventions abroad by portraying those interventions as the equivalent of men protecting women from harm. Ultimately, Cloud's critique is an argument for resistance to visual images that frame the war as a humanitarian effort to save "brown women from brown men." Analyzing the frame and light/dark oppositions in a thematic set of images posted on the Time.com Web site, Cloud argues that the images construct a justification for war via the ideograph <clash of civilizations> in order to "veil" or mask the actual "economic and geopolitical motives" for the U.S. war on Afghanistan. Cloud's essay could be productively paired with Reginald Twigg's essay, "The Performative Dimension of Surveillance: Jacob Riis' *How the Other Half Lives*" (in Section I), to explore further the functions of photographic images employed in the service of surveillance, domination, and control over others.

We invite you to explore the discussion questions below as well as our suggestions for further reading. For students of visual rhetoric interested in exploring more fully the role of media in governing and authorizing, there is a variety of excellent work available. Some scholarship has focused specifically on public policy making concerning the U.S. government's interventions abroad. For example, Cori Dauber's (2001) essay on photojournalism during wartime upends presumptions concerning vivid media portrayals of casualties and captured soldiers during wars. She suggests that, through skillful and timely rhetorical messages, military policy makers could actively reshape audiences' understandings of graphic media representations of killed or captured military personnel rather than assume such images will erode citizens' support for an intervention. Gordon Mitchell (2000) and Davin A. Grindstaff and Kevin M. DeLuca (2004) have also illuminated the roles of media portrayals in authorizing and legitimating wartime actions by the U.S. government. Scholars exploring governing and authorizing in visual rhetoric scholarship have also explored how sex and gender ideologies constrain the ways women in U.S. culture have been encouraged to present themselves in public life. In addition to the Parry-Giles essay in this section, students might also wish to explore scholarship on the role of media in constructing images of the ideal American woman in the Miss America pageants (Dow, 2003; Tonn, 2003).

Discussion Questions

1. Each of the essays discusses pictorial ambiguity as a resource or pitfall. How do each of these authors treat pictorial ambiguity in visual rhetoric? Can you think of other specific examples in which pictorial ambiguity was a powerful resource or posed significant liabilities for image makers?

2. The essays in this section each comment on appropriation and reuse of pictorial images by adversaries or partisans, whose understanding and vision of the pictorial symbols differs significantly from their producer or the people featured in them. In these essays, how would you characterize differences between the meanings of the images for their producers and featured subject, on one hand, and their critical audiences' interpretations and reuses of them, on the other? How do relationships of power and privilege impinge on actions of appropriation and redefinition of images, to judge from these essays?

3. Compare and contrast how the essays in this section treat the underlying and intersecting factors of sex, gender, race, class, and sexuality in visual rhetoric portraying prominent leaders. In what ways do these factors pertain to governing and authorizing as symbolic actions in U.S. culture, both historically and today?

REFERENCES

Dauber, C. (2001). The shots seen 'round the world: The impact of the images of Mogadishu on American military operations. *Rhetoric & Public Affairs, 4*(4), 653–687.

Dow, B. J. (2003). Feminism, Miss America, and media mythology. *Rhetoric & Public Affairs, 6*(1), 127–149.

Grindstaff, D. A., & DeLuca, K. M. (2004). The corpus of Daniel Pearl. *Critical Studies in Media Communication, 21*(4), 305–324.

Mitchell, G. R. (2000). *Strategic deception.* East Lansing: Michigan State University Press.

Tonn, M. B. (2003). Miss America contesters and contestants: Discourse about social "also-rans." *Rhetoric & Public Affairs, 6*(1), 150–160.

SUGGESTIONS FOR FURTHER READING

Benoit, W. L., Klyukovski, A. A., McHale, J. P., & Airne, D. (2001). A fantasy theme analysis of political cartoons on the Clinton-Lewinsky-Starr affair. *Critical Studies in Media Communication, 18*(4), 377–394.

Bostdorff, D. M. (1987). Making light of James Watt: A Burkean approach to the form and attitude of political cartoons. *Quarterly Journal of Speech, 73*(1), 43–59.

DeLuca, K. M., & Demo, A. T. (2000). Imaging nature: Watkins, Yosemite, and the birth of environmentalism. *Critical Studies in Media Communication, 17*(3), 241–260.

Dow, B. J. (2004). Fixing feminism: Women's liberation and the rhetoric of television documentary. *Quarterly Journal of Speech, 90*(1), 53–80.

Ehrenhaus, P., & Owen, A. S. (2004). Race lynching and Christian evangelicalism: Performances of faith. *Text and Performance Quarterly, 24*(3–4), 276–301.

Parry-Giles, S. J., & Parry-Giles, T. (2002). *Constructing Clinton: Hyper-reality and presidential image-making in postmodern politics.* New York: Peter Lang.

Sheckels, T. F., Robertson, T., Muir, J. K., & Gring-Pemble, L. (2007). *Readings on political communication.* State College, PA: Strata Publishing.

BENJAMIN FRANKLIN'S PICTORIAL REPRESENTATIONS OF THE BRITISH COLONIES IN AMERICA

A Study in Rhetorical Iconology

LESTER C. OLSON

Iconology, or the study of visual representation, has been defined in various ways, but those definitions share a common etymology.[1] "To begin with the explanation of the term Iconology," wrote George Richardson in 1778, "it is derived from two Greek words, which signify speaking pictures or discourse of images."[2] Rhetorical iconology emphasizes that such speaking pictures may be used in efforts to influence people to feel, believe, or act in desired ways. Both visual and verbal rhetoric entail a commitment to use a community's representational systems in endeavors to enlist the will of an audience. Both entail the concerns of an advocate and the interests of a public, sometimes at odds, sometimes in agreement. Accordingly, rhetorical iconology is the study of how advocates have used visual representations in attempts to enlist the will of an audience or diverse audiences. At the heart of rhetorical iconology are the ambiguities of appeals for agreement among people whose interests, concerns, values, feelings, and expectations may be in conflict.

This study in rhetorical iconology is focused on a fundamental shift among the images which Benjamin Franklin designed to represent the British colonies in America. "JOIN, or DIE" and "Magna Britannia, or her Colonies Reduc'd" were reproduced widely in the colonies and England throughout the American Revolution.[3] Each of these compositions presented a markedly different vision of the American colonies, the former image suggesting in 1754 that the colonies could form a united community apart from Britain (Figure 1), the latter image suggesting in 1765 that neither the colonies nor Britain could survive apart from each other (Figure 2). This essay attempts to explain the underlying reasons for the fundamental shift in Benjamin Franklin's portrayals of the British colonies in America, by exploring the hypothesis that

SOURCE: Olson, L. C. (1987). Benjamin Franklin's pictorial representations of the British colonies in America: A study in rhetorical iconology. *Quarterly Journal of Speech, 73,* 18–42. © National Communication Association.

"Magna Britannia" was both a deliberative work directed to the British Parliament and an apologetic work directed to a conservative segment of the colonial public. Franklin used the engraving both to advocate the repeal of the Stamp Act in Parliament and also to defend his own reputation in America, where some had accused him of complicity in the Stamp Act, while others had noted the radical implications of his emblem, "JOIN, or DIE," as it had been used anonymously on the masthead of a seditious publication.

Although the rhetorical tradition originates in the study of public speeches about civic matters, this analysis of "Magna Britannia" illustrates how concepts from the rhetorical tradition can illuminate pictorial persuasion, so contributing to a growing body of literature that explores the interdisciplinary value of the rhetorical tradition.[4] The argument proceeds in three stages—first an examination of the historical evidence that "Magna Britannia" was a deliberative work, then an examination of the historical evidence that it was also an apologetic work, and finally, an interpretation and criticism of the engraving in light of those two kinds of rhetorical discourse.

In the process, we will observe how the meanings of these pictorial works were shaped by the points of view of the audiences who viewed them and by the contemporary political circumstances. In the case of "JOIN, or DIE," an image that was in no sense threatening to Britain during the French and Indian war became tainted by radical implications a decade later when the image was appropriated for the masthead of *The Constitutional Courant* during the Stamp Act controversy. In the case of "Magna Britannia," an image that had several associated meanings to Parliamentarians was likely to have had alternative and supplementary meanings to Americans. In both cases, the meanings of these pictorial compositions were shaped not only by the palpable form of the message but also by the points of view of the audiences and by the political circumstances surrounding distribution. It is, therefore, necessary to interpret these images in light of the rhetorical understandings and public address of the period.

This essay complements existing scholarship on the verbal rhetoric of the revolution by investigating the visual rhetoric of the period. Several

Figure 1 "JOIN, or DIE," *Pennsylvania Gazette,* May 9, 1754, p. 2, col. 2. designer: Benjamin Franklin, publisher: Benjamin Franklin and David Hall, media: newspaper, size: 2″ × 2.″

SOURCE: Photograph courtesy of the Library of Congress.

scholars, among them Stephen Lucas, Ronald Reid, John Wilson, Barnet Baskerville, Judy Hample, J. Vernon Jensen, Kurt Ritter, James Andrews, Barbara Larson, Peter D. G. Thomas, and Edmund and Helen Morgan, have investigated the rhetorical and political use of newspapers, pamphlets, broadsides, and speeches during the American Revolution, but the rhetorical and political use of visual works during the period remains to be studied by scholars of rhetoric.[5] Scholarship on the rhetoric of the American Revolution can continue to be invigorated by investigating the pictorial persuasion of the period.

I. The Deliberative Use of "Magna Britannia"

Benjamin Franklin's engraving, "Magna Britannia, or her Colonies Reduc'd," had an enduring significance throughout the American Revolution and proved immensely popular among those critical of the British government's American policies (Figure 2).[6] Originally printed at the end of 1765 or the beginning of 1766,

"Magna Britannia" was distributed by Franklin in England and America on note cards. During the subsequent decade of dissent, various illustrators reproduced the engraving in modified forms in America, France, England and Holland. Sometime between 1766 and 1769 an enlarged broadside version with an accompanying explanation and moral was printed anonymously at Philadelphia and distributed in the American colonies (Figure 3). In December 1768, the frontispiece of a liberal English magazine, *The Political Register,* incorporated the illustration above another pictorial work, "Its Companion." Sometime before 1775 in France, an additional version of Franklin's illustration was printed, modified by the absence of brooms on the ships in the background and by the repositioning of Britannia's spear. Then on November 29, 1774, M. Darly published yet another British version of the engraving, retitled "Brittannia [*sic*] Mutilated" (Figure 4).[7] Finally, probably in 1780, the Dutch adapted yet another version of the print, this one derived from Darly's version but with French and German legends beneath. The idea of the American colonies as the limbs

Figure 2 "MAGNA Britannia: her Colonies REDUC'D," circa January 1766, designer: Benjamin Franklin, media: single sheet, size: $4\frac{1}{8}'' \times 5\frac{7}{8}''$.

SOURCE: Photograph courtesy of the Library Company of Philadelphia.

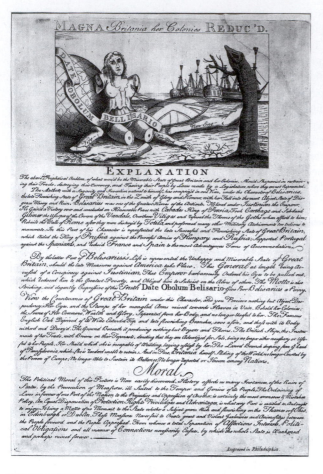

Figure 3 "MAGNA Britania her Colonies REDUC'D," circa 1766–1770, media: broadside, size: $14^7/_8$" $\times$ $9^{13}/_{16}$".

SOURCE: Photograph courtesy of the Library Company of Philadelphia.

of a self-destructive Empire had recurring relevance throughout the imperial dispute.

These illustrations succinctly dramatized a way of viewing the colonies and their relationship to Britain. The colonies are parts, or limbs, of Britannia. The separateness of the colonies, not only from England but also from each other, is emphasized by labeling Britannia's four severed limbs "Virg," "Pennsyl-," "New York" and "New Eng." These colonial parts are subordinate to Britain, since the colonies constitute the extremities while Britain is the head and torso. Yet, because together they form one body, the print underscores the interdependence of the colonies and England, and so identifies the cause of one with the cause of the other. Finally, internal divisiveness within the Empire, especially the use of force to subjugate the colonies, becomes the

equivalent of suicide for the Empire. Although this last association was most emphasized in an accompanying text from the 1766–69 broadside version, each of these ideas depends upon the others. The single pictorial metaphor resonates with a congeries of commonplace ideas and attitudes condensed and consolidated in the single image.[8]

Several letters from Benjamin Franklin to Americans prove that "Magna Britannia" was designed to convince the British Parliament that imposing the Stamp Act with military force was an inexpedient policy. Franklin sent the earliest of these letters on February 24, 1766 to David Hall, a printer and friend of Franklin's in Philadelphia, the publisher of the *Pennsylvania Gazette*. Franklin's letter described how he used the pictorial composition and the letter articulated the engraving's central contention:

I enclose you some of the Cards on which I have lately wrote all my Messages; they are to show the Mischiefs of reducing the Colonies by Force of Arms.[9]

Franklin repeated this information and more in a letter dated March 1,1766, when he wrote to his sister, Jane Mecom:

I congratulate you and my Countrymen on the Repeal of the Stamp Act. I send you a few of the Cards on which I wrote my Messages during the Time, it was debated here whether it might not be proper to reduce the Colonies to Obedience by Force of Arms: The Moral is, that the Colonies might be ruined, but that Britain would thereby be maimed.[10]

In these letters Franklin portrayed himself as having written political messages on the engraving; he professes to have used the engraving as note cards for his political correspondence. He affirmed that the policy issue was whether force should be used to impose the Stamp Act on America and that his appeal was to a "moral" based on an argument from consequence: such a policy was inexpedient because in the process the whole Empire would be maimed. By implication, the primary audience consisted of ministers to Parliament in the House of Commons, since they

BRITTANNIA MUTILATED.
or the Horrid (but true) Picture of Great Brittain, when Deprived of her Limbs. BY HER ENEMIES.
Pub.d Nov.r 29 Act Nov.r 29 1774 by Marly & Strand

Figure 4 "BRITTANNIA MUTILATED," published November 29, 1774, publisher: M. Darley, size: $11^3/_4'' \times 15^1/_2''$.

SOURCE: Photograph courtesy of the Library Company of Philadelphia.

were the representatives who debated the issue, and since Franklin was actively lobbying in Parliament as Pennsylvania's agent. Precisely when "Magna Britannia" was so used is open to some speculation, though Leonard Labaree reasons that it was most likely designed and distributed sometime in mid-January, 1766 when Franklin intensified his lobbying activities against the Stamp Act.[11]

Additional letters were sent to Deborah Franklin, his wife, as well as to Joseph Galloway, Franklin's political ally, who was a prominent member of the Pennsylvania Assembly.[12] In a letter to William Franklin, Galloway alluded to his own letter from Benjamin Franklin and forwarded a copy of the engraving:

I suspect the Print inclosed by Mr. Fn. [Franklin] to me and several others is his own. Quere. It is certainly a good one. Explains the Subject deeply. The Launce [lance] from the Thigh of New Eng[land] pointed at the breast of Brittannica [*sic*], is striking, as is indeed every other Emblem. If you have not one inclosed to you keep it, if you have please return it by the Bearer.[13]

Galloway's letter classifies the engraving as an "Emblem," so identifying it with a tradition of

aesthetic images designed to influence belief. The letter also intimates that the positioning of the lance was important in his interpretation, a comment which warrants speculation about the significance of that placement. As a group, these letters—especially those to David Hall, a newspaper publisher, and to Galloway, perhaps the most influential leader of the Pennsylvania Assembly—suggest that Franklin also directed this pictorial work to a conservative, sympathetic, and influential segment of the colonial public.

An American reprint of the composition, probably published between 1766 and 1769, was inscribed in a contemporary hand:

The above piece was invented by Benja[min] Franklin & a Number of them struck off on card paper on which it is said, he used to write all his Messages to Men in power in Great Britain; he also emplyd [*sic*] a Waiter to put one of them in each Parliament Mans hand as he entred the house the day preceding the great debate of the Stamp Act—The meaning of the spear from N. England your own Sagacity will point out.[14]

The inscription elaborates on the distribution of the emblem and the nature of the audience, by claiming that a waiter gave one to each minister in Parliament as he entered the house. Like Galloway, the anonymous commentator attached significance of some sort to the positioning of the "spear from N. England." But because the author of this inscription is anonymous and because the description was made in America at a remove from the events, the description of the distribution ought to be accepted provisionally.

To date, as Edwin Wolf observes, not a single note card with Franklin's handwriting on it has been found.[15] Although Wolf has located a half-sheet version dated in 1765–1766, it was among the papers of an American colonist, Eugene Pierre Du Simitière (Figure 2). Furthermore, to date no quotations from the memoirs, correspondence, journals, or speeches of *any* minister of Parliament have corroborated that Franklin actually used the engraving to urge the repeal of the Stamp Act. Yet it seems likely that Franklin employed the print in endeavors to influence political policy in Parliament, since nothing expressed with the engraving was more bold or more provocative than what Franklin was willing to state publicly in his *Examination* before the entire House of Commons.[16]

A search of Franklin's correspondence reveals one Briton who definitely knew about the print. That letter was from Mrs. Stevenson, Franklin's landlady in London, and it was dated November 24, 1766, several months after the repeal. But other, more politically noteworthy evidence confirms that Franklin distributed "Magna Britannia" in England toward the conclusion of the Stamp Act controversy. Thomas Hollis wrote to Jonathan Mayhew on June 19, 1766:

> He [Franklin] is certainly a Man of Knowledge, Ability; wishes well to what is right; loves his Country, N. A. [North America] even to partiality; yet, according to old observings, to me, he is a *Trimmer*. His *Card* too, which came forth in such numbers, appeared *not*, if I am well informed, till after the Death of the D. of C. [Duke of Cumberland], and till the Spring, that the leaders in the Ministry had taken party and *resolved* to repeal the Stamp Act.
>
> *All this in Confidence.*
>
> No Measure certainly was *wiser*, than that of securing an Influence over the Public Prints, which influence evidently has been of highest Utility on both sides the water & may & will & must be again.[17]

Hollis's letter proves that "Magna Britannia" was used in England to advocate political policy. Accordingly, the meanings of "Magna Britannia" should be ascertained in light of that rhetorical use and that British audience. Yet, if Hollis was entirely correct, Franklin distributed "Magna Britannia" only after the change from the Grenville ministry to the Rockingham ministry had made the repeal of the Stamp Act policy probable.[18] So Hollis's comment raises additional questions about how, if at all, Franklin was a "Trimmer" when he distributed "Magna Britannia."

II. THE APOLOGETIC USE OF "MAGNA BRITANNIA"

Although commentators on "Magna Britannia" uniformly have treated it as a deliberative work concerned with the Parliamentary debate over a policy to use military force to impose the Stamp Act, the rhetorical uses of the engraving probably were more complex than that.[19] We have evidence that an American audience for Franklin's engraving also existed, since Franklin sent several copies of it to Americans. Indeed, most of the extant evidence about the political use of "Magna Britannia" has been written in the form of letters from Franklin to Americans. What we lack is an interpretation of the engraving from the point of view of that colonial audience, for surely these colonists were not debating whether Parliament should use military force to impose the Stamp Act.

In addition to visualizing some of Franklin's most vital appeals to the British Parliament, "Magna Britannia" also constituted a significant shift among Franklin's pictorial representations of the united American colonies, since the emblem was a marked departure from Franklin's earlier image of America, "JOIN, or DIE." Initially published in the *Pennsylvania Gazette* on May 9, 1754, "JOIN, or DIE" depicted the American colonies as a segmented serpent (Figure 1). Since abbreviations for the colonies appeared beside the parts of the serpent, the image corresponded to the geographical form of the colonies: a long, narrow strip of land separated into individual political units running from North to South in the same sequence as a serpent from head to tail. By keying into the folk belief that a segmented serpent could reunite its parts and survive, the motto emphasized the most salient feature of the suasory appeal: both the colonies and the serpent must join if they would live.

Both "JOIN, or DIE" and "Magna Britannia" show each colony as a part of a larger unity. The colonies were separated even among themselves. But while the implied need to unify the serpent was restricted only to the colonies, the implied need to unify Britannia entailed the union of the colonies with the entire British Empire. While the segmented serpent obscured any relationship of the colonies to England, Britannia's severed body emphasized colonial interdependence with Britain. Most important, while the segmented serpent implied that autonomous colonial action was possible if the colonies would unite, Britannia's severed body implied that autonomous colonial action was impossible. What were Franklin's underlying reasons for this fundamental shift in his portrayals of the British colonies in America?

The appropriation of "JOIN, or DIE" for use on the masthead of a radical publication, *The Constitutional Courant*, may have provided one salient reason for Franklin's shift in the imagery representing America: he may have sought to protect his own reputation from the taint of radicalism that had become associated with "JOIN, or DIE." A second and independent development which may have motivated Franklin was his need to counter allegations from the Proprietary party in Pennsylvania that Franklin had not adequately represented the colony throughout the Stamp Act proceedings. In light of these two political developments, "Magna Britannia" was an apologia in the sense that it was used both to circumvent potential criticism of Franklin for the incipient radicalism of "JOIN, or DIE" and also to counter actual contentions about Franklin's complicity in the passage of the Stamp Act.

Franklin's *Pennsylvania Gazette* originally circulated "JOIN, or DIE" on May 9, 1754, shortly before the Albany Congress in response to the French and Indian war.[20] Before the month of May had ended, the emblem had been reproduced in the *New-York Gazette, The New-York Mercury, The Boston Gazette,* and *The Boston Weekly News-Letter.*[21] By August, the emblem had been alluded to in the *Virginia Gazette* and the *South Carolina Gazette.*[22] Because "JOIN, or DIE" was circulated in opposition to the French and Indians, the serpent device was not initially a symbol of protest or rebellion within the British Empire, but rather it dramatically symbolized the need for well orchestrated action against an outside threat. The British Empire in North America could be saved only by joint defensive action by the colonial militia, so Franklin's idea of union at the time of "JOIN, or DIE" was not radical, but was rather a practical, military necessity. The emblem simply affirmed that the colonies should act as a united political community for vital matters of common defense. Yet, by visualizing the colonies apart from the rest of the British Empire, the emblem suggested that colonial interests were sometimes distinct from British ones; this ambiguity made it possible *later* for the emblem to embody the concerns of a radical political faction within the Empire.

Recognizing the potential to use "JOIN, or DIE" to dramatize colonial opposition to the British government's Stamp Act of 1765, William Goddard appropriated the emblem for the masthead on two of three versions of the *Constitutional Courant,* published on September 21, 1765 and circulated throughout the northern colonies (Figure 5).[23] On October 7, 1765, the *Boston Evening-Post* reproduced "JOIN, or DIE" with a description of the *Courant.*[24] On October 7, the *Courant* also was described in the *Newport Mercury* of Providence, Rhode Island, but without reference to the serpent image.[25] Before the Stamp Act controversy was over, the *Courant* was characterized in England as one of the most radical publications opposing the new tax law.[26] As a consequence, "JOIN, or DIE" had come to symbolize colonial opposition to British law during the sustained intercolonial challenge to Parliamentary sovereignty.[27]

Did this radical use of "JOIN, or DIE" motivate Franklin to publish "Magna Britannia" as a means to demonstrate his own loyalty to government? During the Stamp Act controversy, Franklin knew that the *Constitutional Courant* had been published with "JOIN, or DIE" on the masthead before he published "Magna Britannia," if Leonard Labaree's suggestion of a mid-January, 1766 publication date is correct, since long before then two colonial officials had written to Franklin about the *Constitutional Courant.* Enclosing a copy of the *Courant* with

Figure 5   "JOIN or DIE," *Constitutional Courant,* September 21, 1765, masthead, media: newspaper.

SOURCE: Photograph courtesy of the Massachusetts Historical Society. Reprinted by permission.

"JOIN, or DIE" on the masthead, the Acting Governor of New York, Cadwallader Colden, wrote to Franklin on October 1, 1765:

Sir,

My regard to you makes me give you the trouble of the inclosd Printed Paper [the *Constitutional Courant],* one or more bundles of which, I am well informd, were deliver'd to the Post Rider at Woodbridge [New Jersey] by James Parker, were distributed by the Post Riders in several parts of this Colony [New York], and I beleive [*sic*] likewise in the Neighbouring Colonies: the doing of which was kept Secret from the Post Master in this Place. It is believed that this Paper was Printed by Parker after the Printers in this Place had refused to do it, perhaps you may be able to Judge from the Types. As he [James Parker] is Secretary [*sic*] to the General Post Office in America, I am under a necessity of takeing [*sic*] notice of it to the Secrettary [*sic*] of State by the return of the Packet which is daily expected, and I am unwilling to do this without giving you previous notice by a Merchant Ship which Sails Tomorrow.[28]

Although Colden's letter erroneously attributed the *Courant* to James Parker, rather than to William Goddard, this letter proves that Franklin almost certainly knew about the radical use of "JOIN, or DIE," since Colden enclosed a copy of it with his letter.[29] The letter depicted the publication of the *Courant* as a secretive and seditious act. The letter also suggested to Franklin some potential for political embarrassment, possibly because Franklin was deputy Post Master under the Crown and his personnel had been implicated in the printing and distributing of the

Courant, possibly because Franklin himself had designed the emblem which appeared prominently on the masthead of the seditious publication. Although Colden expressed his personal regard for Franklin, he also intimated that Franklin could vindicate himself by identifying the printer's types.

Although Colden's letter leaves open the question of whether the Acting Governor of New York definitely connected "JOIN, or DIE" with Benjamin Franklin's design a decade earlier, a letter from the Lieutenant Governor of Massachusetts-Bay, Thomas Hutchinson, does not. Hutchinson wrote to Franklin on November 18, 1765:

The riots at N York have given fresh spirits to the rioters here. An uniformity of measures it is said will be effectual and join or die is the motto. When you and I were at Albany ten years ago we did not Propose an union for such Purposes as these.[30]

Not one, but two high ranking colonial officials had informed Franklin that "JOIN, or DIE" had been appropriated for radical purposes during the Stamp Act protests and riots. Further, Hutchinson's letter connected the motto to Franklin's design prior to the Albany Congress. Hutchinson affirmed his own confidence in Franklin's benign intent when he distributed "JOIN, or DIE" in 1754. Even so, recognizing that the radical appropriation of "JOIN, or DIE" had transformed its meanings by emphasizing opposition to the British Parliament, Franklin may have designed "Magna Britannia" to deny the seditious use of his earlier pictorial representation, "JOIN, or DIE," so demonstrating his own continuing loyalty to the government. More important, Franklin's "Magna Britannia" was consistent with most of the American rhetoric during the Stamp Act controversy in that both the rhetoric and the design denied any colonial attempt to gain independence from the Crown. So "Magna Britannia" would not have been simply a personal apologia; the design also would have represented the ethos of responsible opposition to the Stamp Act.

At least two British publications also described "JOIN, or DIE" as radical in its implications, but whether Franklin was aware of these specific developments is open to speculation. The *Annual Register* for 1765 described the emblem and the *Courant,* observing that subsequent to the passage of the Stamp Act:

> Essays soon followed, not only against the expediency, but even the equity of it, in several newspapers, one of which bore the significant title of "The Constitutional Courant, containing matters interesting to liberty, and no wise repugnant to loyalty, printed by Andrew Marvel at the sign of the Bribe refused, on Constitution-Hill, North-America;" and wore the still more significative headpiece; a snake cut in pieces, with the initial letters of the names of the several colonies from New-England to South-Carolina, inclusively, affixed to each piece, and above them the words JOIN or DIE. To these were added caricatures, pasquinades, puns, bonmots, and such vulgar sayings fitted to the occasion, as by being short could be more easily circulated and retained, at the same time that, by being extremely expressive, they carried with them the weight of a great many arguments.[31]

"Rationalis" commented on the publication of the *Courant* in the *Public Ledger* of London on November 16, 1765, and excerpts were reprinted in the *Pennsylvania Journal* on February 20, 1766:

> A printed paper is just now fallen into my Hands, from North-America; the title of which is The CONSTITUTIONAL COURANT: *containing matters interesting to Liberty and no wise repugnant to Loyalty.* It is dated Saturday, September 21, 1765, and marked No. 1, printed by Andrew Marvel, at the sign of the Bribe-Refused on Constitution Hill, North-America: and is a half sheet, containing an introduction and two political

pieces, with an ill executed stamped emblematical device in the middle of the front, representing a writhing serpent divided into eight parts, marked with the following initials, NE. NY. NJ. P. M. V. NC. SC. and over all these words, JOIN OR DIE.[32]

The date of the *Pennsylvania Journal* article on February 20, 1766 proves that news of the report in the *Ledger* already had recrossed the Atlantic before Franklin's earliest extant reference to "Magna Britannia" on February 24, 1766. It is likely that Franklin was aware of the article in the *Ledger,* since he himself occasionally had articles printed in the *Ledger* under pseudonyms during this period.[33]

The reprinted article from the *Ledger* in the *Journal* also suggested how a contemporary British public had interpreted the *Courant:*

> From the extraordinary publication which I have mentioned [the *Courant*], . . . and indeed from all intelligence we receive from that quarter of the world, we must have reason to believe, that union is forming, which, according to the wisest opinions, it must ever be for our greatest interest and security to give no cause for being affected, and therefore the policy must have been erroneous which has contributed thereto.[34]

The article criticized the Stamp Act for inadvertently promoting an intercolonial union which eventually could threaten the British Empire's political stability. The colonial union advocated in "JOIN, or DIE" was interpreted as endangering the British government.

There is, then, reason to believe that "Magna Britannia" was in part a response to the radical appropriation of "JOIN, or DIE." In addition to the personal letters which Colden and Hutchinson sent to Franklin, no fewer than four publications could have informed Franklin that his emblem, "JOIN, or DIE," had been used on the masthead of the *Constitutional Courant,* including the *Courant* itself, the *Boston Evening-Post,* the *Public Ledger,* and the *Annual Register.* Either of the American publications would have reached Franklin in London by the probable publication date of "Magna Britannia" in mid-January or early February of 1766, since these documents were available at least three full months before the likely publication date of

"Magna Britannia." Either of the British publications might have informed Franklin of the radical use of "JOIN, or DIE," since the article in the *Ledger* was available two months before Franklin's earliest extant reference to "Magna Britannia" and since the *Annual Register* may have been available by then. These publications may have suggested to Franklin a need both to protect his own reputation from the taint of radicalism and also to reshape British and colonial perceptions of the appropriate way to represent colonial opinion.

"JOIN, or DIE" and "Magna Britannia" may be connected not only by virtue of their common subject matter, the nature of the American colonial community. They also share certain formal characteristics: both works derive from the aesthetic tradition of emblems and devices. Although many varied and sometimes subtle distinctions were drawn between emblems and devices prior to the eighteenth century, during the period of the American Revolution, some individuals used the terms "emblem" and "device" interchangeably or in the combination "emblematical device."[35] However one chooses to label "JOIN, or DIE" and "Magna Britannia," both works share three features which warrant connecting them as the same general form of appeal: both present a pictorial representation in combination with a motto to develop a moral or lesson. As devices or emblems, then, both works were predominantly deliberative in that they proposed a line of conduct. Yet the differences between the two emblems suggest that "Magna Britannia" was also an apologia for "JOIN, or DIE." In fact, "Magna Britannia" does not resist interpretation as an adept pictorial response to the potential problems created by the radical use of "JOIN, or DIE," since "Magna Britannia" emphatically visualizes the interdependence of the American colonies and the rest of the British Empire.

While the radical appropriation of "JOIN, or DIE" posed a threat to Franklin's political reputation in the northern colonies and in England, members of the Proprietary party assaulted Franklin's political reputation within Pennsylvania. During the winter of 1764, the Proprietary party had initiated a campaign that was successful in preventing Franklin from retaining his seat in the Pennsylvania Assembly, though the Proprietary party was unsuccessful in obtaining enough seats to prevent the Assembly party from dominating the legislature. Franklin's political allies then nominated him to serve as Pennsylvania's agent in London. Subsequently, during the fall of 1764, the Proprietary party initiated a campaign to prevent Franklin from becoming the colonial agent in London. Contending that Franklin could not adequately represent the colony because of a conflict of interests, they observed on October 26, 1764 that Franklin and his son were office holders under the Crown and therefore, "the Remonstrants cannot expect that a Gentleman of his moderate Fortune will sacrifice his Interest for the Sake of the Province, which he must necessarily do, if he but seems to oppose the Measures of the Ministry."[36] On November 1, 1764, twelve members of the Proprietary party, among them John Dickinson, published and signed a *Protest Against the Appointment of Benjamin Franklin as Agent*. They offered seven reasons for their opposition to Franklin's appointment.[37] To these charges, Franklin responded with *Remarks on a Late Protest* on November 7, 1764, less than a week later.[38]

For our purposes, what is important about the exchange is the evidence it provides that Franklin's reputation was under assault even as he assumed the responsibilities as agent, and, as important, that he was aware of these developments, which persisted after his departure for London in November. Franklin never disputed the contention that he faced a conflict of interests in his roles as a colonial agent and deputy Post Master under the Crown; instead, he emphasized that the Crown appointment was proof that he was regarded favorably by the King and his ministry. As Verner Crane has observed, the Crown appointment in the Post Office "did not make Franklin anti-American," as the proprietors later insinuated, but it did "confirm him in his instinctive prudence" and impelled him "to draw the veil of anonymity over much of his writings" during the Stamp Act controversy. While Franklin's use of several pseudonyms also had the advantage in England of making the pro-American arguments seem to originate from several sources and "to come from a less interested source than a colonial agent," Franklin's strategy of anonymity had the serious disadvantage in America of leaving him vulnerable to criticisms both for inactivity and for complicity with the government, criticisms that developed during the continuing controversy over his appointment as agent.[39]

On December 7, 1764, a month after Franklin's response to the *Protest,* William Smith anonymously published *An Answer to Mr. Franklin's Remarks,* thereby extending the attack upon Franklin's political reputation in Pennsylvania. On December 20, 1764 and again on January 10, 1765, Franklin's political ally, John Hughes, wrote in response to the "malicious and scandalous" *Answer.* Hughes deplored the anonymous nature of the pamphlet and offered to pay 10 pounds toward building a public hospital for every charge proven true, if the author of *An Answer* would agree to pay only 5 pounds for every charge proven false.[40] Later, when it was alleged in Pennsylvania that Franklin had helped plan and promote the Stamp Act, Franklin's son, William Franklin, responded vehemently in the *Pennsylvania Journal* of October 3, 1765, that "it is grossly false, and consequently a shameful imposition on the people." William Franklin added, "Not a gentleman of the proprietary party, even among those, who scruple not to aver the truth of it in conversation, can, I am convinced, be found so hardned [sic] as to avow in print, with his name subscribed, that he believes it to be true, or to undertake to produce any proofs in its support."[41] That Franklin was kept informed of such developments is certain. In a letter dated November 11, 1765, for instance, Hugh Roberts urged Franklin to "keep up thy Spirrits [sic] for thou hast yet a numerous set of Advocates who dare to speake their Sentiments with freedom and vindicate thy conduct."[42]

Even after the repeal of the Stamp Act, allegations persisted that Franklin had promoted the Stamp Act to gain personal favor in the eyes of the ministry and to secure places for his political allies. The *Pennsylvania Journal, Supplement* on September 18 and again on September 25, 1766 published lengthy essays purporting to prove that Franklin had been responsible for promoting the Stamp law. Since the Stamp Act had been repealed much earlier that year, the writer's purpose was doubtless to influence voters in the upcoming fall election by discrediting members of the Assembly party. Although the author wrote in the persona of an anonymous observer of political life in England, the writer's own concern about Pennsylvania's form of government was evident in his conclusion:

> As Dr. F[rankli]n has evidently nothing else in view than to obtain a Change of the Government of Pennsylvania, and get himself placed at the head of it; . . . As he is so regardless of your real liberties, as to engage warmly with the weight of all his friends, in protecting and encouraging the most ignominious law, the Stamp-Act; . . . And as he is for every other reason, under such strong suspicions of betraying his constituents, and is certainly known to have deserted them, and not to have served them with any zeal; Whether he can safely be continued as the Agent, and Patron of the Liberties of your province, is a question that I apprehend the people of your side [of] the water will easily solve.[43]

Because the continuing controversy over Franklin's political conduct during the Stamp Act proceedings stood to influence the fall elections, David Hall, though no longer a partner of Franklin in the publication of the *Pennsylvania Gazette,* printed and distributed copies of Franklin's *Examination* in Pennsylvania in an effort to vindicate him. In the *Pennsylvania Gazette* of September 18, 1766, Franklin's defenders announced the publication of the *Examination,* using it as incontrovertible proof that Franklin had acted decisively on behalf of the colonies. As Verner Crane has claimed,

> Dr. John Fothergil and other friends of the Pennsylvania agent rallied to his defense; and in 1767 the new *Pennsylvania Chronicle* devoted much space . . . to his rehabilitation. A long essay by "A Lover of Justice" was inserted to prove that Franklin's activities in aid of repeal, as a lobbyist and writer, had been persistent and effective. In succeeding numbers William Goddard reprinted nine essays contributed by Franklin to London newspapers in 1765 and 1766.[44]

According to Ward Miner, the campaign to restore Franklin's damaged reputation "continued at intervals until June 9, 1769, by which time twenty-four different items had been published."[45] "Magna Britannia," sent by Franklin to several Americans and subsequently distributed in Philadelphia on a broadside, was probably used as additional evidence of his efforts during the Stamp Act controversy.

In summary, by the winter of 1765–66, Franklin recognized that his public image was in question within Pennsylvania, where some believed that he failed to defend the colonies' best economic interests and others thought him an accomplice to the Stamp Act. Elsewhere, in the northern colonies and in England, the previously quiescent implications of his emblem, "JOIN, or DIE," were being described and commented upon as seditious, so making manifest the ideas of faction and sedition. By mid-November of 1765, both of these political developments in America had been related in personal letters to Franklin. In light of these developments, it seems reasonable to infer that "Magna Britannia" was, in part, an apologia directed to a conservative segment of the colonial public.

III. An Interpretation and Criticism

Recognizing that Benjamin Franklin probably designed "Magna Britannia" to fulfill both deliberative and apologetic functions, the design may be interpreted and criticized as an attempt to influence public opinion in Britain and in America by investigating how features in the composition evoked a range of likely meanings and appealed to specific Parliamentary and colonial interests. Attention to the rhetorical functions of the engraving enables one to discern how different audiences may have interpreted identical features of the composition in dissimilar ways. For example, Parliamentarians were likely to see the subordination of the colonial limbs as a tacit recognition of Parliament's sovereignty, so satisfying one of their expectations during the policy debates. In contrast, moderate colonial protestors, who knew about the radical appropriation of "JOIN, or DIE," could see the same subordination of Britannia's limbs as a reminder that all parts of the empire were interdependent and as a denial that the colonies could survive as an autonomous community, so satisfying the colonial expectation that Franklin demonstrate his own moderate tactics to obtain repeal while eliminating the potential taint of radicalism.

When Franklin represented the whole British Empire as one body politic, he almost certainly realized that he was relying upon a metaphor to influence his British and colonial audiences, because Franklin had specified some differences between the human body and a political government in his earlier writings.[46] Franklin therefore used the pictorial metaphor of a human body politic for a strategic reason: the metaphor rendered the interdependence of the parts vital to an extent that a mechanistic metaphor could not have conveyed. Since force would irrevocably harm the well being of the whole body politic, the pictorial metaphor developed Franklin's appeal for moderate conduct both in Britain and in America.

Franklin chose the specific image of Britannia because she represented a shared British heritage; by convention, Britannia represented varying geographical scopes within the Empire, usually denoting England, Great Britain, or, most rarely, the entire Empire. Britannia's image may have obscured the diverse descent of some colonial populations: Franklin estimated that Pennsylvania, for example, was roughly one-third German.[47] Even so, Franklin's use of Britannia emphasized a heritage shared by many Americans and Englishmen in an attempt to reduce the psychological distance between them. Probably for similar reasons, Franklin observed during his *Examination* before the House of Commons that the British colonies in America "consider themselves as a part of the British Empire, and as having one common interest with it; they may be looked on here as foreigners, but they do not consider themselves as such."[48]

Britannia's image also located the imperial dispute precisely in Parliament, either because another of Britannia's conventional referents was the Parliament, or because her head presumably corresponded to the governing part of the body politic.[49] As such, Britannia's image granted Parliament's demand that the colonies recognize its sovereignty. As the head of the body politic, Britannia was placed in a role of both political authority and moral culpability. In that sense, Britannia's image was well adapted to Parliamentarians, who almost unanimously were perturbed by the colonies' protests and riots as an affront to their power. Britannia's image was designed to remind these parliamentarians that they, not the colonies, were morally responsible should the government decide to implement the

Stamp Act with military force, even as her butchered body depicted the dire consequences of that policy.

Britannia's image implicitly dissociated the dispute from the King, so maintaining for the colonists an important distinction between royal and Parliamentary authority. While the colonists had by convention acceded to the authority of Parliament, Franklin and others privately noted that the colonial charters specifically acknowledged the King's sovereignty. To Franklin, the colonies' past compliance with Parliament proved that those laws were prudent and acceptable to Americans, not necessarily that Parliament had a right to pass such laws.[50] Therefore, for a limited group of confidants, as well as for some colonial pamphleteers during the controversy, the dissociation of the dispute from the King may have reduced somewhat the legitimacy of Parliament's American policies.

Finally, Britannia's image obfuscated any colonial responsibility for various legislative acts and for social unrest. Arms and legs could not have been held morally accountable, since the mind dictated the activities of the extremities. In addition, such limb imagery obscured aspects of intercolonial unity, since different limbs served different bodily functions and, more important, since intercolonial unity was possible only through Britannia's torso. Franklin was adapting to the ministers' apprehensions of a united colonial rebellion by noting aspects of intercolonial disunity, much as he had in 1760.[51] At the same time, Franklin also attempted to assuage conservative colonists' concerns about the radical implications of "JOIN, or DIE," since the arms and legs of the Empire could neither form an autonomous community nor survive severed from Great Britain.

Franklin depicted his home colony of Pennsylvania as an arm and hand near an olive branch, while New England in contrast was represented as a leg and foot with a lance beside it directed at Britannia's heart. Both Joseph Galloway and the anonymous contemporary writer attached significance to this positioning of the lance. Both chose to intimate rather than specify its meanings. Both described it as "from New England," rather than near or beside that limb. New England had been the site of two violent Stamp Act riots in which persons had been assaulted and homes destroyed. Pennsylvanians,

in contrast, had protested in comparatively peaceful ways; the vigilance of a group of men known as the white oaks enabled the colony's government to prevent direct acts of violence. This difference between the olive branch and the spear may have ingratiated Pennsylvania to Parliament by reminding its members of that colony's comparatively peaceful protests, while amplifying another difference within the colonial community.

If so, then, "Magna Britannia" seems better adapted to Parliamentarians, who would find some reassurance in evidence of colonial disunity, than to American colonists, who probably would find evidence of divisiveness counterproductive to continued concerted action against the act. Alternatively, the olive branch falling from Pennsylvania's hand may have implied that the normally peaceful Quakers were prepared to separate themselves from the body politic. Seen from this point of view, both the olive branch and the spear emphasized intense colonial dissatisfaction with the tax law, though each colony's means of expressing those sentiments still differed.

"Magna Britannia" amplified the vital interdependence of the colonies and the Empire by emphasizing the harmful consequences of employing military force. By adopting such a policy, Britain would destroy her own means of obtaining nourishment, her resources for military defense, her international stature, perhaps even her life. Franklin amplified each consequence by incorporating background and foreground imagery. It is noteworthy that a similar emphasis on harmful consequence recurs in Franklin's private correspondence as well as his *Examination* before the House of Commons.

Franklin visualized the potential economic consequences of enforcing the Stamp Act, by placing ships with brooms attached to their masts in the background. As a text accompanying the 1766–69 broadside version of the print explained, "The British Ships, the Instruments of her trade, with Brooms on their Topmasts, denoting that they are advertised for Sale, being no longer either necessary or Useful for her people." This background imagery drew upon the economic consequences of the colonies nonimportation agreement to prove that policies harmful to America were disastrous for Britain's own economy.[52]

The placement of Britannia's shield and spear on the ground behind her developed a second harmful consequence: a policy of force to impose the Stamp Act would render the whole Empire less able to defend itself should a French or Spanish adversary seize the opportunity to attack her. Although the London version of the print did not textually amplify this appeal, the version printed at Philadelphia did:

> Her Shield which she is incapable of Weilding, laying useless by her. The Lawrel Branch droping from ye hand of Pennsylvania, which she is rendered unable to retain. And in fine, Britannia herself sliding of the World, no longer Courted by the Powers of Europe; no longer Able to Sustain its Balance; No longer respected or known among Nations.

This language amplified yet a third harmful consequence: "Magna Britannia" visualized the lost international stature of the whole Empire. This consequence was developed both by Britannia's placement in the composition as well as by a comparison to Belisarius. Britannia's torso was propped up beside a globe, a placement that depicted her inability to dominate world politics should she decide to dismember herself. Draped across the globe and Britannia's lap was a banner reading "Date Obolum Belisario"—Give Belisarius a Penny. Although this classical allusion was not explained explicitly in the original London version of the print, presumably because well-educated Parliamentarians could readily grasp the comparison, the Philadelphia version of the print in 1766–69 commented at length upon the comparison of Britannia with Belisarius:

> Belisarius was one of the greatest Heroes of the Antients. He lived under Justinian the Emperor. He Gain'd a Victory over and concluded an Honourable Peace with Cabades King of Persia, Took Carthage and Subdued Gilimes the Usurper of the Crown of the Vandals, Overthrew Vitiges and refused the Thrown of Goths when offer'd to him; Rebuilt the Walls of Rome after they were destroy'd by Tolita, and performed many other Athievements too tedious to enumerate. In this part of his Character is represented the late and Successful and Flourishing State of Great Britain,

which Aided the King of Prussia against the powerful Armies of Hungary and Russia; Supported Portugal against the Spaniards, and reduc'd France and Spain to the most Advantageous Terms of Accommodation.

> By the latter Part of Belisarius's Life is represented the Unhappy and Miserable State of Great Britain, should the late Measures against America take Place. This General at length being Accused of a Conspiracy against Justinian, That Emperor barbarously Ordered his Eyes to be pulled out, which reduced him to the Greatest Poverty, and Obliged him to subsist on the Alms of others. The Motto is also Stricking, and elegantly Expressive of this Truth *Date Obolum Belisario*—Give Poor Belisarius a Penny.

> View the Countenance of Great Britain under this Character, and you Perceive nothing but Abject Despondency: Her Eyes, and the Stumps of her mangled Arms raised toward Heaven in Vain. Behold her Colonies, the source of Her Commerce Wealth and Glory, Separated from her Body, and no longer useful to her.

The comparison to Belisarius synthesized several appeals: it underscored the colonies' assistance in past international conflicts; it suggested the military harm Britain would do to herself by weakening the colonies; it visualized the loss of international stature resulting from conflict within the Empire.

Franklin's final appeal from consequence stressed that the dispute within the Empire could destroy the life of the body politic. This was his most emphatic appeal, and it was amplified in the foreground by the addition of a mutilated oak, the healthy English oak being a conventional symbol of England. A text on the Philadelphia version of the print noted:

> The Famous English Oak Deprived of its Wide Extended Top and late flourishing Branches, save a few, and those with its Body withered and Decay'd. The Ground Beneath it producing nothing but Bryars and Thorns.

This image, like that of Britannia's mangled body, was one of portending decay and death. All of these appeals were designed to dissuade Parliament from a policy of military force and to demonstrate for Americans how Franklin sought to protect colonial interests in the moderate manner of a loyal opposition.

CONCLUSION

Emphasizing the design of "Magna Britannia" in light of its rhetorical functions, rather than the efficacy of the engraving with respect to actual change in public opinion, there were several senses in which Franklin skillfully designed the London version of "Magna Britannia" to influence Parliamentarians. The image conciliated, because it did not challenge but rather recognized Parliament's authority as Britannia's head. The emblem sought to discredit the policy of military force, which the Grenville faction had advocated in Parliament, since the emblem depicted that policy's dire consequences: lost trade, lost defense, lost international stature, lost life of the body politic. The emblem sought to dissuade the country faction from military force by diminishing their financial motivations: although the new tax in America might provide a means for those ministers to reduce the land taxes in Britain, this financial benefit for the landed gentry would be less than the costly consequences of military enforcement for the empire. In the background, ships for sale in "Magna Britannia" reminded the mercantile faction in Parliament that their own economic prosperity depended on the act's repeal.

The arrangement of the pictorial composition reflects a prudent weighing of these appeals. Franklin did not need to make lost economic benefits the central appeal of "Magna Britannia," because the mercantile interests already were convinced of the merits of repeal. As the *Annual Register* of 1766 asserted, during the debate which resumed in mid-January of 1766 over the Stamp Act:

> Petitions were received from the merchants of London, Bristol, Lancaster, Liverpoole, Hull, Glasgow, & c. and indeed from most of the trading and manufacturing towns and boroughs in the kingdom. In these petitions they set forth the great decay of their trade, owing to the new laws and regulations made for America.[53]

So as a reminder, Franklin made a peripheral appeal in "Magna Britannia" to commercial matters, but emphasized matters of authority and imperial unity through the central placement of Britannia's dismembered body.

Yet these appeals to Parliamentarians were also counterproductive, given some of Franklin's other concerns. One of these was what Franklin saw as Parliament's gradual usurpation of the Crown's authority over the colonies. As Verner Crane has argued at some length, Franklin believed that the colonies legally were subject only to the dictates of the King, though by convention they had complied with past Parliamentary policies. "The Sovereignty of the Crown I understand," Franklin wrote in the margin of the Lords' first *Protest Against the Bill to Repeal the American Stamp Act* in 1766. "The sovereignty of the British Legislature out of Britain, I do not understand."[54] Since Franklin himself was apprehensive of Parliament's encroachment on the King's rightful authority, his own choice of Britannia may have been counterproductive to the extent that it reinforced Parliament's sense of rightful authority over America.

Intimately related to what Franklin perceived as the Parliament's encroachment on the King's power over America was Franklin's perception that British subjects in general had come to believe that they, like the King, properly had authority over the colonial dominions. As Franklin wrote to Lord Kames in 1767, "Every Man in England seems to consider himself as a Piece of a Sovereign over America; seems to jostle himself into the [royal] throne with the King, and talks of OUR *Subjects in the Colonies*."[55] Although Franklin recognized that this pervasive attitude of smug superiority posed serious problems for the maintenance of imperial unity, his depiction of Britannia seemed to reinforce such sentiments of rightful domination, for by implication the extremities were less vital and therefore less significant than the head and torso.

A final counterproductive consequence of Franklin's appeal with "Magna Britannia" was that it may have undermined his own efforts to develop what he called a "consolidating Union." Franklin also wrote to Lord Kames on April 11, 1767, "I am fully persuaded with you, that a consolidating Union, by a fair and equal Representation of all Parts of this Empire in Parliament, is the only firm Basis on which its political Grandeur and Stability can be founded."[56] Earlier, during the Stamp Act controversy, Franklin had written in an unpublished pamphlet:

> Representation [is] necessary to consolidate the Empire—to inform government of the State of remote Parts—& them of the Motives & Measures of Government. People in Colonies will never be convinced that they are virtually represented &c.[57]

Yet, while Franklin saw representation as vital to consolidate the Empire, "Magna Britannia" seemed to grant Parliament the authority to legislate without the actual representation of America.

Similarly, while "Magna Britannia" seemed well designed as an apologia to a conservative and moderate segment of the American public, the pictorial work was ill-suited in certain regards to such an audience as well. "Magna Britannia" succeeded as proof that Franklin acted to protect colonial interests to the extent that it demonstrated his own moderate way of obtaining repeal. The work was moderate in its emphasis on colonial subordination and interdependence in the Empire, even as it placed responsibility for just policy upon the Parliament. In these ways, the print also was well designed to counter the radical implications of "JOIN, or DIE" as used in the *Constitutional Courant,* since "Magna Britannia" denied that the colonies could form an autonomous community or that they could survive apart from the Empire. In addition, "Magna Britannia" pointed to the efficacy of the united colonies' non-importation agreement, by placing ships for sale in the background.

Yet, "Magna Britannia" possibly failed adequately to satisfy certain demands of a colonial audience. The emblem did not, for example, maintain a basis to distinguish between internal and external taxes, since all taxes within a single body politic must be internal. Because that distinction provided one of the colonists' chief bases for protesting the Stamp Act, a basis which Franklin himself had relied upon repeatedly during his *Examination,* this implication of the emblem could not have been very satisfying to some colonial protestors.[58] More important, even though "Magna Britannia" indicated to a colonial audience that their unity in the non-importation agreement contributed to the repeal of the Stamp Act, "Magna Britannia" may have focused upon

divisiveness among the colonies, by contrasting Pennsylvania's olive branch with New England's lance. The image suggested disunity in the manner that various colonies objected to the act. In that sense, the print was counterproductive to the extent that it exacerbated a sense of divisiveness among the colonies.

Obviously, Franklin could not in this pictorial work satisfy all the diverse demands that Englishmen and Americans might bring to bear upon it. Certain of these seeming failings can be explained by Franklin's pragmatic sensibility in political life. While he saw Parliament encroaching on the King's authority, while he deplored the pervasive attitude among Englishmen that they had a degree of authority over America, and while he hoped to see the development of a consolidating union, he was also pragmatist enough to recognize that these would not be changed by his lone appeal, no matter what its form, no matter how persistent.[59] Even though Franklin wanted to see the various dominions represented in a consolidated union, he commented several times in his correspondence that such a development was unlikely, and in a letter to Lord Kames, after articulating his doubts about Parliament's sovereignty over America, Franklin added, "On the other hand, it seems necessary for the common Good of the Empire, that a Power be lodg'd somewhere, to regulate its general Commerce; this . . . can be plac'd no where so properly as in the Parliament of Great Britain."[60] Political pragmatism, then, accounts in large part for Franklin's strategic choices in "Magna Britannia."

Franklin's caution and political moderation also go far to explain the seeming shortcomings of "Magna Britannia" for an American audience. Recognizing on the one extreme that his political career was threatened within Pennsylvania by allegations that he did not protect colonial interests and on the other extreme that the radical appropriation of "JOIN, or DIE" developed implications which could taint his own career with hints of inappropriate conduct for a Crown officer, Franklin with "Magna Britannia" demonstrated his loyalty to American interests while circumventing criticism for the incipient radicalism of "JOIN, or DIE."

Roughly a decade later, in 1774–75, when Franklin was being denounced publicly in England because he had sent copies of Thomas

Hutchinson's private correspondence with British government officials to Americans, Franklin sought to justify his conduct by reviewing the political principles that had guided his handling of imperial issues throughout the preceding decade of dissent. In that narrative apologia, written but left unpublished, Franklin's explanation and assessment of his public works during the Stamp Act controversy aptly explains and evaluates his performance with "Magna Britannia," a detail in a campaign with much larger dimensions:

> It has long appeared to me that the only true British Politicks were those which aim'd at the Good of *the Whole British Empire,* not those which sought the Advantage of *one part* in the Disadvantage of the others. Therefore All Measures of procuring Gain to the Mother Country arising from Loss to her Colonies, and all of Gain to the Colonies arising from or occasioning Loss to Britain, especially where the Gain was small and the Loss great; every Abridgment of the Power of the Mother Country where that Power was not prejudicial to the Liberties of the Colonists, and every Diminution of the Priviledges of the Colonists, where they were not prejudicial to the Welfare of the Mother Country, I in my own Mind condemned as improper, partial, unjust, and mischievous, tending to create Dissensions, and weaken that Union, on which the Strength, Solidity, and Duration of the Empire greatly depended. And I opposed, as far as my little Powers went, all Proceedings either here or in America, that in my Opinion had such a Tendency. Hence it has often happened to me, that while I have been thought here too much of an American, I have in America been deem'd too much of an Englishman.[61]

NOTES

1. The word "icon" is taken to mean a visual representation so as to designate a type of image that is palpable in manifest form and denotative in function. The word "image" will be used more generally to include graphic, optical, perceptual, mental, and literary types of visual perception. An "image" need not be representational. For a commentary on types of images, see W. J. T. Mitchell, "What is an Image?" *Iconology: Image, Text, Ideology* (Chicago: University of Chicago Press, 1986).

"Iconology" is taken to mean the study of visual representations in general, rather than the specific techniques developed by either Erwin Panofsky or C. S. Peirce in particular, because this definition facilitates rhetorical analysis at the most fundamental level of symbol or representation, as suggested by Kenneth Burke in *A Rhetoric of Motives* (New York: Prentice-Hall, Inc, 1950; Berkeley: University of California Press, 1969). To American scholars, the word iconology may evoke thoughts of C. S. Peirce's writings, while to British and Continental scholars it is likely to suggest the writings of Erwin Panofsky. Although specific techniques in Panofsky's approach to iconology have been found useful, such as his emphasis on motif as a unit of critical analysis that connects distinct visual works, neither approach is endorsed fully by the choice of the word "iconology," which antedates both scholars' writings by centuries. For Peirce's discussion of his approach, see "The Icon, Index, and Symbol," in *Collected Papers,* 8 vols., ed. Charles Hartshorne and Paul Weiss (Cambridge: Harvard University Press, 1931–58) 2:156–173. For Panofsky's discussion of his approach to iconology, see his *Studies in Iconology: Humanistic Themes in the Art of the Renaissance* (New York: Oxford University Press, 1939), 3–32 and also "Iconography and Iconology: An Introduction to the Study of Renaissance Art," *Meaning in the Visual Arts* (Garden City, New York: Doubleday Anchor Books, 1955), 26–55. For an explication of Panofsky's approach, see David Mannings, "Panofsky and the Interpretation of Pictures," *British Journal of Aesthetics* 13 (1973): 146–162. For an attempt to apply Panofsky's iconographic techniques in a rhetorical analysis of a film, Martin J. Medhurst, "*Hiroshima, Mon Amour:* From Iconography to Rhetoric," *Quarterly Journal of Speech* 68 (1982): 345–370. Medhurst's conception of motif seems to differ from Panofsky's conception of motif, since in practice Medhurst uses motif to denote an image that recurs within a single film while Panofsky uses motif to denote an image that recurs in a series of distinct visual works. To Panofsky, motif provides a technical means of connecting a series of art works that may be otherwise distinct. More important, Medhurst explicitly seeks to modify Panofsky's techniques, when Medhurst asserts repeatedly that the appropriate critical move is "not from iconography to iconology, but from iconography to rhetoric" (Medhurst, 348). Even though all three of Panofsky's levels of analysis explore aspects of visual symbols, Medhurst's comments assume that somehow Panofsky's first and second levels of analysis—preiconographical description and iconographical analysis—can be undertaken without a focus on rhetoric, for Medhurst asserts repeatedly that rhetorical analysis should occur at the third level of analysis, which he alludes to as the rhetoric of visual forms (Medhurst, 348). However, Kenneth Burke has argued at length in *A Rhetoric of Motives* that symbols are by nature rhetorical to the extent that they promote identifications and divisions. If so, it would follow that rhetorical qualities are present at all three levels of analysis, since all three explore aspects of the visual symbol.

For criticism of Panofsky's approach, see Michael Podro, "Panofsky," *The Critical Historians of Art* (New Haven: Yale University Press, 1982), 178–208 and Ernst Gombrich, "Introduction: Aims and Limits of Iconology," *Symbolic Images* (Edinburgh: R. & R. Clark, 1978), 1–25. I am grateful to Mr. Michael Podro for discussing the topics of iconology and metaphor with me at the University of London on 23 February 1984. I am also grateful to Mr. Ernst Gombrich for an interview about his writings and the topic of metaphor on 7 February 1984 at the Warburg Institute of London.

For commentary on the interpenetration of image and text, see Roland Barthes, "Rhetoric of the Image," *Image-Music-Text,* trans. Stephen Heath (New York: Hill and Wang, 1977) and Wendy Steiner, *The Colors of Rhetoric: Problems in the Relation between Modern Literature and Painting* (Chicago: University of Chicago Press, 1982).

For an illustration of how iconology and ideology may be connected in critical analyses of visual works, see David Dabydeen, *Hogarth's Blacks: Images of Blacks in Eighteenth Century English Art* (Surrey, England: Dangaroo Press, 1985) and Sander L. Gilman, "Black Bodies, White Bodies: Toward an Iconography of Female Sexuality in Late Nineteenth-Century Art, Medicine, and Literature," *Critical Inquiry* 12 (Autumn 1985): 204–242.

2. George Richardson, *Iconology: or, a Collection of Emblematical Figures Containing Four Hundred and Twenty Four Remarkable Subjects, Moral and Instructive; in Which Are Displayed the Beauty of Virtue and the Deformity of Vice,* two volumes (London: G. Scott, 1778), 1: i.

3. Edwin Wolf, 2nd, "Benjamin Franklin's Stamp Act Cartoon," *Proceedings of the American Philosophical Society* 99 (December 1955): 388–396 and Albert Matthews, "The Snake Devices, 1754–1776, and the *Constitutional Courant,* 1765,"

Publications of the Colonial Society of Massachusetts (Boston: Colonial Society of Massachusetts, December 1907), 11: 409–453.

4. A bibliography of this literature is available in Martin Medhurst and Thomas Benson, editors, *Rhetorical Dimensions in Media: A Critical Casebook* (Dubuque, Iowa: Kendall/Hunt Publishing Company, 1984), 365–407. Kenneth Burke, to whom the volume has been dedicated, recognized as early as 1950 that cartoons may be used for rhetorical purposes, for he noted in *A Rhetoric of Motives* that "if the Aristotelian concern with topics were adapted to the conditions of modern journalism, we should perhaps need to catalogue a kind of *timely topic,* such as that of the satirical cartoon, which exploits commonplaces of a transitory nature" (62). Subsequent essays by Medhurst and DeSousa explored such topics within the framework of the neoclassical canons of rhetoric. Martin J. Medhurst and Michael A. DeSousa, "Political Cartoons as Rhetorical Form: A Taxonomy of Graphic Discourse," *Communication Monographs* 48 (1981): 197–236; Michael A. DeSousa and Martin J. Medhurst, "Political Cartoons and American Culture: Significant Symbols of Campaign 1980," *Studies in Visual Communication* 8 (Winter 1982): 84–97. For a critique of these essays, John Sullivan, "Taxing the Medhurst/DeSousa Taxonomy: Another Look at Political Cartoons," (Paper presented at the Speech Communication Association, Washington D.C., 13 November 1983). For an account of how the neoclassical canons were employed generally in theories of art during the eighteenth century, Vincent M. Bevilacqua, "Classical Rhetorical Influences in the Development of Eighteenth Century British Aesthetic Criticism," *Transactions of the American Philological Association* 106 (1976):11–28.

Two essays that appear to have contributed historically to the current focus in rhetorical criticism on the interdisciplinary value of the rhetorical tradition are Phillip K. Tompkins, "The Rhetorical Criticism of Non-Oratorical Works," *Quarterly Journal of Speech,* 55 (1969): 431–439 and Thomas O. Sloan, Richard B. Gregg, Thomas R. Nilsen, Irving J. Rein, Herbert W. Simons, Hermann G. Stelzner, and Donald W. Zacharias, "Report of the Committee on the Advancement and Refinement of Rhetorical Criticism," *The Prospect of Rhetoric,* Eds. Lloyd Bitzer and Edwin Black (Englewood Cliffs, New Jersey: Prentice-Hall, 1971), 220–227. Both essays tended to legitimize in general the on-going work by rhetorical critics on forms of communication other than oratory.

5. Stephen E. Lucas, *Portents of Rebellion: Rhetoric and Revolution in Philadelphia, 1765–1776* (Philadelphia: Temple University Press, 1976); Ronald F. Reid, *The American Revolution and the Rhetoric of History,* Bicentennial Monographs (Speech Communication Association, 1978); Kurt W. Ritter and James R. Andrews, *The American Ideology: Reflections of the Revolution in American Rhetoric,* Bicentennial Monographs (Speech Communication Association, 1978); Barbara A. Larson, *Prologue to Revolution: The War Sermons of the Reverend Samuel Davies: A Rhetorical Study,* Bicentennial Monographs (Speech Communication Association, 1978); John F. Wilson, "Jonathan Boucher's Farewell Sermon," *Language and Cognition,* ed. Lawrence J. Raphael, Carolyn B. Raphael, and Miriam R. Valdovinos (Plenum Publishing Corp., 1984), 269–281; Judy Hample, "The Textual and Cultural Authenticity of Patrick Henry's 'Liberty or Death' Speech," *Quarterly Journal of Speech* 63 (October 1977): 298–310; Kurt W. Ritter, "Confrontation as Moral Drama: The Boston Massacre in Rhetorical Perspective," *Southern Speech Communication Journal* 42 (Winter 1977): 114–136; J. Vernon Jensen, "British Voices on the Eve of the American Revolution: Trapped by the Family Metaphor," *Quarterly Journal of Speech* 63 (February 1977): 43–50; Peter D. G. Thomas, *British Politics and the Stamp Act Crisis: The First Phase of the American Revolution, 1763–1767* (Oxford: Clarendon Press, 1975); Edmund S. Morgan and Helen M. Morgan, *The Stamp Act Crisis: Prologue to Revolution* (Chapel Hill: University of North Carolina Press, 1953).

The political use of caricature during the era of the American Revolution has been studied by Herbert M. Atherton, *Political Prints in the Age of Hogarth: A Study of the Ideographic Representation of Politics* (Oxford: Clarendon Press, 1974) and Mary Dorothy George, *English Political Caricature to 1792: A Study of Opinion and Propaganda* (Oxford: Clarendon Press, 1959). Because these admirable books investigate the general use of political prints in England throughout the eighteenth century, neither book focuses in much detail upon specific works, such as "Magna Britannia" or "JOIN, or DIE." John Agresto focuses on an engraving by Paul Revere prior to the American Revolution in "Art and Historical Truth: The Boston Massacre," *Journal of Communication* 29 (1979):170–174.

6. Wolf's essay reproduces these variants of "Magna Britannia", except for the version by M. Darly, which is reproduced here for the first time.

Other essays that comment at length on "Magna Britannia" are Leonard W. Labaree, editor, *The Papers of Benjamin Franklin* (New Haven: Yale University Press, 1959–84), 13:66–72; Frederic R. Kirkland, "An Unknown Franklin Cartoon," *Pennsylvania Magazine of History and Biography* 73 (January 1949): 76–79.

7. Darly's version appears to have been an attempt to reverse the meanings of the work by eliminating implications of self-destruction and by blaming the reduced state of the Empire upon unidentified "ENEMIES." Darly depicted Britannia chained to the trunk of the English oak and he omitted Britannia's spear. The text specifies that she has been deprived of her limbs "BY HER ENEMIES."

8. The topic of visual or pictorial metaphor has been addressed in the following: Virgil Aldrich, "Visual Metaphor," *Journal of Aesthetic Education,* 2 (1968):73–86; Ernst Gombrich, "Visual Metaphors of Value in Art," *Meditations on a Hobby Horse And Other Essays on the Theory of Art* (London: Phaidon Press, 1978); Arthur C. Danto, "Metaphor, Expression, and Style," *The Transfiguration of the Commonplace* (Cambridge, Massachusetts: Harvard University Press, 1983); Lester C. Olson, "An Essay on Pictorial Metaphor and Rhetorical Iconology" (Paper delivered to the Speech Communication Association, Denver, Colorado, 8 November 1985).

9. Labaree, 13:170; Wolf, 389.

10. Labaree, 13:189, Wolf, 390.

11. Labaree, 13:67–68.

12. A transcript of the letter to Deborah Franklin is located in Labaree, 13:176; Wolf, 389–390.

13. Labaree, 13:68; Wolf, 390.

14. Wolf, 390. Although Edwin Wolf is correct in his claim that the exact date of publication of the Philadelphia broadside version must remain at issue, reasoning that it was most probably published between 1767–69, he may err when he dismisses Ford's initial dating of the engraving in 1766, by claiming that "it hardly seems likely that Franklin's London original would have reached any of his American correspondents much before news of the repeal of the act; hence its republication would have lacked a point" (Wolf, 390–392). By that reasoning, however, the *Examination,* which transpired on 13 February 1766, only eleven days before Franklin sent "Magna Britannia" to David Hall, also would not have been circulated in 1766, since it also would have reached America after the repeal of the Stamp Act. Strahan did not send a copy of the *Examination* to Hall until May 1766, but it was printed and distributed

as early as September 1766 to vindicate Franklin's conduct and to influence the fall elections in Pennsylvania. There is reason to believe that "Magna Britannia" could have served similar ends, since a copy was sent to Hall in February 1766 and since it also demonstrated Franklin's effort to obtain repeal. Therefore, the 1766 date for the Philadelphia version remains a plausible one, though even if the print were published later as Wolf suggests between 1767 and 1769, "Magna Britannia" still could have been used as an apologia to vindicate Franklin, since the endeavor to rehabilitate his reputation persisted throughout that period. According to Ward Miner, the campaign to restore Franklin's damaged reputation "continued at intervals until June 9, 1769, by which time twenty-four different items had been published." Ward Miner, *William Goddard: Newspaperman* (Durham, NC: Duke University Press, 1962), p. 73.

15. Wolf, 390.

16. Reproduced in Labaree, 13:124–162. Labaree addresses the extent to which the *Examination* was a preorchestrated affair at 13:128. Labaree's position is endorsed tacitly by G. Jack Gravlee and James R. Irvine in "Franklin Reexamined: A Rejection of Parliamentary Manipulation" *Southern Speech Communication Journal* 48 (Winter 1983): 167–181.

17. Thomas Hollis to John [or Jonathan] Mayhew, 19 June 1766, from the original in the Massachusetts Historical Society.

18. For an analysis of the political factors entailed in the change of government, Peter D. G. Thomas, "The Change of Ministry in 1765," *British Politics and the Stamp Act Crisis: The First Phase of the American Revolution, 1763–1767* (Oxford: Clarendon Press, 1975), 115–130.

19. Wolf, 388–396; Labaree, 13:66–72; Kirkland, 76–79.

20. *Pennsylvania Gazette,* 9 May 1754, p. 2, col. 1.; Matthews, 11:409–453 reproduces all of the serpent icons alluded to in this essay.

21. *New-York Gazette,* 13 May 1754, p. 2, col. 3; *New-York Mercury,* 13 May 1754, p. 2, col. 3; *Boston Gazette,* 21 May 1754, p. 3, col.1; *Boston Weekly News-Letter,* 23 May 1754, p. 1, col. 1.

22. *Virginia Gazette,* 19 July 1754, p. 3, col. 1, *South Carolina Gazette,* 22 August 1754, p. 2, col. 2.

23. *Constitutional Courant,* 21 September 1765, masthead. Miner, 50–52, has proven that Goddard published the *Courant,* though it is often attributed to James Parker; Labaree concurs with Miner (12:287).

24. *Boston Evening-Post, 7* October 1765, p. 3, col. 1.

25. *Newport Mercury,* 7 October 1765, p. 2, cols. 1–3.

26. "Rationalis" *Public Ledger,* 16 November 1765, p. 1, col. 4; also the *Annual Register for 1765,* 5th edition (London: Printed for J. Dodsley in Pall Mall, 1793), 50–51.

27. "JOIN, or DIE," like "Magna Britannia," had an enduring but changing significance throughout the decade of dissent that preceded the American Revolution. During subsequent American reactions to the Coercive Acts beginning in the summer of 1774, the emblem was printed repeatedly on the mastheads of three colonial newspapers: the *Massachusetts Spy,* 7 July 1774 until 6 April 1775; the *New-York Journal,* 23 June 1774 until 15 December 1775; the *Pennsylvania Journal,* 27 July 1774 until 18 October 1775. In all these subsequent cases, "JOIN, or DIE" was employed to promote intercolonial unity against the policies of the British government.

28. Labaree, 12:287–288.

29. Labaree specifies that the version of the *Courant* sent to Franklin was one with a serpent on the masthead. "This was a half sheet, printed on both sides, in the form of a newspaper. The heading was divided in the center by a device nearly identical with BF's 'Snake Cartoon' of 1754" (12:287).

The attribution to Parker was incorrect, see Miner 50–52; Labaree concurs with Miner (12:287).

30. Labaree, 12:380–381.

31. *Annual Register for 1765,* 50–51. The publication date of the first edition of the *Annual Register for 1765* is not known with precision. As early as 10 October 1765, an advertisement in the *Public Ledger* announced that the 1765 volume of the "*Annual Register . . .* is preparing for the Press and will be published about the usual time" (p. 3, col. 4). An advertisement on 30 November–3 December 1765 described the *Register* as "in great Forwardness for the Press," (p. 529, col. 1), and on 18–21 January 1766, the *Public Ledger* announced that the *Register* "is in the Press and will be published about the usual time," (p. 71, col. 3).

The comments in the *Annual Register* on "JOIN, or DIE" were subsequently reprinted with minor changes in Edward Barnard, *The New, Comprehensive and Complete History of England* (London: Printed for the Author and Published by Alex. Hogg at No. 16, Pater-noster Row, 1782), 666.

32. "Rationalis," *Public Ledger,* 16 November 1765, p. 1, col. 4; "From the Public Ledger," *Pennsylvania Journal,* 20 February 1766, p. 1, col. 3.

33. For example, he used the pseudonym "W. S." in the *Public Ledger,* 20 November 1765, p. 4, cols. 2–3. For the attribution of this article to Franklin, see Verner W. Crane, ed., *Benjamin Franklin's Letters to the Press, 1758–1775* (Chapel Hill: Published for the Institute of Early American History and Culture by the University of North Carolina Press, 1950), 35–38.

34. "Rationalis," p. 2, col. 1; "From the Public Ledger," p. 1, col. 3.

35. Frank H. Sommer, "Emblem and Device: The Origin of the Great Seal of the United States," *Art Quarterly* 24 (Spring 1961): 57–76. Although one commonplace basis for distinguishing an emblem and a device was whether the pictorial image depicted a human form, in which case the pictorial composition was classified as an *emblem,* Franklin himself did not distinguish emblems from devices on that basis. When Franklin later chaired a committee, charged by Congress with designing a *device* for the great seal of the United States, Franklin proposed an image which portrayed the destruction of the Pharaoh's army in the Red Sea. Other committee members, Thomas Jefferson and John Adams, also proposed images that included human forms (Sommer, 64).

36. Crane, *Letters,* 24.

37. To discredit Franklin they objected that he was the chief author of measures to change the Proprietary government under the Penn family into a Royal government under the King. They also claimed that "enmity" between Franklin and the proprietors would "preclude all Accommodation of our Disputes with them." They added that Franklin, "as we are informed, is very unfavorably thought of by several of his Majesty's ministers." Further, Franklin's appointment is "so very disagreeable to a very great number of the most serious and reputable Inhabitants of this Province." The authors also affirmed that Franklin's appointment was questionable because it was made in haste. They alleged that Franklin had misused public funds "whereby the Province suffered a loss of L6000," and, in general, they claimed that they "wish to prevent mischief arising from his appointment" (Labaree, 11: 408–412).

For a list of publications against and promoting Franklin's political career in 1764, see Melvin H. Buxbaum, *Benjamin Franklin, 1721–1906, a reference guide* (Boston: G. K. Hall & Co., 1983). For an account of the election campaign, see J. Phillip Gleason, "A Scurrilous Colonial Election and Franklin's Reputation," *William and Mary Quarterly* 3rd Series, 18 (1961): 68–84.

38. Franklin depicted concern for the reputation of the Assembly as the principle reason for his apologia in which he systematically responded to the seven charges, choosing not to dispute the first two charges about his intention to change the proprietary government and instead endeavoring to refute the remaining five charges (Labaree, 11:430).

39. Verner W. Crane, "The Stamp Act Crisis," *Benjamin Franklin: A Profile,* ed., Esmond Wright (New York: Hill and Wang, 1970), 116.

40. *Pennsylvania Journal,* 20 December 1764, p. 3, col. 2 and 10 January 1765, p. 2, cols. 1–3 and p. 3, col. 1.

41. *Pennsylvania Journal,* 3 October 1765, p. 3, col. 3.

42. Labaree, 12:388.

43. *Pennsylavania Journal, Supplement,* 18 September 1766, p. 2, col. 2.

44. Crane, "Stamp Act Crisis," 113.

45. Miner, 73.

46. Franklin commented, for example, "The human body and the political differ in this, that the first is limited by nature to a certain stature, which, when attain'd, it cannot, ordinarily, exceed; the other by better government and more prudent police [policy?] as well as by change of manners and other circumstances, often takes fresh starts of growth, after being long at a stand; and may add tenfold to the dimensions it had for ages been confined to" (Labaree, 9: 78–79). On another occasion, Franklin compared the Empire to a Polypus, noting that "A Nation well regulated is like a Polypus; take away a Limb, its Place is soon supply'd; cut it in two, and each deficient Part shall speedily grow out of the Part remaining. Thus if you have Room and Subsistence enough, as you may by dividing, make ten Polypes out of one, you may of one make ten Nations, equally populous and powerful; or rather, increase a Nation ten fold in Numbers and Strength" (Paul W. Conner, "The Continentalist," *Benjamin Franklin: A Profile,* ed. Esmond Wright, 80).

47. Labaree, 13: 132; Lucas, 13; Merrill Jensen, "America in 1763," *The Founding of a Nation,* (New York: Oxford University Press, 1968), 10.

48. Labaree, 13: 150.

49. Herbert M. Atherton, "The Allegory of Patriotism," *Political Prints in the Age of Hogarth: A Study of the Ideographic Representation of Politics* (Oxford: Clarendon Press, 1974), esp. 89–97.

50. Franklin privately reasoned that if Parliament had the right to legislate for the colonies in all matters, then those colonists, who originally fled to America to obtain religious freedom, could not have done so legally. Reflecting later on his convictions during the Stamp Act controversy, Franklin noted that: "From a thorough Enquiry (on Occasion of the Stamp-Act) into the Nature of the Connection between Britain and the Colonies, I became convinced that the Bond of their Union is not the Parliament but the King. That in removing to America, a Country out of the Realm, they did not carry with them the Statutes then existing; for if they did, the Puritans must have been subjected *there* to the same grievous Acts of Conformity, Tithes, Spiritual Courts, & c., which they meant to be free from, by going thither; and in vain would they have left their native Country, and all the Conveniences and Comforts of its improved State, to combat the Hardships of a new Settlement in a distant Wilderness, if they had taken with them what they meant to fly from, or if they had left a Power behind them capable of sending the same Chains after them, to bind them in America. They took with them, however, by Compact, their Allegiance to the King, and a Legislative Power for the making a new Body of Laws with his assent, by which they were to be governed" (Labaree, 21: 417).

51. Franklin remarked, for example, "I shall next consider the other supposition, that their [colonial] growth may render them *dangerous* [to the British government]. Of this I own, I have not the least conception. . . . Those [colonies] we now have, are not only under different governors, but have different forms of government, different laws, different interests, and some of them different religious persuasions, and different manners. Their jealousy of each other is so great that however necessary an union of the colonies has long been, for their common defence and security against their enemies, and how sensible soever each colony has been of that necessity, yet they have never been able to effect such a union among themselves, nor even to agree in requesting the mother country to establish it for them. . . . If they could not agree to unite for their defence against the French and Indians, who were perpetually harassing their settlements, burning their villages, and murdering their people; can it reasonably be supposed that there is any danger of their uniting against their own nation, which protects and encourages them, with which they have so many connections and ties of blood, interest, and affection, and which 'tis well known they all love much more than they love one another" (Labaree, 9: 90).

52. *Annual Register for 1766,* 5th edition (London: J. Dodsley in Pall Mall, 1793), 35.

The imagery of brooms on the masts of ships was commonplace in political prints during the Stamp Act controversy. Such imagery appears in the background, right of "The Great Financier," published in London in 1765. It also appears in the background of three extant variants of "The Deplorable State of America," published at London, Boston, and Philadelphia. During subsequent disputes over the Townshend Duties, similar ship imagery was used again in England to criticize the government in "Political Electricity," published in 1770. The brooms on the masts would have reminded Britons and colonists during this later conflict with Parliament that the non-importation agreement had proven an effective way to coerce repeal.

For a list of caricatures printed in England during the Stamp Act controversy, Douglass Adair, "The Stamp Act in Contemporary English Cartoons," *William and Mary Quarterly* 3rd series, 10 (October 1953): 538–542. For a list of caricatures printed in the colonies during the Stamp Act controversy, E. P. Richardson, "Stamp Act Cartoons in the Colonies," *Pennsylvania Magazine of History and Biography* 96 (July 1972): 275–297.

53. *Annual Register for 1766,* 35.

54. Crane, "Stamp Act Crisis," 125. As Crane also has pointed out: "when [William] Knox, in his attack on the charter exemptions, contended that the constitution of Great Britain 'acknowledges no authority superior to the legislature, consisting of king, lords, and commons,' Franklin queried: 'Does this writer imagine that wherever an Englishman settles, he is Subject to the Power of Parliamt'? Knox's description of the colonies as subjects of Great Britain he rejected in a note which goes all the way in denial of Parliamentary sovereignty over the colonies: 'The People of G. Britain are Subjects of the King. G. B. is not a Sovereign. Parliament has Power only *within the Realm.*' Again, when the Lords in their first *Protest* referred to the dependency of the colonies 'on the imperial Crown and Parliament of

Great Britain,' Franklin underlined 'Parliament' and supplied this note: 'Thrust yourselves in with the Crown in the Government of the Colonies. Do your Lordships mean to call the Parliament *imperial*[?]'" (Crane, 126–127).

55. There is some controversy about whether this letter to Lord Kames was sent on 11 April 1767 or on 25 February 1767. For Labaree's comment on the issue, see 14:62–64 and 116. Quote from 14: 65.

56. Labaree, 14: 65.

57. Crane, *Letters,* 72.

58. Labaree, 13: 144–145, 153, and 156.

59. On Benjamin Franklin's political pragmatism, see Clinton Rossiter, "The Political Theory of Benjamin Franklin," *Benjamin Franklin: A Profile,* ed. Esmond Wright, 151 and Verner Crane, *Letters,* 129.

60. Crane, "Stamp Act Crisis," 129; also Labaree, 14:69.

61. Labaree, 21: 417.

18

PRESIDENTIAL RHETORIC'S VISUAL TURN

Performance Fragments and the Politics of Illusionism

KEITH V. ERICKSON

I'll go to Japan if that's what you want. But I won't kiss their asses.

—Harry S. Truman
(terHorst & Albertazzie, 1979, p. 48)

A reporter flippantly asked President Reagan what it was like being an *actor* living in the White House, to which he candidly replied: "How could you be president and not be an actor?" (Roberts, 1993, p. 9). Indeed, as Schmuhl (1990) argues, one legacy of the Reagan administration is the lesson that acting, stagecraft, and mediated images can enhance statecraft. There is little doubt that mediated images of Reagan's dramatic appearances at such historically significant sites as Normandy Beach, South Korea's DMZ, and the Berlin Wall captivated American and international audiences as *coup de théâtre*. As Meyrowitz (1985) notes, the presidency is frequently articulated in spectacle form because citizens accept the fact that chief executives "*perform* the role of president rather than *be* president" (p. 303). So doing, "the presidential performer legitimates his claims, authenticates his role, and captivates his audience" (Raphael, 1999, p. 48). Citizens, though, may be ill-equipped to distinguish between political fact and well-chosen, felicitously performed stratagem. As a consequence, such apparently innocent presidential activities as George Bush pitching horse shoes or Bill Clinton reading *The Night Before Christmas* to minority children are rarely recognized as rhetorical illusions that visually define ideological and hegemonic relationships—the "micro-physics of power" (McKerrow, 1989, p. 98).

White House-manipulated photo-opportunities have dramatically altered how presidents are

SOURCE: Erickson, K. V. (2000). Presidential rhetoric's visual turn: Performance fragments and the politics of illusionism. *Communication Monographs, 67*(2), 138–157. © National Communication Association.

portrayed visually (Hart, 1994). Kennedy, for example, charmed the nation with engaging photographs of touch football, quiet contemplation, elegant affairs, international diplomacy, and a youthful family (Schlesinger, 1965). A nonphotogenic Johnson, hoping to emulate his predecessor's visual appeal, staged 222 photo-opportunities and had 500,000 photographs of himself taken (Lammers, 1982, p. 155). Images of Nixon toasting Chairman Mao, Ford celebrating the nation's 200th birthday in New York Harbor, and Carter shuttling peace offerings between Israel and Egypt likewise captured the attention of witnesses worldwide. The Reagan administration, however, truly mastered the art of performing the presidency: "Every moment of every appearance was scheduled, every word was scripted, every place where Reagan was expected to stand was chalked with toe marks" (Regan, 1988, p. 248). Reagan's artful use of dramatized spectacle redefined the rhetorical presidency to the extent that the "moving synoptic moment has replaced the eloquent speech" (Jamieson, 1988, p. 117). Clearly, presidential rhetoric has taken a visual turn.

Presidents stage photo-opportunities to influence, manipulate, entreat, entice, amaze, or otherwise assume power over witnesses. The White House does so knowing that citizens are twice as likely to view rather than listen to a chief executive (Hart, 1987). Moreover, public relations experts recognize that witnesses tend to believe what they see rather than hear inasmuch as "words no longer hold people's attention or their interest" (Ellul, 1985, p. 131). Recognizing this, White House photo-opportunities are staged to stimulate political interest, create social awareness, reach mass audiences, and influence the public's "psychological readiness to acquiesce" (Erickson, 1998, p. 148). Rhetorically performed gestures, however, can "blind" unsuspecting witnesses to deceptive and/or manipulative visual appeals, thereby clouding the distinction between fiction and reality (Miroff, 1988). In addition, this project contends that performance imagery reaffirms power structures by suppressing all but the dominant ideology, minimizing rational discourse, dissipating the public sphere, and disguising politically motivated ends. As such, I demonstrate how mediated presidential performances are capable of hoodwinking the public, mystifying presidential behavior, lessening an administration's accountability, suppressing the public's participation in politics, and reifying ideological authority figures (Debord, 1994; Miroff, 1989). It is these forms of scripted, symbolic gestures that this essay seeks to describe, interpret, and evaluate.

The relative invisibility of presidential performance fragments demands of the critic an imaginative critical lens, one that captures the rhetorical, aesthetic, and ideological implications of mediated images. This essay, therefore, offers an analysis of rhetorically crafted performance images following Corbin (1998), Hariman (1995), McGee (1982, 1984, 1990), and McKerrow (1989). Here, presidential performance images are considered material, symbolic fragments that may be assembled and reconstructed to illuminate their political influence. Specifically, I examine performance fragments from the perspectives of prudential style (Hariman, 1995), McGee's fragmentation thesis (Corbin, 1998), and McKerrow's (1989) critical rhetoric orientation of *symbolism that addresses publics* (p. 101). Critical rhetoric is text-based (as opposed to agent-centered) and oriented to unpacking nonapparent power practices in the dominant ideology's fragmented discourses. I hope, therefore, to unlock the power and ideological constraints imbedded in mediated presidential performance fragments. In addition, I link performance fragments to prudential behavior, thereby identifying "crucial elements of political decision-making typically unseen by other scholars" (Hariman, 1991, p. 35). Integrated throughout this analysis is an ideational critique of the phenomenon.

OVERVIEW: PRESIDENTIAL PERFORMANCE FRAGMENTS

Clinton respectfully commemorated the fortieth anniversary of Central High's desegregation. He did so by symbolically escorting the Little Rock Nine through the school's front door. The gesture, hailed by the Black community, reminded witnesses of the government's historic action taken to redress institutional racism ("Clinton Opens," 1997, p. 4+). Rhetorically prudent, this gesture signaled Clinton's posture toward politically marginalized and disenfranchised publics. By contrast, an imprudent performance may reveal or question a president's intention, sincerity, competence, and/or character, especially when it functions to "promote gesture over accomplishment and appearance over fact" (Miroff, 1988, p. 289). Clinton, for example, joked and laughed with an aide at Secretary of Commerce Ron Brown's funeral. Upon spotting a film crew, however, he quickly dabbed his eyes as if stricken with grief. Rush Limbaugh, conservative talk show host, derided the president's "phony acting" and aired the incident repeatedly. The White House responded that Clinton was merely reacting to allergies ("Grief analysis," 1996). Thus, as these examples illustrate, the rhetorical implications and potential consequences of prudent and imprudent presidential performances are considerable.

A president's stylized aesthetic (the ability to act with decorum to the "irrational novelty of the moment" [White, 1987, p. 20]) is managed by prudence. Kennedy, for example, left a black tie event in Los Angeles to drop in unexpectedly on a high school prom. Displaying masterful prudence, he gracefully greeted and moved among an otherwise thunderstruck crowd (Schlesinger, 1965). Clearly, a president's political style is a vital determinant of a performance fragment's visual appeal insofar as gestures do not prove, but rather aesthetically display, exhibit, and/or illuminate by miming natural performance (Stucky, 1993). To create among witnesses the impression of authenticity or naturalness, presidents stage performance fragments with attention to coherence, sensitivity, and care. Indeed, spectator receptiveness is dependent upon how well presidents articulate performance fragments. Reagan, for example, stood beneath a towering bust of Lenin and scolded Moscow intellectuals for disregarding human rights and religious freedoms. Back home, Reagan's passionate performance was widely applauded, and was subsequently deemed his finest hour (Schieffer & Gates, 1989).

A prudent political style mirrors aesthetic propriety, the rhetorical practice of image management that stimulates the spectator's aesthetic responses (emotions such as pleasure, joy, awe, wonderment). As such, prudent performance fragments appropriate and display mastery of those rhetorical and aesthetic materials that constitute the "standard[s] of rationality devised for a performative context" (Hariman, 1995, p. 27).

Standards applicable to the presidency include charisma, taste, sensitivity, and responsiveness— qualities hopefully principled by *phronesis* (ethicality, practical wisdom, right action, rectitude). Performance fragments uninformed by *phronesis* may rhetorically manipulate, deceive, obfuscate, and/or dominate (McGee, cited in Corbin, 1998). Clearly, presidential imagery that misrepresents political reality not only misinforms but treats witnesses as objects of manipulation and control. Hence, a critical rhetoric critique informed by prudence can identify "how there is a relationship between [political] morality and gesture. . . ." (Hariman, 1991, p. 34).

Critically, deconstructing performance fragments requires an awareness of the aesthetic subtleties of ideology insofar as "power in the West is what displays itself the most, and what hides itself the best" (Foucault, cited in Kritzman, 1990, p. 11). This is especially true of images that synoptically link a president to sites, rituals, and occasions that serve as markers of culture, power, and/or authority. By visually appropriating cultural and political symbols, a president is able to make "strategic choices about how to engage the popular imagination in any political situation" (Bennett, 1983, p. 42). Why? Because the "power of the State stems largely from citizens's emotional investment in its symbols" (Cos & Schatz, 1998, pp. 15–16). On the eve of Clinton's inaugural, for example, he appeared at Monticello, walked by candlelight to the Lincoln Memorial, rang a replica of the Liberty Bell, and with tear-filled eyes accepted the congratulations of Barbra Streisand and Michael Jackson at the Capitol Centre (Howard & Cerio, 1993). In addition, performance fragments influence and shape witness perceptions of political events, myths, and/or dramas. Nixon's dramatic trip to China, for example, encountered fierce press reaction regarding the Shanghai Communiqué, but the "public simply was not interested in the complex analyses of the document after having watched the spectacle of an American president welcomed in the capital of an erstwhile enemy" (Kissinger, 1979, pp. 1091–1092). High drama and exotic visuals simply minimized the "need for the inconvenient particularities of argument and inference" (Farrell, 1989, p. 161). Nor should the fact the trip coincided with the New Hampshire presidential primary go unnoticed.

Similarly, as narrative representations, performance fragments recount, retell, or reshape society's cultural and political realities. Ideologically, visual narratives intrude upon political reality insofar as they "save us the trouble of thinking and having to remember" (Ellul, 1985, pp. 127–128). In addition, presidential performance fragments silence witnesses and defuse the public sphere. Reagan's photo-opportunities, which forbid question asking, deprived the public "the genuine interplay of opinion, question, and argument that forms the basis of decisions" (Regan, 1988, p. 248). Performance fragments, therefore, practice exclusionary politics inasmuch as they relegate citizens to the status of spectator, and thereby blunt the dialectical process upon which democratic discourse depends. Monarch-like, the president seemingly governs high above the political fray (Minogue, 1985). Similarly, presidential rhetoric's visual turn suppresses alternative viewpoints as well as marginalized voices insofar as only the dominant orthodoxy is presented for viewing. Hence, performance fragments express "domination by ignoring, neglecting, and even obliterating the established sites of subordinated people" (Kuper, 1972, p. 422).

Crafted to impress, intrigue, beguile, or otherwise please witnesses, performance fragments "totally elide the distinction between the symbolic and real" (Villa, 1993, p. 227). As such, rhetorically crafted performance fragments constitute political illusions—aesthetically framed images that manipulate the public's emotions and perceptions of political reality. Reagan, for example, visited a Chicago public housing project. There, the fiscally tight-fisted president promised relief, inspected living quarters, reassured residents, and held children. This hegemonic performance fragment depicted Reagan as compassionate and humane even as it disguised his true motivation for visiting Chicago—to attend a sporting event (Regan, 1988)! Finally, performance fragments function as nominalist rhetoric. Ideologically, they name, define, or otherwise give meaning to symbolic gestures and actions. As a consequence, performance fragments enable many witnesses to "believe that they inhabit not only an intelligible, but a satisfying political world" (Miroff, 1982, p. 224). Hence, performance fragments rhetorically manipulate an otherwise inchoate symbolic environment.

PRUDENT PRESIDENTIAL PERFORMANCE FRAGMENTS

Although various exigencies, affairs of state, political ceremonies, and/or diplomatic strategies may prompt presidential performances, political need typically motivates presidents to signal visually: (1) consubstantiality with the mythic presidency; (2) ideological authority, power, and control; and (3) active leadership. Within the context of these rhetorical functions, therefore, this study assembles a text that unmasks performance fragments as powerful instruments in a contemporary president's rhetorical arsenal.

Consubstantiality with the Mythic Presidency

Performance fragments enable chief executives to *affirm visually mastery of the mythic presidency*. Citizen perceptions of the office demand that a president act presidential with such palpable authenticity as to display "true performance" (Hymes, 1975, p. 18). True performance constitutes a prudent adaptation to the standards and traditions of the mythic presidency. Presidents do not imitate their predecessors, however. Nixon correctly observed that what vitalizes the presidency is that "each man remains distinctive" (1978, p. 1078). [Pundits, for example, scoffed at Clinton's early gambit to mimic Kennedy (Alter, 1993, p. 33).] Accordingly, the electorate has witnessed a broad range of political styles and idiosyncratic takes on the mythic presidency, ranging from Johnson's roughshod élan ("a range boss on [a] cattle drive" [terHorst & Albertazzie, 1979, p. 248]) to Reagan's easy grace.

Irrespective of a distinctive style, performing the presidency prudently constitutes a rhetorical balancing act between political necessity and the public's romantic expectation of *phronesis*. [Regrettably, a president as illusionist will likely give every appearance of being a *phronimos* (McGee, in Corbin, 1998).] For example, candidate-Carter both astonished and delighted a post-Nixon electorate by declaring: "If I ever tell a lie, if I ever mislead you, if I ever betray a trust or a confidence I want you to come and take me out of the White House" (Turner, 1976, p. 30). Although inflated for dramatic effect,

Carter's promise nevertheless prudently signaled his principled character and respect for the presidency. Similarly, Johnson threatened to federally enforce civil rights laws in the deep South. Johnson's bold gesture asserted, "I intend to do what is right," an unexpected and courageous performative that thereby impelled nineteen hundred conservative New Orleanians to burst into applause. This authentic performance signaled Johnson's political strength and will to embrace the mythic presidency—the chief executive as a nonpartisan leader and protector of the commonweal (Goldman, 1969, p. 246).

Prudent performances *also facilitate the inventional management of presidential personae.* Even though the media expect chief executives to perform photo-ops with subtle decorum, the White House routinely crafts malleable self-inventions that act out hyperbolic presidential compliments in an "uninterrupted monologue of self-praise" (Debord, 1994, p. 19). Presidents enact a variety of fictive personae (personal and public) in order to heighten their authority and to avoid imposed characterizations. For example, labeled a pro-gun control advocate, Clinton prudently staged a photo-op in a Maryland duck blind where he appeared brandishing a shotgun— an image that deemed him "male bonding with hunters" (Clift & Hosenball, 1994, p. 25). Rhetorically crafted to read as a totality, the underlying stratagem of such image portrayals generally escapes intellectual capture. Typically, presidents enhance their political attributes by posing as bigger-than-life, simultaneously casting themselves as strong, active, decisive, and compassionate. Moreover, if artfully practiced, such prudential performances can "become *realistic,* a straightforward mimesis of dramatic reality" (Lanham, 1976, pp. 147–148). Indeed, prudent performance fragments facilitate a president's ability to realistically enact such roles as world leader, peacemaker, protector of the commonweal, guardian of cultural and political values, commander-in-chief, and chief executive. Clearly, such image fragments function contingently as nominalist rhetoric (McKerrow, 1989). In Bonn, for example, Reagan altered Europe's impression that he was a "nuclear cowboy" (Kondracke, 1982, p. 21). His subsequent remade image, buoyed by visual representations and aphoristic eloquence, depicted him as a humanitarian, diplomat, peacemaker, and world leader.

Reagan's prudent performances both calmed Europe's fears and distanced him from previous positions. From the White House's perspective, Reagan's reenactment of the presidential persona through performance fragments allowed the European audience to identify with him. The mimesis form of the performance fragments provided the medium by which the audience actively, personally, and practically identified "with the verbal and nonverbal symbols of a hero cast as a vision of ideal community" (Chesebro, 1989, p. 14). In this case, the ideal accepted by the European community was the mythic presidency persona. By contrast, chief executives who offer exceedingly intimate images of themselves may appear nonpresidential, as illustrated by Johnson whose imprudent display of an abdominal scar stunned journalists (Culbert, 1983).

Closely related, staged performance fragments *reify and assert a president's popular support.* A grass-roots presidential appearance, for example, may signal presidential popularity as it seduces those easily intoxicated by hoopla, symbolism, and political power. Such performances have the impact of sublimity, a sudden aesthetic shock that transports the spectator to states of pleasure, appreciation, and acceptance. Perhaps Bush's simple reflection expresses it best: "You know, after all the politics, I'm the president. And they [the citizenry] get this sense of, you know, excitement" (Keen, 1992, p. A11). For example, immediately following his 1998 State of the Union Address, Clinton delivered speeches at Urbana, Illinois and La Crosse, Wisconsin. Vice President Gore, with cheerleader effusion and stentorian bombast implored the college audiences to "Stand up! Stand up and show support for your president" ("The Clinton Rally," 1998, p. 22). The subsequent enthusiastic response signaled the public's approval of the president and indifference to media claims of sexual misconduct. [Gore's dramatic posturing affirms McGee's notion of a materialist rhetoric ("rhetoric as object")—its "pragmatic *presence* [being] our inability safely to ignore it at the moment of its impact" (McGee, 1982, p. 45).] To an unsuspecting spectator, accolades dispensed at rallies, graduation exercises, and other celebratory occasions authenticate a president's visually projected popularity. Few performance settings, however, rival parades and motorcades for signaling popularity, commanding attention, usurping public space, and imposing deference to the chief executive. Nixon's travel party in Rome and Belgrade recognized this phenomenon when they intentionally stalled cars to create traffic jams, thereby creating the illusion of a massive presidential welcome (Kissinger, 1979). Similarly, parade imagery suggests a president's populace support, as did Carter's emboldened walk to his inauguration: "A shock went through the crowd. They heard gasps of astonishment . . . [and] some wept openly" (Carter, 1982, p. 17). Carter's spontaneous walk reflected prudent decision-making as he enacted the "right gesture in a public space . . . for political action" (Hariman, 1991, p. 28). In like manner, state orchestrated parades (depending on levels of formality or informality) can visually signal diplomatic respect/disrespect or popularity/unpopularity.

Ideological Power, Dominance, and Control

Presidents use prudent performance imagery to *honor the dominant ideology's wisdom and assert political realities.* The White House, as a signifier of political meanings, attempts to manage and control the citizenry's views of reality by visually imposing interpretive frames that felicitously engage the public's perceptions. As such, a rhetorically staged performance fragment "achieves its effect because it simultaneously blends practical utility with aesthetic pleasure" (Leff, 1984, p. 124). Such performance fragments are complex, occasionally quixotic, and typically suspended between perceptions of accommodation and rejection of the uneven distribution of power. Indeed, administrations create or rhetorically mystify world views to influence the public's definition and perception of reality. Moreover, political reality frequently emerges from the strategic use of visuals that cue spectators' emotive impulses, unspoken agreements, and cultural recollections. Although occasionally disdained by critics, fetching images nonetheless rhetorically influence the public's acceptance of political fantasies insofar as they suppress reliance upon logic and collaborative evidence, and visually stress dominant and underlying ideological themes. Thus,

Clinton's inspired releasing of a bald eagle named "Freedom" at a wilderness site on July 4, 1996, earned him the sobriquet: "Clinton the Environmentalist" (Turque & Rosenstiel, 1996, p. 26).

Prudent performance fragments can *signal a president's ideological dominance over state ceremonies and rituals, sites of political practice and spaces of discourse.* Not surprisingly, sites surrounding the ritualistic practice of asserting or affirming ideology and/or authority are selected for their ability to inspire wonderment and command respect. Ceremonies and rituals enacted at state-erected structures, monuments, and memorials, for example, articulate cherished principles, cultural recollections, and ideological values that define, soothe, and unify witnesses in a form of primitive mystification. They succeed because such prudent performances echo prior events, occasions, and actions. Hence, such ritual performatives privilege the president and symbolically create community, parry dialogue and criticism, all the while imposing political deference and conformity. Indeed, nearly all public events presided over by the president "push" witnesses into and "are operators of, and on, social order" (Handelman, 1990, p. 15). Crafted to beguile the spectator, prudent presidential performance fragments reinvigorate the values, beliefs, and traditions public events intend to evince. They effectively suspend political debate and divisiveness because, as ideological conceits, presidential performance rituals typically express "yearnings for togetherness, for fusion" (Dayan & Katz, 1991, p. viii).

Mediated as rhetorical images, performance fragments can "reassert—even magically reinvigorate—the symbols we believe in but rarely think about" (Combs, 1980, p. 23). For example, by having isolated pan-human virtues, Clinton's prudent oratory at Normandy's D-Day anniversary signaled respect for patriotism, heroic sacrifice, and the price of freedom. So doing, the President eased tension between himself—an alleged draft dodger—and veterans (Walsh, 1994). Presidents can likewise performatively appropriate the public sphere's rules (Foucault's "orders of discourse" [Therborn, 1980, p. 82]) of who may speak, who may assert or participate, and what may or may not be uttered. Kennedy recognized this principle when he declaimed "*Ich bin ein Berliner*" at the Berlin Wall. Chaos nearly erupted, prompting him to observe that "Had I said, 'March to the wall—tear it down!' that they would have" (Schlesinger, 1965, p. 884). This lore-making gesture convincingly established Kennedy's ability to prudently perform a script capable of eliciting emotional responses for political advantage. So powerful was this gesture that years afterward Nixon, in contemplating a visit to Berlin, feared the inevitable comparisons his and Kennedy's appearance would draw (Kissinger, 1979).

Presidential performance fragments frequently *target politically influential and marginalized audiences*. Rhetorically, presidents address such groups to garner political support, and/or to create hegemonic impressions of shared power, cultural accommodation, and political inclusiveness. Thus, administrations routinely attend the conventions of (among others) minorities, educators, physicians, and lawyers. As Laclau observes, "classes cannot assert their hegemony without articulating the people in their discourse" (cited in McKerrow, 1989, p. 95). Thus, Reagan unabashedly portrayed himself as a diversity candidate by busing minorities to, and speaking at, the Statue of Liberty—a political fantasy visually constructed as reality (Nimmo & Combs, 1983). Politically inspired images that target disenfranchised or politically marginalized spectators (women, minorities, gays, children) typically signal compassion, concern, sympathy, or celebrate or reward accomplishment. Eileen Collins, the first female shuttle commander, illustrates this point as she accepted the Clintons' congratulations at a Rose Garden ceremony—her male counterparts went unacknowledged (Walsh, 1994). Similarly, presidents recognize America's diversity by being photographed at minority churches and temples, housing projects, inner-city schools, and by symbolically offering homage to current and past minority leaders. Seldom do such performance fragments positively benefit the disenfranchised even though a prudential performance should "engage the particular with the general good in mind" (Kuypers, 1996, p. 457).

Rhetorical performance fragments can likewise *privilege a president as head-of-state, diplomat, and titular representative of the American people*. As Kennedy put it, making an appearance in a foreign nation is "one of the most powerful weapons we have. . . ." (cited in Schlesinger, 1965, p. 884). In 1969, for example, Nixon's widely broadcast trip to Romania had as its contrapuntal motive the piquing of Soviet sensibilities. Nixon gloated that, "By the time we get through with this trip they are going to be out of their minds" (Kissinger, 1979, p. 156). Similarly, photo-op appearances can help repair diplomatic ill-will. Reagan's sharply symbolic visit to Brazil, Colombia, Costa Rica, and Honduras, for example, offset damage inflicted by U.S. support of Great Britain in its war with Argentina. His adroit performances visually signaled to South and Central American nations sensitivity, non-imperialist intentions, and a desire to mend diplomatic wounds ("Reagan Heads," 1982). Presidential gestures can also warn or threaten nations. Bush's high dudgeon televised address to the Ukranian legislature (prior to meeting Gorbachev) pointedly warned them as to the risks of suicidal nationalism and America's unwillingness to intervene in republic disputes. So doing, Bush aligned himself with Gorbachev, signaled indifference toward internal republic squabbles, visually reinforced his image as peacemaker and world leader, and effectively squelched recklessly shrill political cant (Serrill, 1991, p. 24). Thus, deftly crafted images of a president can signal "who are the powerful and who are the weak . . . [and] reinforce authority" (Kertzer, 1988, p. 5).

In addition, presidents use visual drama to signal diplomatic policy, as did Nixon's initial tour of Europe that established the principle that the United States would consult its allies "before negotiating with . . . potential adversaries" (Nixon, 1978, p. 370). Presidents likewise enact leadership scenes to upstage political opponents. Gorbachev, for example, performed with enigmatic aplomb jack-in-the-box diplomacy. His highly visible performances won the praise and raised the hopes of the world's citizenry, and kept both Reagan and Bush off-guard in one-upmanship contests (Javetski & Fly, 1989, p. 60). Among world leaders, though, performative restraint can ease tensions and help cement relations. Bush and Gorbachev, for example, sustained each other's confidence through mutual applause and flattery. Bush vowed not to be filmed "danc[ing] on the Berlin

Wall" (Talbot, 1991, p. 24)—an act that would have diminished Gorbachev's credibility at home. By contrast, Reagan dangled one foot over Berlin's demarcation line "as if to tempt the totalitarian demons on the other side" (Morganthau & DeFrank, 1982, p. 36). [A splenetic Chancellor Schmidt groused that the penchant of presidents to perform for the cameras from the *safe* side of the wall was "feckless and uselessly provocative" (Osborne, 1978, p. 10).] Too, a presidential state visit can rhetorically inspire a heartened sense of goodwill, create suspense, calm political animosities, and clarify political *agon*—"dramatic conflict between leading characters" (Combs, 1980, p. 55).

Signal Active Leadership

Presidents rhetorically craft images to *alert the populace to presidential initiatives, political agendas, and legislative accomplishments.* Johnson, for example, went to Appalachia to inaugurate the War on Poverty program as "through my eyes . . . all America saw the [impoverished]" (Johnson, 1967, pp. 78–79). Symbolically, such witnessed performances are interpretative frames that visually warrant and synoptically link the public with presidential agendas. As such, Johnson's prudently calculated appeal constituted "an aesthetic sensibility that . . . regulat[ed] the political process" (Hariman, 1991, p. 29). Similarly, symbolism generated by Bush's gestural flummery at the Iwo Jima Memorial, arguing for a constitutional amendment banning flag desecration, was for many citizens an appropriate and rhetorically compelling performance fragment. Bush's action visually signaled patriotism, reverence, and a facile evocation of one of the nation's foremost totems ("How," 1988). In this case, chirping the dominant mantra proved to be powerful politically. As such, his dramatic staging was *"artful as a performance,* not as an artifact" (McGee, 1990, p. 276). Similarly, with breast-heaving pride Johnson signed the 1965 Education Bill at his boyhood school house, a performance that pitched equal opportunity but just as surely positioned him as lawmaker. Axiomatically, it expressed earnestness, concern for minority affairs, and interest in education (Goldman, 1969). However, the significance of Johnson's theatrical appearance was that it affirmed Washington's newly imposed role in public education. Thus, the importance of such performance fragments is that they attach themselves "to a structure of signification" (Greene, 1998, p. 35).

Similarly, chief executives routinely rely on performance fragments to *heighten the public's awareness of salient events, political issues, policy developments, and emergencies.* Clinton clearly appreciates this function: "I need to [travel more to] get the public focused back on the big issues" ("President," 1993, p. A1). Typically, presidents heighten public awareness in spectacle form at sites that visually elicit a "concentration of suggestions: of connotations, of emotions, and of authority" (Edelman, 1985, p. 96). Bush's contrived *rededication* of Mt. Rushmore during the 1992 campaign, for example, visually framed him with the American presidency's foremost icons and the mythic architecture of public memory. Visually arresting, such public event performances rupture the spectator's political structures, instantiate ideological abstractions, and impose on the public's cognition new "versions of social order . . . mediate[d] into collective abstractions" (Handelman, 1990, p. 15). Clinton, for example, effectively alerted the public to the terrorist potential of militia groups. He visited the Oklahoma City bomb site, planted a tree memorializing victims, and orchestrated a high security town-hall meeting in Montana—home to paramilitary groups and the infamous Unabomber. Witnesses applauded Clinton's emblematic appearances for being on-the-job, personally tackling an issue of grave national import in seemingly a timely, concerned, sympathetic, and an authoritative manner. No critic faulted his aesthetically prudent performances as they eased public fears and sparked the nation's collective consciousness. Shortly, previously unknown weekend militia groups came under public scrutiny as they were labeled dangerous radicals (Carney, 1995).

Typically, legislative appeals taken directly to the people fail (Denton & Hahn, 1986). Knowing this, when presidents do go public they stage events and speaking engagements that maximize visual appeal. Typically, going public appearances are short-lived displays that signal presidential activity rather than demands for legislative compliance. However, for spectators absorbed by spectacle illusionism, such performance fragments "are visual forms of rhetorical support, dramatized proofs [authenticating] political reality" (Erickson, 1998, p. 148). As rhetoric, such gestural performances may signal an administration's official stance. For example, a Cassandra-like Clinton ominously warned of dire consequences should his anti-crime package not pass congress. Lacking sufficient support, he posed in Milwaukee with police officers and, in Maryland, dramatically joined a Black congregation who *prayed* for the bill's passage. Politically hardened critics and Washington insiders smirked at this jejune performance even though it gave articulate expression to the bill's salient and revelatory significance (Barnes, 1995).

Likewise, dramatic gestures can *divert the public's attention* by commanding headlines and air time that overshadow competing agents, agendas, exigencies, and/or sensitive operations. Diversionary performances are rhetorically powerful and help to explain why "a person cannot escape from the influence of dominant actors" (McKerrow, p. 94). In one week, Bush was filmed hiking through the Sequoia National Forest, announcing an end to weapons grade plutonium production, attending a baseball game, fishing in Wyoming, and meeting with the president of Mexico in an attempt to divert the public's attention from the Democratic National Convention ("Going," 1992). Similarly, Clinton proposed an education plan and visited Detroit the day the United States Senate initiated impeachment proceedings against him. Essentially, a diversionary performance in spectacle context "blocks, ignores, shuts out, other forms of cognition. . . ." (Polan, 1986, p. 63). Sidestepped or shunted to background status, real issues and problems take backstage. Reagan's administration, for example, recognized that performance fragments offered an opportunity to capture on film rhetorically stirring images symbolizing prosperity and military might. "The idea was to divert people's attention away from substantive issues by creating a world of myths and symbols that made people feel good about themselves and their country" (Maltese, 1992, pp. 198–199). Reagan, for example, only days following the bombing of a U.S. military barracks in Lebanon, ordered the liberation of Grenada. Exhibiting graceful comportment, he later visited the island and acceded to the clamor of a conquering hero welcome. The spectacle's appropriateness, timeliness, grandeur, and commander-in-chief imagery shifted attention from tragedy to triumph while simultaneously giving resonance and meaning to the president's anti-Communist resolve (Stengel, 1986). Thus, Reagan's presence served largely as a soothing response to an otherwise horrific disaster and a lopsided intervention.

IMPRUDENT PRESIDENTIAL PERFORMANCE FRAGMENTS

Presidential performance fragments are subject to uneven media coverage, dotty misinterpretation, and niggling attention that occasionally spike surges of public doubt or mistrust. A dull or embarrassing presidential performance, for example, can signal confusion, incompetence, or insensitivity. Bush's blather at Auschwitz, for example, ("Boy, they were big on crematoriums, weren't they?" [Jacoby, 1997, p. A14]) signaled a shallow appreciation of holocaust horrors. Worse, an infelicitous performance fragment may reveal itself as a rhetorical stratagem. For example, Clinton's forced images of physical vigor soured an outspoken gonzo journalist, which prompted the scatological complaint: "How many miles of this shit-eating jogging are we going to have to watch?" (Thompson, 1994, p. 188). Similarly, silly tableaux and temporary flirtations with the melodramatic ring hollow, and are likely to elicit spectator bemusement. At a New Hampshire truck stop, Bush commandeered an eighteen wheeler, blew its horns, assaulted its gears, and took it for a brief spin. Journalists greeted his return by donning trucker caps inscribed "Shit Happens"—the performance fragment never aired (Schiefer & Gates, 1989, p. 354). In addition, imprudent performance fragments can generate negative press and "morph" into unintended meanings. Bush's center-stage excursion to Japan generated images of a game-playing, albeit a suppliant president in search of jobs, jobs, jobs. The negative chaining fantasies depicting the performance fragment motivated one reporter to lament that "we used to know how to stage photo-opportunities and make handsome and well-engineered lies" (Lapham, 1992, p. 23). Illness aside, Bush's excursion failed to exhibit a "performative sensibility" (Hariman, 1991, p. 27). Thus, it gave critics license to question the president's rationality, grasp of issues, and ability to anticipate the contingent.

Unforeseen circumstances, poor aesthetic judgment, nongraceful demeanor, or an impromptu social blunder may diminish the rhetorical impact of even the most artfully conceived performance fragment. For example, gun shots and tear gas cut short a Bush victory speech in Panama, an incident that failed to "remind Americans at home of an administration success story" (Wines, 1992, p. A1). Austin's categories of infelicitous performatives (abuses and misfires) inform the following analyses (1975). Here, abuses are performance violations while misfires represent performances unsuccessfully enacted.

Performance Fragment Abuses

Blatantly staged or contrived performance fragments lack prudence and will likely signal disregard for truth, hint at deceitful behavior, and heighten questions regarding political manipulation. A particularly brazen, if not racist, photo-op had Clinton playing basketball with a Black teenager during the South Central Los Angeles rioting. Critics jeered: "It's inherently unpresidential, and it's locked in simplistic assumptions" (Krammer, 1993, p. 23). As Burke notes, dramatistic elements must cohere: "It is a principle of drama that the nature of acts and agents should be consistent with the nature of the scene" (1931/1969, p. 3). The tactical need of the moment, for example, cannot justify modifying performances to fit diverse audiences, because they are typically unconvincing. A D-Day photo of Clinton on Normandy Beach, for example, depicted him on bended knee piously forming a cross with loose stones, with an accompanying cut-line that read "Clinton Wishes He had Served." This performance fragment exhibited appalling taste, violated standards of prudence, smacked of hypocrisy, and represented "a canonical example . . . of visual subterfuge" (Messaris, 1994, p. 186).

In addition, critics may question the political and/or ethical elements of *inappropriate, unsuitable, or frenetic performance fragments.* Carter, who showed barely a hint of aesthetic intensity,

uncharacteristically displayed leanings toward ceremonial kitsch by insisting that Israeli and Egyptian delegates sign a peace accord on top of Mt. Sinai—aghast, both nations adamantly refused to surrender to such dizziness (Lasky, 1979). Similarly, Ford was eager to give an anti-crime speech at Yale University though it offered no course work in criminal justice, and would have invited a public and media pillory. One political maven argued that an appearance by Ford would lack sufficient ground-figure realism, and acidly concluded: "A crime speech at Yale is a form of insanity" (Casserly, 1977, p. 78). Performance fragments must also transcend the commonplace lest their salience and ability to inspire awe diminish. Thus, according to a former Clinton aide, the contrived necessity to dart back and forth across the nation trivializes image-making, wearies witnesses, and ultimately loses the "ability of the country to focus on what is really important" (Panetta, cited in Kiefer, 1998, p. A4). Too, frenzied photo-op performances may signal news manipulation, campaigning, showboating, or worse, inattention to matters of state in deference to "hearing the sweet music of compliments and cheers" (Hartmann, 1980, p. 385). Moreover, prudence frequently dictates deference to political reality as opposed to spun-sugar, visual fantasies. For example, even though it signaled the end of the cold war, as a lame duck president Bush declined to engage in elevated drama at the START II arms control pact signing. Bush correctly reasoned that his political status negated the need to festoon the event with self-serving political gestures (Gerstenzang & Goldberg, 1992).

Likewise, *rhetorically insensitive presidential performance fragments* may cast doubt on a chief executive's cultural awareness, reflect chauvinism, and/or spawn ugly American comparisons. When one million gay men and women marched on Washington in 1993, for example, Clinton left town—a hastily called business trip that conveniently denied activists access to the White House and forestalled guilt by association visuals. Within the gay community, however, the president's actions branded him a traitor (Shapiro, 1993). Similarly, Carter jested about catching Montezuma's revenge at a state banquet in Mexico, a remark that "made him look like a country bumpkin," and signaled cultural superiority (Lasky, 1979, p. 387).

Likewise, staging inappropriate ceremonies at emotionally supercharged sites may suggest rhetorical insensitivity. Until 1998, for example, no serving president had visited the holy sites of Jerusalem. [Clinton's canceled visit to the Western Wall in 1994 was considered a "moral victory for Arabs" (Holmes, 1994, p. A12.).] Similarly, no amount of rhetorical bleating could "vanish on command" Jewish "cultural and historical wounds" that surfaced with images of Reagan at Bitburg, a German cemetery containing remains of Nazi SS troops (Farrell, 1993, p. 292). Moreover, a president's camera hungry antics may anger or upset nations. Nixon's visit to Romania, for example, recklessly antagonized the Soviets and signaled support for a Communist dictatorship—a drama-laden trip likened to diplomatic brinkmanship (Rosenfield, 1969). Similarly, Bush shocked Israel and elicited grave criticism from Democrats by meeting and being photographed with the Syrian President, al-Assad, prior to the Desert Storm conflict with Iraq. As Israel's Arens charged: "In the Middle East, the meeting is the message" (Bierman, 1990, p. 25). Finally, images designed to disguise leisure-time activities as official business or working vacations may signal inattention to duty or portray the president as a wastrel. For example, journalists speculated "Who is in charge?" regarding Reagan's frequent (345 days in eight years) trips to, and pictorial horse-back rides at, the Western White House ("A New Round," 1985).

Performance Fragment Misfires

Ineffectual or failed visual dramas may suggest a chief executive's inability to exercise political acumen or display prudent leadership. Carter recounts that his shuttle diplomacy between Israel and Egypt, had it been unsuccessful, "would have greatly dramatized failure" inasmuch as the world awaited the mission's outcome (Carter, 1982, p. 416). Kissinger recognized that diplomacy, as political theater, requires high-profile activities that climax with dramatic yet refrained decorum. Consequently, his legendary grasp of dramatic flair included "agreements that he had prearranged but portrayed as major breakthroughs" (Destler, Gelb, & Lake, 1984, pp. 268–269). Thus, attention-holding summits generally claim substantive accomplishments as opposed to imprudent acts that question the participants' diplomatic skills, political motives, or worse, knowledge. Reagan, for example, exhibited shocking indifference toward diplomatic negotiations by being underprepared at the Reykjavik nuclear arms' reduction summit. Moreover, he engaged Gorbachev in a series of acrimonious leader-of-the-world scenes that quickly became hostile skirmishes marked by mutually exchanged barbs and a climate of disquietude (Schieffer & Gates, 1989).

Likewise, ill-timed and no-win presidential performance fragments may communicate poor judgment or frivolousness. Critics charged Bush with callous indifference following his decision to golf in Maine the day he called up military reservists bound for Iraq (Broder, 1990). Not surprisingly, such rhetorical situations are best left to surrogates or avoided altogether. Clinton, for example, debated visiting the World Trade Center bomb site, but an adviser warned: "There isn't much [you can] do except tie up traffic" (Birnbaum, 1993, p. A6). Moreover, presidents are not always welcome. Clinton was painfully aware of this fact during the 1994 congressional races (Walsh, September 19, 1994). Similarly, Bush's conservative posturing met strident rebuff and charges of perfidy at the hostile Rio Earth Summit ("Bush," 1992). Intriguingly, presidents sometimes attempt to avoid photo-opportunities. At other times they simply miss photo-opportunities. In either case, they do so at considerable risk. For example, a prudent presidential performance at a photo-opportunity can visually legitimize, spotlight, or give prominence to individuals, groups, or organizations—especially marginalized communities. Thus, when Reagan elected not to attend an NAACP convention it was considered a snub, a rejection that symbolically characterized African-Americans as politically unimportant to a Republican president. An annoyed Benjamin Hooks snapped: "It is sufficient just to note that he found a week of play and recreation of higher priority" (West, 1983, p. 517). Similarly, should a president not participate in a host nation's rituals and ceremonies—perfect synoptic moments—it would likely signal cultural chauvinism, disinterest, disrespect, or even a foreign policy change. Carter's decision not to attend Marshall Tito's funeral, for example, inadvertently signaled an implied foreign policy decision to withdraw support for Yugoslavia (Richardson, 1980). Consequently, in a bulletproof vest and to deafening chants of "Get Out," Reagan dutifully attended a rain soaked wreath laying ceremony at Bogotá's statue of Simón Bólivar (Kittle, 1982). Similarly, a good-spirited Ford kept his appointment with Japan's Emperor Hirohito even though his trousers were hopelessly too short. Journalists were "scandalized" by this sartorial gaffe (Fairchild, 1989, p. 192). Finally, student rioters forced Eisenhower to cancel a trip to Tokyo, an episode he called "the greatest triumph of the communists" during his presidency (Lisagor, 1969, p. 20).

IMPLICATIONS AND CONCLUSION

McGee's fragmentation thesis and McKerrow's critical rhetoric perspective proved to be viable platforms from which to expose presidential photo-ops as rhetorically crafted ideological texts. In the spirit of these orientations, presidential images were positioned as discourse fragments symbolizing ideological power. As a critical rhetoric text, this project revealed that performance fragments frequently substitute visual stratagems for leadership, shape hegemonic and ideological power claims, and affix the chief executive to the so-called mythic presidency. Specifically, presidential images were exposed as mystifying political reality, bypassing the public forum, serving partisan interests, and misdirecting the citizenry's attention. I conclude, therefore, that presidents who routinely engage in illusionism govern "on the basis of representation and substitution" (Ellul, 1985, p. 127), a rhetorical practice that numbs the citizenry, dramatizes decision-making, masks authentic voices, exerts political dominance, and usurps the public sphere. As such, performance fragments misdirect, mislead, and/or marginalize citizens as observers of, rather than participants in, the political process (Miroff, 1982). Clearly, such political activity is contrary to the ethical practices of democratic governance (viz., Debord, 1994; Miroff, 1989; Mitchell, 1994; Wise, 1973). This is particularly sobering in light of McGee (cited in Corbin, 1998) who bluntly asserts: "Politics simply isn't informed by ethics any longer" (p. 49).

In addition, this project established that political image-making is tied to the prudential mastery of rhetorical and aesthetic materials. Typically, prudent presidential performance fragments appear natural, improvisational, propitious, and appropriately responsive to mutating rhetorical situations. In time, prudent gestures come to represent a normative "master code for successful performance" (Hariman, 1991, p. 28). Moreover, prudent performances cohere to rhetorical events, instantiate ideological abstractions, legitimate ritual expectations, harmoniously represent the mythic presidency, construct political realities, and reflect the dominant ideology's power structures. Thus, prudence significantly impacts the visual manifestation of ideology, with power emerging as a "byproduct of successful performance" (Hariman, 1991, p. 34).

Solutions? It may be unproductive to speculate about correctives given the media's ferocious appetite for visually arresting images. Moreover, "actions oriented toward change will tend to be conducive to power maintenance rather than to its removal" (McKerrow, p. 94). Indeed, it is unlikely future administrations will refrain from utilizing rhetorical performance fragments as a means of commanding authority and exercising power. However, it is not inconceivable that a media-educated citizenry could deconstruct the physics of performance driven imagery by critically inquiring: "What does this event which we are witnessing really tell us about the president's purpose, his grasp of public affairs, his political skills?" (Miroff, 1989, p. 162). In any event, citizens should hope for that day when responsible journalists will tire of broadcasting shallow, self-serving, and/or deceptive performance fragments. Overdue, such reporters would dramatically assert themselves as neither coddlers of, nor "megaphones for, the man in the Oval Office" (George Reedy, cited in Thompson, 1983, p. 98).

Several observations regarding a critical rhetoric analysis of visual fragments emerged as a result of this project. Hariman (1995) correctly observes that "standards for appropriate performance [are] always negotiated through performance" (p. 74). That is, prudent performatives are neither rule bound nor subject to systematization. Methodologically, therefore, the critic should avoid analyzing performance fragments utilizing a template or formulaic mind-set. Performance fragments must be assembled and contextualized to appreciate fully their ideological underpinnings. Likewise, presidential performance fragments have multiple and sometimes nonapparent rhetorical objectives. Thus, a critic may misread or fail to unpack an image's ideological implications. Prudent stratagems if perceived as politically authentic may escape critical observation. Johnson's tearful address to Congress upon the assassination of Kennedy, for example, described the fallen president as a visionary whose dreams for America would be made manifest under his administration (Johnson, 1971). Critically, the President also articulated the nation's core values, beliefs, and strengths, an ideological move that disguised his true feelings toward Kennedy, comforted a grieving nation, and maintained ideological continuity. Too, a president's motives are inevitably complex (fiscally, psychologically, politically, militarily) and infrequently self-revealing. At times, therefore, imputing subtly disguised motives to a chief executive's performances may border on noetic criticism, especially attempts to tease out discrete rhetorical motives where none is intended. In addition, citizens respond polysemously—uniquely—to aesthetic performance fragments. For example, when Carter taught Sunday school, media critics both scoffed at his phoniness and praised his sincerity (Shogon, 1977). Therefore, interpreting spectator responses offers "no *certainties*," only critical "*possibilities*" (Gray, 1989, p. 344).

Similarly, aesthetic displays are difficult to capture as performance standards are neither fixed nor universal, but temporally contingent. In short, a presidential performance witnessed *now* as a prudent gesture may be critiqued, after-the-fact, as deceitful, shallow, or rhetorically puzzling. Clinton, for example, dramatically pointed his index finger at the American public and tersely snapped: "I did not have sexual relations with that woman. . . ." (Lacazo, 1998, p. 38). Perceived by many as an authentic performance, accusations of sexual infidelity temporarily subsided. Not until the veil of illusionism was lifted, did the public grasp the deceptiveness of the President's performance. Thus, Clinton's confession regarding Monica Lewinsky collided head-on with values associated with the mythic

presidency. Indeed, citizens accustomed to a self-assured Clinton were unsettled when he "dropped the mask" to reveal "the real Bill" (Noonan, 1998, p. 36). Similarly, a performance fragment dismissed as mere performance may fail to recognize the cultural force of ideology. Reagan, for example, announced a tax reform proposal in Williamsburg as its visual images suggested a "new American Revolution" (Kernell, 1986, p. 3). Newscasts redounded with images of horse drawn carriages, period costumes, militia men, and colonial flags. Why? Because such imagery triggers cultural memories and values that reify ideology. In short, witnesses are aesthetically moved by the clangor and symbols of nationalism.

Additionally, a critic must be alert to the power implications of performance fragments that seemingly aid, comfort, assist, or otherwise benefit the spectator. It is, after all, "equally the case that power is not only repressive but potentially productive [helpful]. . . ." (McKerrow, 1989, 101). Note Noonan's (1990) affectionate description of how, at a memorial service, Reagan embraced the relatives of 248 soldiers who had lost their lives in a transport aircraft mishap: "Reagan embodied; he became the nation holding you, he was the nation hugging you back, and there was nothing phony about it, nothing [imprudent]" (p. 262). His Commander-In-Chief performance helped ease the pain of the Christmas tragedy. By contrast, presidents routinely take advantage of horrific events to establish dominance and authority. Chief executives visit "disaster sites to dramatize, in *deus ex machina* fashion, empathy and the healing resources of government" (Erickson, 1998, p. 148). Reagan, for example, passed sandbags at a Louisiana flood site for only 11 minutes before retreating to high ground—time enough, though, to make the evening news (Spear, 1984, p. 17). Moreover, a president's decision *not* to create a performance fragment may have ideological or power implications. Bush, for example, elected not to visit Valdez, Alaska, an oil spill site. Although Bush cited a busy schedule, one pundit allowed that "planting trees makes a better picture than holding up dead otters" (Dowd, 1989, p. A16).

In addition, critics are cautioned against rendering unidimensional or bipolar critical judgments (e.g., power/powerless; freedom/dominance; hegemonic/concordant) as politics is almost never black or white. Clearly, ideology interpenetrates society by exerting its force variously and by degree through gender, race, economic status, affiliation, and a multitude of social issues and policies (Minogue, 1985). Moreover, it cannot be argued that spectators are consistently mesmerized by, or surrender their critical judgment to performance fragments. Nor should we forget that citizens *expect* a president to perform the rituals and routines of centralized authority and governance. For example, Johnson's somber and physically demanding walk behind the horse drawn caisson holding Kennedy's casket (from the Capitol to Arlington National Cemetery) reassured mourners by giving resonance to the continuity of political order (Goldman, 1969). [Deeply touched, the former First Lady thanked him for his bravery and thoughtfulness (Kennedy, 1963).] Finally, performance fragments lend themselves to polysemous critical interpretations. For example, Johnson's aforementioned center-stage walk can be read alternatively as a strategic ploy, simply a display of newly assumed authority. Critically speaking, therefore, mapping the intentions of ideological representations requires keen judgment and discernment.

Finally, as demonstrated by this project, performance fragments may be judged ethical or unethical. A critic essentially judges whether a performance fragment takes authenticity or verisimilitude as an end. That is, does the imaged representation reflect reality or simply the appearance of truth? Is it an authentic representation or a rhetorically crafted fiction? Nixon, for example, helped stem a public outcry by personally inspecting a Santa Barbara oil spill. Although audiences witnessed footage of a sparkling clean beach, it had been "cleaned especially for the event, while miles of beach to the north and south remained hopelessly blackened" (Bennett, 1983, p. 47). Similarly, performance fragments often suppress a president's authentic voice or persona. This is significant insofar as the self-portrait of dominant authorities is "designed to be impressive, to affirm and naturalize the power of dominant elites, and to conceal or euphemize the dirty linen of their rule" (Scott, 1990, p. 18). Critical analyses may reveal a president's

moral choices and political judgments regarding the arts of domination.

Social critics may wish to explore additional means of reading performance fragments. For example, Cloud (1994) would have social critics "seek out counter-ideological information and perspectives whose contradictions with the prevailing constructions of 'reality' expose those constructions as mystifications" (p. 157). Similarly, Greene (1998) argues for a new materialist rhetoric that abandons "a logic of representation for a logic of articulation" (p. 21). Too, drawing parallels between visual imagery and language may sponsor an Althusserian (1971) interpellation critique. Finally, a critique of concordance may judge multi-vocal accommodation accomplished through presidential dramas by "maximiz[ing] the different categories located in the discourse and then . . . recontextualiz[ing] them" (Condit, 1994, pp. 212–213). Regardless of one's critical stance, however, presidential rhetoric's visual turn offers the social critic ample ideological fragments to critique.

Future projects scholars may wish to pursue include: (1) citizen sensitivity to the rhetorical implications of political illusionism; (2) authentic and nonauthentic performative voices; (3) performatives and the privileging of power and ideology; (4) aesthetic implications of prudence and decorum; (5) critical correctives that warn or educate the citizenry to the dangers of mediated illusionism. Scholarship exploring these issues should advance significantly our appreciation and understanding of presidential rhetoric's visual turn. As Butler (1997) notes, the politics of performatives "offers an unanticipated political future for deconstructive thinking" (p. 118).

In conclusion, numerous scholars caution against the political dangers of deriving reality from visual representations, the consequences of which may be the creation of a "culture of images, a society of the spectacle, a world of semblances and simulacra" (Mitchell, 1994, p. 157; Debord, 1994; Miroff, 1989; Polan, 1986). Such an eventuality is possible, they contend, because the public is largely "unaware of [the president's] ontological status as *image*" (Goethals, 1978, p. 26). Unfortunately, few citizens critically discern the symbolic from the real, nor do they willingly surrender visually acquired perceptions of political reality. Indeed, presidential rhetoric's visual turn provides many spectators political satisfaction and reassurance. Citizens, it seems, are as likely as not to applaud felicitous visual stratagems. Interestingly, the polity do not want their president to perform the presidency poorly, seemingly even if such actions adversely affect democratic processes. Critics quick to label performance fragments illusionist rhetoric, therefore, may encounter public resistance insofar as "discrediting an image may actually strengthen its acceptance" (Bennett, 1983, p. 56). Thus, critics of presidential rhetoric's visual turn should construct prudent texts mindful of this irony of the postmodern condition.

REFERENCES

A new round of musical chairs claims Mike Deaver. (1985, April 15). *People, 23,* p. 24.

Alter, J. (1993, Nov. 1). Less profile, more courage. *Newsweek, 122,* p. 33.

Althusser, L. (Ed.). (1971). Ideology and ideological state apparatuses. (B. Brewster, Trans.). In L. Althusser (Ed.), *Lenin and philosophy and other essays* (pp. 127–186). New York: Monthly Review Press.

Austin, J. L. (1975). *How to do things with words.* Cambridge: Harvard University Press.

Barnes, J. A. (1995, May 28). Photo-op cops. *The American Spectator, 28,* pp. 50–51.

Bennett, W. L. (1983). *News: The politics of illusion.* New York: Longman.

Bierman, J. (1990, Dec. 3). Talking turkey. *Maclean's, 103,* pp. 24–25.

Birnbaum, J. H. (1993, March 9). The presidential style is exuberant, informal and totally in control. *Wall Street Journal,* pp. Al; A6.

Broder, D. (1990, Sept. 13). Bush's vacation won't matter unless Persian Gulf policy fails. *Austin American-Statesman,* p. A4.

Burke, K. (1931/1969). *Counter-statement.* Berkeley, CA: University of California Press.

Bush refuses to apologize in Rio. (1992, June 13). *Austin American-Statesman,* p. A17.

Butler, J. (1997). '*Excitable speech': A politics of the performative.* New York: Routledge.

Carney, J. (1995, May 1). Measure of a president. *Time, 145,* pp. 65–66.

Carter, J. (1982). *Keeping faith: Memoirs of a president.* New York: Bantam Books.

Casserly, J. J. (1977). *The Ford White House: The diary of a speech-writer.* Boulder, CO: Colorado Associated University Press.

Chesebro, J. W. (1989). Text, narration, and media. *Text and Performance Quarterly, 9,* 1–23.

Clift, E., & Hosenball, M. (1994, Jan. 10). Shooting down birds—and rumors. *Newsweek, 123,* p. 25.

Clinton opens school doors for Little Rock Nine on 40th anniversary. (1997, Oct. 13). *Jet, 92,* p. 4+.

Cloud, D. L. (1994). The materiality of discourse as oxymoron: A challenge to critical rhetoric. *Western Journal of Communication, 58,* 141–163.

Combs, J. E. (1980). *Dimensions of political drama.* Santa Monica, CA: Goodyear.

Condit, C. M. (1994). Hegemony in a mass-mediated society: Concordance about reproductive technologies. *Critical Studies in Mass Communication, 11,* 205–230.

Corbin, C. (Ed.) (1998). *Rhetoric in postmodern America: Conversations with Michael Calvin McGee.* New York: Guilford Press.

Cos, G. C., & Schatz, R. T. (1998). A communist and a court's decision: The social construction of flag worship argumentation and Chief Justice Rehnquist's dissent in Texas v. Johnson. *Free Speech Yearbook, 36,* 38–51.

Culvert, D. (1983). Presidential images. *Wilson Quarterly, 7,* 158–167.

Dayan, D., & Katz, E. (1991). *Media events: The live broadcasting of history.* Cambridge, MA: Harvard University Press.

Debord, G. (1994). *The society of the spectacle.* M. Imrie (Trans.). New York: Zone Books.

Denton, R. E., Jr., & Hahn, D. F. (1986). *Presidential communication: Analysis and description.* New York: Praeger.

Destler, I. M., Gelb, L. H., & Lake, A. (1984). *Our own worst enemy: The unmasking of American foreign policy.* New York: Simon & Schuster.

Dowd, M. (1989, Sept. 25). Bush as U.N.'s host with the most. *New York Times,* p. A16.

Edelman, M. (1985). *The symbolic uses of politics.* Chicago: University of Chicago Press.

Ellul, J. (1985). *The humiliation of the word.* Grand Rapids, MI: William B. Eerdmans.

Erickson, K. V. (1998). Presidential spectacles: Travel and the rhetoric of political illusionism. *Communication Monographs, 65,* 141–153.

Fairchild, J. (1989). *Chic savages.* New York: Simon and Schuster.

Farrell, T. B. (1989). Media rhetoric as social drama: The winter Olympics. *Critical Studies in Mass Communication, 6,* 156–182.

Farrell, T. B. (1993). *Norms of rhetorical culture.* New Haven: Yale University Press.

Gerstenzang, J., & Goldberg, C. (1992, Dec. 31). Bush, Yeltsin to sign arms pact. *Los Angeles Times,* p. A12.

Goethals, G. (1978). Sacred-secular icons. In R. B. Browne & M. Fishwick (Eds.), *Icons of America* (pp. 24–34). Bowling Green, OH: Popular Press.

Going fishing. (1992, Aug. 10). *New Yorker, 68,* pp. 22–24.

Goldman, E. F. (1969). *The tragedy of Lyndon Johnson.* New York: Alfred A. Knopf.

Gray, P. H. (1989). Performance, postmodernism, and politics. *Text and Performance Quarterly, 9,* 342–347.

Greene, R. W. (1998). Another materialist rhetoric. *Critical Studies in Mass Communication, 15,* 21–40.

Grief analysis. (1996, April 22). *Time, 147,* p. 24.

Handelman, D. (1990). *Models and mirrors: Toward an anthropology of public events.* Cambridge: Cambridge University Press.

Hariman, R. (1991). Critical rhetoric and postmodern theory. *Quarterly Journal of Speech, 77,* 67–70.

Hariman, R. (1991). Prudence/performance. *Rhetoric Society Quarterly, 21,* 26–35.

Hariman, R. (1995). *Political style: The artistry of power.* Chicago: University of Chicago Press.

Hart, R. P. (1994). *How television charms the modern voter.* New York: Oxford University Press.

Hart, R. P. (1987). *The sound of leadership: Presidential communication in the modern age.* Chicago: University of Chicago Press.

Hartmann, R. T. (1980). *Palace politics: An inside account of the Ford years.* New York: McGraw-Hill.

Holmes, C. W. (1994, Oct. 28). Clinton drops out of tour of Jerusalem. *Austin American-Statesman,* p. A12.

How Bush won: The inside story of the campaign. (1988, Nov. 21). *Time, 132,* pp. 8–18+.

Howard, L., & Cerio, G. (1993, Feb. 1). The inaugural moments you may have missed. *Newsweek, 121,* p. 8.

Hymes, D. (1975). *Folklore: Performance and communication.* The Hague: Mouton.

Jacoby, J. (1997, June 7). Read his lips . . . for a price. *Austin American-Statesman,* p. A14.

Jamieson, K. H. (1988). *Eloquence in an electronic age: The transformation of political speech making.* New York: Oxford University Press.

Javetski, B., & Fly, R. (1989, July 17). A July surprise for Gorby? *Business Week,* pp. 60–62.

Johnson, L. B. (1971). *The vantage point: Perspectives of the presidency.* New York: Holt, Rinehart, and Winston.

Keen, J. (1992, Sept. 22). Wheedling, needling on tracks of Bush trip. *USA Today,* p. Al 1.

Kennedy, J. B. (1963, Nov. 25). Letter to Lyndon Johnson [Framed Wall Exhibit, Main Gallery]. Lyndon B. Johnson Presidential Library, Austin, TX.

Kernell, S. (1986). *Going public: New strategies of presidential leadership.* Washington, DC: Congressional Quarterly Press.

Kertzer, D. I. (1988). *Ritual, politics, and power.* New Haven, CT: Yale University Press.

Kiefer, F. (1998, June 19). Clinton as a pacesetter of presidents. *Christian Science Monitor,* pp. Al; A4.

Kissinger, H. A. (1979). *White House years.* Boston: Little, Brown and Company.

Kittle, R. A. (1982, Dec. 13). Reagan's Latin tour . . . Mostly on plus side. *U.S. News & World Report, 93,* pp. 63–64.

Kondracke, M. (1982, July 5). Speech, speech! Author, author! *New Republic, 187,* pp. 21–25.

Krammer, M. (1993, May 31). It's the job, stupid. *Time, 141,* p. 23.

Kritzman, L. D. (Ed.). (1990). *Michael Foucault, politics, philosophy, culture: Interviews and other writings, 1977–1984.* New York: Routledge.

Kuper, H. (1972). The language of sites in the politics of space. *American Anthropologist, 74,* 411–425.

Kuypers, J. A. (1996). *Doxa* and a critical rhetoric: Accounting for the rhetorical agent. *Communications Quarterly, 44,* 452–462.

Lacazo, R. (1998, Aug. 24). When is sex not 'sexual relations.' *Time, 152,* p. 38.

Lammers, W. W. (1982). Presidential attention-focusing activities. In D.A. Graber (Ed.), *The president & the public* (pp. 145–171). Philadelphia, PA: Institute for the Study of Human Issues.

Lanham, R. (1976). *The motives of eloquence: Literary rhetoric in the renaissance.* New Haven, CT: Yale University Press.

Lapham, L. H. (1992, March). Journey to the East. *Harper's, 284,* pp. 7–10.

Lasky, V. (1979). *Jimmy Carter, the man and the myth.* New York: Richard Marek.

Leff, M. (1984). Decorum and rhetorical interpretation: The Latin humanist tradition and contemporary critical theory. *Vichiana* (pp. 107–126). Napoli: Loffredi Editore.

Lisagor, P. (1969, Sept. 12). The lure of faraway places. *Nation's Business, 73,* pp. 19–20.

Maltese, J. A. (1992). *Spin control: The White House office of communications and the management of presidential news.* Chapel Hill, NC: University of North Carolina Press.

McGee, M. C. (1982). A materialist's conception of rhetoric. In R. E. McKerrow (Ed.), *Explorations in rhetoric: Studies in honor of Douglas Ehninger* (pp. 23–48). Glenview, IL: Scott Foresman.

McGee, M. C. (1984). Another philippic: Notes on the ideological turn in criticism. *Central States Communication Journal, 35,* 43–50.

McGee, M. C. (1990). Text, context, and the fragmentation of contemporary culture. *Western Journal of Communication, 54,* 274–289.

McKerrow, R. E. (1989). Critical rhetoric: Theory and praxis. *Communication Monographs, 56,* 91–112.

Messaris, P. (1994). *Visual literacy: Image, mind, and reality.* Boulder, CO: Westview.

Meyrowitz, J. (1985). *No sense of place: The impact of electronic media on social behavior.* New York: Oxford University Press.

Minogue, K. R. (1985). *Alien powers: The pure theory of ideology.* New York: St. Martin's Press.

Miroff, B. (1982). Monopolizing the public space: The president as a problem for democratic politics. In T. Cronin (Ed.), *Rethinking the presidency* (pp. 218–232). Boston: Little, Brown and Company.

Miroff, B. (1988). The presidency and the public: Leadership as spectacle. In M. Nelson (Ed.), *The presidency and the political system* (2nd ed.) (pp. 271–291). Washington, DC: Congressional Quarterly Press.

Miroff, B. (1989). Secrecy and spectacle: Reflections on the dangers of the presidency. In P. Brace, C. B. Harrington, & G. King (Eds.). *The presidency in American politics* (pp. 151–164). New York: New York University Press.

Mitchell, W. J. T. (1994). *Picture theory.* Chicago: University of Chicago Press.

Morganthtau, T., & DeFrank, T.M. (1982, June 21). The upstaged summit. *Newsweek.* pp. 34–36.

Nimmo, D., & Combs, J. E. (1983). *Mediated political realities.* New York: Longman.

Nixon, R M. (1978). *The memoirs of Richard Nixon.* New York: Grosset and Dunlap.

Noonan, P. (1990). *What I saw at the revolution: A political life in the Reagan era.* New York: Random House.

Noonan, P. (1998, Aug. 31). Why the speech will live in infamy. *Time,* p. 36.

Osborne, J. (1978, July 29). Carter in Germany. *New Republic, 179,* p. 10.

Polan, D. B. (1986). 'Above all else to make you see': Cinema and the ideology of spectacle. In J. Arac (Ed.), *Postmodernism and politics* (pp. 55–69). Minneapolis: University of Minnesota Press.

President Clinton targets lobbyists, says he'll travel more. (1993, May 11). *Austin American-Statesman,* p. Al.

Raphael, T. (1999). The king is a thing: Bodies of memory in the age of Reagan. *The Drama Review: The Journal of Performance Studies, 43,* 46–58.

Regan, D. (1988). *For the record.* New York: Harcourt Brace Jovanovich.

Reagan heads south to mend fences. (1982, Nov. 29). *Business Week, 2767,* p. 55.

Richardson, D. B. (1980, July 7). For Yugoslav leaders: 'Instant stature.' *US. News & World Report, 89,* p. 20.

Roberts, S. V. (1993, May 24). Wanted: A national cheerleader. *U.S. News & World Report, 114,* p. 9.

Rosenfield, S. S. (1969, July 6). Nixon's trip plans may affect talks. *Washington Post,* p. A3.

Schieffer, B., & Gates, P. (1989). *The acting president.* New York: E. P. Dutton.

Schlesinger, A. M., Jr. (1965). *A thousand days: John F. Kennedy in the White House.* Boston: Houghton Mifflin.

Schmuhl, R. (1990). *Statecraft and stagecraft: American political life in the age of personality.* South Bend, IN: University of Notre Dame Press.

Scott, J. C. (1990). *Domination and the arts of resistance.* New Haven, CT: Yale University Press.

Serrill, M. S. (1991, Aug. 12). Tag-team diplomacy. *Time, 138,* p. 24.

Shapiro, J. P. (1993, April 26). Gays march, Clinton balks. *U.S. News & World Report, 114,* p. 20.

Shogon, R. (1977). *Promises to keep: Carter's first hundred days.* New York: Crowell.

Spear, J. C. (1984). *Presidents and the press: The Nixon legacy.* Cambridge, MA: MIT Press.

Stengel, R. (1986, March 3). In Grenada, apolcalypso now. *Time, 127,* pp. 17–18.

Stucky, N. (1993). Toward an aesthetic of natural performance. *Text and Performance Quarterly, 13,*168–180.

Talbot, S. (1991, Aug. 5). Good fellas. *Time, 138,* p. 24.

terHorst, J. F., & Albertazzie, R. (1979). *The flying White House: The story of Air Force One.* New York: Coward, McCann & Geoghegan.

The Clinton Rally. (1998, Feb. 9). *U.S. News & World Report, 124,* pp. 20–24.

Therborn, G. (1980). *The ideology of power and the power of ideology.* London: NLRB.

Thompson, H. S. (1994). *Better than sex: Confessions of a political junkie.* New York: Random House.

Thompson, K. W. (Ed.). (1983). *Three press secretaries on the presidency and the press.* Lanham, MD: University Press of America.

Turner, R. (1976). *I'll never lie to you.* New York: Ballantine Books.

Turque, B., & Rosenstiel, T. (1996, July 15). Turning Clinton green. *Newsweek, 128,* p. 26.

Villa, D. R. (1993). Postmodernism and the public sphere. In F. M. Dolan & T. L. Dumm (Eds.) *Rhetorical republic* (pp. 227–248). Amherst, MA: University of Massachusetts Press.

Walsh, C. (1997, June 2–14). Perspectives. *America, 176,* p. 6.

Walsh, K. T. (1994, June 20). Rediscovering his father's generation. *U. S. News & World Report, 116,* pp. 12–13.

Walsh, K. T. (1994, Sept. 19). Pitchmen in angry times. *US. News & World Report, 117,* p. 40.

West, D. M. (1983). Constituency and travel allocations in the 1980 presidential campaign. *American Journal of Political Science, 27,*515–529.

White, E. C. (1987). *Kaironomia: The will-to-invent.* Ithaca, NY: Cornell University Press.

Wines, M. (1992, June 12). Protests disrupt Bush's Panama visit. *Austin American-Statesman,* pp. Al, A9.

Wise, D. (1973). *Lying: Government deception, secrecy, and power.* New York: Random House.

19

MEDIATING HILLARY RODHAM CLINTON

Television News Practices and Image-Making in the Postmodern Age

SHAWN J. PARRY-GILES

Politics in the postmodern media age is a struggle over images (Mitchell, 1994). That struggle forms political reality (Meyrowitz, 1985), as the media mediates the "cultural norms of the postmodern age" (Gold & Speicher, 1995, p. 95). According to Baty (1995), "mass mediated remembrances [act] as the common grounds of political cultural residence" (p. 43). Yet when we consume these televisual images, which Stephens (1998) depicts as "a magic that may come to dwarf . . . other forms of communication" (p. 7), we are invited, via the medium itself, to forget their mediated form (Hart, 1994).

Because of the near invisibility of mediation, scholars often overlook its role in the image-making process. In the scholarship about First Lady Hillary Rodham Clinton (HRC),[1] for example, many writers reduce HRC's image-making failures and successes to her own personality or personal style. Offering such an explanation for HRC's image deficiencies, Campbell (1998) concludes that "Clinton's style of public advocacy typically omits virtually all of the discursive markers by which women publicly enact their femininity" (p. 6). Viewing HRC's image more affirmatively, Muir and Benitez (1996) attribute "positive response[s]" to her own personal attributes, heralding the "charismatic nature of her interactions with audiences" (p. 153). Although acknowledging that the news narratives contain images of women ideologically, Brown (1997) nevertheless ignores the full complexity of mediation practices as she, like the others, holds HRC primarily responsible for her own image construction. According to Brown, "one reason for the instability of Hillary Clinton's television image is her refusal to be silenced" (p. 255).

What such explanations lack is a recognition of the media's role in the complex process of image-making. While HRC, her handlers, and

SOURCE: Parry-Giles, S. J. (2000). Mediating Hillary Rodham Clinton: Television news practices and image-making in the postmodern age. *Critical Studies in Media Communication, 17*(2), 205–226. © National Communication Association.

375

her political enemies contribute to her image, the media's role in that image-making process is rendered invisible or reduced to the stereotypical portrayal of women in the news (Jamieson, 1995). As Vavrus (1998) asserts, "analyses of political rhetoric can be rather anachronistic; often it is inattentive to its mediated forms—as if speeches were typically experienced first-hand, without broadcast or print mediation" (p. 216). Certainly, for most of us, the way in which we "know" Hillary Rodham Clinton is through mediated discourse.

Thus, this study moves beyond the media stereotypes of HRC and addresses how the production practices of television news influence image-making. Although beginning with a review of the stereotypes of HRC in television news, the essay moves on to demonstrate how the visual decontextualization and recontextualization practices of television news editors influence HRC's image. This essay then analyzes the intricacies of the camera strategies involved in covering HRC, which create a more interpersonally-intimate portrayal of the First Lady. Next, this work assesses the role of repetition in reinscribing a reductionistic image of HRC over time and across news networks—practices grounded in economic incentives and product promotion. Such an analysis reveals the ways in which the mediation practices of television news naturalize HRC's image, resulting in a more dominant and evolving collective memory of someone who has been called one of the "most loved and hated presidential wives in American history" (Gould, 1996, p. 641).

TYPECASTING THE FIRST LADY

Much has been written about the news media's reliance on stereotypes in its coverage (Bennett & Edelman, 1985; Gans, 1979; Warnick, 1998). Such an interest in mediated stereotypes merges with a curiosity over first lady archetypes (Gould, 1989) to produce an abundance of attention on the stereotypical images of Hillary Rodham Clinton. In examining the polysemic (i.e., the ideologically complex and conflicting) images of HRC, evidence from three biographical narratives of the current First Lady that were produced by three television networks (CNN,

ABC, and MSNBC) in 1996 and 1998 will be explored. This essay also extends the analysis to include additional network stories surrounding HRC's reactions to President Clinton's August 17th, 1998, confessional.[2] From 1992 to the present, the images of Hillary Rodham Clinton are varied and at times antithetical; HRC is depicted as a career woman turned feared feminist, a sometimes all-powerful First Lady who becomes a more traditional "good mother," and a "stand by your man" wife who is victimized by a cheating husband. As HRC's image shifts from a strong, independent feminist to a good mother and sympathetic wife/victim, her public opinion ratings improve (Burrell, 1997; Jamieson, 1995).

The Many Images of HRC

In the television texts under review, HRC's image centers on her unusual success, first as a student, and then as a lawyer. In an October 18th, 1996, *Nightline* feature on HRC (and Elizabeth Dole), ABC reporter Jeff Greenfield notes that after giving the first student-delivered commencement address at Wellesley College, "a lot of people thought they were looking if not at the future president, at least at a future Senator" (Two women, 1996). Offering a similar construction of HRC's school days, NBC reporter Jamie Gangel asserts in an MSNBC feature on August 4, 1998, that "as an honor student at Wellesley, [HRC's] friends thought she might be the first woman president" (*Time & Again,* 1998). Kathy Slobogin, journalist for CNN, celebrates HRC's professional accomplishments differently in an October 13, 1996, feature, talking about her early work on the "Congressional committee investigating the impeachment of Richard Nixon, one of three women attorneys chosen" (They don't bake . . . , 1996).

ABC's *Nightline* also relies on stereotypical images of feminism in depicting HRC. As Jeff Greenfield reports, HRC represents "a symbol of hard-edge feminism" when she remarked that she chose to practice law rather than to stay home and bake cookies. Continuing, Greenfield explains that for many, HRC and feminism served as an "embodiment of all that was wrong with the sixties" (Two women, 1996). Not surprisingly, HRC personifies feminism, reflecting the media's role in forming a less than positive image of that political construct (Farrell, 1995; Rhode, 1995).

CNN, ABC, and MSNBC also promulgate the stereotype that powerful women are to be feared, a view that is accented by occasional unnamed, unseen voices that heighten the mystery surrounding this seemingly frightening woman. As Bernard Shaw introduces the CNN broadcast entitled, "They don't bake cookies anymore," he explicitly articulates concern over powerful women by claiming, "Americans have a hard time accepting power in the hands of the First Lady." Within that same CNN story, an unidentified and unpictured male quips that HRC's "been portrayed as sort of the boss's wife from hell" (They don't bake . . . , 1996), a cultural cliché that reifies women's private role as wife and the dangerous and mysterious power behind the public man. For the other features, the language likewise connotes a sense of fear. In MSNBC's hour-long feature on HRC, various NBC reporters refer to her as a "political weapon," "high octane Hillary," and a "political animal" (*Time & Again,* 1998). A similar image is also perpetuated in the CNN broadcast when Bernard Shaw refers to HRCs "power monger" persona (They don't bake . . . , 1996). Most significantly, Chris Bury from ABC's *Nightline* refers to Elizabeth Dole as the "anti-Hillary," or the "un-Hillary," and Jeff Greenfield equates HRC with "the political equivalent [of] nitroglycerin" (Two women, 1996). Although the three networks use different means—from explosives to weapons to *ad hominem* attacks—they all communicate the commonplace that power in the hands of women is frightening (i.e., nitroglycerin) (Campbell, 1996).

Creating the sort of "double bind" for women that Jamieson (1995) addresses, the television news texts combine a rhetoric of fear surrounding powerful women with a gendered discourse on first ladies. Images of nitroglycerin thus are juxtaposed with "traditional" first lady images, including metaphors involving lace and high heels. CNN reporter Kathy Slobogin, for example, reveals how praise for HRC is simultaneously "laced with danger" (They don't bake. . . . 1996), furthering the image that in spite of any feminine pretense, women in power are still to be feared. Within such a phrase, the juxtaposition of danger with lace epitomizes the double bind for women

who become so powerful that they lose their femininity. In a different kind of double bind, Bernard Shaw juxtaposes HRC with Elizabeth Dole. According to Shaw, "Elizabeth Dole is high heels above the rest. She was breaking glass ceilings before Hillary Clinton even bumped her head on them" (They don't bake . . . , 1996). Although the networks acknowledge both women's career accomplishments, such achievements are contextualized in very gendered terms. Such messages remind all that even in the work place, high heels represent a standard form of measurement for women, emphasizing that women in power are still judged by feminine prescriptions. The specific language of the television newsmakers functions thus at a more subtle level of image construction (Edelman, 1988).

Early in Bill Clinton's first presidential term, HRC's image defies traditional conceptions of the first lady (Winfield, 1997), as she is equated with images of feminism, power, and fear. However, as her attempts to reform health care failed and she faced allegations concerning Whitewater, the White House associated the First Lady more with children's issues (Farrell, 1995; Muir & Benitez, 1996), constructing a "good mother" image for HRC. ABC's Jeff Greenfield, for example, interviews a Washington Bureau Chief from the *New York Times,* to portray the First Lady as someone who "stays at home, cares for children, cares about her daughter, who she clearly does care about" (Two women, 1996). Although such a comment is not that notable, keep in mind that the "good father" image is not featured in this story, equating instead a "good mother" vision with the office of the First Lady. ABC likewise emphasizes the presence of HRC's "good mother" image, as an unidentified and unpictured woman is overheard stating: "Being [a] mother is extremely important to this woman," a phrase that is juxtaposed in the introduction with images of HRC in a power position (Two women, 1996). HRC's handlers, her friends, and the news stations thus reassure the American public that HRC represents the "good mother" stereotype, revealing the manner in which women must continually negotiate the tasks of motherhood and career. Such a focus on motherhood, though, is not at all surprising; "the central icon of the caring person within western culture is the figure of the mother" (Macdonald, 1995, p. 133).

Offering reassurances of the First Lady as a "good mother," HRC's image also evolves into one of a supportive wife, especially in light of Bill Clinton's extramarital activities. Although HRC's comment that she is not "some little woman standing by my man like Tammy Wynette" evidences "hard-edged feminism" for Jeff Greenfield (Two women, 1996), that same phrase epitomizes her response/non-response to Clinton's affairs for journalists in 1998. Throughout the MSNBC feature, journalists continually refer to HRC as "standing by her man" during the Clinton-Lewinsky scandal. In the same story, *Today* anchor Matt Lauer labels HRC the most "credible defender" of her husband. Gwen Ifill, another narrator in the feature, speaks of HRC's image as that of her husband's "helpmate" more than his "co-president" (*Time & Again,* 1998).

HRC's image, as construed by her own handlers and portrayed by the news media, thus, evolves greatly from early 1992 through 1998. Unlike 1992, victimage images are now much more prevalent in the coverage of HRC. During the MSNBC feature, NBC's news anchor Tom Brokaw announces the allegations of Independent Council Kenneth Starr's office during the January 22, 1998, broadcast. Introducing the segment, Brokaw states, "When a story of this magnitude and this nature explodes across the public landscape, a lot of people are affected, even wounded. Families, wives, the First Lady" (*Time & Again,* 1998). In a separate MSNBC story of August 18, 1998, the day after Clinton's confessional, the theme centers on HRC's "humiliation" in combination with her desire to keep her family together (First lady committed, 1998). In a special story about women who stay with men who cheat, ABC News reporter Jan M. Faust (1998) discusses multiple reasons why women remain, including denial, sadomasochism, and the need to be emotional caretakers or to defend their husbands in the face of heightened criticism. The title of this Internet article is "Standing by their men: Women in the trenches."

Despite the shift in HRC's image from that of successful but feared career woman, to a "stand by your man" kind of First Lady, her critics continue to raise questions about her political motives. In a separate MSNBC story from August 15, 1998, John Palmer comments, "one often hears speculation from those outside the White House that Hillary Clinton's bond with the president is more political than personal, that the couple have a common love for public policy matters that transcends their personal relationship." Thus, even in the context of the Clinton-Lewinsky scandal, the polysemic nature of HRC's image is still visible.

Overall, such images remain more negative than positive. While the journalists acknowledge her educational and career successes, fear and skepticism pervade HRC's stories. As her approval ratings improve (Milton, 1999), she becomes trapped by more traditional images of the first lady. The polysemic nature of HRC's image is not that surprising; Fishburn (1982) contends that images of women in the media range "from the idealized lady of exemplary tastes and behavior to the terrible mother who would destroy us all" (p. 3). These images are obviously influenced by not only the television news coverage but also by HRC herself, White House handlers, and HRC's political enemies. The television news texts promulgate such images. Most importantly, though, these stereotypical images become more salient when examined in relation to the visual representations that help naturalize them.

LAYERS OF SELECTIVITY AND CONTEXTUALIZATION

Much has been written about the agenda-setting function of the news, particularly in relation to the institutional practices that impact the selection of news stories (McCombs & Shaw, 1972). This notion of selection represents a much more complex process than the earliest research on agenda-setting revealed. Beginning with the selection of which issues to cover, multiple layers of selectivity exist for television news organizations. Once a television news network decides to do a story on Hillary Rodham Clinton, for example, those involved must decide which contexts they wish to feature in their story about HRC. On location, a journalist then selects which part of the event(s) to emphasize within the story. Camera operators are also involved in the selection process as they film certain shots of HRC as well as other aspects of the environment (i.e., audience members). Back in the studio, journalists and editors then develop a story about HRC, selecting images from the available footage that exemplifies their narrative. For the texts under review for this essay, an additional layer of selectivity is added. When completing a biographical piece on HRC, the producers select footage from numerous stories on HRC. All of this material is then streamlined into a historical exposé. By the time a piece like CNN's "They don't bake cookies anymore" is aired, CNN's editors and journalists have progressed through multiple layers of the selection process.

This selectivity, though, is largely invisible to the uncritical viewer (Bennett & Edelman, 1985). As Hart (1994) explains, "Television asks us to forget that its pictures have been selected from among an infinite number of alternative images, alternative news frames, alternative camera angles, and alternative dramatis personae" (p. 66). Not only is the selection process rendered virtually invisible, the documentary-style story assumes an aura of realism. Explaining the relationship between selection and realism, Mander (1987) argues that news reporters "pretend to reflect social reality, but in fact offer selected interpretations of discrete events and in so doing reinforce modern empirical prejudice that reality is knowable and coherent" (pp. 54–55). The effect of such presentational forms and selection processes results in what Ellis (1992) calls "the constitution of events for a particular form of comprehension, and the production of a particular point of view for the spectator" (p. 19).

Nowhere is the impact of selectivity clearer than in the visual choices made by television news organizations. For television news, Gunter (1987) maintains that pictures have priority and words are often "built around" visuals (p. 171). The alleged higher order of the visual over the verbal may be explained by the assumption that "moving pictures" represent "actuality" for the journalist because such pictures are believed to "convey the truth in a way best suited to the medium" (Schlesinger, 1978, p. 128). Many like Snyder (1980) critique such visual realism, arguing that "the picture does not provide a 'copy of an appearance,' nor does it attempt to duplicate vision or even to suggest how we might have seen what is shown" (p. 228). The constructed nature of photographs/videotape

images (Jamieson & Campbell, 1983), however, does not lessen their impact or memorability (Graber, 1990; Barnhurst & Wartella, 1998). As Messaris (1992) contends, visuals "convey a message which would probably not go over at all well if it were made verbally" (p. 191). In the end, media visuals reflect the overall norms of news networks, dramatic and deviant stories as well as issues of on-going interest.

Within this section, this essay turns attention away from the verbal to the visual text and examines the photographs and videotaped footage that accompany the verbal messages about HRC.[3] Although HRC and her staff may stage events that accent positive visual coverage of the First Lady, the news media wield significant control over the meaning and use of that visual discourse. Because the visuals become evidence for the news media's contentions and are less subject to ethical standards, the media are primary arbiters of meaning (Messaris, 1997). Journalists achieve this epistemological and ideological role by creating referents for the visuals. First, visuals are decontextualized from their original stories and then recontextualized within alternate stories to substantiate the contentions of journalists.

Visual Evidence

In examining how the visuals reinforce or stand in for the narrative (Barnhurst & Wartella, 1998), I return to the earlier discussion of stereotypes. When discussing HRC's educational success, all three texts incorporate a still photograph of HRC delivering her Wellesley commencement address, originally published in *Life* magazine (They don't bake. . . . 1996; *Time & Again,* 1998; Two women, 1996). The visual images for her success as a career woman are not as prevalent. During the MSNBC story on HRC's early legal accolades, the visuals move from the Wellesley photo to a profile picture of Bill and Hillary Clinton looking into each other's eyes and smiling. Noticeably absent is a visual image of HRC's career achievements in CNN's story. Instead of such positive images, CNN showcases journalist Kathy Slobogin's presence in the story (They don't bake . . . , 1996). Similarly, Jeff Greenfield is shown talking with Ted Koppel after HRC's story airs when the former reviews HRC's accomplishments (Two women, 1996). Again, no images of HRC are provided here to illustrate her positive attributes.

Conversely, the visual images for the negative attributes of HRC's image generally reinforce such negative constructions. In some instances, visual evidence is not offered as with the "anti-Hillary" and "power monger" phrases. In these instances, the words are voiced by the journalists who are pictured on screen (They don't bake . . . , 1996; Two women, 1996). Yet, the news networks are much more likely to evidence the negative stereotypes over the positive ones. Visual evidence for Greenfield's connection of HRC to feminism is accompanied by the HRC interview where she delivers her famous line, "I suppose I could have stayed home and baked cookies . . . ," which is followed by a second infamous quotation, "I'm not sitting here as some little woman standing by my man" (Two women, 1996). When the unidentified male voice equates HRC with the "boss's wife from hell," the accompanying picture features a black and white video shot of HRC speaking to a silent Bill Clinton. Neither are smiling and Bill Clinton is looking away from his wife as she speaks (They don't bake . . . , 1996). A similar kind of visual accompanies Slobogin's "laced with danger" comment in regard to HRC's alleged power in the White House. Again, HRC is talking to her husband. Neither is smiling, and he listens rather expressionlessly. In the end, the video is frozen as it captures both Clintons with a slight, smile on their faces (They don't bake . . . , 1996). Such negative visuals equate HRC's power with talk. HRC talks; Bill Clinton listens, countering the stereotype of women (first ladies) as silent partners (Rhode, 1995).

Not surprisingly, pictorial evidence of HRC's motherhood role and her "standing by her man" image pervade the texts. Many of the photographs show HRC and daughter Chelsea holding hands, hugging, or smiling at one another. In most cases, HRC, not Bill Clinton, is the one engaged in conversation with Chelsea or showing affection to their daughter (They don't bake . . . , 1996; Time & Again, 1998; Two women, 1996). Similarly, pictorial evidence of HRC "standing by her man" is quite predictable. In the September 12, 1998, feature entitled,

"The President and the People," NBC visualizes the "standing by her man" phrase with images of HRC smiling up at her husband adoringly, defending him during the Matt Lauer Today interview in January of 1998, and introducing her husband during a speech that he gave days after the August 17th confessional. In that introduction, HRC states, "I'm proud to introduce my husband, our president." The President and the First Lady are then featured sharing a warm, smiling embrace. Such images are undoubtedly easy to depict because of the archetypal images of motherhood and supportive spouse.

Thus, as the media construct the narrative of HRC, the visual images selected to evidence or reinforce their message are of equal if not more importance. While disagreement exists over whether or not audiences accept and/or reject a news sources' interpretation of an event (Philo, 1990; Robinson & Levy, 1986), many concur that the news industry holds considerable and questionable control over the visuals that air. Even though political figures attempt to control their own image, the image makers (e.g., the television news media) "show us their view of the world whether they mean to or not" by acting as "mediators of information about and images of those parts of society most distant from the lives of the majority" (Gross, Katz, & Ruby, 1988, pp. 18, 27). As Messaris (1997) contends, far less accountability exists for the visual message as compared to the verbal, where there are high expectations for presentational accuracy.

Visual Manipulation

The process of selection takes on a new edge when considering accountability and the use of visual manipulation. In the postmodern age of television, no one referent exists for a photograph or an image in a video segment (Hart, 1994). As a result, the news media wield considerable power in defining the meanings of such visual images, as referents are generated by the signifier (Baudrillard, 1981/1994; Schram, 1991).[4] The news media thus assume considerable authorial influence over the projected "meanings" of such visual discourse. When videotape coverage or a photograph is originally filmed, the visual text is clearly situated within a particular context. Over time, select video footage and photographs of presumably a dramatic nature, are placed in a news organization's video archives, becoming available for the future journalist looking for contemporary visual evidence. These video images or photographs sit decontextualized in video archives. Journalists then take such decontextualized visuals and recontextualize them within a new story. The original meaning is lost and the new context that is depicted by a journalist narrating the story comes to define the referent for the visual text (Hart, 1994; Messaris, 1992).

Such examples of visual recontextualization are difficult to discover without closely examining vast amounts of television news coverage on the same subject over time. One clear example of this practice, though, occurs during the CNN piece about HRC. In the beginning of the feature, Bernard Shaw narrates the introduction while visuals and captions simultaneously appear on the screen. In one clip, the words "WHITEWATER" and "whitewater" are projected on the screen. The visual image that accompanies these captions is of HRC smiling and talking to someone behind her as she sits at a table with a microphone (They don't bake . . . , 1996). The implication is that this is a picture of HRC testifying before the grand jury in the Whitewater investigation. The shot of her laughing likewise implies that she is not taking the situation too seriously. Those who study HRC know, though, that the Whitewater grand jury proceedings were closed to news organizations. The footage shown during this news section derives from HRC's testimony before five congressional committees as head of the President's Task Force on Health Care Reform (King, 1996). Those proceedings were open to the public and are frequently featured in numerous television news accounts. Nevertheless, in the absence of visuals from Whitewater hearings, CNN offers substitute images of a HRC testimony, which stands in for her testimony concerning her own alleged criminal wrongdoing in the Whitewater matter. Other visuals *appear* completely decontextualized as well. For example, during the same CNN story, Slobogin contends that HRC "is a mirror, reflecting our national ambivalence about women's roles." HRC is shown next delivering the famed "I suppose I could have stayed

home . . ." line. Slobogin continues, "and that ambivalence has cost her." The visual image that accompanies Slobogin's last comment is of a group of people holding signs. The sign that is central to the visual reads, "Liar, Liar, Pants on Fire" (They don't bake. . . . 1996). In this scene, the visual implies that the protester's sign is directed toward HRC. Certainly, though, this visual could have been taken from anywhere and the message could be about anyone. Even the camera operator filming the original footage may not know the "intent" of the sign. Thus, CNN clearly creates the referent for the visuals in this feature.

At other times, this seamlessness of the camera editing often conforms to what Messaris (1994) calls "the logic of verbal narration" (p. 18). Within the same CNN broadcast, Slobogin states, "There were other seeds of trouble in Arkansas—trouble with her husband over other women." The first visual evidencing this "trouble" is a black and white photograph of HRC looking down and to her left. She looks perhaps pensive or sad but seems to be watching something to her left intently. The next image is a videotape shot of Bill Clinton dancing with several women (mariachi dancers). Most notably, as he dances with one women, he stares intently at her body (They don't bake . . . , 1996). To begin with, we are led to believe that the pensive look on HRC's face within the black and white photograph is of her thinking about her husband's alleged extramarital activities. The seamless way the shot progresses to one of Bill Clinton dancing furthers the notion that she is actually watching him engage in philandering behavior. The way she looks to her left and the sudden appearance of the video clip further perpetuates a sense that she is on the outside of the event looking in. CNN implies thus that this photograph catches HRC in a scopophilic moment, where we watch her watching him, seemingly unmasking HRC's "staged" persona. Beyond that, the video of Bill Clinton of course stands in for his extramarital activities, which demonstrates again how the television news media supply referents for the visual images.

Most disturbing, though, is a more recent video practice by NBC news. As the news media expend considerable time speculating over HRC's handling of her husband's affair with

Monica Lewinsky, their representatives seek video footage of the First Lady's emotional state. During a September 12, 1998, special broadcast by NBC News entitled, "The President and the People," NBC airs an extremely close facial shot of HRC's profile. In the shot, she appears to be crying or to have recently stopped crying. Jane Pauley narrates:

> Hillary Rodham Clinton knows her husband of 28 years better than anyone. Yet this revelation was news to her too we're told. For most wives the painful details of an affair would be discussed behind closed doors. (The president and the people, 1998)

Like the examples before, NBC creates the referent for this visual as we are led to believe that the close-up shots reflect HRC's emotional reaction to her husband's recent admonition. The video footage, though, is actually derived from the memorial service for those Americans killed in the Tanzania and Kenya Embassy bombings.

C-SPAN aired the ceremony on August 13, 1998, four days before Clinton's confessional. During the ceremony, most of those who spoke also cried, including President Clinton, Secretary of State Madeleine Albright, and Secretary of Defense William Cohen (Ceremony for embassy . . . , 1998). To use HRC's reaction to that ceremony after meeting with the families of loved ones who died in the two African countries, evidences most clearly how the television news media engage in visual manipulation. For NBC, HRC's reactions to the death of the bombing victims stands in for her reaction to her husband's affair as NBC decontextualizes the memorial service close-up shot and recontextualizes it within the Clinton-Lewinsky scandal.

These four examples of the news media's visual manipulation represent a practice that is undoubtedly more widespread than we know. As Messaris (1992) explains, "evidence of rearrangement is not always so obvious" (p. 189). Yet, he contends that this recontextualization practice may be the "most prominent form of visual manipulation" that exists (p. 189)—a practice that allows the television news media to select which images to use in depicting their subjects in questionable ways. Other visual

practices, though, likewise influence image-making, including the use of close-up shots and the positioning of the spectator within the television news visual.

INTERPERSONAL PROXIMITY AND SUBJECT POSITIONING

In attending closely to the television news images, one becomes intrigued by the camera work involved in depicting persons and events. Two prevalent practices are the use of close-up shots and the positioning of the television viewer within the mediated event. This section demonstrates how close-up shots function as the media's way to gauge the honesty of an image-maker. When combined with the interpersonal-conversational dynamics of television news, the camera situates the viewer within mediated conversations, exacerbating the emotional responses we have about the camera's subject (e.g., Hillary Rodham Clinton).

Camera Distancing

As previously explained, audiences generally find visual stimuli more interesting than verbal discourse (Graber, 1990). In order to maintain a viewer's interest, the camera shot tends to be in constant motion; visuals change rapidly through editing, zooming toward or away from the subject, or panning across an image (Messaris, 1992). For MSNBC, as Jane Pauley introduces the segment for *Time & Again* (1998), the camera shot zooms in as she transitions to the feature story. When she prepares the audience for a commercial break, the camera shot distances itself from her. The camera thus functions to draw us into the interaction as the shot moves closer to Pauley, evidencing a strategy of engagement.

This use of mediated proximity creates a sense of intimacy—as television functions as "a delivery system for [such] intimacy" (Hart, 1994, p. 11). Meyrowitz (1982) maintains that "regardless of the size of the image of a person within the television frame, we may react to the picture in terms of distance, not size" (p. 226). The use of close-ups shots of HRC is a common strategy within the television news features. As with all visuals, the close-up shots function as visual evidence. Slobogin of CNN, for example, asserts that HRC "is the least popular First Lady in modern history" (They don't bake . . . , 1996). The visual accompanying this statement is an extreme close-up shot of HRC, which exhibits her face mostly, with only a small portion of her hair visible because of the closeness of the camera's gaze. The black and white photograph that CNN zooms in on for this close-up shot exposes a sad-looking First Lady—a shot again featured without context. In the same story, author Gene Lyons talks about HRC's public relations problems in Arkansas: "A lot of southern women will do their best most of the time to look as good as they can. And a lot of people sort of looked at Hillary with the coke bottle glasses, the unfortunate hairdo and a lot of women just said 'what's wrong with that girl'" (They don't bake . . . , 1996). The accompanying visuals, not surprisingly, showcase HRC with large glasses and with what CNN's producers must have concluded were representations of her "unfortunate hairdo." CNN's camera zooms in on these still photographs to the point of violating any sense of visual privacy. The effect of such visual intrusion though "lures us into believing that we know the people—and hence the women—we invite regularly into our homes" (Jamieson, 1995, p. 145). If these visuals are verbally resituated in a negative context by the journalists, the negative effects are presumably exacerbated by the decreased distance.

Beyond drawing the audience into the story and increasing a sense of "intimacy" for the viewer, such close-ups also serve to test the honesty of the person in question. In the postmodern media age of image-making, the news media are on a continual search for what Schram (1991) depicts as "the real that underlies the appearance" (p. 213). Hunter (1987) attests that the role of photography specifically is to "fix personality, to draw a distinct character from someone's face" (p. 115). The role of the close-up shot helps "fix" that personality. In addition, close-up footage represents an attempt to unmask the image of the image-maker as part of the media's quest for the "real" (Parry-Giles & Parry-Giles, 1999).

In evidencing the "dueling imaging" process (or the competition between HRC's image-making attempts and the news media's mission to capture the real in their own image-making activities), this essay turns to MSNBC's story on the first couple's trustworthiness. In her February 10, 1992, feature on HRC, Jamie Gangel states, "The Clinton strategy—if the American public will trust Hillary Clinton, then maybe they will trust and vote for Bill Clinton" (*Time & Again,* 1998). As Gangel reads this statement, the visual features HRC delivering a speech. Most notably, the camera zooms from a public distance to an intimate one that centers on HRC's face. While the camera operator at the time was probably not attempting to assess HRC's character, those who edited NBC's 1992 story seemingly offered a close-up view of HRC's facial cues in order for the audience to assess her candor. As Graber (1990) maintains, journalists often use close-ups "to permit viewers to make personality judgments" and people often believe that "facial close-ups readily reveal mental states" (p. 138).

In a similar example, CNN uses the close-up shot again as a means to unmask HRC's image. Slobogin states, "Critics say Hillary Clinton has stonewalled, that she gives lawyerly answers rather than candid ones" (They don't bake . . . , 1996). While Slobogin speaks, the camera zooms in on a talking HRC. The camera in these close-up scenes can do what people cannot—enter HRC's intimate space, seemingly penetrating the image-making strategies of people like HRC. Such visual intrusion acts as a mediated character-assessing strategy.[5] Hart (1994) explains that "the character model is ideal for television. With vaults of video footage at their disposal, television producers can find evidence for any claim they might wish to make" (p. 40). Since viewers are instructed to question HRC's image verbally and visually, the audience will most likely oblige and attend to the visual evidence presented. But while attempting to help the audience assess the character and demystify the image, the camera can draw the spectator even further into the conversation.

Spectator Positioning

As Meyrowitz (1982) contends, the "screen becomes an 'extended retina' for the viewer" (226). Because close-up footage creates an intimate distance between the viewer and the object of the camera's eye, the viewer is often situated within the mediated conversation. As Messaris (1994) explains, "it is commonly assumed that because of the real-world association between physical-closeness and psychological intimacy, the audience's sense of intimacy with an on-screen character may be enhanced if that character gets more close-ups" (pp. 32–33). While creating intimacy, such close-up shots also position us within the conversation as the camera's subjects look at us as if we were the recipients of their messages (Messaris, 1992)—rendering the mediation virtually invisible. For many of HRC's close-up shots, the spectator positioning can exacerbate a recoiling response as we seemingly become the recipient of her more pointed remarks.

Three examples serve to exhibit this process of spectator positioning most clearly. First, all three networks feature at least parts of an interaction between HRC and one of Bill Clinton's Arkansas gubernatorial opponents, Tom McRae. As McRae speaks to the media, HRC approaches him with a series of questions and statements. HRC states, "Tom, who was the one person who didn't show up in Springdale? Give me a break. I mean, I think we ought to get the record straight" (*Time & Again,* 1998). HRC continues talking, and the camera zooms in on her. Her voice is raised, she gestures grandly, and most importantly, she speaks toward the camera. Even though she is addressing her husband's opponent and those listening to his press conference, the positioning of the camera situates the television viewers in the conversation so that we become recipients of her anger too.

This practice is furthered during two of the most famous HRC media events—the ones involving cookies/teas and Tammy Wynette. With the former, as HRC is delivering the line, "I suppose I could have stayed home and baked cookies and had teas. . . ." (Two women, 1996), the camera places us within the conversation at a typical personal distance away from HRC. She does not engage in direct address (eye contact with the camera), nevertheless, we are positioned in the conversation as if we are standing beside HRC and other bystanders in the restaurant, watching her deliver what Jeff Greenfield portrays as "hard-edged feminism" (Two women, 1996). When HRC articulates the second infamous line—"I'm not sitting here as some little woman

standing by my man" (Two women, 1996), the camera zooms in for a close-up shot as HRC shakes her fist forward and delivers the unambiguous line quite forcefully. Even though she is looking at journalist Steve Kroft of *60 Minutes,* the camera is situated just over his right shoulder, allowing her gaze to center to the left of the camera. The intimate distancing of the close-up shot coupled with the spectator positioning can create a recoil response just as if we were present during the interviews; we too become the recipients of her anger. Again, because the intimate camera positioning is contextualized as evidence of HRC's aggressive style, the spectator may be more attuned to such instructional cues. Such images resonate perhaps more than the softer visions of first lady as "good mother."

As many contend, politics in the postmodern mediated age are becoming more personalized (Keeter, 1987). Part of the personalization is linked to the mediation practices involved in televised political newsmaking. While such practices can exacerbate an emotional response (Graber, 1990), such a response is not always positive. As Hart (1994) contends, "because [TV] is used more often to vilify, the language of personality generates so many enemies that hell itself cannot contain them" (p. 73). For HRC's image, the constant visual intrusion and the spectator positioning of the camera in the scenes that portray HRC as more assertive undoubtedly impact her public image, especially when such images are shown over and over again.

THE ROLE OF REPETITION AND NEWS RECYCLING

Some scholars attend to the role of repetition within a particular news story (Ellis, 1992), yet the role of repetition across stories is likewise important to the image-making process. In examining the production and reproduction of HRC's image from 1992 to the present, many of the same images re-emerge. Thus, the stereotypes of HRC and the production practices involving selection, recontextualization, close-up shots, and spectator positioning, are rearticulated over and over, reifying HRC's image in the mediated public sphere. As Baty (1995) argues, "Once plot is displayed as a structure trying to effect, or map, the real, then it may be reproduced ad infinitum" (p. 125).

Retelling and Reifying

Predictably, when a television news story airs that synthesizes HRC's public life, the images are quite familiar. Most national journalists-turned-historians often begin with the *Life* magazine photo of HRC delivering the Wellesley commencement address in 1969 (They don't bake . . . , 1996; *Time & Again,* 1998; Two women, 1996). Undoubtedly relying on available footage from local news archives in Arkansas for the pre-1992 years, photographs and visuals that stand in for her role as First Lady of Arkansas are often connected to her interaction with Bill Clinton's opponent (Tom McRae) in the 1990 governor's race (They don't bake . . . , 1996; *Time & Again,* 1998). Some of the longer stories also emphasize HRC's image conversion prior to 1992 when she accepted her husband's last name and/or changed her looks to a more contemporary style (They don't bake . . . , 1996; *Time & Again,* 1998).

The 1992 campaign images are by far the most recycled images of HRC. These images represent the "cookies and teas" comment and the Tammy Wynette reference that were detailed earlier (They don't bake . . . , 1996; *Time & Again,* 1998; Two women, 1996). MSNBC, in fact, airs the cookies and tea line twice in a one hour broadcast. Not only do these two images stand in for the 1992 campaign, but they serve an iconic function as well. As Baty (1995) argues in her discussion of Marilyn Monroe, "the iconic sign enacts the position of the simulacrum: the sign represents the copy with no original" (p. 64). These images of HRC likewise reflect the depiction of the "representative character" of Bellah, et al. (1996):

> It is rather a public image that helps define, for a group of people, just what kinds of personality traits it is good and legitimate to develop. A representative character provides an ideal, a point of reference and focus, that gives living expression to a vision of life. (p. 39)

These two visions of HRC simulate her "essence" and also communicate larger ideological messages regarding the appropriate, and in HRC's case, inappropriate behavior for first ladies and all women in U.S. culture. Their continual reproduction serves to remind us that not only is HRC's behavior in these two contexts delegitimized, but women who dare to act too assertively are likewise cautioned in the process.

Images of HRC's First Lady role are also consistently portrayed across the three networks. Even though she engages in multiple activities in the United States and around the world, the most frequently articulated images are of HRC's 1993 testimony before five congressional committees regarding health care, and her 1996 press conference following her testimony before the Grand Jury on the Whitewater matter (They don't bake . . . , 1996; *Time & Again,* 1998; Two women, 1998). In more recent stories about the First Lady, NBC's January 1998 interview between Matt Lauer and HRC regarding the Clinton-Lewinsky scandal is commonly featured (*Time & Again,* 1998).

Although other images are included in the news narratives about HRC, those referred to above are common images showcased across news networks, over time. The retelling of a similar narrative helps produce a sense of image familiarity for audience members (Bennett & Edelman, 1985). Even those who seldom watch television news are bound to recognize these images because they are so popularized. The consistency across television news networks helps promulgate a sense of realism as the mediation and selectivity involved in production practices are virtually invisible (Schram, 1991). The reproduction of selected images also produces higher levels of comprehension. As Graber (1990) concludes, "visual themes proved to be more memorable than verbal ones" (p. 145), especially when those images are circulated and recirculated within the public sphere. HRC's image thus becomes reified and normalized in the repetitive process.

News Recycling

Multiple motives exist for repeating images over time. Obviously, news organizations want to tell a consistent story. If that story is repeated across networks, HRC's biography appears factual and actual. News networks simply resort to the same iconic images that are reproduced over time.

Economic incentives, though, are undoubtedly a motivating force behind the repetition of television news images. The recycling of stories, or the use of archival news footage for a contemporary story, saves a television station time and money. As MSNBC's feature *Time & Again* reveals, NBC integrates several historical news narratives about a subject and broadcasts them with the intent of telling the mediated history of a particular person, relationship, or incident. Such stories are spliced together into a holistic theme about the subject matter and narrated by Jane Pauley, who offers introductions, transitions, and conclusionary thoughts. Regarding the *Time & Again* (1998) feature on HRC, NBC rebroadcast seven stories over the course of the show that were filmed from one to six years earlier. No new footage is presented; only Jane Pauley's narration offers a contemporary recontextualization of the material. Compared to other hour long news programs, *Time & Again* represents an economical way for MSNBC to fill up news space in the 24 hour news cycle. Most notably, NBC is not the only news organization to disseminate "news as history." In fact, Dan Rather announced on CNN's *Larry King Live* (1998) the production of *60 Minutes II,* which updates one of three stories that aired previously on its parent program, *60 Minutes.*

Such broadcasts also act as a means of product placement. Just as films advertise products in their texts by situating them "naturally" within the storyline (Miller, 1990), news organizations advertise their journalists and their networks in a similar manner. Once again, MSNBC's program *Time & Again* (1998) provides a clear case study. In the introduction of each show, MSNBC features a montage of NBC's changing logos spliced together with images of their prominent historical and contemporary news anchors and reporters. Just as the NBC peacock changes form from 1952 through 1998, so too do the faces of NBC's anchors, as we revisit images of Huntley, Thomas, Brinkley, Chancellor, Gumbel, Pauley, Brokaw. . . . Background voices are likewise heard: "This is Lowell Thomas in New York"; "I'm Chet Huntley, your host." We also see the changing faces of journalists like Tom Brokaw, who is showcased in the introduction and then featured in two different newscasts about Hillary Rodham Clinton. Thus, NBC's news anchors of past and present become the products promoted by the news organization. As the stories air, though, further product placement is visible. The MSNBC logo appears in the bottom left of the picture. Because all of the stories are recycled, a second NBC logo often appears on the bottom right through much of the program—inundating viewers with double images of the NBC symbol. Although economically driven, promotional incentives also naturalize news images as stories are repeated and reified.

In the process of promoting the network and its journalists, news recycling thus sends the message that NBC and its journalists were on the scene of important news as it happened, capturing history. In the introduction for its *Time & Again* series (1998), MSNBC splices the NBC logos and journalists of past and present with visual images and verbal messages of significant historical events; we see images of the first American moon walk and hear John F. Kennedy's famed, "And so my fellow Americans" phrase. In its signoff for the program, Pauley concludes with "and we're history." By recirculating the same stories and situating them within a television news context, news comes to serve as "a primary archive or repository of collective memories" (Zelizer, 1992, pp. 194–195). In the process, the journalists' role as storyteller, and now historian, is legitimized. News personnel become historical authorities because their television news stations archive visual memories that are circulated and recirculated indefinitely (Zelizer, 1992). For Hillary Rodham Clinton, that repository of collective memory shapes the collective response to her, which renders her own actions and image-making less potent within the ideological and reductionistic maze of mediated memory.

COLLECTIVE MEMORY AND HRC

Even though some scholars argue that news is not history (Ellis, 1992; Schlesinger, 1978), others disagree. As Edelman (1988) asserts, "News accounts . . . reconstruct social worlds, histories, and eschatologies, evoking grounds for concern and for hope and assumptions about what should be noticed and what ignored, who are respectable or heroic, and who [are] not respectable" (p. 29). Over time, the rearticulation of these images produces a consistent and normalized story that is naturalized in a culture's collective memory.[6] As Barnhurst and Wartella (1998) maintain, "repetition of the video in the familiar television ritual" represents part of the collective memory (communal) experience (p. 290).

The issue of stereotyping is inherently tied to collective memory. Johnson, et al. (1982) argue that "dominant representations may be those that are most ideological, most obviously confirming to the flattened stereotypes of myth" (208). For HRC, those stereotypes that stand in for her image serve ideological functions as well. Farrell (1995) argues, for example, that the contestation surrounding HRC reflects "deeper questions about the role of candidates' wives and the dilemma of professional women" (p. 700). Those who believe that HRC's mediated images are a backlash against the gains of second wave feminism may be persuaded by Butler's (1990) contention that "those who fail to do their gender right are regularly punished" (p. 273). With HRC, the negative sentiment surrounding her image seemingly dissipates once she is placed in the role of victim during the aftermath of her husband's confessional. As Jane Pauley reports during a September 12, 1998, broadcast: "Once vilified for ambition and political overreaching when she took on health care, now she's admired, for being the faithful loving wife." Evidencing this claim, NBC features a pollster arguing that HRC's popularity "has skyrocketed." NBC then turns to person-on-the-street interviews, featuring one woman's sentiment, "She's more of a woman than most women would be" (The president and the people, 1998). As HRC prepares to enter the New York Senate race of 2000, news reporters and news guests are already predicting that her victimage status will give way to her previous negative images. Republican Pollster Christine Matthews argues on MSNBC's *Morning Line* (1999):

> The First Lady has been benefiting from her victim status in some ways, standing behind President Clinton. Her popularity has been its highest that it has been for quite some time. What we find with the voters, though, is when she takes these strong stands on the issues . . . her popularity plummets . . . When she's out there as a candidate having to take a strong stand on issues, multiple issues, that's when the voters start to stand back and say, "Hey, this is too much, I'm not very fond of this woman."

Within the coverage of HRC, a troubling depiction resonates: we are to fear women with power, yet admire women with the status of victim. Such images reward women who do not challenge the vows of marriage regardless of the circumstance while sending an ominous message to women who aspire to a position of power.

Like stereotyping, the issue of recontextualization is likewise linked to collective memory. Just as visual images often exist without referent until contextualized by television journalists, Nora (1989) argues that memories "have no referent in reality; or rather, they are their own referent: pure, exclusively self-referential signs" (p. 23). The ability to constitute such referents awards the television news media tremendous power in the process of naturalizing the historical and reifying the real. As Zelizer (1995) contends, remembering has "as much to do with identity formation, power and authority, cultural norms, and social interaction as with the simple act of recall. Its full understanding thus requires an appropriation of memory as social, cultural, and political action at its broadest level" (p. 214). Thus, as we understand the complexities of image-making in the visually mediated, postmodern world, we must deconstruct the structure of mediated strategies that naturalize such reductionist images.

Because the news story is generally told from the point of view of the journalist, spectator positioning heightens a sense of identification with the storyteller and thus renders less potent the image-making activities of the subject. While HRC's image is polysemic and always "contentious" (Goodall, 1994; Winfield, 1997, p. 221), journalists arguably wield more power in HRC's image-making process because they are the ones who tell her story, evidence their contentions, contextualize her visual images, and position her within the larger socio-political context.

What is important for all scholars of HRC (and other political figures) to remember is that those images which are circulated in the culture represent the hyperreal Hillary Rodham Clinton. With mass mediated images, it becomes impossible to discern the real from the simulated (Baudrillard, 1981/1994; Fiske, 1996). It becomes necessary then to recall that HRC's "reality" is derived from her "televisuality" (Fiske, 1996, p. 2)—means of production that cannot be ignored in discussions about image-making. In large part, this analysis tells us more about mediation in the postmodern age than it does about Hillary Rodham Clinton as an individual. Nevertheless, such production practices have real-life consequences for those who become the subject of the camera's gaze (Plissner, 1999) and for viewers who witness how political women are treated in the mediated public sphere.

As this essay is written, HRC is considering a run for the U.S. Senate seat in New York. Regardless of her life after the White House, these mediated images remain as part of the collective memory of her. As MSNBC commentators and guests speculate about her senatorial bid, metaphors of "time bomb[s]" are used because of her untested political experience, which parallel suggestions that she may "fatally wound . . ." the Democratic Party in New York were she to lose. These images of doom exist with others that juxtapose her "strong" yet "vulnerable" personae (Hockenberry, 1999). Carl Bernstein summarizes much of the commentary over the past few months concerning HRC's potential bid for the U.S. Senate:

> [the big question is] whether or not the perception and image of Hillary Clinton continues to soften as it has in the last few years. . . . She has gone in the public perception from someone being often portrayed [as] hard as nails to now a figure of some vulnerability. I think if she continues to soften in the eyes of those who are going to judge her, that it's going to be an interesting factor. (Hockenberry, 1999)

As these phrases reveal, images of fear are juxtaposed with calls for vulnerability, evidencing how HRC's polysemic images are archived within the vaults of our news-mediated collective memory. Disturbingly, such depictions reveal how the conflicts over women in politics, in the workplace, in the home, and in relationships are likewise yet to be resolved.

ACKNOWLEDGMENTS

The author thanks the General Research Board, University of Maryland, College Park, MD, and the Faculty and Instructional Development Grant committees, Monmouth College, Monmouth, IL, for funding this research.

NOTES

1. Throughout this paper, I use Hillary Clinton's initials when referring to the First Lady. Although some may find the use of such initials unusual or awkward because few refer to her in that manner, I find other forms of address more problematic. Using "Clinton" creates confusion for the reader as to whether or not I am talking about the First Lady or the President. Using Hillary counters writing convention and represents a practice often reserved for women mostly, creating an air of personalization within a scholarly context, and lessening the respect shown to HRC.

2. These three texts reflect an overview of Hillary Rodham Clinton's childhood and professional career. Because I am surveying the coverage of three major networks, I believe the texts are representative of television news coverage of HRC. The texts also reflect an expanded version of the shorter nightly news stories, and some of the texts under review encompass many of the same stories and visuals used in the nightly news broadcasts. In order to review the changing nature of the coverage of HRC in light of President Clinton's August 17, 1998, confessional and HRC's potential bid for the U.S. Senate seat in New York, I also review recent on-air coverage by ABC, MSNBC, and NBC, as well as survey their respective Internet stories that were simultaneously broadcast and featured on their Internet sites in 1998 and 1999. The examination of television news is warranted because as Morse (1986) maintains, news represents an "indispensable ideological tool in modern Western societies," and television news in particular serves "as an indicator of public attention to issues of concern to American society" (p. 56).

3. For additional analyses of how visual discourse functions rhetorically in political texts, see Edwards & Winkler (1997); Lucaites (1997); Olson (1983); and Olson (1990).

4. See Condit (1989) for a discussion of the interplay between the theory that audiences resist dominant discourses in public texts and the alternative perspective that audiences fully accept the dominant view. Like Condit, I support the view that audience members can offer alternative readings to dominant discourse.

5. For further discussion of how close-up shots function in television news texts, see Campbell's (1987) examination of *60 Minutes.*

6. Zelizer (1995) argues that "collective memory refers to recollections that are instantiated beyond the individual by and for the collective . . . collective memory comprises recollections of the past that are determined and shaped by the group. By definition, collective memory thereby presumes activities of sharing discussion, negotiation, and, often, contestation" (p. 214).

REFERENCES

Barnhurst, K. G., & Wartella, E. (1998). Young citizens, American TV newscasts and the collective memory. *Critical Studies in Mass Communication, 15,* 279–305.

Baty, S. P. (1995). *American Monroe: The making of a body politics.* Berkeley: University of California Press.

Baudrillard, J. (1994). *Simulacra and simulation* (S. F. Glaser trans.). Ann Arbor: University of Michigan Press. (Original work published 1981).

Bellah, R. N., Madsen, R., Sullivan, W. M., Swidler, A., & Tipton, S. M. (1996). *Habits of the heart: Individualism and commitment in American life.* Berkeley: University of California Press.

Bennett, W. L., & Edelman, M. (1985). Toward a new political narrative. *Journal of Communication, 35,* 156–171.

Brown, M. E. (1997). Feminism and cultural politics: Television audiences and Hillary Rodham Clinton. *Political Communication, 14,* 255–270.

Burrell, B. (1997). *Public opinion, the first ladyship, and Hillary Rodham Clinton.* New York: Garland.

Butler, J. (1990). Performative acts and gender constitution: An essay in phenomenology and feminist theory. In S. E. Case (Ed.), *Performing feminisms: Feminist critical theory and theater* (pp. 270–282). Baltimore: John Hopkins University Press.

Campbell, K. K. (1996). The rhetorical presidency: A two-person career. In Martin J. Medhurst (Ed.), *Beyond the rhetorical presidency* (pp. 179–195). College Station: Texas A&M University Press.

Campbell, K. K. (1998). The discursive performance of femininity: Hating Hillary. *Rhetoric & Public Affairs, 1,* 1–19.

Campbell, R. (1987). Securing the middle ground: Reporter formulas in *60 Minutes. Critical Studies in Mass Communication, 4,* 325–350.

Ceremony for embassy bombing victims. (1998, August 13). *C-SPAN.* Purdue Research Foundation.

Condit, C. M. (1989). The rhetorical limits of polysemy. *Critical Studies in Mass Communication, 6,* 103–122.

Dow, B. J. *Prime-time feminism: Television, media culture, and the woman's movement since 1970.* Philadelphia: University of Pennsylvania Press.

Edelman, M. (1988). *Constructing the political spectacle.* Chicago: University of Chicago Press.

Edwards, J. L., & Winkler, C. K. (1907). Representative form and the visual ideograph: The Iwo Jima image in editorial cartoons. *Quarterly Journal of Speech, 83,* 289–310.

Ellis, J. (1992). *Visible fictions: Cinema: television: video* (2nd ed). London: Routledge.

Farrell, A. E. (1995). Feminism and the media: Introduction. *Signs, 20,* 642–645.

Faust, J. M. (1998, August 19). Standing by their men: Women in the trenches. *ABC News.* Retrieved from the World Wide Web: http:\\www.abcnews.com.

First Lady 'committed' to marriage. (1998, August 18). MSNBC. Retrieved August 19, 1998 from the World Wide Web: http://msnbc.com/news.

Fishburn, K. (1982). *Women in popular culture: A reference guide.* Westport, CT: Greenwood Press.

Fiske, J. (1996). *Media matters: Race and gender in U.S. politics.* Minneapolis: University of Minnesota Press.

Gans, H. J. (1996). *Deciding what's news: A study of CBS Evening News, NBC Nightly News, Newsweek, and Time.* New York: Vintage Books.

Gold, E. R., & Speicher, R. (1995). Marilyn Quayle meets the press: Marilyn loses. *Southern Communication Journal, 67,* 93–103.

Goodall, S. (1994). De/reconstructing Hillary: From the retro ashes of the Donna Reed fantasy to a 90s view of women and politics. In S. A. Smith (Ed.), *Bill Clinton on the stump, state, and stage: The rhetorical road to the White House* (pp. 163–186). Fayetteville: University of Arkansas Press.

Gould, L. L. (1989). The historical legacy of modern first ladies. In N. K. Smith & M. C. Ryan (Eds.), *Modern first ladies: Their documentary legacy* (pp. 167–175). Washington, DC: National Archives and Records Administration.

Gould, L. L. (1996). Hillary Rodham Clinton (1947–). First Lady: 1993–. In L. L. Gould (Ed.), *American first ladies: Their lives and their legacy* (pp. 632–648). New York: Garland.

Graber, D. A. (1990). Seeing is remembering: How visuals contribute to learning from television news. *Journal of Communication, 40,* 134–155.

Gross, L., Katz, J. S., & Ruby, J. (1988). Introduction: A moral pause. In L. Gross, J. S. Katz, & J. Ruby (Eds.), *Image ethics: The moral right of subjects in photograph, film, and television* (pp. 3–33). New York: Oxford University Press.

Gunter, B. (1987). *Poor reception: Misunderstanding and forgetting broadcast news.* Hillsdale, NJ: Lawrence Erlbaum.

Hart, R. P. (1994). *Seducing America: How television charms the modern voter.* New York: Oxford University Press.

Hockenberry. (1999, June 7). MSNBC.

Hunter, J. (1987). *Image and word: The interaction of twentieth-century photographs and texts.* Cambridge, MA: Harvard University Press.

Jamieson, K. H., & Campbell, K. K. (1983). *The interplay of influence: Mass media & their publics in news, advertising, politics.* Belmont, CA: Wadsworth.

Jamieson, K. H. (1995). *Beyond the double bind: Women and leadership.* New York: Oxford University Press.

Johnson, R., & Dawson, G. (1982). Popular memory: Theory, politics, method. In R. Johnson, G. McLennan, B. Schwartz, & D. Sutton (Eds.), *Making histories: Studies in history-writing and politics* (pp. 205–252). Minneapolis: University of Minnesota Press.

Keeter, S. (1987). The illusion of intimacy: Television and the role of candidate personal qualities in voter choice. *Public Opinion Quarterly, 57,* 344–358.

King, N. (1996). *The woman in White House: The remarkable story of Hillary Rodham Clinton.* New York: Birch Lane Press.

Larry King Live. (1998, December 3). CNN.

Lucaites, J. L. (1997). Visualizing "the people": Individualism vs. collectivism in *Let Us Now Praise Famous Men. Quarterly Journal of Speech, 83,* 269–288.

Macdonald, M. (1995). *Representing women: Myths of femininity in the popular media.* London: Edward Arnold.

Mander, M. S. (1987). Narrative dimension of the news: Omniscience, prophecy, and morality. *Communication, 10,* 51–70.

McCombs, M. E., & Shaw, D. L. (1972). The agenda-setting function of mass media. *Public Opinion Quarterly, 36,* 176–187.

Messaris, P. (1992). "Visual manipulation": Visual means of affecting responses to images. *Communication, 13,* 181–195.

Messaris, P. (1994). *Visual literacy: Images, mind, & reality.* Boulder: Westview.

Messaris, P. (1997). *Visual persuasion: The role of images in advertising.* Thousands Oaks, CA: Sage.

Meyrowitz, J. (1982). Television and interpersonal behaviour: Codes of perception and response. In G. Gumpert & R. Cathcart (Eds.), *Inter/Media: International communication in a media world* (2nd ed). (pp. 221–241). New York: Oxford University Press.

Meyrowitz, J. (1985). *No sense of place: The impact of electronic media on social behaviour.* New York: Oxford University Press.

Miller, M. C. (1990). End of story. In M. C. Miller (Ed.), *Seeing through* (pp. 186–246). New York: Pantheon.

Milton, J. (1999). *The first partner: Hillary Rodham Clinton.* New York: William Morrow.

Mitchell, W. J. T. (1994). *Picture theory.* Chicago: University of Chicago Press.

Morning Line. (1999, May 30). MSNBC.

Morse, M. (1986). The television news personality and credibility: Reflections on the news in transition. In T. Modleski (Ed.), *Studies in entertainment: Critical approaches to mass culture* (pp. 55–79). Bloomington: Indian University Press.

Muir, J. R., & Benitez, L. M. (1996). Redefining the role of the first lady: The rhetorical style of Hillary Rodham Clinton. In R. Denton & R. L. Holloway (Eds.), *The Clinton presidency: Images, issues, and communication strategies* (pp. 139–158). Westport, CT: Praeger.

Nora, P. (1989). Between memory and history: *Les Lieux de Mémoire. Representations, 26,* 7–25.

Olson, L. C. (1983). Portraits in praise of people: A rhetorical analysis of Norman Rockwell's icons in Franklin D. Roosevelt's "four freedoms" campaign. *Quarterly Journal of Speech, 69,* 15–24.

Olson, L. C. (1990). Benjamin Franklin's commemorative medal, *Libertas Americana:* A study in rhetorical iconology. *Quarterly Journal of Speech, 76,* 23–45.

Palmer, J. (1998, August 15). First Lady is Clinton's first defender. MSNBC. Retrieved August 15, 1998 from the World Wide Web: http://msnbc .com/news.

Parry-Giles, S. J., & Parry-Giles, T. (1999). Meta-imaging, *The War Room,* and the hyperreality of American politics. *Journal of Communication, 49,* 28–45.

Philo, G. (1990). *Seeing and believing: The influence of television.* London: Routledge.

Plissner, M. (1989). *The control room: How television calls the shots in presidential elections.* New York: The Free Press.

Rhode, D. (1995). Media images, feminist issues. *Signs, 20,* 687–710.

Robinson, J. P., & Levy, M. R. (Eds.). (1986). *The main source: Learning from television news.* Beverly Hills: Sage.

Schlesinger, P. (1978). *Putting "reality" together: BBC News.* London: Constable.

Schram, S. F. (1991). The post-modern presidency and the grammar of electronic electioneering. *Critical Studies in Mass Communication, 8,* 210–216.

Snyder, J. (1980). Picturing vision. In W. J. T. Mitchell (Ed.), *The language of images* (pp. 221–246). Chicago: University of Chicago Press.

Stephens, M. (1998). *The rise of the image, the fall of the word.* New York: Oxford University Press.

The president and the people. (1998, September 11). NBC News.

They don't bake cookies anymore. (1996, October 13). *Democracy in America.* CNN.

Time & Again. (1998, August 4). MSNBC.

Two women. (1996, October 18). *Nightline.* ABC News.

Vavrus, M. (1998). Working the Senate from the outside in: The mediated construction of a feminist political campaign. *Critical Studies in Mass Communication, 15,* 213–235.

Warnick, B. (1998). Appearance or reality? Political parody on the web in campaign '96. *Critical Studies in Mass Communication, 15,* 306–324.

Winfield, B. H. (1997). Hillary Rodham Clinton's image: Content, control, and cultural politics—Introductory Note. *Political Communication, 14,* 221–224.

Zelizer, B. (1992). *Covering the body: The Kennedy assassination, the media, and the shaping of collective memory.* Chicago: University of Chicago Press.

Zelizer, B. (1995). Reading the past against the grain: The shape of memory studies. *Critical Studies in Mass Communication, 12,* 214–239.

20

"TO VEIL THE THREAT OF TERROR"

Afghan Women and the <Clash of Civilizations> in the Imagery of the U.S. War on Terrorism

DANA L. CLOUD

1899: Take up the White Man's burden—
Send forth the best ye breed—
Go, bind your sons to exile
To serve your captives' need;
To wait, in heavy harness,
On fluttered folk and wild—
Your new-caught sullen peoples,
Half devil and half child.
Take up the White Man's burden—
In patience to abide,
To veil the threat of terror
And check the show of pride.[1]

2002: The picture that emerges [from rhetoric about war in Afghanistan] is a land teeming with wild-eyed warlords, malnourished children, abused women, mud huts and treacherous mountain terrain whose caverns and underground caves are home to minions of malevolence—basically, a scene out of Lord of the Rings.[2]

SOURCE: Cloud, D. L. (2004). "To veil the threat of terror": Afghan women and the <clash of civilizations> in the imagery of the U.S. war on terrorism. *Quarterly Journal of Speech, 90*(3), 285–306. © National Communication Association.

The phrase "clash of civilizations," popularized in the 1990s by Samuel Huntington,[3] refers to the idea that the United States and its people face an incontrovertible conflict with Others, particularly Islamic Others, whose civilizations are inferior and hostile to Western capitalism. This rhetoric of the clash of societies destined by nature to be enemies is not a recent invention, however. David Spurr has argued that the idea of immutable clash between allegedly superior and inferior civilizations has been part of the rhetoric of U.S. imperialism since at least the end of the 19th century.[4] He writes, "The colonizer's traditional insistence on difference from the colonized . . . establishes a notion of the savage as Other, the antithesis of civilized values."[5] Likewise, rhetorical scholar Robert Ivie has noted that justifications for war often involve representations of the "enemy" as savage and barbaric: "The usual strategy is to construct the image indirectly through contrasting references to the adversary's coercive, irrational, and aggressive attempts to subjugate a freedom-loving, rational, and pacific victim."[6]

The discourse of enmity between "civilized" people and "savages" is not the only dimension of the rhetoric of civilization clash, however. Images of the oppressed in an "inferior" civilization can prompt a paternalistic response alongside an aggressive one. Descriptions of the people of an enemy society as ignorant, abject victims of an enemy regime warrant intervention on the allegedly humanitarian grounds of saving people from themselves. Thus, the idea of the "white man's burden" is a core element in the belief in a clash between white, Western societies and inferior Others requiring policing and rescue.[7]

This article is an attempt to answer the question, "What does the clash of civilizations *look* like?" This question is significant because the imagery of civilization clash has long been as important as verbal political rhetoric in warranting U.S. policies of war and occupation.[8] Although the strategy of contrasting images of Others is not new to political discourse, it was prominent and influential in the political and cultural discourses justifying the 2001–2002 war with Afghanistan that began after terrorist attacks on U.S. targets on September 11, 2001. This article explores the role of widely circulated images of Afghans, with emphasis on those of Afghan women, in national news magazines and their web sites during this war, arguing that images of Afghan women and men establish a binary opposition between a white, Western, modern subject and an abject foreign object of surveillance and military action. These images construct the viewer as a paternalistic savior of women and posit images of modern civilization against depictions of Afghanistan as backward and pre-modern. Through the construction of binary oppositions of self and Other, the evocation of a paternalistic stance toward the women of Afghanistan, and the figuration of modernity as liberation, these images participate in justifications for the war that belie the actual motives for the war. This contradiction has a number of implications for democratic deliberation and public life during wartime.

The main purpose of this article is to document the ways that the imagery of the war on terrorism justifies the imperial thrust of U.S. foreign policy. In addition, however, this study has implications for theory, criticism, and practical politics. For rhetorical theory, this article extends the idea of the visual ideograph introduced by Janis Edwards and Carol Winkler.[9] I argue below that visual ideographs are more than recurring iconic images that shift in meaning depending on context; they also index verbal ideographic slogans, making abstractions such as <clash of civilizations> concrete. For criticism, the essay defends what John Thompson calls "depth hermeneutics," seeking underlying truths veiled by a misleading ideological common sense.[10] Finally, for politics, the article exhorts readers to answer the real (rather than only the image of) clash of war with protest and solidarity across national borders.

This article proceeds as follows: First, it describes the verbal rhetoric of civilization clash, arguing that this phrase and its accompanying imagery operate in an ideographic way, summing up and exhorting conformity to a sense of American-ness established through negation of the self-governing humanity of the Other. The role of images of Afghan women in this discourse is to establish the barbarity of a society in which women are profoundly oppressed. After a brief survey of relevant concepts from the literature on visual rhetoric, the essay proceeds to an analysis of photographs from the website *Time.com* to demonstrate the ways in which these images have warranted the use of force in Afghanistan on allegedly humanitarian grounds. In Kipling's terms, U.S. forces are there to "serve their captives' needs." After analyzing these aspects of the images of Afghan women, I argue that the humanitarian justifications encapsulated in the rhetoric of civilization clash are contradicted by evidence suggesting that other economic and geopolitical motives for U.S. intervention were primary among makers of foreign policy.

\<CLASH OF CIVILIZATIONS\> AS IDEOGRAPH

Huntington argues that civilizations (groups bounded by shared cultural identity and/or religion) rather than races (as biologically defined) or nation states (bounded by political borders) have driven global politics since the end of the Cold War. Following this argument, global conflict erupts because of the existence of competing cultures and competing ways of life—an allegedly secular, democratic capitalism vs. Islamic theocracy and dictatorship.[11] Paralleling George W. Bush in his speech after the terrorist attacks on the World Trade Center and the Pentagon on September 11, 2001,[12] Huntington implies that Islamic societies would be better off if they were to adopt "our way of life." Thus, he describes Islam as the West's Other; the fundamental clash is "between two different versions of what is right and what is wrong, who is right and who is wrong."[13] "So long as Islam remains Islam . . . this fundamental conflict between two great civilizations and ways of life will continue to define their relations."[14] This account offers a significant justificatory narrative for the war against terrorism in Afghanistan and perhaps elsewhere in the future.

As Michael Calvin McGee defined them, ideographs are historically and culturally grounded commonplace rhetorical terms that sum up and invoke identification with key social commitments; examples include \<liberty\> and \<rule of law\>. Ideographs are the link between rhetoric and ideology, vehicles through which ideologies or unconsciously shared idea systems that organize consent to a particular social system become rhetorically effective.[15] The idea of

civilization clash meets this definition. At least since the U.S. incursions into the Caribbean in the 1890s, the rhetoric of the "clash of civilizations" has been a staple of the rhetorics of war and empire. Because of its historical longevity and because it encapsulates a number of key social commitments (to democracy, to a vision of the geopolitical role of the United States, to racial and national hierarchy, and so on) the "clash of civilizations" should be counted among the ideographs of U.S. political life. Henceforward this essay will refer to images of civilization clash and the rhetorical insistence on colonial distance from the Other as constituting the \<clash of civilizations\>, following standard notation style for ideographs.

Celeste Condit and John Lucaites's study of the ideograph \<equality\> demonstrates that the ideological content or meaning of an ideograph can shift over time in response to historical exigencies and struggle among groups attempting to claim the ideograph.[16] In the case of the \<clash of civilizations\>, however, the meaning of the ideograph has remained relatively stable across modern history. Perhaps the exigencies calling the ideograph forth are so similar in each war that when the ideograph emerges in public discourse, the phrase's meaning echoes the reified interpretations of the past. Unlike the ideograph \<equality\>, over which contesting groups successfully struggled, the \<clash of civilizations\> is an ideograph that is often managed and framed by discourses of a hegemonic elite.

Images are central to the constitution of meanings for the \<clash of civilizations\> and should be considered as ideographs in their own right. As Winkler and Edwards have argued, images function as ideographs in public discourse when they are "culturally-grounded, summarizing, and authoritative terms that enact their meaning by expressing an association of cultural ideals and experiences in ever-evolving and reifying form within the rhetorical environment."[17] Either visual or verbal, an ideograph is a commonplace abstraction that represents collective commitment, warrants power and guides behavior, and is culture bound.[18]

Edwards and Winkler's study of editorial cartoons concludes that some iconic or enduring, easily-recognized images (such as the flag-raising at Iwo Jima) are themselves ideographs, subject to appropriation, contestation, and shift in meaning over time. Amplifying Edwards and Winkler's claims, I argue here that photographs and other images can enact ideographs visually and index, or point to, the verbal slogans capturing society's guiding abstractions. The imagery of the <clash of civilizations> may be uniquely suited to this role: In setting up visual binary oppositions between U.S. citizens and enemy Others, it literally constitutes the clash between them. Photographs of self and Other enact the clash when they are set alongside one another. Paradoxically, photographs render the abstraction of the ideograph concrete in what appears in a photograph to be an unmediated experience of reality. Thus, the visual ideograph is, perhaps, even a stronger inducement to national identification than its propositional counterpart.

Racialized images of the savage Other and gendered images of women as victims lurk in Western culture's symbolic repertoire, taking shape as the <clash of civilizations> in perennial justifications for war. As several theorists have noted, gender, nation, and race are closely intertwined in colonialist discourses historically.[19] Among the features of a gendered nationalism is the idea of "saving the brown women from the brown men."[20] Although an enemy nation's men often represent "the enemy," the women (and children) of that same nation often are represented as victims needing rescue from the men of their society.[21] In the <clash of civilizations> rhetoric as it appears in the United States, women's oppression is a marker of an inferior society.

The rhetoric disregards women's oppression in the United States, however, which takes the form of ideological constructions of a domesticated womanhood and economic disparity between men and women. The condemnation on the part of U.S. leaders of women's oppression only in those countries that are the targets of nation building is thus somewhat hypocritical. In a visual rhetoric of abjection, only another society's women are visible as the oppressed. Because the contrasting visibility of self and Other establishes the <clash of civilizations>, it is necessary to understand the strategies and characteristics particular to visual discourse about the U.S. war on terrorism.

VISUAL RHETORICS AND WAR

Building on work in semiotics, argument theory, and other fields, rhetorical scholars have articulated some key propositions in understanding what images do in public discourse. Some scholars have attended to the ways in which images function in and as rational argument.[22] Others, however, have emphasized the ways in which photographic images, especially, can organize perception in less rational ways. Photographic images are marked by metonymy, the reduction of complex situations into simpler visual abstractions. In particular, the photographs examined below exemplify the strategy, identified by Hariman and Lucaites, of the "individuated aggregate . . . a trope whereby the population as a whole is represented solely by specific individuals."[23] They argue that such images, as in the case of Dorothea Lange's 1936 image "Migrant Mother," can characterize "unwarranted victimage and a moral appeal for state action."[24]

In addition to involving reduction and emotion, photographic images deploy a number of other persuasive strategies (such as framing, selection, editing, use of light, or arrangement of subjects), yet the photograph's strategies are masked by the appearance of having captured reality.[25] As Susan Sontag puts it, "Something we hear about, but doubt, seems proven when we're shown a photograph."[26] Finally, images possess the capacity for visceral emotional appeal.[27] In these ways, the process of imagistic persuasion does not always enable rational, conscious processing.

In the naturalization of what are necessarily partial rhetorical fictions, an image of an Afghan man with weapons, for example, reduces the man to the image of the terrorist when he, his life, and his reasons for taking up arms are probably more complex than the snapshot.[28] Metonymically, the connotations of terrorism attach to Afghan men in general.[29] Of most importance for the purposes of this article, images construct paradigmatic oppositions in order to win the identification and disidentification of audiences. In times of war, images of enemy Others, represented as helpless and savage, are foils for images of the national self. This binary construction strengthens national identification, entailing rigid disidentification with and scapegoating of the Other (and a rhetorical and potentially actual "kill").[30] In conveying this opposition, the photographs enact the <clash of civilizations>. In the actual depiction of clash between self and Other, they exhort U.S. viewers to identification with social commitments to war and the values of democracy-cum-capitalism. Such identification entails emotional responses of anger and fear (against the savage enemy) and/or pity and outrage (at the treatment of women).

DARKNESS AND CHAOS: BINARY IMAGES OF AMERICANS[31] AND AFGHANS

The images examined in this essay come from the *Time.com* website, where *Time* magazine cover images and other photographs are reproduced and reorganized. All of these images appeared either on the cover or in the pages of *Time* magazine between September 11, 2001 and September 11, 2002. They have been available to audiences independent of time and place on the *Time.com* web site, where they have been compiled into series of related images, some set to music.

Although the imagery of the war on terrorism may vary by publication outlet, medium, and audience, the images on *Time.com* and in *Time* magazine represent the dominant versions of such imagery. The reach and mass popularity of newsmagazines and their web sites suggest not only that millions of viewers are exposed to these representations, but also that visitors return again and again to the publications, which cultivate through repetition the dominant ideological framings of the <clash of civilizations>. According to the web site, 50 million people, and three million distinctive viewers, visit *Time.com* each month.[32] In print, *Time* magazine reaches 24 million readers worldwide each month, "more than any other news source."[33] Mass public support for the war in Afghanistan on the basis either of anger and fear at terrorists as savages or of concern for the innocents in Afghanistan is rooted in the common sense that is reproduced, in part, by photographs circulated in these mass media.

Appearing as they did in the pages of one of the most widely distributed periodicals in the world and on a web site with millions of daily hits, the photographs examined below were among the most common images circulating in the civic realm in the United States (if not around the world) during this time.[34] On the *Time.com* web site, these images appear in thematic clusters, conveniently arranged in what *Time.com* labels photo essays.[35] They construct paradigmatic binary oppositions, encourage viewers to adopt a paternalistic stance toward Afghan women, and offer images of modernity, aligned with light, in contrast to the darkness of chaos and backwardness. Through these contrasts, the images enact the <clash of civilizations> and take part in a dominant cultural and political rhetoric justifying U.S. intervention on the basis of that ideograph.

Enacting the <Clash of Civilizations> in Binary Oppositions

The overarching strategy of these images is to construct a binary opposition between an American self and enemy Others. Thus, images do not state the ideograph <clash of civilizations> as much as they *become the clash* in visual condensations of the meanings of "American" and "Other." The ideograph <clash of civilizations> is enacted in these images in ways that are more concrete than the linguistic invocation of the phrase. David Spurr explains that the classification of Third World people justifies foreign policy:

> What motivates the classification of Third World peoples is the need to define a coherent stance that ultimately will determine the nature of Western policies toward the Third World: investment or disinvestments, increased credit or higher interest rates, military intervention or diplomatic negotiation, aggressive aid or benign neglect.[36]

The photographs of people who represent entire cultures in conflict encourage viewers to interpret the war as a moral clash between good and evil, and between persons who are essentially reasonable and people who are fundamentally irrational. Metonymizing the conflict in terms of "our way of life" and challenges to it reduces a complex set of geopolitical motives, strategies, and outcomes to a cultural binary. One photo essay from the *Time.com* site clearly reveals this process. "From Shadow To Light" is a compilation of images from *Time* during the year following the attacks.[37] As arranged on the web site, this series of images unfolds in a set order to a score of somber electronic music: A bald man stands looking at the wall of posters seeking World Trade Center victims; a presumably Arab man in a headscarf holds a pistol in front of his face as if ready to aim it; President Bush speaks in an unidentified office with a group of men around a table, presumably his advisers; a band of unidentified Afghan people wander in a desert; two Afghan children, one on a donkey, the other standing in the foreground, look into the camera; a person in a crowd of Muslim protesters holds up a photo of Osama bin Laden; finally, a white American man in a red-white-and-blue tie looks disconsolately downward in front of the New York Stock Exchange (see Figure 1). The series also includes images of police and firefighters engaged in selfless acts of heroism. In this set of photographs, the swift oscillation establishes a fundamental difference between heroic, white, rational U.S. men on the one hand, and scruffy Al Qaeda fighters, represented variously as irrational militants (e.g., demonstrators with pictures of Bin Laden held in the air), as savages in the desert, or as hopeless nomads.

The most significant characteristic to observe about these images is that, as arranged, they set up a compelling series of paradigmatic binary oppositions between the American "self" and the Afghan "Other." The white man in Figure 1 stands in for identification with nation, economic system, and the taken-for-granted combination of the two: America plus capitalism equals democracy. The inverse is implied: anti-American plus pre-capitalism equals barbarity. The arrangement of these images demonstrates the strategy, identified by Burke and Barthes, of constructing identity in terms of its negation.[38] Following the photograph of a bald white man with a serious expression on his face, a photo shows a dark-skinned man (presumably a member of the Taliban) holding a pistol lined up vertically along his face, as if threatening to aim at the white man. The sequence of images

encourages viewers to feel a sense of antagonism and fear toward the gunman. The sequence also alternates between images of clean-shaven white men in ties (including President Bush, the disconsolate man mentioned above, and one other businessman fleeing the WTC scene) and images of unkempt Afghan people. The connotations of these images are of reason—associated with capitalism, adulthood, urbanity, professionalism, and whiteness—and the opposing stereotypes of irrationality—associated with children, idol-worship, and the unmodernized desert. Visitors to the site are likely to identify with the stance of the reasonable American as set against terrifying or pitiable images of Afghan subjects.

Despite Huntington's claims to a non-racial theory of civilization clash, these images of the <clash of civilizations> are about race. The title of the photo essay is notable: In "From Shadow To Light," darkness signifies the chaos and violence of the "uncivilized." The title echoes colonialist representations of Africa as "the dark continent," and the United States, its heroes, and leaders, as the province of light. The metaphorical darkness is also literal and racial: Peoples needing rescue from themselves are almost invariably darker-skinned than their saviors. The coding of racial difference as cultural difference participates in what Stuart Hall would call a discourse of inferential racism.[39] As Ella Shohat and Robert Stam have argued, racist Eurocentrism manifests itself in coded ways emphasizing cultural differences rather than racial ones, thereby masking its racism.[40] Likewise, Etienne Balibar and Immanuel Wallerstein, along with Michael Hardt and Antonio Negri, have noted that racism often refers to moral, cultural, and religious differences, omitting reference to bodies or biology.[41] It is clear in the oscillation between images in the "From Shadow To Light" series that the distinctions between self and Other are not only cultural, moral, and religious, but also racial.

The racialization of this imagery, reminiscent of discourses of slavery and lynching, also is imbricated with gender. The <clash of civilizations> imagery in the "From Shadow To Light" photo essay pits U.S. citizens, figured as white men, against portrayals of Afghan men as terrorists. This confrontation is a direct one, evocative of fear and hostility. When women are the

Figure 1   ["Patriotic Capitalist Mourns."]

SOURCE: James Nachtwey/VII.

Figure 2   ["From Shadow Into Light."]

SOURCE: John Stanmeyer/VII.

Figure 3   ["Eye Contact: Schoolgirl in Afghanistan."]

SOURCE: Photo by Majid Saeedi.

Figure 4   ["Half Devil and Half Child."]

SOURCE: Photo by Majid Saeedi.

Figure 5   ["Hyper-mediated Women's Liberation."]

SOURCE: John Stanmeyer/VII.

objects of the gaze, however, the images seem to argue for intervention toward nation building, an allegedly humanitarian kind of control that is somehow worth the violence visited upon those being rescued.

Gender and Paternalism

In "From Shadow To Light," there is a photograph of a lone woman, dressed head to toe in a burqa, wandering through crumbling desert ruins early in the morning with the sun rising in front of her (Figure 2). As in other examples from the "From Shadow To Light" compilation, she moves visually from darkness into the light of liberation promised by U.S. intervention. This ostensibly humanitarian motive also characterizes an image of a girl or young woman in school (see Figure 3), in a photo essay called "Kabul Unveiled." The photograph offers an extreme close-up view of a young woman, sitting in a schoolroom at a desk, covered almost entirely from head to toe in a yellow burqa. This point of view allows the viewer to peer into the one eye that peeps from under her bright yellow head covering.[42] The photograph conveys a sense of desperation to learn despite the constraints of an oppressive culture. Mandated to cover her head and body, the young woman can read in school, but only with one eye. Through this forbidden eye contact, the viewer is invited to experience a momentary emotional connection, and also outrage and despair over the quite literal containment of her person. Yet the image also foregrounds the point of view of the colonizer: It is the American who is able to subject others to her/his gaze and, thus, defines the Afghan woman as the object of U.S. cultural hegemony. As this example illustrates, and like 19th-century colonial discourses, the photographs in these essays offer a surveying paternal gaze.[43]

Several images in these photo essays visually recall Rudyard Kipling's description in his poem "The White Man's Burden" of those "savages" needing conquering as "your new-caught sullen peoples . . . half devil and half child." One image in a photo essay about the Taliban shows a small boy looking up at a Taliban fighter. Both are standing in profile, but we see only the torso of the fighter, his arm supporting a machine gun, which visually appears to be aimed toward the child (see Figure 4). Here literally a "half devil," a faceless and, therefore, dehumanized Other, is looking down at the child, who is, in turn, looking up at him, implying a potential identification between the two. Thus, the enemy society is metonymically represented as containing both terrorist devils and innocents who may yet aspire to terrorism if not saved in time. The point of view of this photograph also invites two different gazes: a direct look at the faceless gunman as anonymous target of antipathy, and a downward gaze at the now-innocent but potentially vengeful child. The scene evokes Kipling's exhortation to the "white man" to save these people, especially the women and children, from themselves.[44]

War may require vilifying visual frames, but occupation requires a humanitarian flexing of the nationalist frame. The vision of Afghans (and later, Iraqis) as incapable of rebuilding their society or becoming civilized without outside intervention bolsters the argument that the United States cannot just pull out of either Afghanistan or Iraq and leave chaos behind.[45] On this note, Michael Ignatieff has called Afghanistan and Iraq "havens of chaos and terrorism"; he argues that the people of these countries should be dominated for their own good.[46] In this way, the images that compress the <clash of civilizations> into icons of identification and division work alongside political rhetoric and journalism to establish a paternalistic stance toward Afghans and other nations.

A paternalistic rhetoric takes a position sympathetic to, but standing above, Others. To occupy this stance of benevolent but superior caretaker is to adopt the prerogative of telling others what they need and how they should obtain it. As Linda Alcoff explains in "The Problem of Speaking for Others," there is a difference between an ethically legitimate standing in solidarity with the oppressed and the opportunistic use of someone else's oppression as rationale for war.[47] "Kabul Unveiled" is the most prominent of the *Time.com* photo essays demonstrating the paternalism of the <clash of civilizations>. For example, the viewer of Figure 2 literally looks down on the woman in the ruins. The viewer of the photograph of the schoolgirl in yellow (see Figure 3) has the prerogative of entry into her private space and, it seems, her emotional state. On the other hand, she cannot see her inspectors; thus, the photograph constitutes a relationship of inequality, not solidarity.

In the photo essay, the narrative order of the images is significant. Early in the sequence, images of oppression flow from one to the other in a guided tour with clickable arrows to move to the next frame. As the viewer moves through the photographs (assuming that most viewers will look at them in the order presented), however, images of modern liberation are interspersed between the images of women as victims. Finally, photographs of feminists and other unveiled, public women dominate and end the sequence. Taken together, these images encourage viewers to lament the status of Afghan women and support U.S. intervention. The implied before-and-after sequence suggests that before the U.S. attacks, Afghan women wandered in chaos or lived, invisible and indistinct, at the mercy and discretion of irrational and autocratic men.[48]

MODERNITY AS MEDIA AND MARKET

I do not deny the terrible reality of women's oppression in Afghanistan or, to greater or lesser degrees, in any society marked by theism, disparities in wealth between men and women, and oppressive social norms regarding domesticity, dress, and appearance.[49] Although the oppression of women under Taliban rule is well documented, these images do more than represent that reality. They operate within a rhetorical discourse that becomes more forceful when images of oppression are contrasted with images of women granted entry—by the arrival of U.S. forces—into modern, Western-style, market-driven "civilization." Images of modernized Afghan women operate in deliberate contradistinction to the photographs of the oppressed. One such image shows a feminist leader, identified in a brief caption as Soraya, standing in a brightly lit window at the head of a table surrounded by unveiled women engaged in what appears to be a political discussion or meeting.[50]

Indeed, Soraya and these women are the subject of an article in the December 3, 2001, issue of *Time,* whose cover image of the unveiled face of an Afghan woman is labeled "Lifting the Veil."[51] The unidentified woman on the cover of this issue mostly faces the camera but is turned slightly away, making her glance appear somewhat coy. Her expression suggests the shy defiance of one unused to visibility. Hers is a visibility granted literally by the U.S. publication of her image and indirectly by U.S. military intervention. As the photo essays oscillate between images of oppression and liberation, so the December 3 issue of *Time* sets stories about women under Islamic dictatorship against stories about feminist and other women coming out from behind the veil after the arrival of U.S. troops.

The photo essay "Kabul Unveiled" condenses this opposition in its sequence of images, defining liberation as the exposure of women to the consumer market and to the mass media. In an image of a woman in a blue burqa shopping for clothing, shopping becomes a key indicator of modernity.[52] The salesman holds up a blue burqa to the woman, both standing before an entire wall made blue by compressed rows of identical burqas. Thus, the viewing position framed by this image is one of pity and condescension at the eternal homogeneity of Afghan women's lives. The photo invites lamentation from an individualistic, consumer-identified point of view that the Afghan woman has no freedom of consumer choice between one blue burqa and another. The powerful victimage of this image is countered by a subtle humor that encourages the viewer to laugh (figuratively looking down on her) at the woman's predicament rather than considering the complex social and historical contexts of women's covering.[53] Within an individualistic and pro-capitalist rhetoric, women's oppression takes the form of the denial of individuality and access to the market. Significantly, the title of the downloaded image, attributed either by the photographer or the editors, is "shopping.jpg." The woman shopping exemplifies a pitiable absence of fashion choice in contrast to a modern conception of freedom as individual choice in the modern world of market capitalism.

The ideological force of this image is made stronger by its obvious aesthetic appeal. The inescapable beauty of all of these photographs comes, in part, from the ways in which they insert U.S. viewers into a vivid construction of the reality of Afghan women. Talented professional photographers have captured the astonishing blue wall of burqas, the vivid colors surrounding the schoolgirl in Figure 3, and the sense of solitude and hope of the woman in the ruins in Figure 2. In another context, the photographs could dignify and humanize the women who are their subjects.[54]

One remarkable image toward the end of "Kabul Unveiled" shows a female Afghan television announcer reading the news (see Figure 5). The caption of this image reads: "Unveiled: Female TV announcer Shakaba Amid goes on the airwaves without a burka [*sic*] during the news hour for the Islamic State of Afghanistan's TV station, closed by the Taliban for seven years." [55] The photograph is a medium shot of a light-skinned woman sitting at a desk in a television studio, defying tradition by appearing not only in public, but also on television, without the traditional covering of head and face. This single photograph actually represents the woman three times, once in a medium shot of her profile as she reads from news reports, and twice (in waist shots of her still seated as she reads) on television monitors in the foreground. These layers of simulacra offer a sharp modern contrast to the image of the burqa-clad woman making her way through the ruins of a pre-modern world. The photograph implies that Western intervention will continue to civilize and modernize Afghanistan, bringing the country and its women into the hypermodern, technologically advanced media age.

The narrative logic of this sequence, proceeding from oppression to intervention to liberation, again establishes the invasion as a legitimate response to the 9/11 terrorist attacks. There is evidence that many members of the public at large (as opposed to the smaller anti-war publics) were encouraged by framing texts to interpret these images as reasons to support the war and occupation. In the spring and summer of 2002, triumphalism over the liberation of women and the bringing of that nation into modernity and functionality saturated mainstream culture as well. Exhibiting this position, *USA Today* commented:

> Like a throwback to days gone by, men in turbans and robes—and even some 200 women—on Tuesday began their loya jirga (grand council) meeting.
>
> Using a system based on old traditions, Afghans are deciding their future, and the result is important not only to Afghanistan, but to the United States as well.
>
> The battered country has rarely known such a moment of hope and opportunity. The U.S. war on terror ousted the repressive Taliban. Afghans have now come together to create a functioning system.[56]

Despite the article's acknowledgment of Afghans' agency, it attributes credit for their agency to the United States. The tone of the piece is one of jubilant paternalism: Afghans have thrown off the past because the United States ousted the Taliban.

The *San Francisco Chronicle* echoed the images of darkness and light that are part of the <clash of civilizations>: "As women emerge from the shadows, so will Afghanistan itself."[57] Even many prominent and historically anti-war figures on the Left, such as Christopher Hitchens, as well as a number of feminists, uneasily supported the U.S. invasion of Afghanistan on the grounds that women were so oppressed there.[58] Although no critical analysis of ideologies that circulate across texts can establish a direct connection between a particular artifact and public response, the photographs on *Time.com* are part and parcel of this widely circulating rationale that can be summarized as <the clash of civilizations>.

THE <CLASH OF CIVILIZATIONS> AS PRETEXT

Answering the question of whether this rationale is legitimate requires a critical perspective that can unveil realities under rhetorical surfaces. This method, what John Thompson calls "depth hermeneutics,"[59] features the exposure of contradictions between discourses and the truths that they veil. The epistemological assumptions of rhetorical inquiry have shifted away from this method, emphasizing instead how regimes of truth are created in discourse. As I have argued elsewhere, without a concept of an extra-discursive real, we compromise our ability to see phenomena such as imperialism for what they are; further, there is the risk of theorizing judgment and agency out of existence.[60] Thompson's method, although not a novel development in critical theory, articulates a materialist approach that allows criticism to expose reality under rhetorical fictions. Without the assumption of interpretive depth, it would be difficult to make the case for uncovering the contradictions between the humanitarian discourse of the photo essays and the reality of war, between the rhetoric of liberating women and the actual history of U.S. alliance with other oppressive regimes, including Kuwait and Saudi Arabia.[61]

There are other contradictions between the rationale for war of "saving the brown women from the brown men" and the reality of women's lives there. Since the U.S. bombing of Afghanistan, the Northern Alliance has forcibly stopped the fast-growing Union of the Women of Afghanistan from marching in Kabul. The leading women's rights organization, the Revolutionary Association of the Women of Afghanistan (RAWA), opposed U.S. military action there as well as the war in Iraq, arguing that their feminist movement does not need U.S. "help" in the form of bombs and military occupation.[62] Their continuing opposition belies the U.S. justifications for war based on the humanitarian rescue of oppressed women. RAWA's statement on the U.S. war in Afghanistan reads, in part:

America, by forming an international coalition against Osama and his Taliban-collaborators and in retaliation for the 11th September terrorist attacks, has launched a vast aggression on our country. Despite the claim of the U.S. that only military and terrorist bases of the Taliban and Al Qaeda will be struck and that its actions would be accurately targeted and proportionate, what we have witnessed for the past seven days leaves no doubt that this invasion will shed the blood of numerous women, men, children, young and old of our country.[63]

Their predictions were accurate. After the killing of thousands of innocent civilians in Afghanistan, Afghan women are hardly better off than they were before; they regard the U.S. war as akin to the Taliban regime.[64]

The full political case for my belief that U.S. withdrawal would be better than occupation for Afghan people, including women, is beyond the scope of this article. However, accepting the argument that the people of a nation cannot determine the shape of their own society is an example of having been persuaded by the "clash of civilizations" hypothesis and accepting its racialized logic. Further, in the Afghanistan case, it is difficult to dispute that even the women's movement in Afghanistan has no use for the United States or the occupation. Thus, the appeals to the liberation of women, even profoundly oppressed women, must be understood not as legitimate justification but rather as a pretext for the war and occupation.

As McGee noted in his discussion of the ideograph, tightly condensed symbols of a people's commitments can be quite forceful inducements to public consent to their rulers' policies. These images as condensed incantations of the ideograph <clash of civilizations> are no exception. Political discourse has accompanied and invoked the image of Afghan women in the appeal to the <clash of civilizations>. President George W. Bush encapsulated the <clash of civilizations> motive in his 2002 State of the Union Address: "The last time we met in this chamber, the mothers and daughters of Afghanistan were captives in their own homes, forbidden from working or going to school. Today women are free, and are part of Afghanistan's new government."[65] Likewise, in his 2004 State of the Union Address, President

George W. Bush summarized the effects of the U.S. intervention in Afghanistan:

As of this month, that country has a new constitution, guaranteeing free elections and full participation by women. Businesses are opening, health care centers are being established, and the boys and girls of Afghanistan are back in school. With help from the new Afghan Army, our coalition is leading aggressive raids against surviving members of the Taliban and al-Qaida [sic]. The men and women of Afghanistan are building a nation that is free, and proud, and fighting terror— and America is honored to be their friend.[66]

Here Bush shares the narrative strategy of the *Time* photographs and constructs a new image of the Afghan people, not as pre-modern Others but as "friends" in his claim that U.S. forces led to freedom. The phrasing suggests that the women before intervention were Others, but that they now have been folded into U.S. identity as friends. Based on his argument, however, only a subdued or compliant population has the prerogative of becoming a friend. Even in friendship, the Afghan people are claimed by the United States without reciprocal power to define the relationship.

Bush's remarks imply that saving the people, and specifically the women, of Afghanistan was the primary motive and outcome of the U.S. intervention. A closer look at the history of U.S. relations in the region reveals more salient reasons for the U.S. war. Well before the terrorist attacks on September 11, 2001, the balance of power in Afghanistan had shifted, away from "moderates" in the Taliban, who favored open relations with the United States and the United Nations, toward more nationalist and fundamentalist forces.[67] In this new configuration, the regime was much less open to the idea of allowing the United States to run an oil pipeline through Afghanistan from the Caspian Sea, which was a major component of U.S. plans to control the world oil supply. Before this point, the condition of women in Afghanistan and the injustices of Islamic dictatorship had not been of concern to the United States.[68] Thus, there is a contradiction between the rhetoric of moral inferiority and the mercenary motives of the war.[69]

Conquest of another nation for economic gain and geopolitical control is the textbook definition of imperialism.[70] Conservative intellectuals in foreign policy circles expressed the imperialist motives of the intervention explicitly, even as U.S. mass culture offered the humanitarian justifications better designed to win public support. In the influential journal *Foreign Affairs,* Sebastian Mallaby states outright the need for a new U.S. Empire: "A new imperial moment has arrived, and by virtue of its power America is bound to play the leading role."[71] Huntington also admits to this claim: "Culture, as we have argued, follows power. If non-Western societies are once again to be shaped by Western culture, it will happen only as a result of the expansion, deployment, and impact of Western power. Imperialism is the necessary logical consequence of universalism."[72] As in the time of Rudyard Kipling's description of the "white man's burden," the clashing images of <the clash of civilizations> are the surface of U.S. imperialism.[73]

In *Covering Islam,* Edward Said includes the clash of civilizations hypothesis in a category of discourse that "covers, and covers up, Islam."[74] He writes:

> "Islam" has always represented a particular menace to the West. . . . Of no other religion or cultural grouping can it be said so assertively as it is now said of Islam that it represents a threat to Western civilization. It is no accident that the turbulence and the upheavals which are now taking place in the Muslim world (and which have more to do with social, economic, and historical factors than they do unilaterally with Islam) have exposed the limitations of simple-minded Orientalist clichés about "fatalistic" Muslims without at the same time generating anything to put in their place except nostalgia for the old days, when European armies ruled almost the entire Muslim world.[75]

Later, he adds, "'Islam' is only what holds the West's oil reserves; little else counts, little else deserves attention."[76]

CONCLUSION: BEYOND THE IDEOGRAPH

Scholars should understand the workings of images during the war and occupation in the context of the actual economic and geopolitical aims of the United States. The visual manifestations of the <clash of civilizations> during the U.S. war against Afghanistan in 2001–2002 veiled the threat of terrorism with explanations of irrational hatred between superior and inferior civilizations. Metonymic, emotionally charged, and widely circulated images of terrorists and abject women established binary oppositions between self and Other, located U.S. viewers in positions of paternalistic gazing, and offered images of a shining modernity that justified U.S. intervention there. Veiling not only the reasons for terrorism, this discourse also rendered opaque the actual motives for the war and, thus, disabled real public deliberation over its course.

As in any qualitative cultural study, only indirect evidence can be adduced to suggest that such images created identification and solidified public support for war and occupation. President George W. Bush's approval ratings with regard to policy in Afghanistan were high through the end of active hostilities in 2002. In March 2002, a CNN/*USA Today* poll reported that 79 percent of Americans thought the president was doing a good job, with a majority saying they thought the U.S. was winning the war on terrorism.[77] The Associated Press reported in June, 2003, "Since the Sept. 11 terrorist attacks and through the wars in Afghanistan and Iraq, Bush has enjoyed approval ratings of 60 percent or higher in most polls, indicative of the historical trend of the nation rallying around the commander in chief when the nation's security is threatened."[78]

The cultivation of attitudes toward enemy Others in mass media is central to the rallying of public support for war. Most imagery about war is produced, mass mediated, and controlled by a mere handful of multinational media corporations beholden to state power.[79] In this context, the <clash of civilizations> imagery in national newsmagazines and on their web sites has been a powerful inducement to the public's consent. In the interest of fuller deliberation, it is imperative to cut through the pseudo-cultural, pseudo-humanitarian coding of what is, at the end of the day, a racist and imperialist project of war and occupation for the control of oil. In the case of the U.S. war with Afghanistan, the ideograph encouraged consent to repressive violence in the domestic arena (the policing of Arabs, Muslims, and dissenters under the Patriot Act) as well as abroad in acts of outright brutality that resulted in the deaths of many thousands of innocents.[80]

Images in mass media compose a slippery and not always tenable terrain upon which the struggle against the brutality of imperialism is waged. As Kevin DeLuca has argued, the increasing saturation of public discourse with mediated images compels the Left to engage and employ the strategies of visual rhetoric.[81] In *Image Politics,* DeLuca argues that social movement "image events" can "deconstruct and articulate identities, ideologies, consciousnesses, communities, publics, and cultures in our modern industrial civilization."[82] He and others are right that media and politics are intertwined and that the "public screen" has overshadowed more traditional deliberative public fora in which contending groups make arguments and engage in instrumental action toward concrete political outcomes.[83]

But is "imagefare"[84] all there is? Is it enough for movements seeking actual social change (increased standards of living for those struggling, an end to discrimination, the rights of full citizenship, and so on to more radical aims) rather than fleeting moments of shocking representation? This discussion of the possibilities and limits of the public screen raises several other questions for future inquiry—namely how, for which audiences, in what contexts, and under what circumstances oppositional images may seriously interrupt the flow of mass-mediated common sense. The social, economic, and political contexts of that engagement (including the presence or absence of a broader movement) will condition the extent of the Left's influence on an imagistic terrain. A rhetorical situation of pro-imperialist hegemony, I would argue, needs a movement with sufficient strength and visibility to enable public reframing and questioning of images that appear as slices of reality within a taken-for-granted, nationalist system of ideas.[85] To a lesser extent, critical readings of images may enable oppositional interpretation, and we should avail ourselves of opportunities to unpack the workings of hegemonic imagery in broadly accessible venues and language.

At the end of the day, the <clash of civilizations> is not just an image or an ideograph. Thus, the real clash of war requires more than scholarly criticism. Ultimately, the most significant aspect of this discourse is its role in justifying the deadly imperialist adventures of the

United States. In this context, activists must continue to challenge not only the rhetoric of civilization clash, but also its actuality, motives, and consequences. Enabling fully informed deliberation of war and occupation in the U.S. public requires critical unpacking of images and engaging the real necessity of speaking in public alongside others in international solidarity. To this end, we must go beyond scholarly production and emulate the hundreds of thousands of participants, whose numbers spanned nations, races, religions, ages, genders, sexualities, and political beliefs, in the anti-war demonstrations of 2002 and 2003. In image and in deed, these activists have begun the work of deconstructing the <clash of civilizations> in favor of shared humanity, solidarity, and peace.

Notes

1. Rudyard Kipling, "The White Man's Burden," *McClure's Magazine* 12 (February 1899). Available at Jim Zwick, "'The White Man's Burden and Its Critics," http://www.boondocksnet.com/ai/kipling/ and in Rudyard Kipling, *Rudyard Kipling's Verse: The Definitive Edition* (New York: Anchor, 1989), 321.

2. Sean Gonsalves, "War on Terrorism Has Oily Undercurrent." *Seattle Post-Intelligencer,* September 3, 2002, B5.

3. Samuel Huntington, *The Clash of Civilizations* (New York: Simon and Schuster, 1998).

4. David Spurr, *The Rhetoric of Empire* (Raleigh-Durham, NC: Duke University Press, 1993).

5. Spurr, 109–24.

6. Robert L. Ivie, "Images of Savagery in American Justifications for War," *Communication Monographs* 47 (1980): 284.

7. About Kipling's poem, Jim Zwick writes, "Published in *McClure's Magazine* in February of 1899, Rudyard Kipling's poem, 'The White Man's Burden,' appeared at a critical moment in the debate about imperialism within the United States. The Philippine-American War began on February 4 and two days later the U.S. Senate ratified the Treaty of Paris that officially ended the Spanish-American War, ceded Puerto Rico, Guam, and the Philippines to the United States, and placed Cuba under U.S. control. Although Kipling's poem mixed exhortation to empire with sober warnings of the costs involved,

imperialists within the United States latched onto the phrase 'white man's burden' as a euphemism for imperialism that seemed to justify the policy as a noble enterprise. . . . The poem was not quickly forgotten." "The 'White Man's Burden' and Its Critics," at http://www.boondocksnet.com/ai/kipling/.

8. The predominance of images is not a new or "postmodern" feature of the rhetoric of identity and Otherness. Cartoon and photographic images of white men literally carrying black people to schoolhouses characterized the rhetoric of the "white man's burden" through the 1890s. These images are available for viewing at http://www.boondocksnet.com/ai/kipling/.

9. Janis L. Edwards and Carol K. Winkler, "Representative Form and the Visual Ideograph: The Iwo Jima Image in Editorial Cartoons," *Quarterly Journal of Speech* 83 (1997): 289–310.

10. John B. Thompson, *Ideology and Modern Culture* (Stanford, CA; Stanford University Press, 1991).

11. Huntington, 110–120.

12. George W. Bush, "Transcript of President Bush's Address," *Washington Post,* September 21, 2001, A24. In response to the question, "Why do they hate us?" Bush said, "These terrorists kill not merely to end lives, but to disrupt and end a way of life."

13. Huntington, 209.

14. Huntington, 212.

15. Michael Calvin McGee, "The Ideograph: A Link Between Rhetoric and Ideology," *Quarterly Journal of Speech* 66 (1980): 1–16.

16. Celeste Michelle Condit and John Louis Lucaites, *Crafting Equality: America's Anglo-African Word* (Chicago: University of Chicago Press, 1993), 2.

17. Edwards and Winkler, 297.

18. Edwards and Winkler, 297–302.

19. See Nira Youval Davis, *Nation and Gender* (Thousand Oaks, CA: Sage, 1997); Anne McClintock, Aamir Mufti, Ella Shohat, Social Text Collective, *Dangerous Liaisons: Gender, Nation, and Postcolonial Perspectives* (Minneapolis: University of Minnesota Press, 1997).

20. This is Gayatri Chakravorty Spivak's phrase, from "Can the Subaltern Speak?" in *Colonial Discourse, Postcolonial Theory,* ed. Patrick Williams (New York: Columbia University Press, 1994), 66–111, cited material on 92.

21. For this reason, Rahul Mahajan argues that the Left should avoid appeals to innocent women and children in their opposition to war. See his *Full Spectrum Dominance* (New York: Seven Stories Press, 2003).

22. Barbara Biesecker, "Rhetorical Ventriloquism: Fantasy and/as American National Identity," in *Argument in a Time of Change: Proceedings of the 10th NCA/AFA Conference on Argumentation,* ed. James Klumpp (Annandale, VA: NCA, 1998), 168–172; David S. Birdsell and Leo Groarke, eds., "Toward a Theory of Visual Argument," *Argumentation and Advocacy* [Special Issue on Visual Argument] 33 (1996): 1–10; Randall Lake and Barbara A. Pickering, "Argumentation, the Visual, and the Possibility of Refutation: An Exploration," *Argumentation* 12 (1998): 79–93.

23. John Louis Lucaites and Robert Hariman, "Visual Rhetoric, Photojournalism, and Democratic Public Culture," *Rhetoric Review* 20 (2001): 38.

24. Lucaites and Hariman, 40.

25. Susan Sontag, *On Photography* (New York: Farrar, Strauss, and Girous, 1973), 17. Celeste M. Condit, *Decoding Abortion Rhetoric* (Urbana: University of Illinois, 1990), 82. See also Barry Brummett, *Rhetorical Dimensions of Popular Culture* (Tuscaloosa: University of Alabama Press, 1991), 27; Kathleen Hall Jamieson, *Dirty Politics: Deception, Distraction, and Democracy* (New York, Oxford: Oxford University Press, 1992), 16–42; John Fiske and John Hartley, *Reading Television* (London: Methuen, 1978), 48–49; David D. Perlmutter, *Photojournalism and Foreign Policy* (Westport, CT: Praeger, 1998). Perlmutter acknowledges the emotional power of some images but rejects the idea that images override reason or drive policy.

26. Sontag, 5. See also Francis A. Beer and Robert Hariman, *Post-Realism: The Rhetorical Turn in International Relations* (East Lansing: Michigan State University, 1996), 3; Terry Eagleton, *Ideology: An Introduction* (London: Verso, 1991), 58.

27. Emotionally powerful images, such as the photograph of a naked Vietnamese girl fleeing a napalm attack during the Vietnam War or the image of a starving Sudanese child under the watchful eye of a vulture, can evoke outrage, pride, pity, fear, and a host of other emotions. Huynh Cong (Nick) Ut, "Naked Little Girl and Other Children Freeing Napalm Strike," Associated Press, June 8, 1972; Reproduced at http://asap.ap.org/data/interactives/_news/nick_ut/index.html, accessed December 3, 2007. Kevin Carter, "Sudan, 1993," first published in D. Lorch, "Sudan is Described as Trying to Placate the West," *New York Times*, March 26, 1993, A3.

28. One could argue that these images become typical or iconic over time, training audiences in the

appropriate responses. See Robert Hariman and John Louis Lucaites, "Performing Civic Identity: The Iconic Photograph of the Flag Raising at Iwo Jima," *Quarterly Journal of Speech* 83 (1997): 363–392; and "Public Identity and Collective Memory in Iconic Photography: The Image of 'Accidental Napalm'," *Critical Studies in Media Communication* 30 (2003): 35–66. On the other hand, postmodernist scholars argue that the impact of most images in late capitalist culture is fleeting and potentially conducive of resistance. Frederic Jameson, *Postmodernism: Or, the Cultural Logic of Late Capitalism* (Raleigh-Durham, NC: Duke University, 1992); David Harvey, *The Condition of Postmodernity* (New York: Blackwell, 1990); Kevin DeLuca, *Image Politics* (New York: Guilford, 1999).

29. As Roland Barthes explains, there is "a reduction from the object and the image," collapsing signifier and signified in such a way as to lead viewers to think that the image is the thing itself. Rather than distinguishing between metaphor and metonymy, he describes metonymy as a particular kind of metaphor that pretends to stand in for the thing represented (signifier). For Barthes, all images perform this metonymic function, simultaneously transposing reality to representation. See Roland Barthes, *Image—Music—Text* (New York: Hill and Wang, 1977), 19, 51. Elsewhere, Barthes makes a distinction between metonymic images that reduce perspective (most news photographs; he also calls them "unary" images), and others that make incongruous and paradoxical perspectives possible. See *Camera Lucida* (New York: Hill and Wang, 1981), 40–43.

30. Kenneth Burke, "Identification," in *Rhetoric of Motives* (Berkeley: University of California Press, 1969), 19–28; Edward Said, *Orientalism* (New York: Random House, 1979).

31. I use the term "American" advisedly to refer not simply to U.S. citizens, but to the rhetorically constructed national identity that wins the identification of the majority of the people. As a fiction, American-ness is constructed across many discourses including the photographs under consideration here.

32. http://www.time-planner.com/planner/timecom/.

33. http://www.time-planner.com/planner/home.html.

34. I cannot afford to purchase the rights to reproduce a large number of such images; however, to confirm their representativeness, I direct readers to the web sites and archives of *Time* and *Newsweek,* the two largest mass-circulation newsmagazines published in the United States.

35. Although a photo essay traditionally is a series of still photographs accompanied by text in book or article form, *Time* calls these compilations photo essays. Although they more properly are described as image montages set to music, I will use their label advisedly.

36. Spurr, 71.

37. "From Shadow to Light" at http://www.time.com/time/covers/1101020909/.

38. Barthes, "Myth Today," in *Mythologies* (New York: Hill and Wang, 1972), 109–159; Burke, 19–28.

39. See Stuart Hall, "The Whites of Their Eyes: Racist Ideologies and the Media," in *Silver Linings,* ed. G. Bridges and Rosalind Brunt (London: Lawrence and Wishart, 1981), 28–52.

40. Ella Shohat and Robert Stam, *Unthinking Eurocentrism: Multiculturalism and the Media* (New York: Routledge, 1994).

41. Etienne Balibar and Immanuel Wallerstein, *Race, Nation, Class: Ambiguous Identities* (London: Verso, 1991); Michael Hardt and Antonio Negri, *Empire* (Cambridge, MA: Harvard University Press, 2001). I take issue with Hardt and Negri's claims that cultural racism is a new kind of racism. Indeed, the <clash of civilizations>, inherently a culturalist rhetoric, has been a staple of wartime rhetoric since the turn of the 20th century.

42. http://www.time.com/time/photoessays/afghanwomen/.

43. Spurr, 33–60.

44. "In the Taliban's Heartland" [photo essay], http://www.time.com/time/photoessays/taliban/7.html.

45. For example, the *Seattle Times* ran an article on January 2, 2004, by a correspondent who had traveled to Iraq. The article emphasizes quotations from Iraqis who support the continuation of the occupation, even though most Iraqis are opposed to it. An Iraqi police official commented, "I prefer that the Americans stay here for many years so that democracy can stand up and be built stronger. If Americans leave soon, Iraq will be many pieces." Hal Bernton, "Creating Order from Chaos is Half the Battle in Iraq," *Seattle Times,* January 2, 2004, Al, http//www.lexisnexis.com.

46. Michael Ignatieff, "Nation-Building Lite," *New York Times Magazine,* July 28, 2002, 26. Notably, none of this discourse addresses U.S. police brutality, racial profiling, or war as chaotic acts of

terrorism, although in terms of repressive consequences there is a possible analogy there.

47. Linda Alcoff, "The Problem of Speaking for Others," *Cultural Critique* 7 (1991): 5–32.

48. It is not necessarily the case that the images of oppressed women all came from the period before the U.S. intervention; however, all of the images of liberation were published after the war began.

49. I am including the United States in this category.

50. http://www.time.com/time/photoessays/afghanwomen/.

51. Terry McCarthy, "Parlika's Passion," about Soraya Parlika and 200 women activists who gathered to remove their burqas as a political statement.

52. http://www.time.com/time/photoessays/afghanwomen/.

53. It could be that images, as condensed rhetorical forms, are not well suited to the task of critical interrogation of ideologies. Scholarship and social movement discourse may unpack these complexities far more successfully. For example, feminist political theorist Nancy Hirschman has argued that veiling is not necessarily the oppressive sign that Western eyes interpret it to be. She writes, "Fueled by media reports of the oppressive practices of the Taliban in Afghanistan, anti-American fury in Iran, and Saudis demanding restrictions on U.S. women soldiers, many Westerners tend to associate veiling with extreme gender oppression, even seeing the veil as the ultimate symbol of a unified, monolithic Islam. This belies a great diversity in the practice, however, and completely ignores the fact that many Muslim women not only participate voluntarily in veiling, but defend it as well, indeed claiming it as a mark of agency, cultural membership, and resistance." Nancy Hirschman, "Western Feminism, Eastern Veiling, and the Question of Free Agency," *Constellations: An International Journal of Critical and Democratic Theory* 5 (1998): 345–369.

54. See, for example, the work of photographer Alan Pogue, who travels to Afghanistan and Iraq to photograph the targets of war. His images, placed on *Time.com*, might very well unwittingly participate in the <clash of civilizations>. See his work at http://www.austin360.com/aas/life/pogue/020302pogue.html.

55. http://www.time.com/time/photoessays/afghanwomen/.

56. "Afghanistan Begins Again," *USA Today*, June 12, 2002, 12A, http://www.lexisnexis.com.

57. Joan Ryan, "Women Hold the Key to Future of Kabul," *San Francisco Chronicle*, March 31, 2002, D3, http://www.lexisnexis.com.

58. See Hitchens' debate with Mark Danner at Salon.com, November 12, 2003, http:// www.lexisnexis.com. Also "The War, the West, and Women's Rights," *Pittsburgh Post-Gazette*, December 16, 2001, http://www.lexisnexis.com.

59. Thompson, op. cit.

60. Ronald Walter Greene is a prominent representative of the relativist epistemology I describe: "The Aesthetic Turn and the Rhetorical Perspective on Argumentation," *Argumentation and Advocacy* 35 (1998, 19–29); "Another Materialism," *Critical Studies in Mass Communication* 15 (1998): 21–41. I have articulated counterarguments to this position in Dana L. Cloud, "The Materiality of Discourse as Oxymoron," *Western Journal of Communication* 58 (1994): 141–163.

61. Saudi women are required to cover themselves head to foot and are not permitted to drive cars or eat in public. They are allowed education only with their father's permission, yet the U.S. media have not systematically deployed images of these women to warrant the direction of foreign policy (including military intervention) because the Saudi government is a compliant U.S. ally. Donna Abu-Nassar, "Women in Saudi Arabia Making Strides in Loosening Rules but They Still Have a Long Way to Go," *Associated Press Worldstream*, May 8, 2002, http://www.lexisnexis.com.

62. RAWA's documents are available on the organization's web site, http://rawa.fancymarketing.net/. Similarly, although it is beyond the scope of this article, I could support the claim that the U.S. occupation of Iraq is unwelcome and damaging to the Iraqi people; the ongoing and increasingly organized resistance is testimony to the desire on the part of Iraqi people for self-governance rather than U.S. profiteering.

63. At the time of this writing, appointed Afghan President Hamid Karzai has just signed a new constitution for Afghanistan, one that ostensibly guarantees sexual/gender equality. Only time will tell whether everyday life will measure up to the stated values of the document.

64. Sharon Smith, "Using Women's Rights to Sell Washington's War," *International Socialist Review* 21 (January-February 2002): 39–43. See also Nicholas Kristoff's account of the ongoing oppression of women there; "Afghan Women Still in Chains," *Milwaukee Journal-Sentinel*, February 17, 2004, 13A.

65. http://www.whitehouse.gov/news/releases/2002/01/20020129-11.html.

66. Text of President Bush's State of the Union Address as released by the White House, Associated Press, January 21, 2004, http://www.lexisnexis.com.

67. Michael Elliot, "Special Report: The Secret History," *Time,* August 12, 2002, 28–49.

68. Indeed, the Mujahedin, precursors of the Taliban, had the support of the United States during the Cold War for their opposition to the Soviet invasion. In 1997, the *Wall Street Journal* called the Taliban "the players most capable of achieving peace in Afghanistan at this moment in history." Hugh Pope, "Afghani Rebels Win Gains Global Notice— Nation Attracts Formal Recognition, Oil Firms' Interest," *Wall Street Journal,* May 27, 1997, A14. For the business press, the Taliban regime was crucial to secure Afghanistan as "a prime transshipment route for the export of Central Asia's vast oil, gas and other national resources." Unocal and Saudi Arabia's Delta Oil companies planned to use the Taliban control of Afghanistan to facilitate the building of a 2.5 billion-dollar pipeline through Afghanistan and Pakistan to the Arabian coast. A 1998 article heralds the Taliban, despite acknowledging its human rights abuses, as bringing the stability necessary to complete the pipeline deal. In 1998, this situation became untenable after the bombings of U.S. embassies in Tanzania and Kenya. It was clear that the Taliban were not going to be as cooperative as Unocal and others had hoped. Increasingly, the U.S. aligned with Russia against Afghanistan, and there is evidence that even in early 2001, plans were on the table to get rid of Osama bin Laden and re-establish control of the country. In May 2001, an issue of *Military Review* prepared the U.S. military for possible intervention in Afghanistan on the basis of U.S. oil interests threatened by an increasingly unfriendly regime. See Gonsalves, B5; Ian Traynor, "The Unfinished War," *The Guardian U.K.,* February 12, 2002, 4.

69. Lance Selfa, "A New Colonial Age of Empire?" *International Socialist Review* 23 (May-June 2002): 50–57.

70. In the wake of World War I, Russian socialist V. I. Lenin wrote that imperialism is the annexationist, predatory, and plunderous [sic] tendency of capitalism as a world system, in which a handful of "advanced" countries control the fates of the overwhelming majority of the people of the world. See his *Imperialism: The Highest Stage of Capitalism* (New York: International Publishers, 1939). Imperialism is marked by several characteristics: monopolization of capitalist enterprise internal to a nation-state and internationally, the creation of an international financial elite, the export of capital (and not just commodities), and "the territorial division of the whole world among the greatest capitalist powers" (89). These criteria still describe international relations today.

71. Sebastian Mallaby, "The Reluctant Imperialist: Terrorism, Failed States, and the Case for American Empire," *Foreign Affairs* 81 (March/April 2002), http://www.foreignaffairs.org/20020301facomment7967/ sebastian-mallaby/the-reluctant-imperialist-terrorism-failed-states-and-the-case-for-american-empire.html.

72. Huntington, 310.

73. Noam Chomsky, *9–11* (New York: Seven Stories/Open Media, 2001), 79.

74. Edward W. Said, *Covering Islam* (New York: Pantheon, 1981), xii.

75. Said, xiii.

76. Said, xv.

77. "Poll Watch," *The White House Bulletin,* March 26, 2002, http://www.lexisnexis.com. Approval for the war in Iraq was much lower overall, perhaps because the rationale there was the dubious claim that Saddam Hussein was harboring weapons of mass destruction. Discourse emphasizing the oppression of his people was not central to the case. In addition, in 2003 the economy began to sag, resulting in questions about spending priorities.

78. Will Lester, "Bush Approval Numbers High, But Economy, Uncertainty, Tamp Down Re-Election Support," *Associated Press Newswire,* June 25, 2003, http://www.lexisnexis.com.

79. Robert McChesney, *Rich Media, Poor Democracy* (New York: New Press, 2000).

80. In the bombing of Afghanistan, between 2,000 and 4,000 Afghan civilians were killed by U.S. forces. By many estimates, U.S. strikes killed more Afghani civilians than terrorists killed at the World Trade Center. See Traynor, 4. In Iraq, the death toll from the present war and occupation (at the time of this writing) includes more than 500 U.S. troops and between 8,000 and 10,000 Iraqi civilians, more than 1,500 in Baghdad alone; more than 20,000 have been injured (as reported at http://www.iraqbodycount .net/). Hundreds of thousands died in the first Gulf War from the war and from the punishing sanctions that lasted for 12 years.

81. Kevin Michael Deluca, *Image Politics* (New York: Guilford Press, 1999).

82. DeLuca, 17.

83. Kevin Michael DeLuca and Jennifer Peeples, "From Public Sphere to Public Screen: Democracy, Activism, and the 'Violence' of Seattle," *Critical Studies in Media Communication* 19 (2002): 125–151.

84. DeLuca and Peeples, 139.

85. The images released in May 2004 of U.S. soldiers torturing Iraqi prisoners at the Abu Ghraib detention center in Iraq have proved to be something of an exception: images so violent and violating of dominant understandings of civilization and barbarism as to cause public support of the Iraq war to plummet. These images disrupt enthymemes of the United States as rescuer of an inferior civilization and render U.S. agents as barbarous. Interestingly, the image of a hooded Iraqi standing on a crate, holding wires he was told would electrocute him if he fell, seems to mimic images of veiled women in Afghanistan. See Andrew Jacobs, "Shock Over Abuse, but Support for the Troops," *New York Times,* May 2, 2004, "Week in Review," http://query.nytimes .com/gst/abstract.html.

AFTERWORD

Look, Rhetoric!

THOMAS W. BENSON

Let us begin again. How often we students of rhetoric have said that to ourselves, starting over again down the centuries. Usually, we have started over again by looking back to our beginnings. We keep our eyes on the road, but with glances in the rearview mirror. In the many reformings of rhetorical criticism in the 20th century, we have looked back to Herbert Wichelns, whose "The Literary Criticism of Oratory," first published in 1925, was itself a way of starting forward again by looking back. In that 1925 essay, Wichelns refounded the rhetorical criticism of public discourse by starting with a concession:

> Oratory—the waning influence of which is often discussed in current periodicals—has definitely lost the established place in literature that it once had. . . . Yet the conditions of democracy necessitate both the making of speeches and the study of the art. It is true that other ways of influencing opinion have long been practiced, that oratory is no longer the chief means of communicating ideas to the masses. And the change is emphasized by the fact that the newer methods are now beginning to be investigated, sometimes from the point of view of the political student, sometimes from that of the "publicity expert." (Wichelns, 1925/1958, pp. 5, 7)

Then a curious thing happened, but in fits and starts.

Wichelns established rhetoric as the frame for critics of oratory in departments of speech. Before long, the students who followed Wichelns developed a thriving scholarship in rhetorical criticism and soon found themselves going far beyond oratory and public discourse to ask what could be learned from the application of rhetorical approaches to those "other ways of influencing public opinion." These scholars discovered that rhetoric could be a useful way of studying film, fiction, theater, journalism, landscape, performance, poetry, visual arts, architecture, music, photography, evolving electronic media, spectacle, protest, and other nonoratorical modes of human action (see Medhurst & Benson, 1984). There was, naturally, some institutional resistance in the discipline to the rhetorical study of nonoratorical forms. Much of that resistance was put to rest by the 1970 National Developmental Project on Rhetoric, a joint venture of the National Endowment for the Humanities and the Speech Communication Association, which issued its report, *The Prospect of Rhetoric,* in 1970. The project's committee on the scope of rhetoric and its place in higher education explicitly encouraged the study of "theory and practice of forms of communication which have not been as thoroughly investigated as public address" (Ehninger et al., 1971, p. 217), and its committee on rhetorical criticism asserted that "rhetorical criticism may be applied to any human act, process, product

413

or artifact which, in the critic's view, may formulate, sustain, or modify attention, perceptions, attitudes, or behavior" (Sloan et al., 1971, p. 220). In developing these new domains of criticism, rhetorical scholars found that rhetoric had been explicitly present since the beginnings of its study in all the domains of the visual and other arts. They found, as well, that the study of non-oratorical rhetoric was a two-way process— rhetoric had something to teach the study of each of the other modes, and the study of each of those modes rhetorically stimulated new ways of thinking about "traditional" rhetoric, forcing us to question taken-for-granted truths. At the same time, rhetorical studies crafted creative alliances with critical and cultural studies more generally (see Benson, 1978; Prelli, 2006; Rosteck, 1999).

Critical studies in rhetoric are almost always in some sense about power and agency. The theme of power, in the context of visual rhetoric, illustrates something of the complexity of the role of the critic in rhetorical power. Those who developed rhetorical studies in departments of speech in early 20th-century America combined the study of theory, public address, and rhetorical criticism with a practical, daily attempt to translate what they learned into classroom instruction in public speaking for college men and women.

The analysis of public oratory was always, in principle, part of the search for useful lessons, ideals, or rhetorical failures that could guide the practice of public speaking for citizens in training. At the core of the practice was the conviction that in the open contest of free debate, citizens could improve their chances of arriving at reasonable judgments. Speech critics taught public speaking. Visual rhetoric has partly justified itself by pointing to the evident proliferation of rhetorical action or its substitutes into other modes of expression. Democratic institutions depend on continuing critical analysis. But visual rhetoric as a scholarly discipline is almost exclusively a mode of criticism, at least among scholars situated in the disciplines of speech, communication, and English. Most practitioners of visual rhetoric are critics, but most of us are not teaching courses in the production of the sorts of images we subject to critical analysis; in fact, a central if implicit theme of much visual rhetoric is that the citizen is a spectator, a consumer, an agent by proxy at best. Critics of visual rhetoric are not, for the most part, teaching the practical skills of photography, filmmaking, advertising design, cartooning, landscape architecture, or television news broadcasting. The disjunction between criticism and practice in rhetorical studies is reflected thematically in the criticism, which again and again returns to themes of decentered or stigmatized identity, crippled agency, distraction, diversion, nostalgia, self-exhibition, exclusion, and the manipulation of collective memory.

Visual rhetoric in all its forms appears to be more or less exempt from the implicit standard of verbal rhetoric that all argument, in principle if not in practice, is subject to the ethical expectations of reciprocity—all parties are owed an equal chance to speak—and of bilaterality—if we commit ourselves to an argument, we owe our interlocutors the fair chance to win us and our audiences over to their point of view (see Johnstone, 1983). Visual rhetoric, for the most part, does not work that way. On the other hand, the actual conduct and structure of verbal persuasion in a mass society often makes the standard of reciprocity seem a remote and unlikely will o' the wisp. Counterfactual truthiness.

Although most scholars of visual rhetoric work primarily as critics rather than as instructors in the making of visual rhetoric, this does not mean that they are without a sense of the social importance of visual rhetoric. The critical analysis of visual rhetoric is richly connected with a sense of everyday life and public action. The work of the critics in this collection variously contributes to recovering lost vernaculars, exercising an alert wariness about implicit appeals to togetherness that excludes, appreciating the marginalized, making visible the repressed, and tracing the history of official, popular, commercial, and cultural practices, forms, and themes that are outside the canon of public address and its scholarship.

It must also be conceded that most visual rhetoric, at least as it becomes subject to analysis by rhetorical critics, is not purely or merely *visual*. This occurs in three sorts of ways. In one sense, it is evident that rhetorical critics of the visual are dealing with media and genres that are often, themselves, mixed media—photojournalism is captioned and is contextualized in written news stories; motion pictures and television employ images, speech, and other sounds; protest demonstrators carry signs and shout slogans. In another sense, when rhetorical critics analyze visual rhetoric, we often go beyond the visual image itself to create a larger "text" that comprises the image and some other layers of verbal context—whether antecedent information about the production of the image, simultaneous verbal discourse that contextualizes the image, or subsequent verbal commentary that is taken to represent responses to the image or this larger "text." It is then this "text," and not the image by itself, that is the subject of the critic's attention. In a third sense, many of the visual objects that engage rhetorical critics are themselves so heavily invested with generic significance that the visual images seem to come to audiences and to critical analysis pretextualized and overdetermined. What we "see" in a typical frame from a Hollywood film is so heavily invested with narrative context that we see the story in the image. What we "see" in most of the images of television news is so heavily invested with propositional or propagandistic context that it could be drawn from—or easily catalogued in—a pigeon hole in a film stock library: the grieving widow, the first day of school, the hurricane at the beach, the reporter at the fire scene. These three senses of the textualizing of the visual do not constitute objections to the study of visual rhetoric. On the contrary, rhetorical inquiry is precisely committed to understanding how such visual rhetoric works.

Although neither visual rhetoric nor the scholarship of visual rhetoric are purely visual, the visuality of visual rhetoric matters. Visual rhetoric is never entirely reducible to textuality and in fact seems to draw much of its power from the interaction of sight and sense. Another recent book on visual rhetoric employs on its front cover a photograph in which we see

a hand, at the left side of the frame, holding a snapshot of a city skyline, which is being held up against the same skyline, which we see on the right side of the larger, "present" photograph. But in the shot-within-the-shot, we can see the Twin Towers of the World Trade Center, which are missing from the skyline in the background of the "present" photograph. The simplicity and austerity of the double photograph invite reflection, abstracting the scenes without imposing a narrative or a sentiment; we can find but are not especially prompted by the photographer to prefer the comforts of simple irony, patriotic outrage, or ritualized grief. This austerity and abstraction

Figure 1 *Defining Visual Rhetorics* Cover Image.

SOURCE: Used by permission from Lawrence Erlbaum. Photographer: Richard LeFande.

liberate our contemplation and ask us to see and to reflect. At the same time, the remembered day in September 2001, referred to but not pictured in the before-and-after of the double photograph, is remembered with a wide-eyed muteness that takes in the vanity of our search for meaning. The photograph helps us, if we accept its invitation, to become aware of our own predicament. To merely see the concreteness of the scene without reference to its meaning would be a failure of witness. To turn our backs on the silence of the city afternoon and the plain evidence of our eyes, seeking consolation in "meaning," would also be a failure of witness— the witness of our incapacity to experience what is gone, the duty to remember despite our incapacity, the homely curiosity of the photographer holding his earlier photograph against the altered skyline.[1]

The 20 critical essays in the present collection investigate a variety of visual forms— photography, editorial cartoons, public monuments, tattoos, mural art, television news and advertising, postal stamps, prints. They describe images doing the work of social control and of social protest or political change. They are, as a collection, concerned with race and ethnicity, wealth and class, sexuality and gender, memory and forgetting, discernment and distraction, getting and spending, individual identity and collective identification, seeing and showing, realism and illusion, the body, the market, and the state. All have been published within the past 20 years, most within the past 10 years, attesting to a rising level of interest and sophistication in the scholarship of visual rhetoric. All provide a balance of theoretical argument and critical practice, which may make them especially useful in classroom discussion and as inspirations to further investigations. We'll see.

For a generation of American schoolchildren, the first sentence they ever read, and their introduction to "textuality," was an imperative found in a picture book: "Look, look!" Still good advice.

NOTE

1. The World Trade Center photograph, by Richard A. LeFande, appears as the cover photo on *Defining Visual Rhetorics* (Hill & Helmers, 2004). Mr. LeFande, whom I have always known as Louis LeFande, was an MFA student in the Program in Visual Studies at SUNY Buffalo, which was housed in the Visual Studies Workshop in Rochester, New York, in 1970 and 1971, where I was an associate professor and his adviser, and we engaged in some early attempts to formulate a criticism of visual rhetoric. I had been teaching rhetorical theory, public address, rhetorical criticism, and other parts of the "speech" curriculum, including small group discussion and nonverbal communication as well as courses in the rhetoric of fictional and documentary film at SUNY Buffalo since 1963.

REFERENCES

Benson, T. W. (1978). The senses of rhetoric: A topical system for critics. *Central States Speech Journal, 29*(4), 237–250.

Ehninger, D., Benson, T. W., Ettlich, E. E., Fisher, W. R., Kerr, H. P., Larson, R. L., et al. (1971). Report of the committee on the scope of rhetoric and the place of rhetorical studies in higher education. In L. F. Bitzer & E. Black (Eds.), *The prospect of rhetoric* (pp. 208–219). Englewood Cliffs, NJ: Prentice Hall.

Hill, C. A., & Helmers, M. (Eds.). (2004). *Defining visual rhetorics.* Mahwah, NJ: Lawrence Erlbaum.

Johnstone, H. (1983). Bilaterality in argument and communication. In J. R. Cox & C. A. Willard (Eds.), *Advances in argumentation theory and research* (pp. 95–102). Carbondale: Southern Illinois University Press.

Medhurst, M. J., & Benson, T. W. (Eds.). (1984). *Rhetorical dimensions in media: A critical casebook.* Dubuque, IA: Kendall/Hunt.

Prelli, L. J. (Ed.). (2006). *Rhetorics of display.* Columbia: University of South Carolina Press.

Rosteck, T. (Ed.). (1999). *At the intersection: Cultural studies and rhetorical studies.* New York: Guilford.

Sloan, T. O., Gregg, R. B., Nilsen, T. R., Rein, I. J., Simons, H. W., Stelzner, H. G., et al. (1971). Report of the committee on the advancement and refinement of rhetorical criticism. In L. F. Bitzer & E. Black (Eds.), *The prospect of rhetoric* (pp. 220–227). Englewood Cliffs, NJ: Prentice Hall.

Wichelns, H. A. (1958). The literary criticism of oratory. In D. C. Bryant (Ed.), *The rhetorical idiom: Essays in rhetoric, oratory, language, and drama* (pp. 5–42). Ithaca, NY: Cornell University Press. (Original work published 1925)

INDEX

Abbot, Jon, 318
Abject, the, 267–269
Abramson, Daniel, 140–141, 148–150
Abstract Expressionism, 243, 301
"Accidental Napalm" (Ut), 175–195, 178f, 186f, 187f
Adams, Alice, 44
Adams, Ansel, 318, 324n9
Adams, Herbert B., 66
Adams, Noah, 269
Adams, William, 189
Addams, Jane, 232
Adorno, Theodor, 51
"Advantages of Being a Woman Artist" (poster), 241
Adventures of Ozzie and Harriet (TV series), 321
Advertising, 273–277
    by Apple Computers, 276, 279–290
    branding and, 276, 281, 287, 315
    Hariman on, 274
    identity and, 279–295, 313–326
    by Kodak Corporation, 283–284, 313–323
    McLuhan on, 322
    by Pennsylvania Railroad, 273f
    by U.S. Postal Service, 295–308
    See also Consumerism
Afghanistan, 330, 393–406
African Americans, 202, 367
    Apple ads and, 284, 285
    art and, 227, 248
    Civil War and, 100, 106–107, 111–114
    postal commemoratives and, 303–306
    Riis on, 30–32
    See also Civil rights movement
Agassiz, Louis, 111
AIDS, 201, 205–218, 267
AIDS Memorial Quilt, 216, 309n29
Albee, Parker, 120–121

Albright, Madeleine, 382
Alcoff, Linda, 401
Alexander, Elizabeth, 266, 267, 268
Ali, Muhammad, 262–263, 266, 268, 284, 285
Alonzo, Angelo, 207–208, 211–212
Alpers, Svetlana, 62
Althusser, Louis, 370
American Gothic (Wood), 132
Amnesia, 307–308
    See also Memory
Amphigorical logic, 287, 290
Apple computer advertisements, 276, 279–290
Appropriation, 101, 102, 202–203, 275, 329, 331
    Colonial emblems and, 333–356
    comic form and, 241–256
    consumption and, 279–294
    iconic images and, 175–198
    power and, 357–374
    resistance and, 205–226
    respresentative form and, 119–138
    television news and, 375–392
Aristotle, xxii, 43, 74n11, 181
Art Workers Coalition (AWC), 243
Asante, Molefi, 263, 266
Ashcroft, John, 258–259
"Atom-cracking," feminist, 244–245
Audience, 328–329
    presidential photo opportunities and, 357–374
Auslander, Philip, 280
Austin, John L., 16, 366
Authorizing, 327–331
Aztlán, Casa, 201, 227–237, 234f–236f

Baca, Judy, 228, 230
Baldetta, John, 210–212, 216
Baldwin, James, 265

Note: Page numbers with an *f* indicate figures; those with an *n* indicate note numbers.

Balibar, Etienne, 398
Barba, Eugenio, 281
Barclay, Paris, 83
Barker, Francis, 47
Barnett, A. W., 230, 231
Barnhurst, K. G., 386–387
Barrera, Carlos, 232
Barry, Ann Marie Seward, 282
Barthes, Roland
  on metonymy, 408n29
  on myths, 268, 302–303
  on negative identity, 398
  on photography, 62, 121, 176, 182, 185, 189,
    257, 264, 321
Bartlett, Truman H., 72
Barton, Clara, 166
Baty, S. Paige, 124, 125, 288, 375
Baudrillard, Jean
  on *simulacra*, 46–48, 296, 308n5, 387
  on television, 38n7, 380
Baxandall, Michael, 62
Baylin, Anne, 195n2
Beauchamp, Keith, 259
Belisarius, 346
Bellah, Robert, 124–125, 297, 308
Benedict XVI (pope), 55n5
Benitez, L. M., 375
Benjamin, Walter, 16
  on captions, 290
  on photography, 21–22, 24, 189
Bennett, Lerone, 269
Benson, Christopher, 265, 268
Benson, Steve, 130, 131f
Benson, Thomas W., 4–6, 106, 107, 413–416, 419
Berger, Arthur Asa, 284
Berger, Carole, 105
Berger, John, 34
Berlant, Lauren, 81, 87, 92
  on citizenship, 170n13
  on visual *paramnesias,* 160
Bernstein, Carl, 388
Bertelsen, Lance, 120–121
Betsky, Aaron, 298
Bhabha, Homi, 148
Biesecker, Barbara, 101–102, 157–169, 419
Blair, Carole, 101, 139–150, 202, 419
Blair, J. A., 227–228
Blogs, xxiv
Bodnar, John, 99, 299
Body rhetoric, 18–19
  public kissing and, 79–98
  violence and, 257–272
Bond, Julian, 263
Boone, Mary, 244
Bordo, Susan, 44, 55n11, 265

Bosmajian, Haig A., 5
Bostdorff, Denise, 123
Bourdieu, Pierre, 16
Bracero Program, 230
Bradley, Mamie. *See* Till Bradley, Mamie
Brady, Mathew, 68
Brain, Robert, 208
Branding, consumer, 276, 281, 287, 315
  See also Advertising
Brewer, David J., 66
Britton, Andrew, 106
Brokaw, Tom, 386
  on Clinton-Lewinsky affair, 378
  Greatest Generation, 101–102, 161–165, 169
Brooks, Gwendolyn, 263
Brouwer, Dan, 17, 201, 205–218, 419
Brown, Joshua, 106
Brown, M. E., 375
Brown v. Board of Education, 146–147,
    152n18, 265, 358
Brown, Wendy, 164
Browne, Stephen H., 100
Brummett, Barry, 124, 253
Bruni, Frank, 86
Bryant, Carolyn, 258
Bryant, Roy, 258, 261, 262
Buckley, William F., Jr., 205, 206, 210, 212,
    218n4, 221n23
Burgin, Victor, 176
Burke, Kenneth, 4–5, 8
  on artistic symbols, 229
  on "atom cracking," 244–245
  on audience expectations, 109–110
  on cartoons, 350n4
  on conventional form, 107
  on dramatic frames, 241–242, 245, 366
  on form, 305, 311n62
  on negative identity, 398
  on "pure" science, 55n8
  on "representative anecdote," 124
  on symbolic actions, 16
  on symbols, 350n1
Burns, Ken, 100, 105–115
Burton, Marie, 230
Bush, George H. W., 306, 357, 361–367, 369
Bush, George W., 251f, 395, 398, 404, 405
Butler, Judith, 16, 81, 93n8, 223, 267–269, 370, 387
Butsch, Richard, 280

Califia, Pat, 86
Callas, Maria, 282, 285–287
Campbell, Bebe Moore, 263
Campbell, Bill, 306
Campbell, Karlyn Kohrs, 121, 245, 248, 375
Capitalist Realism, 315–316

Captions, for images, 290, 303, 366
Caputo, John, 180
Carmichael, Stokely, 260
Carter, Jimmy, 358, 360–362, 366, 367, 369
Cartoons, 100, 199f, 327f
   Benjamin Franklin's, 333–349, 334f–337f, 340f
   Iwo Jima image in, 101, 119–133
   rhetoric of, xv, 6, 350n4
Casa Aztlán, 229–237, 234f–236f
Castelli, Leo, 244
Celebrate the Century ad campaign, 295–308
Chadwick, W., 243, 244, 246
Chávez, César, 201, 231, 232, 234f, 236
Chesnutt, Charles W., 40n55
Chicago, Judy, 6
Chicago Mural Group, 229
Chicano murals, 201, 227–237, 234f–236f
A Child Is Born (Nilsson), 45–46
Chilton, Edward, 185–187, 186f
Chong, Denise, 183
Chong, Dennis, 141–142, 151n9
Cicero, xxiv
Cirque du Soleil, 82, 83
Civil religion, 296–299, 307–308
Civil Rights Memorial, 101, 139–150,
   143f, 144f, 146f
Civil rights movement
   Lyndon Johnson and, 361
   tactics of, 141–142, 149
   Emmett Till's murder and, 202, 258,
      263–270, 272n57
   See also Race
Civil War
   Montgomery (AL) memorials to, 145, 147
   postal commemoratives of, 297–298
Civil War (TV series), 100, 105–115
Clarke, Eric O., 84–85
"Clash of civilizations," 101, 200, 330, 393–406
Class, 4, 10, 16–17, 108, 164, 363
   Riis's photos and, 22–37
   tattoos and, 208, 220n11
   voyeurism and, 33–37
Clay, Cassius. *See* Ali, Muhammad
Clément, Catherine, 287
Clichés, 85, 119, 377, 405
Clinton, Bill, 124, 188, 357–359, 363–367
   gun control and, 361
   impeachment threat against, 159, 365
   Kennedy and, 360
   Lewinsky affair and, 369, 376, 378, 381–382, 385
   WWII memorial and, 157, 158
Clinton, Chelsea, 380
Clinton, Hillary Rodham, 276, 329–330, 375–388
Close, Chuck, 244
Cloud, Dana L., 101, 200, 330, 370, 393–406, 420

Clow, Lee, 280, 282
Cmiel, Kenneth, 142
Coats, Andrew, 210, 212–213, 216
Cobb, Charles, 269
Coburn, Judith, 289
Cochran, Johnny, 263
Cockcroft, E., 229
Cohen, Lizabeth, 274
Cohen, William, 382
Colden, Cadwallader, 340
Coleman, A. D., 319, 324n8
Collins, Eileen, 363
Comics. *See* Cartoons
Commodification, 273–277
   Baudrillard on, 308n5
   political amnesia and, 307–308
Communication studies, 4–9
Community Mural Movement, 229, 238n3
Condit, Celeste, 388n4, 395
Conquergood, Dwight, 220n14
Conrad, Paul, 128
Consumerism, 273–277
   Barthes on, 302–303
   civil religion and, 296–299
   democracy and, 276, 296, 305, 395–398
   McLuhan on, 321–322
   See also Advertising
Contextualization, xvii, 230, 237, 247, 249, 414–415
   political cartoons and, 122, 132
   presidential rhetoric and, 369, 370
   television and, 376–382, 387
Cook, James, 219n11
Cooley, Thomas M., 70–71
Cousteau, Jacques, 52–53
Crane, Verner, 342, 343, 354n54
Crary, Jonathan, 7–8
Crimp, Douglas, 220n17
Custer, George Armstrong, 108
Cynics, xxi

Daguerreotypes, 1, 62, 65
   by Mathew Brady, 68
   of Lincoln, 18, 61f, 62–69, 73
   by J. T. Zealy, 110–112
Daly, Tom, 110, 115n3
Darwin, Charles, 77n78
Dauber, Cori, 330
Davies, Russell T., 88
Davis, Susan G., 309
Dean, James, 324n12
Debord, Guy, 9, 289, 299, 370
   See also Spectacle
DeCoster, Jeffrey, 187–188, 187f
Dees, Morris, 139–140, 152n20
Dehner, Dorothy, 243

Deleuze, Gilles, 9, 23, 268
DeLuca, Kevin Michael, 87, 175–176, 277, 420
  on image politics, 199, 406
  on Emmett Till, 200, 202, 257–270
  on wartime media, 330
Demo, Anne Teresa, 18, 201–202, 241–254, 330, 420
Democracy, 72
  consumer, 276, 296, 305, 395–398
  oratory and, 413–414
  Vietnam War and, 181, 184–189
  Virilio on, 194
  WWII and, 121, 128, 158, 168
Derrida, Jacques, 7, 38n5
Diamond trade, 273–274
Díaz, Aurelio, 232
Dickerman, Leah, xxv
Dickinson, Greg, 305
Diekmeyer, Peter, 285
Diogenes of Sinope, xxi
Disciplinary gaze, 25–27
Discipline, Foucault on, 23, 38n12, 44, 45, 49
Disney Corporation, 46, 192, 280
Documentary films
  Civil War, 100, 105–115
  during Depression, xxiii
  about Emmett Till, 258, 259
  genres of, 5–6
  about Maya Lin, 150n2
  Miracle of Life, 17, 41–54
  See also Films
Documentary photography, 24, 396
  assumptions of, 107–109
  audience collaboration with, 109–110
  How the Other Half Lives as, 22–37
  reframing of, 100, 111–115
  See also Photography
Dole, Bob, 157
Dole, Elizabeth, 377
Douglas, Mary, 267
Dow, Bonnie, 19, 253
Doxa, 162
Duden, Barbara, 42, 43, 45, 46, 48
Duncan, Hugh, 245
Dylan, Bob, 263–264
Dyson, Michael Eric, 149

Eastman, George, 67, 76n53, 316
Eclipse of Reason (film), 43
Eco, Umberto, 176–177
Edelman, M., 386
Edwards, Janis L., 101, 119–133, 202, 394–396, 420
Edwards, Paul, 287
Ehrenhaus, Peter, 101, 184
Einstein, Albert, 287
Eisenhower, Dwight D., 368

Eisenstein, Sergei, 286
Elizabeth I (queen of England), xxii
Ellis Island museum, 306
Ellis, J., 379
"Emblems," 337–338
Enthymemes, 62–63, 73–74, 74n11, 411n85
Epideictic rhetoric, 230–231, 295–312
Epstein, Jeffrey, 83, 89
Erasmus, Desiderius, 163
Erickson, Keith V., 329, 357–371, 420
Ethnicity. *See* Race
Eugenics movement, 56n17, 70, 72–73, 77n78
  See also Race
Evans, Walker, 317, 324n7
Evers, Medgar, 142
Ewen, Stuart, 315

Falklands War, 363
Faludi, Susan, 253
Family, 223, 283–284
  domestication of, 27–29
  homosexuality and, 80, 90–91
  interracial, 200
  mythology of, 320–321
  photography and, 17, 68, 277, 319–323
  slave, 106–107, 112–113
  WWII and, 161–165, 171n24
Farrell, Tom, 114–115
Faust, Jan M., 378
Feminist "atom-cracking," 244–245
Fields, Barbara, 111, 113, 115
Fierstein, Harvey, 89
Films
  Eisenstein on, 286
  Rebel Without a Cause, 324n12
  rhetoric of, 5–6
  Saving Private Ryan, 101–102, 158–162, 168–169
  See also Documentary films
Finnegan, Cara A., 1–11, 18, 61–74, 417
Fischer, R. A., 121, 134n12
Fishburn, K., 378
Fiske, John, 37
Flores, L. A., 230, 231, 236
Ford, Gerald, 358, 366, 368
Ford, Henry, 303
Forman, Milos, 195n3
Foss, S. K., 230
Foss, Sonja, 101, 106, 133, 309n29
Foster, Hal, 7–8
Foucault, Michel, 7, 16
  Birth of the Clinic, 43–45, 212
  on conformity, 55n11
  Discipline and Punish, 23, 38n12, 44, 45, 49
  on *doxa,* 162
  on heterotopias, 9, 276, 281, 290

History of Sexuality, 41, 44, 56n12
  on knowledge, 93
  on memory, 168
  on sexuality, 41, 44–45
  on "speaking eye," 45, 46, 48, 54
  on surveillance, 9, 23–24
Fowler brothers, 69
Framing, 100, 111–115, 241–242, 245
Franklin, Benjamin, 6, 328–329, 333–349,
    334f–337f, 340f
Franklin, H. B., 192
Franklin, John Hope, 139, 150
Franklin, William, 343
Freeman, Keller, 120–121
French and Indian War, 334–335
Freud, Sigmund, 16
Fuller, Bryan, 83
Fuller, Matt, 205–206, 211, 216
Fuller, Meta, 244
Fuoss, Kirk W., 261
Fury, Gran, 18, 85–88, 86f
Fussell, Paul, 121

Gablik, S., 253
Galloway, Joseph, 337, 345
Galton, Francis, 77n78, 78n100
Gamson, William, 126–127
Gandhi, Mohandas, 285–287
Gangel, Jamie, 376, 383
Gaonkar, Dilip, 7, 8
Gaze, 9
  camera's, 388
  disciplinary, 25–27
  medical, 44–47, 51
  mirrored, 285, 290
  normalizing, 49
  performance of, 34
  visibility and, 16
Gender, 330–331, 370, 387
  Judith Butler on, 16, 93n8, 267–269, 387
  "feminist atom-cracking" and, 244–245
  Kodak advertisements and, 316, 324n6
  paternalism and, 400–401, 403
  race and, 4–10, 29, 164, 396
  Riis's photos and, 24–33
  typecasting Hillary Clinton and, 376–378, 381,
    384, 387
Gillis, John, 297, 298, 309n29
Gilman, Sander, 29
Goddard, William, 339, 343, 352n23
Goffman, Erving, 201, 206–208, 221n20, 315,
    316, 321
Goldberg, Vicki, 120–121
Goldman, Debra, 279, 291n4
Goldsby, Jacqueline, 266, 268

Goldstein, Richard, 83
Golub, Jennifer, 282
Gombrich, Ernst, 107, 120, 350n1
Gonsalves, Sean, 393
Gonzalez, Alberto, 231, 232
Gonzalez, Rodolfo, 201, 231
Goodman, Nelson, 7
Gorbachev, Mikhail, 363–364, 367
Gore, Al, 361
Gottlieb, Andrew, 243
Governing, 327–331
Graber, D. A., 385
Graffiti, 229
Gran Fury, 85–88, 86f
Grand Central Terminal, Kodak's Colorama in,
    313–323, 314f
Graves, John, 158
Greatest Generation (Brokaw), 101–102, 161–165, 169
Greene, Ronald Walter, 370, 409n60
Greenfield, Jeff, 376–380, 384
Gregg, Richard B., 5
Grenada, U.S. invasion of, 365
Griffith, D. W., 40n55
Grindstaff, Davin A., 330
Gronbeck, Bruce E., xxi–xxv, 2, 5–6, 420–421
Gropper, William, 327f
Gross, Larry, 5, 81
Grover, Jan Zita, 209, 219n9
Grundberg, A., 323
Guattari, Félix, 9, 23
Guernica Culture House, 195n3
Guerrilla Art Action Group (GAAG), 243
Guerrilla Girls, 201–202, 241–254, 330
  "Advantages of Being a Woman Artist," 241
  history of, 243–244
  bell hooks on, 253
  international influence of, 253
  posters by, 241, 244, 246, 249–252, 250f, 251f
  publications of, 244, 246–248
  Steinem on, 242
Guevara, Ernesto "Che," 233, 234f, 235f
Guggenheim Museum, 244
Guimond, James, 121
Gulf War, 306, 367
Gun control, 361
Gunter, B., 379
Gutiérrez, José Angel, 201, 231

Haas, Ernst, 318
Habermas, Jürgen, 7, 175, 176
Habitus, 16
Haddock, Jon, 195n3
Halftone process, 64, 68, 313
Hall, David, 336, 337, 343, 351n14
Hall, Stuart, 398

Halstead, Murat, 61–62
Halttunen, Karen, 69
Hamberger, Lars, *45–46*
Hamer, Fannie Lou, 260, 270n14
Hammerback, J. C., 232
Handy, Bruce, 321
Hariman, Robert, 396, 421
    on "Accidental Napalm" images, 102, 175–195,
        276–277, 329
    on advertising, 274
    on prudent performance, 358, 362–364
Haring, Keith, 244
Harold, Christine, 200, 202, 257–270, 277, 421
Harper, Phillip Brian, 88
Hart, R. P., 379, 383, 384
Hartley, John, 265
Hartnett, Stephen, 69
Harvey, David, 308n7
Haskins, Ekaterina V., 102, 201, 276, 295–308, 421
Hauser, Gerard, 92, 151n11
Hausman, Carl, 122
Hawkins, Peter S., 309n29
Haymarket Riot (1886), 24, 73
Heller, Steven, 290
Helmers, Marguerite, 415–416, 415f
Helms, Jesse, 247, 251
Heraclitus, xxi
Hermeneutics
    depth, 394, 403
    physiognomic, 69–70
    of suspicion, 175
Heterotopias, 9, 276, 284–286, 290
Hidalgo, Miguel, 234, 235
Highfill, Holly, 230
Hill, Charles A., 415–416, 415f
Hirohito (emperor), 368
Hirsch, J., 320
Hirschman, Nancy, 409n53
Historical re-vision, 157–174, 247–248, 252–254
Hitchens, Christopher, 403
HIV disease. *See* AIDS
Hocus Focus, 289, 291n11
Hollis, Thomas, 338
Homosexuality, 159
    company benefits and, 283, 284
    marriage and, 80, 90–91
    military service and, 123f, 124
    narrative of risk and, 51
    public kissing and, 15, 79–93, 329
    stigmatization of, 83, 85, 92
hooks, bell, 152n21, 253
Hope, Diane S., 1–11, 200, 277, 313–323, 417
Horkheimer, Max, 51
How the Other Half Lives (Riis), 16–17, 22–37,
    28f, 31f, 32f, 35f, 330

Howells, William Dean, 21
Hudson-Weems, Clenora, 264
Hughes, John, 343
Huie, Bradford, 261–262
Hulser, Kathleen, 108
Human rights, 181, 192
Hunter-Gault, Charlayne, 265–266
Huntington, Samuel, 394, 395, 398, 405
Hutchinson, Thomas, 340, 348–349

Icon(s)
    collective memory and, 188–195,
        288, 295
    definitions of, 120, 349n1
    image-making and, 375–376
    Olson on, 120, 349n1
    Osborn on, 122, 130, 131
    photographic, 102, 177–178, 189–195
    postal, 296–299
Iconology, 333–349, 349n1
Identity, 275–276
    advertising and, 279–295, 313–326
Ideographs
    "clash of civilations" and, 395–396
    McGee on, 101, 120, 125–129, 395, 404
    verbal, 132
    visual, 101, 125–133, 394–396
Ifill, Gwen, 378
Ignatieff, Michael, 401
Illusionism, politics of, 329, 357–371
Image vernaculars, 61–74
Imperialism
    Lenin on, 410n70
    Mexican Americans and, 233, 235
    Vietnam War and, 182, 188, 195
    war on terror and, 394, 403, 405–406
Indiana, Gary, 244
Ingres, Jean-Auguste-Dominique, 249–250
Inouye, Daniel, 164–165
Interracial relationships, 200
Intertextuality, 22, 23, 33, 37
Iraq, 401, 405
    Abu Ghraib prison in, 411n85
    Gulf War and, 306, 367
Irigaray, Luce, 246
Irmas, Deborah, 220n11
Italian Americans, 302
Ivie, Robert, 394
Iwo Jima editorial cartoons, 101, 119–133
Iwo Jima Memorial, 364, 395–396

Jabbar, Kareem Abdul, 264
Jackson, Jesse, Jr., 265
Jackson, Jesse, Sr., 257, 265
Jameson, Fredric, 299, 299, 309n22

Jamieson, Kathleen, 121, 358, 377
Jay, Martin, 7–8
Jenks, Chris, 125
Jensen, R. J., 232
Jhaveri, Hemal, 84
Jim Crow laws, 248, 260, 264
   See also Race
Jobs, Steve, 280, 282
Johnson, Lyndon, 358, 360, 361, 364, 369, 370
Johnson, R., 387
Jones, Rose, 53
Jung, Carl Gustav, 289
Juxtaposition, 9, 47, 100
   incongruous, 244–249, 252–254
   strategic, 242, 249–252, 250f, 251f

"Kahlo, Frida" (Guerrilla Girl), 246
Kahlo, Frida (Mexican painter), 233–234,
   234f, 235f
Kairos, 81, 82
Kammen, Michael, 99, 168
Kaplan, Amy, 24
Kaposi's sarcoma, 210, 221n19, 222n26
Kelley, Robin D. G., 264, 266, 269
Kennedy, John F., 358, 359, 369, 370, 386
   Berlin Crisis and, 362–363
   Clinton and, 360
   iconic photographs of, 74n4
Kent State killings, 189, 190
Kerr, Norman, 316, 318–319
Kielwasser, Alfred, 86
Kimberly Agreement, 274
King, Martin Luther, Jr., 149, 259, 284
   Civil Rights Memorial and, 141–142, 144, 147
   papers of, 272n54
   postal commemorative of, 306
   Emmett Till's murder and, 200, 264, 265
Kipling, Rudyard, 393, 395, 401, 405, 406n7
Kissing, 15, 18, 54, 79–93, 329
Knight, Robert, 80
Kodak Corporation, 67, 76n53
   advertising campaigns of, 277, 283–284, 316
   Colorama of, 313–323, 314f, 318f–320f
Koestenbaum, Wayne, 284
Kooning, Elaine de, 243
Kooning, Willem de, 243
Koppel, Ted, 379–380
Kramer, Hilton, 244
Krasner, Lee, 243
Kress, Gunther, 121
Kristeva, Julia, 267
Kroft, Steve, 384
Ku Klux Klan, 37, 40n55, 150n1, 270
Kuhn, Annette, 164
Kuhn, Thomas, 7

"*La marcha*" (Raya), 235, 236f
Labaree, Leonard, 337, 339
LaBruce, Bruce, 79–80
Lacan, Jacques, 7, 16
   mirror stage of, 9
   on visibility, 166
Lamarck, Jean-Baptiste, 43
Lancioni, Judith, 18, 100–101, 105–115, 421
Lange, Dorothea, 396
Lauer, Matt, 378, 380
Lavater, Johann Caspar, 69
LaWare, Margaret R., 101, 201, 227–237, 421
Lawrence v. Texas, 81
Lawson, James, 142
Leap, William, 86
Lears, T. J. Jackson, 73
Leary, Kevin, 121
LeFande, Richard A., 415f, 416n1
Leff, Michael, 245
Lehnus, Donald J., 308n11
Lenin, Vladimir, 410n70
Leonardi, Susan J., 291n9
Lesbianism. *See* Homosexuality
Lester, Paul Martin, 121, 194
Levin, Joe, 139, 152n19
Levine, Lawrence, 114
Lévi-Strauss, Claude, 288
Levy, Anita, 25, 28–29
Levy, Steven, 289
Lewinsky, Monica, 369, 376, 378,
   381–382, 385
Lewis, William, 272n57
Limbaugh, Rush, 359
Lin, Maya, 139–150, 140
Lincoln, Abraham, 18, 61–74, 108
Lincoln Memorial, 99f, 134n12, 169, 359
Lingus, Alphonso, 264
Lippard, Lucy, 253
Lippert, Barbara, 281
Lithography, xxii
Long, Beverly, 22
Longinus, xxii
Lorde, Audre, 263
Lotringer, Sylvere, 194
Louganis, Greg, 82
Louis XIV (king of France), xxii
Lozano, Rudy, 234f
Lubin, David M., 68
Lucaites, John Louis, 102, 175–195, 276–277,
   329, 395, 396, 421
Luckovich, Mike, 127f
Lynchings, 202, 259–261, 266–267, 269
   murder versus, 270n7
Lyons, Gene, 383
Lyotard, Jean-François, 308, 311n66

Magic lantern shows, xxv
Mahajan, Rahul, 407n21
Mailer, Norman, 159
Malcolm X, 259, 266
Mallaby, Sebastian, 405
Mander, M. S., 379
Manovich, Lev, 9
Mao Zedong, 358, 359
Marchand, Roland, 315
Marcuse, Herbert, 289
Mariette, Doug, 127
Marling, Karal Ann, 129–130
Marriage
  gay, 80, 90–91
  interracial, 200
  See also Family
Martin, Emily, 48–49, 55n4, 55n9
Martin, James, 287
Maslin, Janet, 279, 290
Matthews, Christine, 387
Matzer, Maria, 283
Mayenova, Maria, 130–131
Mayhew, Jonathan, 338
McClellan, George, 108
McCullough, David, 108–114
McGee, Michael C., 8, 364
  fragmentation thesis of, 358, 368–369
  on ideographs, 101, 120, 125–129,
    132, 395, 404
  on materialist rhetoric, 361
McKerrow, R. E., 358, 368
McLuhan, Marshall, 5, 315, 321–322
McNally, Joe, 183f
McRae, Tom, 384
Medhurst, Martin J., 6, 349n1
Memory, 99–102, 317
  Aristotle on, xxii
  collective, 168–169, 188–195, 288,
    307–308, 386–389
  Foucault on, 168
  political amnesia and, 307–308
  postal commemoratives and, 295–308
Mendel, Gregor, 77n78
Menzel, Peter, 324n14
Messaris, Paul, 120, 122, 132, 274–275,
  286, 288, 382–383
Meta-narratives, 9, 308
Metaphor, 2
  cartoons and, 119–129
  Colonial emblems and, 333–356
  marketing and, 279–294
Metonymy, 408n29
Metropolitan Museum of Art, 244, 250f
Metz, Christian, 9
Mexican-American murals, 201, 227–237, 234f–236f

Mexican-American War, 231
Meyer, Richard, 86, 87
Meyrowitz, J., 357, 382, 383
Michel, Neil, 101, 139–150, 202, 422
Milam, J. W., 258, 261–262
Miller, Jeremy, 281
Miller, Toby, 163
Mimesis, 361
Mimicry, 242, 246–247, 252
Miner, Ward, 343–344, 352n14
Minh-ha, Trinh T., 111–112
Minor, Robert, 10, 199f
Miracle of Life (film), 17, 41–54
Mirzoeff, Nicholas, 282
Miss America pageants, 331
Mitchell, Gordon, 330
Mitchell, Joan, 243
Mitchell, S. Weir, 56n18
Mitchell, W. J. T., 120, 133
  on critical public art, 139, 150
  on mixed media, 177
  on "pictural turn," 7, 8
Montanus, Neil, 318
Moody, Anne, 264
Moore, Joan W., 237
Moore, Liz, 243
Morgan, Robin, 253
Morin, Richard, 129f
Morris, Charles E., III, 18, 79–93,
  201, 329, 422
Morrison, Toni, 263
Morse, John T., 66–67
Mount Rushmore, 132, 364
Movies. *See* Films
Ms. magazine, 195n2
MTV, 82, 83, 85
Mug shots, of criminals, 68–69
Muir, J. R., 375
Mulryan, Dave, 284
Mulvey, Laura, 9
Munch, Edvard, 179
Munsterberg, Hugo, 115n4
Murals
  African-American, 227
  Chicano, 201, 227–237, 234f–236f
  See also Posters
Murder of Emmett Till (film), 259
Museum of Modern Art, 244, 248
Museums, 244, 248, 285, 306–307
Mutchnick, Max, 87–88
Muybridge, Eadweard, 67
Myrdal, Gunnar, 149
Myths
  Barthes on, 268, 302–303
  civil religion and, 297

family, 320–321
  Lévi-Strauss on, 288
  transnational, 308

NAMES Project AIDS Memorial Quilt, 216, 309n29
Narrative
  meta-, 9, 308
  performance fragments and, 360
  photography and, 323
  of traumatic events, 182–185, 190,
      192–195, 261–262
National Endowment for the Arts (NEA), 247
National Endowment for the Humanities
    (NEH), 413
Negri, Antonio, 398
Nelson family, 321
Newton, Julianne H., 275
Nickel, D. R., 317, 320, 321
Nicolay, John G., 71
Nietzsche, Friedrich, 45
Nike Corporation, 192
Nilsson, Lennart, 17, 41–54
Nixon, Richard, 358–363, 367, 376
Nochlin, Linda, 247–249
Nolke, Virginia, 301
Nolte, Carl, 121
Noonan, P., 369
Nora, P., 387

Oakar, Mary Rose, 165
O'Hara, Scott, 217, 222n28
Oklahoma City bombing, 364
Oldenburg, Claes, 244
Olson, Lester C., 1–11, 417
  on Franklin's illustrations, 102, 328–329,
      333–349, 334f–337f, 340f
  on icons, 120, 349n1
Operation Desert Storm, 306, 367
"The Opposition" (Gropper), 327f
"Optical unconscious," 189
Oratory, xxiv, 5, 413–414
  presidential, 329, 357–371
Orozco, José Clemente, 232
Orvell, Miles, 67
Osborn, Michael, 122, 130, 131

Palmer, John, 378
Panofsky, Erwin, 7, 349n1
Panopticism, 9
Paramnesias, visual, 160
Parks, Gordon, 318
Parks, Rosa, 215, 284
Parody, visual, 101, 119–120, 130–132, 202
Parry-Giles, Shawn J., 276, 329–330, 375–388, 422
Paternalism, 29, 400–401, 403

Patlán, Raymond, 229, 232
Patton, Cindy, 212, 217, 219n8, 224n41
Pauley, Jane, 382, 386, 387
Pavis, Patrice, 280–281
Peeples, Jennifer, 175–176
Peirce, Charles S., 7, 69, 349n1
Performance, 15–19
  of desire, 33–37
  of the gaze, 34
  intercultural, 281
  kairotic, 82
  political, 357–371
  prudent, 358, 362–364
  rhetorical, 144–150
  surveillance and, 21–37
Peterson, Merrill D., 67
Pfeffer, Naomi, 48–49
Phelan, Peggy, 166, 207–209, 216–217
Photography
  as art form, 317, 321, 323
  Barthes on, 62, 121, 176, 182, 185,
      189, 257, 264, 321
  Walter Benjamin on, 21–22, 24, 189, 290
  captions for, 290, 303, 366
  color, 313–314, 317–318
  of criminals, 68–69
  daguerreotypes and, 62, 65, 68
  Derrida on, 38n5
  family, 17, 68, 277, 319–323
  halftones and, 64, 68, 313
  history of, xxiii
  iconic, 102, 177–178, 189–195
  Lucaites on, 396
  of lynchings, 259, 260, 266–267, 269
  magic lanterns and, xxv
  physiognomy and, 62, 67–74
  Sontag on, 22, 110, 319–320, 323, 396
  Trachtenberg on, 63, 108, 180
  See also Documentary photography
Phrenology, 62, 67–70
Phronesis, 360
Phuc, Kim, 181, 183–185, 183f, 188–195
Physiognomy, 62, 67–74, 70, 72–73
Picasso, Pablo, 285, 287
"Pittsburgh, 1916" (Minor), 10, 199f
Plato, xxi–xxii
Podro, Michael, 350n1
Pogue, Alan, 409n54
Politics
  of illusionism, 329, 357–371
  image, 199, 406
  of subversion, 241–254
  visibility, 79–98, 208–209
  See also Cartoons
Pollack, Della, 144, 151n14

Pollock, Jackson, 243, 301
Pope, Rebecca A., 291n9
Porter, Eliot, 318
Poster, Mark, 290
Posters, xxii–xxiii
    advertising, 273f, 314–317, 314f
    by Guerrilla Girls, 241, 244, 246,
        249–252, 250f, 251f
    "Read My Lips," 85–88, 86f
    See also Murals
Powell, Kimberly, 249
Powers, L. D., 232
POZ magazine, 205–206, 210–211, 218n2
Presidential rhetoric, 329, 357–371
Prostitution, 29, 39n50, 219n9
Public address studies, 62–64
Public Art Workshop, 229
Public sphere, 175–195
    dissent and, 185–188, 186f, 187f
    "public screen" and, 271n15
    Warner on, 171n32, 191–192
Pullman Strike (1894), 24, 73

Quaid, Dennis, 89–90

Race, 370, 398
    affirmative action and, 306
    eugenics movement and, 56n17, 70, 72–73, 77n78
    gender and, 4, 10, 29, 164, 396
    hooks on, 152n21
    Jim Crow laws and, 248, 260, 264
    Kodachrome and, 324n8
    lynchings and, 259–261, 266–267, 269, 270n7
    Riis on, 30–33, 31f, 32f
    stigma of, 29, 39n50, 163–164
    See also African Americans
Rather, Dan, 386
Ratzinger, Joseph, 55n5
Rawls, John, 51–53
Raya, Marcos, 232–237, 236f
"Read My Lips" campaign, 85–88, 86f
Reagan, Ronald, 283, 357, 359–361, 363–365,
        367–369
Realism
    Capitalist, 315–316
    commericial, 316, 321
    critiques of, 379
    Howells on, 21
    photographic, 24
    Socialist, 316
Rebel Without a Cause (film), 324n12
Reinelt, Janelle, 219n6
Religion, civil, 296–299, 307–308
Rembrandt, 47, 50
Renault, Dennis, 123f

Re-vision, historical, 157–174, 247–248, 252–254
Revolutionary Association of the Women of
        Afghanistan (RAWA), 403–404
Reynolds, Nancy, 207–208, 211–212
Rhetoric
    in *Apologia,* 328, 338–344
    body, 18–19, 79–98, 257–272
    Burke on, 5
    of cartoons, xv, 6, 350n4
    critical studies of, 413–416
    as deliberative genre, 335–338
    of difference, 231
    epideictic, 230–231
    exhibition, 167, 172n45
    iconology and, 333–349
    materialist, 361
    oratory and, xxiv, 5, 413–414
    photographic framing and, 105–115
    presidential, 329, 357–371
"Rhetorical consciousness," 2, 7, 8
Rich, Frank, 80, 82
Richardson, George, 333
Riis, Jacob A.
    background of, 24–25
    eugenics movement and, 72–73
    How the Other Half Lives, 16–17, 22–37,
        28f, 31f, 32f, 35f, 330
    magic lantern shows by, xxv
Riley, Richard W., 301
Rilke, Rainer Maria, 248
Rivera, Diego, 6, 233
Roalf, P., 232n3
Roberts, Hugh, 343
Robichaud, Nancy, 281
Rockwell, Norman, 6, 320
Rodin, Auguste, 72
Roeder, George, 121
Rogovin, Mark, 230
Román, David, 218n5
Romo, Ricardo, 234, 235
Ropes, John C., 66
Rorty, Richard, 7
Rosen, Lisa, 85
Rosenfield, Lawrence, 230, 274
Rosenstone, Robert, 106
Rosenthal, Joe, 119–123, 125–129
Rosteck, Thomas, 245
Rudnick, Paul, 83, 85
Rueckert, William, 242
Runyon, Marvin, 299

Said, Edward, 405
Sanders, Clinton, 208
Sandoval, Alberto, 218n5
Savage, Augusta, 248

Savedoff, Barbara, 65
Saving Private Ryan (Spielberg), 101–102, 158–162, 168–169
Sawday, Jonathan, 47, 50–51
Sayre, Henry, 151n14, 243
Scafetta, Joseph, Jr., 302
Scarry, Elaine, 190, 260
Schmidt, Helmut, 364
Schmuhl, R., 357
Schnabel, Julian, 244
Schorr, Bill, 123f, 127, 130f
Schram, S. F., 383
Schumer, Charles, 258–259
Schwartz, Barry, 64, 67, 75n16
Scopic regime, 9
Scott, Linda M., 107
Scott, R. L., 199
Searle, John R., 16
Seidman, Steven, 82–83
Sekula, Allan, 69
Self-stigmatization. *See* Stigmatization
Sellars, Peter, 281
Sender, Katherine, 89, 97n75
Serra, Valentino, 318
Shaw, Bernard (TV personality), 377
Shay, Jonathan, 182
Shelley, Cameron, 18–19
Shields, Ronald E., 276, 279–290, 422
Shohat, Ella, 111, 398
Shugart, Helene A., 84
Shulman, Jessica, 284
Silent Scream (film), 43, 55n6
Simulacra, 307, 385, 402–403
    Baudrillard on, 46–48, 296, 308n5, 387
    Jameson on, 299
    Mitchell on, 370
Siqueiros, David Alfaro, 232
Slobogin, Kathy, 376, 377, 379, 381, 383
Sloop, John M., 18, 79–93, 201, 329, 423
Smith, D. K., 199
Smith, Roberta, 244
Snyder, J., 379
Social stratification, 25–27
"Soldiers of Misfortune" (DeCoster), 187–188, 187f
Solomon-Godeau, Abigail, 22
Sommese, Lanny, 15f
Sons of Italy, 302
Sontag, Susan, 22, 110, 319–320, 323, 396
Southern Poverty Law Center (SPLC), 139–140, 142, 143f, 144f, 145, 150n1
"Speaking eye," 45, 46, 48, 54
Spectacle, 9, 289, 299, 365, 370–371
    critique through, 175–176
    lynching as, 260–261, 266–267, 269
Speech Communication Association, 413

Spellman, Francis Joseph, 185–187, 186f
Spielberg, Steven, 101–102, 158–162, 168–169
Spinoza, Benedict de, 257
Spivak, Gayatri Chakravorty, 407n20
Spurr, David, 394, 397
Stafford, Barbara Maria, 45, 48
Stallybrass, Peter, 33–36
Stam, Robert, 111, 398
Stamp Act, 334–348
Stange, Maren, 22, 25
Stayskal, Wayne, 124
Steele, Shelby, 265
Steinem, Gloria, 242
Stephens, Mitchell, 375
Stereotypes, 387
    Hillary Clinton and, 376–378, 384, 387
    Cornel West on, 148
Stern, Madeleine, 70
Stieglitz, Alfred, 316–317
Stigmatization, 17, 29, 414
    AIDS and, 201, 205–218
    etymology of, 207
    Goffman on, 201, 206–208
    homosexuality and, 83, 85, 92
    meanings of, 219n10
    race and, 29–30, 39n50, 163–164
Stoddard, Tom, 222n26
Stormer, Nathan, 17–18, 41–54, 101, 423
Strikes, labor, 10, 24, 199f
Strine, Mary, 22
Stuart, David, 126–127
Stuart, Otis, 80, 82
Stuber, Adolph, 317, 318
Sturken, Marita, 189
Surveillance, 16, 79–98
    double, xxiii
    Foucault on, 9, 23–24, 44
    performative dimension of, 21–37
    politics of, 23–24
    Riis's photos and, 17
Sweet, Ozzie, 318

Tagg, John, 26
Tarbell, Ida, 64–65
Tattelman, Ira, 86
Tattoos
    class and, 208, 220n11
    history of, 208, 219n11
    HIV/AIDS, 201, 205–218
Tehrani, Alex, 289
Television
    Baudrillard on, 38n7, 380
    Hillary Clinton and, 276, 329–330, 375–388
    collective memory and, 386–388
    contextualization and, 376–382, 387

history of, xxiii–xxiv
Nelson family on, 321
news recycling on, 384–386
Templeton, John, 284
Terrorism, war on, 80, 393–406
Thomas, Clarence, 249
Thompson, John, 394, 403
Tijerina, Reies, 201, 231
Till Bradley, Mamie, 258, 259, 262, 263, 265, 267, 268
Till, Emmett, 200, 202, 257–270
Titian (Tiziano Vercellio), 250
Tomb of the Unknown Soldier, 309n29
Tomkins, Calvin, 244
Tompkins, Phillip K., 5
Torres, Sasha, 259
Toscani, Oliviero, 221
Trachtenberg, Alan, 63, 107, 108, 180
Trade unions, 10, 24, 199f
Trauma narratives, 182–185, 190, 192–195, 261–262
Truman, Harry S., 357
Tulloch, John, 280
Turner, Frederick Jackson, 73
Turner, Kathleen J., 6
Turner, Ted, 285
Turning Point Project, 290
Twigg, Reginald, 16–17, 21–37, 330, 423
Tyler, Kathy, 287

Unconscious, "optical," 189
Unions, trade, 10, 24, 199f
United Farm Workers, 232, 234–235
United Nations, 181
Untold Story of Emmett Louis Till (Beauchamp), 258
U.S. Postal Service (USPS) commmemoratives, 276, 295–308
Ut, Nick, 178f, 183
Utopias, heterotopias and, 285

Valverde, Juan de, 50–51
Van Leeuwen, Theo, 121
Varnedoe, Kirk, 253
Vavrus, M., 376
Vega, Salvador, 232
"Veritatis Vietnam" (Chilton), 185–186, 186f
Vernacular, 18
definition of, 309n28
myth and, 393–412
visual culture and, 61–78
Vesalius, Andreas, 47
Vietnam Veterans Memorial, 101, 106, 139, 147, 300, 309n29
Vigée-Lebrun, Élisabeth, 248
Villa, Pancho, 234

Virgin of Guadalupe, 201, 228, 233
Virilio, Paul, 194
Visibility, 79–98
of AIDS, 209–210, 267
gaze and, 16
Lacan on, 166
medical imagery and, 41–60
politics of, 82–86, 208–210
risks of, 220n15
self-stigmatization and, 17
stigmatization and, 205–218
technology and, 18, 312–326
Visual rhetoric, xvii, 1–11
definitions of, 2–3, 415–416
manipulations of, 378–386
public sphere and, 176
resistance and, 199–200
scholarship of, 415f
scholarship on, 3–9, 414–416
visual studies versus, 6–8
Visual turn, 7, 8, 357–358
Visuality, xvi–xvii, xxiv–xxv, 2, 7–8, 62, 415
Voyeurism, 16, 21–40
Ehrenhaus on, 184
Riis's photos as, 17, 23, 33–37
Sontag on, 22

Wagner, Richard, 286
Walker, Francis A., 62, 67
Wallerstein, Immanuel, 398
Walters, Suzanna, 83, 84
Walzer, Michael, 180
Warner, Charles Dudley, 66
Warner, Michael, 81, 87, 92, 171n32, 191–192
Wartella, E., 386–387
Washington, George, 63, 75n16
Washington Monument, 169
Weibe, Robert, 72
Wells, Samuel R., 69, 71
West, Cornel, 148
West, Nancy Martha, 315, 317
Wetenhall, John, 129–130
White, Allon, 33–36
White, Hugh, 270n7
"White Man's Burden," 39n50, 393, 395, 401, 405, 406n7
Whitewater investigation, 381, 385
Whitney, Henry C., 66
Whitney Museum of American Art, 244
Wichelns, Herbert, 416
Williamson, Judith, 279, 288
Wilson, Woodrow, 66
"Wingspread" report, 5
Winkler, Carol K., 101, 119–133, 202, 394–396, 423

Wiseman, Frederick, 6
Wittgenstein, Ludwig, 7
Wolcott, James, 159–160
Wolf, Edwin, 338, 351n14
Wolf, Michelle, 86
Wollstonecraft, Mary, 44
Women Artists in Resistance (WAR), 243
Women in Art (WiA), 243
Women in the Military Service (WIMS) Memorial,
     165–169, 167f
Women Students and Artists for Black Art
     Liberation (WSABAL), 243
Women's International Terrorist Conspiracy from
     Hell (WITCH), 243
Women's Liberation Organization, 243
Wood, Grant, 132
Working Women's Society, 29

World Trade Center, 323n3, 367, 395, 398, 415–416
World Trade Organization (WTO), xxiv, 200
World World II Memorial, 101–102, 157–169,
     157f, 170n8
Worth, Sol, 5, 120
Wright brothers, 303
Wright, Frank Lloyd, 285, 303
Wright, Mose, 261

Ybarra-Frausto, Tomás, 229
"Year of the Woman" (1992), 304

Zadan Craig, 83
Zapata, Emiliano, 233, 234f, 235f
Zealy, J. T., 110–112
Zelizer, B., 386, 387
Zwick, Jim, 406n7

ABOUT THE EDITORS

Lester C. Olson is Professor of Communication at the University of Pittsburgh, where he specializes in public address, rhetoric, and visual culture. His books include *Emblems of American Community in the Revolutionary Era: A Study in Rhetorical Iconology* (1991) and *Benjamin Franklin's Vision of American Community: A Study in Rhetorical Iconology* (2004). His book on Franklin was recognized with awards from the Rhetoric Society of America and the National Communication Association, the two largest communication and rhetoric societies in the United States. His essays concerning visual rhetoric can be found in the *Quarterly Journal of Speech* and the *Review of Communication.* He earned his Ph.D. from the University of Wisconsin–Madison in 1984.

Cara A. Finnegan is Associate Professor in the Departments of Speech Communication and Art History at the University of Illinois at Urbana-Champaign. Her research explores the social, political, and historical role of visual communication in the American public sphere. She is the author of *Picturing Poverty: Print Culture and FSA Photographs* (2003). Her essays on visual rhetoric have appeared in journals such as the *Quarterly Journal of Speech, Rhetoric & Public Affairs,* and *Rhetoric Society Quarterly.* She is a former recipient of the National Communication Association's Diamond Anniversary Book Award and its Golden Monograph Award.

Diane S. Hope is the William A. Kern Professor in Communications at the Rochester Institute of Technology. She publishes in the areas of visual communication and the rhetoric of social change. She was awarded the National Communication Association's Excellence in Research Award from the Visual Communication Division in 2007 for her book, *Visual Communication: Perception, Rhetoric and Technology* (2006). She edited Earthwork (2001), a special issue of *Women's Studies Quarterly* devoted to women and the environment and was general editor of *Women's Studies Quarterly* from 2002–2005. Her publications have appeared in various journals and edited collections. She directs the Kern Communication conferences on Visual Communication: Rhetoric and Technology, and Communication and Social Change at the Rochester Institute of Technology.

About the Contributors

Thomas W. Benson is the Edwin Erle Sparks Professor of Rhetoric at Pennsylvania State University. He is the author or editor of 13 books, including *Reality Fictions: The Films of Frederick Wiseman,* with Carolyn Anderson; *Writing JFK: Presidential Rhetoric and the Press in the Bay of Pigs Crisis;* and *The Rhetoric of the New Political Documentary,* with Brian Snee. He is the former editor of the *Quarterly Journal of Speech, Communication Quarterly,* and *The Review of Communication.*

Barbara A. Biesecker is Associate Professor of Rhetoric in the Department of Communication Studies at the University of Iowa. She teaches and writes at the intersections of contemporary rhetorical theory and criticism, feminist theory and criticism, and cultural studies. In addition to her book, *Addressing Postmodernity: Kenneth Burke, Rhetoric and a Theory of Social Change,* she has contributed essays to several edited volumes and has published her work in journals such as the *Quarterly Journal of Speech, Philosophy and Rhetoric,* and *Rhetoric and Public Affairs.* She is completing a book-length manuscript on the rhetoric and politics of remembering World War II; coediting a collection of essays on rhetoric, politics, and materiality; and editing the new Forum Series for the *Journal of Communication and Critical/Cultural Studies.* She is the 2007 recipient of the National Communication Association's Douglas Ehninger Distinguished Rhetorical Scholar Award.

Carole Blair, Professor of Communication Studies at the University of North Carolina, earned her BA and MA at the University of Iowa and her PhD at Penn State. Her research, with Neil Michel (Axiom Photo Design, Davis, California) and Bill Balthrop (University of North Carolina), focuses on the rhetorical and cultural significance of U.S. commemorative places and artworks. Her research has been published in journals and anthologies across disciplines (communication studies, landscape architecture, English, philosophy, sociology). She has received the National Communication Association's Doctoral Dissertation Award, Golden Anniversary Monograph Award (twice) and Charles H. Woolbert Research Award, and the outstanding article award from the Organization for the Study of Communication, Language and Gender. She teaches related courses on visual and material rhetorics, rhetoric and public memory, and rhetorics of place, as well as contemporary rhetorical theory and criticism.

Dan Brouwer is Associate Professor in the School of Human Communication at Arizona State University. His research interests span theories of publics and counterpublics, the rhetoric of social movements, rhetorical criticism, and cultural performance. Recurrent research topics include HIV/AIDS and queer politics. He is coeditor (with Robert Asen) of the book *Counterpublics and the State,* and he is currently working on a coedited book project (also with Robert Asen) on publics and publicity. Recent essays have appeared in the journals *Critical Studies in Media Communication, Rhetoric and Public Affairs,* and *Western Journal of Communication.* A sabbatical leave during 2006–2007 permitted Dr. Brouwer to lecture on issues of publics and social controversy at l'Université Stendhal Grenoble 3 (France), Roskilde Universitetscenter (Denmark), and the University of Copenhagen.

Dana L. Cloud (PhD, University of Iowa, 1992) teaches in the Communication Studies Department at the University of Texas, Austin. She has published one book (*Rhetorics of Therapy*, 1998) and is completing a second on the labor movement. Along with many book chapters, she has published numerous articles on the subjects of ideology, popular culture, rhetorics of race, gender and sexuality, social movement studies, public sphere studies, and Marxist and feminist theory, in outlets such as the *Quarterly Journal of Speech, Communication and Critical Cultural Studies, Rhetoric and Public Affairs, Critical Studies in Media Communication,* and *Western Journal of Communication.* A longtime activist against the death penalty and for workers, women, minorities, immigrants, and GLBTQ persons, she is a member of the International Socialist Organization. She lives in Austin with her spouse Kathleen Feyh and daughter Samantha Hutchinson-Cloud. More information may be found at http://uts.cc.utexas.edu/~dcloud .

Kevin Michael DeLuca is Associate Professor at the University of Georgia. Author of the book *Image Politics: The New Rhetoric of Environmental Activism,* he explores humanity's relation to nature and how people's relationships to nature are mediated by technology. He has published essays on environmental politics, social movement practices, the rhetorics of violence and bodies, social theory, and media. He uses his privileged position to cultivate sublime experiences and to think. Once in a while, he understands something briefly.

Anne Teresa Demo is Assistant Professor in the Department of Communication Studies and Rhetoric, Transmedia, and the School of Art and Design at Syracuse University. Her work explores the relationship between rhetoric, identity, and U.S. cultural politics through two primary research concentrations. Her primary area of research has focused on the visual rhetoric of contemporary immigration policy and politics. Her secondary research examines the role of visual rhetoric in social movements. She has published articles in the *Quarterly Journal of Speech, Critical Studies in Media Communication, Rhetoric and Public Affairs, Environmental History,* and *Women's Studies in Communication.*

She received her PhD in 2000 from Pennsylvania State University.

Janis L. Edwards (PhD, University of Massachusetts, 1993) is Associate Professor of Communication Studies at the University of Alabama, where she teaches courses in rhetoric and political communication and serves as the Undergraduate Program Coordinator. She also facilitates the UA Visual Studies Consortium. Her research interests concentrate on politics and gender, visual studies, and public memory. She is the author of *Political Cartoons in the 1988 Presidential Campaign: Image, Metaphor, and Narrative,* and her essays have appeared in publications such as the *Quarterly Journal of Speech, Communication Quarterly, PS Political Science and Politics,* and *Women's Studies in Communication.* She has twice served as Chair of the National Communication Association's Visual Communication Division and received the division's first research excellence award. She is also an award-winning visual artist who has exhibited widely in California, New York, and other locales.

Keith V. Erickson is Professor of Speech Communication, University of Southern Mississippi. His research interests include visual rhetoric, presidential communication, and rhetorical theory. He has published 6 books and 40 articles, including essays in *Communication Monographs, Quarterly Journal of Speech, Communication Education, Rhetoric Society Quarterly, Communication Quarterly, Communication Studies, Western Journal of Speech Communication,* and *Journal of Language and Social Psychology.* He is past editor of the *Southern Communication Journal* and *Texas Speech Communication Journal.* He also served as President of the Southern Communication Association and International Society for the History of Rhetoric. He is presently investigating the visual implications of first lady international travel.

Bruce E. Gronbeck is the A. Craig Baird Distinguished Professor of Public Address, Department of Communication Studies and the Project on the Rhetoric of Inquiry, at the University of Iowa. In addition, in the Obermann Center for Advanced Studies, he directs the University of Iowa Center for Media Studies and Political Culture. His scholarship is focused on relationships between and among rhetoric, media, politics, and culture. He has authored or edited a dozen books on presidential campaigning, democracy and engaged citizens, media studies (theory and criticism), rhetorical criticism, and public communication generally. He holds a PhD from Iowa as well as honorary doctorates from Concordia College (MN), Uppsala University (Sweden), and Jyväskylä University (Finland).

Robert Hariman is professor in the program in rhetoric and public culture, Department of Communication Studies, Northwestern University. His publications include *No Caption Needed: Iconic Photographs, Public Culture, and Liberal Democracy* (2007, coauthored with John Louis Lucaites); *Political Style: The Artistry of Power* (1995); three edited volumes, *Popular Trials: Rhetoric, Mass Media, and the Law* (1990), *Post-Realism: The Rhetorical Turn in International Relations* (1996, coedited with Francis A. Beer), and *Prudence: Classical Virtue, Postmodern Practice* (2003); and numerous book chapters and journal articles in several disciplines. Current work on visual culture includes frequent posting at the blog, http://www.nocaptionneeded.com.

Christine Harold (PhD, Penn State, 2002) is Assistant Professor in the Department of Communication at the University of Washington. She teaches courses in rhetoric and cultural theory. Her research focuses on the relationship between consumer culture, rhetoric, and the possibilities for political engagement within contemporary capitalism. Her book, *OurSpace: Resisting the Corporate Control of Culture* (2007), examines culture jamming as a response to corporate power. It advocates an "open content" ethic as one way to promote a more robust and democratic public culture. She is currently at work on a second book, tentatively titled *De/sign*, about the intersections between design, mass consumption, and environmental sustainability.

Ekaterina V. Haskins is Associate Professor of Rhetoric at Rensselaer Polytechnic Institute. She is the author of *Logos and Power in Isocrates and Aristotle* (2004). Her research on classical

and contemporary rhetoric has been published in the *Quarterly Journal of Speech, Rhetoric Society Quarterly, Philosophy and Rhetoric, Space and Culture, Journal of Communication Inquiry, American Communication Journal,* and a number of edited collections. Her scholarship received several awards, including the Karl Wallace Memorial Award from the National Communication Association, the Everett Lee Hunt Award for Outstanding Scholarship in recognition of her book, and the Rhetoric Society of America's Kneupper Award for Best Article. Her research interests include rhetorical theory and history, visual rhetoric, and rhetorics of public memory and national identity.

Judith Lancioni is Associate Professor in the Department of Radio, Television, and Film, College of Communication, Rowan University, Glassboro, New Jersey. She teaches television scriptwriting, film and television theory and criticism, and feminist film criticism. In addition to her article on the ideological implications of reframing in *The Civil War,* she has also presented three conference papers on the Burns film and is currently working on a book on the subject. In addition, she has published articles on the ethics of reality television, dramady and postfeminism in *Desperate Housewives,* and the Cinderella myth in *Billy Elliot.*

Margaret R. LaWare is Associate Professor in the Department of English/Program in Speech Communication at Iowa State University, where she is also a Women's Studies affiliate. She received her PhD in Communication Studies from Northwestern University and has taught at SUNY Plattsburgh. One of her research areas focuses on issues of diversity and community as communicated visually, through public art and public space. She has also written about gender issues and feminist rhetorical communication within the framework of responses to war and militarization. Her articles have appeared in such journals as *Advocacy and Argumentation, NWSA Journal, Basic Course Annual,* and *Women & Language,* as well as in edited volumes.

John Louis Lucaites is Professor of Rhetoric and Public Culture in the Department of Communication and Culture, Indiana University. His publications include *No Caption Needed: Iconic*

Photographs, Public Culture, and Liberal Democracy (2007, with Robert Hariman) and *Crafting Equality: America's Anglo-African Word* (1993, with Celeste Condit), as well as three coedited volumes: *Martin Luther King, Jr. and the Sermonic Power of Public Discourse* (1993, with Carolyn Calloway Thomas), *The Contemporary Rhetorical Theory Reader* (1999, with Celest Condit), and *Rhetoric, Materiality, and Politics* (forthcoming, with Barbara Biesecker). He is the senior editor for the University of Alabama's book series on Rhetoric, Culture, and Social Critique and the editor of the *Quarterly Journal of Speech* (2008–2010). He cosponsors a blog on rhetoric and visual culture with Robert Hariman titled "No Caption Needed" (http://www.nocaptionneeded.com) and is a contributing editor at "The BagNewsNotes" (http://bagnewsnotes.typepad.com/bagnews).

Neil Michel is a partner at Axiom, a creative services firm in Davis, California. He received his MA from the University of California, Davis in 1993. He is currently director of eMedia at *Prosper Magazine,* a monthly business/lifestyle magazine and Web site (ProsperMag.com) based in Sacramento, California. As a commercial and editorial photographer, his work has appeared nationwide in books, brochures, newspapers, and magazines, including *The New York Times, San Francisco Chronicle, Washington Post, San Jose Mercury News, Sacramento Bee, The Chronicle of Higher Education, Science Magazine, Journal of the American Medical Association, Landscape Architecture Magazine, Triathlete Magazine,* and *Running Times.* His academic work blends rhetoric, cultural studies, and photography. His research on the history and evolution of American memorials appears in numerous journals and anthologies. In November 2005, he and coauthor Carole Blair received the National Communication Association's prestigious "Golden Anniversary Monograph Award" honoring their article on Mount Rushmore.

Charles E. Morris III is Associate Professor of Rhetorical Studies in the Department of Communication at Boston College. He is the editor of *Queering Public Address: Sexualities in American Historical Discourse* (2007) and coeditor, with Stephen H. Browne, of *Readings on the Rhetoric of Social Protest* (2001/2006).

His essays have regularly appeared in the *Quarterly Journal of Speech,* as well as *Rhetoric & Public Affairs, Communication and Critical/ Cultural Studies,* and *Women's Studies in Communication.* For his work on GLBT history, he has received the Karl Wallace Memorial Award and Golden Monograph Award from the National Communication Association.

Shawn J. Parry-Giles is Professor of Communication at the University of Maryland. She also serves as the Director of Graduate Studies and the Director of the Center for Political Communication and Civic Leadership with the same department and institution. She studies rhetoric and politics, featuring the rhetoric of U.S. presidents and first ladies. Specifically, she studies presidential war discourse, women, media, and politics, as well as popular culture and politics. She has authored or coauthored three books: *The Prime-Time Presidency: The West Wing and U.S. Nationalism, Constructing Clinton: Hyperreality and Presidential Image-Making in Postmodern Politics,* and *The Rhetorical Presidency, Propaganda, and the Cold War, 1945–1955.* She is currently working on a book that examines the U.S. news coverage of Hillary Rodham Clinton from 1992–2000, culminating in her 2008 presidential bid.

Ronald E. Shields, Professor and Chair in the Department of Theatre and Film, Bowling Green State University, serves as editor of *Theatre Annual: A Journal of Performance Studies.* In 2006, he received the Leslie Irene Coger Award for Distinguished Performance from the National Communication Association. During 2004, he was honored by the Central States Communication Association as the Outstanding Performance Studies Scholar and was also a recipient of an NEH fellowship to Princeton University. Recent publications include essays in *Text and Performance Quarterly, JACA (Journal of Communication Administrators),* and as a contributor to the edited volume *More Than a Method: Trends and Traditions in Contemporary Film Performance* (2004). An active stage director, his current research and creative work links musicology and performance studies and explores the nexus of visual rhetoric, 17th-century Venetian opera, and the performance of culture.

John M. Sloop (PhD, University of Iowa, 1992) is Professor of Communication Studies at Vanderbilt University. The author of three books, including *Disciplining Gender* and numerous journal articles and book chapters, he writes about public issues as a way of understanding and challenging commonsense assumptions. He is currently working on a book that investigates the ideological links between humans, transportation, and a variety of media technologies. He enjoys running, blogging, and listening to music.

Nathan Stormer, Associate Professor, University of Maine, earned his PhD in Rhetoric from the University of Minnesota with minors in Feminist Studies and Cultural Studies (1997). He is interested in the interrelation of the body and discourse and in rhetorical theories of culture, particularly the intersections of social space, cultural memory, and performativity. His primary research area is the history of medical antiabortion discourse in the United States. In addition to journal articles on the subject, he has published the volume *Articulating Life's Memory: U.S. Medical Rhetoric About Abortion in the Nineteenth Century* (2002).

Reginald Twigg completed his PhD in Communication at the University of Utah in 1997, where his areas of research focused on rhetoric, cultural studies, and critical theory. He has published essays in the field, applying critical theory to cultural texts and practices, such as interior decorating, documentary narratives, lifestyles as rhetoric, and spheres of argument. Having taught at both the University of Utah and the University of Maine, he has spent the past decade in the computer software industry. Today, he manages the document image capture software business at IBM, where he also conducts and publishes research on enterprise information taxonomies, business process ontologies, and software metadata models. With prior work assignments in the United States and Europe, he currently resides in Southern California.

Carol K. Winkler is Professor of Communication Studies and Associate Dean for Humanities at Georgia State University in Atlanta, Georgia. Her most recent book, *In the Name of Terrorism: Presidents on Political Violence in the Post–World War II Era* (2006), analyzes internal administration documents, presidential speeches, and memoirs to discover how the term *terrorism* has evolved into an ideological marker of American culture. Her research on argumentation, ideology, and foreign policy rhetoric appears in *Rhetoric and Public Affairs, Quarterly Journal of Speech, Political Communication and Persuasion, Terrorism, Controversia: An International Journal of Debate and Democratic Renewal,* and numerous anthologies.